**Macroeconomic Theory**

# Macroeconomic Theory

**Gardner Ackley**
*University of Michigan*

The Macmillan Company

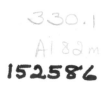

Sixteenth Printing, 1971

Library of Congress catalog card number: 61–5091

THE MACMILLAN COMPANY
866 THIRD AVENUE, NEW YORK, NEW YORK 10022
COLLIER-MACMILLAN CANADA, LTD., TORONTO, ONTARIO

Printed in the United States of America

TO THE MEMORY OF MY PARENTS
HUGH M. AND MARGARET ACKLEY

# Preface

This book is the product of some fourteen years of teaching a semester course—"The National Income"—at the University of Michigan. It is hard to say at what point I began writing this book, but mimeographed parts of it have been used in the course since at least 1955.

The course is elected, in about equal proportions, by advanced undergraduates and first-year graduate students, and the text is therefore aimed at this group. However, considerable flexibility of student level is provided in that many more specialized and difficult portions are placed in chapter appendices which may be omitted without damage to continuity. Also, the last three chapters, which contain the most advanced material, can be eliminated in a purely undergraduate course. Some instructors might prefer to omit Chapters IV and XI, which can be done without interfering with the argument.

Flexibility is further allowed by the use of related readings. Students, in my course, purchase J. M. Keynes, *General Theory of Employment, Interest and Money*, of which all chapters except 4, 6, 14, 16, 22, and 23 are assigned. A considerable selection from the vast post-Keynesian literature is also assigned or given as additional reference. My strong view is that, although Keynes' classic is quite unsatisfactory as a textbook, it should be carefully read by every serious student of economics.

I have tried to make my course, and therefore this book, primarily theoretical. To be sure, in teaching one attempts to develop the relevance of the theory to the diagnosis of current economic conditions and to current discussions of public policy. It is possible that this book could be used in a course which focusses primary attention upon such applications. In this case, it should be supplemented not by further readings in theory but by the *Economic Reports of the President*, and similar policy-oriented materials.

Although this book is primarily theoretical, there has been no hesitation at some points to introduce empirical matters. Note particularly the discussion of the consumption function (there is also some empirical discussion of the aggregate production function). One might complain that I have not introduced equivalent empirical (or at least statistical) discussion in connection with other topics, particularly investment. My defense would have to be that the consumption function is at the heart of modern macroeconomics; that investment theory is in less adequate shape for empirical testing; and that, in any case, while an introductory course in theory should surely introduce the student to the relation of theory and fact it need not attempt to test every proposition.

There is very little in this book that is original, nor should there be. Still, when writing a book such as this, it would be quite impossible that one "should not secretly cherish the belief that he has made some trifling modifications in economic analysis which seem to partake of the nature of contributions. However, it is not worthwhile to give these more specific comment. If such modifications are of any significance the fair-minded student will note the fact; if not, the less said about them the better."*

My intellectual debt to J. M. Keynes, like that of all students of my generation, is unmistakable. Yet this book tries to be much more than another "Guide to Keynes." I am impressed that Keynes' work represents more an extension than a revolution of "Classical" ideas and the tide of post-Keynesian literature has carried macroeconomics far beyond the high-water mark of Keynes' own great contribution.

Certain sections in this book incorporate excerpts from my previous publications, as follows: "A Third Approach to the Analysis and Control of Inflation," which first appeared in *The Relationship of Prices to Economic Stability and Growth: Compendium of Papers Submitted by Panelists Appearing before the Joint Economic Committee, March 31, 1958*, is incorporated with considerable changes in Chapter XVI. Similarly, in Chapter XIX, I have incorporated passages, with minor alterations, from "The Wealth-Saving Relationship," which first appeared in *Journal of*

---

* F. M. Taylor, *Principles of Economics*, Preface to 9th ed. (Ronald, 1925).

*Political Economy*, LIX (April 1951). In Chapter XX, brief excerpts appear from "The Keynesian Analysis of Italian Economic Problems," first published in the *Banca Nazionale del Lavoro Quarterly Review*, September 1957. I am grateful to the University of Chicago Press and the Banca Nazionale del Lavoro, publishers of the two journals, for permission to use these materials. I am also grateful to the Survey Research Center of the University of Michigan for permission to use the chart which appears on page 293.

To Howard S. Ellis, my first teacher of theory, is due my interest in theory and a passion for analytical rigor. Others whose inspiration I feel compelled to acknowledge are former teachers, E. M. Hoover, Jr., Leonard L. Watkins, Z. Clark Dickinson, I. L. Sharfman, and Arthur Smithies. Colleagues who have given both stimulus and invaluable assistance are Richard A. Musgrave, Daniel B. Suits, Warren L. Smith, George Katona, and James N. Morgan. Professor Henry Oliver, of Indiana University, read the entire manuscript, and made numerous extremely helpful suggestions. Hundreds of students have permitted me to sharpen my ideas on them, but I should particularly acknowledge the help of former students William P. Yohe, Heinz Köhler, and Enrique Jarabo-Paya, who have served as assistants with parts of the writing. Further, I am grateful to the Ford Foundation for research help; to the Conference Board of Associated Research Councils and the U. S. Department of State for a Fulbright year during which some of this writing was done in Rome; to the secretarial staff of the Department of Economics, University of Michigan, and particularly to Mrs. Evelyn Uhlendorf, for the efficient typing of interminable drafts. Finally, I must acknowledge the patience of my wife and family; and the academic environment provided by the University of Michigan. Without all of these, this book would have been impossible.

Gardner Ackley

# Contents

PART THREE

## THE KEYNESIAN MACROECONOMICS

## PART FOUR

## SOME EXTENSIONS

# Concepts and Measurement

PART ONE

# Basic Concepts

*Chapter I*

Macroeconomic theory is a somewhat unattractive and awkward name for one of the more important branches of economic analysis. Another somewhat more descriptive title in fairly common use is "income and employment analysis." If we say, further, that this book is basically concerned with the problems of unemployment, economic instability, inflation, and economic growth, the reader will perhaps obtain a better idea of our subject matter. Nor will he need to be reminded that these problems are among the most significant economic problems which contemporary Western society faces—indeed, they would find a prominent place in any list of leading social and political problems of a democratic system.

But to say that the book concerns these problems of economic policy may be misleading. Lest the reader expect that he may find here the solutions to these problems, he should immediately be warned that this book attempts to supply a theoretical framework for the analysis of these hard and complex problems; it does not provide solutions. Solutions involve far more than theory. There are many difficult questions of fact that must first be resolved; and even solid facts and sound analysis are not enough, for solutions also require value judgments. Based on the facts, the analytical framework, and the basic social preferences among competing objectives which society must ultimately express, solutions to these problems further require that the appropriate social policies be embodied in feasible and effective political, economic, and administrative institutions.

Theory can help by indicating which facts are relevant, what some

3

of the social choices must be, and what are the requirements of the institutional arrangements. Sound theoretical analysis is only one element in the solution of problems, but it is a crucial one. Much social policy, past and present, with respect to these particular problems suffers more from faulty analysis and muddy thinking than from lack of facts or unwillingness to choose among competing objectives. Unfortunately, economic analysis has often posed the wrong choices—has indicated as alternatives things which need not be considered alternatives. And it has led generations of scholars to collect and to pore over facts whose relevance is questionable. Thus theory has an important role to perform in connection with these major problems of our society. But it still supplies only one part of the solution to economic problems.

Macroeconomic theory has flowered rapidly in the past twenty years, although its origins stretch much further back. The field is now large enough that no one book can hope to cover it all. This book is therefore confined to fundamentals. It is an introduction, no more. While occasional references are made to the history or evolution of ideas, no systematic treatment is given to this aspect.

## THE MEANING OF "MACROECONOMICS"

"Macroeconomics" is, of course, to be distinguished from "microeconomics." Macroeconomics deals with economic affairs "in the large." It concerns the over-all dimensions of economic life. It looks at the total size and shape and functioning of the "elephant" of economic experience, rather than the working or articulation or dimensions of the individual parts. To alter the metaphor, it studies the character of the forest, independently of the trees which compose it.

More specifically, macroeconomics concerns itself with such variables as the aggregate volume of the output of an economy, with the extent to which its resources are employed, with the size of the national income, with the "general price level." Microeconomics, on the other hand, deals with the *division* of total output among industries, products, and firms, and the *allocation* of resources among competing uses. It considers problems of income *distribution*. Its interest is in *relative* prices of particular goods and services.[1]

---

[1] Some economists may prefer to define microeconomic theory as relating to the behavior of individual firms and households. If we do so, we must realize that much of traditional price and distribution theory involves aggregates. The concept of "industry," for example, aggregates numerous firms, or even products. Consumer demand for shoes is an aggregate of the demands of many households, and the supply of shoes is an aggregate of the production of many firms. The demand for

Most, but not all, of the content of traditional economic theory, until the last twenty-five years, has consisted of microeconomics. Price and value theory; the theory of the household, the firm, and the industry; most production and welfare theory are of the microeconomic variety. However, monetary theory and business-cycle theory also have a long history, and are clearly macroeconomic.

Actually, the line beween macroeconomic and microeconomic theory cannot be precisely drawn. A truly "general" theory of the economy would clearly embrace both: it would explain individual behavior, individual outputs, incomes, and prices; and the sums or averages of the individual results would constitute the aggregates with which macroeconomics is concerned. Such a general theory exists; but its very generality leaves it with little substantive content. Rather, to reach meaningful results, we find that we must approach macroeconomic problems with macroeconomic tools, and microeconomic problems with microeconomic tools.

One may immediately wonder how a meaningful macroeconomics is possible. It is, after all, true that total output (for example) is the sum of individual outputs. How then can we explain the total except as we simultaneously explain the individual parts? The answer to this question raises some points which are far from elementary, and to which we shall frequently have to return in the course of this study. Nevertheless, it is appropriate to comment briefly on this question early in our discussion. Consequently, this chapter concludes with a brief treatment of the question: Is a meaningful macroeconomics possible? Before turning to this, however, we take up some methodological matters, relating to types of economic variables, functional relationships and parameters, economic models, and statics and dynamics.

## MACROECONOMIC VARIABLES

A variable is easily defined—it is a measurable (or scaleable) magnitude which varies, and in whose variation we have an interest, either

---

and supply of labor in a locality or an industry are clearly aggregative concepts. Our usage here is to confine the scope of macroeconomics to aggregates relating to the whole economy, together with subaggregates which (a) cross product and industry lines (such as the total production of consumer goods, or total production of capital goods), and which (b) add up to an aggregate for the whole economy (as total production of consumer goods and of capital and government goods add up to total production of the economy; or as total wage income and property income add up to national income). Macroeconomics uses aggregates smaller than for the whole economy, but only in a context which makes them subdivisions of an economy-wide total. Microeconomics also uses aggregates, but not in a context which relates them to an economy-wide total.

because of its direct importance or because of its effect on other variables. We need not here list the variables in which macroeconomics is interested. But it is useful, right at the beginning, to stress some characteristic types of variables, and their differences. The most important such distinction (the neglect of which has been the cause of infinite confusion) is between stock and flow variables. A stock variable has no time dimension, a flow variable does. The weight of an automobile is a stock variable; its speed is a flow variable. The population of cars is a stock variable; traffic is a flow. The weight of a car is 2,200 lbs.; the number (population) of cars is thirty million—not 2,200 lbs. per day or month, or thirty million cars per year or minute. To be sure, a stock must be measured at some point in time. The weight of a car may change (by accretion of mud, or using up of gas or tires); the car population may increase or decrease by the difference between production and scrappage. But the *magnitude* of the stock has no time dimension. A flow, on the other hand, can only be expressed per unit of time. Speed is 60 miles per hour (or one mile per minute, or 1/60 mile per second, or 1,440 miles per 24 hours—all the same speed but expressed in different time units). Traffic is measured as so many cars passing a given point per hour, or so many car-miles per day, or in some other way that inevitably requires the statement of a time unit or else the measurement is meaningless. To say that speed is one mile, or that traffic is fifty cars is meaningless.

All this may seem very obvious; but almost no other single source of confusion is more dangerous in economic theory—not only to beginners but sometimes to advanced students in the field. Money is a stock; expenditures or transactions in money a flow; income is a flow, wealth a stock. *Saving* is a flow ($100 per month); *savings* is a stock ($10,000 accumulated as of July 1, 1959). Investment is a flow ($55 billion dollars per year in the United States in 1958); the aggregate of investments is a stock (in manufacturing it totaled, perhaps, $140 billion on January 1, 1958). (Unfortunately, while the use of "saving" and "savings" is now fairly standardized, the cumulative total of investments is often merely designated as "investment"; only the context can show whether the author means the flow or the stock. Fortunately, the words "capital" or "capital stock" are often applied to the stock concept, thus avoiding the confusion.)

Is "price" a stock or a flow variable? Price does not need a time dimension (although rate of price change does); but it obviously is not a stock magnitude. Actually it can be thought of as a ratio between two (actual or potential) flows—a flow of cash and a flow of goods. In the ratio, the time unit appears both in numerator and denominator and hence cancels out.

Other ratio variables appear in economics. Such ratios may express relationships between stocks, between flows, or relationships of stocks to flows. An example of the first is the concept of "liquidity," as measured, for instance, by the percentage of liquid assets to total assets of a person or firm. An example of a flow ratio is the ratio of saving to income. Examples of ratios between a stock and a flow are the various "velocity" concepts: ratios between a flow of money transactions or income and a stock of money. Since the time dimension does not cancel out, velocity must be expressed in terms of a time dimension: the money stock "turns over" twelve times a year (or once per month or three times per quarter-year).

Upon encountering any variable, the student should spend a moment determining for himself whether it is a stock, a flow, or a ratio concept, and, if the latter, whether a ratio between stocks, flows, or a stock and a flow. Much confusion will be saved by this exercise.

We have seen that flows must be expressed in terms of a time unit. What unit we choose is obviously immaterial, although the one-year unit is often a natural one in income analysis. But whether we express income as per year, per month, per day, or per second, we must have in mind that the flow is either an instantaneous rate at some point of time, or is an average of such instantaneous rates over a period of time. We can say that as of 10:03 A.M. on Monday, May 26, 1959, consumer disposable income was at the rate of 331 billion per annum. If we say that, for the year 1958, consumer disposable income was at the rate of 316.5 billion per annum, we really mean that this was the average rate of income flow during that year. A car can be traveling at the rate of 60 miles per hour at some particular instant, or it can travel 60 miles per hour for an eight-hour day—meaning not that the speedometer was at 60 every moment in that day but that it traveled 480 miles in eight hours, or an average speed of 60 miles per hour. Since most economic flows cannot be read from speedometers or similar measuring devices, we in practice must measure them over a period of time. John Doe received $731 in income payments during March, 1959. His March income was thus at the rate of $731 per month, or $8,772 per annum. Conceptually, however, we speak of rates of flow as of any instant of time, expressing that flow in terms of any convenient time unit.[2]

---

[2] A convenient simplification often used in economic theory is that of "period analysis." In period analysis, we assume that flows (such as income) are not capable

Several crucial problems in economic theory involve relationships between flows and stocks. Except for mere revaluations, stocks change only through flows. The stock of capital goods increases through an excess of new construction and manufacture over wearing out. Savings accumulate through the act of saving (or decrease through dissaving). But it makes a great difference whether stock changes are fast or slow; the effect on the stocks is the same, but, quite obviously, the flows involve current transactions and thus affect other current rates of flow. Some of the trickiest problems in (dynamic) macroeconomic analysis involve just this point (for example, the "acceleration" theory of investment, the relationship of stock and flow theories of the rate of interest, and many problems involving the slippery concept of "hoarding"). We shall have something to say about this matter at later points.

## FUNCTIONAL RELATIONSHIPS AND PARAMETERS

Economists have come increasingly to use the language and apparatus of mathematics. This reflects the increasing precision with which economists have formulated their concepts. Thus, economists talk of functional relationships among their variables instead of the earlier and often vague discussions of "tendencies" or "causes."

The existence of a functional relationship among two or more variables simply means that the values or magnitudes of the variables are somehow uniquely related. A change in one variable is associated in some regular and predictable way with a change in another. We can first simplify by assuming a functional relationship among two variables only. A familiar relationship of this sort is the demand schedule of microeconomic price theory. This relationship is one between price and quantity demanded. Given the demand schedule (function), then corresponding to each price there is some unique quantity which buyers will take. Quantity demanded is a function of price—in this case, an "inverse" function (when price rises, quantity drops, and vice versa), as opposed to a "direct" function (in which case the variables both move together, as with most supply func-

---

of continuous change, but, rather, change only at certain intervals (the ends or beginnings of "periods"). Thus, income (like other flow variables) changes only in stairstep fashion. We say: "Income moves as follows: 100, 90, 85, 82.5 . . ." If we think of these magnitudes each as the cumulation of income payments over the duration of the period, then the flow takes on the same dimension as a stock, and we (seem to) avoid stock-flow difficulties. Some authors work almost invariably in period analysis terms (whether explicitly or not). We shall not use it except at specific points in our analysis, clearly calling attention to the fact that we are doing so. It is the author's conviction that analytical results which depend on the very special assumptions of period analysis have often been quite illegitimately generalized.

tions). A functional relationship may, but need not, express the simple idea of cause and effect: *A* varies *because B* varies. In the microeconomic demand schedule the relationship is presumably of this sort: the market price "determines" or "causes" the amount demanded.

We express the idea of functional relationship symbolically as:

$$D = f(P)$$

where $D$ is the quantity demanded of some commodity, and $P$ its price. The notation $f$, followed by the parentheses, simply means "function of." (It does not mean that $P$ is multiplied by $f$.) Often, where there are several functional relationships involving the same variables, particular functional relationship may be designated by Greek letters, or by repeating the variable which appears on the left, as

$$D = \Phi(P),$$

or

$$D = D(P)$$

These are to be understood in the same way as the "$f$" notation above.

This simple two-variable (price and quantity) demand function, however, only isolates for special attention two out of many relevant variables. Amount demanded of a particular good depends not only on its price, but also on prices of other goods and on consumer incomes (among other things). That is,

$$D_1 = D(P_1, P_2, P_3 \ldots P_n, Y)$$

where $D_1$ is the quantity demanded of the particular good, $P_1$ is its price, $P_2, P_3 \ldots P_n$ are the prices of other goods whose prices may also influence the demand for the good in question, and $Y$ represents consumer incomes. Actually, we could also spell out still other variables, such as the advertising expenditures made by producers of the particular good and by producers of other goods, the quality of each of these goods (if this were scaleable and could thus be treated as a variable), the interest rate, etc.

Now, when we use the simple two-variable (price-quantity) demand function, we must actually mean that we are holding the values of these other variables constant, and are concerned with what happens to quantity demanded when the price of the particular good changes, all other variables remaining unchanged. This is sometimes expressed by adding the phrase *ceteris paribus*, "other things equal." For each change in the value of one of the other variables we will have a new functional relationship between price and quantity. In other words, the ordinary demand curve shifts when one of these other variables changes. So long as we confine our attention to a single functional relationship, it is obviously possible to consider the values of all except one of the variables on the right-hand side of the equation as fixed—that is, we treat these other variables as "parameters," or external circumstances—subject to change, to be sure—but not of interest to the problem at hand. For example, we may be interested in finding the effect on quantity demanded ($D_1$) of a change in $P_1$, or $P_2$, or $Y$, or advertising expenditures, or any other variable, *considered by itself*—other things being equal.

But when we combine this demand function with other functions, in a system of relationships simultaneously determining a number of variables, we cannot use *ceteris paribus* with respect to (i.e., we cannot "suppress," or treat as a parameter) any potential variable in one equation which appears as a true variable in another equation in the system. That is, we cannot assume to be given something that we are, at the same time, considering as subject to change. This means that we must frequently treat functions involving more than two variables.

The idea of one variable depending on two or more others which may vary simultaneously always provides difficulties for the beginning student. Yet it is necessary, even in the simpler macroeconomic models, to deal with this kind of situation. The student must, therefore, master this notion from the beginning.

Perhaps a simple numerical example will help. Using the example of the demand function, and concentrating only on three variables (treating the others as parameters), we might have:

$$D_1 = D(P_1, Y)$$

where the symbols have the same meaning as before. Some selected values of a particular function are shown in Table 1–1 which follows. The data are arranged in two different ways, to facilitate comparison.

It can be seen most easily from the first arrangement that if income is held constant at any particular level, quantity demanded varies inversely with price. From the second arrangement it can be clearly seen that when price is held constant at any particular level, demand varies directly with income. It can also be seen that the effect of a given price change is different depending on the level of income. A reduction of price from 10 to 9 increases amount demanded by 4 units when income is 100, by 6 units when income is 200, by 9 when income is 300, and by 10 when in-

**TABLE 1–1.  Hypothetical Demand Function with Three Variables**

| First Arrangement | | | | Same Data Rearranged | | | |
|---|---|---|---|---|---|---|---|
| Combination | Y | $P_1$ | $D_1$ | Combination | Y | $P_1$ | $D_1$ |
| a | 100 | 10 | 50 | a | 100 | 10 | 50 |
| b | 100 | 9 | 54 | e | 200 | 10 | 80 |
| c | 100 | 8 | 59 | i | 300 | 10 | 100 |
| d | 100 | 7 | 65 | m | 400 | 10 | 110 |
| e | 200 | 10 | 80 | b | 100 | 9 | 54 |
| f | 200 | 9 | 86 | f | 200 | 9 | 86 |
| g | 200 | 8 | 94 | j | 300 | 9 | 109 |
| h | 200 | 7 | 104 | n | 400 | 9 | 120 |
| i | 300 | 10 | 100 | c | 100 | 8 | 59 |
| j | 300 | 9 | 109 | g | 200 | 8 | 94 |
| k | 300 | 8 | 121 | k | 300 | 8 | 121 |
| l | 300 | 7 | 136 | o | 400 | 8 | 133 |
| m | 400 | 10 | 110 | d | 100 | 7 | 65 |
| n | 400 | 9 | 120 | h | 200 | 7 | 104 |
| o | 400 | 8 | 133 | l | 300 | 7 | 136 |
| p | 400 | 7 | 149 | p | 400 | 7 | 149 |

come is 400. Likewise, income change has a different effect on quantity demanded at different levels of price.

Actually, this need not be the case. Suppose the demand function were as follows:

$$D_1 = 70 - 5P_1 + .3Y$$

*The student should calculate tables like those above for this demand function.* He will see that each change of 1 in price will always change amount demanded (in the opposite direction) by 5 units, regardless of income; and each change of 100 in income will always change amount demanded (in the same direction) by 30 units. (This is, in several respects, the simplest kind of function, and later numerical examples will therefore use this kind. Quite obviously, however, there is no reason to suppose that actual functions are of this simple character.) The student should also calculate the values to see that

$$D_1 = 100 - 5P_1$$

represents the *ceteris paribus* price-demand function when income is treated as a parameter—i.e., is held constant at $Y = 100$. If $Y = 200$, this demand curve shifts to become

$$D_1 = 130 - 5P_1$$

Further,

$$D_1 = 20 + .3Y$$

represents the *ceteris paribus* income-demand function when price is treated as a parameter—i.e., is held constant (at $P_1 = 10$).

Economic relationships that we shall use have often been classified as (1) "behavioral"—i.e., reflecting the voluntary choices of economic subjects; (2) "institutional restraints"—i.e., reflecting the operation of laws or rules of behavior (examples: required bank reserves as a fraction of deposits, tax collections as a function of income, etc.); (3) "technical"—i.e., reflecting technological relationships; and (4) "identities" or "definitions."

## ECONOMIC MODELS

An economic model consists simply of a group or set of economic relationships, each one of which involves at least one variable which also appears in at least one other relationship which is part of the model. A simple and familiar microeconomic model combines supply and demand relationships to determine price and amounts exchanged of a single commodity. Formally, this appears as

(1) $$D = D(P)$$

(2) $$S = S(P)$$

(3) $$D = S$$

where $D$ and $S$ are amounts demanded and supplied, respectively, of some commodity, and $P$ is its price. (Here we have—perhaps quite legitimately—suppressed other variables than price in both supply and demand equations. This means that we assume that these other variables can reasonably be imagined as holding unchanged when price, supply, and demand of this commodity change.)

To write down this model in the form of equations does no more (and actually a little less as we have done it so far) than we do when we draw the supply-demand diagram of Figure 1–1. In this familiar diagram we summarize what we know (or think that we know) about the behavior of buyers and sellers of this commodity in the two curves. When we find their intersection at $X$, "determining" price at $P_o$ and amounts supplied and demanded at $S_o$ and $D_o$, we are using equation (3).

For the equations to say as much as the diagram does, we would have

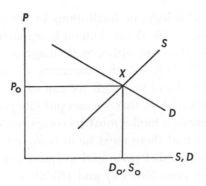

**Figure 1–1.**

to specify something about the "slopes" of the functions—that amount supplied is an increasing function of price and amount demanded a decreasing function:

$$\frac{dS}{dP} > 0, \frac{dD}{dP} < 0.[3]$$

Neither in the diagram nor in the equations (with the added specification of slopes), do we attempt to say very much in detail about this market. Our diagram has no units shown on either axis, because we do not pretend to know the quantities involved. Our equations are similarly vague. What use, then, is our model? Since we do not specify our functions (beyond the matter of slope), we cannot use it to predict actual prices and quantities. However, even with the limited information that we have, we can predict (for example) that any event which tends to reduce supply (disaster to some suppliers, rise in the price of another good which can be produced with the same facilities, etc.) will tend, *ceteris paribus*, to raise prices and reduce amounts exchanged; a tax on the commodity will raise the price to buyers inclusive of tax, lower the net proceeds to sellers, and reduce amounts exchanged; and so on. If we knew more about the particular market—e.g., that the upward slope of the supply curve was very slight, and the downward slope of the demand curve rather sharp, we could make somewhat more specific predictions. If we knew still more—so that we could put units on our axes in the diagram, or spell out numerical equations, we could make still more specific predictions.

A model, then, uses what we know or think we know about economic

[3] The symbol $\frac{"dS"}{dP}$ is the slope of the supply curve; "$> 0$" means that it is positive, or slopes upward to the right. Correspondingly, $\frac{"dD"}{dP}$ is the slope of the demand curve; "$< 0$" means that it is negative, or slopes downward to the right.

behavior patterns, technology, or institutions to permit us to make predictions—more or less specific depending on how much or little we know. We could, of course, dispense either with diagrams or equations, and reason entirely verbally. It is only that diagrams or equations prove to be a most convenient shorthand in which we can express anything about a relationship between variables that we can put into sentence form.

To be useful, of course, a model must be complete. Mathematically, we express this by saying that there must be as many equations as there are unknowns. We cannot predict price and quantity (or even the direction of their change) from equations (1) and (3) alone.

Economic models, then, are succinct statements of economic theory. Theory, in turn, is simply a generalization or abstraction of experience and observation. We see thousands of farmers producing and supplying wheat. We can observe many things about these farmers and their productive activities: the colors of their eyes, the numbers of their children, their various productive techniques, the numbers of acres they farm, and millions of further details. We choose, however, to make one significant abstraction about their behavior. We select from among all of our observations one relationship which we think is most relevant and significant— that they tend to grow more wheat at a higher than at a lower price. We throw away all of the rest of our information (we could not, in any case, remember or record very much of it), and summarize our "knowledge" about the supply of wheat in a simple function. Frequently, perhaps, our abstractions and generalizations from experience and observation are erroneous, or unnecessarily incomplete. But that is simply the difference between bad or inadequate and better or more complete theory.

Much more could be said about the nature of economic models and economic theory than these few words (and some of what little has been said is debatable). But rather than to discuss these matters further in this general form, we prefer to get on to some specific macroeconomic models, and let further points or arguments arise from our development and use of them.

## EQUILIBRIUM, STATICS, AND DYNAMICS

Equation (3) in the market model used in the last section expressed a condition of equilibrium—that amounts supplied and demanded be equal. This concept of equilibrium now requires brief discussion.

The concept of equilibrium is familiar in a general way to all beginning students of economics. A system can be said to be in equilibrium when all of its significant variables show no change, and when there are no pressures or forces for change which will produce subsequent change in the values of significant variables. (Perhaps it is better to say that the forces for change are in balance, rather than that they are absent.) In the market model of the previous section we reason that if price is at $P_o$, then it is simultaneously possible both for sellers to find a market for all that they wish to sell at the market price and for buyers to find suppliers for all that they wish to buy at the market price. At no other price are both conditions fulfilled. Thus, with price at $P_o$, both buyers and sellers are satisfied, and none will have reason to change the price—to offer higher or lower prices. Price $P_o$ will remain in effect, unchanged so long as the demand and supply conditions summarized in equations (1) and (2) continue to prevail.

States of equilibrium need never be realized in the economy for equilibrium analysis to be a useful tool of thinking. Corresponding to any given set of external circumstances, there may be some pattern of economic variables which, if once achieved, would show no further tendency to change. Assuming for the moment that there are forces in an economy (or in a particular market) which push it toward equilibrium when it is not in that state, a description of the equilibrium position is a description of the directions in which economic variables are headed. Of course, the external circumstances which determine the equilibrium may always be changing, so that equilibrium is never attained. Nevertheless, it remains useful to know the directions in which variables are headed at any given time, whether they are expected ever to reach their equilibrium values or not.

There are circumstances in which disequilibrium produces only a tendency for further change, which may not be in the direction of equilibrium. Even in this circumstance, however, it is useful to be able to identify the equilibrium which, if it could be obtained, would lead to cessation of further change.

States of equilibrium may be of several sorts. Since economic variables are of both stock and flow varieties, full equilibrium would be one in which all stocks as well as flows were stable. This would necessarily mean that the net flows which add to the stocks would, in equilibrium, be zero. (This does not mean that all flows would be zero. The stockpile of iron ore at a blast furnace may be constant even though the furnace is operating at full speed, if only it is added to as fast as it is used.) Such a concept of full equilibrium for the economy as a whole is that of the Classical "stationary state," in which the community's stock of capital is just maintained, with zero net saving and investment. Such a state of full or "stationary" equilibrium has questionable relevance to our economic society. Nevertheless, it is important to recognize that this is the only full equilibrium, and that so long as saving and investment are positive, changes are occurring in the economy's stock of capital, which may ultimately affect the rates of current flows.

A more immediately applicable concept of macroeconomic equilibrium is that of short-run or flow equilibrium, in which flows (but not stocks) are stable and have no tendency (at least in the short run) to further change. Of course, if this flow equilibrium involves positive or negative net change in stocks, full stock-plus-flow-equilibrium is not achieved, and the growth or shrinkage of stocks may contain the seeds of later change in flows. But because annual accretions of most stocks are relatively small (compared with the total size of such stocks) we may frequently find it useful, in short run analysis, to ignore the changes in stocks, whose effects will show up only over a considerable period of time.[4]

We might illustrate these two concepts from another field. Corresponding to each rate of gasoline intake (as controlled by accelerator pressure), there will be some equilibrium speed of a car. A change in accelerator pressure will not immediately cause the speed to reach its new equilibrium rate. But soon it will do so. When it does, the speed of the car is in short run equilibrium. But driving the car at any speed depletes its stock of gas. Sooner or later (if the stock is not replenished), the tank will be empty and the long run equilibrium—of zero speed—will be achieved. But both short run and long run equilibrium concepts, while not independent, are useful in proper context.

A third possible variety of equilibrium is one to which substantial attention has been paid in recent macroeconomic literature. This is the moving equilibrium in which stocks grow, but only in the same proportion with the growth of the current flows. Thus all relevant stock-flow ratios are constant, and the accretion of stocks has no tendency, even ultimately, to affect the rates of current flows. This may be called "proportional growth." In later chapters we consider some models both of proportional and nonproportional growth.

The branch of economic analysis which confines its attention to equilibrium positions is called "statics." The most useful variety of statics is the so-called "comparative statics," which compares equilibrium positions corresponding to two or more sets of external circumstances. Our supply-demand exercise in the previous section was, of course, of this variety.

Static analysis, whether simple or comparative, concentrates only on equilibrium positions. It does not concern itself with the time it takes for

---

[4] While this assumption *may* be appropriate with respect to the stock of plant and equipment, it obviously is not with respect to inventories. Business cycle analysis cannot possibly ignore changes in inventory stocks.

an equilibrium position to be achieved, nor with the path by which variables approach their equilibrium states. This is *one* concern of dynamic analysis.

"Dynamics" is concerned essentially with states of disequilibrium and with change. Whether the disequilibrium involves the absence of short-run (flow) equilibrium or the condition and movement of an economy not in long-run (stock-plus-flow) equilibrium, study of movement and change is the province of dynamic analysis. This is sometimes oversimplified by describing dynamics as the study of the movement of economic variables from one equilibrium position to another. Although such study is an important and useful exercise in dynamic analysis, it retains the tie to the equilibrium concept. A broader and more significant dynamics would include as well the movements of a system which is never in equilibrium, either because no equilibrium exists, or because the movements of the system are not in the direction of equilibrium, or because of continuous changes in external circumstances—productive techniques, population, consumer tastes, government actions, to name the more outstanding ones. Study of the "business cycle" may fall in this broadest category of dynamics. Whether the study of the moving equilibrium of "proportional growth" should be called statics or dynamics is a matter of taste.

A more formal and sophisticated definition makes the essence of dynamics to be that it studies systems or models involving *relationships which hold over time*—i.e., relationships in which the value which obtains *now* for a variable may depend not only on the simultaneous values of other variables, but also or instead on *previous* values of other variables (or even previous values of the same variable). Examples are behavior patterns involving *lags* (the investment expenditures that I make today depend on yesterday's value of the interest rate); or *habituation* (my consumption expenditures today depend, among other things, on my yesterday's level of consumption); or *cumulants* (my savings today are the cumulative total of all my past saving and dissaving).[5] A system which involves one or more such relationships is a dynamic system.

Of course, one special state of any dynamic system may be that of no change, or equilibrium—which occurs when the previous values which determine today's values produce results which are exactly the same as those of the day before. Thus today's values will produce again the same results tomorrow, and so on. A dynamic analysis of an equilibrium situation is therefore possible.

The above definition of dynamics would seem, in contrast, to leave as

---

[5] Any of these or other dynamic relationships can be formulated in period analysis terms, but none has to be.

the province of statics only the analysis of systems in which all causal relationships are simultaneous. However, this unnecessarily restricts the scope of statics. If equilibrium is a state of no change over time, then, so long as equilibrium prevails, the time dimensions of a relationship can be ignored. For example, if the interest rate is constant, it makes no difference whether we recognize that my investment depends on yesterday's interest rate as opposed to today's, for both yesterday's and today's interest rate are the same. We can simply say that investment (undated) depends on the interest rate (undated). Habituation, likewise, has no independent role when there is no change, and habituation can be ignored. Thus, in an analysis which restricts itself to equilibrium positions, the time aspect drops out. To use statics, we do not have to deny that some of our relationships hold over time; this fact simply makes no difference, so long as we confine our attention to equilibrium positions. But the existence of relationships that hold over time obviously cannot be ignored when we deal with disequilibrium and change—which brings us back to our initial identification of dynamics with disequilibrium and change.

However, the more complete view of equilibrium as a special state of a dynamic system leads us to the discovery that not all dynamic systems are capable of achieving equilibrium. This is true even though there may *exist* an equilibrium for such a system. There may be some pattern of variables which, if once achieved, would repeat itself endlessly in the absence of new disturbance. Yet, if the system starts with some pattern other than the equilibrium one, it may show no tendency to approach equilibrium, but only generate endless change. Such an equilibrium is, therefore, not very meaningful. It is called an "unstable" equilibrium. A "stable" equilibrium, on the contrary, is one which the system's movements tend to approach or reach. If a stable equilibrium is disturbed, it will be reestablished. Not so an unstable one.

Now if we confine our analysis only to equilibrium positions, we are obviously unable to distinguish between stable and unstable equilibria. If it were not for this, we could defend statics as a good approximation— saying that we are not interested in, or can afford to ignore, what happens "on the way," but are only interested in final destinations. However, because we find it easy to construct plausible economic models which are unstable, or systems which are only barely stable (take a long time to settle down when disturbed), and because we seem to observe in the real world some movements which resemble the results of these models, we now think that the method of statics is not merely incomplete but potentially misleading.

Nevertheless, because statics is simpler, and because it provides a convenient, even necessary, starting point for dynamics, the primary method of this book is statics. Still, dynamic analysis will not be entirely neglected.

## IS A MEANINGFUL MACROECONOMICS POSSIBLE? [6]

We return, finally, to a question introduced earlier in this chapter. One part of the answer to the question whether a meaningful macroeconomic theory is possible lies in the fact that macroeconomic reasoning can take account of many limitations and relationships which are not applicable to individual parts. For example, for any individual or group of individuals, income and expenditure on currently produced output obviously can and usually will be different magnitudes; but for a whole society, income and expenditure (properly defined) can be shown always to be equal. Any individual can save without investing, or invest without having previously or currently saved; but, carefully defined, saving and investment must be identical for the whole economy. One country's imports may well exceed its exports; but for all countries combined, total imports and exports must obviously be equal. One individual can reduce his stock of cash by paying out in excess of his receipts. But unless the community's total money stock is changed, society cannot. One firm or industry can increase its output and employment by bidding workers away from other industries; when there is full employment, industry as a whole cannot increase total labor input.

Exploration of the meaning and implications of these "macroeconomic truisms" comprises an important part of macroeconomic theory.

However, macroeconomics would be (and sometimes is) sterile if confined solely to definitional relationships among macroeconomic variables. It must also seek relationships among economic variables which express motivation and behavior. Theories involving such relations must rest, obviously, upon hypotheses concerning the behavior of the individual workers, families, and firms which comprise the economy. Are aggregative theories of behavior possible?

We know, of course, that individuals do react in certain generally similar ways to given changes in the circumstances that confront them. For example, *other things equal*, most families will spend more on the purchase of consumer goods if their incomes increase. But the increased expenditures will be of different magnitudes. An increase of $1,000 in the income of a family whose income was previously $2,000 may produce a different increase in expenditure than the same increase received by a

[6] For a fuller treatment of this question, see Chapter XX, below.

$20,000 family. An income increase received by a thrifty family may go largely to augment savings; by another family it may all go into higher consumption spending. Or, the same family may react in very different ways to the same income change at different times. We could not hope to have a theory which would predict at all accurately how individual families would respond to higher incomes; but the law of large numbers is a help when we deal with aggregates—the vagaries of individual behavior tend to be swallowed up in a regularity of mass behavior. When we deal with aggregates for the whole economy, we obviously take maximum advantage of the greater regularity of mass than of individual behavior.

However, differences of individual behavior may be more than random. There may be—indeed there probably are—systematic and measurable differences of consumption behavior as income changes (to continue the illustration) as between farm and urban families, between families whose primary income source is profits and those depending primarily on wages, between high and low income families, etc. Even if each group of families behaved in an entirely regular and predictable way in response to an income change, there might still be no systematic or predictable response of aggregate consumer expenditures to a change in aggregate consumer income. If a given change in aggregate income were received at one time primarily by one sector, and at another time primarily by another sector, no reliable generalization could be made as to the effect on total consumer expenditures of any given change in aggregate consumer income.

For a regular aggregative relationship to exist, it is obvious that income distribution must either be unchanged as among the sectors with different responses, or income distribution must change only in some systematic and regular way as aggregate income itself changes.

Suppose, for example, that there are two consumer sectors, each with its own perfectly regular and stable income-consumption schedule, as in Table 1–2, which follows:

**TABLE 1–2. Hypothetical Consumption Functions of Two Sectors**

| Sector Income | Sector Consumer Expenditures A | B |
|---|---|---|
| 100 | 80 | 90 |
| 150 | 105 | 135 |
| 200 | 130 | 180 |
| 250 | 155 | 225 |
| 300 | 180 | 270 |
| 350 | 205 | 315 |

A given aggregate income of 300 for the two sectors combined might consist of 100 for Sector A, 200 for Sector B; 150 for each sector; or 200 for A and 100 for B. As can be seen from the above table, the corresponding total consumer expenditures would be 260, 240, and 220. An aggregate income of 500 might be distributed 350 A, 150 B, total consumption 340; or, 250 A, 250 B, total consumption 380; or, 150 A, 350 B, total consumption 420. There is obviously no unique relationship between aggregate consumption and aggregate income.

But if theory or observation should tell us that aggregate income were always distributed half to A and half to B, a perfectly regular relationship between the totals would obtain. Or, if theory or observation should tell us that, as aggregate income changed, its distribution between A and B would alter in some regular and systematic way, again we would have a stable relationship between aggregate income and aggregate consumption. Now, however, our aggregate consumption-income relationship would be a compound or product of two kinds of "laws"—laws relating to the consumer behavior of the several sectors, and laws relating to the distribution of income. And the aggregate response of consumption change to income change might resemble the response of neither group to income change.[7]

The lesson of all this is simple: theories relating two or more economic aggregates can be derived from theories of individual behavior only if the composition of the aggregates is constant, or if the composition changes in some regular way as the size of the aggregate magnitudes changes; empirical regularities of individual and small group behavior are consistent with an empirical regularity of aggregate behavior only under the same circumstances.

Fortunately for the existence of a meaningful macroeconomics, both observation and theory (including important parts of microeconomic

[7] For example, suppose that the laws determining income distribution result in the following relationship

$$(1) \qquad\qquad A = 40 + .4(A + B)$$

where $A$ and $B$ are the two sector incomes. Aggregate income is $(A + B)$. The sector consumption functions shown in the table above are

$$(2) \qquad\qquad C_A = 30 + .5A$$
$$\text{and } (3) \qquad\qquad C_B = .9B$$

where $C_A$ and $C_B$ are sector consumption expenditures. Substituting from (1) into (2) and (3), and combining, we have

$$C_A = 30 + .5[40 + .4(A + B)]$$
$$C_B = .9[(A + B) - (40 + .4\{A + B\})]$$
$$(4) \qquad C = C_A + C_B = 14 + .74(A + B)$$

Equation (4) thus gives us a relationship between aggregate consumption and aggregate income.

theory) tell us that the composition of many of our most useful aggregates is sufficiently stable or systematic to permit of meaningful aggregative theories and measurements.

Macroeconomics is aided by one further important principle—many variables that are extremely important for explaining individual behavior tend to "cancel out" when we deal with aggregates. This can be illustrated again by reference to the consumption-income relationship. Consumption behavior of the individual family depends not only on income but very importantly on many other things—for example, age of the family head; size of the family; the age of its automobile and other durable goods; whether it owns or rents its dwelling; the incidence of sickness, births, weddings, college-age children; and so on. To "explain" individual or small-group consumer expenditures we would need to include these variables and many more. But for the explanation of aggregate behavior many of these variables cancel out, at least in the short run. The age structure of the total population changes only very slowly, as does the percentage owning homes. Births, deaths, and sickness will this year alter the expenditure patterns of many families, but the incidence of these in the total population is quite predictable and stable; some families have obsolescent cars and furniture, but others have new, and so on. These variables cannot be totally overlooked in dealing with aggregate behavior, particularly when we deal with longer periods; but their importance at one time is slight, and they can frequently be safely ignored. This is one of the most significant of all of the advantages of macroeconomics. Economic behavior is invariably complex and multivariate; even in macroeconomics we shall find it necessary to include a number of variables; but we can usually deal safely with systems involving fewer variables than are relevant for microeconomic theory.

In particular, much of microeconomics has to do with relative prices of different goods and services. Higher prices for one good both attract resources to its production, and cause buyers to transfer their purchases in other directions. It is the fluctuation of these price relationships that mold and alter the structure of resource use. But it is always *relative* prices that are the concern—price of good A relative to prices of goods B, C, D, etc.; the wage rate in firm or industry A relative to that paid elsewhere; the price of the services of a factor of production (affecting factor income) relative to the prices which the income recipient must pay for particular consumer goods or consumer goods in general; and so on. But, again, the effects of relative prices may largely cancel out in dealing with the economy as a whole. If one price rises relative to others, other prices have fallen relative to the first. If one industry or product has gained or lost customers or resources in response to a change in relative prices, another has lost or gained, in a way which may leave the aggregate magnitudes largely unaffected. Yet it is these internal changes which are of basic concern in microeconomics.

This is not to say that relative prices do not have relevance in macroeconomics, although most macroeconomic theory has up to now largely neglected them.[8] But, at least as a first approximation, the neglect of relative prices—which are the cornerstone of microeconomic analysis—can be justified. Since any price is relative not only to prices in general, but often significantly to many other individual prices, neglect of relative prices at one stroke reduces tremendously the number of variables with which macroeconomics must deal.

In short, then, macroeconomic theory can meaningfully exist, at least as a first approximation of reality: (a) because it can rely upon certain macroeconomic truisms; (b) because the composition of many aggregates is relatively stable, or varies systematically with changes in the magnitudes of the aggregates; (c) because many of the variables most significant in explaining individual economic behavior, including particularly relative prices, at least roughly cancel out when dealing with the whole economy. This is not, however, the last that we shall have to say on these matters.

[8] For examples of concern with relative prices see: A. P. Lerner, "The Relation of Wage Policies and Price Policies," reprinted from *American Economic Review* in *Readings in the Theory of Income Distribution* (Selected by a Committee of the American Economic Association), Blakiston Co., 1946, pp. 314–29; and G. Ackley and D. B. Suits, "Relative Price Changes and Aggregate Consumer Demand," *American Economic Review*, XL (December 1950), 785–804.

# National Income and National Product

*Chapter II*

Two of the most significant variables in macroeconomic analysis are national income and national product. These variables measure the total performance of an economy better than do any others. Hence it is essential to understand what these concepts are, and something about how they may be measured. It is even more important, however, to understand what lies behind these totals—to see how national income and product grow out of and are related to the diverse productive activities taking place in business firms, governmental units, and households; and to understand how the figures for national income and national product rest upon figures in the individual accounts and then in the consolidated sector accounts of the various units that make up the economy.

A grasp of the general concepts of social accounting is essential to the understanding of macroeconomic theory. The "macroeconomic truisms," referred to in the last chapter, derive largely from the social accounts. Practical applications of macroeconomic theory to problems of forecasting, fiscal policy, or even to a detailed understanding of economic history, will require more intimate acquaintance with income and product concept and measurement. Since this book deals primarily with theory, some of the finer details of concept and measurement will be omitted. The student who is interested in national income concepts and measurement will find a large and rapidly growing literature.[1] This book makes no pretense at

[1] The best recent general treatments of the theory of national income and product accounting include: C. S. Shoup, *Principles of National Income Analysis* (Houghton Mifflin, 1947); H. C. Edey and A. T. Peacock, *National Income and Social Accounting* (Hutchinson's University Library, 1954); J. P. Powelson, *Economic Accounting*

covering the subject exhaustively. Even some of the major theoretical issues are barely touched upon here.

Our procedure in this chapter is, first, to develop the general concepts of national income and national product. Second we see how these concepts are related to each other in a hypothetical simple economy in which all economic activity goes through the market place (there is no production in households or government—indeed, no government exists), and in which there are no international transactions of any kind. In the following chapter, we see how national income and product are related, and how they might be defined and measured, in a complex economy like that of the United States.

As indicated, we might, if our interest were in the pure theory only, stop short of this last step. However, a more detailed understanding of the accounts is necessary even for the relatively simple applications which we shall want to make to problems of policy. Further, a knowledge of the accounts will prove useful in many other kinds of economic analysis, quite unrelated to the problems we shall discuss. Indeed, there is scarcely a problem in economics which cannot be illuminated through use of the data provided by our modern social accounts. Consequently, no serious student of economics should fail to acquire a reasonable familiarity with the structure of these accounts, the concepts used, what kinds of data are available and for what periods, and some idea of the statistical sources and reliability of the estimates. Chapter III provides an introduction to these useful tools, but no more than that. It is written largely in terms of the concepts used in the official United States income and product accounts, and no attention at all is paid to the sources of the data or the means of estimate.

## THE CONCEPT OF NATIONAL INCOME

We may define an individual's income as the amount of his earnings from the productive services currently rendered by him or by his property. National income is nothing more than the sum of all individual incomes. Income is obviously a flow concept, measured, in practice, by recording and summing the individual income transactions occurring during a period of finite length.

Defining income as earnings distinguishes it from income receipts. In-

(McGraw-Hill, 1955), Chaps. 14–20; *A Critique of the United States Income and Product Accounts,* Studies in Income and Wealth, vol. 22, National Bureau of Economic Research (Princeton University Press, 1958), especially George Jaszi, "The Conceptual Basis of the Accounts: A Re-examination."

come may be earned during a period, but not received—either because it is taxed away before receipt or is somewhere retained, possibly to be paid (and received) at a later date. Income receipts may exceed income, either through delayed payment of past earnings in excess of current retentions, or through simple "transfer payments" which do not represent payment for productive services, past or present. (Relief payments or veterans' benefits are examples of "government transfer payments"; bad debts of consumers to business are a type of "business transfer payments"; gifts of goods or money among individuals are "interpersonal transfers.")

Income must clearly be distinguished from mere asset transformations. If I sell a house, a bond, or a patent right, the proceeds of sale are obviously not income. Or, if a debt is repaid, the amount of the repayment is not income. All that has happened is that one form of wealth (house, bond, patent right) has been transferred into another form— usually cash. On the other hand, the current flow of services from the house, interest from the bond, and royalties from the patent are income.

A special problem is presented by capital gains, arising from the sale of assets at prices higher than their purchase costs. This difference represents neither an asset transfer nor true income, except perhaps to the person who is in the business of buying and selling assets and whose ability to buy for less than he sells is the source of his livelihood. In theory, as well as in practice, the borderline between this case and the true capital gain (which is of the nature of a windfall) is hard to draw, but we need not become entangled here in this problem. The ordinary capital gain does not represent earnings from current productive services; hence it is not income.

Theoretically, we should deduct from gross earnings any costs which the individual incurs in order to permit the earning of his income: for the worker, the cost of tools which he must himself supply, union dues, travel to work; for the property owner, brokerage fees, bank charges, safe-deposit box rentals (to the extent that the box is used to keep securities rather than the family jewels). In practice few of these are deducted. The reason is that the borderline is impossible to draw clearly between outlays made in order to permit the earning of income and outlays which represent merely the use or enjoyment of income. Does not one incur travel expense to work at least in part because *as a consumer* he prefers to live at a distance from his place of employment? Suppose he chooses to live thirty miles in the country. Is the worker's union membership a purely economic or partly a social and political grouping? Should we then deduct his dues to social, political, or religious organizations, membership in some of which may also enhance his ability to earn? If cost of tools is to be deducted, why not work clothing—not only overalls but the bank president's Homburg? Where do we stop? In order to work one must be clothed; but also one must eat. Indeed, in order to be efficient, one must also have some entertainment and relaxation. This line of argument might soon have us concluding that all consumer expenditures—or at least some minimum subsistence budget—is part of the cost of earning, and should be deducted in computing net income. The convention we must adopt—indeed it is implicit in our basic Western code of values—is that we earn in order to consume, not consume in order to earn. Even in the light of this doctrine, we could perhaps distinguish certain minor classes of individual outlays (such as employees' purchase of tools) for deduction from income, but most national income accounting does not do so.

When we come to income earned from ownership of a business enterprise, however, outlays made in order to earn income are all-important, are fairly easily defined, and they must obviously be deducted. Business income is, of course, only one species of individual income—corporate profits are really the individual earnings of the stockholders. However, it is completely obvious that the gross receipts of a business are not the income of its owners. Unlike most consumer expenditures, most business outlays can clearly be said to be incurred in order to earn income. (Even here there are some ambiguities—e.g., in connection with operation of the family farm, which is often described as a way of life as much as a means of livelihood.) Thus, all national income estimators recognize that business expenses must be deducted in order to arrive at that part of national income which represents earnings (profits) from the ownership of enterprise.

Some of the specific problems connected with this calculation of profit income will be indicated below; for now, it is enough to recognize that national income is the sum of all (a) wages, salaries, commissions, bonuses, and other forms of employee earnings (before deduction of taxes or social security contributions); (b) net income from rentals and royalties; (c) interest income; and (d) profits, whether of a corporation, partnership, or proprietorship, whether paid out to owners or retained in the business, and before deduction of taxes based on income.

We can also subdivide national income by the sector in which it is earned: wages and salaries and supplements thereto, for instance, are paid by business firms; by governments; by private non-profit organizations; by households; by foreign or international residents, firms, or organizations. Each of these sectors could be further subdivided in any convenient way, e.g., the business sector by industry.

A concept related to national income is that of disposable personal income. This is, first, a receipts rather than an earnings concept, and it is computed after taxes have been deducted. Thus, to go from national income to disposable income we must add receipts which are not payments for current productive services (government and business transfer payments), and we must deduct both earnings not currently received and all taxes (social security contributions of employees and employers, corporate profits taxes and retained corporate earnings, and personal taxes). It is this figure that consumers can "dispose of"—spend as they choose or save.[2]

A third income concept is also used in the U.S. income accounts, namely "personal income." This is disposable income plus personal taxes, or current personal income receipts after social security contributions but before taxes. It is the only *monthly* income figure, and is available fairly promptly after the end of the month to which it relates. (Disposable income estimates are made quarterly, fairly soon after the end of the quarter; while national income and national product estimates are available only after a substantial lag.)

## THE CONCEPT OF NATIONAL PRODUCT

National product is the economy's total current output of goods and services, valued at the market prices they command. This is also a flow concept, measured in practice by accumulating transactions over a period of time.

The main difficulties in computing national product lie in the avoidance of double counting. We should not count as output the bread, the flour that went into the bread, the wheat that produced the flour, and the fertilizer that helped grow the wheat. Despite all the steps in the process, we end up only with bread—bread is the product, not bread plus flour plus wheat plus fertilizer. In other words, we want to count only "final products," excluding "intermediate products." Final products might be limited to consumer goods and goods sold to the government (collective consumption). In practice, however, we also include output of new capital goods as part of final output.

---

[2] Actually, this is somewhat misleading. The total after-tax income of unincorporated enterprises is included in disposable income; yet here, as in the corporation, there are retained earnings, sometimes even involuntarily retained. Further, the consumer's freedom to dispose is often severely limited by contractual arrangements (mortgages, life insurance policies, installment contracts, etc.).

There is much to be said for the idea that new capital goods are not final products. They are certainly not wanted for their own sake, but only to produce (directly or indirectly) other final products. The machine services which contribute to the production of bread are essentially like the flour. Machine methods are more productive than hand methods; therefore machinery is produced and used. But sooner or later this production of machines means that more bread will be produced than otherwise. Having counted the production of the bread, this argument would have it that we should not also count the production of machinery. Of course, machinery services are unlike flour in that the machine will render services over a period of years. What is produced this year in the form of a new machine is an instrument which will contribute to production of bread for many years to come. But this does not really make much difference. The value of the machine (or of the resources that went into the production of the machine) is sooner or later included in the value of the bread, and should not be counted in addition to the counting of the bread. In fact the value of the machine—and the resources that produced it—is *derived from* the value of the bread, in just the same sense as is the value of the flour.

The argument that we should not include capital goods in national product would be particularly convincing if (a) all production of capital goods merely went to replace other capital goods as they wore out, and if (b) this wearing-out occurred smoothly over time. Suppose, for example, that ten machines are used in bread-making, each machine lasting ten years, with one wearing out and being replaced each year. Here we can clearly see that the value of the bread includes the value of the machines in exactly the same way as it does the flour, and we should probably not even be tempted to count both bread and machines as final product. It would be clear that to do so would be double-counting of the same nature as adding bread and flour.

Of course, we rarely have so even a correspondence of wearing out and replacement. Suppose all ten machines wear out and must be replaced in a single year; then none for the next nine. If we count only bread as a final product, we will fail to recognize that in the tenth year, either the total production of the economy is in a real sense greater than in the other nine (if bread output is maintained constant, while machine production also occurs), *or* that any dip in bread output in the tenth year (if resources are diverted from bread-making to machinery-making) does not represent a real decline in production.

Even if all production of machinery were merely for replacement purposes, it would therefore give us a more accurate picture of the year-to-year trend of production if we were to add together the production of bread and the production of machinery. We would have to call this a *gross* national product, however, to recognize the element of double-counting. *Net* national product would deduct, each year, some allowance for the using up of machine services. In our simple and extreme example in which all machines wore out at once, the calculations would be as in Table 2–1 which follows (we assume bread output continues unchanged in the year of machine replacement):

**TABLE 2–1.  Hypothetical Gross and Net Products, Totals and by Years**

| Year | Bread Output | Machinery Output | Gross Product | Depreciation | Net Product |
|------|------|------|------|------|------|
| 1 | $200 | — | $200 | $40 | $160 |
| 2 | 200 | — | 200 | 40 | 160 |
| 3 | 200 | — | 200 | 40 | 160 |
| 4 | 200 | — | 200 | 40 | 160 |
| 5 | 200 | — | 200 | 40 | 160 |
| 6 | 200 | — | 200 | 40 | 160 |
| 7 | 200 | — | 200 | 40 | 160 |
| 8 | 200 | — | 200 | 40 | 160 |
| 9 | 200 | — | 200 | 40 | 160 |
| 10 | 200 | 400 | 600 | 40 | 560 |
| Ten-Year Total | $2000 | $400 | $2400 | $400 | $2000 |

It is clear that either the gross or net product column gives a better picture of the year-to-year movement of productive activity in the economy than does the measurement of bread output alone. It must, however, also be recognized that, taking the ten-year period as a whole, the sum of the bread output column is the same as the sum of the net product column. Sooner or later, counting the bread also counts the value of the machines.

In addition to the possible mere unevenness of replacement, account must also be taken of the permanent growth, over time, in the total stock of capital goods, through new production of plant and equipment in excess of replacement. One could still argue that the enlargement of the stock of capital goods would, sooner or later, contribute to an enlarged output of "true" final products, and that it is enough to count these final products if and when they emerge. But if net investment is usually positive (new production exceeds replacement) we are continually late in recognizing this if we wait for the final output to increase. More important, the well-known volatility in investment activity—and in the use of productive services in creating new capital—would not be reflected.

Thus almost all analysts prefer to say that gross product of a year is the output of "true" final goods, plus the production of new capital goods. Net product is the output of consumer and government goods, plus the *net increase in our stock of capital goods*—new production of capital goods in excess of replacement.

However, it must be recognized that in practice we have no measure of what capital goods are used for replacement of others which wear out or become obsolete. The best we can do is to subtract from gross national product the current bookkeeping allowances which are made for depreciation, in order to give us an approximation of net national product. Since the current allowances in no sense precisely measure "wearing out" or "using up," but only an arbitrary accounting provision therefor, net national product is also a somewhat arbitrary figure. The one thing we can rely on is that the total depreciation allowances taken with respect to any capital good will exactly equal its cost. Thus at some time (although not necesarily at precisely the right time) our net national product account will have shown a deduction which recognizes that the total value of the machine is included in the value of the final output. Even if not precise, we still get, in this way, a more accurate view of the year-to-year fluctuations of productive activity than we would if we merely measured final products exclusive of capital goods.

A problem closely related to the one just discussed has to do with inventory changes. Suppose that in some year we produce more wheat than we use in the production of flour (which is then used for bread). Our output this year can be said to include not only the final product, bread, but also the unused wheat. Again, we could have refused to count this extra wheat this year, reasoning that it would, another year, permit more bread to be made. Instead, we count as this year's product the final goods output plus the increase in inventories of intermediate goods (or less any inventory decrease: if we use up our first-of-year stock of intermediate goods in producing final goods, we choose to say that our output this year is the output of final goods less the decrease in inventories).

Since there can also be changes in inventories of *final* goods (if we sell more than we produce, or vice versa) we can equally well define national product as current *sales* of consumer, government, and capital goods, plus any increase in inventories either of final or intermediate goods. In fact, this is always the way we go about it. National product is measured as sales of final goods plus inventory increase.

One further adjustment remains. We may export some of this year's output (of intermediate as well as final goods). This obviously is part of our national product, and should be added to our domestic sales plus inventory increase. Likewise, we must take account of imported materials used in producing domestic products. A $100 suit of clothes made from British woolens does not represent $100 worth of U.S. production. We ought to deduct from the value of the suit the value of the cloth—this much is not part of our national product but rather of the British product. Instead, the usual practice is to deduct our imports from our exports. We count the full $100 of suit production as part of our domestic consumer goods final output, but we deduct the value of the cloth from the value of the tobacco we ship to Britain. The total national product is correct, although the breakdown is in this respect misleading.

We have argued above as though all national product were produced in business, and were therefore either sold or accumulated in business inventories. Actually we must recognize that production also occurs in government, of output which is not sold, but which nevertheless should properly be counted. Also, some production occurs in households, for household use. This, too, should be counted, although we shall see that there are serious problems of definition and of valuation in both government and household production. First, however, we shall consider the accounts for a hypothetical simple economy in which neither household nor government production occurs.

## NATIONAL INCOME AND PRODUCT IN A SIMPLIFIED MARKET ECONOMY

Our assumptions in this section are as follows:

1) Production occurs only in business firms;

2) The firms are individual proprietorships or partnerships—thus there is no possible distinction between net income of the firm and of its owners;

3) Businesses produce only what they sell and sell all that they produce. There are no changes in inventories of finished goods, raw materials, or work in process;

4) No government exists—there are no government expenditures, taxes, subsidies, or social insurance contributions;

5) The economy has no international economic relations—it is a "closed economy."

Since all production takes place in business firms, all national income is earned in the business sector. This consists of the wages and salaries (and other forms of employee compensation) paid; the contractual payments of interest, rents, and royalties for services of property; and the profits accruing to the owners of enterprises. These incomes can be thought of as constituting a flow from business to persons. This flow is shown on the right side of Figure 2–1.

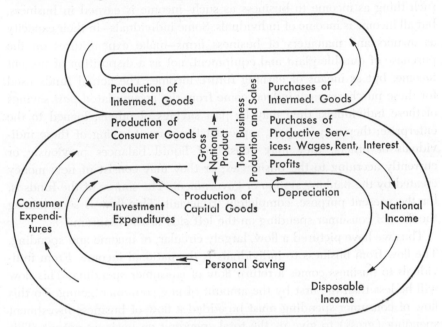

Figure 2–1.

Gross national product will likewise originate entirely in the business sector. It will consist of the value of the production of consumer goods plus the value of the production of capital goods. Since, by assumption, there is no change in inventories, production of these goods is identical with their sales. This identity of production and sales leads also to the concept of national product as expenditure. Gross national product then consists of consumer expenditures on (or purchases of) consumer goods from business, plus business' own purchases of new capital equipment.

Consumer purchases from business must obviously be made largely by means of and out of the incomes earned in business. Thus the flow of expenditure from consumers to business will constitute a return flow, comparable in size with the income flow from business to consumers. If the return flow of spending is identical in size with the income flow, consumers will be saving nothing; if the spending flow exceeds the income flow, consumers will be dissaving; if it is less than the income flow, it will indicate consumer saving in the amount of the difference. This flow is shown on the lower left side of the diagram.

The flow of spending on new capital goods is of a different sort. It does not come "out of" business income in any sense comparable to the relation of consumer spending to consumer income. Indeed, there is no such thing as income to business as such—income is earned in business, but all income is income of individuals. Some individuals—in their capacity as owners and managers of business firms—make expenditures on the purchase of durable plant and equipment, not as a disposition of present income, but as means of earning future income. The actual funds used for these purchases may indeed come from the accumulated *past* savings of these individuals; they may be past savings of others, loaned to the enterprise; they may, in part, represent the current saving of these individuals or others; they may consist of liquid balances previously or currently accruing to the businesses; or they may consist of new money created by the banking system or government. The source of the funds is, for the present purpose, completely irrelevant. This flow is seen joining the flow of consumer spending on the left side of the diagram.

Thus we have pictured a flow, largely circular, of income and spending. The flow from business to individuals is the national income. From individuals to business comes a return flow of consumer spending. This flow will be less than the first by the amount of any consumer saving. To this flow of consumer spending must be added a flow of business investment spending (gross) to give us the total spending on business output. This flow is the gross national product. We now have only to consider the relationship between the size of the business inflow of spending and the business outflow of income.

A little reflection will show that these two flows can differ only by the amount of depreciation charges. All that business "takes in" comes from the two types of final spending—on consumer and on capital goods. To be sure, individual firms also make sales to other business firms—of intermediate goods; the farmer sells wheat to the miller, the miller sells flour to the baker, the baker sells bread to the retailer. But these flows are entirely within the business sector; what is an inflow for one business is necessarily an outflow for another. This "loop" is shown on the top of the diagram. Only the purchases by consumers and the sale of new capital goods constitute a flow from without business into business.

Similarly, the net outflow from business consists only of incomes. Individual firms may purchase intermediate goods from other firms; but such purchases stay within the business sector. Finally, we must recognize that all that "comes in" to a business must also "go out" either as purchases from another firm or as income, except for the amount charged for depreciation. This relationship derives from the fact that *profit* is computed as a residual. Profit consists of the difference between revenues from sales and all costs. Costs in our simple model consist only of purchases of intermediate goods (which cancel out for the business sector as a whole), contractual incomes paid (wages, salaries, interest, royalties, etc.), and depreciation. The flow of sales into the business sector as a whole must equal the flow of incomes (contractual and residual) plus depreciation.

The relationships among these flows are summarized in the diagram. In this diagram the magnitudes of the several flows are measured by their widths. A measurement at the upper left of the circle—consumer plus capital goods spending—equals gross national product. A measurement on the right equals both net national product and national income. In this simple model it is clear that net product and national income are identical.

It can also be seen that the two reductions in the circular flow corresponding to depreciation allowances and personal saving must exactly equal the one augmentation of the flow through business investment in new capital goods. If we call the sum of depreciation and saving "gross saving," it is clear that it must equal gross investment. Or, net investment (gross investment less depreciation) must equal saving.

We can summarize this algebraically as:

(1) $$GNP \equiv C + GI$$

(2) $$NI \equiv GNP - D$$

(3) $$NI \equiv C + S$$

Where

$$GNP \equiv \text{gross national product}$$

$$C \equiv \text{consumer spending}$$

$$GI \equiv \text{gross investment (purchases of new capital goods)}$$

$$NI \equiv \text{national income}$$

$$D \equiv \text{depreciation}$$

and

$$S \equiv \text{personal saving}$$

The first equation merely says that total expenditure arises from and is equal to the spending of consumers on consumer goods and the purchases by business of capital goods. The second equation expresses the fact that total incomes are equal to the (gross) value of output less depreciation. The third equation shows that incomes are either spent or saved.

Substituting equation (3) into equation (2), and rearranging, gives us

(4)                              $$GNP \equiv C + S + D$$

Comparing equations (1) and (4) shows that $GI$ (gross investment) must equal $S + D$ (gross saving).

Or, we can substitute equation (1) into equation (2), giving us

$$NI \equiv C + GI - D$$

or

(5)                              $$NI \equiv C + I$$

where

$$I \text{ (net investment)} \equiv GI - D$$

Comparing equation (5) with equation (3) we can see the equality of (net) investment and (net) saving.[3]

When we simplify things to this point, we can almost convey verbally why it is that $S$ and $I$ must be equal. Equation (5) says that income arises from and is equal to the sum of consumer and investment spending. Equation (3) says that income is either consumed or saved. That income which arises from other than consumer spending (i.e., investment) must necessarily equal that income which is not spent on consumer goods (i.e., saving).

In this simplest of all possible formulations, one may perhaps be able to grasp, *in words*, the equality of saving and investment. When we complicate even to the extent of recognizing that "net investment" is not a kind of spending but only an abstraction, verbalization of the equality begins to escape us; and when we get to the complicated relationship which exists in a more nearly "real" world, no one can possibly explain in words why saving equals investment. But, as we shall see, it is just as

---

[3] The student may wish to prepare a diagram, like that on p. 33, or equations like those above for the slightly more complicated case in which some national product is not sold to consumers but is added to business inventories. Also, he may introduce imports (by consumers or business), and exports (by business).

unmistakably so in the real world as in this very simple world with which we have been dealing.

A good deal of macroeconomic theory uses or implies a set of social accounts no more complicated than that set forth above. Much, for example, of Keynes' *General Theory of Employment* implies this system of accounts, as does most other purely theoretical literature. The reason for using accounts which omit government is easy to understand. Economic theory traditionally deals with free-market, private behavior—the actions of households in earning and spending their incomes; and of businessmen in hiring factors, producing, and selling. All of these activities are oriented to the market and are affected by the market. Government actions—in taxing, borrowing, and spending—are not market-determined. Government decisions are made by a political process. This process is studied by another branch of social science—political science.

To be sure, government action is increasingly becoming market oriented, in the sense that taxing, spending, borrowing, and lending decisions are tempered or even dictated by a desire to offset or prevent market results that fail to conform to certain social standards. But in order to know what government action may be called for in order to achieve desired social ends, one must first understand the market forces operating by themselves. Hence it is often useful to assume an economy with no government, and this is what the pure theory usually does. An economy with no government has very simple accounts: national product (net) equals national income. If we further assume no corporations, national income and product also equal disposable income.

But when we desire to test theoretical generalizations against the facts, or to apply theoretical solutions to practical situations, we must work within the framework of a society in which government—and the corporate form—are extremely important. In this context we need to work with social accounts far more complex than those we have so far developed. Since we shall want both to test our theories against the data, and to apply them to a few concrete problems of policy, we must learn more about social accounts of the real world. These are the subject of Chapter III.

# The United States National Income and Product Accounts [1]

*Chapter III*

We have now reviewed the concepts of national income and national product, gross and net. We have considered the relationships among these concepts in a highly simplified economy, but only by implication has there been any discussion of how one might go about measuring either income or product. In the succeeding sections we shall consider how we might measure product and income originating in the business, government, household, and rest-of-world sectors of an actual economy. In the process, we will not only discover the relationship between income and product in such an economy, but also set up a system of national accounts which will trace the principal economic flows among the major segments or sectors of the economy. We begin with the accounts of the business sector. This is the sector in which most output and income originate. It also provides most of the complexities of measurement.

[1] The material in this chapter is largely based upon the present practices of the United States Department of Commerce, which estimates and publishes official national income and product data for the United States. The methodology of the Department is fully explained in two basic publications, which should be owned by every economics student. *National Income, 1954 edition,* discusses in detail the basic concepts and methodology underlying the estimates, and presents basic data from 1929 through 1953. *U.S. Income and Product* (published in November, 1958) presents revised estimates beginning with 1946 and extending through 1957. More important, it presents a number of entirely new and important breakdowns of product and income, embodies several conceptual changes, and brings the methodological and statistical discussion up to date. See also the interesting *The National Economic Accounts of the United States: Review, Appraisal, and Recommendations,* by National Accounts Review Committee (National Bureau of Economic Research, 1958).

## THE BUSINESS PRODUCT AND INCOME ACCOUNT

In the latest revision of the U.S. income and product accounts, a summary table for the "business sector" no longer appears. The dropping of this sector account can be defended on grounds of simplification, but a loss is also involved. As the authors of *U.S. Income and Product* admit, "The business account eliminated here is useful as a conceptual bridge relating national production and its accounting to their business analogues." [2] Since we are particularly interested in establishing this "conceptual bridge," we retain the business sector account in our presentation.

Conceptually, we can derive all of the data necessary for our business income and product account through a manipulation and consolidation of the ordinary profit and loss or income statements of business firms. A profit and loss statement has the primary purpose of telling the owners of a business how much profit (or loss) was made during a particular period. Its basic form involves three headings: (a) gross revenues from sales plus other "nonoperating" income; (b) cost of goods sold; and (c) profit [equals (a) minus (b)]. Since (a)—sales—equals the sum of (b)—costs—plus (c)—profit—we can set up a two-column, balanced account involving revenues on one side (the right) and costs and profits on the other (left).

$$\left.\begin{array}{c} \text{Cost-of-goods-sold} \\ plus \\ \text{Profit} \end{array}\right\} \quad equals \quad \left\{\begin{array}{c} \text{Sales} \\ plus \\ \text{Other income} \end{array}\right.$$

What we now proceed to do is to break down each of these items into its possible subcategories in a way which will facilitate our further manipulations. These breakdowns are made in accordance with a standard accounting form, as follows:

*Cost of goods sold:*
  purchased materials and services:
    from other domestic businesses
    from abroad
  wages and salaries and
    supplements thereto
  depreciation
  taxes (except on profits)
  interest paid
  bad debts and contributions

*Sales:*
  to persons
  to other domestic
    businesses
  to government
  to abroad
*Other income:*
  interest received
  dividends received
  subsidies

[2] *Op. cit.*, p. 51.

*Profit*
    corporate profit:
        corporate profits taxes
        retained earnings
        dividends
    *or:* proprietors' income
    *or:* rental income of persons

The breakdown of sales on the right is by type of purchaser. By defining each type sufficiently broadly we can put every buyer in one of these four classes. The breakdown of costs on the left is by object rather than on some functional basis; a functional category like "factory overhead" or "advertising expense" can always be redivided into such items as wages and salaries, depreciation, and purchases. A three-way breakdown of profit is appropriate if the firm is a corporation. If it is a partnership or proprietorship, we use the heading "proprietors' income" or "rental income of persons." The latter is the heading used for the "profit" share when it arises from the rental of real estate by a person for whom this is merely an incidental source of income. (A corporation which rents property earns "corporate profits"; an unincorporated business having property rental as a principal source of net income earns "proprietors' income.") These noncorporate profit incomes are not subdivided, because such enterprises make no formal division between business saving and disbursement of profit to owners; and taxes paid on these incomes are treated as personal taxes.

The first thing to note about this statement is that the costs listed do not represent, in all cases, the *outlays made* on the various object headings in the course of the period. Rather they are the *costs assignable to the sales* of the period. The difference between these two concepts involves, first, capital goods, and, second, inventory change.

When men are hired to work on construction of new facilities, or when new capital equipment is purchased, we do not enter these outlays under "wages and salaries" or "purchased materials." Rather, we enter in this period's accounts only a bookkeeping assignment of a portion of previously incurred costs for the construction or acquisition of capital goods, an entry called "depreciation." The methods of spreading original cost over useful life vary, but one important principle governs: the sum of the allocations to individual periods must precisely equal the original cost less scrap value—no more, no less. If the machine is still in use after its entire original cost has been "written off," no further entries of depreciation are made. So far as the books are concerned, the current services of that machine are free. If the machine has to be junked or replaced before its full cost has been written off, the remaining cost (less scrap value) is usually entered as a cost in the last year of its service life. (In each of these cases it would be possible, at the end of the useful life of an asset, to recalculate its annual cost and revise the previously reported profits or losses of all the previous years; but this is simply not practicable.)

The second difference between the actual outlays of a period and what is called cost of goods sold arises in connection with changes in inventories. Suppose, for instance, that in some period there was no production—no wages were paid nor materials used—but goods were sold (from previous inventory). We do not want to call the entire sales proceeds profits; rather we wish to charge wages previously paid and materials previously purchased as costs of these sales. Or, if we produce during this period more output than we sell—to make an extreme case, we sell nothing—we do not wish our accounts to show that we necessarily made heavy losses. Consequently, we show as costs not the current *outlays* on labor and materials, but rather outlays chargeable to this period's sales. Inventory changes need not be only in finished goods; they may consist of raw materials or goods in process. The treatment is nevertheless basically the same. If we buy a two years' supply of a raw material this year, we do not charge it all against this period's sales; we charge only that which was "used" in producing the goods sold this year.

Although the particular accounting methods of handling this problem vary, in effect they all involve a cost-of-goods-sold figure which consists of the actual *outlays* during this period, *less any increase in the value of inventories* (or plus any reduction in inventories).

The first change we wish to make in the accounts is to make this inventory adjustment show up explicitly, in order to convert the account from a *sales and cost-of-goods account* to a *production and current outlays account*. We do this by adding any inventory increase to both sides of the account. On the right-hand side, this gives us a new entry: "inventory increase" (which may, of course, be negative); on the left-hand side, the heading "cost-of-goods-sold" becomes merely "current outlays." Current outlays will be larger than cost-of-goods-sold if inventories have increased and vice versa. But both sides of the account have changed by the same amount, and the totals remain equal. (The student should set up in his notes an account in the form shown on page 39–40, and actually perform this manipulation and the others that will be decribed below.)

Further manipulations require that we consolidate into one grand account all of the individual firm accounts that have now been prepared in the form indicated.

Before we do this, however, it is necessary to call attention to two kinds of business firms whose (imaginary) accounts are also consolidated. The first such "firm" is the owner of the owner-occupied house, who is conceived to sell to himself, as occupant, the services of his house. Each such firm has an imaginary account in the standard form:

Wages, etc.                                                            Sales:   to persons
Purchased materials and services
Depreciation
Interest
Taxes
Rental income of persons

Sales, in this case, is an estimated *gross rental value* of the owner-occupied house, based on comparable rents for tenant-occupied houses. Wages and purchased materials are actual outlays for maintenance and upkeep; depreciation is based on original cost and estimated life; taxes (property taxes) and interest (on mortgage) are the actual outlays of the owner-occupant; while rental income is the imputed net difference between the imputed rental value and the actual and imputed costs. These individual—if imaginary—profit and loss accounts are treated exactly as any other accounts in the consolidation and further manipulations which we are now about to discuss.

The second unusual kind of "firm," the accounts for which are included in the business sector, is the *government enterprise.* A government enterprise is an activity or agency of local or central government which is engaged in the production of goods or services and their sale at prices which at least roughly cover their cost. This definition is not entirely precise, but in practice, the line is not hard to draw. The state university is not a government enterprise because its tuition docs not come close to covering its costs. The Federal Post Office is such an enterprise, despite its deficit of hundreds of millions of dollars. Municipal power plants, water, or sewage systems; state toll highways; and Federal lending, transportation, or insurance activities are clear examples.[3]

The reasons for including the activities of these enterprises in the

[3] For a list of 47 Federal agencies so classified, see *National Income, 1954 Edition,* p. 66, footnote 6 to Exhibit 1.

business sector are indicated at a later point. Here we are only interested in understanding their accounting treatment. This treatment—in the U.S. accounts—is extremely rudimentary. The accounts of each government enterprise can be organized in a modified version of the standard form, as follows:

| | |
|---|---|
| Wages, etc. | Sales: to persons |
| Purchased materials and services | to other domestic businesses |
| Current surplus of government enterprises | to government |
| | to abroad |

The obvious deficiency of this account is its lumping together in a "current surplus" of what would be depreciation, interest, taxes, and profit in a business firm. If records were more adequate, a further breakdown of this item could be estimated. In a socialist economy, in which such enterprises were more important, a breakdown would be mandatory. For the United States this treatment is adequate for most purposes, in view of the relative insignificance of such enterprises.

For each firm, including the two special kinds just discussed, there will have been entries under some or all of the individual headings in our standard accounting form on page 39–40, or one of the variants appearing above. We now aggregate all of the entries which have been made under each heading, giving us a single consolidated account, which has consolidated entries under each of the standard headings. The totals at the foot of each column of the consolidated account will, of course, still be equal. On the right-hand side of this consolidated account we are now approaching the gross national product concept; we have all "business" sales plus the aggregate inventory increase of all business (plus "other income," which we shall soon eliminate). But the total far exceeds business gross national product because it includes all sales of intermediate goods: the farmer's sale of wheat to the flour mill is there, along with the mill's sale to the bakery, the bakery's sale to the retail store, and the retailer's sale to the consumer. We want to eliminate all except the last of these.

All except the last of these transactions also appear on the left side of the account under "purchases from other domestic business." When the farmer sold to the mill, this went into the farmer's sales (to other business), but the identical entry also went into the mill's purchases (from other business). Now that we have consolidated, the totals of these intermediate transactions necessarily become equal on both sides of the account. No individual firm is likely to sell to other businesses the same amount as it buys from other businesses. But for all firms combined the totals must be equal because they are the same transactions looked at from opposite sides.

Thus, we can immediately strike something close to a business gross national product account by eliminating from both sides the identical total of interfirm sales of intermediate goods. This completely eliminates the entry on the left side: "purchased materials and services: from other domestic businesses." But does it also completely eliminate the item on the right-hand side, "sales to other domestic businesses?" A moment's reflection will show that it does not. This entry actually consists of two parts, only one of which cancels out against the item on the left. These two parts are: (1) sales of *intermediate goods* to other domestic businesses, and (2) sales of *capital goods* to other domestic businesses. From the standpoint of the seller, there is no distinction. But the *buyer* had entered as "Purchased materials and services"—to be currently charged off against sales—only the noncapital goods. Purchase of capital goods never gets directly into the profit-and-loss account; rather, the current charge against sales in computing profit takes the form of a depreciation allowance.

Thus, after our cancellation, there remains on the right side: "Sales to business on capital account."

A few further subtractions from both sides gives us an account which will add up to gross national product originating in business.

The first adjustment subtracts from both sides the value of materials purchased abroad. On the left, this is done by eliminating the remaining item of purchased materials and services: "from abroad." On the right, this item as such does not appear. As indicated above (on p. 32) we subtract business' imports from its exports, making the heading now read "Sales: net to abroad."

Except for "Other Income," we now have, on the right, the business gross national product, consisting of the sales of "true" final goods (consumer and government goods), sales of capital goods, net sales abroad, and the increase in inventories (which picks up the goods—of all types—produced but not sold).

We get rid of "Other Income" very simply: (1) subtract interest received by business from interest paid by business—the item on the left now represents the net interest payments by business to nonbusiness; (2) subtract dividends received by business from dividends paid, leaving net dividends paid; (3) enter subsidies as a negative item on the left side.

We can now rearrange the items which remain on the left side in a way which separates the income from the nonincome items. With some changes in nomenclature, our table now appears as follows (if the student has performed all of the manipulations as they have been described, he should be able to reconcile fully his account with Table 3–1 below):

**TABLE 3–1. Consolidated Business Income and Product Account**

| | |
|---|---|
| *National income originating in business:* | *Consolidated net sales:* |
| Compensation of employees | to persons |
| Wages and salaries | to government |
| Supplements ᵃ | to abroad |
| Net interest | to business on capital |
| Net dividends | account |
| Corporate undistributed profits | |
| Corporate profits tax liability | *Increase in inventories* |
| Proprietors' income | |
| Rental income of persons | |
| *Adjustments to market price:* | |
| Indirect business tax liability ᵇ | |
| Business transfer payments ᶜ | |
| Current surplus of government | |
| enterprises | |
| Less: subsidies | |
| *Net national product originating in* | |
| *business* (subtotal) | |
| *Depreciation* | |

| | |
|---|---|
| *Charges against business gross* | *Business gross product* |
| *product* (total) | (total) |

ᵃ Supplements include employer contribution to social insurance, employer contributions to private pension and welfare funds, and miscellaneous kinds of "other labor income."

ᵇ All business taxes not based upon business profits. This includes, of course, all real estate taxes, even those paid by owner-occupants. Also included are minor nontax liabilities.

ᶜ Includes bad debts (interbusiness bad debts cancel out; this leaves net bad debts by persons to business), charitable contributions by business, prizes, etc.

It is clear from the above account that for the business sector gross national product equals national income plus certain "adjustments," and plus depreciation. Or, net national product equals national income plus the adjustments.

National income and net national product can be seen to be two different ways of measuring the results of business' productive activity. To the extent that the adjustment items exist—indirect business taxes, transfer payments, etc.—these measures are numerically different, although both relate to the same activity. The one measurement—on the product side— is a measurement based on the prices at which products are sold. When we add up national product, we add up sales prices at which goods were sold. The other measurement—national income—expresses the results of productive activity in terms of the earnings of factors of production. Indeed some prefer to say that we have only one concept, called national income or national product indifferently, but valued alternatively "at market prices" or "at factor cost." National income (or product) at factor cost is what we have simply called "national income"; national income (or product) at market prices is what we have simply called "national product."

Having traced their derivation from the profit and loss account we can easily see why these measures, whatever we call them, will be different. Despite our consolidation, cancellations, and adjustments, the right-hand side of our account can still be thought of as essentially a consolidated sales figure. It represents a flow of dollars into business firms in payment for goods produced. After certain deductions are made, these total proceeds from sales are available to be paid or attributed as earnings or incomes of the participating factors of production. Such incomes are contractual—in the case of wages or interest—or, in the case of profit, residual. Since one is residual, their sum must, by definition, exhaust the total to be paid or attributed. The sales proceeds exceed the incomes only because (1) some part of the sale price of goods is represented by a bookkeeping charge called *depreciation*—which is income to no one, but which must be deducted, along with the contractual incomes, before profit appears; (2) some part of the sale price of goods is represented by *taxes* which business must pay; (3) some part of sale price is represented by payments (or losses) which are labeled *transfers* rather than income because productive services are not provided in return; and (4) in the case of goods sold by government enterprises, there is a gap (positive or negative) between selling prices (less intermediate purchases) and factor costs (wages) which is not the earnings of any factor of production.[4] The prices at which goods are sold must be high enough—in relation to prices of factors—to absorb these four charges. (If taxes must be paid

---

[4] Some part of this might correspond to the interest and profit of an ordinary business, and could be attributed as earnings of an unidentified factor of production: government or the people collectively. We do not know how much of it should be so treated, and we choose to recognize in the accounts only factor incomes which correspond to what natural individuals can recognize as their own incomes. In a socialist economy, it would be different.

by business, prices will either have to be higher for what business sells, or incomes must be lower.) On the other hand, to the extent that *subsidies* are paid, either selling prices could be lower or factor prices higher than in their absence. Subsidies, then, reduce the gap between national product and national income, and could, theoretically, even make it negative.

This relationship of national income and product, we can see, does not represent any economic tendency or "law"; it is simply true by definition. It is the residual character of profit that kept the individual firm accounts in balance; this residual definition of profit also keeps the consolidated account in balance, despite all of the adjustments; it therefore is responsible for the definitional character of the relationship between national income and product.

Discussion of three further problems in the business sector—*imputations*, the *inventory valuation adjustment*, and *capital consumption allowances* (other than depreciation)—is postponed to a later point.

## PRODUCT AND INCOME IN GOVERNMENT

We can organize our discussion of national product and income originating in government around the simple statement of government receipts and expenditures which appears in Table 3–2 below. This is a consolidated statement, netting out all transactions among various levels of government. The social insurance funds are likewise consolidated with

TABLE 3–2.   Government Receipts and Expenditures Account

| | |
|---|---|
| Purchases of goods and services:<br>   from business<br>   from abroad<br>   wages, salaries, and supplements<br>Transfer payments:<br>   to persons<br>   foreign<br>Net interest paid<br>Subsidies<br>Less: current surplus of government enterprises<br>Surplus or deficit (—) on income and product account | Taxes:<br>   personal tax receipts<br>   corporate profits tax accruals<br>   indirect business tax accruals<br>Contributions for social insurance:<br>   employer<br>   personal |
| Government outlays<br>  and surplus (total) | Government receipts<br>  (total) |

other government accounts. This statement omits all transactions in existing assets (government purchase or sale of land or buildings). Government lending transactions are also excluded from the account, as are
the current accounts of government enterprises. However, the purchases
of capital goods by the government enterprises, and the interest payments on any obligations of these enterprises, are included in the
general government budget on the expenditure side. The current surplus
of these enterprises constitutes a source of government revenues. However
it is entered as a negative item on the expenditure side, instead.

Most of the entries in this account need no explanation. The surplus
or deficit item, on the left, is simply a balancing item, designed exactly
to reconcile the other items of receipts with the expenditures. Because
of many peculiarities of definition (a few already suggested), this surplus (or deficit) does not correspond either with the ordinary concept
of budget surplus or with the surplus in the so-called "cash budget."
Thus it is expressly labeled "surplus or deficit on income and product
account." It can easily be reconciled with either of the former concepts,
however.

Purchases from business, on the left, are obviously the same item as
sales to government in the business account. This duplication of an item
in the business account also holds true of the corporate profits tax and
indirect business tax entries on the right. Transfer payments to persons
include the outpayments of the social insurance funds, as well as direct
relief, veterans' benefits, etc. Foreign transfer payments consist of net *cash*
transfers abroad; transfers of currently purchased *goods* are not included,
and, of course, loans and repayments are disregarded. The interest paid
item is net—that is, interest received by government has been deducted,
as in the case of business.

One peculiarity of the government account which needs to be noted
is that the time periods to which the several entries relate are not the
same. For example, the entry for corporate profits taxes represents the
taxes currently accrued on this year's income, not the actual payments
which the government receives this year, which will be based, in part, on
the previous year's income. The current accrual is, of course, the figure
that is relevant for, and appeared in, the business sector account. Yet,
in the case of personal taxes, the current receipts figure is used. This
seems to presume that the figure which is relevant for consumer behavior is that representing current payments, not currently accruing
liabilities (to the extent that these differ). Other items in the government account are not on a current cash basis: for example, government

purchases are entered in the year of delivery of goods to the government (which is the date at which their sale is recognized by business) although payment may fall in the following year.[5]

These timing differences—as well as the exclusion, already noted, of certain kinds of transactions—prevent this account from serving as a cash account, and the deficit or surplus from representing the net absorption or release of money by government.

Other breakdowns of many of these items are, of course, possible. For example, taxes and purchases can be broken down as among Federal, state, and local. Or, expenditures can be broken down on a functional basis, or as among durables, nondurables, services, and construction.

The government sector account is not designed to give, as a *total*, the government's contribution either to national product or income. That would be possible, but only through consolidations and "nettings-out" which would sacrifice useful detail. Since government product (largely services) is not sold, it obviously does not show up on the receipts side, as was the case of business product. Nevertheless, it is clear that at least some activities of government are truly productive and should be included in the national product. But which activities? And how should they be valued?

With respect to the first question, most economists would agree in principle with Professor Simon Kuznets—who has stressed the point [6]— that many government services can best be thought of as intermediate goods: these services contribute to output which has already been counted in the business sector, but are not themselves final products. Unfortunately, no thoroughly satisfactory criterion has yet been suggested for this distinction, and, to date, no U.S. national product estimates recognize it.[7] For purposes of international comparisons of economic welfare, or comparisons in one country over periods of time long enough for the scope of government activity to have materially changed, this may constitute a serious limitation. Its importance for income theory— particularly short-run theory—is, however, probably slight. Thus, at least in practice, our first question is answered: all general government services are treated as part of final output.

---

[5] In general, the business sector account is consistently on an accrual basis, the personal account on a cash basis; this means that the government account—which reflects entries from each of the others—will necessarily be on a mixed basis.

[6] For a brief treatment, see his *National Income: A Summary of Findings* (National Bureau of Economic Research, 1946), pp. 131–133, and the reference there given.

[7] To be sure, those services which government *sells* to business, at a price related to cost, have been treated as intermediate goods by virtue of the inclusion of government enterprises in the business sector.

But how shall they be valued? Since they are not sold, and there is no basis for imputing a market price to them, they must be valued at cost. In the official U.S. national product accounts, this cost is labor cost only; nothing more. To be sure, the goods and services which government purchases from business for public use are valued at market prices. But these have already been counted as part of the business product. No "value added" is recognized by their employment in the rendering of government services, except to the extent of labor costs incurred in government. Thus the contribution of public school education to national product is valued at the salaries paid to teachers, janitors, and administrators. (The materials, supplies, and equipment, if purchased from business, are, however, in the national product as final products of the business sector.) One could argue that public school education is "worth" more than this; if it were provided by a profit-making business firm, it might be sold—i.e., the market might value it—at a price in excess of the public cost.

However, the attempt to impute a hypothetical "market value" to government services is doomed to failure. The very reason that education is a public function is (at least in part) that society has determined that this function could not be satisfactorily provided by private business. This is even more true of such governmental functions as preservation of order, public health, national defense, or provision of roads. By the very nature of its status as a government service no analogy with a market price charged by private business is possible.

It might, however, be possible to measure the cost of government output in a more inclusive way, making its valuation more comparable to the valuations used for private output. The Appendix to this chapter discusses some of the problems of valuation, and suggests a possible improvement in the method of valuing government output.

Thus *national product* (gross and net) originating in government, as now officially measured, consists of wages, salaries, and supplements paid to government employees.

One might suppose that *national income* originating in government would include the above items of "earnings," plus the interest payments made to holders of government bonds. Whatever is the productive service rendered by the owner of a private bond (variously described in economic theory as "abstinence," "waiting," or "sacrifice of liquidity") which entitles his return to be said to be "earned," he surely performs exactly the same service when he holds a public bond. In the private case, however, his return is paid for out of additional production; in the public case, it may or may not be. The private borrower must see the opportunity for profitable use of the funds he borrows before he assumes the interest charge—must see, in other words, the opportunity to increase his returns by more than his costs. A share of this surplus he pays as interest. Even if his forecast should be wrong—and earnings prove insufficient to cover the interest payments—still, the inclusion of interest on this unproductive use of funds is merely offset in the national income by a negative profit figure.

Governments sometimes borrow funds for productive investment purposes, in which case the interest payments can in some very real sense be said to be paid out of additional production, and thus "earned." However, there can be no identification of government borrowing (interest payments) and productive public investment. Productive public investment is often financed from current tax revenues; in this case there are no interest payments that might represent earnings on government capital. More important, we know that borrowing not only can be used, but in fact typically is used, to finance unproductive deficits—mostly those associated with war. In no sense can it be said that war creates additional production out of which government interest can be paid.

National income originating in government is thus measured as being identical with national product—i.e., wages, salaries, and supplements paid. Interest is not included.[8]

The reasons for treating the government enterprise as part of the business sector should now be clear. Unlike the product of general government, its output is sold, and can be measured by a market-registered sale value rather than by an incomplete accounting of cost. Materials purchased by such enterprises should not be treated as final products of the business sector (as would be the case if the enterprises were included in general government); and the sales of such enterprises to regular business firms should be treated as intermediate rather than final products. Although the absence of depreciation accounts and interest payments for the government enterprises makes the procedure still quite imperfect, it is obviously a better procedure than to include the government enterprises with general government.

---

[8] Since the government interest payments are shown on a *net* basis, the deduction is somewhat less than the gross total of government interest payments. In effect, interest payments by business to government are treated as merely "passing through" government on their way to households, and are included in the national income. For further explanation of the rather puzzling treatment of interest in the national accounts, see below, pp. 53–4.

## PRODUCT AND INCOME IN HOUSEHOLDS

The principal matter which needs special explanation in connection with the personal sector account is the definition of this sector. It includes not only households in the usual sense of the term, but also nonprofit institutions serving consumers, such as nongovernmental but nonprofit schools, colleges, and hospitals; voluntary associations, such as churches, country clubs, and "funds" (like the Red Cross); trust funds benefiting consumers; and private pension and welfare funds. When the institution (e.g., the hospital) pays wages and buys supplies, these are treated as personal consumption expenditures. The charges made by the private nonprofit hospital, as well as the gifts it receives from private households to cover its deficit, are treated as interpersonal transfers, and never appear in the account (gifts from business, however, appear as business transfer payments). When a private pension or welfare fund makes payments to its beneficiaries, these, too, are treated as interpersonal transfers and never show in the accounts. However, when an employer pays into the fund, this is treated as personal income ("supplements to wages and salaries"); likewise, the interest on the fund's investments is treated as personal income at the time it is earned by the fund. These peculiarities of definition of the personal sector can be defended (that is, if we are limited in the number of sectors we can recognize); but they need to be remembered by the user, if he is not to be misled.

The form of the personal account appears in Table 3–3 below. Like the government account, it is not constructed to show national product or national income as a total. Instead it shows the sources and disposition of aggregate household income.

Most of the items have previously been encountered in the business or government accounts. One important new item is wages, salaries, and supplements paid in households, which appears both on the right as a personal receipt, and on the left as a personal expenditure. Another new item is "personal saving"—a residual item, in the amount necessary to balance the two sides of the account. Since personal income includes the entire earnings of unincorporated enterprises, personal saving includes unincorporated business saving. Since consumption expenditures do not include purchase of new houses (these are treated as sales to business on capital account) any payments out of income for such purchases will be included in personal saving. There are other peculiarities of definition that keep personal saving from corresponding exactly to the simple concept that this heading might normally bring to mind. Nevertheless, it does measure the increase in the net worth—the assets less liabilities—of the household sector, as that sector is defined in the accounts.

TABLE 3–3.   Personal Income and Outlay Account

| | |
|---|---|
| Personal consumption expenditures:<br>    purchases from business<br>    wages, salaries, & supplements<br>    purchases abroad<br>    interest paid<br>Personal taxes<br>Personal saving | Wages, salaries, and supplements<br>    from: business<br>            government<br>            households<br>            abroad<br>    less:   employee and employer<br>                social insurance con-<br>                tributions<br>Rental income of persons<br>Proprietors' income:<br>    business and professional<br>    farm<br>Dividends<br>Personal interest income<br>Government transfer payments<br>Business transfer payments |
| Personal Outlay and Saving (total) | Personal Income (total) |

A few words are necessary to explain the treatment of interest in the personal account. On the receipts side appears an entry "personal interest income." On first encounter one might suppose that this represented the sum of the two items of interest outpayments already encountered in business and government sectors, plus, perhaps, any interest payments made entirely within the household sector. It is the latter payments that one might suppose were shown on the left or payments side of the personal account, as "interest paid." Both surmises would be incorrect. To see why, consider the following simple numerical example. (This discussion ignores interest from abroad, since we have not yet reached the rest-of-world sector; however, the principles here set forth can very easily be expanded to include that sector.)

### BUSINESS SECTOR

| Payments of interest | |
|---|---|
| to households | 70 |
| to government | 20 |
| to business | 100 |
| total | 190 |

Receipts of interest
    from households          25
    from government      35
    from business        100
    total                       160
Net interest payments                     30

## GOVERNMENT SECTOR

Payments of interest
    to households          50
    to business           35
    total                       85
Receipts of interest
    from households          10
    from business         20
    total                       30
Net interest payments                     55

## HOUSEHOLD SECTOR

Payments of interest
    to households           5
    to government        10
    to business           25
    total                     40
Receipts of interest
    from households          5
    from government      50
    from business        70
    total                   125
Net interest payments                    −85

We may note that the sum of net interest payments by the business plus the government plus the personal sectors is $30 + 55 − 85 = 0$. This is obviously not the figure that we wish to have appear as personal interest income. Another total is that of net outpayments by business and government plus payments of interest by households to households: $30 + 55 + 5 = 90$. Yet interest receipts by households clearly total 125. To reach this total, we must add to the net outpayments of business and government sectors the *total* or gross interest payments by the household sector: $30 + 55 + 40 = 125$. The figure which we insert on the left or payments side of the personal account as interest paid is, then, the total interest paid by households. Personal income, on the right, includes the net outpayments by the other two sectors, plus the gross outpayments by the household sector.

What is the logic of this treatment? In effect, it is to make interest payments by households "pass through" business and government directly to other households. To this flow of interest from households to households (passing through the other sectors) is added the interest income which originates in business or government—i.e., those outpayments not offset by inpayments. Note the distinction between the treatment of interest paid by households to business for the service of extending credit and all other payments by households to business for other goods and services. In the latter case, we register a sale by business to consumers. Out of the proceeds of this sale certain incomes are directly or indirectly generated, which, of course, return to the household sector. In the case of interest, the payment never registers in the business account, but passes directly through to other consumers. To evaluate this treatment would require discussion of alternatives, which would occupy more space than the matter merits here. Our objective is merely that the student should understand what has been done.

Now we are ready to ask what, if any, national product and national income originate in the household sector. As is the case with government, no goods or services are sold by households; but production does occur in households, some of which we can measure and include. That which we include, as gross and net product, is the sum of (1) the services of household employees—valued at wages, salaries, and supplements paid; and (2) the services of extending credit by households to households, measured by the total of household interest payments (remembering that these are treated in effect as though they were all within the household sector). The same sum, considered as earnings of employees plus earnings from the extension of credit, also measures national *income* originating in households. These services and earnings can clearly be seen to be nonduplicative of any output or income measured in another sector.

It is clearly arbitrary to include in the national product only those services performed in the home by hired employees, but not the same services when performed by family members. Kuznets has estimated that the value of housewives' services may be as great as one-fourth of the national income as otherwise measured. Not to recognize the value of these productive services is a source of serious bias in the national product, over a period in which productive activities are shifting from the home to the market place. A meal prepared at home is valued in the national product at its *ingredient* cost—these ingredients are final products when sold to the household, and no value is added by the labor of the housewife. The same meal eaten in a restaurant will be valued at a market price which includes not only cost of ingredients, but also labor cost, capital charges, and profit. Production of clothing, laundry, food preservation, and meal preparation—to name only the more obvious ones—have shifted significantly from the home to the market. At the same time, housewives have increasingly entered the labor market as employees receiving a monetary income. Failure to include the value of services rendered in the household by family members thus not only (1) understates the national product and income, and (2) gives a false impression of the proportion of total output originating in business, but also (3) biases seriously all measures of the long-period trend in national product, and all comparisons of national product or income between countries in which different proportions of total production move through the market place.

The reasons for not attempting to estimate the value of housewives' services for inclusion in the national product are basically two. In the first place, the statistical foundation for such estimates is very poor. We would thus add a very large, but unreliable, figure to a national product that was otherwise fairly precise. Second, although we must recognize that these services are productive, they are nevertheless of a different character than the market-valued services. This is perhaps reflected in the fact that most housewives are insulted by the notion that their services have a value equal to the wages of a laundress for six hours a week, of a cook for ten hours, a dishwasher for four hours, a baby-sitter for twelve, and so on. Home life is—fortunately—more than mere production. The motivations, the choices, the rewards are more than purely economic.

In the household we see that the line between production and consumption is a vague one. If I raise vegetables in my back yard, as a source of food, perhaps this is production—even though I receive other benefits and pleasures, and even though the vegetables I raise may actually cost more than ones I could buy. Is it still production when I raise flowers instead? If I decided that golf would give me the same benefits as flower-raising, no one would classify the golf as production. Many millions of man-hours are devoted to shaving; is this production? How about shoe-shining, newspaper reading, entertaining the baby, playing the piano?

At the beginning of our discussion of national income, we asked whether travel to work, necessary food and clothing were consumption or part of the cost of earning an income. We have come full circle and are back at the same kind of question. Economic activity is not all of life; nor can we neatly compartmentalize life into economic, political, religious, aesthetic, and other spheres.

For the above reasons, national product originating in households includes only the services of hired employees.[9] This deficiency clearly calls for caution in making long period or international comparisons.[10] However, it is probably not serious for most applications of national income and product data in short run income analysis, forecasting, and policy making. The very fact that these household services are non-market-oriented means that we can safely ignore them in an analysis which concerns itself with market-oriented production and the employment and income associated with this production. To be sure, to the extent that there are genuine marginal comparisons made by the consumer between rendering services in the household and rendering or seeking them through the market, our data will be biased even in the short run. But the error will be slight, far less than would be introduced by any attempt to estimate the value of home-supplied services.

## FOREIGN TRANSACTIONS ACCOUNT

The 1958 simplification of the structure of the national income and product accounts referred to on page 39 no longer requires specific consideration of the "rest-of-world" as a sector of the U.S. economy. The new, simplified system dispenses with a business sector account, and does not attempt to show national product and income by sector of origin. Thus, it presents only a simple "Foreign Transactions Account," which does not isolate the U.S. income and product originating in rest-of-world. Since we have retained here the sector-of-origin concept, we need a somewhat more elaborate rest-of-world account.

Why should we treat the rest-of-world as a sector of the U.S. economy? There would be no need to do so were it not for the fact that some factor services, the remuneration for which should clearly be included in national income and product, have not been elsewhere counted. Specifically, the wages and salaries, interest and profits which U.S. na-

---

[9] We can note briefly that the production occurring in the home, whether the labor is provided by family members or employed workers, also uses capital: appliances, the house itself. We have already included in the national product an estimate of the value of the services of the house, even when owner-occupied. However, no allowance is made for the value of the services of owner-used appliances, furniture, automobiles, etc. This omission is often criticized. Any representation of the value of these services raises the same kinds of problems as were raised in connection with government capital goods. It might be possible if handled in a way similar to that suggested in the Appendix for government goods.

[10] See Simon Kuznets, *Economic Change* (Norton, 1953), pp. 145–215.

tionals earn from activities abroad are part of current earnings, but not otherwise included in our tabulation of national income. While we are at it, we also correct what would otherwise have been an overstatement of U.S. income by putting these factor earnings from abroad on a *net* basis: that is, for example, we should include in U.S. national income the dividends which a U.S. resident receives from his ownership of stock in a foreign concern; but we should not include (although up to now our treatment has so implied) the dividends paid by an American corporation to a foreign stockholder. Wages and salaries, interest, royalties, and branch profits (the business account treated above included only the domestic production of American companies with branches abroad) also need to be put on a net basis.

The net total of these factors payments constitutes not only the national income but also the gross and net national products originating in the rest-of-world sector, since, so far as our economy is concerned, these factor services are final products.

Since we wish to isolate these particular transactions, which form part of the U.S. income and product, we set up our rest-of-world account in the form shown below. It is drawn up from the standpoint of rest-of-world, and this explains the nomenclature. The account includes not only the counterpart of net U.S. sales of factor services abroad, but also the counterparts of the other international entries appearing in the other sector accounts, and a balancing item, which, from the standpoint of the U.S. can be called "net foreign investment."

TABLE 3–4.   Rest-of-World Account

| | |
|---|---|
| Net purchases of factor services (by rest-of-world from U.S.): | Net disinvestment (by rest-of-world) in U.S. |
|   Wages and salaries | Transfer payments from U.S. government |
|   Interest | |
|   Dividends | |
|   Branch profits | |
| Net purchases from (U.S.) business | |
| Net purchases from (U.S.) government | |
| Net purchases from (U.S.) households | |
| Net current payments to the U.S. (total) | Sources of net current payments (total) |

As with the other sector accounts, various degrees of "netting-out" or cancellation are possible in constructing this account. The form shown above is highly netted-out, because all sales to the United States have been subtracted from the corresponding purchases. The new "Foreign Transactions Account" of the Department of Commerce is a rearrangement which does not break transactions down by sectors; but it does show the totals of both imports and exports of goods and services. It is drawn up from the standpoint of the United States, rather than rest-of-world. It does not permit one to determine the national income or product originating in rest-of-world.

**TABLE 3–4A.  Foreign Transactions Account**

| Exports of goods and services (from U.S.) | Imports of goods and services (to U.S.)  Transfer payments by U.S. government  Net foreign investment |
|---|---|
| Receipts from abroad | Payments to abroad |

Either of these accounts is, essentially, a simplified rearrangement of a customary "balance-of-payments" account. There are, however, a few differences in coverage. The principal difference is that unilateral transfers abroad in the form of goods are not included in the national income and product accounts. If from the government, they are simply included in government purchases, and no notice is taken of their destination. If from consumers (e.g., "CARE" packages), they are treated as any other consumer expenditure. (In the customary balance of payments account these are treated as merchandise exports, balanced by an entry under unilateral transfers.) Cash transfers by government (but not loans) are shown explicitly; but cash transfers by consumers are treated simply as consumer purchases abroad, along with such items as tourist expenditures.

One further peculiarity of the treatment of international transactions in the national income and product accounts is that U.S. monetary gold stocks are treated as part of the rest-of-world sector. Sale of gold to the Treasury is treated as a business sale to rest-of-world.

There are several alternative ways of treating international transactions in social accounting. The United Nations' recommended social accounting system even introduces a different basic concept of national product, which rests on an alternate treatment of some of the international items. Likewise, there are a number of rather fine conceptual problems that might delay us. However, we spend no time on these matters, primarily because (1) for the U.S. economy, the rest-of-world sector has an extremely small impact; and (2) we shall assume a closed economy in our theoretical discussion in the rest of this book. The student specializing in international economics, however, should familiarize himself with the treatment of international transactions in the U.S. accounts and the problems and alternatives to such treatment. He will also, of course, wish to develop the special applications of the theory of output and employment relevant to an open economy.

## COMBINING THE SECTOR ACCOUNTS

From the accounts of the several sectors we are now ready to accumulate the total national income. From the business sector, we have wages, salaries, and supplements; net interest; corporate profits, income of unincorporated enterprises, and rental income of persons. To this we add the wages, salaries, and supplements earned in government, and the same items earned in households, plus household interest payments. From rest-of-world, we add net factor earnings.

Similarly we can accumulate the sector national products into a total national product. The gross national product tabulated by sector of origin would appear as follows:

1. Business output:
   a. sales to consumers
   b. sales to government
   c. net sales abroad
   d. sales to business on capital account
   e. change in inventories
2. Government output
   a. wages, salaries, and supplements
3. Household output
   a. wages, salaries, and supplements
   b. interest paid
4. Rest-of-world output
   a. wages and salaries
   b. interest
   c. dividends
   d. branch profits

The above breakdown of national product is not, however, the one most useful for analytical purposes. Instead, we almost invariably rearrange these items into a tabulation of gross national product by type of expenditure (figures in parentheses following the entries refer to item numbers in the tabulation immediately above):

I. Consumer expenditures
   A. on business products (1a)

      B. on household services (3a and 3b)

      C. on imports (not appearing in previous tabulation)

  II. Government expenditures

      A. purchases from business (1b)

      B. purchases from abroad (not appearing in previous tabulation)

      C. wages, salaries, and supplements (2a)

  III. Gross private domestic investment

      A. sales to business on capital account (1d)

      B. change in inventories (1e)

  IV. Net exports of goods and services (1c + 4 − IC − IIB)

Here, although the same items are represented, the classification is by type of *purchaser* of the national product. National product is output; it is also expenditure. Here we classify expenditures by the sector which is the source of the spending, rather than by source of the output. This classification reflects the modern theoretical approach, which argues that output is determined by *demand*. If goods are demanded, they will be produced (and resources will be employed to produce them) up to the capacity available; if there is no buyer, output will not occur. To understand the level of output, therefore, we should classify it by type of purchaser, and examine the factors that explain each type of purchase.

The four major types of buyers of final goods are, in order of importance today, consumers, government, business, and rest-of-world. We call business expenditures "gross private domestic investment." To call inventory change a type of "expenditure" may be slightly unrealistic in the case of the unexpected accumulations of unsold goods which may sometimes be included here. Even these, however, do represent expenditures by the business firm that bought or produced them.

"Net exports of goods and services" is the appropriate expenditure component of gross national product insofar as international transactions are concerned. Only with respect to these international items is the expenditure approach more than a simple rearrangement of the breakdown by sector of origin. In the sector-of-origin arrangement, we find net business sales abroad and net sales abroad of factor services. But when we treat GNP as expenditure, we include as part of consumer and government expenditures their respective net imports. Thus, all of the business sector's net exports and the net export of factor services cannot be included in the expenditure tabulation of the GNP, but, rather these items less the consumer and government imports. This difference is, of course, the "net export of goods and services."

Each of the major types of expenditure can, of course, be further subdivided, and, for analytical purposes, it should be, when such further subdivision separates classes of expenditure the explanations of which may draw upon separate considerations. National income and product data have, of course, many uses other than those with which this book is immediately concerned. The breakdowns which are needed for one purpose are not necessarily those most useful for another. Actual U.S. data can be broken down in fine detail in accordance with several classificatory schemes. The main breakdowns in which the summary data are published (and the estimates for 1958) are shown in Table 3–5.

Before we turn to these actual data for a recent period, by way of bringing together and summarizing this chapter, there are three special topics related to the business sector whose discussion was previously postponed. We now turn to these matters.

## SPECIAL PROBLEMS IN THE BUSINESS ACCOUNT

### Imputations

So far, we have discussed only one kind of imputation which is included in the U.S. national product accounts—the imputed rental value of owner-occupied homes, and the corresponding factor income which results (after deducting associated costs). Although this is the single most important imputation, others are in the aggregate at least as large.

Of these others, the simplest to understand are the items of wages paid "in kind," in the form of employer-supplied food, lodging, and (in the case of military personnel) standard clothing. When an employer furnishes such items, the money wages which he pays are presumably less than they would otherwise be. Thus, national income is understated if the value of these wages in kind is omitted, and shifts in the extent of such "free" services can produce fictitious changes in national income. Thus, it seems reasonable to add the estimated value of these "free" goods to wages and salaries. (Only the more obvious sorts of pay "in kind" are recognized, the sorts as to whose valuation there can be least debate, and which represent clearly *divided* situations—some employers doing it one way and some the other.)

Corresponding to the addition of wages and salaries in the income total is the treatment of sales to consumers in the product total. The goods and services supplied "free" were purchased (or produced) by business but not sold, and would, in the absence of a correction, have been treated as intermediate goods—not part of final output. But they differ from the raw materials used up in producing other final goods—rather they are themselves final goods. Unless they are so reclassified their value is nowhere recognized.

Thus, in the business account, wages and salaries and sales to consumers are both increased by the identical figure—an estimate of the market value of these goods supplied to workers. In the household account, wage and salary incomes and personal consumption expenditures rise, too, by the same amount. We imagine, in other words, that the wages were really paid in money form, but the recipients then immediately turned around and used this money to buy these goods and services from their employers.

A similar imputation occurs to account for food and fuel produced and consumed on farms (by farm owners). Here, however, the income item that is increased is net income of unincorporated enterprises, and the expenditure (product) item is again consumer expenditures. It is as though farmers had sold this produce on the market and then turned around and repurchased it for their own consumption. Clearly the income and product totals are both improved by these imputations.

The remaining large imputations arise in connection with the activities of financial intermediaries, including banks, life insurance companies, and investment trusts. These are rather complicated, and will only be sketched here.

The problem in accounting for operations of commercial banks arises because the explicit charges which banks make for the services they perform for their customers are substantially inadequate to cover the costs of these services. Banks operate at a profit, nevertheless, because they receive interest on their loans and investments, but pay little or no interest to their depositors. To the extent that customers of banks are final consumers, this means that the services received are substantially undervalued. The imputation made here pretends that all interest received on the banks' loans and investments is paid out to bank depositors, and that service charges of exactly equal amount are made for bank services. To the extent that bank deposits are owned by other businesses, there is no effect on total national income and product, although national product originating in banking is increased and that originating in other industries is reduced. However, to the extent that bank deposits are owned by households, both national income and national product are increased—by an increased (imputed) interest receipt and by increased (imputed) consumer purchase of services from banks.

In the case of life insurance, the problem is to define and value the services which insurance companies provide to consumers. This is obviously not measured by the premium payments made, for the premiums are in large part saving rather than consumption. Here again, the imputation involves the pretense that all investment income of insurance companies is directly received by the policyholders, who then buy services from the companies, these services valued at their cost (wages and salaries, purchased materials, depreciation, taxes, and, in the case of stock life insurance companies, the profits accruing to the stockholders). The "saving" of the companies is thus transferred to the household sector, and "personal saving" must therefore be understood to include the increase in the policy reserves of life insurance companies. In the personal sector accounts, both premium payments and benefit payments are, of course, ignored.

The details of the general types of imputations sketched out above are rather complicated, but these paragraphs at least should warn the reader of the existence of these imputations, which are sufficiently sizable to make a real difference if he wishes to use national income and product data on household interest income, personal saving, etc.

### Inventory Valuation Adjustment

As is the case for the matters treated in the last section, the details of the inventory valuation adjustment are extremely complicated; but even the fairly casual user of the accounts can and should understand the general purpose and effect of the often sizable entries under this heading.

The entry "inventory valuation adjustment" appears on the left-hand or income side of the business account, in connection with corporate profits and income of unincorporated enterprises. But to understand it, we need to know that it has been made also on the right hand or product side of the business account, although it does not explicitly show up there. (It would be useful if the adjustment were specifically shown on both sides of the account, but there is a technical reason which makes this impossible in the case of unincorporated businesses.) We shall develop the *logic* of the adjustment as it relates to the product side of the account, even though its existence there is concealed.

On the product side of the business account, we have the entry "change in inventories." The entry that appears here is not (except by coincidence) the figure that would have been derived from the accounts of business firms. The business accounts show inventory change over a period as a difference between the ending and beginning values of goods in inventory. This difference will be the product of changes both in "prices" and in physical quantities. By "prices" we mean the bases for valuation that businesses use. Some businesses may use actual cost, others cost or market whichever is lower, others market prices. Where "cost" is used, and no track is kept of the individual pieces in the stock, the cost of an inventory may be estimated by the LIFO (last-in-first-out), FIFO (first-in-first-out), or an "average" method. We need not go into the details of these methods here (although the calculation of the adjustment requires separate estimates for the inventory holdings valued by each of them). Whatever the method used, the change in the value of the inventory from beginning to end of the period is nevertheless the product of a unit change and a "price" change.

What we now need to understand is that any change that occurs in the level of "prices" at which inventories are valued during a period will give rise to a completely false estimate of that part of national product which is not sold but is added to inventories. To demonstrate this, consider the following examples:

(1)

| | | |
|---|---|---|
| Ending inventory | 120 units at $.75 = | $90 |
| Beginning inventory | 100 units at $1.00 = | $100 |
| Change in inventory (book value) | | − $10 |

(2)

| | | |
|---|---|---|
| Ending inventory | 80 units at $1.50 = | $120 |
| Beginning inventory | 100 units at $1.00 = | $100 |
| Change in inventory (book value) | | + $20 |

(3)

| | | |
|---|---|---|
| Ending inventory | 120 units at $1.20 = | $144 |
| Beginning inventory | 100 units at $1.00 = | $100 |
| Change in inventory (book value) | | + $44 |

In example (1), physical inventory has increased by 20 units, yet inventory value has declined. We can see that there has been, this year, some output which went into inventory. The national product consists not only of the output that was sold, but also of some output which ended up in increased business inventories. Yet the book value figures would have us believe that this year's sales were greater than production. In the second example, we have the reverse. If we believed the value figures, we would conclude that output this year was greater than sales. In fact, some of this year's sales were of goods produced in an earlier year.

Note that in each case, the appropriate direction of the inventory change is independent of whether we value it at beginning or ending "prices." In case (1), for example, we know that twenty units of output were produced in addition to the output that was sold. This output has a positive, not a negative, value, whether we value these units at the higher, beginning-of-year prices, or at the lower, end-of-year prices. In the one case we would have an inventory increment valued at $20 (20 units at $1.00), in the other, valued at $15 (20 units at $.75); either of these gives a more accurate picture than the —$10 shown by the books.

Thus we want to substitute some other figure for the book value change, one which will recognize the true direction of the physical change in inventories. But how should we value the physical change? A moment's reflection will provide a general principle, if not an actual method. That output which goes into inventory should be valued on a basis comparable to the valuation basis used for the goods that were sold. How are the goods sold valued, during a year in which prices change? They are valued, of course, at the actual prices at which they are sold. This means that the total year's sales are valued at an *average* price, each price weighted by the number of units sold at that price. Suppose, for example, that the price level of goods sold fell twenty per cent, by a smooth trend, from beginning to end of the year. Suppose, further, that (physical) sales were the same each day of the year. Then the aggregate goods sold would be valued at an average price which in this case was ten per cent below the beginning-of-year price. If the goods which are not sold are to be valued on a comparable basis, they, too, should be valued at some kind of an average "price," although in this case the average is not of sales prices but of inventory valuation bases. Assuming for simplicity that in the above examples the change in valuation basis was evenly spread from beginning to end of year, the change in inventory, valued at average "prices" would be, in each example, as follows:

(1)                    + 20 units at $.875 = + $17.50

(2)                    − 20 units at $1.25 = − $25.00

(3)                    + 20 units at $1.10 = + $22.00

If we then substitute these values as measures of the inventory change for the year, we have made an "inventory valuation adjustment." This adjustment is in the amount that it was necessary to add to the book value change in order to convert the book value change in inventories to the corrected value. The size of the inventory valuation adjustment was, therefore, in each case as follows:

(1)                         $17.50 − (−$10) = $27.50

(2)                         −$25.00 − $20 = −$45.00

(3)                         $22.00 − $44 = −$22.00

It will be noted that, whenever "prices" have risen during the year, the inventory valuation adjustment will be negative (whatever has happened to physical inventories); when prices have fallen, it will be positive. Only if prices have not changed will the adjustment be zero. This last result is, of course, what we want, for, if prices have not changed, the book value change will correctly reflect the physical change, valued at average (constant) prices.

Having made an inventory valuation adjustment on the product side of the business account, it is obviously necessary to make it on the income side as well. Here, however, we show it explicitly. It can be thought of as being a measure, on the income side, of the amount of inventory profit or loss. (However, the terms inventory profit and loss can be used in various meaningful senses; the inventory valuation adjustment corresponds to only one of these senses.)

The above paragraphs attempt to explain in very simple terms the underlying philosophy of the inventory valuation adjustment. The student should be warned, however, that this is not the way it is computed (for example, we have no direct measure of physical inventory change; we first must estimate that before we can revalue it at average prices). He should also be warned that there are some nasty theoretical problems as well as some very complicated statistical ones involved in computing the adjustments. However, he should be able to understand what the adjustment is for; and, in a general way, how to interpret any actual inventory valuation adjustment which he encounters in using national income and product data.

## Capital Consumption Allowance

In Table 3-5, it will be seen that a more comprehensive item, "capital consumption allowance," has replaced the item "depreciation," which we have so far used to measure the difference between gross and net national products (in the business sector). The largest component of this new item is still depreciation; but it also includes "accidental damage to fixed capital," which is perhaps self-explanatory; and an item "capital outlay charged to current expense." Although this entry is not of major importance, the student should understand what it signifies. Business expenditures for construction and producers' durables have actually been entered in the product account at a larger total than that which would result from a mere consolidation of individual firm capital accounts. The national product total includes some purchases which the business firms which make them have treated merely as current expense. The largest expenditures in this category are the drilling expenses of oil and gas producers, which are typically charged, in private accounting, entirely against current revenues, rather than "capitalized" and charged over the useful life of the oil or gas well. Other items which the national product accountant wishes to include in new capital goods are, for example, the dies used for stamping automobile body parts. Because of the rapid style changes in this industry, such dies are typically charged to current expense, although they are of a type that, in other industries, would be used for many years, and be capitalized in their accounts. If these items are to be treated as capital goods in the national product account, a compensating entry has to be made on the left or income side of the account. The entry needed on the left side of the national product account to reflect their inclusion on the right side in gross private domestic investment is called "capital outlay charged to current expense," and, as has been seen, it is grouped with depreciation and accidental damage to form the total capital consumption allowance.

This treatment does not, of course, affect the size of the national income or the net national product. One might suppose that the logic which supported the inclusion of these items in gross national product might have dictated a recalculation of depreciation and an adjustment to business profits, but this further step has not been taken.

The present context is a good one for noting the nonrecognition of depletion allowances in the national product accounts. Rather, what the private accountant labels depletion is here merely treated as part of business profits. (Depletion allowances result from the capitalization of wasting natural resources. When one purchases or discovers a mineral deposit, he customarily charges its original cost or discovery value over the estimated useful life of the asset.) Since the value of neither new discoveries or of purchases of resources is included in the national product accounts as "investment"—nor should it be, if production is defined in any usual manner—then it is logically correct to refuse to recognize current charges which write off the value of the discovery or purchase. Once again, however, the item headings in the product and income accounts—especially the items of corporate and personal saving—get distorted from their natural or usual meanings.

## ILLUSTRATIVE DATA FROM THE UNITED STATES ACCOUNTS

Table 3–5, which appears on the following page, presents actual national income and product data for the year 1958, in substantially the

**TABLE 3–5. United States National Income and Product, 1958 (billions of dollars)**

| | | | | |
|---|---|---|---|---|
| Compensation of employees | $256.8 | | Personal consumption expenditures | $293.0 |
| Wages and salaries | 239.4 | | Durable goods | 37.6 |
| Supplements to wages and salaries | 17.4 | | Nondurable goods | 141.9 |
| Employer contributions for social insurance | 8.1 | | Services | 113.4 |
| Other labor income | 9.3 | | Gross private domestic investment | 54.9 |
| Proprietors' income and inventory valuation adjustment | 46.6 | | New construction | 35.8 |
| Business and professional | 32.4 | | Residential nonfarm | 18.0 |
| Farm | 14.2 | | Other | 17.7 |
| Rental income of persons | 11.8 | | Producers' durable equipment | 22.9 |
| Corporate profits and inventory valuation adjustment | 36.7 | | Change in business inventories | –3.8 |
| Profits before tax | 37.1 | | Net exports of goods and services | 1.2 |
| Tax liability | 18.2 | | Exports | 22.6 |
| Profits after tax | 18.9 | | Imports | 21.3 |
| Dividends | 12.4 | | Government purchases of goods and services | 92.6 |
| Undistributed | 6.5 | | Federal | 52.2 |
| Inventory valuation adjustment | –.4 | | National defense (less sales) | 44.1 |
| Net interest | 14.3 | | Other | 8.1 |
| NATIONAL INCOME | 366.2 | | State and local | 40.5 |
| Plus: Indirect business tax and nontax liability | 39.0 | | | |
| Business transfer payments | 1.7 | | | |
| Statistical discrepancy | –2.1 | | | |
| Current surplus of government enterprises minus subsidies | –1.0 | | | |
| NET NATIONAL PRODUCT | 403.8 | | | |
| Plus: Capital consumption allowances | 37.9 | | | |
| Depreciation charges | 34.7 | | | |
| Accidental damage to fixed business capital | .7 | | | |
| Capital outlays charged to current expense | 2.5 | | | |
| GROSS NATIONAL PRODUCT | $441.7 | | GROSS NATIONAL PRODUCT | $441.7 |

Source: *Survey of Current Business,* July 1959.

form in which these data are presented (in summary tables) by the U.S. Department of Commerce.

Here all the sector accounts are combined into one grand account. On the right hand, or product, side we have the business gross product plus the gross (same as net) products originating in the other sectors, but rearranged, as indicated above on page 61 by kind of buyer or user of the output. By now, the student should have no trouble interpreting every entry on the product side.

The left-hand or income side is based on the form of the business account, but includes as well the incomes originating in the other sectors. When we recall that in the other three sectors national income is measured as identical with (gross and net) product, we see that adding the products originating in the other sectors to that originating in business and adding the incomes originating in other sectors to that originating in business does not disturb the balance of the account. Therefore, also, the differences which appear between gross and net national products and national income are the differences which arise in the business sector only, where valuations at factor prices differ from valuations made at market prices.

There are a few entries on the income side which need a word of explanation. Under "compensation of employees" it should be noted that employ*ee* contributions for social insurance are included in "wages and salaries"; employ*er* contributions are treated as a "supplement." The "other labor income" heading consists of employer contributions to private pension and welfare funds, plus a few miscellaneous types of labor income, such as directors' fees and workmen's compensation payments.

The "statistical discrepancy" results from the fact that items on the left- and right-hand sides of the account have been independently estimated, from various sources. The discrepancy is arbitrarily assigned to the income side, as part of the reconciliation between income and product. It may, of course, be positive instead of negative.

The final note of explanation relates to the item "current surplus of government enterprises minus subsidies." Our discussion has kept these items separated, but in the accounts they are always reported as a combined total. (These two items likewise appear on the left side of the government sector account, where they are also consolidated into one.)

With these explanations, the student should now be able to understand each entry in this account, why it appears where it does, and from which sector account or accounts it was derived.

## SAVING AND INVESTMENT

In the previous chapter, we derived the relationship which must exist between saving and investment in a simple hypothetical economy with no government, no corporations, no international trade, and no change in inventories. A similar relationship (i.e., equality) must exist between broader concepts of saving and investment, as we measure these in our real world income and product accounts. As in the previous case, the equality is based simply on the way we define our terms and make our measurements. It does not represent any economic "law" or "tendency" (which might or might not be exactly true); it is true by definition.

Return briefly to the accounts of the four sectors. The entries in these sector accounts can be simplified and regrouped as follows:

---

### Business Account

| | | | |
|---|---|---|---|
| BPI | Personal income payments: wages and salaries (after social insurance deductions), dividends, interest, rental income, income of unincorporated enterprises, transfers | C | Sales to consumers |
| | | G | Sales to government |
| | | X | Sales abroad (net) |
| | | GPDI | Sales to business on capital account plus inventory change |
| CS | Corporate saving | | |
| IVA | Inventory valuation adjustment | | |
| SIC | Social insurance contributions, employee and employer | | |
| BT | Business taxes | | |
| S | Current surplus minus subsidies | | |
| CCA | Depreciation, etc. | | |

### Government Account

| | | | |
|---|---|---|---|
| G | Purchases from business | BT | Business taxes |
| GM | Purchases abroad (net) | PT | Personal taxes |
| GTA | Transfers abroad | SIC | Social insurance contributions |
| GPI | Personal income payments: wages and salaries, interest, transfers to persons | | |
| —S | Current surplus minus subsidies | | |
| GS | Government surplus | | |

*Household Account*

| C | Purchases from business | BPI | |
|---|---|---|---|
| HPI | Personal income payments: | GPI | |
| | wages and salaries, interest | HPI | Personal income |
| HM | Purchases abroad (net) | RPI | |
| PT | Personal taxes | | |
| PS | Personal saving | | |

*Rest-of-World Account*

| RPI | Net personal income pay-<br>ments:<br>wages and salaries, inter-<br>est, dividends | NFI | Net foreign investment |
|---|---|---|---|
| | | GTA | Government transfers<br>abroad |
| BP | Branch profits | | |
| X | Business net exports | | |
| —GM | Government net imports | | |
| —HM | Household net imports | | |

From the business account, we have the following equation:

(1) $BPI + CS + IVA + SIC + BT + S + CCA = C + G + X + GPDI.$

The two sides of this equation are precisely equal because of a definition of profit as a residual item which precisely balances the books.

From the government account, we have:

(2)  $G + GM + GTA + GPI - S + GS = BT + PT + SIC.$

This equation is true because of the definition of surplus ($GS$) as a balancing item.

From the household account, we have:

(3)  $C + HPI + HM + PT + PS = BPI + GPI + HPI + RPI.$

This account is balanced by the definition of personal saving ($PS$) as a residual.

From the rest-of-world account, we have:

(4)        $RPI + BP + X - GM - HM = NFI + GTA.$

This account is balanced by the definition of net foreign investment.

If we add these four equations together, we will find most items either appearing on both sides of the resulting equation, or appearing twice on the same side with opposite sign. Most items therefore cancel out, and we are left with this equation:

(5)     $PS + CCA + CS + IVA + BP + GS = NFI + GPDI.$

The items on the left may be called items of gross saving. They are:

| | |
|---|---|
| PS | Personal saving |
| CCA | Capital consumption allowance |
| CS | Corporate savings (domestic) |
| IVA | Inventory valuation adjustment |
| BP | Branch profits (foreign) |
| GS | Government surplus |

Those on the right may be called gross investment. They are:

| | |
|---|---|
| NFI | Net foreign investment |
| GPDI | Gross private domestic investment |

Why are gross saving and gross investment equal? Their equality is the result of no economic "law" or tendency; it results from the way in which we have defined our terms and balanced our accounts. To explain it in words would be almost impossible; but we know that it is so.

Other rearrangements of the several sector accounts are possible. One presentation, sometimes referred to as the "Nation's Economic Budget," rests on a rearrangement of equation (5).

$$(6) \quad (GPDI - CCA - CS - IVA - BP) + NFI - GS - PS = 0.$$

The grouping within the parentheses is treated as the "excess of expenditures over receipts" of the business sector of the economy, and the three remaining terms as the "excess of expenditures over receipts" of the rest-of-world, government, and personal sectors. Obviously the sum of these sector "excesses" must be zero (except for statistical discrepancy).[11]

## SUMMARY

In this chapter we have considered one of the ways which has been developed for reflecting, in quantitative form, the productive activities of an economy, and the distribution of the income that arises from this production. These national income and product accounts are set up in a way designed to yield an unduplicative total of output and income, and to show the breakdowns of these totals among categories that are presumed to be significant for economic analysis.

Quite obviously this arrangement is only one of a vast number of possible ways of measuring economic activity. Implicitly, the scheme rests on a whole range of theoretical propositions, which make these par-

---

[11] This form of presentation was used in many of the Economic Reports of the President in the years 1946–52. It is also used, e.g., in G. Colm, *The American Economy in 1960* (National Planning Association, 1952), p. 29 and passim. And it appears (without being called a "budget") in *U.S. Income and Output*, pp. 220–21.

ticular computations and breakdowns relevant. Even the concept of what is an unduplicative total rests on certain theoretical preconceptions. Other summaries of activity are possible, however, even based on essentially the same theoretical preconceptions (reflecting, however, slightly different theoretical emphasis). Among these are "input-output" analysis and "moneyflow" accounting. Since these organizations of data contribute little to the type of macroeconomic theory employed here, we refer the interested student to other sources for their explanation; [12] however, the relationship of each to the national income and product accounts is easy to understand.

The essential arrangement employed in the national income accounts is one which visualizes consumers, government, business firms, and rest-of-world as "demanders" for the total output of the economy. Their purchases (or expenditures) are identical in value with the value of the output. This same value sum is available, after certain deductions, to be paid or attributed as income to those participating in production. These incomes, in turn, provide the basis for consumer purchases, and the share that is taxed away provides the basis for government purchases (although neither type of purchase is necessarily limited by the resources arising from current income).

In much of the subsequent theoretical analysis, a highly simplified system of accounts is used (which recognizes little or no government nor even, perhaps, the corporate form). The student should be able to discern, however, (1) that this simplification does not involve matters of basic principle; but (2) that when the theory is applied to concrete situations, it must be modified to take account of the complexities of the real world, as reflected in the actual income and product accounts.

## APPENDIX

### The Valuation of Government Output

National income and product statisticians value the goods and services produced in the business sector at market prices, but government output is valued only at labor cost. It is clear that no market price can be imputed to government services (as we impute a market price for the services of owner-occupied houses). But can we not get a better measure of cost—one more comparable with the valuations used in the private sector? To answer this question, we must first isolate what the precise difference may be between the valuation basis

[12] See, for example, Powelson, *op. cit.*, Chaps. 24 and 25; and National Accounts Review Committee, *The National Economic Accounts of the United States.*

for goods and services sold in the market and those produced in government and valued at labor cost. The price of the market-valued service includes total cost plus profit, total cost being composed of current materials, labor, depreciation, interest, and indirect taxes. The profit element may be thought of as including a return on capital supplied by owners, plus some reward for uncertainty-bearing or successful innovation, and, in some cases, wages of management. Occasionally it may be negative, but on the average, and for goods and producers which persevere in production, it is positive.

The value assigned to the government service includes only labor cost, but the current materials and services purchased are counted in the business product as final goods. There is no depreciation, interest, or profit; and no indirect taxes. The inclusion of indirect taxes in the value of the private product, without inclusion of a corresponding amount in the value of government output is an obvious source of bias, although it is hard to see how to adjust for it. Potentially more serious would seem to be the failure to include any capital cost (at least depreciation and interest, if not profit) in the valuation of public services, particularly since many government services rely heavily on fixed capital. This needs further discussion.

The noninclusion of depreciation actually turns out on analysis to make no difference in the *net* valuations of the public versus the private service, *taken over the whole life of the assets used.* To see this, we must recall that private capital goods are, in effect, counted twice in the gross national product, but only once in the net product. In the private gross product, we enter the cost of a new bank building—in the year in which it was built; we also enter in the national product each year the value of the banking services performed with the aid of the building. This value of banking services obviously includes the value of the services of the building; this is the element of double counting. We eliminate this by subtracting depreciation each year—in an amount which, over the life of the building, will exactly subtract the original cost. What is left, when we get through, is a total net product over the life of the building which consists of the value of the banking services; the value of the building originally went into national product, but this was exactly offset by subsequent subtractions.

Compare with this the treatment of the courthouse building. When built, by a private contractor, it enters the gross national product as a business sale to government. Since the annual value of judicial services is not represented by a market price which includes the value of the building's services, there is no occasion for the subsequent subtraction of depreciation to eliminate the double counting. To be sure, we might, if estimates were available, add depreciation on government capital into the value of the gross product originating in government, then subtract the identical figure each year in calculating net product. This would improve the gross product measurement; it would clearly not affect net product, nor would it have much effect on the short-run, year-to-year pattern of the gross product.

Thus the absence of depreciation charges is not, basically, the source of any undervaluation of government services. The difference rests rather in the remaining elements: interest and profit. In the private case the value of the goods or services which are produced through the use of capital goods includes a return on capital—it recognizes capital's productivity. This is not true in the public case.

Perhaps a very simple numerical example contrasting the bank and courthouse will help clarify this. Assume each building cost $100 and has a ten-year life, depreciating by $10 per year. The annual market value of the banking services rendered through use of the building is $50. Over the ten-year life of the bank building, gross national product is thus $600: $150 in the first year and $50 in each of the subsequent nine. Net national product is $140 in the first year; $40 a year for nine years thereafter, or $500 in total. The value of the bank building went into national product in the year of its construction; an identical total was thereafter subtracted from the current value of banking services, leaving, for the period as a whole, only the value of the banking services.

Let us assume that the $50 annual market value of banking services breaks down as follows:

| | |
|---|---:|
| Wages and salaries | $15 |
| Purchased materials | 10 |
| Depreciation | 10 |
| Interest | 10 |
| Profit | 5 |
| Total | $50 |

For the judicial services rendered in the courthouse, assume also that annual wages and salaries are $15 and purchased materials are $10.

The gross and net national product in the government case includes the original price of the building ($100) plus $25 annually for wages and materials. (In the case of the bank, the purchased materials were intermediate goods, thus not counted in the national product except as included in the value of banking services; when the same materials are sold to the government, they are treated as final goods.) Over the life of the building, gross and net products are thus $350; $125 in the first year, $25 a year thereafter for nine years.

The difference in net products—$150, or $15 per year—consists of the annual interest and profit which a market price yielded to those who provided the capital and took the responsibility for the operation of the bank. In other words, in the private sector, valuations recognize the productivity of capital and entrepreneurship; in the public sector neither is recognized. There appears to be no easy conception of public entrepreneurship, to which a value might be imputed. However, it might be possible, and would be desirable, if capital accounts could be constructed for the government sector, to impute as part of the value of the national product originating in government a return—at say 3 per cent—on the depreciated value of the government capital used. These capital accounts would also permit us to include in gross national product (although not in net) an annual depreciation charge on government capital goods. Data for this are not presently available. Perhaps a first step, and a highly desirable one, would be to develop capital accounts for the government enterprises, and to improve our knowledge of the subsidy (or "profit") which these enterprises involve. General government capital accounts could then follow.

The above discussion should automatically have indicated why government interest payments do not measure the services of government capital, and why government interest is excluded from national product and national income. Overwhelmingly, government debt has been incurred to fight wars (and to a much lesser extent, provide relief in depressions). The amount of debt outstanding bears no relationship to the stock of real, productive government capital. Postwar national product originating in government does not exceed prewar national product originating in government by an amount which bears any relationship (unless coincidentally) with the growth in the government's annual interest bill. Indeed, during the war period, government productive capital—at least of the normal sort—probably declined, as roads and public buildings were not replaced or maintained. Periods of intensive government capital formation, on the other hand, have often been periods in which the public debt (and hence the interest bill) was declining, as taxes were used to finance both public works and debt retirement, in addition to current services.

# Output and Employment [1]

*Chapter IV*

## "REAL" NATIONAL PRODUCT

In Chapter II, the concept of national product was first introduced as a collection of goods and services. The national product consists of (the current flow of) those particular goods and services which can be identified as "final goods"—those going to consumers or government, plus those goods which constitute the net addition to stockpiles and to productive capacity in the form of structures and equipment. In order to summarize this collection of goods and services—and to compare its size at one time with its size at another—we express each good in terms of its money value, then add these values. We are all aware, however, that a money value total can change either through a change in the level of prices at which the various units are valued, or through a change in the numbers of units, or both. Here we are concerned with separating that part of the change in the money value of national product which is due to price change from the part which is the "real" or physical change.[2]

Anyone who has ever considered this problem knows that there is an unavoidable ambiguity—the so-called "index number problem"—which inheres in the very conception. Of course, if the physical output of each

---

[1] The reader who is in a hurry can skip this chapter without serious break in the argument. Or, he can omit the fourth and sixth sections, "Real National Income" and "Short-Run Relationship of Employment and Output."

[2] For two very interesting treatments, see Kenneth Arrow, "The Measurement of Price Changes," and H. E. Riley, "The Price Indexes of the Bureau of Labor Statistics," in *The Relationship of Prices to Economic Stability and Growth*, Compendium of Papers Submitted by Panelists Appearing Before the Joint Economic Committee, March 31, 1958, pp. 77–87 and 107–116. The first is a masterful exposition of index number theory, the latter a careful description of index number practice.

78

good in our collection should change in the same proportion as each other output, then we could be certain of the proportion of change of the aggregate output. It is clearly in whatever proportion the physical magnitudes of all individual outputs changed. We could then multiply the original dollar GNP by the percentage by which physical output had changed, divide this into the actual dollar GNP figure for the second period, and use the quotient as a measure of the change in prices—an "implicit" price index.

Normally, however, all outputs do not change in identical proportion: the product mix changes. Physical quantities of some products increase, of other products decrease, or all increase or decrease but in different percentages. In order to say what has happened to the total physical quantity involved, we must weight each of the several physical movements by its importance—that is, its economic value. An increase of ten per cent in the output of electric locomotives probably outweighs a decrease of 20 per cent in the output of jackknives. But by how much? What is the net movement of the output of locomotives plus jackknives? Plus 9 per cent, 8 per cent, or 2 per cent? To answer this question we can use the relative market values of locomotives and jackknives. The question is: Which set of relative market values shall we use—that which prevailed at the beginning of the period over which we are making the comparison, that which prevailed at the end, or some combination of the two? Only if relative prices of locomotives and jackknives did not change —both prices went up or down in exactly the same proportion—would we have no trouble in establishing the net movement of the physical total of locomotives plus jackknives.

Suppose, for example, that the facts are as shown in the following table.

**TABLE 4–1.  Assumed Outputs, Prices, and Values of Locomotives and Jackknives: Proportional Price Changes**

|  | Time 1 | Time 2 | Percentage Change |
|---|---|---|---|
| Outputs: |  |  |  |
| locomotives | 20 | 22 | +10% |
| jackknives | 3,000,000 | 2,400,000 | −20% |
| Prices: |  |  |  |
| locomotives | $ 500,000 | $ 800,000 | +60% |
| jackknives | $1 | $1.60 | +60% |
| Values of output at current prices: |  |  |  |
| locomotives | $10,000,000 | $17,600,000 | +76% |
| jackknives | 3,000,000 | 3,840,000 | +28% |
| total | $13,000,000 | $21,440,000 | +64.9% |

TABLE 4–1.  Assumed Outputs, Prices, and Values of Locomotives
and Jackknives: Proportional Price Changes (Continued)

|  | Time 1 | Time 2 | Percentage Change |
|---|---|---|---|
| Values of output at time 1 prices: |  |  |  |
| locomotives | $10,000,000 | $11,000,000 | +10% |
| jackknives | 3,000,000 | 2,400,000 | −20% |
| total | $13,000,000 | $13,400,000 | + 3.08% |
| Values of output at time 2 prices: |  |  |  |
| locomotives | $16,000,000 | $17,600,000 | +10% |
| jackknives | 4,800,000 | 3,840,000 | −20% |
| total | $20,800,000 | $21,440,000 | + 3.08% |

Here we have no difficulty in arriving at the conclusion that physical output of locomotives plus jackknives rose by 3.08 per cent. The raw figure of total value rose by 64.9 per cent; but this increase was mostly due to inflation. Valued at constant prices and using either set of prices, the net increase in output was only 3.08 per cent. We could reach this result in still another way. We could "deflate" the total current values of output—$13,000,000 and $21,440,000—by a price index number which had the values of 100 at time 1 and 160 at time 2. (To "deflate," we divide $13,000,000 by 1 and $21,440,000 by 1.6.) This gives us deflated values of output (in time 1 prices), of $13,000,000 and $13,400,000, again an increase of 3.08 per cent.

There is no ambiguity of meaning in the case of identical proportionate price change. In effect, 500,000 jackknives remain the equivalent in value of one locomotive, whatever their absolute prices may be. Thus we can say that the total outputs at time 1 and time 2 were respectively 26 locomotives (20 actual and 6 equivalents) and 26.8 locomotives (22 actual and 4.8 equivalents), an increase of 3.08 per cent. Or, if we prefer, the outputs were 13 million jackknives (3 million actual and 10 million equivalents), becoming 13.4 million at time 2 (2.4 million actual and 11 million equivalents), again an increase of 3.08 per cent.

But suppose, now, that instead of the prices moving in identical fashion, they, too, move in divergent pattern. Suppose the locomotive price rises by 100 per cent and the jackknife price rises by only 10 per cent. Assume that the change in physical outputs was exactly as before. Our table now becomes as follows.

TABLE 4–2.  Assumed Outputs, Prices, and Values: Nonproportional
Price Changes.  Two Quantity Indexes

| | *Time 1* | *Time 2* | *Percentage Change* |
|---|---|---|---|
| Outputs: | | | |
| locomotives | 20 | 22 | +10% |
| jackknives | 3,000,000 | 2,400,000 | −20% |
| Prices: | | | |
| locomotives | $ 500,000 | $ 1,000,000 | +100% |
| jackknives | $1 | $1.10 | +10% |
| Values of output at current prices: | | | |
| locomotives | $10,000,000 | $22,000,000 | +120% |
| jackknives | 3,000,000 | 2,640,000 | −12% |
| total | $13,000,000 | $24,640,000 | +89.5% |
| Values of output at time 1 prices: | | | |
| locomotives | $10,000,000 | $11,000,000 | +10% |
| jackknives | 3,000,000 | 2,400,000 | −20% |
| total | $13,000,000 | $13,400,000 | + 3.08% |
| *Quantity Index 1* | 100.00 | 103.08 | + 3.08% |
| Values of output at time 2 prices: | | | |
| locomotives | $20,000,000 | $22,000,000 | +10% |
| jackknives | 3,300,000 | 2,640,000 | −20% |
| total | $23,300,000 | $24,640,000 | + 5.75% |
| *Quantity Index 2* | 100.00 | 105.75 | + 5.75% |

Here we see the problem: if we value the outputs at initial prices, we
conclude that the total physical increase was just over 3 per cent; valued
at final prices it is almost 6 per cent. Which is correct? Both are correct—
they merely measure different things. The former test measures the
change using the value standards prevailing at time 1, and the latter
using those prevailing at time 2. At time 2 relatively more importance
is attached to locomotives than at time 1, as reflected in the increase
in the relative price of locomotives. Since this is the output which increased, the total increase appears larger when judged by standards
which make locomotives more important, jackknives less important.

What we have done above is, in effect, to compute two alternative
forms of a "quantity index." (There are various other forms of quantity
index which we could also compute.) By dividing either of these quantity
indexes into the original dollar values in current prices, we get, of course,
a measure of the average change in prices—an implicit price index. These

two implicit price indexes for time 2 (time 1 = 100) are 183.88 and 179.23. But we can also derive a price index directly, then use this to "deflate" the original dollar values, giving us an implicit quantity index. Two commonly used price index number formulas (among a great variety of other possibilities) are used in the table which follows.

TABLE 4–3.   **Two Price Indexes Computed and Used to Deflate Current Dollar Values**

| | Time 1 | Time 2 |
|---|---|---|
| Prices: | | |
| locomotives | $       500,000 | $    1,000,000 |
| jackknives | 1.00 | 1.10 |
| *Index 1* | | |
| Price relatives (time 1 = 100) | | |
| locomotives | 100 | 200 |
| jackknives | 100 | 110 |
| Price relatives weighted (multiplied) by time 1 market values: | | |
| locomotives | $1,000,000,000 | $2,000,000,000 |
| jackknives | 300,000,000 | 330,000,000 |
| weighted sum | $1,300,000,000 | $2,330,000,000 |
| weighted average * (Price Index 1) | 100 | 179.23 |
| Deflated value of total output using Price Index 1 | $     13,000,000 | $     13,747,698 |
| Implicit quantity index using Price Index 1 | 100.00 | 105.75 |
| *Index 2* | | |
| Price relatives (time 2 = 100) | | |
| locomotives | 50 | 100 |
| jackknives | 90.91 | 100 |
| Price relatives weighted by time 2 market values: | | |
| locomotives | $1,100,000,000 | $2,200,000,000 |
| jackknives | 240,000,000 | 264,000,000 |
| weighted sum | $1,340,000,000 | $2,464,000,000 |
| weighted average * (Price Index 2) | 54.38 | 100 |
| (Price Index 2 shifted to time 1 = 100) | (100.00) | (183.88) |
| Deflated value of total output using Price Index 2 | $     23,905,848 | $     24,640,000 |
| Implicit quantity index using Price Index 2 | 100.00 | 103.08 |

* Weighted sum divided by sum of the weights.

It will be noted that a price index using time 1 as the basis of price relatives and time 1 market values as weights produces the same measure of output change as a quantity index using time 2 prices as weights (it can be demonstrated algebraically that these have the identical formula); while an index using time 2 price relatives weighted by time 2 market values produces the same result as a quantity index using time 1 prices.

## GRAPHIC APPROACH TO THE PROBLEM OF REAL OUTPUT

Let us review in a simple graph what we have done up to this point. In Figure 4–1, we measure physical outputs of the two commodities

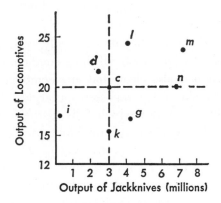

Figure 4–1.

along the horizontal and vertical axes. The points marked *c* and *d* correspond to the outputs at times 1 and 2 in our example. If the only information we had related to the individual quantities, we could say very little about the comparison of any two aggregate quantities. We could say only that the combinations represented by the points labeled *l, m,* and *n* were greater *than* combination *c,* and that combinations *i* and *k* represented a smaller total output. That is, if we have more of one commodity and no less of the other (case *n*), or more of both (cases *l* and *m*), we are clearly better off. If we have less of one and no more of the other (case *k*) or less of both (case *i*) we are worse off. But combinations (like *d* or *g*) involving more of one commodity but less of the other cannot be compared without more information.

Relative market values provide more information. The sloping "expenditure line," *ab*, in Figure 4–2 shows all of the combinations of locomotives and jackknives that could have been purchased for $13,000,000 at the initial prices. These include the combination of 26 locomotives and zero jackknives (point *a*), 7 million jackknives and twelve locomo-

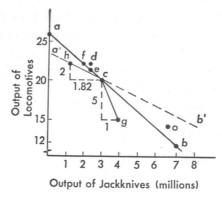

Figure 4–2.

tives (point *b*), and the combination actually bought: 20 locomotives and 3 million jackknives (point *c*). All these combinations have the same value. On this basis it is also clear that any combination which falls to the right of the expenditure line represents a larger total value, and thus a "greater" quantity, while any which falls to the left is a lesser value and hence a "smaller" quantity of total output. Combination *d*, that which was purchased at time 2 (consisting of 22 locomotives and 2.4 million jackknives) is thus a larger quantity than combination *c*. For example, combination *e* is equivalent in value to combination *c*, but combination *d* contains no fewer jackknives but more locomotives. Alternatively, combination *f* is also equivalent to combination *c*, but combination *d* contains no fewer locomotives but more jackknives.

A combination like *g* is clearly inferior to combination *c*. This combination involves 4 million jackknives (1 million more than combination *c*), but only 15 locomotives (5 fewer than combination *c*). The loss of 5 locomotives was accompanied by a gain of only one million jackknives. And, at the relative values prevailing in time 1, the loss has greater value than the gain. In effect, the trade of 5 locomotives for 1 million knives would have been at a relative price of 200,000 knives per locomotive, instead of the 500,000 knives per locomotive ratio which prevailed at time 1, which is shown by the slope of the expenditure line *ab*, as compared with the slope of the line segment connecting points *c* and *g*.

Thus, if we use time 1 prices, we conclude that output increased between time 1 and time 2 (points *c* and *d*). What picture would we get if we used time 2 prices? At these prices, 1 locomotive is worth 909,091 jackknives. Substitution at this rate is shown along the line segment between points *c* and *h*. This line, extended, becomes a second expenditure line $a'b'$. All points on this line are equivalent to the initial combination $c$, when time 2 relative values are used. Point $h$ is thus a combination of the same value as point $c$ on this basis. Point $d$ involves the same number of locomotives (22) as point $h$, but a much larger number of jackknives. Obviously it is superior to point $h$. That is, using time 2 values, the combination bought at time 2 is larger than the combination bought at time 1. By our second test, combination $d$ appears to represent even more of an increase than by our first test (i.e., it falls farther to the right of the second than of the first expenditure line). This, of course, is the conclusion we reached before, which showed the quantity increase as 3.08 per cent valued in time 1 prices and 5.75 per cent valued in time 2 prices.

Thus we have a general graphical technique for comparing two combinations of quantities. We draw two expenditure lines through one of the points, the lines having slopes determined by the two sets of relative prices.[3] If a second point falls to the right of both lines, we can be sure that it represents a larger total quantity; if it falls to the left of both lines, then, by either test, it is a smaller quantity.

There remains the intermediate case, illustrated by point $o$ in Figure 4–2. This combination is seen to be superior to combination $c$ if we use one set of prices (expenditure line $ab$), inferior if we use the other (expenditure line $a'b'$). That is, if we had computed the percentage change in quantities, we would have come out with a quantity increase—i.e., a positive percentage—using one set of prices, and a decrease—a negative percentage—using the other set.

In summary, we have concluded that if we know only physical quantities, the only comparisons that are unambiguous are those in which either all quantities increase or all decrease. In this case we can decide which combination is bigger, though we cannot say by how much. If some quantities increase and others decrease, we cannot decide which combination is "bigger"—i.e., preferable. Use of market values as weights permits us not only to say how large was the increase in quantity when all individual quantity changes were in the same direction, but it even permits us to judge the net increase or decrease when individual quantities change in opposite directions. Use of prices as weights thus reduces the ambiguity in quantity comparisons. But if the relative prices change,

---

[3] The one expenditure line ($ab$ in Figure 4–2) connects all the combinations that could be purchased at the initial prices with the sum actually expended in the initial situation. The second expenditure line ($a'b'$ in Figure 4–2) connects all combinations that could be purchased at time 2 prices with whatever sum would be required to purchase the initial combination of quantities at time 2 prices.

we may still have ambiguity, not only as to the magnitude of net change, but, in some cases, even as to direction of change.

This ambiguity would be removed if we were able to draw the indifference map of consumers.[4] An indifference curve passing through the initial combination $c$ in Figure 4–2 would divide the area into two parts: all combinations above and to the right of the indifference curve would be superior (i.e., larger) combinations; those below and to the left inferior. The use of the double index number test presented above is a substitute for the use of indifference curves, and finds its ultimate rationale in consumer indifference theory.[5]

The trouble with the use of indifference curves is, of course, first, that it is practically (although not conceptually) impossible to establish their shape for any single individual, and, second, that here we need a social indifference curve representing the preferences of a group, and this concept has never been given any fully satisfactory meaning. Neither of these difficulties destroys the rationale referred to above and in the footnote. But the greatest difficulty—and one that does invalidate the rationale referred to—is that the whole argument assumes that the same indifference map (preference surface) exists at time 2 as at time 1. But, in fact, tastes change over time. Indeed, we are often trying to compare the values of two different sets of people, a generation or more apart. It is silly to assume that they have the same preferences. Even in the course of a shorter period—a year or two—tastes change. Almost the same persons may compose the population, but merely through the passage of time, they are *different people*. In the very process of living and consuming, we learn and therefore we change. The deliberate efforts of sellers are only one element in the dynamics of taste, most visibly (although most superficially) evident in the world of fashion.

Recognition of this fact destroys the indifference curve rationale for our index number procedure. We compare two dissimilar collections of goods. Which pile of goods is bigger (i.e., preferable) depends on the

---

[4] For an elementary treatment of indifference curves, see P. A. Samuelson, *Economics, An Introductory Analysis* (4th ed., McGraw-Hill, 1958), pp. 446–52.

[5] Assume that (a) the combinations actually purchased at times 1 and 2 represented points of consumer equilibrium (tangency of the appropriate expenditure line and an indifference curve); and (b) that the indifference curves (i.e., tastes) were unchanged as between times 1 and 2. It can then be demonstrated geometrically that, even if we do not know the shape of the indifference curves, any combination to the right of *both* expenditure lines $ab$ and $a'b'$ of Figure 4–2 must lie on a higher indifference curve, and any combination to the left of both must lie on a lower indifference curve. Combinations between the two lines can be assessed only if we know the exact shape of the indifference curve through point $c$.

tastes of the persons making the comparison. The comparison is essentially subjective.

If the phonograph record collection at our house consisted of more "classical" records and fewer of "progressive jazz," I would consider it a bigger (i.e., better) collection. My sons would consider it a worse one. All index number comparisons are essentially of this sort. The "index number problem" is not soluble because at bottom it represents a matter of tastes. We can neither give clear meaning to any concept of average or aggregate tastes (i.e., define a social as opposed to an individual in-difference curve); nor, even if we could, can we assume that tastes are constant over time.

The unavoidable ambiguity of comparisons of the size of two piles of goods at two different times arises not only because of differences in and changes in the tastes of those making the evaluation. An equally serious difficulty arises from changes in the goods included in the two piles. There are a great many goods in the gross national product of 1960 that were completely unknown in 1910 (and many of the 1910 goods are no longer produced). How does one determine how many electric light bulbs equals one kerosene lamp? Is a Ford Falcon more or less than a surrey-with-a-fringe-on-top? Even where goods do not wholly disappear, their quality changes. How do we assess the "changed quantity of output" involved in the fact that huckleberries are now larger (but less tasty) than they used to be; that pens will now write through butter; that the modern automatic washing machine saves hours of the house-wife's time, permitting her to taxi her children (who used to walk) to school?

Some quality improvement gets recognized in our official price indexes. But enough does not that some economists have argued that the "creeping inflation" of 1955–58 may be largely or even entirely illusory; if only our indexes had more completely reflected quality improvements, the price level would not have risen.[6]

All of the difficulties of measuring real GNP become more pronounced the farther apart in time (or space) are the points being compared. From one year to the next, essentially the same persons compose the population; their tastes have changed but little; new goods are relatively few, as are quality changes. Equally important, changes in the prices

---

[6] See, for example, Richard and Nancy Ruggles, "Prices, Costs, Demand, and Output in the United States, 1947–57," *Relationship of Prices to Economic Stability and Growth*, Compendium of Papers Submitted by Panelists appearing Before the Joint Economic Committee, March 31, 1958, pp. 297–308, esp. pp. 298–300.

and quantities of individual goods will be primarily in one direction—relative prices do not change much in the short run, nor does the product mix. We can be reasonably confident that whatever change is reported in real GNP, the "true change" is very close to that reported. As we compare periods farther apart in time, the individual price and quantity changes will be considerably more disparate. It will thus make much more difference which set of weights we use for our price or quantity indexes, and whatever the result, it will be more difficult to interpret. Further, changes in the population and its tastes make the meaning of any result questionable. Still, whatever the method of correction, a measure of output which has been corrected for price changes is for most purposes more meaningful than one not so corrected.

For example, we can be sure that real GNP in the U.S. did not rise by 133 per cent between 1940 and 1947, which is what the uncorrected dollar figures tell us. There was a considerable inflation of prices. The correction used by the Department of Commerce tells us that the rise in real output was, instead, 37.2 per cent. Whether it was 37.2 or 25.3 or 44.3 per cent, we are sure that it was very much less than 133 per cent. To take another example, the uncorrected dollar estimates for GNP are 419.2 billion for 1956 and 440.3 billion for 1957, a rise of 21.1 billion, or 5.0 per cent. Corrected for price change, the Department of Commerce reduces the increase to 4.8 billion (in 1954 prices), or 1.2 per cent. But, because relative price changes were small and the product mix was much the same in the two years, all of the possible methods of computation will yield measures of the change of real GNP between these two years which will be very close together. We can be quite sure that there was an increase in real GNP which lay between, say, 0 and 2.0 per cent.

## THE DEPARTMENT OF COMMERCE PROCEDURE

Prior to 1951, anyone who wished to estimate real GNP for the United States was forced to deflate the dollar GNP figures of the Department of Commerce either by a wholesale or a consumer price index or some kind of average of the two. Now the Department of Commerce provides an estimate of real GNP, prepared not by using an existing price index but essentially as a quantity index using base period weights. The dollar outputs composing the GNP are divided into the finest product breakdown possible—that is, the finest breakdowns for which separate price indexes are available. Each separate component of GNP is then deflated to a 1954 base, and the resulting deflated components are then added together to give the estimate of real total output in 1954 prices. Retail prices are used for each type of consumer goods; machinery prices, construction costs, etc., for each component of gross investment; government contract prices for each kind of government purchases. Exports and imports are separately deflated and their difference equals net exports in constant prices. For the services of government employees, a simple index of man hour employment in government is used to expand the dollar figure for 1954. In other words, an index of *input* rather than *output* of government employment is used, assuming, in effect, constant productivity.

By dividing the corrected figures into the original dollar figures, we get an implicit price index, whose movements generally resemble but do not coincide with any other price index, nor with any weighted average of existing price indexes.

The Commerce method is obviously only one of several possible ones for obtaining an estimate of real GNP. Even with this method, a somewhat different year-to-year pattern of movement would be given by a shift of the base of the deflation procedure to another year. Nevertheless, for purposes of estimating the real output of the economy, the new series is obviously superior to anything previously available. We now have deflated GNP on an annual basis back to 1929, and on a quarterly basis back to 1947.

## "REAL" NATIONAL INCOME

One might suppose it possible to prepare an estimate of real national income, separate and apart from the estimate of real product. The national income represents the aggregate earnings of factors of production, and these earnings can change in dollar terms merely through inflation or deflation. Could we not deflate each type of factor income by some index number of factor prices to provide us a measure of real income? Brief consideration will show that the whole approach must be abandoned. Consider the wage share, for example. If we deflate aggregate wages and salaries by an index of wage and salary *rates*, we come out with a measure of time worked—of *input* not *income*. To be sure, some of any change in wage and salary rates that we observe merely represents inflation or deflation of pay rates; but some of it represents change in productivity, too. Could we not separate out that part of wage change which represents productivity change, and call the balance a pure price change? Only by a procedure which essentially requires a deflation of *goods* prices, so that we come back to a concept which, in effect, measures output rather than income.

It is interesting to note, however, that Keynes, in his *General Theory* [7] proposed to deflate national income or output by an index of wage rates, an index based upon the movement of the price of unskilled common labor. In effect, he deliberately proposed measuring output in terms of input. His "output measured in wage units," represents, alternatively, an index of employment. Keynes, of course, was familiar with the concept of a real output that could change independently of labor input, primarily through the slow process of the improving productivity of labor. But Keynes was impressed with the ambiguities introduced into the measurement of real output by the "index number problem." Further, his theory was essentially a short-run theory, and in the short run, productivity changes are minimal. At least input (measured as employment) had no ambiguity of definition.

Of course, Keynes was wrong in claiming that employment was an unambiguous concept, for a man-hour of the services of an engineer or surgeon is not the same thing as the man-hour of a ditch-digger, and the input-mix of engineer and ditch-digger man hours may change. Keynes proposed to deal with this problem by weighting the engineer hours and ditch-digger hours according to their relative remuneration. But the relative remunerations may also change. Keynes realized that here the "index number problem" had slipped in by the back door; but he did not think the problem was as serious in this context as in the measurement of output, and he may have been correct.

Few economists have followed Keynes' example of dispensing with the concept of real output; nor shall we. Ambiguous as the concept of real output may be, we shall use it, just as we shall use the concept of total employment, even though that is ambiguous, too. And, when we consider periods of any considerable duration, we shall have to face up to the problem of changing productivity. This, of course, we must measure by comparing the movements of real output and real input.

## THE MEASUREMENT OF EMPLOYMENT
## AND UNEMPLOYMENT

We indicated in the last section an ambiguity in the concept of employment arising from changes in the input-mix of labor hours, and the fact that the input hour of an engineer or executive is not equivalent to

[7] See Chap. 4. pp. 37–45.

that of a farm hand or truck driver. In the broad measures of employment that are familiarly used in the United States, no account is taken of this problem. Indeed, our comprehensive employment measures do not even take account of variations in hours worked.

The basic United States measure of employment is one provided by the Bureau of the Census, based upon a scientific sample of the entire population. This sample, whose composition slowly changes (⅛ is new each month), is interviewed once each month, providing (by "blowing up" the sample findings) a monthly estimate of total employment. A person is defined as employed if, during the survey week, he was at any time at work for a private or governmental employer, or was self-employed, or an unpaid family worker for fifteen hours or more (as in a family business or farm). He is also counted as employed, even if not at work, if he has a job but was not at work because of vacation, illness, labor dispute, bad weather, or because he was taking time off for various other reasons.

As is clear from the foregoing, the concept of employment that dominates this measurement is an essentially social rather than primarily an economic one. A man who is on vacation or on strike is not a social problem (as an unemployed person might be); even if he is working half-time, he at least does not present to society the same problem that a completely unemployed worker does. The definitions clearly reflect their origin in the "great depression" of the thirties, when such measurements first began to be made.

One can assume that, in most respects, this measure of employment may at least move parallel with the concept of productive labor input. The number of workers on vacation, however, does vary seasonally, as does the number temporarily out-of-work because of bad weather; neither of these seasonal variations is reflected in the official employment figures. And the percentage of the total employed working part time (and over-time) varies considerably, and in a way systematically related to the variation of the number classified as employed. Thus, the Census figure is a far from perfect measurement of the concept of employment needed for the purposes of the economist.

For particular branches of the national economy we have somewhat better measures of employment. In manufacturing, particularly, we can combine a measure of weekly average man-hours worked with one of number employed to produce a rather accurate measure of current labor input. These data come from a sample of firms (rather than of the population), and are collected and published by the Bureau of Labor

Statistics. Although they may have some slight longer-term bias (because of the problem of inclusion of new firms in the sample), their shorter period movement comes much closer to what the economist is after. Unfortunately, however, these data are limited to manufacturing. The Department of Commerce does, however, prepare an estimate of the annual full-time equivalent number of employees in all activities. Combined with the estimated number of entrepreneurs, we thus have a fairly good estimate—on an annual basis—of the labor input involved in producing the national output.

As fuzzy as the measurement of employment may be, the measurement of unemployment is even worse. For this we need not only define employment, but also the status of being "in the labor force." The difference between those in the labor force and those employed is the number unemployed. To be in the labor force, when not employed, is essentially a state of mind. There is the problem of the seasonal worker for whom there are no off-season employment opportunities in his home locality (or using his kind of skills). There are the housewife, the retired worker, the student, who will be in the labor force if the "right job" comes along; otherwise not.

Although there are some most interesting conceptual problems, some of which have substantial relevance to the concept of "full employment," we shall here only note that a person is classified as unemployed in the Census Bureau estimates if he is (1) over fourteen years of age, not an inmate of an institution, nor in the armed forces; (2) not classified as "employed" (see above); and (3) either actively seeking work, or not seeking it (a) because he has a job but has been laid off, (b) because temporarily ill, or (c) because of a belief that no job is available in his line of work or in his community.

Alternative measures of unemployment, based on social insurance data, have fatal limitations of coverage.

## SHORT-RUN RELATIONSHIP OF EMPLOYMENT AND OUTPUT

Assuming that we had accurate measures both of real output and of labor input, how should we expect these measures to be related one to the other? For the individual productive unit producing a single commodity, we assume output to be a unique function of inputs. Assuming the *composition* of aggregate output to be reasonably stable, or to be systematically related to the size of aggregate output, we should also find a relationship between inputs and output at the aggregate level. What do we assume about the nature of the individual and hence of the aggregative output functions?

Our conventional theory tells us that, given the techniques of production employed, and given the inputs of other factors of production, output is a direct but non-linear function of employment. As employment increases, output should increase; but beyond some point, at a lower rate than the increase of input.

That is, representing output by $O$, and inputs of labor, capital, and natural resources by $N$, $K$, and $L$, respectively, our aggregate production function is

$$O = f(N, K, L)$$

We specify concerning the nature of this function only that an increase in any one of the inputs (the others held constant) causes output to increase; but further increases in any input cause smaller increases in output than earlier increases. That is, the marginal products of labor, capital, and "land" are all *positive*, but declining.[8] However, if all inputs increase together in the same proportion, output may increase (a) in that same proportion (constant returns to scale), (b) in greater proportion (increasing returns to scale), or (c) in lesser proportion (decreasing returns in scale). Figure 4–3 illustrates the case of constant returns to scale.

Given constant inputs of other factors, e.g., $K_1$ and $L_1$, output responds to increasing employment of labor along curve $O_1$. This curve shows continually diminishing marginal (and average) products of labor. (The marginal product of labor is the slope of the output function; the average product at any point is given by the slope of a line from the origin through that point.) But if a doubling of labor input—e.g., from $N_1$ to $2N_1$—is accompanied by a doubling of other inputs, the average product of labor is unchanged. The whole function moves upward to $O_2$, offsetting the tendency for the average product of labor to fall. If all inputs triple, output also triples (curve $O_3$). For any *constant* input of other

---

8 Technically speaking, we can write

$$\frac{\delta O}{\delta N}, \quad \frac{\delta O}{\delta K}, \quad \frac{\delta O}{\delta L} > O$$

where $\frac{\delta O}{\delta N}$, etc., are "partial derivatives." Further, the second partial derivatives

$$\frac{\delta^2 O}{\delta N^2}, \quad \frac{\delta^2 O}{\delta K^2}, \quad \frac{\delta^2 O}{\delta L^2} < O.$$

The first inequality states that all marginal products are positive, the second that they all decline as inputs increase.

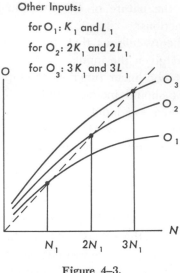

Figure 4–3.

factors, marginal and average products of labor decrease as more labor is used. Given any particular input of labor, labor's marginal and average products increase as inputs of the other factors increase. Changing returns to scale would be represented in the figure by the broken line having either upward or downward curvature.

The production function discussed above relates, of course, to a given body of technical knowledge. Technological change can increase the output associated with any given set of inputs. Or, putting the same thing in another way, technological innovation can reduce the inputs of one or more factors necessary to produce any given output. It may reduce all inputs, or it may reduce the necessary input of one factor, increasing that of another. For such an innovation to be adopted, it must reduce inputs having a greater value than the value of any necessary increase in other inputs; that is, it must reduce cost.

In any event, there has occurred, in Western economies, both a continuous improvement of productive techniques, and a rate of growth of capital which has much exceeded the rate of growth of the labor force. These factors have more than offset the expected diminishing returns to labor as population has grown, and have produced, as we all know, an increasing average productivity of labor—an increase in output much more than proportional to the growth of labor input. In the United States, this increase has apparently averaged about two per cent per year for many decades.

But in the short run (and most of the theory of this book is short run), the quantity of capital employed in production is stationary and so are techniques. Thus, we should assume diminishing returns to labor: a less than proportional expansion and contraction of output as employment expands and contracts. This is what most macroeconomic theorists have in fact assumed. The only trouble with this assumption is that it seems to be inconsistent with the facts.

To be sure, the "facts" are not available in a form which *directly* tests the predictions of the model, for the relationship we are interested in is a timeless one, while the facts consist of observations made over a period of time. Nevertheless, it is difficult to conclude from a careful study of available data that the timeless relationship could be that described above. If anything, the facts suggest the opposite conclusion— that the average product of labor is constant or conceivably *increases* as more labor is hired. One rather simple statistical test of the relationship between labor input and output in the U.S. economy is to compare monthly data on total man-hours of production workers in manufacturing industries and the output of manufactured goods. A statistical regression equation, covering the period 1951–56, suggests that the average product of labor (at least within the observed range of variation) is constant; output is simply proportional to labor input. A second simple test relates total quarterly U.S. employment to total real GNP. A statistical regression covering the years 1947–57 likewise shows a constant average product of labor as employment rises.[8]

---

[8] In using data covering a relatively short time period, it is certainly safe to represent the effects of technological improvement and increased capital per worker merely as a steady upward trend. We can then eliminate this trend so as to disclose the short-run relationship in which we are interested, that is, the relative fluctuations of employment and output. Thus we "fit" to the data a multiple regression in the form

$$O = a + bN + cT$$

For our first test, $O$ represents the Federal Reserve Index of Manufacturing Output (not seasonally adjusted), $N$ is employment of production workers in manufacturing, multiplied by average weekly hours (both from the Bureau of Labor Statistics), and $T$ represents time, measured from the middle of the period (January 1, 1954 = O). All data are monthly, 1951–56. The coefficients, $a$, $b$, and $c$ take on the values that provide the best "fit" to the statistical data (by the customary criterion of minimizing the mean squares of residual variation). The regression is

$$O = .885 + .246N + .4064T$$

(The coefficient of correlation is .950; standard errors are: constant term 8.63, employment coefficient .0054, trend coefficient .0181.)

The final or trend term shows that, on the average, manufacturing output tended to rise by roughly four-tenths of an index point per month (roughly 3.5 per cent per annum) over this period, quite independently of changes in man-hour employment. This was the net result of capital accumulation, technological improvement, etc. The

How are we to explain this inconsistency between the data and the expectation based upon the traditional theory of production? Reasons even for an increasing average product of labor are, indeed, not hard to find.

In the first place, some labor input is of an "overhead" variety—not responsive to short-run variations in output. This category includes not only the services of managerial and clerical employees, but also those concerned with maintenance, tool-making, inspection, research, etc. Although their number may be largely constant in the short run, it will have to grow more-or-less in proportion to any longer-run growth of output. A related factor is the tendency for employers to keep many workers on the payroll, even if not fully occupied, during what are expected to be temporary reductions of output, simply to avoid the possibility of their taking another job during a layoff and being lost to the firm, thus requiring investment in the recruitment, hiring, and training of new workers when output again increases. These two factors influence the results of both of our statistical tests, although they perhaps have more influence on the GNP comparison. Both overhead labor and labor "hoarding" are probably more important in nonmanufacturing industries than in manufacturing.

A third factor which might create the appearance of an increasing average product of labor is relevant only to the GNP comparison. It is the fact that our measure of total employment is not adjusted for changes in the work-week. When employment declines, the input of labor declines in greater proportion, because hours of work are also reduced, and vice versa.

---

coefficient of the employment term (.2464) indicates that, on the average, every increase of a million weekly man-hours produced a rise of about a quarter of a point in the output index. The constant term is, for all practical purposes, zero. This means that the production function, in effect, passes through the origin: output is proportional to labor input.

The second statistical analysis is much more aggregative. For $N$ it uses total employment in millions (as measured by the Bureau of Census, and uncorrected for man-hours worked), and $O$ is real GNP in billions of 1954 dollars (measured by the Department of Commerce). Data are quarterly for the period 1947 through 1957, and are seasonally adjusted. The resulting regression equation is

$$O = -38.9 + .63N + 2.27T$$

Although the negative constant term might suggest that the average product of labor rises as employment increases, and that the marginal product of labor, instead of being less than the average product, exceeds it, the negative constant is very small, and not statistically significant. We should rather say that, after adjusting for trend, output appears to be proportional to employment. (Standard errors are as follows: constant term 88.43, employment coefficient .144, trend coefficient .26. The coefficient of correlation is .9998.)

The above factors—overhead labor, the "hoarding" of labor during slack periods, and changes in average hours worked per employee— relate mainly to our measurements, not to the "true" relationship between actual labor input and output. But there are other, more basic reasons for the possible existence of a constant (or even rising) average product of labor as employment rises.

The traditional expectation of diminishing returns to labor relates to the case in which the input of one factor (labor) is increased or de- creased while inputs of others (of which capital is the most important) remain constant. In fact, although the stock of capital goods *in place* may be constant in the short run as employment changes, capital goods *in use* are usually not. Rather, use of capital goods in production may expand and contract with the use of labor. The customary elementary discussion of production theory, summarized on pages 92–94, typically uses examples involving very simple technology—e.g., variation of farm labor input on a given number of acres, or of fertilizer input with con- stant manpower and acreage. Industrial examples are occasionally used, to be sure: for instance, variation in the number of loomtenders in a textile mill with a constant number of looms operating, where each man can tend more or fewer looms, but with lesser efficiency (greater lost machine time) the smaller the proportion of men to machines.

However, a case perhaps more typical—in many kinds of production— is that of rather constant proportions necessarily obtaining in the short run between inputs of labor and of other factors. When output declines men are laid off; but machines are idled, too, and in the same propor- tion, because each machine is designed to be operated, and can only be operated by a fixed crew. When output revives, more men are added, while the amount of capital *in use* expands proportionately. As the tradi- tional theory recognizes, a proportional expansion of all inputs together does not necessarily lead to diminishing returns. There may even be increasing returns "to scale" as all inputs increase together, at least up to some point, both for the firm and the economy.

In recent years a rather considerable revolution in production theory has occurred in economics. Instead of the old assumption that all inputs are freely variable in whatever proportions may be convenient or profit- able, the assumption of constant proportions among inputs has increas- ingly been substituted. This is the assumption made in "input-output analysis," "activity" or "process analysis," or "linear programming." There may be choice among two or even more competing processes; but given the selection of any process, inputs must be combined in fixed proportions. This emphasis is not unrelated to the growing concern of economics with the concept of plant "capacity," and the popularity of theories of "acceleration," both of which will occupy us at later points in this book.

It appears, at least superficially, that the empirical evidence on short-run variations of employment and output is consistent with the fixed proportions view.

However, some warnings and qualifications need immediately to be posted.

In the first place, the plausibility of fixed proportions among capital and variable inputs is greatest for manufacturing activity. But manufacturing accounts, even in the United States, for only 26 to 28 per cent of total employment and 30 to 32 per cent of national income. In services, trade, agriculture, mining, finance, transportation and communications, and government, production functions involving use of inputs in fixed proportions are relatively few. However, in many or most of these activities the importance of labor as an "overhead" factor is extremely great. If theater attendance picks up, the "output" can expand very considerably with little or no increase in employment. To an important extent, the number of employees in services of all kinds, trade, finance, transportation and communications may be quite independent of considerable short-run variations in output. Output per worker may increase or decrease almost in proportion with the change in total output. (This is also true in government, except that "output" is there conventionally measured solely in terms of employment.) In agriculture, output variations in the short run depend more upon weather than employment; and even such short-run employment variation as occurs is masked by the traditional family organization of agriculture. Fewer or more days per year or hours per day of farm effort are not reflected in the employment statistics.

Thus it is not surprising that employment and output data should fail to display the short-run diminishing returns to labor so commonly assumed in almost all macroeconomic theory up to the past decade. Instead, it is quite understandable that the average product of labor should be constant or appear to rise with increasing output. Nor are these data sufficiently refined to permit testing of the more plausible hypothesis that diminishing marginal returns appear at least at *peak* levels of employment. This hypothesis would rest upon the observation that when plants are operating at peak levels, beyond the points of maximum efficiency for which they were designed, costs rise, and plans to add new plant capacity are pushed. It is well-known that overtime labor is less-efficient; that when labor shortages threaten, workers are hired who are at other times considered unemployable; that many businesses have reserve or stand-by capacity which consists of semiobsolete (and therefore less productive) equipment; that even trade and service establishments have, at some point, to hire extra help, and, given the size and arrangement of the physical premises, this help is often far less efficient.

Output may expand proportionately or even more than proportionately to labor input throughout a wide range of short-run output variation. It is still plausible to suppose that at some point (within the range of experience) diminishing returns set in.

## ASSUMPTIONS OF SUBSEQUENT CHAPTERS

In the chapters that follow, the reader will observe that we employ the traditional assumption of a diminishing average (and marginal) product of labor as aggregate employment expands.

The reasons for continuing the use of the traditional assumption are several. In the first place, these are the assumptions made both by the Classical writers and by Keynes; the assumption does not, therefore, enter into the differences between their views. It is more convenient and will avoid confusion if we discuss Keynes' criticisms of the Classical analysis without the complication of trying to revise or correct *both* arguments on a matter that is not a point of issue between them. Second, the assumption of diminishing rather than constant returns does not make any great difference in results, so long as the diminution is moderate. The reader can easily enough supply the appropriate modifications in the argument as he goes along, if he prefers to believe that a constant average (and marginal) product of labor is a superior assumption. Finally, the traditional assumption is preserved because the writer suspects that, at least at high levels of employment and output, this is still a realistic assumption, for reasons already indicated.     */5d586*

It was suggested in the last paragraph that the assumption of diminishing returns does not make much difference in results so long as the diminution is of moderate dimension. The writer is convinced that it does make a great deal of difference to the analysis if diminishing returns are considerable, especially when we relax our highly aggregative approach. This will be a principal theme of Chapter XX, below.

Such expressions as "moderate" versus "considerable" diminishing returns are obviously vague. Perhaps Figure 4–4 can give them somewhat greater content. In part A, there is shown the short-run supply curve (marginal cost curve) of a firm subject to diminishing returns as its

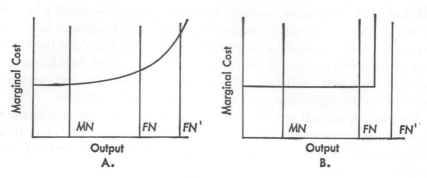

Figure 4–4.

variable input is increased. As is traditional, it is assumed that marginal costs rise only moderately at first but at an increasing rate as output increases. If this is the shape of the typical firm's supply curve, we can also think of it as the shape of the aggregate supply curve of the economy. It shows how efficiency declines (i.e., costs rise) as output is progressively increased, through the employment of additional short-run variable inputs—i.e., labor—with a fixed stock of capital and fixed endowments of natural resources.

If there were no limit on the total supply of labor, there might be no limit on output either. That is, the curve might become steeper and steeper, but never vertical. More reasonably, we could assume that at some point the marginal product of labor would reach zero—that is, the supply curve of output would become vertical. But in fact, there is a limit on the total quantity of labor available, which ordinarily sets a limit on total output far short of the point at which the aggregate supply function might otherwise become vertical. However, it makes a great deal of difference (especially when we consider aggregation problems) whether this limit to output comes at a point where the short-run aggregate supply function is fairly flat—as, for example, at the point marked *FN*—rather than where it is quite steep—as, for example, at *FN′*.

We shall assume that the output limit of full employment of labor comes at a point more like *FN* than like *FN′*. Then the range of output variation in which we are interested, between some minimum level of employment, *MN*, and full employment, *FN*, involves only moderate changes in labor efficiency.

In part B we show the short-run supply curve of the economy on the assumption of constant returns to the variable inputs up to some point of absolute capacity, set by the available stock of capital equipment.

This is the alternative assumption which we have discussed earlier, and which seems at least as consistent with available data as that of part A. Actually, however, so long as the full-employment limit is *FN* (rather than *FN'*) in each figure, the difference between the two views is not striking. Quite obviously, however, if part B were the relevant one, and the limit on labor supply were *FN'*, this would make quite a bit of difference for the theory. It is somewhat less obvious that *FN'* of part A would involve similar problems.

It is quite possible that for some economies, or for certain historical episodes, the relevant full-employment limits are like *FN'*. We shall consider these cases in Chapter XIX. For now, we assume that part A is the relevant pattern (i.e., "moderately" diminishing returns), with a full-employment limit like *FN*. This assumption is certainly more consistent with the data reviewed earlier than would be the assumption of a limit like *FN'*.

# The Classical
# Macroeconomics

*PART TWO*

## Say's Law and the Quantity Theory of Money

*Chapter V*

### IDENTITIES VERSUS THEORIES

Chapters II and III were concerned with *accounting* relationships among a number of macroeconomic variables. The latter part of Chapter IV considered macroeconomic relationships of an essentially *technological* sort—particularly between inputs and output. We are now ready to consider some more strictly *economic* relationships among macroeconomic variables. First, however, a methodological point.

The equality which we discovered in Chapter II among total spending, the money value of total output, and (under simplified assumptions) total income was only a definitional identity. It implied nothing whatever as to causation. Its existence does not mean that we can conclude that output *determines* spending, or that spending *determines* output. In effect, all that this identity reflects is the equality between amounts purchased and sold. The equality between saving and investment is of precisely the same character, although one stage removed from the identity of purchases and sales.

Despite the fact that these accounting relationships imply nothing as to causation, it is of course possible to postulate causal relationships, direct or indirect, among the same variables. This moves us from the realm of accounting into economics. The difference can probably be seen more clearly if we consider at first not broad aggregates like total output and total spending, but instead consider some analogous microeconomic concepts, such as sales and purchases of a single commodity. For each commodity we obviously find an identity between amounts bought and sold in any

105

given period of time (or their rates of sale and purchase at any given time)—either in physical or value terms. This reflects the fact that every purchase is also a sale. Suppose we define amount sold as "supply," represented by $S$; amount bought as "demand," represented by $D$. We have, then, a relationship between supply and demand; supply and demand must be equal. $S \equiv D$. But this does not tell us whether supply determines demand or demand determines supply, or whether both are determined by something else. And it tells us nothing about the commodity or its market except what is obviously true of all commodities and all markets.

We also have, however, a "theory" about this market. This theory postulates certain kinds of behavior by buyers and sellers. It may tell us, for example, that amount supplied is a direct function of a third variable, price; amount demanded is an inverse function of price. These are statements about behavior—embodying, actually, rather complicated hypotheses. The supply hypothesis rests on certain technological assumptions concerning relations of inputs and outputs, on certain institutional assumptions about the way production is organized (in private firms, or public enterprises that behave in certain ways), and on certain hypotheses about motivation of these firms (usually, some variant of the profit maximization hypothesis). The demand relationship rests on some fairly elaborate suppositions regarding the technological and psychological substitutability among goods in satisfying buyers' wants; on the assumption that income payments are at least in part independent of the price of this good; and probably many others.

We use these supply and demand hypotheses to explain the determination of market price, and of quantities bought and sold. They are put together with certain further assumptions about buyers' and sellers' *behavior in the market*—behavior that leads to a clearing of the market, through adjustment of price to eliminate any excess of amount supplied over amount demanded or *vice versa*. These further assumptions may be quite complicated, involving, at least implicitly, the form and frequency of price quotation by sellers (or buyers) and perhaps sellers' inventory policies. Also involved are assumptions regarding the information possessed by buyers and sellers concerning what is happening in the market.

We summarize all these theories (often with insufficient clarity as to what we are summarizing) in a single diagram, like Figure 5–1. In it we show supply and demand functions, intersecting at a point which "determines" price and quantity.

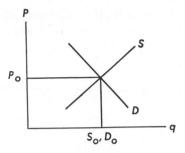

**Figure 5–1.**

Now it should be clear that the relationship we have here described between amount bought and amount sold is a different one from the definitional identity. Here we have amount sold as a function of price:

$$\overline{S} = S(P)$$

amount bought as another function of price

$$\overline{D} = D(P)$$

and an equilibrium condition

$$\overline{S} = \overline{D}$$

which corresponds to the intersection in the diagram. Note that we did not write

$$\overline{S} \equiv \overline{D}$$

Clearly, we have introduced some subtle difference of definition which makes $S$ and $D$ here mean something other than what they meant in the formulation that finds them identical. This is why we did not use the same symbols. Rather, $\overline{S}$ represents the quantity that sellers wish to supply, and will sell if they get a chance. $\overline{D}$ represents the amount that buyers desire to purchase, and will purchase if they can. As functions of price, these amounts can clearly be different, and are different, at most (or even conceivably at all) prices, although amounts *actually* bought and sold must be identical. To write as a "condition of equilibrium" that $\overline{S}$ must equal $\overline{D}$ is to say that if the price were to be at any level other than the $P_o$ in the diagram, either buyers or sellers (or both) must be disappointed—must be buying or selling more or less than they would wish to buy or sell at that price. This disappointment would lead them to do something different than they are in fact doing: that is, any price other than $P_0$ would not represent an equilibrium situation. Since S necessarily always equals D, if $\overline{S}$ were unequal to $\overline{D}$, either $\overline{S}$ would be unequal to S or $\overline{D}$ unequal to D.[1] Equilibrium requires that both buyers and sellers be satisfied with their behavior, i.e., that

$$\overline{S} = S \text{ and } \overline{D} = D$$

or, since

$$S \equiv D$$

equilibrium requires that

$$\overline{S} = \overline{D}$$

If (as is usual) we assume that a stable equilibrium exists, and if our concern is only with equilibrium, we neglect the distinction between $\overline{S}$ and S, $\overline{D}$ and D, and we never are confused as to whether we should say that supply equals demand or is merely identical with demand. (Strangely, however, in a strictly analogous piece of analysis, some economists have argued endlessly whether saving equals investment or is merely identical with investment, apparently believing that if it is one relationship it cannot also be the other!)

Later on we shall come back to this case of a single market to illustrate some points we shall want to make as to the meaning of equilibrium and the nature and relationships of statics and dynamics. For now, however, our purpose is merely to indicate that *we can simultaneously postulate both definitional and behavioral relationships among the same variables.*

Returning now, to aggregates, we should be able to see that the identity that the national accounts give us between aggregate spending and aggregate output implies no theory of causation—it does not imply that one determines the other; but neither does it preclude a theory, simple or complex, concerning these same aggregate variables. Say's Law is a very simple theory of this kind. It asserts a very simple relationship between output and spending. It is that output determines spending. If there were an autonomous increase in output, there would be a cor-

[1] Whether we think that the price can ever actually be other than $P_0$, even temporarily, depends on the assumptions we make about the speed of response by sellers and buyers. Presumably these responses are not instantaneous, and other prices can in fact prevail. But even if we should assume instantaneous response and the price always at equilibrium, we can nevertheless speak meaningfully about potential differences between $\overline{S}$ and $\overline{D}$, at prices other than $P_0$.

responding increase in spending. (As we shall see, a newer theory suggests just the reverse: that spending determines output. While perhaps closer to the truth than Say's Law, this, too, is an oversimplification.)

## SAY'S LAW

The ideas which we shall discuss under the name of "Say's Law" constitute in part a convenient "straw man," reconstructed by modern economists to represent the thinking of their "Classical" predecessors. The same is true of other theoretical constructs attributed to the "Classical Economists," meaning by this term essentially the English and American economists in the main orthodox tradition, from somewhere around the time of David Ricardo (1772–1823) to, say, 1930. No single "Classical Economist" ever held all of the ideas now attributed to this mythical scholar. To the extent that he considered macroeconomic problems at all, his ideas were probably both less rigorously framed, and more realistic, than the artificial summary we attribute to him. The main fact, however, is that his ideas about macroeconomic matters were at best rudimentary. He had not considered in detail the kinds of problems that concern us today. To some extent this was because the society and the economy he lived in did not pose these problems for him. For most of the macroeconomic questions which were asked, his answers were probably adequate. But, mostly, the questions that we consider important did not get asked.

If it is, then, *historically* somewhat inaccurate to talk about (and often to use as whipping boys) the macroeconomic theories of the "Classical Economists," it is nevertheless *analytically* useful to do so. To assemble and to sharpen up a Classical Theory helps us to understand better our own theories, which are, after all, in the main merely improvements upon or extensions of Classical ideas. Further, it helps us to understand the logic of these Classical ideas, much of which is still useful, even if incomplete.

Thus, it is not important whether the student can find in the writings of Ricardo or Mill or Taussig any particular formulation that we attribute to the Classical economists. Nor is it particularly important for our purpose that these same writers may have had insights which crudely anticipated our later formulations.

Say's Law (named after J. B. Say, the French economist, 1767–1832) is usually summarized as "supply creates its own demand." This principle is easily seen to be true in a barter economy, although its application was not supposed to be limited to that circumstance. More fully set forth, what Say appears to have had in mind can be expressed in this way: people work not for its own sake (indeed, work is unpleasant), but only to obtain goods and services that yield satisfactions. In an economy that practices division of labor and exchange, one obtains most of these goods and services not directly (as did Robinson Crusoe) by his own efforts; rather he produces goods in which his efficiency is relatively the greatest and exchanges the surplus above his own use for the products of others. The very act of production therefore constitutes the demand for other goods: a demand equivalent to the value of the surplus goods each man produces. How then can there ever be a general overproduction of goods? Each man's production (supply) constitutes his demand for other goods, and hence the aggregate demand must in some sense equal the aggregate supply. Total output may be limited by the fact that, at some point, for each individual, the satisfactions of a little more leisure will outweigh the sacrifice of a little more of goods that might have been obtained, but such "unemployment" will be "voluntary," not "involuntary." [2]

It is necessary again to distinguish this theory from the definitional identity among national product, national income and total expenditure. The identity exists at any level of income, output, or spending. What Say's Law implies is that any increment of output will generate an equivalent increase in income and in *spending*. Thus income and product can always be at a "full-employment" level. If they should be at a lower level, with some resources unwillingly idle, additional production will generate an equivalent amount of additional income, *which will all be expended in the purchase of the added product*. And since no one will be content at less than "full-employment," additional production *will take place* until the "full-employment" level is reached.

To be sure, Say's Law admitted that individuals might not correctly direct their production in accordance with one another's wants. The man producing shoe laces might produce more than people want to buy at the price (in terms of other goods) he had assumed would exist when he brought the product to market. As a result, the surplus shoe laces would buy fewer potatoes and less beer than he had anticipated. His adjustment to this would involve either a decision in favor of more leisure, or a decision to produce some other product, more in demand.

---

[2] For an excellent statement of Say's Law, see F. M. Taylor, *Principles of Economics* (9th ed., Ronald, 1921), pp. 196–205. For a fuller discussion see J. A. Schumpeter, *History of Economic Analysis* (Oxford University Press, 1954), pp. 615–25.

But this is merely the temporary maladjustment of relative outputs which the market will promptly correct.

Although framed in terms of a barter economy, it was believed that the Law held true for an economy using money. Aside from the occasional eccentric miser, people do not desire money for its own sake. If they sell their output or services for money, the money will promptly be spent against other goods. The money is merely a convenient medium of exchange, avoiding the awkwardness of barter, but nothing more.

The notion that people do not desire money for its own sake, and will therefore not hold idle balances, actually is part of another related but quite separable idea, the "quantity theory of money" to which we now turn. It was suggested above that a money economy behaved in the same way as a barter economy, because rational individuals will not hold idle money. Suppose, however, that for some reason not comprehended in the simple concept of rationality implied above, members of this economy should desire to add to their stocks of money—to lay out in the purchase of goods less money than they have received in payment for the goods they have sold. Even this would create no general surplus of supply over demand for goods if only selling prices are flexible, and respond by dropping whenever amount supplied tends to exceed amount demanded, or rising in the opposite case. This flexibility of prices would result from competition among sellers and among buyers, together with the desire of sellers to sell at the highest possible price and buyers to buy at the lowest. Suppose that at some particular point in time each income recipient should add one-tenth of his current income receipts to his cash balance, paying out only nine-tenths of what he has just received.[3] If only all money prices are competitive and flexible, and fall by one-tenth, the full previous output can still be sold, each good at a real price (in terms of other goods) which is unchanged both for buyers and sellers. So long as no further desire to add to cash balances now appears, the economy can continue to function at the new, 10-per-cent-lower price level, with each participant receiving a money income which is 10 per cent less, but which will buy the same quantities of goods as before, and as it is spent, will provide others with adequate incomes to purchase the (now-10-per-cent-lower-priced) goods which he is offering.

---

[3] We overlook here some difficult definitional problems related to stocks and flows. If one wishes to be more rigorous about this at this point, he should probably think of this in period terms, with one set of inpayments and one set of outpayments per period. However, for present purposes, we need not be completely rigorous, since nothing crucial is involved.

If, at some later time, members of the economy should desire to get rid of the idle cash previously laid by (again assume simultaneously, for simplicity), all prices must rise by 11 per cent, reflecting the excess of money demand over supply at the lower price level.

General hoarding and dishoarding were not, however, assumed to occur in ordinary circumstances. Rational men had no use for idle cash. Therefore they did not hoard it; and, having not previously hoarded, they could not dishoard. Thus the source of price level fluctuations was not ordinarily to be found here. Rather, people normally passed along promptly all the cash they received, and price level fluctuations arose primarily from changes in the *quantity* of cash in circulation. Suppose each individual found in his backyard a little cache of money (a gold mine?). This money, once discovered, would not be held idle, but would flow against goods and services, raising all money prices, although, again, leaving real prices unchanged. Or suppose some members of the society had authority to print money (a government, a commercial bank?) and augmented their spending by use of new cash. The general price level would again rise, in proportion to the increase in money supply. Prices, then, are proportional to the supply of money.

The notion that members of a money-using economy do not willingly hold idle cash balances is something both more and less than Say's Law. This idea was primarily used to provide an explanation for the absolute level of prices. In a barter economy there are only relative prices: the price of a shirt is seven apples; the price of an apple is three nuts; twenty-one nuts will buy one shirt; etc. Given a money, which people do not desire for its own sake but use merely as a medium of exchange, then all prices (expressed in terms of this medium) will rise and fall together with changes in the stock of money. That is, we have an absolute level of prices, which depends on the quantity of money.

Say's Law, on the other hand, asserts something about involuntary unemployment, arising from a deficiency of aggregate demand for goods. Although Say's proposition (that such deficiency cannot occur) is obvious for a barter economy—which, as we have seen, has no absolute price level—for a money-using economy Say's Law is far from obvious. Rather, Say's Law describes a result which depends on several specific behavior assumptions the correctness of which is subject to challenge, and upon a fairly complicated theory of markets. We shall attempt, in the next several chapters, to spell out all aspects of the "Classical Theory" which produces Say's result. We shall see how, and under what circumstances, this result can be expected to work out in a money-using, labor-hiring, and saving-investing economy. First, however, it would be useful to go into somewhat more detail regarding the aspects of money use involved in the quantity theory.

## CASH BALANCES AND THE QUANTITY THEORY

To do so, let us consider the behavior over time of the cash balance of an individual member of a money-using economy. His balance might look somewhat like the diagram in Figure 5–2. At time point 0, this indi-

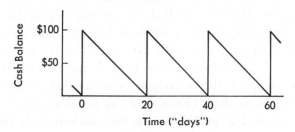

**Figure 5–2.**

vidual receives cash in the amount of $100, presumably in payment for productive services. Just prior to this receipt, his cash balance had been zero. Now it becomes $100. His next receipt of $100 will come 20 time units ("days") later. The particular balance pattern assumed in this diagram has our individual spending one-twentieth of this cash each day, reducing his balance to zero just before his next pay period. This is not the only way a balance can behave. A balance pattern more familiar to most of us is one which replaces the straight downward-sloping line with a highly curved one, the balance rapidly approaching zero soon after pay day. However, the straight-line assumption simplifies calculations without missing any essential principle.

We can say that our individual holds a cash balance that varies from $100 to 0. On the average, he holds $50 (in the straight-line case). This average balance ($50) is equal to one-half his income ($100), if we state his income as per pay period. If we state his income as a "yearly" rate, and there are four pay periods in a "year," his average balance is one-eighth of his income. (Since income is a flow, and cash balance a stock concept, the size of any ratio between them must depend on the time unit used to express the income flow. This unit is obviously a matter of indifference, except for the convenience and custom of the annual unit for reckoning.)

This individual holds no cash for its own sake. His only reason for holding cash at all is to bridge a gap in time between receipts and outpayments of funds. Yet we find him, in fact, holding cash, and doing so quite "rationally" and "willingly." He can be described as having a "demand for cash" equal to one-eighth his "annual" income. (In the curvilinear case, his average balance would be less, and his demand for cash a smaller fraction of his income.) We call this demand a "transactions demand," indicating that he holds cash only to make necessary transactions.

There is a second way in which we can describe our man's cash holding behavior. It is to say that the average dollar he receives is held for ten days. Some dollars are held for one, two, three, eighteen, nineteen, and twenty days. But the average dollar is held ten days. (If we had assumed a curvilinear time path of his balance, the average period would be less.) Alternatively we can say that the average dollar he receives is passed along (turns over) in ten days. Since ten days is half his income period, and there are four such periods per year, we can say that the average dollar he receives is turned over at a rate equivalent to eight times per year. This is its (partial) "velocity."

It should be obvious that to describe his demand for cash as equal to one-eighth his income (annual) or to describe the velocity of his cash receipts as eight times per year are merely alternate ways of expressing a single phenomenon. Likewise, it should be clear that we can use another time period and get different numerical results. (For example, it is sometimes convenient to think of the payment period as our time unit. If so, his demand for cash is half his income, and the velocity of his cash is two.)

To fill out the picture on this matter of money use (or money holding) we need to see what happens to the money which our friend passes along—and where the money came from that he gets. To do this, we shall change our example a little bit. Suppose that the diagram on page 113 represents the total cash-balance position of *all* income recipients in our economy. Let us suppose that all wages, salaries, interest, and profits are paid out to individuals on the same day. They receive, in the aggregate, $100 of income on days 0, 20, 40, etc. Where does the cash come from, and where does it go when they release it? Assume all business is organized in one giant firm (and that there is no government). The pattern of the business cash balance is obviously a mirror image of that of income recipients. Figure 5–3 shows this relationship between the cash balance of business and that of consumers.

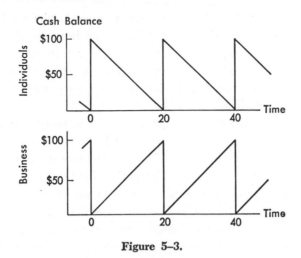

**Figure 5–3.**

As the figure is drawn, business cash balances are reduced to zero as incomes are paid out on day 0. Thereafter, as consumer balances shrink, business balances grow. By day 20, when consumers are out of cash, business has accumulated, through sales to consumers, exactly enough cash to pay the incomes then due, and the sequence is repeated thereafter.

Now our business also has a cash balance. Its average size is also obviously $50. Its balance also turns over eight times per year. The total cash in circulation is clearly $100. Every dollar of this sum is always either in the balance of business or of consumers. It bounces back and forth between them mediating sales of productive services from individuals to business, and sales of goods from business to individuals.

The total "demand for money" on the part of business plus consumers is obviously $100. This is all a "transactions demand." This demand can be described as one-fourth of a year's income. The total transactions in this economy are $800 per year, so the demand for money can also be described as equal to one-eighth of a year's transactions. Another way of describing these relationships is to say that the "transactions velocity" of this money is eight times per year. Or we can say that the "income velocity" of this money is four times per year: the average dollar makes four circuits per year from an income recipient, through business, and back to an income recipient again.

It should also be noted that had the shrinkage of consumers' balances followed a path which was *concave* upward, business balances would have grown by a path which was *convex* upward. The smaller average demand for money by consumers would have been precisely offset by a larger average demand by business; the faster turnover by consumers offset by a slower turnover by business. In either circumstance, however, there is no idle money. *Minimum* cash balances are zero both for business and consumers.

The matters described in the preceding paragraphs are elementary. Yet it is vitally important to see them clearly.

We can complicate this picture of money use in many ways. All income payment dates do not coincide. The period for income payment is not the same for all types of incomes. Business is not organized in one giant firm, but in separate firms having intermediate transactions among themselves, each one holding necessary transactions balances. All of these complications can be incorporated without alteration of principle. Even the fact that people save and lend, and deal in existing assets, and that business gets cash not only from sale but from borrowing can also be brought in. (Other problems, however, cannot be so easily handled: particularly, perhaps, the assumption not only of stationary conditions, but of *certainty* regarding the timing and amount of future payments. More of these things later, however.)

We turn now to brief consideration of some of the factors that determine the amount of transactions cash necessary to accomodate any particular level of transactions or income. One of these factors is, quite obviously, the "payment habits" of the community. Suppose, in our simple example, that the pay period were cut to ten days. Suppose $50 of income were paid out each ten days instead of $100 each twenty days, as in the figure below. Exactly the same level of annual income payments and volume of business sales could now be accomplished with half the previous stock of cash. The demand for cash would now be only one-sixteenth of a year's transactions, only one-eighth of a year's income. The income velocity of money would now be eight, its transactions velocity sixteen. This case is shown in Figure 5–4.

The payment habits that are relevant here are not only those relating to frequency of income payment, but also those relating to frequency of settlement of bills for goods. (Suppose, for example, we introduce charge accounts, which need be settled only once per year. The same factor operates more significantly in the intermediate transactions in the business sector.)

A related determinant of velocity is the degree of business integration. If business is vertically integrated, less cash is needed than if business

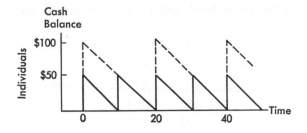

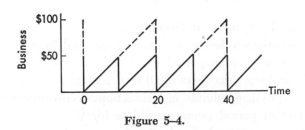

**Figure 5–4.**

is vertically disintegrated, each "layer" holding a necessary cash balance. For discussion of these points the student should consult the section on "determinants of velocity" in any standard money and banking text.[4]

Given the payment habits and the industrial structure of the community, the amount of cash needed for transactions obviously depends only on the money volume of these transactions. If our highly simplified economy considered earlier doubled in size—twice as much production and real income—twice as much money would be required to mediate the enlarged volume of transactions, assuming the price level remained the same. Aggregate income would double to $200 per period and sales of goods to $200, meaning that $200 of cash would have to be available to make the income payments, with average balances of business and consumers each now $100 instead of $50 as before. Alternatively, if prices fell by 50 per cent, the doubled volume of goods and real income could be moved with the same $100 total supply of cash.

Now we are ready for a restatement of the quantity theory. If we assume given payment habits and a given vertical structure of production, if we assume that prices are perfectly flexible in either direction, if we assume that people have no desire for idle (non-zero minimum)

---

[4] A further significant determinant, less often discussed, is the degree of "over-lapping" of payment dates. See Howard S. Ellis, "Some Fundamentals in the Theory of Velocity," *Quarterly Journal of Economics*, May 1938, LII, 431–72; reprinted in *Readings in Monetary Theory* (Philadelphia, 1951), pp. 89–128.

balances, then the price level will be proportional to the quantity of money in circulation.

More formally, we can state the proposition in terms of any of the four following formulations: [5]

$$MV = P_t T$$
$$MC = Y = P_o y$$
$$M = m P_t T$$
$$M = lY = l P_o y$$

The symbols have the following meanings:

$M =$ quantity of money in circulation

$V =$ transactions velocity of money, expressed in number of times per year or other period

$P_t =$ the average price level of all transactions

$T =$ the "physical volume" of transactions occurring during the year or other period (same period as for V)

$C =$ income or "circular" velocity of money, times per period

$Y =$ money national output (or income)

$P_o =$ the average price level of final output

$y =$ the physical volume of final output

$m =$ transactions demand for money expressed as a fraction of the money value of transactions for the period

$l =$ transactions demand expressed as a fraction of money income

It is clear that $V \equiv \dfrac{1}{m}$, and $C \equiv \dfrac{1}{l}$.

Consider now the first formulation. Assume that people never hold idle balances, that money stays in balances only long enough to make necessary payments; assume that the institutional factors which determine this minimum period are given. Then $V$ is constant, and $MV$ is proportional to $M$. If prices are perfectly flexible, $T$ can always be at the maximum level permitted by the technology and the willingness to work of the community. At any given time this level can be taken as constant. Hence $P_t$ is proportional to $M$. An increase or decrease in $M$ would produce a proportional increase or decrease in prices.

[5] These equations are to be understood as equilibrium conditions, not as identities. If $V$ were defined (measured) as $(P_t T)/M$ (or $C$ as $Y/M$), then the equations are true by definition, and therefore devoid of predictive or explanatory value. As theories, these equations assert propositions that are capable of being found untrue, as a definitional identity cannot be.

Consider now the second formulation. The same reasons that make $V$ constant apply as well to $C$, with one necessary addition. Added is the plausible view that, at any particular time, the volume of final output is a constant fraction of the total volume of transactions. Thus, if money stays in all balances only the necessary minimum period of time, and if the number of balances the average dollar must go through in making a complete circuit from one income recipient to another is given, $C$ will be a constant, of course smaller than $V$. Again assuming competition and flexible prices, $y$ can be taken always to be at its maximum level, and $P_0$ therefore proportional to $M$.

The third and fourth formulations are obviously only alternative statements of the first and second. Instead of using a velocity (times per year that money turns over), they use a "demand for money," expressed as the fraction of total money value of transactions or money income that people need to hold in cash form. However, these formulations assume as constant exactly the same technological and behavioral characteristics as do their counterparts using velocity, and reach identical conclusions. At the root of all of these formulations is the idea that no one—consumer or business—holds "idle" cash. He holds some cash (slowing down what would otherwise be an infinite velocity of circulation), but only because there is imperfect coincidence between his discrete lumps of inpayment and his discrete lumps of outpayment.

People hold cash by necessity, but they hold as little and for as short a time as they can.

A second root idea is, of course, that of flexible, competitive prices. Additional cash bids up prices—rather than increasing the physical volume of output or transactions—because output and transactions were already at their maxima. How do we know that they were? Because if they had not been, someone unable to sell all that he wished, would have offered his supply at a lower price, and prices would have fallen—output expanding—until output had reached its maximum.

We shall see, in the next chapter, that the idea summarized in the last paragraph needs to be greatly expanded, and somewhat qualified, in a society in which people sell their services to a business which in turn sells goods.

Before turning to this topic, however, we should recognize that we can easily make the quantity theory into a theory of output, simply by assuming rigid prices.

## THE QUANTITY THEORY WITH RIGID PRICES

If prices are rigid, at too high a level for maximum output, it should be obvious that, based on our other assumptions, an increase in the quantity of money will raise output, not prices. A reduction in the quantity of money will, with inflexible prices, create unemployment rather than simply lower prices. Since it is clear to almost everyone that in the real world, prices are not as flexible (particularly in a downward direction) as this theory assumes, it is not surprising that monetary policy has often been advocated as a means of stabilizing employment and output. If there is unemployment, we may conclude (based on this theory) that it is only because of sticky prices and wages. But, if we do not think that we can get the wages and prices to fall, or that it would take too long, we can eliminate unemployment by increasing the supply of money instead.

Of course, there have been those who said—in one and the same breath—that unemployment was due only to sticky wages and prices; but that monetary expansion would not cure it. Rather, an increase in $M$ would only cause inflation. This is obviously poor logic unless we accept the implicit assumption that prices are rigid in a downward direction, but completely flexible upward, even when output is well below maximum. A more plausible argument might be that prices are sticky in either direction when output is below maximum, but flexible upward when full employment exists.

However, to appreciate more fully what may be involved in any of these special cases, we need to examine more explicitly the price and wage theories which are a part of the Classical analysis, and which, for want of a better, are largely retained in the modern systematic theoretical formulations. That is the task of Chapter VI. In Chapter VII we develop the further complications that arise as a result of the processes of saving and investing.

## SAY'S LAW INCONSISTENT WITH
## THE QUANTITY THEORY? [6]

In a long series of articles appearing in the economics journals beginning about 1942, several economists, the most persistent being Don Patinkin, have argued that Say's Law and the quantity theory are inconsistent, and that an economic model which includes them both is

---

[6] This section can easily be omitted by the reader not interested in purely doctrinal controversies.

untenable. In short, Classical theory, which tried to include them both, committed a grave logical error.[7]

Much of the argument in support of Patinkin's position is highly formal and mathematical. However, the essence of Patinkin's argument is a simple enough matter. Patinkin points out that Say's Law depends on the proposition that goods are produced to exchange for other goods; the quantities of other goods that can be received in exchange are what motivates production. That is, the supply and demand for each real commodity depend only on *relative* prices—what each good will buy of each other good. (In mathematical language this is expressed by saying that the supply and demand equations for goods are homogeneous in degree zero in absolute prices: all absolute prices can be doubled or halved or multiplied by 999 or .001 without changing any seller's or buyer's behavior with respect to the production or consumption of any real good.)

But if goods are to be sold in the first instance for money, the supply schedule for each good can be thought of as constituting a demand schedule for money. Similarly, the demand schedule for each good constitutes a supply schedule for money. At each possible (relative) price for each good, there would either be an excess supply of the good, an excess demand for the good, or, at one particular relative price, an exact balance of supply and demand. Put otherwise, at each possible (relative) price, there would be a net demand for money, a net supply of money, or, at some particular relative price, neither. We can now aggregate all of the net supply or demand schedules for money—those relating to the supply and demand schedules for each good—to get an aggregate net demand schedule for money (counting net supply as negative net demand). If Say's Law holds, the supply and demand schedules for each good are independent of absolute prices (depending only on relative prices); hence, so is the excess supply or demand schedule for each good, and so also the aggregate net demand schedule for money which derives from all of these. The aggregate net demand for money depends only on relative prices and is independent of absolute prices.

But the quantity theory appears to provide a second demand schedule for money—one which makes the demand for money depend not on relative but on absolute prices. The two are said to be "obviously" inconsistent.

[7] For an excellent annotated bibliography of this controversy, see S. Valavanis, *Kyklos* (1955), pp. 351–68. Valavanis' article provides a penetrating critique of the Patinkin position.

To be sure, one can, first of all, point out that the demand for money schedule implied by the supply and demand schedules for individual goods is necessarily expressed (as they are) in flow terms, while the quantity theory demand is in stock terms. One seems to avoid this difficulty if he reformulates the argument as follows. The net demand for money derived from the supply and demand schedules for individual goods is zero at some particular set of relative prices (whether such a set exists and whether there is only one such set is another question). The net quantity theory demand for money (to *add to* existing balances) is zero at some particular absolute price level. We thus have two conflicting conditions for zero net demand for cash.

However, further reflection must show that the first of these two conditions is a necessary but not sufficient condition for a zero net demand for money. Suppose that all markets are in equilibrium—relative prices are such that, in the market for each good, supply equals demand. Thus there is no dissatisfied buyer or seller, and there is no net demand for cash. This first condition would be fulfilled at an infinite number of sets of absolute prices, all producing the same set of relative prices. But, in fact, in a money-using economy, not all of these sets of absolute prices are possible. That is why we need the second condition. Given the institutional and structural limits on velocity, only a certain range of absolute prices is possible, a range from zero up to the maximum level that the existing quantity of money can support.

Now we need one further assumption, one thoroughly consistent with Say's Law. It is that money, unlike real goods, has no utility in and of itself. It is, *per se*, not wanted. Why then is it held at all? Simply because this cannot be avoided when money is used as a medium of exchange. There is some maximum limit to velocity. This limit and the quantity of money select the absolute price level. It is the highest of all of the *possible* price levels referred to in the last paragraph.

Patinkin fails to distinguish between the implications of the two functions of money—as a unit of account, and as a medium of exchange. As a unit of account, absolute money prices indeed have no relevance in a Say's Law economy. Double all prices, or cut them all by nine-tenths, and no one's behavior with respect to supply and demand for goods need be altered. What counts are only *relative* prices. But money also serves the other function, and there is no way of avoiding this so long as income cannot accrue and be spent continuously and simultaneously. People who have no desire for money *per se* (as shown by their zero minimum cash balances just before pay day) nevertheless willingly hold (i.e., demand) money during the intervals between pay days, having (in the simplest case) an average demand for money equal to half their money incomes (measured per pay period). There is no inconsistency in this description of their behavior!

If money were only a unit of account and did not have to circulate, the quantity of money would make no difference. All the world's work could be done with one dollar (or any other quantity of money—in fact, its "quantity" would have no meaning). Yet to recognize that money does have to circulate, and thus (given the structural and institutional factors that limit its velocity) to recognize that its quantity must be related to the price level is not to violate the assumption that money is not wanted for its own sake.

In short, Say's Law, *taken by itself*, is consistent with any absolute price level. The quantity theory selects which absolute price level will prevail (depending on the quantity of money and the institutional and structural factors which determine its velocity). There is no inconsistency between the underlying assumptions of Say's Law and the quantity theory so long as every economic agent has a *minimum balance* of zero. This indicates that money *per se* is not wanted. This assumption is, in fact, shared both by the quantity theory and by Say's Law. Rather than being inconsistent, they are instead completely consistent and complementary ideas.

# Wages, Prices, Employment, and Production

*Chapter VI*

## THE CLASSICAL FULL-EMPLOYMENT EQUILIBRIUM

The various formulations of the quantity theory all state that, at any given time, and with any given stock of money, aggregate price-times-quantity is a constant. More can be sold only at proportionately lower prices. It is further implied that, if prices are flexible, they will fall whenever there are idle resources, this fall in prices somehow automatically promoting or accompanying an expansion of physical volume of output. We need to examine more specifically how price flexibility promotes full employment in an economy in which men work for wages.

Actually, Classical *price theory*, (as opposed to *monetary theory*) implies that the volume of employment and output is determined in the first instance not by the *level* but by the internal *structure* of prices. Specifically, any particular producer's output and employment decisions depend on a relationship between his costs and the prices buyers will pay for his output. We shall simplify this part of the analysis very greatly by assuming (1) that perfect competition prevails in all industries; and (2) that each industry is vertically integrated: it hires only labor and produces final output (using a given stock of capital goods and natural resources); there are no intermediate goods. These assumptions can be removed with no major change in results, but they greatly simplify the analysis. We further assume, as is customary, that sellers attempt always to maximize profits.

In a purely competitive industry we know that profit maximization can be described by the equality of price and marginal cost. Each

124

seller's output will be carried to the point where his (rising) marginal cost equals the (for him) given price. What, now, is the relation of wage rates to marginal cost? Assuming labor as the only variable input, marginal cost—the addition to total cost for an additional unit of output—is necessarily equal to the wage rate divided by the marginal physical product of labor. If the last worker adds ten units of output, the marginal cost of this output is one-tenth his wage; if he adds eight units, marginal cost is one-eighth his wage. Suppose the price of output is $5 per unit, and the wage rate $30. Output will be carried to the point where the last worker adds 6 units to output. To say that output is carried to the point where price equals marginal cost is thus, under these assumptions, equivalent to saying that input is carried to the point where the wage equals the value of the marginal product of labor. The one formulation of the profit maximization principle is simply an algebraic rearrangement of the other. To continue our example, the point where price ($5) equals marginal cost ($30 ÷ 6 units), is also the point where the wage ($30) equals the value of the marginal product (6 units at $5). More formally, if

$$P = MC$$

and

$$MC = \frac{W}{MPL}$$

then

$$W = P \cdot MPL$$

where $P$ is the price per unit of output, $W$ the wage per unit of input, $MC$ marginal cost of output, and $MPL$ the physical marginal product per unit of labor. The product $P \cdot MPL$ is the value of the marginal product. We can also rearrange the above expressions in the form

$$MPL = \frac{W}{P}.$$

This states that output (or input) is carried to the point where the marginal product equals the "real wage"—the money wage deflated by the price level of output.

As any of these formulations indicates, it is the relationship of wages to prices that determines hiring and output, not the absolute level of either one. Thus, if both wages and prices should rise or fall in the same proportion, there would be no incentive for the firm to hire fewer or more workers or to produce a different output.

We assume that for any given enterprise (with given capital and natural resources), marginal costs rise (marginal product declines) as output increases. Since total output is the sum of output in all firms, we can then assume that the law of diminishing returns applies in the aggregate sense as well: as more workers are hired in the total economy, aggregate output increases, but in continually smaller proportion than the increase in input.

We need one more concept to round out our theory—that of the supply curve of labor as a whole, as a function of the real wage. Presumably this rises to the right—that is, more labor will be supplied at a higher than at a lower real wage. However, it might be vertical, or, even, backward-bending (if a higher real wage rate makes some workers wish to take a part of their potential increase in real income in the form of leisure).

Suppose, now, that at given levels of money wage rates and prices, employers find it profitable to employ fewer workers than wish to work at that real wage. If there is full and free competition, the unemployed workers will offer their services at lower money wage rates, rather than remain idle. Whether and to what extent this results in additional employment and output now depends on what happens to prices. If prices should fall in the same proportion as money wages, there would be no incentive for employers to increase employment and output. If they should not fall at all, or should fall in smaller proportion than did wages, employers would find it profitable to increase output, absorbing some of the unemployed.

In his *General Theory of Employment, Interest and Money*, John Maynard Keynes contended that Classical theory provided no satisfactory explanation of what would happen to the level of selling prices in the face of a general wage reduction.[1] Certainly it was inappropriate to extend to the entire economy—as some Classical writers had carelessly done —an assumption which was appropriate in dealing with a single firm or industry—namely, that there was no relation between wage rates paid and money demand for the product, so that prices could be assumed constant as wages fell. Rather, Keynes thought that the logic of the Classical position should require prices to fall in the same proportion as wages. Thus, if there were unemployment and flexible wages, we might expect a general deflation of wages and prices which would continue indefinitely, since there would be no increase in employment, and the unemployed would continually bid the money wage level downward.

[1] See Chapter 2, "The Postulates of the Classical Economics."

The view of Keynes obviously ignores another rather significant strand of the Classical analysis—one we have already considered—the quantity theory. For if prices were to fall as fast as wages, with no increase in output, idle balances would automatically be created in the hands of business or consumers or both. Since rational people are not willing to accumulate idle balances, this could not happen. Real spending would necessarily increase as prices fell, thus preventing as large a decrease in prices as in wages.

Put in another way, we can say that—with a given quantity and velocity of money—prices must fall if an expanded output is to be sold. But in order to provide incentive for an expansion of output, wages must fall relative to prices—i.e., they must fall proportionately more than prices. If wage rates are flexible, money wages *will fall* by whatever amount will provide the necessary profit margin below that price level at which the maximum output can be sold.

We might, rather crudely, think of the sequence of events in these terms: unemployment causes a reduction of the money wage. With given prices, this induces producers to increase employment and output. But larger output can be sold only at lower prices—with a given $M$ and constant velocity. So prices are bid down, too, but by less than wages have fallen. Although this reduction in prices takes away some of the incentive to increase output, it will not take it all away. For if prices fell as much as wages, there would be no incentive for employers to provide an increase in output, and therefore no reason for prices to fall at all. Further, with lower prices but no increase in output, there would necessarily be idle balances. But if prices fall less than wages, there will be both an incentive to increase output, and a market for a larger output.

If the initial fall in money wages (with the accompanying smaller reduction in prices) were insufficient to eliminate all unemployment, money wages would fall further, prices in turn falling some more (but again by less than wages), until full employment and maximum output were reached, at which point wages, prices, employment and output would stabilize.

Perhaps a numerical example will clarify this. Suppose that the quantity of money is fixed at $50 and its circular velocity is 2. This means that money income can be at the rate of $100. It cannot be at a higher rate, and it will never be at a lower. This could involve a number of possible combinations of prices and quantities, a few of which are shown in Table 6–1 below.

TABLE 6-1.   Possible Combinations of $P$ and $y$
with Given $M$

| $P$ | $y$ | $P \cdot y$ |
|---|---|---|
| $2.0 | 50.0 | $100 |
| 1.2 | 83.3 | 100 |
| 1.0 | 100.0 | 100 |
| .93 | 107.5 | 100 |
| .833 | 120.0 | 100 |
| .667 | 150.0 | 100 |
| .5 | 200.0 | 100 |

Each of the possible outputs shown in Table 6-1 requires the input of some particular quantity of labor, in some such fashion as shown in Table 6-2.

TABLE 6-2.   Aggregate Production Function

| $y$ | $N$ | $MPL$ |
|---|---|---|
| 50 | 18.5 | 2.7 |
| 83.3 | 32.4 | 2.4 |
| 100 | 40 | 2.2 |
| 107.5 | 43.5 | 2.15 |
| 120 | 50 | 2.0 |
| 150 | 67.6 | 1.7 |
| 200 | 107.6 | 1.25 |

Suppose that the initial price level is $1.00 and the initial wage level $2.20. The real wage is then 2.2. From Table 6-2, we can see that the most profitable output is 100, requiring 40 units of labor input ($N$). From Table 6-1, we find that exactly 100 units can be sold at $1.00 each with the given supply and velocity of money. In other words, this particular combination of $W$, $P$, $y$, and $N$ satisfies the requirements both of profit maximization and of the quantity theory.

Suppose, however, that there are more than 40 units of labor seeking employment, and that the money wage is now bid down, by their competition, to $2.00. If prices did not fall, the real wage would drop to 2.0, and the point of maximum profit would shift to 120 output and 50 input (see Table 6-2). But this is not possible; more units of output cannot be sold at the same price as before. Therefore, prices have to decline as output expands; and consequently it is not profitable to expand output as far as 120. Rather, with a wage of $2.00, we might find prices declining to $.93, with an output of 107.5 (Table 6–2). The real wage would now be 2.15, which is just sufficient to induce an employment of 43.5 and an output of 107.5, which in turn (see Table 6–1), can just be sold at a price of $.93. Again, we have a combination that satisfies both quantity theory and profit maximization requirements.

Assuming, however, that there were more than 43.5 labor units seeking employment, wages might be bid down further. Suppose, for example, that the supply curve of labor were as represented by the data in Table 6–3 below.

TABLE 6–3.   Supply of Labor

| Real Wage | Supply of Labor |
|---|---|
| 2.4 | 56 |
| 2.2 | 53 |
| 2.15 | 52 |
| 2.0 | 50 |
| 1.7 | 46 |
| 1.25 | 40 |

By comparing this table with Table 6–2, we can see that "full employment" will require an output of 120 units. At this output, and at no other, the demand and supply of labor will be equal, at a real wage of 2.0. We can calculate from Table 6–1 how far the money wage would have to fall in order to produce this equilibrium. We see that the only price level at which 120 units can be sold (with given $M$ and $C$) is $.833. If the real wage must be 2.0 to make employers willing to produce this output, the money wage must then fall to $1.667 (2.0 × $.833). If competition from unemployed workers can reduce wages this far, unemployment will be eliminated. At these values of $W$, $P$, $y$, and $N$, we satisfy not only the profit maximization and quantity theory requirements, but also the requirement for stability of the money wage: that the number of jobs equals the number of job-seekers. It will be noted that a drop of $.533 or nearly 25 per cent in the money wage was necessary to accomplish a drop of about 9 per cent in the real wage.

Thus, we answer the question posed at the beginning of the chapter in this way. The volumes of employment and output depend directly on the structure and not upon the level of prices—they depend on the real wage, which is a ratio of wages to prices. But, in order to widen the gap between wages and prices—i.e., to lower the real wage ratio—it is necessary to reduce the absolute level of money wages. Competition among unemployed in the first instance reduces the money wage. This leads to a reduction both of the real wage and the price level.

A general functional representation of this theoretical system would be as follows:

$$(1) \quad y = y(N)$$

$$\left(\frac{dy}{dN} > 0, \text{ but declining as } N \text{ increases}\right)$$

$$(2) \quad \frac{dy}{dN} = \frac{W}{P}$$

$$(3) \quad N = N\left(\frac{W}{P}\right)$$

$$\left(\frac{dN}{d\frac{W}{P}} > 0\right)$$

$$(4) \quad M = lPy$$

where

$y = $ output
$N = $ employment
$W = $ money wage rate
$P = $ price level
$M = $ quantity of money
$l = $ fraction of income that needs to be held in cash balances to satisfy the transactions demand for money.

Equation (1) is the aggregate production function of the economy. We must specify as to its shape only that output increases less than in proportion to labor input. Equation (2) expresses the profit maximization condition—that the real wage equals the marginal product of labor. Equation (3) represents the supply curve of labor, and equation (4) is the quantity theory.

## GRAPHICAL REPRESENTATION OF CLASSICAL MODEL

Graphically we might represent this model as in Figure 6–1. Part A of Figure 6–1 shows the usual production function, subject to diminishing returns. For each level of labor input there is a corresponding output. Part B shows the intersection of supply and demand curves for labor.

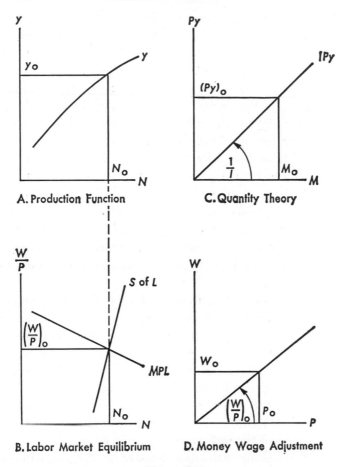

A. Production Function

C. Quantity Theory

B. Labor Market Equilibrium

D. Money Wage Adjustment

Figure 6–1.

The demand curve, the marginal product of labor, is, of course, merely the *slope* of the production function in part A. It declines as employment increases because the production function is concave downward—i.e., because the slope of the production function decreases. Corresponding to each production function there is one and only one marginal product curve. A change in the height of the production function, with no change in its slope, will leave the marginal product curve unchanged. (This is a rise in the *average* productivity but not the *marginal* productivity of labor.) But any change in slope of the production function curve will alter the marginal product curve.

The intersection of the two curves in part B defines the point of full employment, $N_0$, and the real wage, $(W/P)_0$, necessary to secure full employment. If the real wage were somehow maintained higher than that which corresponds to the intersection of the two curves, there would be an excess of supply over demand for labor. If the real wage were lower than corresponds to the intersection, the condition would be one of labor shortage. Assuming labor market competition, the former condition results in a rapid decline in the money wage; the latter in a rapid rise in the money wage. Stability of the money wage is obviously a condition of equilibrium. Therefore, equilibrium requires a real wage of $(W/P)_0$.

We find the equilibrium price level in part C of the figure. Here the diagonal line, $lPy$ (whose slope is $1/l$), shows the amount of money required for each level of money income, or read in the other direction, the level of money income which each possible quantity of money can support. If the actual stock of money is that shown by the vertical line marked $M_0$, then the money income cannot exceed $(Py)_0$. Since we know $y_0$ (from part A), we can immediately compute the equilibrium price level $P_0$.

Part D permits us to find the necessary level of the money wage. In part D we plot the equilibrium real wage found in part B as a diagonal line. Any real wage is a *ratio* of price to money wage; therefore corresponding to each real wage are numerous possible combinations of $P$ and $W$, all of which fall on a straight line through the origin whose slope measures the real wage. Given the equilibrium real wage and the equilibrium price level, there is only one money wage consistent with both of these. This is read off in part D as the vertical coordinate of the intersection of equilibrium price, $P_0$, and the real-wage angle (from part B).

A better understanding of the model and of the diagram will come from analyzing the effects on the equilibrium values of the several variables of various changes in parameters. For example, we may consider the effects of an increase in $M$; a shift in the production function; or a shift in the supply schedule of labor.

An increase in the quantity of money permits an increase in the product of $P$ and $y$ as shown in part C of Figure 6–2. The previous output, $y_0$, could now sell at a higher price, $P_1$. If money wages did not rise this would induce employers to try to increase output, bidding against each other for workers. Since no more workers are to be had (indeed, fewer) the money wage must rise far enough to eliminate the excess demand. (The gap between demand and supply at the new price and old wage is shown in part B of Figure 6–2). There will be an excess demand until the old real wage is restored by a proportionate rise in money wages. What this new money wage level must be can be found in part D.

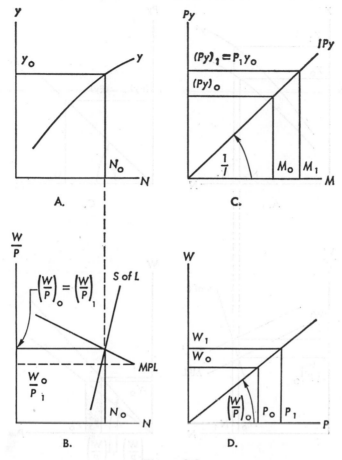

**Figure 6–2.**

The result of monetary increase, then, is to raise wages and prices in equal proportion, leaving output, real wages, and employment unaffected. The results of a decrease in $M$ can easily be worked out.

The next shift we shall consider is a change in the production function. The change shown in Figure 6–3 involves an increase in both the average and in the marginal products of labor.

The new production function, $y'$, gives a new marginal product curve, $MPL'$. The equilibrium real wage is increased from $(W/P)_0$ to $(W/P)_1$, as is the equilibrium volume of employment, from $N_0$ to $N_1$. Output is enlarged to $y_1$, both because of the higher production function and because of the larger employment. If $M$ and $l$ are unchanged, the larger output can be sold only at a lower price, $P_1$. Despite the drop in prices,

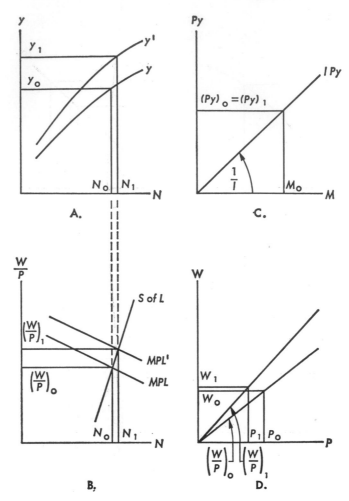

**Figure 6–3.**

the money wage (in this example) can nevertheless rise to $W_1$. (Depending on the slopes of the various functions, the new money wage might be lower rather than higher; however, the real wage will certainly be higher —prices will fall more than wages.)

The effects of an increase in the supply of labor will only be summarized. They are: a lower real wage, a larger employment, a larger output, a lower price level, and a lower money wage. The interested student can check these results on a diagram of his own.

It will be noted that we can divide this analysis into two parts—a "real" and a monetary. The real wage and the levels of employment and output are determined by "real" factors alone: the marginal productivity of labor and the marginal disutility (or other "real" factors underlying the supply) of labor. Money wages and prices are determined solely by monetary factors. Changes on the "real" side can affect prices and wages, but changes on the monetary side have no effect on the "real" magnitudes. This presumably justifies the Classical tradition of developing the theory of output and employment entirely in real terms (Say's Law), leaving the theory of absolute prices to a chapter at the end of the book, or to a separate treatise on monetary theory.

## THE EFFECT OF RIGID WAGES

We consider now the effects of an absence of perfect labor market competition—i.e., a limitation or absence of any tendency for money wages to fall so long as men are unemployed. This might result from an organization of workers which refuses to accept a reduction of money wages when unemployment develops, or which actually forces the money wage upward when there is no excess of demand over the supply of labor. Or it might result simply from custom, legislation, a government wage policy (e.g., President Herbert Hoover's exhortations to employers not to cut wages in 1930 and 1931), or to (misplaced?) social sympathy on the part of employers. Any of these can create unemployment, if the money wage is held or raised too high.

Consider the situation shown in Figure 6–4. Here there is an equilibrium money wage, $W_0$, consistent with full employment. But suppose that the wage is artificially fixed at $W_1$. To simplify exposition, suppose that the money wage was originally $W_0$, but was pushed up to $W_1$. What will be the new levels of $P$, $N$, $y$, and $W/P$?

In the first place, we can easily see that prices must rise, at least somewhat. For if prices did not rise, the real wage would be higher than before, and employers would produce less; and a smaller output with no increase in price would be inconsistent with a constant $M$ and $l$. Prices must rise. Second, we can see that prices could not possibly rise as much as did wages. For if prices rose in the same proportion, the real wage would be unchanged, employers would want to produce as much as before; but for them to sell the same quantity, at a higher price, is also inconsistent with a constant $M$ and $l$. The new $Py$ must be the same as before; therefore $P$ must rise and $y$ must fall.

The diagram is not well adapted to finding directly the new equilibrium levels of the other variables, although this can be done by a process of successive approximation. However, the new equilibrium must, we have

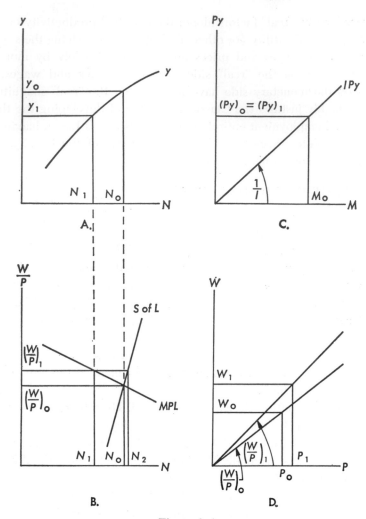

**Figure 6–4.**

shown, involve both a higher price and a higher real wage than before; therefore it necessarily involves less employment and output. It can be seen that the solution shown in Figure 6–4 is consistent with all of the requirements of the model.

The results of an arbitrary increase in the money wage (from $W_0$ to $W_1$) are higher prices, a higher real wage, smaller employment and output, and a volume of unemployment equal to $N_1N_2$. (Note that the sum of new employment plus unemployment is greater than the previous employment.) Those workers still employed are clearly better off.

## MONETARY POLICY AND FULL EMPLOYMENT

Clearly, monetary policy can be used to offset the effects of too high a money wage. If employment drops off because the money wage fails to decline in response (say) to an increase in the average productivity of labor, monetary expansion can permit the full employment level to be restored. It should be clear that in this particular case an expansion of $M$ need not in any meaningful sense be inflationary. Prices merely have to be prevented from falling in response to larger output. On the other hand, if money wages are artificially pushed upward, the monetary authority would have the difficult choice between "ratifying inflation" or permitting unemployment to develop. Since it could be supposed that the inflationary solution might tempt workers to try again, while the "discipline" of unemployment might teach them better manners, the choice would be a difficult one.

Another policy question discussed by means of these analytical tools was what the long run objective of monetary policy should be. Assuming flexible wages, the fruits of economic progress (higher productivity) might be passed along either through (a) with a constant $M$, falling wages and prices, with prices falling more; (b) with moderate increases in $M$, constant money wages and a more slowly falling price level; or (c) with more substantial increases in $M$, a constant price level and rising $W$. Choice among these rested on such considerations as justice to the nonproductive members of society, effects on distribution of existing wealth through price level changes, psychological effects on workers, inventory gains or losses for employers, etc.

We shall pursue none of these questions in the present context; for, as we shall see, these Classical analytical tools have certain weaknesses which make them not fully suitable for application to public policy. Of their logical completeness and consistency, however, there can be no doubt. This reconstructed "Classical theory" cannot be attacked except by attacking the assumptions on which it is based. Keynes was surely wrong in attacking it as logically incomplete or inconsistent. However, there is still another aspect of the matter which needs to be explored, and was explored in the Classical literature, namely, the problem of saving and investment in relation to employment, output, and the price level. This is the subject of Chapter VII.

# Saving, Investment, and the Rate of Interest

*Chapter VII*

## THE QUANTITY THEORY AS A THEORY OF DEMAND

The simple quantity theory developed in Chapter V implies that if only prices are flexible, the maximum level of output is automatically assured. In the preceding chapter we have tried to take this idea apart somewhat by looking more closely into the mechanism by which a reduction in prices would create an incentive for employers to add to their payrolls, and, of course, to their output. We saw that both the absolute level of prices and the structure of prices (the wage/price ratio) are involved in the maintenance of full employment.

In order for a free economy to attain full employment, it is necessary for employers always to be provided with adequate incentive to hire and to produce. This is the *sellers'* side of the problem, with which we concerned ourselves in Chapter VI. But it is also necessary that there be *buyers* for their output. In the last chapter we did not look very carefully at this side of the question. In effect we accepted the quantity theory as a very simple theory of aggregate demand, without much examination of precisely what kind of behavior this involved on the part of buyers, and whether this kind of behavior could reasonably be expected to occur. The present chapter continues our development of the Classical theory, with particular attention to the demand side.

The quantity theory formulations assume that people do not desire money as such. Therefore they will not willingly hold any more of it than they need. They must hold some—i.e., hold the average dollar for a while—because of the lumpiness of transactions. In other words money, even

138

though nothing more than a medium of exchange, nevertheless has to be held in the very process of mediating exchanges. But that is all. No rational reason for holding cash in excess of this amount (i.e., for longer periods) being recognized, then, assuming men to be rational, they will hold no more. If, somehow, some should find themselves with larger cash balances than they need, they would get rid of the excess. Any individual who has more cash than he needs can immediately get rid of it, by buying something. But the economy as a whole does not get rid of cash this way. What one person gets rid of finds itself in someone else's cash balance. How then would idle money—money in excess of transactions needs—work itself out? By increasing the transactions needs. The attempts to spend the idle money would drive up output, or, if that is already at its maximum, prices. Suppose there is unemployment; wages fall; prices fall too; their fall would create idle balances if output did not expand. But because idle balances are shunned, output would expand, prices falling less.

Implied here, then, is a theory of aggregate demand. People spend on goods whatever cash they get hold of. Money "burns holes in peoples' pockets"; if they have it, they spend it. Money turns over automatically against goods, at a predetermined, maximum speed.

This view is what Hansen [1] has called the "naïve version" of the quantity theory. It is a possible one, but, on inspection, not too plausible. Fortunately for the quantity theory, a "more sophisticated version" (as Hansen calls it) is also available. This chapter is concerned with the development and implications of this more sophisticated version.

First, however, we might note an even less realistic version of the quantity theory, which still seems to have currency in some quarters. This is the version which explains prices by means of the quantity of money quite without reference to such mundane matters as spending or money-holding. Prices, it is said, are merely a ratio—a ratio between a quantity of cash and the value of a quantity of goods. Change one term of the ratio —the quantity of cash, and the ratio (i.e., the price level) must automatically change. This mystical kind of explanation deserves little attention.

The Swedish economist, Wicksell, was among the first to emphasize that economists accept an explanation for *individual* prices which runs in terms of supply and demand: if they wish to use the quantity of money to explain the general price level (which is only an average of all indi-

---

[1] Alvin H. Hansen, *Monetary Theory and Fiscal Policy* (McGraw-Hill, 1949). Chapter 3 of this work can profitably be read along with the present chapter.

vidual prices), then they must somehow show how M enters into the determination either of supply or demand for goods. It is this spirit of his approach which makes Wicksell an important forerunner of our modern theories. As we shall see, Wicksell met the challenge he set for economists. He did show how the quantity of money affected prices, through affecting the demand for goods; and he left the *conclusions* of the quantity theory unshaken. But in the process he developed an analysis of aggregate demand into which modern ideas can be fitted with little trouble.

## SAVING AND INVESTMENT

The principal difficulty with the naïve quantity theory is that it takes no consideration of the saving process. People do not, as a rule, automatically spend on goods and services whatever they have available to spend, and as rapidly as they can. Most of us *save* something. Now merely because we save—i.e., spend for consumption less than our incomes—does not mean that we desire to accumulate cash. But most savers do not, at least *directly*, purchase capital goods. Rather, our current saving goes into life insurance policies, security purchases, savings bank deposits, saving and loan association shares, or repayment of mortgage or other debt—to name only the most significant types. We do not need to hold more cash just because we save; if we are not misers we normally will not. Why save in the form of cash when we can save in a form which yields a return? But if we may save in one of these other noncash forms, can we be sure that the flow of cash against goods is not interrupted? We may buy a security with our saving, but the security is not output, and it probably is not even a *new* security, in connection with the issuance of which some current investment spending on new output might be assumed to occur. Rather, we frequently buy an existing share of stock or a bond from some other security holder. (Of the total of securities bought and sold in any given week or year, a very small proportion consists of new securities.)

In the face of all this, can we still be sure that, even if people do not willingly hold idle cash, aggregate spending on newly produced output is nevertheless a fixed multiple of the quantity of cash? Still another part of Classical theory implies an answer of "yes" to this question.

Let us begin by ignoring the existence of a market for old securities. Assume that a person buying a security is "married" to it, and there exists no market for its resale. (We shall soon remove this assumption. Classical theory thought its removal made no difference. Modern theory, however, finds crucial difficulties arising in this connection.) We shall further assume away all intermediate financial institutions—life insurance companies, savings banks, saving and loan associations, investment trusts, etc. Securities must be sold directly to individual savers. Next, we shall simplify things further by assuming that only one kind of security is used—a perpetual bond. There are no shares sold—entrepreneurs either borrow all of the funds needed by their enterprises, through sale of the standard bonds, or, if they supply any funds themselves, it is through direct investment in the physical properties of their enterprises. Further, there are for the moment no commercial banks, at least none with fractional reserves.

A saver, then, has three things he can do with the margin between his income and his consumption expenditure. He may add to his cash balance; he may—as an entrepreneur—purchase capital goods directly; or he may buy a bond newly issued by an entrepreneur. Our assumption is that the rational saver will not do the first of these. The reason is that wealth accumulated in the form of cash is barren—it yields no return; the other forms of wealth have a positive yield, and are therefore preferred. Relatively few savers do the second (although they account for a fair fraction of total saving); most savers do the third.

We shall have much more to say later about the assumed unqualified preference for earning assets over cash. However, this is an essential element in any version of a Classical model. Note that the assumption here is not necessarily that people save in order to obtain a return on their savings; nor that they save more or less if the rate of return is higher or lower. The assumption is rather that, if a return on savings is available, it will be preferred to no return. It is also true that most Classical writers thought of saving as an increasing function of the interest rate, but that is a separate matter.

The issuers of the bonds which savers may buy are, of course, the entrepreneurs who wish to acquire capital goods at a rate in excess of that possible from their own saving. They are willing to incur an obligation to pay interest because they see an opportunity—through use of the capital goods—to earn a margin over all of their costs, including the interest payments which they contract to make.

The bond market therefore provides a means whereby the nonspending of income by savers can be translated into spending in excess of income by entrepreneurs. What Classical theory had to say about this market was that—barring certain interferences—it worked quite like any other market, bringing about an equality between lending or bond purchase (which could be assumed to equal saving) and borrowing or bond sale (which could be assumed to equal investment). The equality of saving and lending arose from the rational consumer's preference for a positive return over no return; the equality of borrowing and investing from the reasonable proposition that entrepreneurs will not incur an interest obligation unless they have some productive use for the funds borrowed; they will not pay interest for the privilege of holding idle cash. The equality of lending and borrowing was maintained through fluctuations in the market rate of interest.[2]

For the market rate of interest to succeed in equating lending and borrowing—and therefore saving and investment—it is necessary that competition exist on both sides of the market. Further, it is necessary (a) that either savers will save more at higher rates of interest than at lower rates, and/or that investors will desire to borrow more at lower than at higher rates, and (b) that there exist some rate greater than zero at which the amount saved equals the amount invested. Economists generally assumed that both saving and investment were interest-elastic, and the possibility that condition (b) might not be fulfilled never entered their minds. The usual picture of the capital market looked like Figure 7–1. Although individual economists may have emphasized the interest-

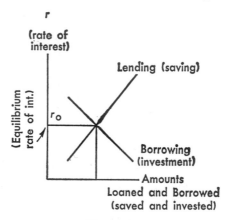

Figure 7–1.

elasticity of one instead of the other of these curves, and even have suggested that the other was interest-inelastic (that is, in the figure, a vertical line), there were excellent reasons advanced why both schedules were interest-elastic. If *either* of them should be sufficiently interest-elastic,

[2] In connection with this equality of saving and investment, see above, pp. 105–109, and below, pp. 320–326.

condition (b) (an intersection in the positive quadrant) is assured. We turn to a brief discussion of the two schedules, starting with the borrowing (investment) schedule.

Although it is recognized that some borrowing may be by consumers—to finance expenditures in excess of income—and although it is possible to develop a consistent theory of interest on the assumption of consumer borrowing alone, most borrowing is rather for the purpose of investment: to permit the borrower to add to his productive capital of machines, buildings, inventories. We can easily dismiss consumer borrowing by making it a subtraction from gross saving, and say that the saving schedule shows the *net* saving made available at each rate of interest by consumers in the aggregate, including both savers and dissavers. Borrowing then is only for investment purposes (government borrowing is assumed at zero until later).

The basic factor underlying the borrowing schedule is the productivity of additions to capital, or, the "marginal productivity of capital." The fruits of business borrowing are capital goods. These capital goods will add to total production in the future, because "roundabout" production methods—i.e., those using capital—are more productive than direct methods—those not using capital; and more roundabout methods are more productive than less roundabout. But by the familiar principle of diminishing marginal returns, the larger the use of capital goods, the less the increment of production from their further use—the greater the use of capital, the smaller the marginal product of capital.

The idea that the borrowing schedule reflects the diminishing marginal productivity of capital conceals a Pandora's box of analytical difficulties, as we shall see in a later chapter. However, for the present, the notion probably has sufficient familiarity and plausibility that we can accept it as in some sense correct that the return available to investors declines as their aggregate rate of investment increases. Since it is from this return that interest must be paid, the higher the rate of investment, the lower the rate of interest that borrowers can afford to pay. They would like, of course, to borrow at the lowest possible rate—at zero if they could. But competition for available funds will force them to pay what is necessary; and they will pay it, carrying investment to the point that further investment would no longer yield a return in excess of the interest rate.

The assumed interest-elasticity of the saving schedule was variously described as reflecting savers' "time preference," "impatience," the "increasing marginal disutility of abstinence," etc. Some of these ideas reflect a view that saving in any positive quantity is sacrifice. A positive rate of interest is necessary to produce any saving—to induce people to make the sacrifice; and beyond this, a rising rate of interest is necessary to secure increasing amounts of sacrifice. Others would deny that the saving schedule cuts the vertical axis. They might still, however, assume a schedule sloping upward to the right. Saving (wealth accumulation) produces certain psychological returns which would successfully compete with current consumption even at a zero rate. However, as additional income is shifted from consumption to saving, a declining marginal utility from added saving must compete with a rising marginal utility from decreased consumption. The level of saving at which the margins are equated depends on the height of the additional reward for saving that interest provides.

Today most economists believe that other motives for saving—and changes operating through these other motives—swamp in their effect the possible changes in saving that might flow from changes in the rate of interest. The interest-elasticity of saving is therefore frequently taken as zero. An *a priori* case can even be made for a backward-sloping saving schedule. Since this question is not an essential one for our theory, we shall have little further to say about it. Only if saving were highly responsive to moderate changes in the interest rate would it make much difference in what follows. We shall generally assume a saving schedule which slopes steeply upward, except where analytical convenience requires us to use a completely vertical saving schedule. Even in such instances, we shall (generally in footnotes) point out the extent to which a positive interest-elasticity would qualify the results.

Given these forces on the supply and demand sides (and the fact of an intersection), it seems clear how the interest rate—if free to fluctuate—would necessarily settle at a point where saving and investment were equal. For, if the rate were higher than this, saving and lending would exceed borrowing and investment. Some savers, unable to find a borrower, and preferring a lower return to none at all, would bid the rate down. If the rate were below the equilibrium level, investors would seek more funds than savers would provide. Competition among borrowers would force the rate up.

The level of the equilibrium rate would depend on the slopes and relative positions of the saving and investment schedules. Other things equal, the more thrifty the population, the lower the rate; other things equal, the greater the marginal productivity of capital, the higher the rate. In equilibrium the rate of interest would equal both the marginal productivity of capital and, as well, the "marginal rate of time preference" or the "marginal disutility of saving" (or some similar marginal rate, depending on what formulation was used to explain the slope of the saving schedule).

If the interest rate fluctuates freely, settling at whatever level equates saving and investment, then the act of saving does not require any qualification of the quantity theory, thought of as a theory of aggregate demand. All money which individuals acquire gets spent. They may not *themselves* spend it all (if they are savers). However, because the saver wishes to hold his savings in a form which produces a positive yield, the rate of interest will adjust to the point where someone else (an investor) will want to spend precisely the amount that the saver did not choose to spend. The total flow of money against goods is not interrupted. Aggregate spending on goods in money terms (the sum of price-times-quantity) is a constant multiple of the quantity of money. Therefore there is always a price level at which full employment is possible.

## A RESALE MARKET FOR BONDS

Now this argument has been conducted under some very rigid assumptions. We can soften this rigidity somewhat by recognizing, first, that different borrowers might have to pay different rates of interest at any given time because of different degrees of risk of default on their interest contracts.[3] We might call the "pure" rate of interest the rate which would have to be paid by a completely riskless enterprise. (There might or might not be any such enterprise.) The actual rate paid by any given enterprise is then the pure rate plus a risk premium—designed to compensate the lender for the particular risk of default which he assumes. The actual rates paid, and their dispersion and average, might fluctuate with changing lender judgments concerning risk premiums. But given the risks of default, the whole family of market rates would move up or down together, reflecting changes in the "pure" rate, due to changed conditions of thrift or productivity.

We can also introduce variations in rate based upon differing maturities of the loan. However, for simplicity, we shall continue to assume only perpetual loans, but introduce greater realism by providing a resale market, in which existing bonds may be traded. (Through this device, borrowing for any particular term is possible. The borrower simply repurchases his debt certificates when he wishes to reduce his indebtedness.)

In order to deal adequately with the resale market, we need to intro-

---

[3] Since we have assumed perpetual borrowing, there is no problem as to risk of default on the principal.

duce a few mechanical relationships, which are perhaps obvious to most readers, but need to be spelled out clearly. When a borrower issues a bond, in, say, one-hundred dollar denomination, he can sell it for one hundred dollars only if the number of dollars of interest per year which he promises to pay is exactly equal to the market rate of interest times one hundred dollars. If he promises to pay three dollars per year, and the market rate is six per cent, he could not expect to sell his $100 (perpetual) bond for more than $50. No one would buy his security except at a price which yielded a return equal to the market rate. But what is the market rate? It is found by dividing the contractual (coupon) rates which various bonds promise to pay by their market values. If (ignoring differential risk) perpetual bonds promising to pay $4 per year are selling for $100, bonds promising to pay $5 per year are selling for $125, bonds promising to pay $6 are selling for $150, and so on, then we say that the market rate is 4 per cent. New bonds can yield no less, and need yield no more. This market rate changes when the prices of bonds change. If the $100 bonds rise to $120, the $125 bonds to $150, the $150 to $180, etc., we say that the market rate has *fallen* to 3⅓ per cent. In other words, *the level of bond prices and of the market rate are two ways of describing one and the same set of facts.* In many contexts it is easier to formulate the theory in terms of changes in bond prices than in terms of changes in interest rates; but it should be clear that any formulation in terms of the one may always be translated into terms of the other.

When we recognize the existence of sales and purchases of old as well as of newly issued securities, we must reformulate our theory of the interest rate by saying that the level of bond prices is determined by the total supply and total demand for bonds, including in supply the old bonds offered for sale by previous owners as well as new bonds offered for sale to finance new investments; and including in the demand for bonds not only that by current savers, but by others as well. As already indicated, Classical theory assumes that this reformulation makes no difference. Let us see why.

The current supply of bonds is made up of the newly issued bonds, sold to finance investment, together with sales of previously-issued bonds by their existing holders. These other sellers may be consumers, who sell securities which they have held, in order to finance dissaving. (Unless they actually dissave, they can merely buy fewer bonds per period, but need sell none.) The dissaving may occur to meet an emergency; or to acquire now goods which might otherwise have been purchased at a later date. There are always a number of consuming units which are dissaving.

Their sale of securities absorbs current saving by other consumers who buy these securities. If there should be a net increase in the amount of dissaving, its effect will be to depress bond prices (raise interest rates)— as more old securities are dumped on the market—in just the same way as would a reduction in positive saving. But the fact of dissaving, or a change in the amount of dissaving, does not interfere with the market equality of saving and investment. Net saving (positive saving less dissaving) is kept equal to investment through variation in the interest rate.

Other sellers of old securities may be businesses, which have been holding them as an income-yielding financial reserve, but now need funds to expand inventories, meet growing payrolls, or replace worn out equipment. These sales finance investment (in inventories of finished goods, raw materials, or work in process; or in plant and equipment) just as do sales of new securities. A net increase in sales from business reserve portfolios depresses bond prices (raises interest rates) in just the same way as any other increase in investment. We should recognize, of course, that just as some businesses may need to call upon their reserve funds by selling securities, other businesses may be purchasing securities, not out of current saving, but in connection with a temporary disinvestment in inventories or in capital goods (depreciation allowances in excess of replacement expenditures). It is not only saving which should be considered net (positive saving less dissaving) but investment, too. Again, there is no reason why fluctuating bond prices (interest rates) should not preserve equality between net saving and net investment.

Another very large volume of "second-hand" sales and purchases will be by individuals (or businesses) whose opinions regarding risk premiums on individual issues differ from the market's opinion. If I hold a security which the market values highly (high price equals low risk premium) but I believe it more risky than another, cheaper issue, I will sell mine and buy the other. A large volume of such transactions may take place as individual security holders move from those issues which they believe the market overvalues to those they believe the market undervalues. But it is clear that this type of transaction cannot influence the general level of bond prices (although it will influence the structure of bond prices). For to say that the "market" overvalues a security I own is to say that someone else is willing to pay a higher price than I think correct. I sell to him. Suppose he is a saver; I have diverted his saving from investment. I then buy another issue which I think is undervalued. This may be a new issue, in which case the diverted savings are re-channelled into investment. If it, too, is an old issue, the seller, who apparently thought the issue *over*valued, has funds to invest in a new issue, or to put in the hands of some other security holder, who in turn can buy a new issue, etc. In short, *so long as no one who has been a security-holder desires to shift to idle cash instead,* total spending will be maintained. Since we assume that no rational wealth-holder would prefer idle cash to a positive return, second-hand sales create no problem. This is so even though the volume of second-hand sales may dwarf the volume of new issues. New saving and investment might even both be zero, yet a substantial reshuffling of existing securities might proceed, with a substantial volume of current bond transactions.

We could consider still other sources of bond demand or supply, but all with the same effect. So long as barren cash is never preferred to income-yielding wealth, the existence of a market in old securities, just as the fact of saving itself, appeared to require no qualification of the quantity theory as a reasonable theory of aggregate demand. The money that is in circulation all moves, and at a predictable rate, in the purchase of goods. Aggregate demand equals money stock times velocity.[4]

Should the thriftiness of the population increase—i.e., its desire to spend income on current output weaken—the reduction of the interest rate that this automatically brings about will both dampen the desire to save and attract extra investment. The rate will fall until the previous volume of demand is restored. Should the incentive to spend on investment in new facilities weaken, the resulting drop in the rate of issuance of new securities will lower interest rates until the potential drop in spending has been offset. At least, these results seem to follow if we assume no willingness anywhere to accumulate idle cash.

## SAVING AND INVESTMENT IN RELATION TO THE QUANTITY THEORY

Nevertheless, although the result is the same as with the naïve theory, the conception is a very different one. Consider now, for instance, the effect of an increase in the quantity of money. If the demand for money

---

[4] To be sure, an increase in the volume of second-hand security dealings may require somewhat larger cash balances in the hands of the traders. That is, some extra money gets tied up in mediating purely financial transactions, thus raising interest rates and reducing investment relative to saving. This problem attracted great attention of monetary theorists in the late twenties and early thirties. However, it was pointed out that the organization of financial markets permitted tremendous volumes of security transactions to be handled with very small balances—that the "velocity of the financial circulation" was exceedingly high. Thus the security markets "absorbed" very little in the way of funds. Even if some funds were absorbed in this way, it would still cause no problem if prices of goods and services were fully flexible (downward).

is a constant fraction of money income—i.e., if income velocity is constant—then if $M$ increases there can be no equilibrium until aggregate price-times-quantity has increased in the same proportion, presumably through an increase in prices (assuming flexible money wages and a previous full-employment equilibrium). However, this version of the quantity theory sees changes in $M$ having their primary impact *by way of the capital market,* rather than through the direct spending of the balances by whoever holds them.

Precisely how do changes in the money supply come about? One important way is through changes in the volume of commercial bank lending to business. Assume that commercial banks have idle reserves, and can lend "new money" to business firms. If business not only borrows (to finance investment) all of the funds provided by savers, but also new money, then there will be an aggregate demand for goods (and for resources to produce goods) in excess of supply. All resources were previously fully employed in producing consumer goods and capital goods. If new investment demand is added which is not matched by any added saving (i.e., any reduction in consumer demand), total demand for goods and productive factors will exceed supply. This will bid up prices. This is why and how an increase in $M$ leads to an increase in $P$. This is how Wicksell connected a change in $M$ to a change in the demand for goods and services and thus in the prices of goods and services.[5]

A simplified version of Wicksell's analysis is illustrated in Figure 7–2.

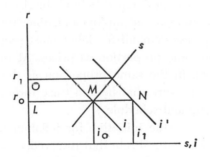

Figure 7–2.

In this figure $s$ is the supply curve of saving, and $i$ the original investment schedule. At $r_0$, amounts saved and invested are equal. If, now, the investment schedule shifts to $i'$, the equilibrium rate (Wicksell called it the "natural rate") rises to $r_1$. Suppose however, that banks meet the addi-

[5] See K. Wicksell, *Lectures on Political Economy,* L. Robbins, trans. (Routledge and Kegan Paul, 1955), Vol. II, esp. pp. 159–208.

tional demand for funds at the old market rate, $r_0$, or at only a slightly higher rate. This is very likely to happen, for the banks—and particularly individual banks in a system—have no way of knowing what the "natural rate" is. As a consequence of their lending, the quantity of money rises at the rate $MN$.[6] The increase in investment demand (as the borrowers spend the new money) represents a net increment of total demand for goods, for there has been no equivalent reduction in consumer demand (increase in saving). The excess of demand over supply bids up prices.

How far and how long will prices rise? As long as the market rate stays below the natural rate, there will continue to be an excess of aggregate demand for goods over supply and prices will rise. Only when bank lending and money creation cease (perhaps because the banks have run out of excess reserves) will the inflation cease. For then the market rate must move up to equal the natural rate, and investment will again just be offset by saving (partly through some expansion in saving, if saving responds to the interest rate, and the rest through some trimming back of the rate of investment).

How far will prices have risen? They must have risen in the same proportion as the money supply, for otherwise there would be idle balances, which would not willingly be held but instead would be depressing the rate of interest below the natural rate, and thus forcing a continuance of inflation.

Money wages must, of course, have risen in exactly this same proportion, too. So long as wages lagged behind the rise of prices, employers would have incentive to increase employment. Since no additional workers are to be had, the excess demand for labor must sooner or later bid up money wages in the same proportion as prices. At this point, all prices and wages have risen in the same proportion as the supply of money. (The student should be sure that he can trace through fully the effects of a drop in the investment schedule.)

In the above example, the initiative for inflation did not come from the banks; rather it was natural rate that rose, reflecting, perhaps, technological innovations or some other source of a higher marginal productivity of capital. The banks merely reacted passively. It was Wicksell's view that this was the normal situation. However, we can also see how the banks might take the initiative. Assume the market rate and natural rate

---

[6] If we hold to our assumption of only one kind of security, the banks will buy bonds at the rate $MN$, in addition to purchases by savers at the previous rate $LM$. If the banks did not buy, the increased supply of bonds would depress bond prices (raise interest rates) to the equivalent of $r_1$. It must be noted that $S$ and $I$ are flows. $MN$, the increase in money supply, is also necessarily expressed as a flow.

as equal and that no change occurs in either the investment or saving schedule. Banks, however, have excess reserves. Suppose that they enter the bond market as buyers, adding their demand to that of savers. So long as they remain in the market, bond prices will be "artificially" raised above the equilibrium level (or, the market rate depressed below the natural rate). During this time, aggregate demand for goods and services will exceed supply and wages and prices will be bid up. When the banks cease to add to the demand for bonds—and to the supply of funds to finance inflationary investment spending—prices will stop rising, and the rate of interest will return to its equilibrium level.

It is interesting to note that Wicksell saw clearly what many even today continue to confuse, namely, that if prices of goods and services are bid up by excess demand, the rise in price does not of itself eliminate the excess demand. If, starting from a full employment equilibrium, entrepreneurs armed with new money come into the market seeking to invest in plant and equipment, they can do so only by bidding goods (or resources to produce goods) away from other uses, through offering higher prices. If we make certain plausible assumptions as to lags, the investors are *able to bid resources* away from consumers, because consumers cannot and will not pay the higher prices, since their money incomes are, *for the moment,* unchanged. Thus, prices rise to clear the market by diverting goods and resources from consumption into investment. "Forced saving," this process is called; consumers are forced, by higher prices without increase in money incomes, to consume less. But Wicksell saw clearly that this was only a temporary diversion. The sale of goods and resources at higher prices automatically creates extra money income in just the amount of the price rise. Consumers now come back into the market with money incomes which have, in the aggregate, risen by the same amount as prices. Their real income position is unchanged; whatever they previously wanted to consume they still want to consume, and the rise in their money incomes permits them to pay the higher prices. Thus the initial rise in prices did not eliminate the excess demand, except during the lag between the paying of higher prices and the consequent realization of higher money incomes. Unless the source of excess demand is eliminated (for example, by a rise in the interest rate to its natural level, which will reduce both consumption and investment demand), the rise in prices can cumulate indefinitely. (This notion of an inflationary "spiral" that provides its own fuel in the form of higher money incomes is an important strand of the modern analysis of inflation.)

Wicksell also saw the reverse—that if a deficiency of aggregate demand

develops as a result of a drop of investment relative to saving, which is
not corrected by a drop in the interest rate, the resulting fall in wages
and prices will not correct the deficiency of demand, except temporarily,
for money incomes and goods prices, and wage costs, will all have fallen
in proportion. The deficiency of demand will still exist until either real
consumption or investment demand increases. This requires (given the
saving and investment schedules) that the banks stop absorbing funds—
i.e., stop maintaining the market rate above the natural level.

Thus we must understand the saving and investment schedules in the
Wicksellian diagram as being defined in real terms. In Figure 7–2 the
shift of the investment schedule from $i$ to $i'$ produces (at $r_0$, or at any
interest rate below $r_1$) an "inflationary gap" in the market for goods. The
resulting rise in prices does not eliminate the gap because it leaves the
$s$ and $i$ schedules unchanged. If the added investment, $i_0 i_1$, occurs, through
a bidding away of goods or resources, actual saving (which has to equal
investment) will of course rise, too. (This is the "forced saving," or
sacrificed consumption, referred to above.) But desired or attempted saving stays as shown by the schedule.

Here we have another example of the difference between accounting
identities and conditions of equilibrium. We know from Chapter II that
actual saving and investment must at all times be equal. For the purpose
of this identity, saving is defined simply as income less consumption. But
if we speak of desired or intended saving, which we think of here as a
function of the interest rate, we can imagine this differing from investment. However, when it does, actual saving will differ from desired
saving, and savers will attempt to eliminate this difference. Only when
actual and desired saving are equal is the situation one of equilibrium.
Under Wicksell's assumptions, this occurred only when the market and
natural rates were equal—i.e., when the banks were neither creating nor
retiring money.

Wicksell and other economists of his time and later saw this distinction
between desired and actual saving, some more clearly than others. Surely
it is useful, and necessary, to define saving and investment in ways that
permit them to be different, and even to discuss states of disequilibrium
in which, defined in this way, they are unequal. But it is necessary always
to remember that *actual* saving and investment can never differ. This was
not appreciated by economists who talked about differences between $s$
and $i$, and the *accumulation* over time of such differences. If $s$ exceeds $i$,
they said, the excess saving accumulates. Eventually the accumulation of
excess saving gets big enough to force its way through into investment.

A whole family of business cycle theories developed along this line. It should be clear that this is a confusion of the worst sort. If desired or intended saving is not equal to investment, the difference is a frustration, a disappointment, a surprise. It is not and cannot be a cash balance, a fund of "free capital," a "pool of uninvested saving," or any of the other even more vaguely described magnitudes that figure in the business cycle theories of Tugan-Baronowsky, Spiethoff, and some others. Here is where an appreciation of the accounting identity is most helpful.

## SAVING AND HOARDING

Another consequence of this more sophisticated version of the quantity theory is the light that it begins to throw on "hoarding" and "dishoarding." The naïve quantity theory implies that all persons have a choice between spending—i.e., buying goods—and holding idle cash, a choice which, if rational, always was supposed to favor spending over adding to cash balances. Hoarding and nonspending were synonymous; hoarding and spending antithetical. The more sophisticated view of the matter recognizes that people can save in the form of adding to bond-holdings as well as in the form of adding to cash balances. If they choose not to hold idle cash it is not necessarily because they are unable to control their impulse to spend; it is because, having determined to save, they prefer to hold an income-yielding form rather than a barren form of wealth. Suppose, nevertheless, that wealth-holders should develop a desire (however irrational this may seem) to hoard—to hold cash instead of bonds. Not only can they fail to buy new bonds with their current saving, but they can, as well, dump on the bond market all or some part of their existing security holdings, the fruit of earlier saving. This act not only reduces the current market demand for bonds (new saving no longer flows into the bond market) but also increases the market supply of bonds. Bond prices fall, *reducing investment, but without reducing saving* (in the sense of desired or intended investment and saving). The drop in aggregate demand for goods threatens unemployment, which leads to a deflation of money wages and prices. The deflation will continue so long as the hoarding does. When hoarding stops, prices must have fallen in the same proportion as velocity has fallen. Prices will then, of course, remain at their lower level, to which money incomes are also adjusted.

If some equally irrational reason should now lead to dishoarding, the process would be reversed. Demand for bonds would now consist not only of saving but of the idle cash balances which their holders now wished to convert into interest-yielding form. The market rate of interest would be depressed below the natural rate, and while this was the case, an excess of aggregate demand would bid up wages and prices. When the dishoarding stopped, the rate of interest would return to its "natural" level, and prices would stop rising, remaining, however, at their higher level. Again, it is via the money market and the rate of interest that hoarding or dishoarding affect the price level.

Although this concept of the role and mechanism of hoarding and dishoarding provides no explanation of why these should occur, this setting of the problem is one that invites possible explanations—including one which we shall develop in a later chapter.

Note again that this version divides into *two* decisions what the naïve theory treated as a single decision. The simple quantity theory pictures individuals choosing between spending their incomes as they are received and accumulating cash. The more sophisticated version sorts out two decisions: (1) shall I spend or save? And (2) in what form—cash or securities—shall I hold my accumulated savings (both that saving which I am currently making, and the accumulation of my past saving decisions)? These two decisions are, of course, not completely unrelated, nor are the acts by which they are carried out completely unrelated. If I dissave by spending an accumulated cash balance, I am dishoarding as well. Further, changes in some factors (e.g., my increased fear or uncertainty about the economic future) might simultaneously affect both decisions (e.g., that I should save more, and that I should convert my present and past savings from bonds into cash). Likewise, it may be that one whose savings are held in cash form will be under greater temptation to dissave; he avoids the time, effort, and possible embarrassment of first cashing a security. Nevertheless, there is no necessary connection between saving and hoarding; I can save without hoarding, hoard without saving, or even save and dishoard, hoard and dissave. Therefore it is a most useful step to sort out for separate analysis the saving and the hoarding decisions. The more sophisticated quantity theory permits us to do exactly this.

Wicksell's analysis not only contributed to this separation, but it also gave us, as has been stressed, a rudimentary theory of aggregate demand for goods. This demand consists of two main divisions: consumer demand and investment demand. Each of these demands was conceived to be interest-elastic: the lower the interest rate, the greater the investment demand; and the greater consumer demand, too (the latter idea is, of course, merely a restatement of the idea that saving depends negatively on the interest rate). Separate external forces influence the volume of investment and consumer spending decisions—in the one case, the host of factors summarized in the concept of the marginal productivity of capital, in the other case, the social and institutional factors determining the thriftiness of the population. But a single rein was available to keep these two forces pulling in balance, and to prevent them from either running away or slowing down. This rein was a freely fluctuating rate of interest. If there were an increase in either of the two components of demand, the resulting rise in the rate of interest would prevent any increase in aggregate demand, through cutting back on both elements of demand, and in the process, shifting some resources from the satisfaction of the demand that had not increased to the demand that had. If either type of demand declined, the resulting fall in the rate of interest would stimulate them both, and shift resources to the one which had not declined.

If, however, for any reason (particularly expansion or contraction of the money supply by the banks) the rate of interest were prevented from performing this regulatory function, aggregate demand, consumption plus investment, would be altered, producing inflation or deflation in the process.

## SAVING, INVESTMENT, AND EMPLOYMENT

In Chapters V and VI, we saw that if wages were inflexible, they could be set at a level too high for full employment, given the quantity of money. In that case, the quantity theory became not a theory of prices, but a theory of output. A reduction in the supply of money would create unemployment and lower output; an increase in the supply of money when there was unemployment would lead to larger output rather than only to higher prices.

Introducing inflexible wages into the Wicksellian scheme converts it from a saving-investment theory of prices to a saving-investment theory of output. Starting from a full-employment equilibrium, suppose investment opportunities deteriorate. If the market rate of interest would immediately drop (i.e., bond prices rise) to the new, lower natural rate, aggregate demand would be maintained. Saving would decrease (i.e., consumption increase), and the lower rate would also stimulate investment. But if the banks should prevent bond prices from rising, by standing ready to sell bonds from their portfolios at the previous level of bond prices, investment would drop, without any offset. The total consumption plus investment spending would decline.

Because Wicksell assumed completely flexible wages and prices, no unemployment except of a very temporary sort occurred in his analysis. Prices fell as fast as did money demand. The decline in investment was balanced by what we should call, by analogy, "forced consumption," as the decline in prices occurred in advance of the decline in money incomes. Actual consumption, in real terms, increased as much as investment declined. But because the schedule of intended or desired saving did not shift to the left, the excess of saving over investment remained, and the deflationary gap did not disappear (until the interest rate fell to its new, lower "natural" level).

But if wages and prices should not decline, the drop of aggregate money demand would become a drop in aggregate real demand, too. Workers would become unemployed, and real as well as money income would be cut. Do we then have a continuing downward spiral: this time of output and employment, instead of prices? Are Wicksellian price spirals converted by sticky wages into employment and real income spirals?

Wicksell and the other Classical writers did not try to answer this question. They may not have believed that wages and prices really were completely flexible. But they did not try to analyze very specifically or clearly what would happen if wages did not decline. Had they done so in the spirit of Wicksell's aggregate demand analysis, they would surely have made some interesting discoveries, one of the first of which probably would have been the "Keynesian" "consumption function."

There are several other problems to which the Wicksellian analytical tools might have been applied which would also have forced some "modern" ideas into the open. But it was not done. And when Keynes tackled the theory of unemployment he did so from a new tack, not utilizing—and even specifically rejecting—the approach which stemmed from Wicksell. However, this is getting ahead of our story.

In the next chapter we attempt to provide a summary of the Classical ideas considered in the present and previous three chapters.

# Summary of the Classical Theory

*Chapter VIII*

## THE CLASSICAL EQUATIONS

In Chapter VI, we presented a generalized functional representation of a Classical theory, but one which did not yet include consideration of saving, investment, and the interest rate. It was as follows:

(1) $$y = y(N) \qquad \text{(production function)}$$

(2) $$\frac{dy}{dN} = \frac{W}{P} \qquad \text{(profit maximization)}$$

(3) $$N = N\left(\frac{W}{P}\right) \qquad \text{(supply of labor)}$$

(4) $$M = lPy \qquad \text{(quantity theory)}$$

We also presented a graphical equivalent of this four-equation system.

Adding the saving-investment analysis appears to require no change in the above four equations. We add:

(5) $$s = s(r) \qquad \text{(saving function)}$$

(6) $$i = i(r) \qquad \text{(investment function)}$$

(7) $$s = i \qquad \text{(equilibrium in capital market)}$$

where $s$ is saving, $i$ investment (both defined in "real" terms), and $r$ the rate of interest. A set of equations either identical with or closely resembling this has frequently been used to represent the "Classical," in contrast to the "Keynesian" system.

Since none of the new variables, $s$, $i$, and $r$, in equations (5), (6) and (7) appears in the previous equations, we seem merely to have two separate equation systems: the original set, (1)–(4), and the new set, (5)–(7). Each set can be solved independently of the other. To the previous graphic analysis, we now merely add our saving-investment diagram, which is independent of the other diagrams. In other words, the rate of interest and the division of the national output between consumption and investment seem to be independent of the factors influencing the size of national output, of the quantity of money, and of the level of wages and prices. Rather, the rate of interest depends alone on productivity and thrift. Economic theory can thus be divided into three watertight branches: employment theory and the real wage [equations (1)–(3)]; the price level [equation (4)]; and the rate of interest and volume of saving and investment [equations (5)–(7)].[1]

## WICKSELL'S FORMULATION

But this formulation neglects Wicksell's contribution, which lay in showing the *interrelations* among money, the rate of interest, and the price level. The "sophisticated" quantity theory, that is, visualizes the monetary factors affecting the price level *via the rate of interest*.

This requires us to combine in some way equation (4), the quantity theory idea, with equations (5), (6), and (7), which relate to the capital market and the determination of interest rates. One way to do this is to eliminate equations (4) and (7) and to replace them with the following:

$$(8) \qquad\qquad s + DH + \Delta M = i$$

where $\Delta M$ is the rate of addition to the money supply, and $DH$ represents "dishoarding"—the rate of use of cash balances to buy securities. (If $\Delta M$ is negative, it represents a decrease in the money stock; if $DH$ is negative, it signifies "hoarding," an increase in cash balances.) The meaning of equation (8) is as follows: The supply of funds to the money market (or the demand for bonds) consists of three parts: current saving ($s$); dishoarding ($DH$); and any increase in the supply of money ($\Delta M$). The sum of these three sources of funds (demand for bonds) must equal $i$, the demand for funds (supply of bonds). The rate of interest must adjust to clear the money market—that is, we assume that bond prices adjust freely to find the level at which supply equals demand. Since $s$ and $i$ are

---

[1] As we noted earlier, the separation between the first two branches is watertight in only one direction: changes in the volume of employment and output can influence prices, although changes in the supply of money cannot influence employment or output.

flow variables, $\Delta M$ and $DH$ must also be thought of in these terms. If the magnitudes of the current flows of $s$ and $i$ are expressed in terms (say) of annual rates, then $\Delta M$ and $DH$ must also be current flows, expressed as annual rates.

The quantity theory asserts that people will not willingly hold *idle* balances—balances in excess of transaction needs. Thus "dishoarding" occurs only when people find themselves with actual cash balances $(M)$ greater than current transactions demands $(lPy)$.

$$(9) \qquad\qquad DH = M - lPy$$

The interpretation of equation (9) when "hoarding" occurs is that, if transactions requirements $(lPy)$ *exceed* actual cash holdings, people will become demanders of funds on the money market—they will borrow, but not for investment purposes, they will sell their existing holdings of old securities, or they will retain in cash (fail to lend) some part of their current saving. If we have some other theory about motives for cash-holding (leading to possible "hoarding" or "dishoarding"), we can substitute it for that embodied in equation (9). In the next chapter, for example, we shall consider another such theory.

Although there is a serious "scale" problem raised by equation (9), it is not significant in the present context, and is therefore deferred to the next chapter, where its importance is crucial.

Equation (8), together with (5), (6), and (9) [or a variant of (9)], constitutes what is often called a "loanable funds" theory of interest. The "loanable funds" approach to the interest rate, and its contrast with other approaches, have been the source of more confusion than almost any other single topic in recent economic theory. This confusion is unnecessary, although it is easy enough to understand how it has developed. One important part of the difficulty originates in the failure to be clear about stocks and flows. These confusions will be discussed in detail in the appendix to the following chapter.

If we now look back at our revised model, consisting of equations (1), (2), (3), (5), (6), (8), and (9), we can see that, as before (see p. 131) relationships (1), (2), and (3) determine the level of output $(y)$, the level of employment $(N)$, and the real wage $(W/P)$. The remaining relationships must therefore determine the absolute price and wage levels $(W$ and $P)$, the amounts saved and invested $(s$ and $i)$, the amount of dishoarding $(DH)$, and the rate of interest $(r)$. For present purposes, the change in money stock $(\Delta M)$ is taken (as well as $M$ itself) to be independently or autonomously determined.

Substituting into equation (9) the output level determined by (1), (2), and (3), and knowing the money stock ($M$), we can find a necessary relationship between the price level ($P$) and the rate of dishoarding ($DH$): corresponding to each possible value of $P$ there is a value of $DH$ (and vice versa). From equations (5), (6), and (8) we could determine the rate of interest ($r$), but only if we knew $\Delta M$ and $DH$. The former ($\Delta M$) is autonomous; but $DH$ depends on $P$, which is still not determined. Thus we cannot solve for $r$, $P$, or $DH$. There are certain *combinations* of these variables that are possible: if we know $P$, then we know $DH$, and can solve for $r$. Or, if we know $r$, we know what $DH$ has to be, and therefore $P$. But the system is not determinate; it has no unique solution, so far as the levels of prices and interest rates are concerned (it is, however, determinate with respect to $y$, $N$, and $W/P$).

Put another way, we have a system of seven equations, but we have eight unknowns: $y$, $N$, $W$, $P$, $R$, $s$, $i$, $DH$.

We can also observe that this system is not an equilibrium system. Equation (8) permits $s$ to be unequal to $i$. But if $s$ is unequal to $i$, some savers or some investors or both must be unsatisfied, or surprised. For we know that actual saving and investment must be equal, and if desired or intended saving and investment diverge, some desires or intentions are frustrated. In Wicksell's description of the process, for example, so long as $i$ exceeds $s$, "forced saving" is occurring, consumers will be trying to raise their consumption, leading to further changes, without limit.

To make the system determinate, we must do one of two things. One is restore the equilibrium character of the model by adding a further equation, which defines equilibrium. This would involve restoring equation (7):

(7)                                     $s = i$

The combination of (7) and (8) would thus require that, in equilibrium, $\Delta M + DH = 0$. That is, any money creation must be exactly balanced by (willing, intended) hoarding. But not only must their net sum be zero in equilibrium, each term must also be zero. For, unless $\Delta M = 0$, $M$ will be constantly changing, and so, therefore [see equation (9)], must be either $DH$ or $Py$. Equilibrium therefore further requires that $\Delta M = 0$. Since the sum $\Delta M + DH$ must be zero, this also means that $DH = 0$. Equation (9) therefore collapses into our old friend

(4)                                     $M = lPy,$

the equation for the quantity theory.

Thus we come back to exactly the same set of equations as that with which we began (p. 157). The "sophisticated quantity" theory gives the same results—in equilibrium—as the naïve one.

This result should not surprise us. For Wicksell's analysis differed from the simple quantity theory only in the *process* by which its results were achieved, not in its results. *In equilibrium,* prices were proportional to the money supply, and both were constant in time. *In equilibrium,* there were no idle balances flowing into the capital market nor additions needing to be made to cash balances in order to finance a larger money volume of transactions.

However, this solution—to make our formal system a static or equilibrium system—loses the whole benefit of Wicksell's notable insights. Is there an alternative?

The alternative is, unfortunately, a very difficult one. It is to construct an explicitly dynamic model. To do this, we must make a number of further assumptions about the disequilibrium behavior of savers, investors, producers, and workers. To reduce these to a set of equations is not a simple assignment. If it is done, we have a dynamic model which can tell us not only the ultimate effect of a displacement of equilibrium, but also show us what happens along the way: how long it takes, and what time patterns the several variables follow in the meantime. Moreover, it should be observed that there are many such dynamic models possible, all with the same equilibrium solution, but with different patterns and time sequences, each corresponding to some particular set of assumptions about lags, and about the disequilibrium behavior of workers, employers, consumers, and banks. The particular dynamic model implicit in Wicksell's description of the inflationary or deflationary process is actually a rather complicated one. A dynamic equation system embodying it could, however, be constructed, although it will not be attempted here.[2]

It was suggested earlier that lack of clarity as to the units in which the loanable funds theory of interest was expressed was a source of wrong or misleading conclusions regarding interest theory. Closely related to this is the second source of confusion—attempting to reason about interest rates in terms of a loanable funds theory either without realizing that it is a dynamic theory with no equilibrium significance, or without being sufficiently rigorous about the particular further dynamic assumptions which are made—and which have to be made—if we are to use the loan-

[2] A very simple "quasi-Wicksellian" model of the inflationary process is presented below, in Chap. XVI, pp. 431–434.

able funds approach to say anything definite or meaningful about interest rate determination. Wicksell (if read sympathetically) was not guilty of this confusion; many other writers have been and still are.

## FULL-EMPLOYMENT UNLESS WAGES RIGID

To repeat what has been emphasized before, it should be clear that the Classical model which we have reviewed is a full-employment model. Should there be a divergence between the number who want work at the going real wage and the number employers will hire at that wage, we have seen that adjustments will occur which will remove this discrepancy, by altering the real wage in the appropriate direction and extent. These adjustments will occur if there is no "rigidity" or "stickiness" of money wage rates. If the demand should exceed the supply, money wage rates can immediately rise; if supply exceeds demand, they can immediately fall.

The way in which money wage rate adjustments would restore full employment was often carelessly stated by some Classical writers, and their formulations are properly subject to criticism. Some writers simply ignored the fact that it was the relationship of wages to other prices that was relevant. They referred to the "law of demand"—more will be demanded of anything at a lower than at a higher price. If there is a labor surplus, wages have merely to fall, and the surplus will disappear. But the "law of demand"—although often carelessly phrased in terms of absolute prices—really is talking about relative prices. More of a consumer commodity, for example, is demanded at a lower than at a higher price because of "substitution" and "income" effects. If $P_a$ falls while $P_b$, $P_c$, etc. remain unchanged, there will be substitution of good $A$ for goods $B$, $C$, etc. If $P_a$ declines while the prices that determine money incomes remain unchanged, people will be able to buy somewhat more both of good $A$ and of all other goods. In the case of a single commodity, it is appropriate enough to assume that a reduction of $P_a$ is a reduction relative to all other prices and relative to money incomes. This is also true if we are talking about the wage of one group of workers. It is obviously not true if we are talking about the general level of the money wage rate.

Classical writers were therefore wrong when they either assumed that the money wage is all that counts, or, though recognizing that it is the real wage that is relevant, assumed that prices could remain unchanged when wages fall.

But we have seen that there does exist a complete and logical version of the Classical argument. A reduction of the money wage will lead to a reduction of the real wage, too, though a smaller reduction. This will be consistent with an increase in the hiring of labor and an increase in the level of output. The conclusion depends, however, on the quantity theory assumption—that people use money only as a medium of exchange, and will not hold more than they need for this purpose.

On the other hand, a money wage which is set too high and refuses to fall, can cause unemployment. And this seems to be the only possible cause of unemployment in the Classical system.

Consider other possible sources of trouble.

A drop in the supply of money because of reduced bank lending activity (i.e., a reduction in the aggregate of outstanding bank loans and investments) will cause deflation. But if money wages are flexible, they will fall, too, and the new equilibrium will leave the real wage, output, and employment unaffected.

Panic hoarding could also cause deflation. Although irrational, this might occasionally occur; but it would not cause unemployment unless wages were rigid.

Difficulties arising from a change in the propensity to save or a change in investment opportunities met a double line of defense. Increased thriftiness, for example, which means a reduction in the demand for consumer goods, would ordinarily be met by an automatic fall in the rate of interest. This decline in the interest rate would both stimulate investment and check the increase in saving. Exactly the same would be true if the source of trouble were a decline in opportunities for investment.

But, if the first line of defense, a flexible interest rate, should for any reason fail, there was another defense. The interest rate might fail, for example, if the banking system became a net seller of securities as their prices began to rise. By doing this, the banks would prevent the full necessary fall in the rate of interest. (To the extent that the banks sold securities, they would be reducing the supply of money in the hands of the public.) The rate of interest not having fallen sufficiently, the aggregate of consumer and investment demand would be reduced. A loss of jobs would now be threatened. To avoid this, money wages, if flexible, would decline; and prices, too. Sufficient decline in wages and prices could maintain full employment. Thus the double line of defense—(a) interest rates; but, if they fail, (b) wages and prices. Once again, rigid wages—in combination with the failure of the interest rate to adjust because of bank (mis)behavior—could cause unemployment.[3] As has

---

[3] Note carefully conceptual difficulties partially glossed over in the preceding paragraphs. *While* the banks are reducing the money supply (i.e., *while* $\Delta M$ is negative),

already been pointed out, the theory of *how much* unemployment would result from artificially maintained money wages was not worked out in Classical economics.

## MONETARY AND FISCAL POLICY IN CLASSICAL ECONOMICS

Thus it is proper to say that wage rigidity is the cause of unemployment —and the only cause—recognized in the Classical system. Whether the *need* for wage reductions to maintain employment arises from some action in the monetary sphere (hoarding or money contraction), or whether its origin is some disturbance of saving or investment propensities in combination with a perhaps entirely passive response by the banking system, the flexibility of money wages could apparently always provide a complete and automatic corrective.

It might be thought undesirable as a practical matter to throw all burdens of adjustment on the level of money wages. If so, the need for wage adjustments could be greatly reduced by preventing the banks from interfering with the saving-investment process—either through a 100 per cent reserve system (elimination of fractional reserves), or through central bank actions designed to offset the actions of the commercial banks. Keeping $M$ stable would prevent shifts in saving propensities or investment prospects from requiring wage and price changes. The interest rate alone would then maintain equilibrium. However, controlled variations in the stock of money would be necessary to stabilize wages and prices against the effects of shifts in the supply of labor, or its productivity, or against changes in the public's demand for money resulting either from changes in the "objective determinants of velocity" or from irrational hoarding or subsequent dishoarding.

Monetary policy, in short, was seen as a useful instrument for avoiding

---

full employment can be preserved only by *falling* prices and wages. But this is a disequilibrium situation. Once the banks stop subtracting from the money supply, there will have been a certain total cumulative reduction in the public's money-holdings. The new equilibrium is one involving a stable, *lower* wage and price level, which has fallen in the same percentage as the reduction of $M$. The maintenance of the interest rate above its "natural" level occurs only so long as the banks are *in the process* of reducing the money supply (selling their bonds to the public in return for part of the public's cash). Once the banks stop being net sellers of bonds, the interest rate will fall to its new "natural" level. The excess of saving over investment, because of a market rate above the natural rate, and the process of reducing the money supply are alternative descriptions of a disequilibrium situation, characterized (if wages are flexible) by *falling* wages and prices. Even if the wage decline is not sufficiently rapid to maintain full employment during the *process* of deflation, once the money supply stabilizes (the market rate falls to the new natural rate), then money wages and prices can continue to decline until full employment equilibrium is restored.

the necessity for price and wage fluctuations—for maintaining stability of the unit of value in a changing environment. External forces of change would otherwise require inflation or deflation of the price level (particularly in a system with fractional reserve banking). Deflation would probably also involve unemployment, because of the admitted difficulty and slowness of downward wage adjustments. These could be completely avoided by intelligent monetary policy.

The instruments of monetary policy are various, and there is no need to go into details here. However, a few remarks are necessary to help clarify the difference between monetary and fiscal policy. Some instruments of monetary policy aim directly at the commercial banks—for example, changes in bank minimum reserve requirements. A rise in reserve requirements will force any banks which were at the previous minimum to reduce their loans and investments, by selling securities from portfolio in excess of new purchases (retiring old loans faster than new ones are made), thus reducing the supply of bank money in the hands of the public. A reduction of reserve requirements permits (although it does not force) banks to increase their loans and investments, thus increasing the supply of bank money. Other types of measures may operate to affect bank reserves, and thus to force or to permit bank expansion or contraction; but they could operate equally well if there were no commercial banks, or in a system with a requirement that banks maintain 100 per cent reserves against deposits. The typical instrument of pure monetary policy is of this sort—open market sales and purchases of securities. When the central bank (or treasury acting as a central bank) buys securities on the open market, it either buys them from the non-bank public, becoming a net supplier of funds and directly increasing the public's cash; or it buys from a bank, in which case the bank's reserves are increased and it is enabled to (and, it is hoped, will) expand its loans and investments, thus increasing the money supply. If the central bank sells on the open market, it either sells to the public, absorbing current saving and extinguishing money, or it sells to a commercial bank, absorbing reserves, thus requiring or inducing the bank to reduce its loans and investments.

Fiscal policy involves alterations in government expenditures for goods and services, or the level of tax rates. Unlike monetary policy, these measures involve direct government entrance into the market for goods and services (in the case of expenditures), and a direct impact on private demand (in the case of taxes). Monetary policy operates less directly, by affecting the interest rate and thus the public's willingness to invest or save (consume). Yet, despite its greater directness, fiscal policy was seen to have no place in the arsenal of stabilization measures, except as it might incidentally serve as an instrument of monetary policy.

To illustrate, suppose that there should be unemployment as a result of an increased propensity to save, offset by commercial bank net sales of securities so that the interest rate falls but very little, thus requiring declines in money wages that are impossible to secure. Proposals may be made for increased government spending to create jobs for the unemployed. Were this new spending to be financed by higher taxes, the private spending of taxpayers would be reduced by as much as government spending increased (it was assumed). But if it were to be financed by selling bonds to the public, it was argued that this could only raise interest rates and thus cut back private investment spending (and/or increase private saving) by as much as government spending increased. The government bonds would have to compete with the bonds issued by private investors for the available supply of saving, thus driving down bond prices (raising interest rates) to choke off any net increase in demand.[4] Only if the increased government spending were financed by new money creation (the printing press or borrowing from banks with excess reserves) would there be a net increase in demand. But this would be using government finances—awkwardly and unnecessarily—as an instrument of monetary policy, a means for increasing the supply of money. Exactly the same effect could be secured by central bank open market purchases of bonds—the conventional instrument of monetary policy. By this means the supply of money can be increased, but without any diversion of resources from public to private use.

Said R. G. Hawtrey in 1925, commenting on proposals for public works expenditures to relieve unemployment in England: "Here, then, is the real virtue of the proposal. If the new [public] works are financed by the creation of bank credits, they will give additional employment. . . . But then the same reasoning shows that a creation of credit unaccompanied by any expenditure on public works could be equally effective in giving employment. The public works are merely a piece of ritual, convenient to people who want to be able to say that they are doing something, but otherwise irrelevant. To stimulate an expansion of credit is

---

[4] Actually, there is some inconsistency here. If the banks are the source of the trouble, stabilizing the rate of interest by standing ready to sell bonds at only slightly above previous bond price levels, they presumably stand ready, too, to buy at only slightly lower bond price levels. Thus the banks might well purchase the new government bonds without much rise occurring in interest rates. In this case, the new government spending would not be at the expense of equivalent private spending. Here again, however, the fiscal measure works only because it becomes an indirect means of monetary policy.

usually only too easy. To resort for the purpose to the construction of expensive public works is to burn down the house for the sake of the roast pig." [5]

One of the most striking changes made by modern macroeconomic thought is that it largely reverses the previously conceived roles of monetary and fiscal policy. Today, monetary effects are recognized, and monetary policy is still seen to be important; but the emphasis is on fiscal measures in securing economic stabilization (or, if badly used, in creating instability). This is the case even where fiscal measures are used in a way which has no effect, direct or indirect, on the quantity of money.

[5] "Public Expenditure and the Demand for Labour," *Econonomica*, V (March 1925), pp. 43–44.

# The Keynesian Macroeconomics

*PART THREE*

# Some Obstacles
# to Full Employment

*Chapter IX*

In this chapter, we shall consider some qualifications of the Classical model, which were first suggested by J. M. Keynes, in *The General Theory of Employment, Interest and Money.*[1] The first of these—"liquidity preference," or "speculative demand for money"—can be added to the Classical model without changing its full-employment character, so long as we continue to assume wage flexibility. However, a special case of this qualification—the "liquidity trap"—might create a situation in which full employment would be impossible even with perfect wage and price flexibility.

The second qualification of the Classical model is even more serious. It is the possibility of what we might call an "inconsistency" between saving and investment. If this situation prevails, then the Classical correctives fail (even though wages are perfectly flexible), and full employment may become impossible.[2]

Finally, we consider some difficulties of wage-price flexibility which have been long understood, but which assume particular importance in the light of Keynes' extensions of Classical thinking.

We conclude the chapter with the recognition that these obstacles to full employment rather thoroughly destroy the notion of an economy

[1] See *General Theory*, Chaps. 13 and 15.

[2] There is a relationship, which some economists claim is implicit in Classical analysis, which might theoretically rescue the economy from unemployment due to a "liquidity trap" or "inconsistency," if only wage rates are thoroughly flexible. This is the relationship of consumer spending to wealth—the so-called "Pigou effect." We have not considered this as part of the Classical model (nor is it needed in the Classical model). It is not discussed in the present chapter, but in Chap. XII.

whose automatic responses will invariably prevent the development of unemployment, or quickly correct it if it should arise. Since the Classical doctrine fails to consider the economics of less-than-full employment, it is necessary to develop new theoretical tools appropriate to such a situation. This new theory must take the levels of employment and output as primary variables.

In this chapter we shall concentrate on situations posing the threat of unemployment, rather than those involving possible inflation. This asymmetry of treatment is deliberate, and is designed to assist in the development of succeeding chapters. It does not represent any judgment that the economy is necessarily disposed more toward unemployment than inflation. At a later point, we shall devote a chapter to the subject of inflation. It is probably true, nevertheless, that new analytical tools are more needed to help us understand unemployment than inflation. The student will find it a very useful exercise to work out for himself in each instance the argument of this chapter as it would apply to a situation the reverse of that for which it is developed—i.e., for an increase rather than for a decrease in aggregate demand.

## LIQUIDITY PREFERENCE: THE SPECULATIVE DEMAND FOR MONEY

In Chapter VII, we showed that the Classical theory was not necessarily invalidated when we recognized a resale market for bonds—when, that is, we took account of the fact that the supply and demand for bonds include sales and purchases which do not represent current investment and saving. It is clear that many sales and purchases do represent mere rearrangements of asset portfolios, both by businesses and by consumers. However, no matter how extensive these rearrangements may be, it is clear that so long as no one who sells an old security prefers to hold idle cash instead, the interest rate should still maintain equality between saving and investment, or a constant level of aggregate demand. Only if the *banking system* should become a net buyer or seller of bonds (i.e., a net source of cash or a net absorber of cash) would the equality of saving and investment be disturbed, requiring an inflation or deflation of the general price and wage level.

Keynes suggested, however, that *private nonbank investors* might at times become net absorbers or releasers of cash, and thus disturb the smooth functioning of the securities market. Thus, even if the banks could be made to behave, and the supply of money were held constant, there was still room for trouble to develop.

Keynes' idea was not merely that, at times, there might occur spontaneous or autonomous changes in the public's demand for money. This possibility had been recognized by a number of writers in the Classical tradition. Hoarding, although irrational, might nevertheless occasionally appear, and require deflation of prices if unemployment was to be avoided. But hoarding, in this view, played an autonomous, nonsystematic role, like the weather, or "acts of God." Some writers even recognized that whenever times were bad and people became uncertain of the future, hoarding might generally be expected to appear, worsening an already bad situation. But even in this view, hoarding could not be considered the *cause* of the bad times, only a factor which would intensify them, if otherwise caused. What Keynes argued was that there exists an inherent tendency for hoarding and dishoarding to occur in a way that is systematically destabilizing.

Let us review the Classical argument once more. As the Classical writers saw the functioning of the capital market, the interest rate would automatically fluctuate to reflect changes either in the saving or investment schedules. In Figure 9–1, an increase in thriftiness, for ex-

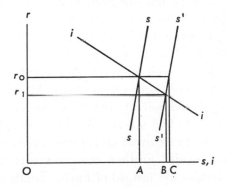

Figure 9–1.

ample, represented by a shift of the saving schedule from $ss$ to $s's'$, should lead to a reduction of the interest rate from $r_0$ to $r_1$. Had $r_0$ been maintained, intended saving, $OC$, would have exceeded intended investment, $OA$. But the drop to $r_1$ discourages saving to $OB$, and encourages investment, also to $OB$. As compared to the initial situation, saving has increased (i.e., consumption has decreased) by $AB$. The increase of investment, also $AB$, has just offset the decrease in consumption.

Wicksell had noted that the banking system might tend, under the circumstances referred to here, to become a net absorber of funds, by selling bonds from bank portfolios as bond prices started to rise—thus preventing much rise in bond prices (or by maintaining their loan rate unchanged, and only making such loans as were called for at that rate). What Keynes saw was that ordinary, private wealth holders might tend to play the same role as Wicksell's banks. If so, keeping the quantity of money constant would not be enough to prevent a saving-investment disturbance. *In what follows, we shall assume a constant M, in order to concentrate attention on the role of nonbank lenders.*

What Keynes pointed out was quite simple. An increase in thriftiness or a decrease in investment prospects would indeed naturally tend to reduce interest rates. That is, it would tend to raise bond prices. If there were no resale market for bonds, there would be no problem. But when we introduce the resale market, and recognize that the volume of outstanding bonds is very large compared with the quantity of new issues, we have to consider how the holder of an existing bond is likely to behave as he sees bond prices advance. Naturally, he will be pleased: his asset is now worth more. If he thought that the advance in prices was permanent, he would certainly not be led to do anything about it. However, suppose that he has observed that, in the past, bond prices have had their ups and downs but that no permanent trend in their level has appeared; suppose that he sees nothing in the present situation to indicate that the level of bond prices is likely to be permanently higher. Then he may very well interpret the present rise as a temporary thing, likely to be reversed later on. If this is his expectation, he will be better off if he should sell his bonds at the present, higher-than-normal price, and wait to buy others until the expected decline in price had occurred. His sale (to a current saver) will represent saving to which no investment corresponds.[3] Further, current savers, too, may see the bond price rise as temporary; instead of buying bonds with their current saving, they may merely hold their cash, and wait for the expected decline in price.

To be sure, holding cash instead of a bond involves foregoing an interest return. The Classical writers had assumed that foregoing an available return was irrational, and would, therefore, never occur. But this conduct is not irrational if interest rates are expected to rise (bond prices fall) very much. Keynes points out that an expected rise in the rate of interest by the square of itself will wipe out the expected gain from holding a bond. If a bond paying $5 per year coupon and now

---

[3] In the sense of intended or desired $s$ and $i$, of course. Actual $s$ and $i$ are always equal.

selling for $100 should have dropped in a year to $95, the capital loss of $5 would have wiped out the $5 of interest. If it were expected to fall by more than this, the net advantage is clearly in holding barren cash. Keynes called this a "speculative demand" for money.

The adjective "speculative" is significant. For Keynes is here calling attention to a general phenomenon of whose existence and consequences economists have long been aware. In markets for durable, standardized commodities, where stocks are large relative to current new supply and demand, speculation inevitably occurs, and its role is agreed to be highly beneficial in ordinary circumstances. Its role consists of reducing temporary price fluctuations, as speculators buy when prices fall below normal and sell when above, thus reducing the amplitude of the price fluctuations which would otherwise occur.

In the wheat market, for instance, the annual supply comes onto the market at harvest time, while demand—by ultimate consumers—has little, if any, seasonal pattern. But the price does not go nearly to zero right after harvest—which it would have to do in order to increase consumption sufficiently to take all this glut of wheat off the market. Nor does it soar high enough to choke off all demand in the months when no new supply is forthcoming. Rather, seasonal price fluctuations are almost completely smoothed out by speculators, who buy during the crop months, when prices fall below levels expected to prevail later, and sell (from inventory), during the remainder of the year, when prices are higher than their normal average. As a result of this action the seasonal pattern of wheat prices is smoothed out, until (ideally) the difference between low and high is little more than the cost of carrying wheat in inventory, including interest.

Speculation in the wheat market not only smooths out prices and consumption over the course of the year, but over longer periods, too. A bumper crop in one year, due to unusually favorable weather, will lead to some price decline. But speculators, sensing (or guessing) that prices will be higher in subsequent years, buy wheat and thereby prevent as large a price decline as would otherwise have occurred. In the year of a relatively small crop, prices rise; but, to the extent that stocks exist, the rise will be moderated by the release of inventories, to get the benefit of the higher-than-normal prices.[4]

[4] It is probably unnecessary to remind the reader that the wheat "speculator" often is a person who also has other interests in the wheat business—a farmer, a dealer, or a flour miller, for instance—who needs to hold inventories of wheat in connection with his other activities, but can easily alter the size of his inventories in response to speculative considerations.

As the wheat example may remind us, however, speculators may sometimes be wrong in their estimates of future prices. They may expect
higher (or lower) future prices than can in fact be justified by ultimate
supply and demand conditions. In response to this expectation, they may
hold the present price too high (low), by absorbing wheat into inventories (selling from stocks). Thus, in Figure 9–2, SS and *DD* may repre-

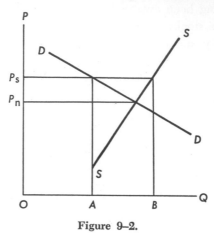

Figure 9–2.

sent the long run supply and demand conditions for wheat. An average
price of $P_n$ would keep production and consumption in balance. Speculators, however, because of mistaken views about either supply or demand (overestimate of future demand, underestimate of future supply),
may hold the price in the neighborhood of $P_s$, standing ready to absorb
into inventories the current average excess, *AB*, of production over consumption. So long as the conviction prevails that the long-run normal price
is at or above $P_s$, speculators may continue to pile up inventories, and
keep the price above the level which can adjust consumption to production.

Of course, sooner or later, this mistaken view will be overthrown, and
prices allowed to fall. The continued piling up of inventories will sooner
or later convince speculators that current prices are too high, and they
will unload. As they do, prices will have to fall below $P_n$ for a time,
until the previous surplus is worked off. (If they had held the price too
low, by selling from inventory, sooner or later the exhaustion of stocks
would convince them of their mistake. As they tried to rebuild necessary
stocks, the price temporarily would rise above $P_n$.)

Mistaken views like these do not often arise from a *changed expectation* by speculators as to the normal price level for a commodity. More

frequently, it is the normal price which changes; while speculators, not appreciating the extent of the fundamental changes in supply or demand conditions, cling to a now obsolete view of the normal price. Thus they tend to delay the readjustment of price levels—up or down— by selling from or buying for inventory at price levels close to those that have previously been considered normal.

What Keynes asserts is that the bond market is a perfect example of a speculative situation of this kind. The "commodity" involved is highly durable. The existing stock is extremely large relative to the new flows of investment and saving—i.e., new supply and demand for bonds. The market is close to a perfect market, in which a definite price always exists and any individual can buy or sell to the limit of his resources without appreciable influence on the price. People do observe the interest rate to have been generally stable, fluctuating within a narrow range in the past—with trends nonexistent or insignificant for long periods. Naturally they develop concepts of normal prices, and naturally they behave in a way which prevents wide fluctuations from developing.

This very phenomenon of speculation, which Keynes developed to explain the behavior of *nonbank* lenders, actually provides the most cogent rationale for the kind of behavior which Wicksell described for the commercial banks. Why do the banks tend to sell from their portfolios as interest rates start to fall and to buy when they start to rise (thus, in each case, limiting the fall or rise)? Because banks, too, like to avoid capital losses and make capital gains. They, too, have developed concepts of normal rates of interest, and behave rationally in the light of these concepts. Thus Keynes' theory is broad enough to include Wicksell's (although Keynes made no reference to this).[5]

We have seen that speculation—if mistaken—tends ultimately to be self-correcting in any commodity market; but what Keynes further recognized was that the self-correcting mechanism is either absent or very slow and painful in the case of the interest rate. This, however, is anticipating later discussion. For the moment, our concern is with the existence and the operation of the speculative demand for money, not its ultimate significance for the economy.

[5] There is, of course, the difference that bank operations involve the creation or destruction of money, those by nonbank lenders its activation or inactivation. The difference is not as great as might appear at first sight, however. In fact, before it became common to count banknotes or bank deposits as "money," changes in their volume were often referred to as causing changes in the effective velocity rather than in the volume of "money" (i.e., reserve money, usually gold).

## THE SUPPLY AND DEMAND FOR MONEY, RECOGNIZING SPECULATION

What we have presented in the above paragraphs can be seen to represent a theory about hoarding or dishoarding behavior of wealth-holders. When interest rates are below those considered normal (i.e., bond prices above normal) people will sell bonds from their portfolios, accumulating idle cash; they will hoard. When bond prices are below normal, people will use idle cash to buy bonds; they will dishoard. In the appendix to this chapter we consider the possibility of formulating this interest theory specifically in terms of hoarding and dishoarding behavior—i.e., in "loanable funds" terms. In the body of the chapter, however, we will formulate it the way Keynes did, in terms of supply and demand for cash balances—i.e., in stock rather than flow terms.

We assume, to start with, that we can take the prevailing concepts of "normal" bond prices as given, at any particular time. The levels of these "normal" interest rate concepts are obviously not determined by stable characteristics of human nature or social organization (although tendencies for the normal rate concepts of different individuals to coincide or differ may be affected by these more stable factors). Rather, the particular concepts of normal prevailing at any given time reflect experiences of the immediate and more distant past, as perceived by each individual, modified by any information, reasoning, or hunches that he may have about the way in which the future may differ from the past.

A change in the current market rate will often, to some extent, cause a revision of one's concept of what future rates will be. What we must assume for Keynes' idea to have validity, and it is an entirely reasonable assumption, is that a change in the present rate will not ordinarily lead to an equivalent change in the expected future rate. If the latter were the case, the concept of a normal rate would have no meaning, and there could be no speculative demand for money.

Given each wealth-owner's idea of the normal rate, and the amount of resources each one commands, we can imagine drawing up a schedule showing—for each level of the current rate—what would be the aggregate desired volumes of cash holdings and of bond holdings. At "high" present interest rates, presumably the desire for cash would be small, the desire to hold bonds very large. That is, bonds would appear to be "cheap," and almost everyone would prefer to hold the asset which both yields a return and is expected to rise in price, or, at worst, not fall. The only persons still preferring cash would be those few who thought that bond prices—although already low in the judgment of others—were, nevertheless, likely to fall enough to wipe out the yield. On the other extreme, at very "low" interest rates ("high" bond prices), almost everyone would expect a fall in bond prices and would therefore prefer to be a cashholder. For each intermediate rate between these extremes we could also find the aggregate volume of preferred or desired holdings, both of bonds and cash.[6]

The results of this hypothetical survey of the preferred asset form for each wealth-holder might be summarized in the form of a schedule showing, at each interest rate, the "demand for bonds," or the "demand for cash," or the "preferred asset ratio" (or in some other way). This one set of facts is clearly capable of different kinds of summary. Keynes chose to use the "demand for cash" form. A graph of this schedule might look like Figure 9–3. The curve is shown as concave upward, on

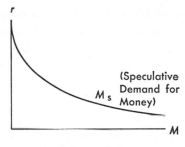

Figure 9–3.

the assumption that the distribution of concepts of normal is rather bunched around a prevailing level, few holding extreme views on either side of this range.[7]

Clearly, the more alike are the normal rate concepts of wealth-holders,

[6] Assuming each wealth-holder to possess a single-valued expectation of the future bond price, that is, to be certain that his expectation were correct, he would always desire to hold a portfolio which was either all cash or all bonds. Assuming instead, that each one has some idea of a *range* of probable future rates, each rate within this range held with a different degree of certainty, we might find not only all-bond or all-cash portfolios, but also mixtures of bonds and cash, with the proportions in each form varying in accordance with where the current market rate stands in relation to the whole distribution of expected rates. Although it is sensible and realistic to reformulate the theory in terms of uncertainty; it is easier to work with the theory formulated in terms of single-valued expectations; and it produces no real difference of result (at this stage of analysis).

[7] Theoretically, this should make the curve S-shaped. At some point, far to the right, the curve should become concave downward, and possibly even vertical. It does not seem likely that this portion of the curve would ever become relevant.

the flatter the curve will be; the more diverse their expectations of the future course of interest rates, the steeper the curve.

We have been describing in these paragraphs the demand for money as an asset—as an alternative to holding bonds. This demand for money has to be seen as a demand which is additional to the "transactions demand for money" envisaged in the Classical quantity theory. That demand was for so-called "active balances." People hold such balances with the notion of using them. Such active balances bounce around from one holder to another, mediating transactions. Although at some point in his payment cycle, each individual will have a zero demand for an active balance (just before his "pay day"), at all times the aggregate transactions demand for cash is positive, and is a fairly stable proportion of the dollar value of transactions or of the dollar volume of income or output.

But this new demand for money is a demand for "idle balances," or for money as an asset rather than as a mere medium of exchange.

Thus the total demand for money has two parts—a transactions demand, which is proportional to the level of money national product (or income), and an "asset" or "speculative" demand, which is, *ceteris paribus*, a function of the interest rate.

Equilibrium with respect to money holding requires that the *actual* money holdings or cash balances of the public in the aggregate equal the *needed or desired* cash balances. When only the transactions demand was considered, equilibrium therefore required a certain level of $Py$, money national income or product. That is, the price and output levels had to be such that people willingly held the entire stock of money. Now we hypothesize that the demand for money depends both on the level of money national income and on the level of the interest rate. This means that the *combination* of $Py$ and $r$ must be such as to make the public willing to hold the money stock. Obviously there must be a whole range of possible combinations of $Py$ and $r$ which meet this requirement. For example, a low $Py$ means a low transactions demand; but this could be offset by a sufficiently low $r$, giving rise to a large speculative demand. Or, a somewhat higher $Py$ would be consistent with equilibrium with respect to money-holding if $r$ were also somewhat higher, and the speculative demand correspondingly reduced. Put in another fashion, we can see that any given increase in the supply of money to be held by the public might be absorbed either through a sufficient rise in $Py$ or by a sufficient fall in $r$, or by some combination.

We can begin our further analysis of this matter—so long as we do not stop there—by assuming either one of these determinants of demand to be given, and by considering the other as variable. For example, we could temporarily assume a given interest rate and consider price or output levels as the variable which equated supply and demand for money. Equally well, we can assume the transactions demand as temporarily given, and consider $r$ the variable which equates supply and demand, which is what we now do.

In Figure 9–4, three ways of representing this are shown. In part A,

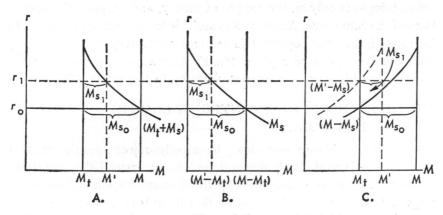

**Figure 9–4.**

we represent the total demand for money, $(M_t + M_s)$, as the sum of a transactions demand which is constant plus a speculative demand which depends on the interest rate. Given the total supply of money $(M)$, there is only one interest rate $(r_0)$, at which total supply and demand are equal.

In part B, on the other hand, we have subtracted the given transactions demand $M_t$ from the total supply, and show $r_0$ as the rate which equates the demand for idle balances $(M_s)$ and the supply of idle balances $(M - M_t)$.

Finally, in part C, we have subtracted the speculative demand from the total supply of money, giving the curve $(M - M_s)$, which can be thought of as the supply of transactions balances. Only at rate $r_0$ is the supply of transactions money equal to the given demand, $M_t$. These are obviously three alternative representations of the same set of facts. Which form we use will depend on convenience in representing the problem at hand.

If, now, we consider the effect of a change in the supply of money $(M)$, *keeping transactions demand constant*, then we can see that the rate of interest will have to change to secure equilibrium. For example, if the supply of money were reduced to $M'$, the equilibrium interest rate—given the transactions demand—will rise to $r_1$.

At times in his *General Theory*, Keynes appeared to assume that a change in the supply of money would have no effect, direct or indirect, on the transactions demand. Thus his analysis appeared to stop with what we have just summarized. This led to the rather peculiar view of the interest rate as a "purely monetary phenomenon"—the rate of interest depends only on the supply of money, and on people's expectations of the future rate. Actually, Keynes' whole analysis, sympathetically interpreted, does not support this extreme view. We, too, shall shortly relax the assumption of a given $M_t$. First, however, we must consider another possible source of interest-elasticity in the demand for money.

## ANOTHER SOURCE OF AN INTEREST-ELASTIC DEMAND FOR MONEY

Many economists—in our view, incorrectly—reject speculation as a source of an interest-elastic demand for money. Instead they substitute another reason or other reasons why the demand for idle balances may respond to the interest rate. Suppose that there is no expectation on the part of any wealth-holder that the interest rate will diverge from whatever it may be at the time (or, at least, no expectation that it may diverge—in an upward direction—by enough to make it worthwhile to lose interest while waiting for the rate to rise). Still, it might be worthwhile to hold an idle balance instead of to hold securities if the return to be gained from holding securities is insufficient to pay one for the trouble and inconvenience (and cost, in terms of brokers' fees, etc.) of investing in securities. Consider, for example, a business firm which must accumulate a fund to meet expected future payments of dividends or taxes. If the available return is very low and the period relatively short before the funds are needed, and the sum involved is relatively small, it may not be worth the cost and inconvenience of buying, and then, in a short while, selling, securities. If the rate of return were higher, it might overbalance this cost and inconvenience. We can recognize that the total wealth-holdings (in forms other than real goods) of consumers and businesses are made up of individual holdings of various sizes, from very small to very large, and the needs for cash to meet obligations are at varying distances in the future. We may further recognize that the costs and inconvenience are in part independent either of the size of the fund involved or of the length of the period for which it might be invested. Then, the higher the rate of interest, the more of these individual funds will it pay for their owners to put in an interest-yielding form; the lower the rate of yield, the fewer funds will it pay to invest, and the greater will be the desired holding of cash. This is clearly another possible reason why rational individuals might hold idle cash, in an aggregate amount which varies inversely with the rate of interest.

A second reason is somewhat closer to Keynes'. Suppose that individual wealth-holders have no reason to assume that the rate of interest is any more likely to change in one direction than the other, but they recognize that it will probably change. If they hold cash, they can neither benefit nor lose by whatever change may occur in the interest rate. If they hold bonds, they stand either to lose or to gain; they take a risk. Suppose further that the majority of individuals have an aversion to risk: they would rather have $1 "for sure" than a fifty-fifty chance of having either $.50 or $1.50. The mathematical value of the risky alternative is exactly the same as the "sure thing"; but they prefer the latter to the former.

However, holding bonds, whose prices may change, not only involves risk, but it also involves return. The higher the available return, the more individuals there will be for whom the prospect of return makes them willing to assume risk; or, for any individual, the larger the percentage of his wealth that he is willing to commit in the risky form, and the smaller percentage he will prefer to hold in cash. Once again, the demand for cash as an asset—the demand for idle balances—bears an inverse relationship to the rate of interest.

We can substitute either or both of these reasons for an interest-elastic demand for money for Keynes' speculative demand, leaving the subsequent analysis at least formally unchanged.

But the omission of the speculative element has the consequence that we must picture the liquidity preference schedule as a stable schedule, the level of which changes only very slowly over time. For its slope and level depend, in this view, only upon relatively stable characteristics of economic structure (e.g., the size distribution of individual wealth-holdings and the costs of buying and selling securities), or of basic attitudes (e.g., the degree of aversion to risk).

Keynes' speculative demand requires no such stability of the schedule. If the rate of interest has commonly been in the 8 to 15 per cent range, the level of the schedule will reflect this; if it has commonly varied in the 1.5 to 5 per cent range, its level will be much lower, for wealth-holders will have very different expectations as to its probable future range of variation. Yet the elasticity of the schedule may be very much the same in either case. If past variation has been in the 8 to 15 per cent range, it is very unlikely that the rate can, in the short run, be moved outside of these limits; for the expectations of speculators will lead them to act in a way which will hold it in this range. The schedule might become almost infinitely elastic at 8 per cent. But in the other case, it might become highly elastic only at a level of 1.5 per cent.

Keynes' view as to the significance of speculation does not rest upon the previous existence of any particular range of interest rates. His point is, simply, that, at any time, wealth-holders will have, quite reasonably, formed certain expectations as to rates of interest likely to prevail in the near future. These expectations prevent the rate of interest from operating in the way Classical economics assumed—that is, they prevent it from in the first instance automatically adjusting to stabilize the aggregate demand for goods. If the interest rate varied automatically and freely to equate saving and investment, shifts in saving or investment schedules could have no effect other than to change the rate of interest and the division of a given total output between investment and consumption. But if the adjustment of the rate of interest is limited by speculation, the impact of shifts in saving or investment schedules will be on the aggregate demand for goods, leading, if wages and prices are flexible, to inflation or deflation; or, if they are rigid, to an increase or decrease in output and employment.

## SPECULATIVE DEMAND FOR MONEY ADDED
## TO THE CLASSICAL MODEL

We have seen earlier that it is appropriate to suppress any variable in an equation only if the context in which we use that relationship is one in which the suppressed variable can really be taken as given. We can properly say: *"Ceteris paribus,* the larger the quantity of money the lower the rate of interest," only if it is realistic to assume in our larger framework of analysis that prices and output are given. Neither in Keynes' own model nor certainly in the modified version of the Classical model which we are now developing is it proper to assume $P$ and $y$ both as given when $M$ and $r$ change. Thus we cannot, except temporarily, assume the transactions demand, which depends on $Py$, as given. Now consider what happens when these are free to vary.

We noted above that a number of possible combinations of $r$ and $Py$ might be consistent with an equality between the supply and demand for money. But when we combine the monetary analysis with the other parts of our extended Classical model, we can see that only one of these many combinations of $Py$ and $r$ is really possible in equilibrium. The level of $y$ cannot be lower than that which corresponds to full employment, for, if it were, there would be a falling money wage, and a falling price level. Since full equilibrium in the economy requires that wages and prices show no tendency to change, this means that full equilibrium is necessarily a state of full employment. There is thus some equilibrium level of real wage, $W/P$, consistent with full employment and the equilibrium levels of $N$ and $y$. But what will determine the absolute levels of $P$ and $W$? In the original Classical model, the equilibrium level of $P$ could be determined by the money supply. Now, however, the transactions demand is only part of the total demand; we must know $r$ before we can determine $P$ (or must determine both $r$ and $P$ simultaneously). There is another relationship which supplies the key. Given the saving and investment schedules, there is only one level of $r$ at which real desired saving and investment are equal. At any other level of $r$ either savers or investors or both would necessarily be disappointed. This gives us the equilibrium level of $r$, and means that the volume of speculative balances is also determined—that quantity of cash which wealth-holders wish to keep idle at this equilibrium $r$. Subtracting this from the total $M$ leaves the amount available for transactions balances. Knowing the equilibrium $M_t$ and $y$, we can then determine $P$. And there is some $W$, which, taken together with the $P$ of the last sentence, makes employers willing to hire just the amount of labor which seeks employment.

If we want to think of the finding of the equilibrium levels of all variables as the solution to a system of simultaneous equations, we can set up the model in symbolic form as follows:

(1) $$y = y(N)$$

(2) $$\frac{dy}{dN} = \frac{W}{P}$$

(3) $$N = N\left(\frac{W}{P}\right)$$

(4a) $$M = lPy + L(r)$$

(5) $$s = s(r)$$

(6) $$i = i(r)$$

(7) $$s = i$$

where all symbols have meanings previously defined, and where $M$ is autonomous and $l$ determined by the economic structure.

The above equation system differs from the Classical one set forth on page 157 only in one respect: the demand for money—the right side of equation (4a)—consists not only of the transactions demand $(lPy)$ but also the speculative demand, which we have determined to be a function of the rate of interest $[L(r)]$.

As before, we can think of the simultaneous solution of (1), (2), and (3) as giving us the equilibrium levels of $y$, $N$, and $W/P$. Simultaneous solution of (5), (6), and (7) provides us with the equilibrium interest rate, $r$. Inserting into equation (4a) the autonomously given $M$, the level of $y$ from the first group of equations, and the level of $r$ from the last group, allows us to solve for the equilibrium $P$. Then, knowing both $P$ and $W/P$, we can solve for $W$.

It is not very helpful, however, merely to see that there may exist a unique equilibrium solution for all variables. Rather, we want to be able to say how the equilibrium values of these variables are affected by some change in a parameter—e.g., by a shift in the production function, or a change in the quantity of money. We could do this by assuming specific numerical parameters for each of the above equations, and solving them simultaneously for the specific numerical equilibrium values of the variables; then we could change one parameter and solve again. More elegantly and more generally, we can specify the signs of derivatives and use differential calculus to get generalized answers. Instead, however, a graphical solution which any student can follow will be used. For this purpose we have constructed Figure 9–5. This figure modifies and expands the diagrammatic apparatus of Chapter VI.

Parts B, C, E, and F are taken from the diagrams used in Chapter VI. The only difference is that part E relates to the transactions demand for money, which is now recognized as only part of the total demand. Part A is the familiar saving-investment diagram and part D, one of the forms of the supply and demand for money analysis developed in the second section of this chapter.

From parts B and C of the figure we can, as before, find the equilibrium real wage, employment, and output. Part A shows that saving-investment equilibrium requires an interest rate $r_0$. This rate, given the speculative demand schedule for money, means that the amount $M_{s_0}$ will be held in speculative balances. Part D shows that these holdings are consistent with a transactions demand of $M_{t_0}$, given the supply of money, $M_0$. This is consistent with a $Py$ of $(Py)_0$ (part E). Given $y_0$ (part B), this means

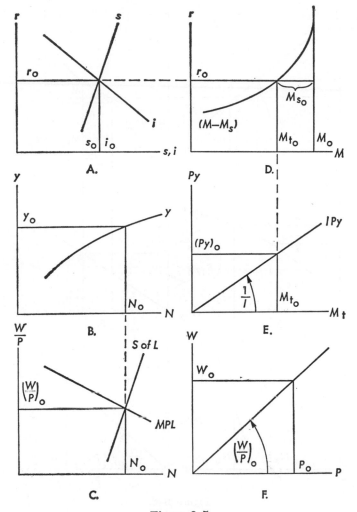

**Figure 9–5.**

that the equilibrium price level is $P_0$. This is shown, in part F, to require a wage level $W_0$ in order to be consistent with the real wage $(W/P)_0$ found in part C.

This apparatus permits us to predict the effect, in comparative statics terms, of any shift of a parameter. For example, assume an increase in thriftiness occurs. In Figure 9–6, the solid lines show an initial equilibrium situation. The broken lines show the new equilibrium associated with the shift of the saving schedule from $s$ to $s'$ (in part A). In terms of comparative statics, we can see that the result is not only a lower

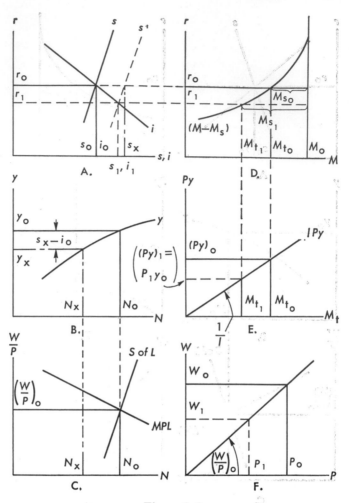

**Figure 9–6.**

interest rate (which is all that the classical model required), but also a lower price and wage level, *even though the quantity of money is unchanged.* The reason for this is that the lower equilibrium interest rate, $r_1$, is associated with a larger demand for speculative balances. This can be accommodated only at a lower price level (so long as the quantity of money is unchanged).

The student should carefully work through the diagrams, making sure that he understands every part of them, and should try to explain the whole process in words. He should then try some other parameter shift—e.g., an increase in the quantity of money, or a rise in the profitability of investment (upward shift in the $ii$ schedule). Table 9–1 summarizes the comparative statics predictions of this model for three cases. The student should first confirm for himself the result shown in cases a through c, then attempt to fill in the missing lines, d through g. We shall comment in the next section on the particular significance of these results.

**TABLE 9–1.  Effects of Parameter Shifts in Expanded Classical Model**

| Parameter Shift | $y$ | $N$ | $\dfrac{W}{P}$ | $r$ | $M_s$ | $M_t$ | $P$ | $W$ | $s$ | $i$ |
|---|---|---|---|---|---|---|---|---|---|---|
| a) Saving schedule shifts to right | — | — | — | ↓ | ↑ | ↓ | ↓ | ↓ | ↑ | ↑ |
| b) $M$ increases | — | — | — | — | — | ↑ | ↑ | ↑ | — | — |
| c) $S$ of $L$ schedule shifts to right | ↑ | ↑ | ↓ | — | — | — | ↓ | ↓ | — | — |
| d) Investment schedule shifts to right | | | | | | | | | | |
| e) $l$ increases (schedule swings downward) | | | | | | | | | | |
| f) Production function shifts upward (both level and slope increasing) | | | | | | | | | | |
| g) $M_s$ schedule shifts upward (more $M_s$ desired at each $r$) | | | | | | | | | | |

Although the diagrams may permit us to find and to understand the comparative statics results—the change in variables necessary to produce a new equilibrium—we may also want to have some idea how these results are brought about. Are we sure that prices and interest rates will in fact tend to fall in the case pictured in Figure 9–6, so that the new equilibrium will be achieved? This is asking, of course, for some explanation of the dynamics of the model. Without being at all rigorous in our presentation, we can sketch several possible varieties of disequilibrium behavior that may satisfy curiosity on this point.

Suppose that, in the case described in Figure 9–6, neither output, the interest rate, nor the price level should immediately fall, but temporarily stayed at $y_0$, $P_0$, and $r_0$. Would forces develop which would require them to fall? The demand and supply of money would still be equal, since the demand (which depends on $Py$ and $r$) would not have changed. But saving ($s_x$) would now exceed investment ($i_0$). One interpretation (with a Wicksellian flavor) of what might now happen would run thus: a drop in consumption demand for current output (increase in saving), with no increase in investment demand and no decrease in the supply of output, would cause unsold goods to pile up. The excess of amounts supplied over amounts demanded would cause a reduction of prices. This would, if money wages remained unchanged, mean a higher real wage, and thus create a deficiency of demand for labor as compared with supply. To avoid unemployment, wages would rapidly be bid down, preventing any rise in $W/P$ and any decline in employment or output. But if wages and prices fall, this will reduce the transactions demand for money and leave larger balances than people want to hold for speculative purposes at the initial rate of interest. In the effort to get a return on these idle balances, some people will buy securities, forcing up their prices and forcing down the rate of interest. Until $P$, $W$, and $r$ have fallen, respectively, to $P_1$, $W_1$, and $r_1$, there will, therefore, be disequilibrium in one or all of the goods, labor, or money markets. In each case, disequilibrium produces a movement in the proper direction—that is, in the direction that will eliminate the disequilibrium.

A slightly different sequence might assume that employers could and would cut back output as fast as demand (consumption plus investment) declined. The increased saving (reduced demand for consumer goods) would then cause a reduction of output, throwing workers out of their jobs. For example, if $r$ did not fall, output might be cut back by the difference $(s_x - i_0)$, as shown in Part B of Figure 9–6. This would create unemployment as employment was reduced to $N_x$. It would also reduce the transactions demand (as $y$ fell even though $P$ did not). The idle balances thus created would flow into the capital market, reducing the rate of interest. A downward pressure on money wages resulting from unemployment would simultaneously reduce costs, and competition would then force employers to reduce prices. In the new equilibrium, output, employment and the real wage would be restored to their initial values, but money wages and prices and the interest rate would all be lower.

Still other sequences can be imagined. These sequences differ as a result of the assumptions made concerning the relative speeds with which the various adjustments occur; consequently they differ with respect to other aspects of the disequilibrium process: for example, who gets hurt in the meantime. If employers lag in cutting back output, their selling prices will fall faster than their costs, and profits will turn to losses. Consumers will gain, as prices fall ahead of incomes. On the other hand, if output is cut back fast enough, profit margins may be protected even though wages lag; but workers will be temporarily unemployed. However, we are still not ready for a systematic and rigorous analysis of dynamic processes.

## THE SIGNIFICANCE OF SPECULATION

So long as the only change which is made in the Classical model is the addition of the Keynesian speculative demand for money, it is not necessary to change very many of the Classical conclusions. It still seems to be true that, in equilibrium, so long as money wages and prices are flexible:

a) Full employment is guaranteed.

b) Any change in the quantity of money will cause prices and wages to change in the same direction and proportion.

c) The rate of interest changes only if saving or investment schedules shift.

What is changed, primarily, is the degree of stability of the price and wage levels. If, in the strict Classical model, the quantity of money were held constant, prices (and wages) would have to change only in response to (a) shifts in the supply of labor or its productivity, or to (b) changes in "velocity"—that is, to changes in the fraction of money income which is needed to be held in cash to mediate transactions. Changes in the supply of labor and in the economy's aggregate production function could be expected to occur rather slowly and predictably. They were not apt to cause trouble. And if it were desired to stabilize prices (or money wages) in the face of these shifts, monetary policy seemed quite capable of doing the job. Changes in the "objective determinants" of velocity were of the same character—slow and smooth, offering no challenge which monetary policy could not meet. The only source of sudden or sharp trouble might be changes in velocity reflecting irrational shifts in the demand for money. One could easily enough argue that either (a) since people are rational, this will not occur—no one would want to acquire a barren cash balance (and, since they are not acquired, they could not be released); or (b) hoarding or dishoarding do occur, but they are a product of instability that has some other origin (e.g., a badly functioning banking system).

Changes in saving propensities, or investment incentives, it has to be emphasized, would be taken care of in the strict Classical model by the interest rate alone, assuming a proper monetary system.

Thus the economy could be counted on to work pretty successfully, if only the banks were not allowed to cause trouble. Of course, the worst trouble they could cause would be price level instability. But it was generally agreed that instability of prices was always unfortunate, and, if it were a downward movement, likely to cause some unemployment because of the stickiness of money wages.

Now what significant change does the speculative demand for money make? Simply this: even if the quantity of money is stabilized, changes in investment and saving propensities will require price and wage changes. This is important, for the instability of the incentives for investment (if not saving) have long been recognized. Investment is essentially postponable; it depends on an uncertain estimate of future demand stretching many years ahead; it is strongly affected by technological change and other "external" factors. Thus, to show that the interest rate cannot be counted on to handle saving-investment problems means that a much heavier load is placed on the wage-price mechanism to avoid unemployment. To be sure, monetary policy might still avoid the necessity for wage-price changes, but the instability and unpredictability of saving and investment poses a bigger challenge to monetary policy than did productivity changes, or alterations in the "objective determinants" of velocity. Thus, the speculative demand for money, which shows the fallibility of the interest rate mechanism, constitutes a serious blow to the supposedly self-regulating character of the economy.

## THE "LIQUIDITY TRAP"

But this is not the worst of it. Keynes further pointed out that, in an extreme form, the speculative demand for money might make automatic full employment impossible, *even if wages and prices were entirely flexible*. Someone later gave the name "liquidity trap" to this case. It is possible, Keynes argued, that, at times, the speculative demand for money schedule becomes infinitely elastic, or nearly so. Suppose, for sake of argument, that the speculative demand for money is infinitely elastic at a rate of 2 per cent. This means that bond prices higher than a level which reflects 2 per cent yield are considered by every wealth-holder as prohibitively high. No one would be willing to hold bonds (in preference to cash) at a bond price level any higher than this. At this level most wealth-holders are right on the margin, holding cash or bonds indifferently, but ready to sell their bonds, and unwilling to buy, at bond prices any higher than those which presently prevail. Suppose, further, that, at present, the investment outlook is such that there is less investor demand for funds at 2 per cent than savers wish to supply at that rate. This means that 2 per cent is too high a rate for full employment. Insufficient aggregate demand means unemployment and falling wages and prices, releasing funds from transactions balances, funds which should bid down the rate of interest and restore full employment. But the interest rate expectations of wealth-holders rule out this result. No amount of deflation and release of cash from transactions balances can drive the interest rate below 2 per cent, and 2 per cent is too high for full employment. (Incidentally, in this case, monetary policy is helpless, too.) In other words, there is an impasse, a "trap." Figure 9–7 helps us visualize this

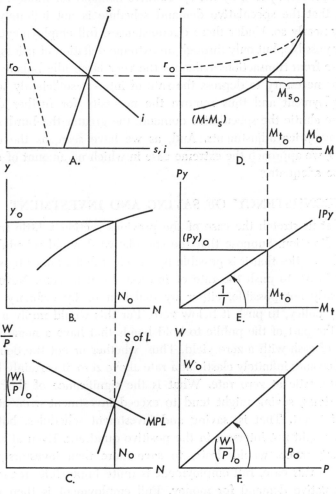

**Figure 9–7.**

situation. Assuming the situation shown by the *solid* schedules in parts A and D, then, as before, full employment is possible, at the levels for the several variables indicated by the subscripts zero. Now suppose that, instead, the liquidity preference schedule is that shown by the broken line in part D. (Continue to ignore the broken schedule in part A.) An interest rate of $r_0$ is necessary for full employment, but such rate cannot be achieved, even if the wage and price level (and thus the transactions demand) should approach zero. It is impossible to show what would happen. All we know is that full-employment equilibrium is not possible.

The case just described is, admittedly, an extreme case, but it dramatizes the problem posed by the speculative demand for money. Suppose, instead, that the speculative demand schedule is not infinitely elastic, but only nearly so. Under these circumstances, full employment is theoretically possible; but only through an extreme deflation of prices, enough to release from transactions balances the very large idle balances which would be necessary to depress the rate of interest sufficiently to restore full employment and thus remove the necessity for further deflation. The more elastic the speculative demand, the greater the burden placed upon wage-price adjustments. And, as we have seen, as the elasticity increases, we approach the extreme case in which no amount of deflation would be adequate.[8]

## AN "INCONSISTENCY" OF SAVING AND INVESTMENT

Now let us stretch the case of the previous section a little further in another direction. Suppose that the speculative demand schedule is not extremely elastic—that it is possible by sufficient deflation, or by sufficient increase in $M$, to push the rate of interest down to zero. Nevertheless, it is clearly not possible, either by deflation or by ordinary tools of monetary policy, to push it below zero. For this would imply a willingness on the part of the public to hold bonds that have a negative yield, in place of cash with a zero yield. Thus, whether or not the demand for money becomes infinitely elastic at a rate above zero, it certainly becomes infinitely elastic at zero rate. What is the significance of this? Simply that, at times, saving might tend to exceed investment even at a zero rate of interest. That is, saving and investment schedules, both quite inelastic, might not intersect in the positive quadrant. Even at zero rate of interest, savers would desire to save more than investors want to employ. In this case, full employment is quite impossible, regardless of the speculative demand for money. Full employment is then not prevented by expectations of future rates of interest which are inconsistent with the conditions of thrift and productivity. Rather, it is an inconsistency between saving and investment at any (positive) rate of in-

[8] The reader should recall that we are here ignoring the "Pigou effect," which will be treated in Chap. XII.

terest. The diagrammatic treatment of this case is included in Figure 9–7, using the broken instead of the solid investment schedule in part A, but ignoring the broken schedule in part D.

Again, we need not labor the extreme case to see the relevance of the considerations advanced. What this view emphasizes is the relative interest inelasticity of saving and investment schedules. If both are inelastic, then only moderate shifts in either one can cause substantial changes in the rate of interest which would equate $s$ and $i$ (Wicksell called this rate the "natural" rate). This means that a larger burden is placed on wage and price adjustments than would be the case were saving and investment schedules highly elastic. In order for wide changes to occur in the interest rate in the face of speculative concepts of "normal" rate, large changes must occur in the transactions demand for money, changes requiring very extreme inflation or deflation of the price level. Thus there may be situations in which the reductions in the interest rate necessary to maintain full employment are simply not feasible.

The view that saving and investment schedules are highly inelastic is, of course, an empirical judgment. It could be a very mistaken one. However, it has been many years since the idea of an elastic saving schedule gained much support, and such evidence as is available on investment—and it is scanty and difficult to interpret—is at least as consistent with the hypothesis of a low as of a high interest elasticity. Specifically, it was Keynes' empirical judgment that the investment schedule, while elastic, was not infinitely so—even at a zero rate of interest, investment would be at a limited, not an infinite, rate—a rate possibly appreciably less than the rate of saving at zero $r$. Most writers who have pressed the view of a highly-elastic investment schedule have used entirely *a priori* arguments; some, almost mystical arguments. One can, equally well, state that the view that saving or investment schedules are highly elastic is also an empirical judgment, which could be very wrong.

## AUTOMATIC FULL EMPLOYMENT?

In this chapter we have pointed out some difficulties with the supposedly self-adjusting full-employment mechanism envisaged by Classical theory. They are:

1) The possibility that investment and saving schedules are quite inelastic, perhaps even (at times) not having a positive intersection. In any case this throws a large burden on the interest rate, requiring

large fluctuations in the rate if changes in aggregate demand are to be avoided.

2) The quite normal tendency for wealth-holders to speculate on future bond prices means that the interest rate cannot be expected in the first instance to fluctuate in a way which will maintain stable aggregate demand even if the interest rate adjustments required are minor. Point (1) suggests that they may be major.

3) Failure of the interest rate in the first instance to stabilize aggregate demand means that inflation or deflation must occur, to induce, through changes in the transactions demand for money, the interest rate changes that could not occur in the first instance. The greater the required changes in the interest rate (point 1), and the more elastic the speculative demand (point 2), the greater the extent of the wage-price changes required. If the saving and investment schedules lack positive intersection, or if the speculative demand schedule is infinitely elastic at too high a rate, no amount of deflation can secure full employment.

Ignoring extreme cases, we still are justified in doubting the effectiveness of wage-price flexibility (instability) as a means of securing income and output stability (at full employment) in a progressive economy. This would be the case even without any special emphasis on some institutional features of industrialized, western economies which convince us that wage-price flexibility is an inadequate defense. Without going into detail, we need mention only the existence of trade unions and minimum wage laws (as well as rigidities in many industrial prices). Quite apart from organized institutional opposition to wage-cutting, there is a general social reluctance—on the part of employers as well as the public—to condone money wage reductions, even if temporary unemployment for many workers should be the cost of the failure to cut wages. And not often is the theoretical argument understood which makes this the cost.

It somewhat misses the point to argue that a general cut in money wages will be followed by a cut in prices, too, so that real wages will decline by less than might otherwise appear, and thus to condemn opposition to wage cuts as short-sighted or irrational. The point missed is that wage bargains are not struck between a single employer and a single spokesman for all workers. Rather, thousands of individual wage negotiations are required, each of which is quite independent of the others. No group of workers is large enough to take account of the effect of any wage reduction which it may negotiate on the prices its members pay.

A 20 per cent money wage reduction is a 20 per cent real wage reduction, for what happens to prices would have happened anyway. No group can be sure that other wages will be cut or that prices in general will fall. It is not irrational, from that group's point of view, to oppose or to attempt to delay money wage reductions.

Even without unions and union contracts, wage scales cannot be revised frequently. With union contracts, usually fixing wage rates for a year or more, a general change of money wage rates—in either direction—takes a long time to accomplish. Wage contracts expire at different dates. Those workers whose contracts are up for renewal at any one time naturally do not want their wages cut before those of other workers, even if they could be sure (which they cannot) that the other workers would be cut later, too.

This is not to say that without strong unions, wage flexibility could not be much greater than it is today. And if wage flexibility could clearly be shown to be the only or even the best way to stabilize demand and secure full employment, then the fact that unions are economically and politically powerful should not deter us from condemning their effects. But most economists have come to doubt (1) that wages would be nearly as flexible as the theory requires even without strong unions; (2) whether, in any case, wage flexibility is *an effective instrument* for economic stability; and, certainly, (3) whether it is the *best instrument* for maintaining economic stability.

The slowness or stickiness of downward wage adjustments requires recognition of one further point. Because wage-price changes are slow, they almost invariably lag behind their source. That means that if wages and prices are falling today in response to actual or threatened unemployment, one can be fairly sure that they have not yet fallen as far as they will fall later. A person contemplating a postponable expenditure (a durable consumer good, or an investment in plant or equipment) should wait for the expected further price change to occur and thus benefit by it. This, of course, means a further reduction of consumption and investment, intensifying the pressure for deflation. Thus we have another reason for doubting the effectiveness of even that degree of wage-price flexibility which is the greatest degree we could hope for quite apart from institutional obstacles.

What, then, is left of the Classical optimism? Not very much. Whether we merely conclude that—with present institutions—automatic full employment is not to be expected; or whether we go further and argue that even with maximum "reform" of present institutions (100 per cent bank reserves, no monopolies in labor or commodities) we could not expect automatic full employment; all should agree that we need a theory which is relevant to a less-than-full-employment situation. This theory was not developed by economists in the Classical tradition. Its development will occupy most of the rest of this book. In its development, we shall use most of the analytical tools and concepts already considered, plus some further, new ones. Because this theory is more general and more realistic, we shall also need, in using it, to sharpen up some tools already introduced, in particular, the investment schedule. We shall also want to develop the dynamics of this theory somewhat more rigorously and more extensively than has been done for the Classical model.

## MONETARY MANAGEMENT AND THE RATE OF INTEREST

Our above analysis has been conducted primarily with reference to the assumption of a given supply of money, except occasionally where we have referred to single once-and-for-all shift in the monetary stock. That is, we have, so far, been concerned with alterations in the rate of interest—and accompanying changes in other variables—produced by shifts in the private economy, *reacting against a constant supply of money*. Yet, in all modern economies, there exists an active central bank, attempting to pursue a monetary policy designed to achieve certain objectives of economic stablization. Such banks keep careful, daily watch of economic developments, and, when seems appropriate, are prepared to alter the supply of money either to neutralize or to reinforce the movements that would have taken place without their intervention. For example, when unemployment threatens, or begins to appear, the central bank may not wait for reduced economic activity and a deflation of the wage and price level to reduce transactions demands, thus to push down the rate of interest, encouraging investment and reducing saving. Rather, it will probably take vigorous steps to expand the supply of money, so that the rate of interest will fall further and faster than market forces alone could accomplish. Or, if the central bank is concerned about inflation, it may not be willing merely to let increasing transactions demand raise the rate of interest, but may take steps to reduce the quantity of money.

We can analyze the effects of this intervention in the previous terms if we wish; but we are likely to miss a most important aspect of the process if we do. In the previous terms we can imagine an increase (or decrease) in $M$ causing the rate of interest to fall (rise) as we move along a *given* asset-demand-for-money schedule. Indeed, if the central bank acts to increase the supply of money by buying securities on the open market, the very process of putting the new money "into circulation" involves a bidding up of bond prices, as bond-holders are induced to sell to the central bank at prices sufficiently higher than have previously prevailed so that former bond-holders now prefer cash.

But if it is known that the central bank is prepared to take monetary action to lower (raise) the interest rate, it may hardly be necessary for the bank to buy (sell) a single security to accomplish the change that it seeks to achieve. Once the "financial community" understands that the central bank intends to lower (raise) interest rates, the whole liquidity preference schedule is sure to shift, and in a way which will accomplish the desired change in the interest rate with perhaps very little effort on the part of the bank.

Suppose that in the situation pictured in Figure 9–8 the initial stock of public holdings of idle cash balances is $M_0$ and the rate of interest $r_0$.

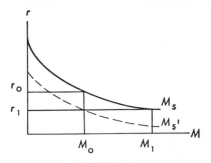

**Figure 9–8.**

Some wealth-holders are cash-holders at $r_0$ because they fear the possibility of a rise in the rate of interest. Others are willing to hold bonds. If all wealth-holders' expectations were unchanged, the stock of idle balances would have to be increased to $M_1$ in order to push the rate of interest down to $r_1$, by causing more and more wealth-holders to fear that present bond-price levels were unsafe, too high to be long maintained.

But if all wealth-holders were aware of the central bank's intention and ability to push the interest rate to $r_1$ and to hold it there for an indefinite period, the whole liquidity preference schedule might be shifted downward to $M'_s$, permitting the rate of interest to fall to $r_1$ *with no increase in M*. Since the intentions of the central bank are frequently made evident to the market in other ways than by its buying or selling of securities, such shifts in the $M_s$ schedule can be expected to occur as monetary policy shifts from one of "tight money" to "moderate ease" or to "active ease," as these terms have come to be employed. That the schedule will probably not shift to the extent indicated in the figure is due to the fact that the bank may not make clear how far it expects to go (in fact, it may not itself know, when it changes its policy, how far it may be necessary or desirable to pursue its policy—and might deliberately conceal its intention if it did), and because speculators may recognize that future changes in monetary policy—called for by future changes in underlying economic conditions (saving and investment schedules)—may induce the bank shortly to reverse its policy. Speculation then comes to center not so much on what economic conditions would do to the interest rate if $M$ were constant as to center on what Federal Reserve policy is likely to be.

However, even if the central bank were able completely to conceal its intentions from the market, we could still expect shifts in the $M_s$ schedule. Suppose, for example, that expectations concerning the future rate of interest were initially unchanged and the central bank, by open-market purchases, gradually increased $M_0$ to $M_1$, pushing the rate of interest from $r_0$ to $r_1$, and then held the money supply stable. In the process of getting the rate of interest down to $r_1$, many wealth-holders were moved from bonds into cash as bond prices rose, for they considered the new bond-price levels unsafe. But as the rate of interest remained at $r_1$ and gave increasing evidence that it would stay there, many of these newly-liquid wealth-holders could be expected to overcome their fear of the new higher level of bond prices. If the rate is to stay at $r_1$ they are needlessly sacrificing a return that is available to them. They would now want to move back into securities. The bank could accommodate this desire by selling them securities at the new higher bond-price level, letting the stock of idle balances gradually shift back toward $M_0$. That is, it may take *purchases* to *push* the rate down, but it does not necessarily require that the money stock be permanently enlarged in order to *hold* it down, once expectations have been adjusted to the new state of affairs.

The import of all this is that it is misleading to analyze economic changes on the assumption of a given liquidity preference schedule, assumed to stay put in the face of changes in monetary policy. In fact, a principal determinant of the level of the schedule is the public's expectation of what monetary policy will be.

Central bankers (particularly in the last few years) have talked a certain amount of nonsense about their "neutrality" in the market, except under those special, occasional circumstances when their intervention is needed to engineer a major alteration of the interest rate. The fact of the matter is that the very existence of a central bank makes its influence on the rate of interest a paramount one. Everyone knows that the bank can make the rate whatever it wants it to be (within *wide* limits), and that it will act to achieve what it considers to be objectives of national economic policy. This means that—within *narrow* limits—the level of the rate of interest is determined by monetary policy. (This is, of course, not to say that the policy pursued is always the wisest policy—only that there can be no such thing as neutrality of the central bank in any meaningful sense of the term.)

Despite our insistence on this point, we shall, in most of what follows, proceed to ignore it. We ignore it, for we are interested in an analysis of what would happen if there were no monetary intervention. In order to judge whether intervention is required or to predict what its effects may be, it is essential to be able to predict what would happen if intervention did not occur. This is as true of fiscal policy or any other kind of macroeconomic policy as it is of monetary policy. If our interventions were always perfectly executed, we might banish all instability. It would still be true, however, that tendencies to instability were present in the economy and it would still be essential to understand them, in order to guide the intervention.

One postscript can now be added to our discussion of the other sources (than speculation) of an interest-elastic demand for money. If these were the only or even the primary sources of the interest-elasticity of the demand for money, the liquidity-preference schedule would be, as previously indicated, a rather stable schedule, shifting only slowly, in response to changes in the size-distribution of individual wealth-holdings, in the costs of dealing in securities, or changes in the degree of risk aversion by wealth-holders. Such an analysis is quite incapable of explaining the interest-rate changes that we observe in the market as a result of changes in monetary policy (or in the public's comprehension of what that policy is). It thus misses a very large aspect of the reality of interest rate determination.

## APPENDIX

### Hoarding and Dishoarding in a "Loanable Funds" Analysis

Many economists have tried to incorporate Keynes' innovation regarding the speculative demand for money into a loanable funds framework of analysis. In other words, they have sought to incorporate flows of speculative hoarding and dishoarding into the analysis of interest rate determination, along with (the flows of) saving, investment, and money creation. Instead of Keynes' analysis which uses *stock* concepts—the supply and demand for money—they wish to substitute a *flow* analysis of the rate of interest. Let us see briefly what are the problems involved in this method of formulation. The transition from Keynes' way of putting the matter to a loanable funds framework often appears simple; it is not.

In Figure 9–9, we show one way in which a graphic representation of the loanable funds theory—incorporating Keynes' ideas of speculative demand— has frequently been presented. Part A is the same as part B of Figure 9–4. It shows the Keynesian supply and demand for idle balances (given the transactions demand). At interest rate $r_1$, the demand for balances would fall short of the supply by $BC$. This is why it is not an equilibrium: people would be holding idle balances in the amount of $AC$, but would wish to hold only $AB$. At such low security prices, very few want idle cash. At $r_2$, also not an equilibrium, desired holdings, $AD$, would exceed actual holdings, $AC$, by an amount $CD$, because many would be fearful that security prices so high must be only a temporary condition.

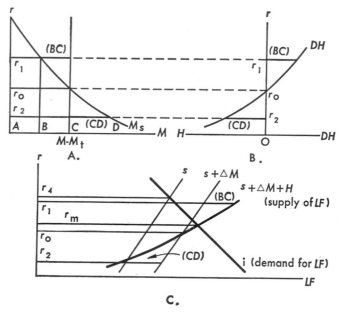

**Figure 9–9.**

If we now assume that, at all interest rates other than $r_0$—that is, at all interest rates at which actual idle balances diverge from desired balances— people respond by selling or purchasing securities, in the attempt to bring actual balances into equality with desired balances and actual security holdings into equality with desired holdings, then we derive the hoarding-dishoarding curve of part B. In this diagram, dishoarding is measured to the right from the zero point in the center, and hoarding (negative dishoarding) to the left. At interest rate $r_1$, there would be dishoarding in the amount of $BC$, as people tried to use unwanted balances in this amount to buy "cheap" securities. At $r_2$, there would be hoarding of $CD$, as people, whose actual cash balances were less (and whose security holdings more) than those they desired to have at these abnormally high security prices, dumped securities on the market for cash.[9]

In part C, we combine the hoarding-dishoarding analysis with the other sources of supply and demand for loanable funds. The supply consists of the saving schedule, $s$, shown as responsive to the interest rate, plus new money $\Delta M$ (here taken as autonomous), the total of these two sources being shown as the line $s + \Delta M$, to the right of and parallel with $s$. The complete supply includes also the dishoarding, which, at some interest rates, is a positive amount to be added to the other sources. At $r_1$, this additional source of loanable funds is in the amount $BC$. At $r_0$ neither hoarding nor dishoarding occurs, so the total supply of funds consists of $s + \Delta M$. At rates below $r_0$ there will be hoarding (negative dishoarding) which must be subtracted from the supply of loanable funds (it could alternatively be represented as an addition to the demand). At $r_2$, this will be in the amount $CD$. The total supply, $s + \Delta M + DH$, is shown by the heavy line rising to the right in the diagram. This supply can be matched with the demand (for investment), to produce the market interest rate $r_m$.

Although this result is plausible, it is the author's contention that it is seriously misleading, if not wrong. Let us consider some of the difficulties.

1) The first is a "scale problem," mentioned in the previous chapter, but postponed for treatment here. The analysis summarized in part A of Figure 9–9 is a stock analysis. It shows a stock of money and a demand for that stock— an actual versus a desired stock. Part B translates the difference between these two stocks into a flow. But this cannot be done without more information than is supplied by the theory about desired stocks. For example, at rate of interest $r_1$, we know that (given the transactions demand) the public would be holding more cash than it desired to hold—would hold an excess in the amount $BC$. What we need to know in order to convert this statement into one that deals with flows is this: given an actual stock in excess of the desired stock, *how fast* will wealth-holders release the excess? Suppose the difference between people's desired and actual cash-holdings is 500 million dollars. Will they release this unwanted cash in purchase of securities at the rate of 50 million per day for ten days, 5 million per day for a hundred days, 500 million for one day, or at the rate of 1 billion for a half day?[10] The answer to this question will deter-

---

[9] In the above discussion, and in the figure, we show dishoarding as the difference between $M - M_t$ and desired idle balances, $M_s$. In our earlier analysis (p. 159) we represented dishoarding ($DH$) as the difference between $M$ and $lPy$—that is, $M - M_t$. Here, we are only recognizing the additional proposition that not all the difference between $M$ and $M_t$ flows to the loan market: given each rate of interest, some part of the difference between $M$ and $M_t$ will be retained in the form of idle balances. In short, we now represent dishoarding as

$$DH = M - lPy - M_s$$

where

$$M_s = L(r)$$

[10] The reader must not suppose that if they release it at the rates specified above it will all be "released," and no excess stock of cash exist, in respectively, 10, 100, 1 or ½ days. Unless or until the rate of interest (or some other variable) changes, the

mine the magnitude of the dishoarding flow, which is to be added to the flows of saving and money creation in constituting the total supply of loanable funds.

Actually, our problem here is both on the behavioral and on the purely technical level. The numerical size of the flows of saving and money creation depends, of course, on the time unit in which these are expressed. Flows of 50 million per day, 350 million per week, and 1,500 per month are all identical in size. If we add to the flow of saving (which can be indifferently expressed as a magnitude of 50, 350, 1,500 or any other figure), a difference of 500 between an actual stock and a desired stock of idle balances, we get a total in which the relative importance of the dishoarding item seems to depend on the arbitrary choice of unit in which the saving flow is expressed. To avoid this absurd result, we must (1) specify the speed at which idle balances are released (this is the behavioral aspect); and (2) express this flow of released balances in terms of the same time unit in which the saving and the money creation flows are expressed (this is the technical aspect).

What difference do these matters make? A great deal. If the release of idle balances is very fast (e.g., the entire difference between actual and desired cash pours into the market in a single day), then, in part C of Figure 9–9, we would have to show $s$, $i$, and $\Delta M$ as very small amounts—curves pinched up close against the vertical axis. This would cause the determination of $r_m$ to be dominated by the slope of the $DH$ part of the curve. If, on the other hand, the release of idle balances proceeds very slowly, then the importance of the dishoarding analysis shrinks into insignificance, and the rate of interest is dominated by the slopes of the saving and investment schedules (and the rate of money creation). This is a major substantive problem: is the rate of interest, in the short run, dominated by people's willingness to hoard-dishoard, or is it dominated by their willingness to save and invest?

2) A second difficulty with this analysis is its disequilibrium character. That it represents disequilibrium should be clear from the fact that we assumed the transactions demand for money to be given. Since the transactions demand depends on $Py$, this means that we have assumed prices and outputs as given. Yet, at any interest rate other than $r_0$, saving and investment would be unequal, meaning that some savers or investors would be frustrated, disappointed, or surprised, leading them to change their behavior, and thus the aggregate demand for goods.

No one can object to a disequilibrium analysis; this is the essence of dynamics, and an adequate dynamics, we have already agreed, is fundamental. However:

a) the user of the analysis must understand that it is a disequilibrium analysis, a temporary snapshot of a necessarily changing situation; some who have used this presentation have apparently not so realized; and

---

excess will remain unchanged. If I buy a security with an idle balance, someone else has the cash; the nonbank public cannot change the quantity of cash that it holds. However, the *attempt* to change this quantity can, and presumably does, cause interest rates, prices, or some other variable to change so that the same total quantity of cash is now the *desired* quantity, given the new values of the other variables.

b) analysis of a disequilibrium is primarily useful if it is a *process* analysis, that is, if it shows what will happen next; in this case we want to know, if the interest rate is, in fact, $r_m$ today, what will it be tomorrow? Who has been disappointed or surprised, what will he be led to do, and how will this affect the future course of the interest rate?

3) The third difficulty with this analysis is with the realism of its assumptions. We have implicitly assumed that the interest rate adjusts very rapidly, while income, output, and prices (which determine the transactions demand) change only with a lag. If this were not so, we could not legitimately have held $M_t$ as given while the interest rate adjusts. This much is probably fairly realistic —income, output, and the general price level (although not all individual prices) do move sluggishly. But if we restrict our analysis to a very short period, in which income, output, and prices can be taken as given, then we should examine carefully the behavior we have assumed on the part of savers and investors. By drawing the saving curve as an upward-sloping line, we assume that savers respond instantaneously to changes in the interest rate, although only with a lag to changes in income. Rather, we would argue, if there is any adjustm3nt of saving to the interest rate it is probably at least as slow to appear as the adjustment to income change. Likewise, one might argue that the adjustment of investment to the interest rate is also lagged. Without going into detail at this point, or indicating what difference an alternative assumption would make, the author merely asserts that he finds these dynamic assumptions exceedingly improbable and unrealistic.[11]

A correct and meaningful analysis of disequilibrium situations in loanable funds terms is possible, and, if properly conducted, even helpful, *particularly if it is a process analysis*. But the kind of analysis reflected in Figure 9–9 seems dangerously incomplete, often conducted without full realization of what is being done, and probably quite unrealistic. As in the previous chapter, we conclude that dynamic analysis is difficult, and that we are not yet ready for it.

What is the alternative? For the present, it is to deal with equilibrium situations only. How would Figure 9–9 look in equilibrium? Accepting the implausible assumptions already commented on,[12] we draw Figure 9–10 as representing an equilibrium position of this model. For equilibrium to exist, desired or intended $s$ and $i$ must be equal. This means that the sum of $\Delta M + DH$ must be zero. More than this, it means that $\Delta M$ and $DH$ must each be zero, that is (a) the banks must be satisfied with their portfolios and be neither increasing or decreasing $M$, and (b) private nonbank wealth-holders must be satisfied with their portfolios, and must be attempting neither to hoard nor dishoard. The other assumptions of our semi-Classical model also require that full employment must prevail; otherwise there could be no equilibrium of money wages and prices.

We must avoid two incorrect conclusions about this equilibrium situation, which have often been mistakenly drawn from the equivalent of Figure 9–10.

[11] See, however, G. Ackley, "Liquidity Preference and Loanable Funds Theories of Interest," *American Economic Review*, XLVII (September 1957), pp. 662–73.

[12] Incidentally, their implausibility at once disappears when the analysis is turned into an equilibrium one.

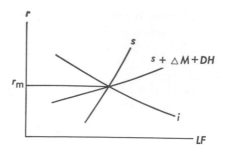

Figure 9–10.

One is this: since, in equilibrium, $r$ must be such as to equate $s$ and $i$ (dishoarding and $\Delta M$ each equal to zero), this means that the Keynesian speculative demand for money (hoarding-dishoarding) analysis has no contribution to make and can be disregarded or eliminated. The other is this: since, in equilibrium, $s$ and $i$ are necessarily equal (otherwise money income would be changing), then the rate of interest can be described as a purely monetary phenomenon, adjusting to whatever level will make dishoarding zero—i.e., make wealth-holders satisfied with their portfolios, given whatever ideas they may have as to "normal" rates of interest. In the present quasi-Classical model, the first of these statements is "less wrong" [13] than the second; but each is wrong. The fact is that we are analyzing the rate of interest as part of a complete macroeconomic model, which is the only analysis of the rate of interest that is worth the paper it is written on. In this model there are three kinds of behavior specified as dependent upon the rate of interest: (a) that of savers; (b) that of investors; and (c) that of wealth-holders in adjusting their portfolios. Obviously, equilibrium requires that the rate of interest be such as to make (a) savers satisfied with what they are in fact saving; (b) investors satisfied with what they are in fact investing; and (c) wealth-holders satisfied with the division that in fact exists of their portfolios between cash and bonds. A rate of interest consistent with any two of these, but not the third is not an equilibrium rate; something will have to change, whether the rate of interest or the price level or some other variable, until all three conditions are satisfied. It is simply not meaningful to give priority to one or two of these relationships over another. Further, since the model assumes mutual interdependence among numerous variables, it is no more correct to say that it is the rate of interest which adjusts to maintain equilibrium in saving, investing, and wealth-holding, than that it is the price level, or the real wage, or the supply of labor which maintains such equilibrium. Perhaps the most serious shortcoming of the usual loanable funds analysis of the interest rate is that it implies that the determination of the interest rate can be discussed apart from the other macroeconomic variables and relationships that make up the complete

[13] In the sense that it is less misleading in its conclusion. From a methodological standpoint, each is equally wrong. And when we abandon other Classical assumptions (e.g., perfect wage and price flexibility), the first proposition is also misleading in its conclusion.

model. Even if we assume certain lags, so that *in the very short run* the burden of adjustment falls only on the interest rate, a more complete analysis requires recognition of the interdependence of the interest rate, price level, income level, and all the rest.[14]

[14] For a treatment of loanable funds vs. liquidity preference theories that meets most (but not all) of the objections raised above, see W. L. Smith, "Monetary Theories of the Rate of Interest: A Dynamic Analysis," *Review of Economics and Statistics,* XL (Feb. 1958), 15–21.

# The Consumption Function

*Chapter X*

As the preceding chapters have repeatedly emphasized, the optimism of Classical macroeconomic analysis rested upon a belief in the efficacy of two fundamental correctives—the rate of interest, as a defense against saving-investment disturbances, and a flexible wage-price level, as a defense against any other threat to full employment (including a failure of the interest rate). We have shown in the last chapter, however, that the ability of the interest rate to perform its stabilizing function is much more limited than Classical writers recognized. We have also indicated some of the difficulties of relying upon wage-price flexibility, quite apart from the fact that in some circumstances, perhaps implausible because of their extreme character, no amount of wage-price flexibility could maintain full employment. Thus, it was concluded, an analysis which covered situations of unemployment seemed called for.

In order to simplify our analysis and to bring certain new ideas into sharp relief, we shall temporarily assume that the Classical correctives are not working at all. That is, we shall assume the interest rate to be completely inflexible—either held constant by an infinitely elastic speculative demand for money at the prevailing rate, or stabilized by a (perverse) kind of monetary policy. We shall further assume that money wages and prices are absolutely rigid, having no tendency at all to decline regardless of the extent of unemployment. Since we are here considering only situations involving less-than-full employment, we also rule out rising wages or prices.

Each of these simplifying assumptions will be removed in Chapter XIV.

## THE CONSUMPTION FUNCTION HYPOTHESIS

We can introduce our subject by reverting to a question raised at the end of Chapter VII, in connection with a discussion of Wicksell. Wicksell had shown that, in the face of a drop in investment, a failure of the interest rate to decline would reduce the aggregate demand for goods, leading to a downward spiral of wages and prices that must continue without limit so long as the interest rate failed to adjust to its new, lower "natural" level. The question was then raised as to what would happen if money wages were rigid and failed to decline. The drop in aggregate demand would then become a drop in real demand, too. Workers would become unemployed, output would fall, and all incomes which depended on the level of output would decline. So long as the interest rate failed to decline, a continued deficiency of aggregate demand would prevail; but would output and employment then drop without limit?

The source of the deficiency of demand was an excess of intended saving over investment. The sum of the goods consumers and investors wanted to buy had been reduced. Wicksell saw clearly that a mere drop in prices would not necessarily change aggregate demand for goods and services, because the level of money incomes would drop in the same proportion and leave the situation unchanged in "real" terms for all. And if real income was unchanged there was no reason for consumers to wish to save any less nor investors to invest any more than before. Now, however, we are dealing with a drop in real as well as money income. Is it reasonable or realistic still to assume the same excess of saving over investment as before? A moment's reflection will suggest that it is not. If saving is to stay the same while aggregate real income declines, real consumption expenditure must drop by as much as income, the rate of saving being fully protected at the expense of consumption. A more reasonable *a priori* assumption would perhaps be that, with falling income, both saving and consumption would decline. Thus falling income might be expected to reduce the excess of saving over investment. Is it not possible, therefore, that *sufficient* fall in income and employment might remove all excess of saving over investment, and let income stabilize at some lower, but still positive level?

It is easily shown that this is the case, and that the extent of the necessary decline in income will depend on the extent to which a decline in income is shared between saving and consumption.

Suppose that we postulate a relationship of simple proportionality between consumption and saving, such as that ⅘ of income is consumed and ⅕ saved, whatever the level of income. Table 10–1 illustrates levels of saving and consumption at various levels of income under this assumption.

TABLE 10–1.  **Hypothetical Consumption Function**

| If Real Income Is at the Rate of | Real Consumption Will Be at the Rate of | Saving Will Be at the Rate of |
|:---:|:---:|:---:|
| 200 | 160 | 40 |
| 160 | 128 | 32 |
| 120 | 96 | 24 |
| 80 | 64 | 16 |
| 40 | 32 | 8 |
| 0 | 0 | 0 |

Suppose that investment and saving had initially been equal at a rate of 40, with income at 200. Investment now drops to 32. Income must decline to 160 before the excess of saving over investment disappears. If investment should drop further, to 24, income must fall further, to 120. But unless investment should drop to zero, the downward spiral of income will not be unlimited—even though the interest rate fails to decline. In other words, if the interest rate fails to decline (or to decline enough) to eliminate the excess of intended saving over investment, a drop in real income may accomplish this result instead. This is because we have made saving (and consumption) a function not only of the interest rate but also of real income. Naturally, we need not confine our model to declines in investment. A rise in investment will produce a rise in real income (if the interest rate fails to rise or to rise enough), until the gap between saving and investment is eliminated by higher saving out of the higher income.

The numerical example we have used can be stated algebraically, as follows:

(1)                                            $s = .2y$

(2)                                            $s = i$

where $s$ and $y$ are real saving and real income, respectively, and $i$, the real volume of investment. We mean by $s$ and $i$, of course, desired or intended saving and investment.[1] Substituting from (1) (the saving sched-

[1] For specific discussion of the problem involved in this usage, see Chap. XIV, pp. 320–326.

ule) into (2) (the condition for income equilibrium), we have

$$.2y = i$$

or

$$y = 5i$$

Thus, if $i = 40$, $y = 200$; if $i = 24$, $y = 120$. The advantage of the algebraic statement is that we can now deal with levels of investment other than those shown (for saving) in the table. For example, if $i = 27.5$, $y = 137.5$.

Another way of expressing what has just been done is to work with consumption rather than saving. We must find, given any level of investment, at what level of income the consumption which would result from that income would, when added to the given level of investment, just produce that level of income. For example, if investment were at the rate of 16, income could not be 120. For at an income level of 120, consumption would be 96, which would mean aggregate expenditure, $c + i$, of 112 and thus aggregate income of 112. But in order for consumption expenditures to have been 96, income had to be 120, not 112. But neither could income be 112, for at that income level consumption would be 89.6 (⅘ of 112), which together with investment of 16, would yield total expenditures of only 105.6. Only at an income level of 80 would the resulting consumption (64) plus the given level of investment (16) add up to the level of income necessary to produce that level of consumption.

Algebraically,

(1a) $$c = .8y$$

(2a) $$y = c + i$$

where $c$ is real consumption expenditure, again in the sense of desired or intended consumption.[2] Substituting from (1a) into (2a) gives:

$$y = .8y + i$$
$$.2y = i$$
$$y = 5i$$

as before. That this is a mere reformulation of our previous model can be seen by recognizing that:

[2] This makes equation (2a) an equilibrium condition rather than a definition of income. The sum of actual, realized consumption and investment is identical with income. The sum of the desired or intended expenditures does not equal income by definition, but only in equilibrium. (See below, pp. 320–326.)

(3)                                  $s = y - c$

Substituting from (1a) into (3) gives us:

$$s = y - .8y = .2y$$

which is equation (1). Substituting from (2a) into (3) gives:

$$s = c + i - c = i$$

which is equation (2).

The same model can also be presented graphically, as in Figure 10–1, parts A and B.

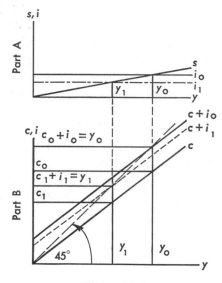

Figure 10–1.

In part A of the figure, the saving function is shown as the upward slanting line through the origin. Saving (measured vertically) is proportional to income (measured horizontally). Investment, $i_0$, is shown as a horizontal line, because it is here assumed to be independent of the level of income. (Although we still may suppose that it depends on $r$, we have assumed $r$ held constant. For the same reason, we have only a single saving schedule rather than a whole family of them, one for each possible level of $r$.) Income can remain only at $y_0$, where saving equals investment. If investment should fall to $i_1$, income would be reduced to $y_1$.

Part B is only slightly more complicated. It sets the model up in the manner of equations (1a) and (2a). Here consumption is shown as a function of income, by the slanting line through the origin labeled *c*. The broken diagonal line rising at a 45° angle from the origin is a construction line. A 45°-angle line (assuming equal units on both axes) connects all points whose distances from the vertical and horizontal axes are the same. Since the vertical axis measures expenditures (*c* and *i*) and the horizontal axis income, the line connects all those points in the quadrant at which income equals expenditures. The *c* function would coincide with this line if 100 per cent of income were consumed. If it does not coincide, the vertical distance between the 45° angle line and the *c* function is the amount of saving, represented more directly in part A. Above the *c* function and parallel to it is a second solid line marked $c + i_0$. This shows what the total of expenditures would be at each possible level of income when investment is given at the (constant) level $i_0$. Income equilibrium requires [equation (2a)] that $c + i = y$. The only level of income at which this condition is satisfied, when $i = i_0$, is shown by the intersection of the $c + i_0$ line with our 45° construction line, for this line connects all the points where the vertical measurement ($c + i$) equals the horizontal measurement ($y$). At a lower level of investment, $i_1$, income equilibrium requires the lower income level $y_1$.

The relation between parts A and B can be easily seen, and it is clear that they are alternative ways of representing the identical set of facts. Although the diagrams are unnecessary to the argument, they are very convenient, and simpler than algebra if we wish to use curvilinear functions.

What is the relationship between the graph and the formula for the consumption function?

A straight line can be described by two properties: its slope and its intercept (traditionally, its vertical intercept).

An infinite number of straight lines can have the same slope (i.e., be parallel); an infinite number can pass through any given intercept; but only one can have a given slope and intercept. The slope of our consumption function is .8. For every increase of 10 in income (horizontal distance), consumption rises (vertical distance) by 8. Algebraically, we write this $\Delta c/\Delta y$ or $dc/dy$. Keynes gave the name "marginal propensity to consume" to this slope. The "marginal propensity to save," or slope of the saving function, is, of course, .2. (Since that portion of an increment of income that is not consumed is necessarily saved, we know that $\Delta c/\Delta y + \Delta s/\Delta y$ must equal 1.)

The intercepts both of consumption and saving functions are, in this case, zero, since both pass through the origin.

It is not necessary to use such simple saving or consumption functions as these. Suppose that the formula for the consumption function is:

$$c = 10 + .75y$$

some values of which are shown in Table 10-2.

**TABLE 10-2.  An Alternative Hypothetical Consumption Function**

| Income | Consumption | Saving |
|--------|-------------|--------|
| 200 | 160 | 40 |
| 160 | 130 | 30 |
| 120 | 100 | 20 |
| 80 | 70 | 10 |
| 40 | 40 | 0 |
| 0 | 10 | —10 |

Substituting the above formula for $c$ into the equation

$$y = c + i$$

produces

$$y = 10 + .75y + i$$

$$.25y = 10 + i$$

$$y = 40 + 4i$$

Thus, if investment is 10, income will be 80; if investment is 30, income will be 160; if investment is 23.5, income will be 134. The first two of these results can be confirmed by reference to the table. The saving function, which can be used instead of the consumption function, would be found as follows:

$$s = y - c$$

$$s = y - (10 + .75y)$$

$$s = -10 + .25y$$

Graphical representation of income equilibrium where the consumption (saving) function is of this type is as shown in Figure 10-2.

In this case, of course, the slope of the consumption function, or marginal propensity to consume (MPC), is .75. The marginal propensity to save is .25. The intercept of the consumption function is 10. (Algebraically

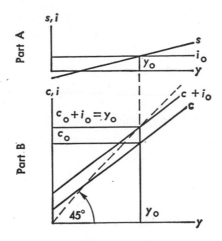

**Figure 10–2.**

we can find the intercept by substituting zero for $y$ in the consumption function.) The saving schedule intercept is $-10$.

We can also introduce the concept of "average propensity to consume" (APC), and "average propensity to save" (APS). Instead of concentrating on *increments* of income, these concepts are concerned simply with the proportions of total income consumed and saved. That is, they are $c/y$ and $s/y$. If the consumption function is our first one

$$c = .8y$$

Then

$$\frac{c}{y} = \frac{.8y}{y} = .8$$

In our second consumption function,

$$\frac{c}{y} = \frac{10 + .75y}{y} = \frac{10}{y} + .75$$

In the first case, the average propensity is constant and equal to the marginal propensity. In the second case, the average is not constant but, rather, declines as income increases, approaching, as a limit (as $y$ approaches infinity) the value of the MPC, i.e., .75.

The APS can be calculated as .2 in our first case, and $\dfrac{-10}{y} + .25$ in the second.

These cases illustrate the first three of the following general rules about the relationships between marginal and average quantities in economics:

(a) if marginal exceeds average, average is rising; (b) if marginal is less than average, average is falling (these relationships hold whether the marginal is rising, falling, or constant); (c) if marginal is constant and equal to average, average is likewise constant; (d) if marginal is rising or falling and at some point equals average, average at that point has reached a maximum or minimum.

Graphically, the APC at any point is measured as the slope of a line from the origin to that point on the consumption function; the APS, similarly.

In our first example, we found an algebraic solution

$$y = 5i$$

In our second,

$$y = 10 + 4i$$

The numbers 5 and 4 are called "multipliers," because any change in investment will produce, as can be seen from the formulas, changes in income respectively 5 and 4 times as great as the change in investment.

It is easily seen what determines the size of the multiplier. Represent the consumption function in general terms as

$$c = a + by$$

where $a$ and $b$ are constants. (The case $a = 0$, $b = .8$ represents our first consumption function; $a = 10$, $b = .75$ was our second.) Substituting this generalized expression for $c$ into the condition for income equilibrium gives us

$$y = a + by + i$$

or

$$y(1 - b) = a + i$$

$$y = \frac{a}{1 - b} + \frac{1}{1 - b}(i)$$

The "multiplier," $1/(1 - b)$, thus depends on the value of $b$, which is the slope of the consumption function, or the marginal propensity to consume. We can either describe the multiplier as

$$\frac{1}{1 - \text{MPC}}$$

or, since $(1 - \text{MPC})$ equals the MPS, the multiplier can be described as the reciprocal of the marginal propensity to save.

Although the algebra of more complex consumption functions becomes awkward, the relationships summarized among MPC, APC, MPS, APS, and the multiplier are unchanged. Figure 10–3 shows several additional types of conceivable consumption functions.

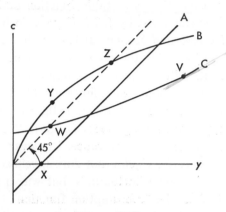

**Figure 10–3.**

Function *A* has a constant MPC of 1, and an APC $< 1$, which rises (from a negative figure) to zero (at point *X*) and approaches 1.[3]

Function *B* has a MPC which declines steadily from a magnitude in excess of 1 to 1 (at point *Y*), and thereafter to successively lower magnitudes. The APC is always higher, declining to 1 (at point *Z*), and thereafter continuing to fall.

Function *C* has a MPC which steadily rises, although it is still less than 1 within the limits shown. The APC falls from ∞ (at the intercept) to 1 (at point *W*) and thereafter continues to decline until *V*, when APC and MPC are equal. Beyond *V*, MPC exceeds APC, and APC rises.

The student should confirm each of these observations. He should then draw the saving function which corresponds to each of these consumption functions and work out the relationships of MPS and APS for these functions.

Of course, if the consumption function is curvilinear, the MPC (or MPS) is constantly changing, and consequently so is the multiplier. Thus, if there is an appreciable increment of investment, the effect on income cannot be calculated from the multiplier which relates to the previous level of income, but to some kind of an "average multiplier" which recognizes the changing MPC over the range of income. In fact, if

---

[3] Negative levels of *c* have no economic meaning. Perhaps schedule *A* should start at point *X*.

the consumption function departed appreciably from linearity, the multiplier concept would not be very useful.

## A *PRIORI* ANALYSIS OF THE CONSUMPTION FUNCTION

The idea that consumption is a stable function of income was given its first full and clear statement by J. M. Keynes, in his *General Theory of Employment, Interest, and Money*.[4] It is easy, however, to find others who had come close to stating the same idea earlier.

As Pigou points out,[5] Alfred Marshall expressly recognized the existence of a relationship between aggregate income and saving, although admittedly in the context of long-term growth, rather than short-term fluctuation. Others, perhaps stating the idea of the latter context, nevertheless failed to recognize its crucial relevance. However, J. M. Clark, in his *Strategic Factors in Business Cycles*, not only specifically formulated the idea in the context of income fluctuations, but was quite clear as to its relevance.[6] Nevertheless, the "consumption function" is properly considered a Keynesian invention, for it lies at the heart of Keynes' theoretical system.

Had earlier economists been specifically asked how they might suppose a man's consumption expenditures would behave as his real income changed, it is likely that they would have given an answer like Keynes'. But, in the short run, *aggregate* real income was simply not a variable with which they needed to be concerned. Flexible interest rates and wage rates would keep real income constant at the limits set by the economy's productive power. In the longer run, aggregate and per capita income might increase as the productive power of the economy grew. But with many other factors operating in the long run, there was hardly any occasion to isolate for particular scrutiny the relationship of consumption to income. Thus the novelty of the consumption function lay as much in the question as in the answer.

Keynes' specific formulation of the relationship between consumption and income on the individual (and also on the aggregate) level, contained several propositions, advanced with different degrees of definiteness and not considered to be equally essential. Two points were definite and essential:

---

[4] Chaps. 8, 9, and 10. For Keynes' development of the simple income model presented above, see his Chaps. 1, 3, 5.

[5] A. C. Pigou, *Employment and Equilibrium* [Second (rev.) ed., Macmillan, 1952], p. 100.

[6] National Bureau of Economic Research (1934), esp. pp. 80–5, but also 48–9, 167–8, 177–8, 188, 202–3.

1) Real consumption expenditures are a stable function of real income.

2) The marginal propensity to consume is positive, but less than one.

Not essential to his argument, and less positively stated were the further hypotheses:

3) The marginal propensity to consume is less than the average propensity (which means that the latter declines with rising income).

4) The marginal propensity, itself, probably declines as income rises.

Although Keynes refers incidentally in the course of his discussion to a few bits of statistical evidence, one who reads his argument can only conclude that his consumption hypotheses were based largely upon introspection and the most casual observation. On no more solid base he propounded what he called his "fundamental psychological law." Keynes may also have seen intuitively that his function is consistent with the behavior of a "rational" consumer of given tastes; nevertheless, he failed to provide any detailed *a priori* argument showing how the behavior he described would necessarily follow from the usual psychological assumptions which economists make. However, numerous later economists have sought to derive the consumption-income relationship from or integrate it with the general analysis of consumer preference which constitutes an important cornerstone of microeconomics.

One might reason crudely, for example, from the notion of diminishing marginal utility of particular goods as their quantities increase, to diminishing marginal utility of goods in general. Indeed, the idea of a diminishing marginal utility of income was specifically formulated by Marshall and other writers. By itself, however, this will not support the proposition that only a portion of an increment of income would be consumed. It needs to be supplemented by some concept of a diminishing (but positive) marginal utility of saving. Income must either be consumed or saved, and the optimum division between the two must involve equal marginal utilities of consumption and saving. An increase in income will be divided so as to maintain this equality, at a lower level of marginal utility for each; this will involve both more consumption and more saving. Although various explanations can be developed for a diminishing marginal utility of saving, the basic idea that consumption and saving are competitive sources of utility is already implicit in the Classical interest rate analysis, with its view that the margin between consumption and saving will be shifted by a change in the interest rate. In fact, a single formulation of the conditions for utility maximization will permit derivation both of the interest elasticity and the income elasticity of saving.[7]

The reason for not attaching much importance to the *a priori* argument in support of Keynes' consumption function is illustrated by the fact that the same kind of derivation supports the view that $c$ should change in response to a change in the current interest rate $r$. Yet, today, hardly anyone supposes that this relationship is of any practical importance. It is, indeed, useful to know that a particular relationship is consistent with a body of *a priori* theorems. But the *a priori* argument can tell us nothing as to the *quantitative dimensions* nor *the stability* of the relationship. What is important about the consumption function is that it is (apparently) a reasonably stable relationship and that it can account for large fluctuations in total expenditure (if the MPC were of the order of .005 or .05 we should pay little attention to the consumption function). The stability and the quantitative magnitude of the consumption function can only be established empirically.

We shall return very briefly at one future point to the *a priori* argument. No other use will be made of it. For the same reason no effort will be made to establish *a priori* propositions about the relation of APC and MPC. This is a very important question, but *a priori* analysis is not likely to be very helpful. However, we should note that Duesenberry and Friedman (among others) have supported by *a priori* analysis, as well as empirically, their positions that the basic long-run relationship between consumption and income is one of proportionality (APC = MPC). Their arguments differ considerably, as does the form of their "short-run" or "temporary" consumption functions. However, it is equally possible, by reference to a slightly altered set of *a priori* assumptions, to derive the hypothesis of a "basic" or "long-run" MPC less than APC.

It should be noted that the *a priori* analysis rests on the assumption of a consumer with given tastes, who never learns nor develops, and who lives apart from a changing world which continually brings him new goods, new pressures to consume in particular ways, new standards by which to judge the satisfactions to be derived from consumption. It is, and properly should be, an abstract timeless analysis of rational behavior using a minimum of psychological assumptions. As such, it can supply hypotheses, but cannot derive "laws" of behavior that are valid at any instant of time, much less generalizations that can be used to predict or describe behavior which is observed over time in a changing world.

[7] For a sketch of this derivation, see the appendix to this chapter.

## EMPIRICAL SUPPORT FOR THE CONSUMPTION FUNCTION HYPOTHESIS: BUDGET STUDIES

Keynes' consumption function hypothesis was, as already noted, based neither on an extended chain of reasoning from *a priori* postulates nor upon any statistical study. It was neither a good example of inductive nor of deductive reasoning. Yet there were certain statistical data available to Keynes (of which he must have been aware although he never mentioned them) which appear to be consistent with all aspects of his hypothesis.

At various times over the past 100 years, and in various countries, comparative studies have been made of family budgets. For a group or "cross-section" of families at a given time, data have been collected regarding size and disposition of income. These data have been used to support the empirical hypotheses, often called "Engel's Law," which describe the changing disposition of income at different levels of income (as income rises, the percentages spent on food and housing decrease, on clothing and household operation remain about constant, on education, health, and recreation expand).[8] These data also ordinarily reveal the *total expenditures* on all objects (or the savings) of the families covered by the study. Almost without exception budget studies show a relationship between family income and total family consumption like that which Keynes postulated for the total economy: low-income families typically dissave; high-income families typically spend less than income. As one moves along the distribution from lower to higher incomes, average consumption rises, but by less than income; and the higher the income the less the rise in consumption from a further increment of income. The MPC is positive, less than one, and declines as income rises.

Data from a recent budget study are plotted in Figure 10–4. The data relate to a scientific sample of 12,500 urban U.S. families, for the year 1950.[9] Each dot represents the average income and the average consump-

---

[8] Ernst Engel (1821–96) was a German statistician, whose conclusions were first published in 1895 in *Bulletin de l'Institut international de statistique.* The text states the "law" as Engel did, although subsequent research shows that only the conclusions regarding food and housing are indisputable. H. S. Houthakker, "An International Comparison of Household Expenditure Patterns, Commemorating the Centenary of Engel's Law," *Econometrica,* 25 (October 1957), pp. 532–51, refers to an earlier and more restricted version of Engel's Law, published in 1857, and referring only to food expenditures. Houthakker summarizes 40 surveys from 30 countries, all of which confirm this narrower version of the Law.

[9] The study was made by the Bureau of Labor Statistics and the Wharton School of Finance and Commerce of the University of Pennsylvania, and published by the latter under the title *Study of Consumer Expenditures, Incomes, and Savings.* Data are from Vol. XVIII (1957).

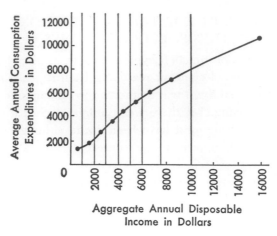

**Figure 10–4.**

tion expenditure of the families whose incomes were within the income brackets shown by the vertical lines. The curved line connecting the dots shows, therefore, the average relationship of consumption to income. This general pattern is typical of the findings of most other budget studies.

What the figure fails to show, and a fact that needs emphasis, is that consumption behavior, regular in terms of *averages*, is nevertheless very diverse as among individual families. For example, for the income bracket $4,000 to $5,000, in the study charted, the average income was $4,462 and the average consumption expenditure was $4,450. But individual consumption spending ranged very widely around this average. Some families in this income bracket may have spent as little as $1,500; others, $8,000 or more. Income "explains" the average consumption of a group, but many other factors must influence the expenditures of individual families within the group. Still one might argue that we are only interested in average or aggregate behavior, and the individual diversity should not disturb us. (Yet this diversity has been made a fundamental point in the analyses of some writers.)

The fact that all budget studies seem consistent with Keynes' hypothesis gives us some reason for confidence in it. Such studies even may provide us with a means for estimating the numerical magnitude of the aggregate consumption function. At the very least, some argue, they provide us with an estimate of the marginal propensity to consume. Almost all budget studies estimate the slope of the income-consumption relationship in the United States as being in the range of .6 to .8. To be sure, there is almost invariably some curvature; but, other than at extreme incomes, the slope is within the range just suggested.

We may well ask, however, whether it is legitimate to transfer estimates based on budget study data to the aggregate consumption function in which Keynes was interested. At best, it is a highly questionable procedure. The data we have been discussing come from a cross-section analysis; they show how consumption *differs* as income *differs,* as between families at different income levels. But Keynes' hypothesis relates to how consumption *changes* as income *changes,* and on the *aggregate,* not the individual family level. To go from the former to the latter requires some rather drastic assumptions about behavior that we have no obvious reason to make.

In the first place, there is the aggregation problem. When aggregate income changes, we would first have to know, in order to use budget study data, *whose* incomes changed. Did high-income or low-income families get most of the increase? To the extent that we wish only to estimate the marginal propensity to consume, and to the extent that the curvature of the relationship is fairly minor (i.e., marginal propensities are quite similar), we might neglect the aggregation problem. Or we can assume that when aggregate income changes the change is distributed among families in different income brackets in about the proportion that these income brackets bear to the total distribution. Then we could try to derive not merely a marginal propensity (slope), but the level of the aggregate function as well.

But even if we had no aggregation problem, would it be legitimate to transfer data about income *differences* to the situation of income *change*? If we were trying to predict the average consumption of 100 families, whose incomes have formerly been $5,000, and now become $6,000, we might predict that the new average consumption behavior would be like that of the average of the other $6,000 families—at least after some period of adjustment. But suppose that the whole distribution of income moves up at the same time: $5,000 families typically become $6,000 families, $6,000 families $7,200, and $10,000 families $12,000. Can we still safely predict that the *new* $6,000, $7,200, and $12,000 families will now behave as the *former* $6,000, $7,200, and $12,000 families had *previously* behaved? We can only if we think that it is *absolute* income that explains why families (on the average) consume as they do. A $4,000 family, in the distribution charted previously, typically just broke even—spent all its income; while a $6,500 family typically saved about $500. Was this because it typically *required,* in some absolute sense, $4,000 to house, clothe, and educate a family? Is it only income above this level that can be balanced against the desire to save, with the balance typically resulting, at incomes of $6,500, in saving of $500? But clearly it does not *require*

$4,000 to support a family. Lower income families in this same distribution lived on considerably less. And, if we go back a few generations, we find that families typically saved money at real incomes considerably below the levels at which families nowadays typically break even. In fact, a careful study of successive budget studies over a series of years reveals that the "breakeven point" in the distribution has steadily moved up as the average income of the group has increased. This is also reflected in the fact that, although the marginal propensity to consume derived from budget studies is always considerably below the average propensity, the average propensity for all families included in a budget study is strikingly similar for studies taken as much as fifty or more years apart, in which period average income has increased two or more times.

These facts have led many economists to argue (Duesenberry was one of the first to make the matter explicit) that it is not *absolute income* but *relative income* that determines a family's consumption. Families with relatively low incomes typically dissave, while those with relatively high incomes typically save, regardless of how high or low the average of all the incomes in the distribution may be. There is considerable support for Duesenberry's relative income hypothesis.[10] We need not specifically accept or reject it to recognize that, in order to be able to reason from cross-section data to the effect of changes in aggregate income on aggregate consumption, we must make some specific assumption as to whether it is relative income or absolute income or some combination that determines family consumption. If, or to the extent, that it is relative income that determines family consumption, cross-section data tell us nothing about the effect of a change in aggregate income which does not alter income distribution.

Budget study data are of vital importance in the study of consumption behavior. But they do not provide us directly with clear evidence on the relationship of aggregate consumption to aggregate income.

## EMPIRICAL SUPPORT FROM TIME SERIES DATA: 1929–41

Fortunately for Keynes' hypothesis, we need not get bogged down in complicated arguments as to how to transform budget study data in a manner relevant to aggregate consumption. We now have aggregate data

[10] J. S. Duesenberry, *Income, Saving and the Theory of Consumer Behavior* (Harvard University Press, 1949). For a contrary view, see J. Tobin, "Relative Income, Absolute Income, and Savings" in *Money, Trade, and Economic Growth* (Macmillan, 1951), pp. 135–56. See also the discussion in M. Friedman, *A Theory of the Consumption Function* (Princeton, 1957), especially pp. 167–82.

on consumption and income from our national income and product accounts. Such estimates first became available on a comprehensive basis for the United States in 1942.[11] One of the first uses to which these data were put by economists was to test for the existence and stability of Keynes' consumption function.

Data for the years 1929–41 are plotted in Figure 10–5. The dollar

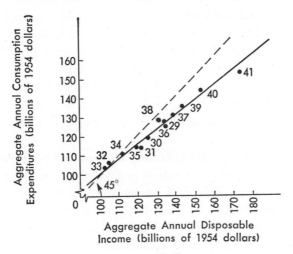

Figure 10–5.

figures have been corrected for price change and are expressed in 1954 prices. Each dot in the chart shows the combination of aggregate disposable income and aggregate consumption expenditure which prevailed in some one of these prewar years. It is obvious that there is an extremely close relationship. It is no wonder, then, that these data engendered considerable enthusiasm for the Keynesian hypothesis. (The data shown in the chart are the most recently revised estimates for those years, rather than the estimates available during or just after the war. However, the picture shown is little changed from that which the first estimates revealed.) Not merely had Keynes guessed correctly that there existed a general tendency for consumption to follow income, but, indeed, it appeared that the relationship was most precise. If there were other factors which also influenced consumption, their total influence must be insignificant.

11 Beginning in 1934, national income estimates had been available for 1929 and subsequent years. But national *product* data (including consumption expenditures) became available only as a result of wartime efforts to provide a complete system of national accounts for use of the war mobilization agencies.

The line in the figure is one fitted to the data by the method of least squares.[12] Its equation is

$$c = 26.5 + .75di$$

This means that the slope of the function (the marginal propensity to consume) is .75. The height of the function is given by the constant term. If the relationship were extended back to a zero income (and no one argues that it would hold under these impossible circumstances), consumption would be at the annual rate of $26.5 billion in 1954 prices. Another way of putting it is that annual consumer expenditures appear to be divisible into two parts: one part ($26.5 billion) is independent of income; the second part consists of three-fourths of whatever disposable income may be. The average propensity to consume declines with income, these data suggest, becoming unity at an income of about $106 billion in 1954 prices.

It will be noted that no dot falls very far from the computed consumption function. In fact the consumption that one would have estimated for any of these years if he had known only its income and used this relationship would in no year have been off by more than 2.5 per cent; in 8 of the 13 years it would have been within about 1 per cent.[13]

Thus, the data are strikingly consistent with all of Keynes' guesses about the relationship, with one exception. The relationship appears to be stable; the marginal propensity is less than one (three-fourths); the marginal propensity is less than the average (which declined from 1.015 in 1933 to .88 in 1941). But there is no suggestion at all that the marginal propensity declines with rising income.

In the immediate postwar period in the United States many economists, viewing these data, were convinced that Keynes' armchair reflection had stumbled upon one of the truly stable and predictable relationships in economics, and one of vital importance for economic policy. For it should now always be possible to know just exactly how much investment (or government expenditure) would be necessary for full employment. By

[12] This means that we have found that line, among all the possible lines, which has the following property: if we measure the difference between actual consumption in each year and the consumption estimated by this line for the income of that year, and if we square each of these deviations, the sum of these squared deviations is at a minimum.

[13] The coefficient of correlation ($r$) for this regression is .9917. A coefficient of 1.0 would mean perfect correlation (all dots exactly on the line). If we exclude 1941— as already showing some effects of wartime abnormalities—the equation becomes

$$c = 18.66 + .816di$$

where $r$ is .9943.

estimating full-employment income and calculating what consumption could be expected at that income, the difference equaled the necessary amount of nonconsumption expenditure. If government expenditures were set at the required level, full employment could be always maintained, and instability and the waste of resources forever eliminated.

There is still much that is valid in this view. But a number of events have occurred and a number of second thoughts have occurred to economists, which have destroyed some of the rosy enthusiasm with which Keynesians looked at the world in those first postwar years.

Before we consider some of these specific problems, a few words should be said about the nature of the relationship represented in the above figure. The reader will note that we have plotted consumption expenditure against disposable income, not national income or gross national product. He will also note that the data are corrected for price change—i.e., are in real terms. Some implications of these decisions are examined below, along with some other problems.

## SOME STATISTICAL PROBLEMS

### Real or Money Income?

Keynes' proposition was specifically formulated in terms of real income. That is to say, Keynes thought that a fifty per cent increase in retail prices, money income remaining unchanged, would affect a man's consumption (in terms of real quantities purchased) in the same way as a reduction of one-third in money income, prices remaining unchanged. On the other hand, a one-third increase in money income would have *different* effects both on real consumption and on the money value of consumption, depending on whether prices changed or not. To illustrate, suppose that the fundamental relationship is

$$(1) \qquad \frac{C}{P} = 50 + .6\frac{Y}{P}$$

where $Y$ and $C$ are money income and the money value of consumption expenditures and $P$ is the price level. Multiplying both sides by $P$ gives:

$$(2) \qquad C = 50P + .6Y$$

The money value of consumption is thus a simple function neither of real income nor of money income alone, but of money income and the price level.

The following sets of hypothetical observations are consistent with the above consumption function:

| Observation | Y | P | C | $\dfrac{Y}{P}$ | $\dfrac{C}{P}$ |
|:---:|:---:|:---:|:---:|:---:|:---:|
| a | 100 | 1 | 110 | 100 | 110 |
| b | 200 | 1 | 170 | 200 | 170 |
| c | 200 | 1.5 | 195 | 133.3 | 130 |
| d | 350 | 1.5 | 285 | 233.3 | 190 |
| e | 350 | 2.0 | 310 | 175 | 155 |
| f | 400 | 4 | 440 | 100 | 110 |
| g | 400 | 1 | 290 | 400 | 290 |

If we plot these observations (last two columns) in a quadrant whose axes are $C/P$ and $Y/P$ respectively, they will trace out a straight-line consumption function, as in part A of Figure 10–6. On the other hand, if

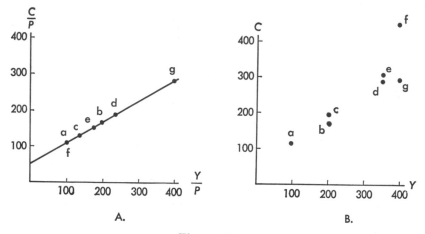

Figure 10–6.

we plot these observations (first and third columns), as in part B, with axes of $C$ and $Y$, only an irregular relationship appears. Thus, if the fundamental relationship is one in real terms, data expressed in money terms may well fail to reveal it.

What Keynes asserted was that people were not subject to money illusions. They could and did "see through" the "veil of money" to the real magnitudes involved. This is an assertion of fact that might be wrong. We all know people who are subject to money illusions. There was Mr. A, for example, who, when his money income increased by 20 per cent during World War II (during a period in which prices increased at least as much), thought that now, being so much better off, he should begin to save some portion of his pay, instead of spending it all as before. A more familiar figure, perhaps, is Mrs. B, who continually complained, during the same period, how the rise in prices was forcing her family into debt, ignoring the fact that her husband's pay had advanced by at least as much as prices had risen. Both kinds of money illusion are possible—the kind that sees only figures on the pay check and ignores the figures on the price tags, and the reverse. No doubt both exist, at least in the short run, and at times one kind of illusion may predominate. However, no one has advanced any consistent theory about their existence or their effect on consumption, and almost (but not quite) all statistical studies have worked with "deflated" data—that is, income and consumption data corrected for price change.[14]

Actually, for the prewar period to which the data in Figure 10–5 refer, it makes very little difference for the "goodness of fit" of the consumption function whether we use deflated or undeflated data. There are two reasons, either or both of which can explain this apparent paradox.

1) The closer the "real" consumption function approaches proportionality—i.e., one which goes through the origin—the less difference it makes whether we use raw or deflated data. The above hypothetical example used a relatively low marginal propensity (.6) with average propensities between .725 and 1.1. It also used extreme fluctuations in prices. But if the average and marginal propensities are the same, then price change makes no difference at all. (Consumption is a constant percentage of real income; if real consumption and real income are each multiplied by the price level, whatever it is, the measurement of the average and marginal propensities is unaffected.) The U.S. data suggest a marginal propensity not so far below the average as our hypothetical example assumed. Thus moderate price fluctuation should cause only minor distortion of the relationship. And price fluctuation in the 1929–41 period was of moderate proportion.

2) But even if there is considerable difference between marginal and average propensities, we would still have a stable relationship between the respective money values if or to the extent that the price level moved in systematic relationship to real income. Suppose, for example, that the price level moves up when real income increases and down when it decreases, in some fairly systematic, linear fashion. It can be shown that, in this case, the relationship of money income and money value of consumption would not be strictly linear, but it would be a stable relation-

[14] For an interesting analysis which shows what difference this makes (but without any hypotheses as to *actual* behavior), see E. Cary Brown, "Analysis of Consumption Taxes in Terms of the Theory of Income Determination," *American Economic Review*, XL (March 1950), pp. 74–89.

ship to the extent that both real consumption and the price level were stable functions of real income. During the prewar period there was a definite (although not perfect) relationship of the price level to the level of output—prices falling with declining income during the depression, and rising slightly with the recovery and more sharply with the beginning of the war period. This is another reason why, in the prewar period, the relationship is little affected by the failure to use deflated data.

What may be more surprising is the fact that in the early postwar years (and this unavoidably gets us ahead of our story), the correlation between money values of consumption and money income is on the whole closer than between the real values. How this can occur can easily be seen from the following hypothetical example. Assume a very narrow fluctuation of real income. Suppose, however, some irregular fluctuations occur from year to year in real consumption, due to factors other than income. These fluctuations need not be large, percentagewise, to produce an almost total absence of correlation between real consumption and real income, as in part A of Figure 10–7.

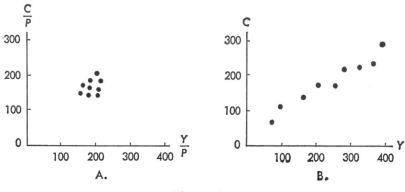

Figure 10–7.

Suppose, however, that prices vary considerably over this period. This price variation means that the *money* values of consumption and income will be fanned out considerably, as in part B. (High prices will push *both* money magnitudes, $C$ and $Y$, out from the origin, or low prices pull them both in toward the origin, producing what may be a purely spurious increase in the coefficient of correlation.) Something of this sort seems to have occurred in the immediate postwar years in the U.S., when a considerable inflation of prices imposed a greater correlation between money values than existed between the real values of consumption and income.

Thus we have the rather strange situation that, in the prewar period, the correlation is little or no better in real than in money terms; while in the postwar period, the correlation is better in money terms. Nevertheless, in the absence of some reasonable theoretical basis for making the money value of consumption expenditures depend upon the money value of income, we will continue to assume that, to the extent that income determines consumption, it is *real income* that determines *real consumption.*

## Total or Disposable Income?

Keynes' "psychological law" related to a man's behavior as his income changed; but to what concept of income should we refer? Do we mean his disposable income, or should we take account of his total earnings, before taxes, and including his share of the undistributed profits of a business (corporate or otherwise) of which he is sole or part owner? To believe that it is disposable income that counts is to argue, as we usually do, that a reduction in a man's taxes will affect his consumption in the same way as an equivalent increase in his after-tax income arising from higher before-tax earnings. We can imagine people for whom and special circumstances under which we might argue otherwise, but no better generalization than this appears reasonable so far as taxes are concerned. With regard to undistributed profits, however, the question is harder. Disposable income (in the official U.S. statistics) includes the total earnings of proprietorships and partnerships, not merely the *withdrawals* from the business by the owners. To make consumption a function of this income concept implies that unincorporated business saving is indifferently substitutable for "personal" saving. Suppose that in each of two years a farmer's income is the same but in one of them half of his income is left in the business to purchase new machinery and make a necessary addition to the barn, while in the other year all of it is available for family use. The view that uses the U.S. disposable income concept would imply the same consumption expenditures each year.

The only relevant statistical evidence on this point comes from an analysis by Klein and Margolis of cross-section data.[15] The authors present tables and graphs showing the cross-section relationship between total incomes and total saving (business plus personal) for owners of unincorporated business. This relationship differs sharply from the same

[15] L. R. Klein and J. Margolis, "Statistical Studies of Unincorporated Business," *Review of Economics and Statistics,* Vol. 36 (February 1954), pp. 33–46.

relationship for all other groups: at each income level, the total saving (business plus personal) of this entrepreneurial group is much the highest. But when *personal saving* alone is plotted against the entrepreneurs' *withdrawals from the business* the relationship is rather similar to the income-saving relationship for owners of incorporated businesses and for hired managers and officials. This suggests that consumption expenditures of the entrepreneurial group depend more closely on withdrawals than on total earnings.

On the other hand, use of disposable income as the relevant variable makes the opposite assumption for corporate saving. Suppose that in each of two years a corporation's dividend rate is the same, but in one year profits were greatly in excess of dividends, while in the second, the corporation lost money but paid dividends from accumulated previous earnings. The view that uses the U.S. disposable income concept would again imply the same consumption expenditures by the stockholder. We may doubt that this would be the case for the principal stockholder of a privately-held company; for the average stockholder who feels remote from the management of his company's affairs and may not even read its financial statements, the assumption is probably reasonable enough.[16] No statistical evidence is available on this point.

### Aggregate or Per Capita?

The data in Figure 10–5 are not corrected for changes in the population. Yet one might well argue that they should be. For the effects which Keynes expected from a rise in aggregate income were those resulting from a rise in the level of the individual consumer's *ability to consume*. A rise in aggregate income which merely represented a larger population with the same average income per capita as before would presumably have quite different effects on consumption than would the same rise in aggregate income with a stable population and growing per capita income. Thus, if the time span of the comparison is considerable, or if population is growing rapidly, putting both income and consumption data on a per capita basis should provide a better estimate of the particular relationship whose stability is assumed. Thus, many students of the consumption function make this correction. (It would, however, make very little difference in the appearance of Figure 10–5. Although the units are different, the slope of the regression and the pattern of scatter around

---

[16] The only author who pays much attention to this question is R. F. Harrod, in *Towards a Dynamic Economics* (London: MacMillan, 1949), pp. 47–8.

the line would appear much the same.) Some students prefer a *per family* correction since the family is the usual consuming unit.[17]

### Which Direction of Causation?

The very high correlation which exists between consumption and income in national income accounts needs to be interpreted with caution. Specifically, it needs to be recalled that there is a double relationship between consumption expenditure and income. There is the relationship summarized in the consumption function: consumption is high or low, rises or falls, *because* income is high or low, increases or decreases. But there is another relationship: since consumption expenditures constitute about two-thirds of total output, consumption is a major factor in determining income—when consumption is high or low, rises or falls, income necessarily tends to be high or low, to increase or decrease. The latter relationship cannot be forgotten in assessing the high correlations we find. Naturally there is a high correlation between total income and something which constitutes the largest part of the total. There would be good correlation even if consumption changes were completely unrelated to income changes.

To see the weight of this consideration, visualize the following experiment. Place in one hat, on separate slips of paper, a selection of "large" numbers—ranging evenly between, say, 800 and 1,200. Place in a second hat a selection of "small" numbers—ranging evenly, say, between 160 and 240. Make successive random paired drawings from the two hats— first a number from one hat, then from the other. Add together each pair of numbers. Call the large number "consumption": call the total of the two "income." It is clear that, in our experiment, income does not "determine" consumption; consumption depends on a random drawing. But there will still exist a good correlation between consumption and income; for the size of consumption dominates the size of income. If you draw a relatively large value for consumption, income will be relatively high even if the other number is relatively low. You are correlating a total with its own largest component.

How could we show that the correlation in this experiment failed to prove the existence of a "consumption function"—i.e., a dependence of

---

[17] The regression equation for per capita consumption on per capita disposable income, both in 1954 prices, for the years 1929–1940, is

$$c = 171.6 + .79di$$

The coefficient of correlation is .9946. (Cf. fn. 13, this Chap.)

consumption on income, over and above the opposite dependence of income on consumption? A moment's reflection suggests the answer. If the causation were entirely one way (consumption determines income but not vice versa), we should expect to find no correlation between "consumption"—the larger random number—and the smaller random number, which we may call "saving" (or, if we prefer, "investment"). There is no reason why a relatively large number drawn from one hat should be associated with a relatively large one drawn from the other. A scatter diagram of the paired values drawn from the hats would appear as in Figure 10–8, part A. But if there were *also* a dependence of consumption

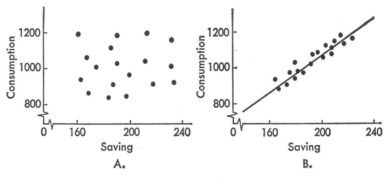

Figure 10–8.

on income, the scatter would look like part B, approaching a perfect correlation (all points falling on the line), as the dependence of consumption on income approached a perfect dependence.

It is simple to demonstrate that the existence of a consumption-income (and therefore a saving-income) relationship implies a consumption-saving relationship, if it is not intuitively obvious. If

$$c = a + by$$

and $s$ (saving) is defined as $(y - c)$, then

$$c = a + b(c + s)$$

$$c(1 - b) = a + bs$$

$$c = \frac{1}{1 - b}(a + bs)$$

or

$$c = A + Bs$$

where

$$A = \frac{a}{1-b}, \text{ and}$$

$$B = \frac{b}{1-b}$$

Thus, our assessment of the existence and stability of the consumption function (independently of the reverse relationship) can best be made by looking at data showing the relationship of $c$ and $s$. In Figure 10–9, we

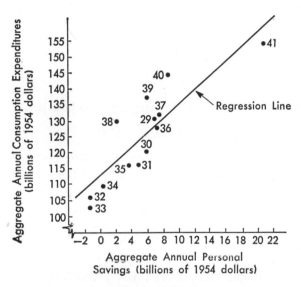

Figure 10–9.

present data for the period 1929–41, previously presented in Figure 10–5, but in the new form. It is clear that there does exist some considerable relationship between consumption and saving, and therefore a relationship between consumption and income which is entirely independent of the fact that income depends on consumption.

The equation for the regression line in Figure 10–9 is

$$c = 108.86 + 2.51s$$

From these coefficients, we can derive an equation for the conventional consumption function. We showed above that

$$A = \frac{a}{1-b} = 108.86$$

and

$$B = \frac{b}{1-b} = 2.51$$

From the second equation we get

$$b = 2.51 - 2.51b$$

$$3.51b = 2.51$$

$$b = .7151$$

Substituting in the first equation, we get

$$108.86 = \frac{a}{1 - .7151}$$

$$a = 31.0$$

Thus our indirectly estimated consumption function is

$$c = 31.0 + .715di$$

which is seen to be very close to the previous direct estimate, which was $c = 26.5 + .75di$. The new constant is slightly higher and the new slope slightly lower. If this regression line is drawn in Figure 10–5, it will be barely distinguishable from the one already shown. It can be argued that the present estimate comes closer to being an "unbiased" estimate than the previous one.[18]

## THE LONG PERIOD CONSUMPTION FUNCTION

One of the most debated problems with respect to the nature of the consumption-income relationship has been whether the basic relationship is one of proportionality or, as Keynes thought, and as the data suggest, one in which the proportion of consumption to income could be expected to decline as income rose. The question has its main relevance to the long-term prospects of a developing economy. Thus, if in 20 or 25 years, it

[18] The treatment in these paragraphs is in essence equivalent to that proposed by T. Haavelmo, "Methods of Measuring the Marginal Propensity to Consume," *Journal of the American Statistical Association*, 42 (March 1947), pp. 105–22. Haavelmo's reasoning in support of his approach is quite different from that set forth here, and may be harder for the reader who is not an econometrician to follow. Actually, in the present instance, the reduction of "bias" by this technique is not a significant matter. But it is important that this method provides a better measure of the standard error of a forecast of consumption. The standard error of an estimate of consumption based upon our direct regression of consumption on income is 1.682. This means that the chances are two out of three that the "true" estimate of consumption would be within $1.682 billions of the estimate given by that regression equation. Our regression of consumption on saving has a standard error of estimated consumption of $6.264 billions, nearly four times as great.

is possible to double the productive power of our economy, can we count on consumer demand expanding in the same proportion as income, i.e., consumption doubling, too, assuming full employment? If so, it means that other sources of aggregate demand (investment and government) need also expand only in the same proportion in order to maintain full employment. On the other hand, if consumer demand would expand in smaller proportion, maintenance of full employment would require that other sources of demand should rise in greater proportion than income. This either means an expansion in the relative as well as the absolute scope of public expenditure, a prospect which many find unattractive, or else an expansion of the share of total output going into investment. Since the purpose of investment is basically to produce goods to satisfy other final demands, many economists see problems in an expansion of investment relative to total demand, which means an even greater expansion relative to the other elements of demand that in the last analysis must justify the investment. Table 10–3 illustrates in a crude way some of these relationships.

**TABLE 10–3.** Illustrative Sequences of Proportional and Nonproportional Development of Consumption

|  | Now | With Doubled Output |
|---|---|---|
| A. Proportionality |  |  |
| Total output ($y$) | 100 | 200 |
| Consumption ($c$) | 70 | 140 |
| Investment ($i$) | 15 | 30 |
| Government ($g$) | 15 | 30 |
| Ratios: |  |  |
| $c$ to $y$ | .7 | .7 |
| $i$ to $y$ | .15 | .15 |
| $g$ to $y$ | .15 | .15 |
| $i$ to $(c + g)$ | .176 | .176 |
| B. Nonproportionality |  |  |
| $y$ | 100 | 200 |
| $c$ | 70 | 110 |
| $i$ | 15 | 60 |
| $g$ | 15 | 30 |
| Ratios: |  |  |
| $c$ to $y$ | .7 | .55 |
| $i$ to $y$ | .15 | .3 |
| $g$ to $y$ | .15 | .15 |
| $i$ to $(c + g)$ | .176 | .429 |

Earlier we suggested that not much light could be thrown on this question by *a priori* analysis proceeding from simple axioms about rational behavior. It is, however, possible to consider some aspects of this problem quite apart from any empirical data. Specifically, we can see that any view that the consumption function is both linear and nonproportional produces ridiculous implications when such a function is assumed stable over long periods of time. Suppose, for example, that the consumption function used in part B of Table 10–3 is $c = 30 + .4y$ (this function passes through the two points shown in the table). It has been somehow established that this is the function which prevails "now," and, since we suppose it to reflect stable characteristics of human nature and social institutions, we also suppose (in the absence of any better knowledge) that it will still prevail in 20 or 25 years, when productive power will again have doubled, just as it has doubled in each of the several preceding 20 to 25 year periods.

The last clause should suggest the ridiculous implications of this hypothesis. If the consumption function, linear and nonproportional, is stable for forward projections over a long period and over considerable variation of income, then it should be stable for backward projections, too. A mere 20 or 25 years ago, total output (at full employment) was only half what it is today, i.e., 50. At an income of 50, $c = 30 + .4y = 50$. That is, total output would have been consumed, with nothing available either for government or investment. Go back another 25 years and consumption would greatly have exceeded income.

It is clear, even without looking at a single statistic, that a consumption function cannot be linear, nonproportional, and stable over long periods of time in a developing economy. Yet this conclusion appears not to have generally occurred to economists until they were shocked into it by a new set of data.

In 1946, Simon Kuznets published estimates of national income and product for the United States, by overlapping decades, from 1869 to 1938. His estimates are shown in Table 10–4, and are plotted in Figure 10–10.

As is clear from the column (3) of the table, the average propensity to consume stayed relatively stable (between .84 and .89) over a very large growth of total (and also of per capita) income. It rose above .89 only when per capita income fell, in the last two decades. Had the relationship derived from the 1929–41 national product data prevailed as well in 1869–78, per capita consumption in this early decade would have

**TABLE 10–4.** National Income and Consumption Expenditure, in 1929 Prices, 1869–1938

| Decade | National Income (billions of dollars) (1) | Consumption Expenditures (billions of dollars) (2) | "Average Propensity to Consume" (3) | National Income Per Capita (dollars) (4) |
|---|---|---|---|---|
| 1869–78 | 9.3 | 8.1 | .86 | 215 |
| 1874–83 | 13.6 | 11.6 | .86 | 278 |
| 1879–88 | 17.9 | 15.3 | .85 | 326 |
| 1884–93 | 21.0 | 17.7 | .84 | 344 |
| 1889–98 | 24.2 | 20.2 | .84 | 357 |
| 1894–1903 | 29.8 | 25.4 | .85 | 401 |
| 1899–1908 | 37.3 | 32.3 | .86 | 458 |
| 1904–13 | 45.0 | 39.1 | .87 | 502 |
| 1909–18 | 50.6 | 44.0 | .87 | 517 |
| 1914–23 | 57.3 | 50.7 | .89 | 546 |
| 1919–28 | 69.0 | 62.0 | .89 | 612 |
| 1924–33 | 73.3 | 68.9 | .94 | 607 |
| 1929–38 | 72.0 | 71.0 | .99 | 572 |

SOURCE: Columns (1) and (2) are from S. Kuznets, *National Product Since 1869* (National Bureau of Economic Research, 1946), p. 119. Columns (3) and (4) are from *idem., National Income: A Summary of Findings* (National Bureau of Economic Research, 1946), pp. 53 and 32.

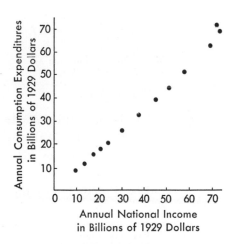

**Figure 10–10.**

been about $395,[19] almost twice as large as per capita national income, which was $215. Kuznets' new data might be consistent with the view that consumption is a stable function of income, with a marginal propensity less than one (and equal to the average propensity). But they were not consistent with the consumption function derived from annual data for the pre-World War II period. Some reconciliation of the two sets of data was obviously required. Perhaps there existed a "long-run" consumption function involving a proportional relationship, and a "short-run" function involving an MPC < APC. But exactly how were the two to be related?

One of the first attempted reconciliations was provided by Arthur Smithies.[20] He reasoned that what might have happened was that the consumption function—basically a nonproportional response of consump-

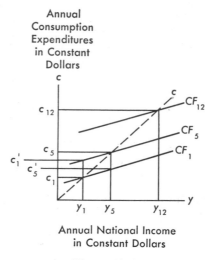

Annual
Consumption
Expenditures
in Constant
Dollars

**Figure 10–11.**

tion to fluctuations in income—had been drifting slowly upward over the decades, as income had slowly grown, and that the upward drift of the function had just happened to offset the tendency for the APC to decline as income grew. That is, in Figure 10–11, the basic consumption function, as of the decade 1869–78, could be represented by the line $CF_1$. Average

---

[19] This figure is derived as follows. A regression was fitted to data for *per capita* consumption and *per capita* national income (not disposable income), both in 1929 prices, for 1929–41. Inserting a per capita income of $215 in this function produces estimated consumption of $395. The regression equation is

$$c = \$289.57 + .49ni$$

[20] "Forecasting Postwar Demand: I," *Econometrica*, Vol. 13 (January 1945), pp. 1–14.

annual income in that decade was $y_1$, producing average annual consumption of $c_1$. But the function was constantly shifting upward. By the decade 1889–98, it had already moved up to position $CF_5$. If income were now to be $y_1$ (as it might in a severe depression), consumption would now be, not $c_1$ but $c'_1$. But, through economic growth, the average level of income by this decade had moved up to $y_5$, producing average consumption of $c_5$. Had there been no upward shift in the consumption function, income $y_5$ would have instead produced consumption $c'_5$. By the decade 1924–33, the function had shifted to $CF_{12}$. Coincidentally, average income had grown, by this decade, to $y_{12}$, producing an average consumption of $c_{12}$. The data estimated by Kuznets consisted of points like $c_1y_1$, $c_5y_5$, and $c_{12}y_{12}$. By coincidence, these all fall on the broken line, whose equation is roughly $c = .9y$. To Smithies, however, it was mere coincidence that the upward drift of the consumption function had just about exactly offset what would otherwise have been a decline in the APC as a result of income growth. Income could have grown without such an upward shift's having occurred. Or the upward shift could have occurred in the absence of any such growth in income.

Several reasons might be suggested for the upward drift in the consumption function. Smithies pointed out that the American population in this period had been moving steadily from rural to urban residence. Since all cross-section data show that, at any given income level, farmers consume less and save more than urban people at that same income level, the shift of population to cities should be expected to raise the total consumption function. A second reason for upward shift (though not suggested by Smithies) was that the age distribution of the population had been changing over this entire period. Larger and larger percentages were in the older age brackets. Since people in these brackets consume but typically do not earn, the total relationship of consumption to income should be raised by an increase in their relative weight. Another trend factor suggested by Smithies was the constant introduction of new consumer commodities in this period, and the incorporation of these into the customary standard of living. Like the previous two factors, this was essentially independent of income growth. But, it did have the effect, he thought, of elevating consumption relative to income above what it would have been had the assortment of available goods been more stable.

To test his trend hypothesis, Smithies did the following. Taking annual data for 1923–40 (with both consumption and income corrected for price and population change), he fitted an equation of the form

$$c = a + by + dt$$

where $t$ represents time. If there were an upward trend, the coefficient $d$ would be positive. If a downward trend, negative, if no trend, zero. He obtained the following regression equation:

$$c = 76.58 + .76di + 1.15(t - 1922)$$

This equation gives a marginal propensity to consume of .76; in addition, consumption per capita in constant prices tended to rise by $1.15 per year, quite independently of any change in income. In 1922 consumption per capita would be $76.58 (in 1929 prices), plus 76 per cent of per capita disposable income. In 1872 ($t = -50$), consumption would be $76.58 + .76di + ($1.15 × -50), or $19.08 + .76di; in 1952 ($t = 30$), consumption would be $76.58 + .76di + ($1.15 × 30), or $111.08 + .76di.

When Smithies substituted in his equations the levels of income estimated by Kuznets for the earlier decades, together with the appropriate value of $t$ for these decades, he obtained hypothetical consumption quite close to Kuznets' own direct estimates. The function, fitted to recent data, also "explained" the earlier data. The reconciliation "worked."

Smithies' student, James Duesenberry,[21] was not satisfied with the explanation which made the basic consumption function nonproportional. After showing that neither changing residence nor changing age distribution could have produced nearly the upward shift which was necessary for Smithies' hypothesis, Duesenberry advocated the position that the basic relationship was one of proportionality between income and consumption. He defended this as consistent with *a priori* theory, including relevant

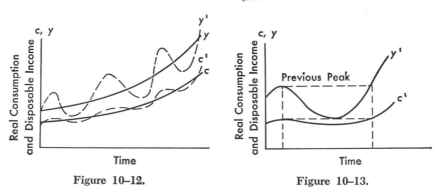

Figure 10–12.                                        Figure 10–13.

borrowings from modern sociopsychological theory. Why, then, do we observe an apparent nonproportionality in the short run? This merely reflects a *lag* in the adjustment of consumption to short term income fluctuations. Consider Figure 10–12. If income should grow steadily over time,

[21] See his *Income, Saving, and the Theory of Consumer Behavior* (Harvard University Press, 1949).

as shown by solid line $y$, consumption would grow in the same proportion, as shown by solid line $c$ (where $c$ is at each time a constant fraction of $y$). But income growth is not steady; it is bunched in spurts and dips, as shown by broken line $y'$. Consumption responds to these spurts and dips in income as along $c'$. If we view the whole history, it is obvious that consumption fluctuates in proportion to income. But if we look at any little piece of history, composing only a single "cycle," we lose sight of the longer-run proportionality, and conclude instead that the relationship is nonproportional.

The behavior of $c'$ and $y'$ in a single (idealized) cycle is shown in Figure 10–13.

The reason why $c$ falls less than $y$ in the depression, Duesenberry argued, is that consumers adjust their consumption not only to current income but to previous income, particularly previous peak income. All during the decline consumers are trying to protect their consumption standards acquired during the previous boom. As income falls, they reduce consumption as little as possible (thus reducing saving sharply). When, during the subsequent recovery period, income rises toward its previous peak level, consumption moves up slowly, too, with much of the increase in income going to restore the saving rate. Only when income moves into new high ground does consumption respond more vigorously to current income. There is, in short, a "ratchet effect." Consumers find it easier to increase consumption than to reduce it. This ratchet can be seen quite clearly in the $c'$ line of Figure 10–12, where consumption rises almost in stair step fashion.

Duesenberry proposed a consumption function of the following unusual form:

$$\frac{s_t}{y_t} = a\,\frac{y_t}{y_0} + b$$

where $s$ and $y$ represent saving and income respectively, the subscript $t$ refers to the current period and o to the previous peak. This equation thus says that the average propensity to save ($s_t/y_t$) is a function of the ratio of current to previous peak income. If this latter ratio is constant (e.g., if income grows steadily at 3 per cent per year, $y_t/y_0$ is always 1.03), then the average propensity to save is constant. But if income falls below the previous peak, the average propensity to save falls. Duesenberry's estimated equation, fitted to data for 1929–40, is

$$\frac{s_t}{y_t} = .25\,\frac{y_t}{y_0} - .196$$

Converting Duesenberry's equation to the more customary form, we get:

$$\frac{s_t}{y_t} = 1 - \frac{c_t}{y_t} = .25\,\frac{y_t}{y_0} - .196$$

$$\frac{c_t}{y_t} = -.25\,\frac{y_t}{y_0} + 1.196$$

$$c_t = 1.196 y_t - .25\,\frac{(y_t)^2}{y_0}$$

Still another attempt to reconcile conflicting indications about the basic form of the relationship of consumption to income is that provided by Milton Friedman.[22] Friedman's argument is that the essential form of the consumption function is one of proportionality. "Permanent" consumption is proportional to "permanent" income. But the actual, observable, "measured" income of any period, for any individual or economy, consists of the sum of permanent and transitory components. Likewise, actual, "measured" consumption consists of its basic, permanent component plus a random, transitory component. Friedman assumes (with little basis, some argue) that the transitory elements of consumption and income are uncorrelated with their corresponding permanent elements, and, further, are uncorrelated with each other.

Figure 10–14, which is for a cross-section of the population, shows the

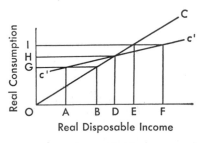

Figure 10–14.

basic consumption function (assumed to be the same for any small sample of families) as the line OC through the origin. This shows the permanent consumption that would correspond to any permanent income. Income OD is the average measured income for the whole community. The particular families with this average income have an average transitory income component of zero—some are families with higher permanent in-

22 *A Theory of the Consumption Function* (Princeton University Press, 1957).

come and negative transitory income components, others are families with lower permanent income and positive transitory income components. The *average* permanent income of such families is, nevertheless *OD*, equal to their average measured income. These families have an average permanent consumption *OH*, which, since the transitory elements of their consumption are randomly distributed, averaging to zero, is also their average measured consumption.

But families having measured income below the average—for example, having measured income *OA*—will include a higher than average proportion of families whose transitory income components are negative. Low-income families include many victims of temporary bad luck, just as high-income families include many with temporary windfalls. The average permanent income of families having measured income *OA* is *OB*. How do we know? Because that is the average permanent income necessary to produce permanent consumption (equal to average measured consumption) of *OG*. If we merely relate measured consumption to measured income we mistakenly associate consumption *OG* with income *OA*. Similarly, those with measured income *OF* have average permanent income *OE*, producing average permanent (equal to average measured) consumption *OI*. The apparent consumption function is *c'c'*, with an MPC considerably below the APC. Instead, in the true, basic function, which is exposed only by long-term income change, APC = MPC.

Friedman further considers the consistency of his hypothesis with data from time series. Approximating the "permanent" income of any year as an extrapolation of previous measured incomes, with current year's income having a weight of .33, preceding year's income a weight of .22, and the 15 previous years having rapidly declining weights, an estimated consumption proportional to this income concept is shown to produce an excellent fit to the actual consumption data for the nonwar years 1905–51. Elsewhere, however, he argues that, in practice, a three-year time horizon gives a good approximation of permanent income: a rise of income that persists for three years is considered permanent. This, however, is an empirical result: "This is not an issue that should be decided a priori; the data themselves should dictate the appropriate number of years." [23]

[23] Already a considerable volume of critical literature has developed with respect to the Friedman hypothesis, most of it rather highly technical. Particularly subject to criticism would appear to be the assumptions that "permanent" and "transitory" income are uncorrelated, and that "transitory consumption" is uncorrelated with "transitory income." See, among others: M. R. Fisher, "Explorations in Savings Behavior," *Bulletin of the Oxford University Institute of Statistics,* XVIII (August 1956), pp.

Finally, mention should be made of an essentially similar, although independent, theory of consumption behavior, developed by Franco Modigliani and Richard Brumberg, which makes the proportion of income saved depend on lifetime average income, again making saving relatively insensitive to current income.[24] Unfortunately, there is not space to develop their interesting argument here.

We shall not here develop further nor attempt to choose among these or other explanations of the "true," long-run relationship of consumption to income. We present these examples of theories about the "true" long-run relationship only to show that the theory of consumption is still very much in a state of disagreement (if not of confusion). This is in striking contrast to the optimistic view of many Keynesians in 1946 that we knew all that we needed to know about what determines aggregate consumption, and how and why.

## WAR AND POSTWAR CONSUMPTION BEHAVIOR

The optimistic appraisal of the stability of the Keynesian consumption function received one jolt from recognition of the problem of reconciling short-run and long-run considerations. It received a further jolt as the postwar period unrolled, disclosing irregularities of consumer spending that found no simple explanation. Figure 10–15 presents the basic information about war and postwar consumption patterns. Because the period covered is now somewhat longer, it is advisable to put these data on a per capita basis. They remain expressed in constant prices, however.

During the war period, consumer expenditures, although remaining high (consumers in the aggregate were not seriously deprived during the war), were still far below the levels that might have been expected on the basis of the prewar relationship of consumption to income. This, how-

---

201–77 (also see May 1957 issue of same journal for a symposium commenting on Fisher's work); I. Friend and I. B. Kravis, "Consumption Patterns and Permanent Income," *American Economic Review*, XLVII (May 1957), pp. 536–55; H. S. Houthakker, "The Permanent Income Hypothesis," *ibid.*, XLVIII (June 1958), pp. 396–404; R. Eisner, "The Permanent Income Hypothesis: Comment," M. Friedman, "Comment," and H. Houthakker, "Reply," *ibid.* (December 1958), pp. 972–93; H. W. Watts, "Long-Run Income Expectations and Consumer Saving," *Studies in Household Economic Behavior*, by Dernberg, Rossett, and Watts, Yale Studies in Economics, Vol. 9, Yale University Press, 1958; *Consumer Behavior: Research on Consumer Reactions*, ed. Lincoln H. Clark (Harper Brothers, 1958), paper by M. Friedman, and comments by J. Tobin, J. Morgan, I. Friend, and G. Orcutt, and reply by Friedman, pp. 444–69.

[24] "Utility Analysis and the Consumption Function: In Interpretation of Cross-Section Data," in *Post-Keynesian Economics*, K. Kurihara, ed., Rutgers University Press, 1954. Yet another hypothesis proposed to reconcile these two sets of data is found in G. Ackley, "The Wealth-Saving Relationship," *Journal of Political Economy*, LIX (April 1951), pp. 154–61, esp. pp. 156–8.

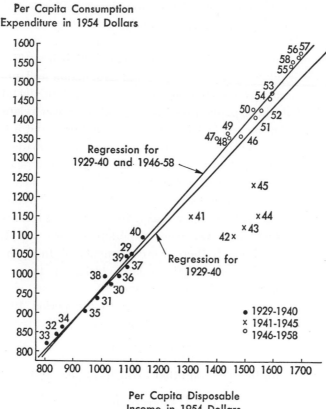

Per Capita Consumption
Expenditure in 1954 Dollars

Regression for
1929-40 and 1946-58

Regression for
1929-40

• 1929-1940
x 1941-1945
° 1946-1958

Per Capita Disposable
Income in 1954 Dollars

**Figure 10–15.**

ever, could be easily enough explained. Rationing and price controls, and limitations on the production of many consumer goods, together with patriotic appeals to save, prevented consumers from bidding for the goods they otherwise would have wanted to purchase at the high-income levels being experienced. Presumably, the purchases they desired to make were shown by the extension of the prewar regression line. The difference between the desired and the actual purchases represented the "inflationary gap" in the consumer sector, a gap that was, on the whole, successfully repressed from having its expected effect on price levels.

Although much of interest can be learned from a careful study of consumption during the war period, we shall pass directly to the postwar experience. The year 1946 was the first full postwar year. It will be noted that aggregate consumer expenditure in that year was already higher that would be expected on the basis of an extension of the prewar pattern.

Yet durable goods had not yet returned to volume production; this meant that nondurable spending was considerably higher than usual relative to income.

Nondurable spending continued "abnormally" high in 1947 and 1948, but to this was added a rapidly expanding production and purchase of durable goods, so that total consumption rose substantially above any level which could be explained on the basis of a prewar relationship of consumption to income. At first there was speculation about a temporary postwar "bulge" in consumer spending, as consumers made good the replacement of durables that would normally have been replaced during the war, when durable goods were not available. The fact that even *nondurable* spending was excessive (by past standards) relative to income made this explanation rather shaky. In any case, it increasingly became apparent that what we were experiencing was no temporary "spending spree" (although there were elements of this), but a permanently higher level of consumption relative to income than could have been predicted on the basis of prewar data.

We can, of course, fit a single function to the period 1929–40 and 1946–58. The equation for this function is

$$c = 104.9 + .86di$$

This compares with the function fitted to 1929–40 per capita data:

$$c = 171.6 + .79di$$

The higher slope indicates that the function which includes both periods comes much closer to making consumption proportional to income. It is also clear that the function including both prewar and postwar behavior provides a good explanation of the observed variation of consumption. The coefficient of correlation for this regression is .9978. This means that almost 100 per cent (99.55 per cent) of the observed variation in consumer expenditure over these years can be "explained" by differences in income among these years, leaving less than 0.5 per cent to be explained by other factors which operated differently.

It is apparent from Figure 10–15 that the deviations of actual consumption from consumption estimated by our 1929–40, 1946–58 regression line are small both in absolute and in percentage terms. In only four of the 25 years does the deviation exceed 2 per cent of the estimated expenditures; in ten years, the deviation is less than 1 per cent. It must be recalled, of course, in evaluating these deviations, that the association of consumption and income is two-directional: income influences consumption spending; but "abnormally" high or low consumption also tends to make income abnormally high or low, reducing the apparent magnitude of the abnormality of consumption.

Still, the evidence surveyed leaves room for considerable satisfaction with the relationship which Keynes postulated. A highly regular relationship does exist between aggregate consumption and aggregate disposable income. Only when we push somewhat deeper below the surface, do problems of interpretation and understanding continue to raise their ugly heads. In the following chapter, we focus on the problem of interpreting the short-run behavior of consumer spending, and propose a tentative hypothesis. This chapter can be omitted by a reader not interested in the details of consumption function analysis. In Chapter XII we present an analysis of other factors which have been suggested as possible influences on consumption spending.

## APPENDIX

### Consumption and Maximization of Utility

On page 219, reference is made to a possible derivation of the consumption function from an analysis of the way in which a "rational" consumer maximizes utility over time. This appendix sketches this derivation.

Briefly, we can conceive of a consumer's receiving utility or satisfaction from current consumption and from the contemplation of expected future consumption; from the mere possession of his current wealth (as a source of safety, prestige, and a fund for heirs) and from the expectation of future wealth; and, perhaps, also directly from the mere receipt of current and the expected receipt of future income (as a source of power, prestige, etc., quite apart from the consumption and saving it permits). Present consumption has a double connection with expected future consumption. A reduction of present consumption will permit greater expected future consumption both (a) through enabling future dissaving and (b) through the larger future income (and thus potential consumption) which the larger wealth will earn. Further, a reduction of present consumption, permitting greater future wealth and income, increases expected future satisfactions from the mere possession of wealth and receipt of income.

Formally, we can conceive of current utility, $U_t$, as a function of three series of variables, stretching into the future:

$$(1) \qquad U_t = f(c_t, \frac{c_{t+1}}{1+m}, \frac{c_{t+2}}{(1+m)^2}, \cdots,$$

$$w_t, \frac{w_{t+1}}{1+m}, \frac{w_{t+2}}{(1+m)^2}, \cdots,$$

$$y_t, \frac{y_{t+1}}{1+m}, \frac{y_{t+2}}{(1+m)^2}, \cdots)$$

where $c_t$, $w_t$ and $y_t$ are the current period's consumption, wealth, and income, respectively, and $c_{t+1}$, $w_{t+1}$, and $y_{t+1}$ are next period's expected consumption, wealth, and income. The symbol $m$ is the rate of time discount, reflecting the idea that future satisfactions are discounted relative to present ones both through ignorance and shortsightedness ("impatience") and, perhaps, more rationally, because of the uncertainty of the future. For simplicity, we have assumed both that the same discount rate applies to all future years and that the same rate is applicable to expected future consumption and to the mere expected possession and receipt of future wealth and income. The first partial derivative of $U_t$ with respect to each term shown is positive, its second partial derivative negative. (This means that an increase in any term within the parenthesis will increase $U_t$; but a further increase will always add less to $U_t$ than the previous increase. In other words, each source of utility is subject to a diminishing marginal utility.) We have the additional relationships:

$$(2) \qquad\qquad y_t \equiv c_t + s_t$$

$$(3) \qquad\qquad w_{t+1} \equiv w_t + s_t$$

$$(4) \qquad\qquad y_t \equiv e_t + w_{t-1} \cdot r_t$$

$$(5) \qquad\qquad c_t \leqq y_t + w_{t-1}$$

Equation (2) merely expresses the budgetary relationship among the income, consumption, and saving of any period (saving alone among the variables can assume negative values); (3) shows that wealth accumulates through saving (or decreases through negative saving); while (4) makes each period's income the sum of its labor income, $e_t$, and its property income, where $r_t$ is the current rate of interest in any period. The last equation (5) expresses the budgetary restraint (for simplicity we exclude the possibility of consumer borrowing). We assume $e_t$, $e_{t+1}$, etc. are autonomous (that is not quite correct because one can invest in himself through education, training, etc.), and that current beginning-of-period wealth, $w_{t-1}$, is given. Of course, $r_t$, $r_{t+1}$, etc., are also given, so far as the consumer is concerned, and we assume that the discount factor, $m$, is given by the consumer's "tastes."

Using relationships (2), (3), and (4) we can convert our utility function (1) into one in which the only variables are current and future consumption. That is, future wealth and income can be expressed in terms of factors taken as given, together with consumption, present and future. For example, by substitution, we derive

$$w_t = w_{t-1} + e_t + w_{t-1} \cdot r_t - c_t$$

$$(6) \qquad\qquad w_t = w_{t-1}(1 + r_t) + e_t - c_t$$

From this we obtain

$$(7) \frac{w_{t+1}}{1+m} = \frac{1}{1+m}([w_{t-1}\{1 + r_t\} + e_t - c_t][1 + r_{t+1}] + e_{t+1} - c_{t+1})$$

From (4) and (5) we obtain

$$(8) \qquad \frac{y_{t+1}}{1+m} = \frac{1}{1+m}(e_{t+1} + [w_{t-1}\{1 + r_t\} + e_t - c_t]r_{t+1})$$

Similar, more complicated expressions can be substituted for $w_{t+2}/(1+m)^2$, $y_{t+2}/(1+m)^2$, etc.

Thus, equation (1) becomes an expression in which the only variables are $c_t$, $c_{t+1}$, $c_{t+2}$, . . . The consumer attempts to maximize $U_t$ through selection of a time pattern for $c_t$, $c_{t+1}$, etc., subject to the series of budget restraints (for each period) implied in equation (5). The mathematical formulation of this maximum is rather complex. But it is obvious that the optimum value for $c_t$ will depend on the consumer's current wealth, his current and expected future labor incomes, the current and expected future rates of interest, and his time discount factor, $m$.

Having found the optimum $c_t$, we can then ask how it will be affected by changes in any of the parameters. It can be demonstrated that an increase in $y_t$ will necessarily increase $c_t$ but by less; it also can be shown that an increase in $r_t$ will decrease the optimum $c_t$. Further, an increase in $w_{t-1}$ will also increase $c_t$.

The effect of a change in $e_t$ is, as noted, to raise $c_t$ by less than the increase in $e_t$. This result follows whether or not the change in $e_t$ also involves proportionate changes in the whole series of expected future labor incomes, $e_{t+1}$, . . . However, if we make certain further, perhaps plausible assumptions, we may be able to show that if an increase in $e_t$ is an increase relative to $e_{t+1}$ . . . , it will cause current consumption to increase in a smaller *proportion* than income; while if $e_t$, $e_{t+1}$, . . . all change in identical proportion, $c_t$ will change in the same proportion.[25] Other elaborations of assumptions may produce other kinds of more detailed *a priori* hypotheses.

Some writers prefer to include as variables in the analysis consumer "needs" in present and future periods, in order to recognize the obvious fact that changing size of family, changing social status, and even changing intensity of enjoyments can be expected over the consumer's life cycle. It is then possible to investigate the effects of changes in the expected future time pattern of income, given various plausible expected time patterns of "needs." One reason for not including "needs" is that it is not, even conceptually, an objectively measurable or scaleable concept. However, suggestive further extensions of the analysis are possible if this variable is explicitly introduced rather than merely taken as a parameter which affects (in an unspecified way) the shape of the function.

[25] M. Friedman, *op.cit.*, assumes that an increase in "permanent income" will yield a proportional increase in consumption, but an increase in "transitory income" will have zero effect on consumption—i.e., it will all be saved. It is difficult to reconcile this either with "rational" behavior, or with the "real world" behavior of consumers.

# Short-Run Consumption Behavior [1]

*Chapter XI*

## THE PROBLEM OF SHORT-RUN BEHAVIOR

We noted at the end of the previous chapter that, taking the prewar and postwar years together, a linear regression of consumer expenditure on disposable income provides an excellent fit to the observed data for these years. The marginal propensity to consume is estimated at .86, only slightly below the average propensity at moderate levels of income.

But probing below the surface suggests problems. We have already noted what some of these are. They relate primarily to the reconciliation of short-run and long-run evidence on consumer behavior. If we take the prewar years alone, the marginal propensity appears substantially lower than when we combine both periods. For 1929–41 it is about .73, becoming .79 if we omit 1941.[2] It is also interesting, and puzzling, to note that if we take the postwar years alone, we also get lower marginal propensity. A regression fitted to the years 1946–57 gives the following result:

$$c = 186.3 + .81di$$

Again, the marginal propensity appears substantially below the average propensity, and well below the longer-term marginal propensity of .86. Short-run consumer behavior does differ from longer-run behavior.

---

[1] This chapter has benefited considerably from discussions with Professor Daniel B. Suits. Professor Suits has recently completed (1959) a statistical analysis of short-run consumption behavior which, although it takes off from analyses quite similar to ones presented in this chapter, breaks important new ground. His results will presumably be published as a monograph by the National Commission on Money and Credit.

[2] All of these marginal propensities are on a per capita basis. In aggregate terms, each should be raised roughly by .02.

And in many if not most of the contexts in which we wish to apply the consumption function to questions of economic policy, it is the short-run behavior of consumption in which we are interested. For example, if we are trying to design fiscal measures to stabilize the volume of employment and output at a high level, it is usually next year's consumption with which we are concerned—or even the level of consumption expenditure in the next six months. Particularly in the postwar period, the short-run behavior of consumption in relationship to disposable income has sometimes been rather erratic.

To be sure, if we plot quarterly consumption and disposable income data, we find that the correlation of the two remains strong. This is done in Figure 11–1.[3]

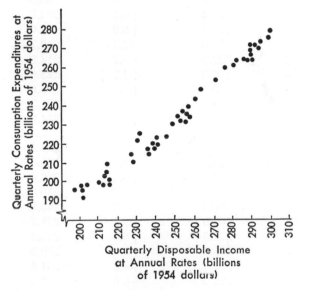

Figure 11–1.

Nevertheless, when we look more closely at quarter-to-quarter changes, problems of erratic behavior become apparent. Table 11–1 presents relevant data for some selected postwar periods.

Several things will be noticed at once. first, five of the twenty-two quarter-to-quarter changes of consumption and income are *in opposite directions*. Second, where changes are in the same direction, the extent of change in consumption exceeds that of income in ten cases. Thus in

---

[3] Data are for the years 1946–58. Quarterly data are expressed in seasonally-adjusted annual rates and in 1954 prices. They are not corrected for population change.

TABLE 11–1.   Disposable Income, Consumption Expenditures, and
Changes in Each, Selected Quarters

(billions of dollars, in 1954 prices, seasonally adjusted annual rates)

| Year | Quarter | Real Disposable Income | Change | Real Consumer Expend. | Change |
|------|---------|------------------------|--------|-----------------------|--------|
| 1948 | 1 | 203.5 |        | 198.1 |        |
|      | 2 | 211.7 | +8.2  | 199.0 | +0.9  |
|      | 3 | 215.3 | +3.6  | 199.4 | +0.4  |
|      | 4 | 215.1 | −0.2  | 200.6 | +1.2  |
| 1949 | 1 | 212.9 | −2.2  | 199.9 | −0.7  |
|      | 2 | 213.9 | +1.0  | 203.6 | +3.7  |
|      | 3 | 214.0 | +0.1  | 204.8 | +1.2  |
|      | 4 | 214.9 | +0.9  | 209.0 | +4.2  |
| 1950 | 1 | 228.0 | +13.1 | 210.7 | +1.7  |
|      | 2 | 227.3 | −0.7  | 214.2 | +3.5  |
|      | 3 | 232.0 | +4.7  | 225.6 | +11.4 |
|      | 4 | 236.1 | +4.1  | 217.0 | −8.6  |
| 1951 | 1 | 230.9 | −5.2  | 222.3 | +5.3  |
|      | 2 | 236.3 | +5.4  | 214.5 | −7.8  |
| 1953 | 4 | 255.9 |        | 234.1 |        |
| 1954 | 1 | 254.4 | −1.5  | 233.4 | −0.7  |
|      | 2 | 254.8 | +0.4  | 236.4 | +3.0  |
|      | 3 | 257.0 | +2.2  | 239.0 | +2.6  |
|      | 4 | 260.9 | +3.9  | 243.2 | +4.2  |
| 1955 | 1 | 263.0 | +2.1  | 248.7 | +5.5  |
|      | 2 | 271.5 | +8.5  | 253.7 | +5.0  |
|      | 3 | 276.5 | +5.0  | 259.9 | +6.2  |
|      | 4 | 281.4 | +4.9  | 261.8 | +1.9  |
| 1956 | 1 | 282.0 | +0.6  | 263.2 | +1.4  |

only seven cases is the "marginal propensity to consume," as here measured, both positive and less than one. To be sure, these irregularities tend
to disappear if we take the movement of six-month or nine-month periods,
but not in all cases.

Consider first the behavior of consumer expenditures during the recession of 1949. Between the four quarters of 1948 and 1949, disposable
income declined 0.2 billions; yet consumer expenditures increased by 8.4
billions. Clearly, consumers behaved contrary to expectations during this
recession; and this unusual behavior is perhaps the primary reason why
the recession was an extremely mild one.

Consider next the six quarters concluding in mid-1951. There was, first, a sharp recovery of disposable income. (Incidentally, this is the largest quarter-to-quarter change shown in the whole table.) But consumer expenditures, already high with respect to income as a result of the behavior just summarized, rose only 1.7 billion. But in the next two quarters, and particularly in the third quarter of 1950, consumption spurted upward, greatly exceeding the moderate rise in income. The third quarter of 1950 and the first quarter of 1951 were the periods of "scare buying" associated respectively with the outbreak of the Korean War and the intervention of the Chinese Communists. In the quarters following each of these episodes consumption dropped sharply despite rising income. Over the five quarters from the first of 1950 to the second of 1951, income rose by 8.3 billion, consumption rose 3.8 billion.

The third episode on which attention is focused in the table is the recovery from the 1953–54 recession. In each of the four quarterly changes between the first quarter of 1954 and the first quarter of 1955, the change of consumption exceeded the change of income. The other irregularities are apparent enough. From the first quarter of 1954 to the first quarter of 1956, income rose 27.6 billion, consumption, 29.8 billion. Consumer expenditures clearly led the way out of the 1954 recession and strongly supported the early part of the 1955–57 boom.

These changes could not have been predicted by "consumption function" reasoning. Other episodes in the postwar history are almost equally puzzling. In fact, dependence upon the consumption function led to serious errors of forecast and bad policy advice on numerous occasions in the postwar years. For short-run purposes we need to know more about the dynamics of consumer behavior.

## IS THERE A "LAG" IN THE CONSUMPTION FUNCTION?

The possibility that income may influence consumer expenditures only with some lag has been frequently suggested in the writings of economic theorists. There is some suggestion in Keynes' own discussion of his "psychological law" that it may operate with a slight lag. Other writers have made much more of the point.

One source of lag is associated with the school of thought of D. H. Robertson. Robertson's argument concentrates on flows of cash. Cash cannot be spent before it is received. Cash receipts are not continuous but periodic. Thus the average lag of consumption change behind income change is one "day," a period whose length can perhaps be identified with the payment period of our Figure 5–3. Robertson's argument that money cannot be spent before it is received assumes a zero cash balance at the beginning and end of each period—which need not be true— and the absence of book credit facilities. In any case, a lag which derives from this source must be short, since Robertson's "day" is defined as being so short that income earned within it cannot be spent before the next day, and most persons are paid weekly or bi-weekly.

Thus, most of those who believe the lag to be significant refer to institutional or psychological reasons for slowness in the adjustment of spending to change in income. Institutional reasons include such facts as the existence of long-term leases (a higher income may cause the family to seek a new apartment—when the present lease expires); the annual model change in automobiles (if a man is promoted to a higher salary bracket, he may also move from the Chevrolet to the Pontiac class—but he will wait for the new model); or, more generally, the existence of durable goods (higher income may cause the family to graduate to a larger size of refrigerator—but if the present one is new, it will probably not be replaced at once).

Psychological reasons for a lag run all the way from (a) the necessity for an income increase to persist for a while before it can be recognized as more than a random fluctuation to (b) the necessity for a family to become identified with the new ways of thinking and standards of good taste associated with a higher income level. In general, the *habitual* nature of much consumer behavior is stressed in this view.

Except for the Robertsonian concept, the lag should probably be represented as a complex one—some effect of income change realized immediately, another part lagged for a short period, and still more lagged considerably. Thus it is an oversimplification to represent the idea as

$$c_t = f(y_{t-1})$$

Still in the same line of emphasis is the Duesenberry formulation already discussed, which stresses the previous peak level of income as having a persisting influence in maintaining consumption expenditures during a period of cyclical decline. Duesenberry's formulation uses a lag, but one of irregular length.

Although theoretical dynamic models using a simple lag of consumption behind income are widely used, it is extremely difficult to verify the existence of a lag. Certainly the lag is not apparent in annual data. The reader can confirm this merely by plotting a scatter diagram in which each point plotted represents one year's consumption expenditure and the previous year's income. But might a lag of a quarter-year appear?

Lloyd Metzler [4] made the following test. He plotted in a scatter diagram quarterly consumption expenditures against the same quarter's income payments; then he repeated, except that each quarter's consumption was matched with the previous quarter's income. It was readily apparent that the relationship with current income was much closer than the relationship with lagged income, and Metzler concluded that any lag must be of very short duration.

Metzler's test, however, is subject to the valid objection, previously noted, that the consumption-income relationship is a two-way relationship. Abnormally high or low current consumption may raise or reduce the current quarter's disposable income; but it obviously does not raise or lower the previous quarter's disposable income. One of the two plottings picks up both kinds of relationship between consumption and income and the other does not. The proper test is to plot, first, each quarter's consumption with that same quarter's saving; then each quarter's consumption with the difference between the previous quarter's income and the current quarter's consumption. The hypothesis to be tested suggests that any quarter's income is divided into planned consumption expenditure and planned saving. But the consumption plan is not carried out until the following quarter,

$$y_{q-1} = \bar{c}_{q-1} + \bar{s}_{q-1}$$

$$\bar{c}_{q-1} = c_q$$

$$\bar{s}_{q-1} = y_{q-1} - c_q$$

where the bars above the symbols mean planned, as distinguished from actual current magnitudes. Thus, we should plot $c_q$ against $(y_{q-1} - c_q)$, which, for short, we can call "Robertsonian" saving.

The two scatter diagrams are presented as the two parts of Figure 11–2. The data are seasonally-adjusted quarterly aggregates for 1947 to 1958, expressed as annual rates, and corrected for price changes.

It is not readily apparent which correlation is better. Computing coefficients of correlation shows that the relationship of quarterly consumption with the same quarter's saving is slightly but not significantly superior to the relationship with "Robertsonian" saving. (The coefficient of correlation for part A is .63, for part B, it is .61.) The lag hypothesis cannot be said to have been confirmed by the data.

But the surprising thing about the diagram is that, on a quarterly basis,

---

[4] "Three Lags in the Circular Flow of Income," in *Income, Employment, and Public Policy* (Norton, 1948), pp. 11 ff.

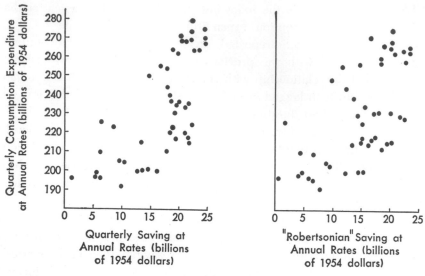

**Figure 11–2.**

the correlation of consumption and saving is as low as it is. Removing, as we do here, the influence of current consumption on current income, the irregularity of postwar short-run consumption behavior shows up most starkly.

### THE CONSUMPTION "RATCHET"

Figure 11–3 shows part A of the previous figure on a larger scale, and includes a line connecting, in serial order, each quarter's observations with the previous and subsequent quarters' points. The slope of this line shows the direction of each quarterly change in consumption and saving. If, in successive quarters, consumption is unchanged, but saving changes, the line segment will be horizontal. (This corresponds to MPC = 0, MPS = 1.) If consumption changes but saving is unchanged, the line segment will be vertical. (This corresponds to MPC = 1, MPS = 0.) If consumption and saving move in the same direction the line segment will slope upward to the right. (This is Keynes' case: 0 < MPC < 1.) If they move in opposite directions, the line segment will slope downward to the right. (This means an MPC either greater than one or else negative.)

Study of the figure discloses the following results: twenty-six of the forty-six line segments slope downward to the right (opposite variation in consumption and saving), three are approximately horizontal (saving

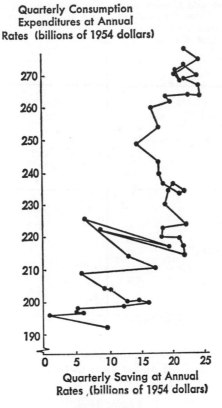

Quarterly Consumption
Expenditures at Annual
Rates (billions of 1954 dollars)

Quarterly Saving at Annual
Rates ,(billions of 1954 dollars)

Figure 11–3.

changing with constant consumption), one is approximately vertical (consumption changing with constant saving), and sixteen slope upward to the right (saving and consumption moving together).

The pattern of line segments appears to suggest that quarter-to-quarter changes in consumption and saving tend to be in opposite directions. But over time, the *levels* of both consumption and saving move jerkily upward, imparting a generally positive slope to the scatter as a whole. The negative quarter-to-quarter relationship is confirmed by the scatter diagram appearing in Figure 11–4, which shows the pattern of concurrent changes in consumption and saving. Only the northeast and southwest quadrants would be consistent with the Keynesian hypothesis; yet these are underpopulated areas.

An inverse movement of consumption and saving could arise in the following circumstances: (a) consumption rises when income falls, (b) consumption falls when income rises, (c) consumption rises by more than

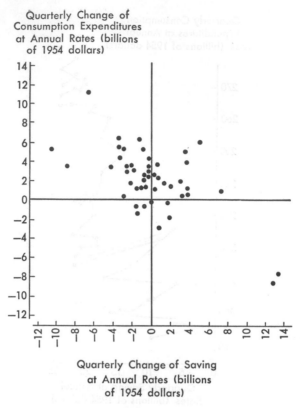

Quarterly Change of
Consumption Expenditures
at Annual Rates (billions
of 1954 dollars)

Quarterly Change of Saving
at Annual Rates (billions
of 1954 dollars)

Figure 11–4.

income, (d) consumption falls by more than income, or (e) with income unchanged, consumption rises or falls. Cases (a) and (b) imply a negative marginal propensity to consume, cases (c) and (d) a marginal propensity to consume greater than one. Since inverse movements seem to be typical of short-run behavior, should we therefore conclude that the short-run marginal propensity to consume is either negative or greater than one? This would probably be a misleading description. Rather, it would seem more correct to summarize this evidence as showing that there occur *short-run changes in consumption expenditure which are unrelated to income*. In any short period, say a month or a quarter, income changes are necessarily small. Thus, if there are irregular or random fluctuations in consumption, up or down, saving will almost necessarily move in the opposite direction, and by roughly the same amount. If we took even shorter periods, say a day or a week, changes in consumption (or errors in measuring it) would necessarily be offset by almost identical movements, but with opposite sign, in saving.[5]

These irregular changes in consumption (if they are not merely errors of measurement) of course give rise to changes in income. In the short run, consumption determines income more than the reverse.

If these irregular fluctuations in consumption were of a purely random variety, they would tend to average out to zero, the longer the time span being considered. Thus we might suppose that annual data would show a much closer correspondence between changes in consumption and in saving, and still closer correspondence would appear if we used two- or three-year totals of consumption and saving. The longer the period used, the more stable should be the correspondence of consumption changes and saving changes, with the ratio of the two changes approaching a magnitude something like .8 or .9 in consumption to .2 or .1 in saving as the periods compared became of the order of half-decades or decades.

But are the irregularities of consumption purely random, and, if they are, how long a period before their effect is roughly cancelled out?

We can get some evidence on this by looking at annual data. In Figure 11–5 we show annual data for consumption and personal saving, for the years 1929–41, and 1946–58. Data are per capita, corrected for price change. Again we have used line segments to connect most of the successive years' observations. The regression line in the figure is fitted to the data for these years, excluding 1941. This regression converts to a customary consumption function having the following formula

$$c = 135.7 + .84di$$

quite consistent with the formula obtained from our direct regression of consumption on disposable income, which was (see p. 248)

$$c = 104.9 + .86di$$

But several conclusions are immediately apparent from the figure:

1. The "fit" of the regression to the data is rather poor. Many individual years lie at considerable distance from the average relationship.

---

[5] An alternative approach to short-run consumer behavior is provided by Arnold Zellner, "The Short-Run Consumption Function," *Econometrica*, 25 (October 1957), pp. 552–67. (Zellner also reviews other earlier studies.) Zellner uses postwar quarterly data, and fits consumption functions using various combinations of income, lagged income, lagged consumption, previous peak income and liquid assets. Our principal objection to his treatment is that he arbitrarily rejects all equations in which the marginal propensity to consume turns out to be negative. On the basis of the analysis above, there seems to be no valid reason for this arbitrary rejection.

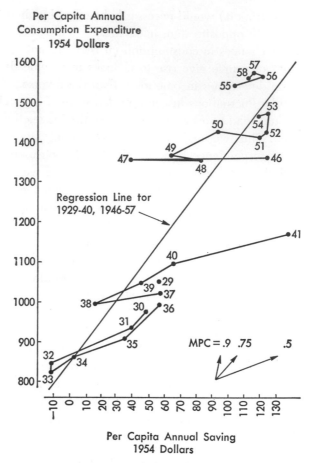

Per Capita Annual Saving
1954 Dollars

**Figure 11–5.**

2. The slope of the regression line corresponds to the slope of very few of the year-to-year line segments. Most year-to-year segments are considerably "flatter" than the average relationship.

3. There are still a few cases of inverse movement of consumption and saving—notably 1948–49, 1950–51, 1954–55, and 1956–57.

What study of the figure suggests is that the annual consumption-saving relationship is one in which consumption and saving rather typically move in the same direction, but with changes in saving roughly as large as changes in consumption. A key on the figure shows the slopes of line segments corresponding to marginal propensities to consume of various magnitudes. A preponderant number of the year-to-year changes have magnitudes ranging between MPC = .5 and MPC = .7.

Superimposed on this relatively "flat" year-to-year relationship are certain upward and downward shifts, all concentrated in a relatively few years. One sees that the years 1930–36 trace out a rather consistent pattern of year-to-year change, but at a level considerably below the 1929 level. The year 1937 marks a transition to a higher level of consumption relative to saving, which is completed in 1938 and prevails consistently through 1941. The period 1946–54 represents again a fairly consistent pattern of year-to-year variation, but at a level far above the prewar relationship. Compare, for example, the years 1929, 1936, and 1937 when per capita real saving was about the same as in 1947–49. But consumption levels are far higher in the later years. A third major shift in the level of the relationship seems to have occurred between 1954 and 1955.

In short, the data suggest a medium-term relationship involving a MPC of roughly .5–.7, but which has shown several rather sharp and discontinuous shifts of level.[6]

The only statistical study using annual data that has suggested a marginal propensity to consume as low as .5 is one by Lawrence R. Klein and Arthur S. Goldberger. Their consumption function appears as follows: [7]

$$C_t = -22.26 + .55W_t + .41P_t + .34A_t + .26C_{t-1} + .072L_{t-1} + .26N_t$$

where $C$ is aggregate consumer expenditures, $W$ is aggregate employee compensation after taxes, $P$ is aggregate entrepreneurial and dividend income after taxes, $A$ is farm income after taxes, $L$ is personal liquid asset holdings (all of the foregoing in billions of 1939 dollars), and $N$ is total population, in millions of persons. The function was fitted to data for the years 1929–41 and 1946–52, by a method which we will not discuss here. Population is introduced as a separate variable rather than putting the other variables on a per capita basis, for reasons which we need not discuss. Likewise, we will ignore for the present the use of liquid asset

---

[6] If we fit separate regressions of consumption on saving to the years 1930–36, 1938–41, and 1946–54, we get the following results

| | |
|---|---|
| 1930–36: | $c = 857.0 + 2.29s$ |
| 1938–41: | $c = 1000.0 + 1.06s$ |
| 1946–54: | $c = 1316.3 + .91s$ |

If we translate these to formulas using disposable income, we get

| | |
|---|---|
| 1930–36: | $c = 260.5 + .70di$ |
| 1938–41: | $c = 485.4 + .51di$ |
| 1946–54: | $c = 689.2 + .48di$ |

[7] *An Econometric Model of the United States, 1929–1952* (North-Holland, 1955), p. 90. (We have combined some terms for simplicity in presentation.)

holdings as an explanatory variable (whose influence in this equation is actually very minor). What we have left is an equation in the form

$$c_t = a(di_t) + b(c_{t-1}) + d$$

except that separate marginal propensities to consume have been computed for the three main income groups: wage earners, profit recipients, and farmers. These marginal propensities are respectively .55, .41, and .34. Since wage earners receive roughly two thirds of total income, the weighted average of these propensities is close to .5.

What, now, can we make of the term $c_{t-1}$, the coefficient of which was found by Klein and Goldberger to be .26? Klein and Goldberger explain the introduction of the previous year's consumption as follows:

> It is generally recognized that consumers do not react immediately to changes in income; hence some lagged, as well as current, values of income are used [by others] as variables. In our model, the influence of the past on present consumer behavior will be represented by lagged consumption, not lagged income. Our hypothesis will be that consumer behavior tends to be repetitive to some extent, but that adjustments will be made in accordance with the income situation and other variables.[8]

However, in our view of the matter, the role of $c_{t-1}$ is rather different. If it is correct that for considerable periods the "medium-term" consumption function remains fairly stable, with a MPC of approximately .5–.7, but is subject to discontinuous shifts, the $c_{t-1}$ variable plays the role of recognizing these shifts, after they have occurred. Once the level of the consumption function has shifted (say) upward, its new higher level is reflected in a higher value of $c_{t-1}$, raising the level of $c_t$ associated with any given value of disposable income. Of course, in the years in which the shift is occurring, the formula will produce a poor estimate. But since these years are few, the formula produces good estimates of consumption most of the time. In effect, the Klein-Goldberger formula says: "If you tell me the level at which consumption was *last* year, I will predict *this* year's consumption by applying a marginal propensity of about .5 to whatever change may occur in disposable income."[9]

---

[8] *Ibid.*, p. 8.

[9] If we fit a regression in the simple form $c_t = a(di_t) + b(c_{t-1}) + d$ to annual data for the years 1929–40 and 1946–58 (all data per capita and in 1947–49 prices), we obtain the following:

$$C_t = .72di_t + .17c_{t-1} + 82.2$$

The coefficient of correlation is .9337.

It is difficult to explain fully why the marginal propensity to consume is so much higher and the coefficient of lagged income so much lower than Klein-Goldberger's.

This formula, interpreted in this way, does not attempt to *explain* the shifts in the level of consumption, but recognizes the shifts once they have occurred.

Perhaps we should describe the matter in terms of a consumption "ratchet," reminiscent of Duesenberry's idea. Every few years, during the longer-term growth of income, the whole level of consumption relative to saving (and thus relative to income) moves sharply upward. Such upward shifts usually have occurred during periods of relatively high income, although Duesenberry's "previous peak" concept definitely does not fit every case. Whatever the cause of the shift, it seems to be irreversible, and subsequent declines or increases of income are shared roughly equally between consumption and saving, until another shift occurs. Each shift "takes off" from a platform provided by the previous one, thus the "ratchet" idea.[10]

## SUMMARY

In this chapter we have demonstrated that the very short-run fluctuations of consumer spending cannot be explained by income changes. On a quarter-to-quarter basis, consumption change is as likely to *cause* income change as to be the passive result of a change in income.

We considered but rejected the hypothesis that short-run variation of consumer spending could be considered to be the result of the previous year's or quarter's change in disposable income. No simple lag system appears to improve the explanation of short-run consumer behavior.

We considered the possible explanation that there were purely random short-run fluctuations in consumption, which averaged out to zero as the time span of the comparison were sufficiently extended. We showed, however, that the time span would have to be very considerably extended to produce an acceptably regular relationship of consumption to income. On an *annual* basis, the most reasonable description of consumer behavior (if we confine our explanation to *income*) is that there is a rather "flat" medium-term consumption function, having a MPC of about .5–.7, whose position is reasonably stable for periods of 4 to 6 years, but which ap-

---

To be sure, our data are per capita, cover a somewhat different period of years, and are deflated by a different price index; still, the variation is rather pronounced. One reason is the exclusion of liquid assets, whose growth over the period is assigned some of the weight given above to income.

[10] An intriguing exception seems to have occurred between 1929 and subsequent years. Without better data for the earlier years we cannot be sure whether 1929 was merely exceptionally high, or whether the function really shifted downward, perhaps partially explaining (or explained by some other factor accounting for) the seriousness of the "great depression."

pears to shift erratically upward from time to time, as income increases, producing *on the average* (but only over considerable periods of time) a relationship having a slope of perhaps .85 or even .9, with the growth of consumption in the longer run approaching a proportional relationship to income. These erratic shifts were not explained.

However we may explain these shifts, it is clear that current disposable income alone does not fully explain consumption spending in either the short run (e.g., by quarters), or in the medium run (e.g., by years). This result should not be surprising, even though few economists in the Keynesian tradition have so far accepted it. When we consider our own spending behavior, it is clear that it is not determined by income simultaneously received. This is obviously true when we refer to periods as short as ten minutes, one month, or even one year. The pattern of our consumption at any given time is surely determined by an income *level* which stretches from some distance in the past some distance into the future. It is *longer-run income* that is important. Duesenberry, Friedman, and others have given specific formulations of this relationship which appear to be oversimplified. But the fundamental notion which underlies their formulations is surely correct. Whatever particular combination of income *history, current level and change* of income, and future income *expectations* may finally be settled upon as the best explanation of current consumption, it is clear that the relationship of consumption and income is far more complex (at least in a wealthy society) than most Keynesians have believed.

In Chapter XII, we shall consider a number of factors other than income which have been suggested as further explanatory variables for consumer spending. It is possible that some of these factors may either (a) help explain the short-run *timing* of consumption spending—i.e., the erratic shifts that we have disclosed in the quarterly or annual relationship; or (b) improve our understanding even of the longer run behavior of consumption spending.

# Other Influences on Consumption Spending

*Chapter XII*

It was shown in Chapter X (and more fully developed in Chapter XI) that, despite early Keynesian enthusiasm for the use of income as the complete explanation of consumer spending, further analysis leaves numerous unanswered questions. Either there is an erratic, unexplainable element in spending, particularly important in the short run, or there are other systematic factors influencing consumption that need to be brought into the analysis. We consider in this chapter a number of possible further explanatory factors that have been suggested.

These factors are divided into several categories for convenience of treatment. Keynes, who never claimed *exclusive* causal importance for income, discussed other factors under the headings "objective" and "subjective." We employ a somewhat more detailed classification, based only in part on Keynes' distinction. We first treat a number of factors which are "objective" in the sense that the variables considered are commonly considered to be "economic" ones, capable of appreciable short-run variation, and can, at least conceptually, be quantitatively measured or scaled in a form which might permit their incorporation into a statistical consumption function. Some of these objective factors might be expected to influence individual behavior with respect to consumption in general, and they are discussed first, followed by discussion of certain factors which are particularly relevant to durable goods expenditure. We then consider subjective or psychological factors, including the important elements of expectations and attitudes. Under the heading of "structural factors" we consider some aspects particularly relevant for the problem of aggregation. Even though the consumption propensities of particular groups or types of spending units might be stable, a change in the relative weights of the several groups can alter the aggregate relation between consumption and income (or other explanatory factors). Finally, we consider some factors which clearly affect consumption's role in the total economy by affecting the size of disposable income (the income variable relevant for individual behavior) in relationship to total output or GNP. The most important of these is fiscal policy. The chapter ends with a section which proposes a summary evaluation of the Keynesian consumption function in the light of post-Keynesian research and analysis.

## SOME "OBJECTIVE FACTORS" INFLUENCING CONSUMPTION

### The Rate of Interest

Although we have seen that an *a priori* case can be made that rational consumers will save more at high than at low interest rates, almost no one today believes this factor to be significant. There is no empirical evidence which clearly supports this Classical idea.[1]

### Sales Effort

The fact that an increase in total consumer demand for one good or class of goods may merely be at the expense of reduced demand for others is sometimes overlooked by those who extoll the virtues of advertising and other selling efforts as a means for increasing aggregate demand. Nevertheless, it is quite possible that an increase or decrease in the amount of selling effort may affect the total volume of consumer expenditures, given the level of income. Reasons for paying little attention to this in the theory of aggregate demand are perhaps, first, that there is no independent measure of the volume of effective selling effort; second, that this volume probably does not fluctuate much in the short run; and, third, that it has not (in the past, at least) been considered subject to social control.

### Relative Prices

Just as selling effort has often been dismissed from consideration as a factor influencing aggregate demand—in the belief that it can only

---

[1] Evidence sometimes adduced showing that savings held in one particular form— e.g., savings deposits in banks—are responsive to interest rates paid on such deposits is clearly meaningless for this purpose. For evidence from consumer surveys on the effect of higher interest rates on personal saving see *Consumer Optimism Weakening*, Foundation for Research on Human Behavior (July 1957), pp. 36–48, summarized in G. Katona, *The Powerful Consumer* (McGraw-Hill, 1960), p. 223.

*shift* demand from one product to another—so economists have usually ignored relative prices of different categories of goods as a factor affecting aggregate consumption. It can be demonstrated that this dismissal is unnecessary and illegitimate and that relative prices might well influence aggregate expenditure; [2] but there have been few specific hypotheses advanced as to the kinds of relative price changes that might affect aggregate consumption. Thus, as is the case with selling effort, we can admit a possible influence, but have no very specific hypotheses as to whether this influence is important or in what direction it operates.

### Capital Gains

Keynes gave specific recognition to the possibility that consumption spending might be influenced not only by income but by capital gains. In fact, he speculated that the American boom of the late twenties might have been intensified and prolonged by consumer spending which reflected the realized and unrealized capital gains which were being made in the stock market. At least one economist has attempted to include capital gains in a statistical consumption function.[3] Perhaps this involves an indirect recognition that consumption may be influenced by the stock of wealth, an idea to which we now turn.

### The Volume of Wealth

The total wealth position of consumers has been advanced as a possible important influence on consumer expenditure. The argument in this respect has been almost entirely *a priori.* Its original complete formulation was by Pigou,[4] who reasoned from an abstract model of consumer behavior. The proposed relationship follows directly from our *a priori* formulation developed earlier, in the appendix to Chapter X, which makes current utility depend on the stock of consumer wealth, current and future (the larger current wealth, the larger, *cet.par.,* will be future wealth, too). Since we hypothesized a diminishing marginal utility for each of the variables in the function, it should be immediately evident that the larger the stock of wealth, the lower its marginal utility; and therefore, the less the strength of the desire to add to future wealth through reducing current consumption. Put simply, the hypothesis is that,

[2] See G. Ackley and D. B. Suits, "Relative Price Changes and Aggregate Consumer Demand," *American Economic Review,* XL (December 1950), pp. 785–804, and, below, Chap. XX, pp. 576–580.

[3] Jan Tinbergen, *Statistical Testing of Business-Cycle Theories, vol. II, Business Cycles in the United States of America 1919–1932* (League of Nations, Geneva, 1939), pp. 35–40.

[4] See A. C. Pigou, *Employment and Equilibrium* (London, 1941), especially pp. 96–130. See also D. Patinkin, *Money, Interest, and Prices* (Row, Peterson, 1956).

other things equal, the more savings a man has, the less the strength of his desire to accumulate more. If two men were identical in their needs, tastes and incomes, but one had already (through past saving, inheritance, gift or windfall) acquired a large fortune, his incentive to *add* to his fortune by current saving will be less than the other man's desire to accumulate a fortune. Suppose that A's and B's incomes are both $10,000 (after taxes) and that they are in all other respects identical except that A has wealth of $100,000 and B has wealth of only $10,000. We might expect A to save, say, $1,000 and B to save more, perhaps $1,010, $1,200, or $2,000. The difficulty is that the *a priori* argument, even if we accept it with all of its limitations, cannot tell us whether $100,000 of additional wealth will increase a man's current consumption by $10 per year, $50, or $1,000. That is, it can provide no indication as to the quantitative magnitude of the effect. Yet this is what makes the variable of crucial or of trivial importance.

This can be illustrated by referring to one of the several contexts in which the influence of wealth has often been considered relevant.[5] Suppose that aggregate demand is insufficient to provide full employment, but that wages and prices are perfectly flexible, free to fall without limit so long as the supply of labor exceeds demand. This fall in wages and prices will increase the total (real) value of the public's holding of wealth. Part of consumer wealth is in the form of goods, land, or equities. The prices of such wealth can be expected to fall much in line with the fall in other prices, so that its real value will not increase. But some part of consumer wealth has a fixed money value. We refer, of course, to money itself and to certain forms of debt, particularly public debt.[6] A deflation of prices will, therefore, increase (in real terms) the wealth of consumers, to the extent that its money value is fixed. If a rising (real) value of wealth stimulates consumption, then there always is some fall in prices which will be adequate to stimulate consumption sufficiently to eliminate any deficiency of aggregate demand.

Thus, some assert, we have, in flexible prices, an infallible cure for deficient aggregate demand. This is called the "Pigou Effect," in honor of the first economist clearly to state the hypothesis.

But here is where the quantitative magnitude of the effect becomes important. Suppose that aggregate demand in an economy is presently

[5] For other contexts see G. Ackley, "The Wealth-Saving Effect," *Journal of Political Economy*, LIX (April 1951), pp. 154–61, and below, Chap. XIX, pp. 555–559.

[6] The price of private debt will not fall along with the price level either, but this should (tend to) cancel out, as the increased wealth of the creditor is offset by the decreased wealth—or increased negative wealth—of the debtor.

70, consisting of 50 consumption and 20 government expenditure and investment. With full employment, total output and income *could* be 100 (measured in present prices). Let us assume that the consumption function is

$$c = .5y + .2w - 85$$

where $c$ and $y$ are real consumption and income, and $w$ is the real value of consumer wealth (all measured in terms of present prices). Total wealth, $w$, consists of 250 in the form of money and government bonds, whose real value fluctuates in inverse proportion to the price level, $P$, and 250 in the form of goods and equities, whose prices are assumed to fluctuate with changes in prices of current output, so that their real value is constant. Inserting $y = 70$ and $w = 500$ into the above consumption function produces $c = 50$.

By how much would the price level have to fall in order to raise total real demand to 100, that is to raise real consumption from 50 to 80? We can calculate as follows:

$$c = 80 = .5(100) + .2(250 + \frac{250}{P}) - 85$$

$$80 = 50 + 50 + \frac{50}{P} - 85$$

$$65 = \frac{50}{P}$$

$$P = .769$$

Prices would have to fall by about 23 per cent, raising the real value of liquid wealth from 250 to 325, or the total value of wealth from 500 to 575. The increase in consumption resulting from this would be $.2 \times 75 = 15$. This would be subject to a multiplier of 2 (because the MPC = .5), accounting for the total necessary increase of 30 in consumption.

Suppose, however, that the consumption function were

$$c = .5y + .01w + 10$$

with the same initial values of $y$, $w$, and $c$ (70, 500, and 50). We can again calculate the fall in $P$ necessary to restore full employment, i.e., to raise $c$ to 80.

$$c = 80 = .5(100) + .01(250 + \frac{250}{P}) + 10$$

$$80 = 50 + 2.5 + \frac{2.5}{P} + 10$$

$$17.5 = \frac{2.5}{P}$$

$$P = .143$$

In this case prices would have to fall to about one-seventh of their original level. If the wealth effect were weaker, or if the ratio of liquid wealth to (full employment) consumer income were lower than we have assumed, the necessary fall in prices would be all the greater. While we might contemplate with equanimity a fall in prices of 23 per cent, a fall in prices of 86 per cent or more is another thing. Yet the *a priori* argument cannot tell us which of these or any other is the figure to expect.[7]

Thus, many economists would hesitate to claim, on the basis of the "Pigou Effect" alone, that social policy should be directed toward maximizing the degree of price flexibility in the expectation of solving thereby all problems of full employment. This is particularly true when we consider some of the problems of price flexibility raised above, on pp. 196–197, and, as well, some of the incidental social effects of wide price fluctuation, particularly on the distribution of wealth and income. Since the bulk of the liquid assets are owned by the relatively better-off segment of the community, this doctrine amounts to saying that, if there is an unemployment problem, we need to shift further the concentration of wealth into the hands of these already wealthy persons, in order to make them so well off that they will no longer feel so great a need to save.

This doctrine appears all the more dangerous to those who deny any *a priori* expectation of a positive wealth-effect on consumption. One psychologist, for example, points out that the wealth-effect argument assumes given tastes; yet the subject matter of the analysis is the accumulation of wealth, that is, a *change* in circumstance and position that can hardly help affecting one's "tastes." It is quite consistent with psychological theory that one's "taste" for wealth should increase the more of it one has, as one learns of its advantages.[8] Thus, the whole *a priori* basis of the wealth-effect is subject to challenge.

[7] Thomas Mayer, "The Empirical Significance of the Real Balance Effect," *Quarterly Journal of Economics*, LXXIII (May 1959), 275–91, approaches a measurement of the empirical significance of the Pigou effect by translating the changes in the real volume of wealth affected through price level changes into income (at 6 per cent), and applying to these an MPC of .7. His conclusion (after considering a number of qualifications) is that the Pigou effect is in practice of little empirical significance. See also A. Hansen, "The Pigouvian Effect," *Journal of Political Economy*, LIX (December 1951), 535–6.

[8] See G. Katona, *Psychological Analysis of Economic Behavior* (McGraw-Hill, 1951), pp. 91–3.

As we shall see in a later chapter, there are other contexts in which the wealth-effect may be relevant in addition to the one discussed here. Indeed, if a positive wealth-effect exists it might be more applicable in these other circumstances. In the relatively short-run context of "business cycle" fluctuations it would appear to have very little relevance, if only because, except in a few cases, cyclical price fluctuations have never been of substantial magnitude.

## The Stock of Money

One portion of total consumer wealth is held in the form of money. As such, the wealth effect already discussed would presumably be applicable to any change in consumer money-holdings, if such change were not offset by equivalent change in other wealth. Yet some economists argue (or imply) more than this—namely, that a change in consumer money-holdings which represents a mere change in the composition of a given (real) total of wealth will affect consumption. For example, in time of depression or unemployment, the central bank may engage in open market purchases of securities. These purchases are made either from the general public or from banks; if from the latter, it is hoped that such purchases may succeed in causing the banks in turn to purchase securities from the general public. In either case, the policy has the effect of increasing the public's liquidity. Former bond-holders become cash-holders. Such policy may well, as we have already seen, lower the rate of interest and thus affect investment and conceivably consumption. What we are now considering is the view that—whatever the effect through the interest rate on investment and consumption—a mere liquidity increase will also stimulate consumption directly.

The basis for this belief is far from clear. Reference is sometimes made to the fact that it is easier for a person to dissave if his wealth is in liquid form. He is then not protected from the temptation to spend beyond his income by the inconvenience and possible embarrassment or loss of first having to cash a nonliquid asset. One can grant the possible correctness of this without conceding that the effect would be of major importance. In the first place, it applies only to potential dissavers (who are, however, a fairly large fraction of the total body of consumers), not to those who could reduce their current saving without having to cash assets; in the second place, the "consumers" whose portfolios may be shifted in a more liquid direction by central bank open market purchases include, in important measure, trust funds, pension plans, insurance companies, endowed institutions, and a relatively small number of generally wealthy persons, for whom the dissaving temptation is hardly relevant.

Most frequently, the argument that consumption depends on money stocks (regardless of total wealth) is often merely a recrudescence of the naïve quantity theory, transplanted into the language of modern income analysis, and based on little more than a mystical belief that money tends to turn over at a constant rate against goods. More money, more spending. As we have seen in earlier chapters, a clear and logical structure of argument can be developed to support this conclusion, given a number of assumptions (some of which are of questionable realism). But the "sophisticated" quantity theory does not rest on any view that people are unable to avoid spending money if it is in their pockets or bank accounts. Rather it rests on the view that rational individuals do not prefer a barren form of wealth-holding to one which yields a return. That is, the "sophisticated" quantity theory works through the interest rate and investment, rather than through any direct effect on consumption.

But Keynes has made clear that in some circumstances rational consumers may willingly increase their cash holdings. No one is required to sell a bond to the central bank and hold cash instead. How then can the bank succeed in putting more cash into circulation? Simply by bidding bond prices high enough that some institutions or individuals who formerly preferred bonds to cash as a form of wealth-holding are shifted into the group who think bond prices unsafe and prefer cash. In the course of this process interest rates are lowered, and investment spending perhaps increased. A rise in consumption may thus result, through the income effect. But apart from this, is there any reason to suppose that the wealth which speculators have decided would be safer in cash form will now be dissipated by dissaving, or that positive saving will be reduced?

### Empirical Studies of the Influence of Liquid Assets

In recent years the possible influences of wealth and the stock of money or other liquid assets on consumption have been the subject of much theoretical discussion, and have even served as the basis for public policy recommendations. Yet the empirical validity of these arguments has been extremely difficult to establish. Several types of tests or measures of this influence have been attempted, but with results that are far from conclusive, owing to the peculiar difficulty of finding and interpreting relevant evidence.

The first type of evidence we have is from aggregate time series. No valid annual estimates covering any substantial periods of time exist for total consumer asset holdings. What we do have are estimates of consumer money-holdings and their total holdings of "liquid assets," usually defined to include currency, demand and time deposits, government securities, and saving and loan shares. Most statistical analyses have used this intermediate liquid-assets concept.

Some economists have used this series on liquid asset holdings as an *index* of *total* consumer wealth, on the supposition that changes in this series are closely correlated with changes in total wealth-holding. Whatever results are obtained can then either be interpreted as showing the influence of total wealth (as represented by liquid assets), or, alternatively, as showing the independent influence of liquid assets. As previously noted, the interpretation makes considerable difference for policy, for we can imagine changes in liquid asset position that leave total assets unchanged. Further, changes in holdings of money proper occurring as the result of the actions of the monetary authorities may not affect even the total of liquid assets, for increased or decreased money holdings may represent mere swaps for government securities held by the public, which are also "liquid assets." Thus whatever findings emerge have to be interpreted with care.

One principal difficulty with the use of time-series evidence on liquid assets and consumption is the fact that year-to-year fluctuations in such holdings are usually relatively small. During the war period, 1941–46, however, there was a very large jump in the level of consumer asset holdings. Again, after the war, the year-to-year fluctuations were relatively small. Since we have already observed that there was a considerable shift in the level of the simple consumption function between prewar and postwar, it is, of course, possible that this shift in the level of the simple function was caused by the large jump in liquid assets. But it is likewise possible that the difference in the levels of consumption between prewar and postwar that is not explainable by income alone is explained by some *other* factor whose level also shifted from the one period to the other; or that the war was responsible for a basic change in attitudes or tastes. One can improve the "fit" of a consumption function using both prewar and postwar data by simply inserting, along with income, a "dummy variable" which is given an arbitrary value of zero for all prewar years and a value of one for all postwar years. One cannot be positive that liquid assets are much more than such a dummy variable.

The studies using time series that will be presented here probably escape this difficulty. We refer first to the Klein-Goldberger statistical consumption function referred to above. The function, fitted to data for the years 1929–41 and 1946–52, is repeated here for convenience

$$C_t = -22.26 + .55W_t + .41P_t + .34A_t + .26C_{t-1} + .072L_{t-1} + .26N_t$$

where all data are expressed in billions of 1939 dollars, and $C$ represents consumer expenditures; $W$, $P$, and $A$ are the after-tax (disposable) incomes of wage earners, property holders, and farmers, respectively; $L_{t-1}$ is end-of-previous-year liquid-asset holdings; and $N$ is population. The coefficient for liquid asset holdings—0.072—is relatively low. It implies that an increase of one billion dollars in liquid asset holdings is associated, on the average, and other things equal, with an increase of 72 million dollars in consumer expenditures.[9]

The second study of the role of liquid assets is one by Zellner (also referred to earlier), using quarterly data entirely from the postwar period. Zellner's coefficient for liquid assets is much higher than Klein-Goldberger's, as for example in the following function

$$C_t = -21.91 + 0.708Y_t + 0.368L_{t-1}$$

where $C$, $Y$, and $L$ are consumption, disposable income and liquid assets, in 1947–49 prices. Data used were for 1947 through the first quarter of 1955. The liquid assets coefficient is almost seven times its standard error, and thus clearly significant. Other forms of functions fitted by Zellner give liquid asset coefficients ranging from 0.219 to 0.396. Zellner, in attempting to explain the difference between his estimates and Klein-Goldberger's, refers to several possible factors, including the possibility that the influence of liquid assets on consumption is greater in the postwar than in the prewar period,[10] and also the possibility that "the effects of a change in liquid assets may be exhausted *within* the period of a year; therefore the full effects of such a change do not show up when annual data are employed." [11] Over the period used by Zellner, liquid assets varied between 174 and 197 billions (in 1947–49 prices), considerably less than the variation of disposable income (175 to 228 billions). And since the coefficient applicable to liquid assets was only about half that applicable to income, this means that income was the most important explanatory factor. Still, liquid assets appeared to account for an ap-

---

[9] Although the Klein-Goldberger function uses both prewar and postwar data, it is probably free from the difficulty discussed in the previous paragraph because of the fact that the lagged consumption term—$C_{t-1}$—picks up most of the shift in level from prewar to postwar periods.

[10] This is supported by Suits (see fn. 1, Chap. XI).

[11] *Op.cit.*, p. 565.

preciable part of the variation in consumer spending. However, if we accept the thesis of Chapter XI, that the short-period (e.g., quarterly) fluctuations of consumption are essentially erratic or random, we should put little reliance on Zellner's statistical findings, since he arbitrarily rejected all forms of consumption functions which yielded a negative marginal propensity to consume, even though such functions were fitted by statistical techniques which are theoretically superior to the techniques used in functions which he accepted.

A second source of evidence concerning the influence of liquid assets on consumption comes from cross-section or budget-study data. Particularly from the studies of the Michigan Survey Research Center, we can assemble information on the asset positions of different spending units in a scientific sample of the population, along with data on the incomes and spending and saving behavior of these spending units. Here again, however, the only really usable asset data relate to liquid assets (other than currency), although we can also sort these units on the basis of their ownership of homes, automobiles, or unincorporated businesses.

Before considering this evidence, we should note carefully four conceptual difficulties which limit the conclusions we can draw from budget-study evidence. Suppose that we sort families into two groups, within any income bracket: those having large liquid (or total) asset holdings and those having small holdings. The hypothesis is that, other things equal, the families with larger asset holdings would be found to be spending relatively more and saving less. Yet we might find exactly the contrary and still not reject the hypothesis. For the families in the two groups— even though identical in income and all other measurable respects—may be different kinds of people, i.e., have different tastes. The large asset holders may save more (not less) because they are more thrifty, more provident, more cautious than the others, and this is precisely why they have already succeeded in accumulating the larger asset holdings. Certainly, there is no reason to suppose that all families are alike in their feelings about the usefulness of having the protection of large asset accumulations. The hypothesis which is to be tested is that if *all* families (or a random distribution of all families), thrifty and spendthrifty alike, were to hold more assets than they do, they would save less. The data do not permit us to test this hypothesis directly.

Second, any statistical explanation of the differences in spending and saving among families needs to call upon a large number of demographic variables (age, marital status, number of children, rural or urban residence, etc.), and possession of liquid assets is highly intercorrelated with many of these other factors, as well as with income. Properly to sort out the *separate and independent* influence of liquid assets is very difficult.

Third, we need to beware of the interpretation given to any positive correlation between liquid assets at the beginning of a period and the spending of a subsequent period. If consumers plan to purchase expensive durable goods for cash (rather than on credit), they must first accumulate a liquid balance to make the necessary payment. The larger-than-normal cash balance may thus be *caused* by the subsequent expenditure rather than the other way around. If we compared cash balances at the end of a period with spending during the preceding period, we might find just the opposite—persons who have just made large purchases have reduced their cash balances below normal. Perhaps the best test would be to use an average of beginning and ending liquid assets to find whether the persons with larger average balances spend more of their incomes than those with smaller asset balances. This has never been tried.

Finally, whatever relationship we may discover between interfamily *differences* in asset holding and interfamily *differences* in spending cannot automatically be assumed to reveal what would happen if there were an increase in total liquid asset holdings. The problem here is identical with that of going from a budget-study consumption-income relationship to a consumption function predicting the result of a change in aggregate income—the problem of the "relative income" versus "absolute income" interpretation of cross-section data, discussed on pages 223–224.

With all these reservations one may wonder whether cross-section data have any usefulness at all for this purpose. Probably they can make some contribution. Although some users of these data may have ignored the problems just described, we should not neglect the evidence the data provide so long as we keep the necessary reservations in mind.

The studies by L. R. Klein and J. N. Morgan [12] are the only ones to which specific reference will be made here. Using variance analysis, Morgan discovered that possession of liquid assets was negatively associated with consumption, rather than positively, as the hypothesis suggested. This he interpreted as the result of the circumstance covered by our first qualification above—possession of liquid assets is a test which sorts high-savers from low-savers. But he found that for lower-income families, and particularly for families with declining incomes, possession

[12] In *Contributions of Survey Methods to Economics,* L. R. Klein, ed. (Columbia University Press, 1954).

of liquid assets is positively associated with spending. He notes, however, that this may reflect in part the third of our qualifications—assets have been accumulated to finance a subsequent large purchase.[13] Klein fits cross-section consumption functions to data for certain carefully defined and relatively homogeneous classes of consumers. He finds significant liquid asset coefficients in the range of .21–.25. Confining the analysis to those units with income *decreases,* the coefficients are higher: .25–.31; while for those with income increases the coefficient is between zero and .06.[14]

Although the evidence surveyed, both from time series and cross-section studies, is far from conclusive, it is at least consistent with the hypothesis that consumption spending is appreciably affected by the possession of liquid assets (money? total wealth?). Nevertheless, the picture is sufficiently unclear that one may properly remain skeptical whether it provides an adequate basis for policy recommendations, particularly because the evidence does not specifically bear on the contexts to which the policy recommendations relate—i.e., the effect of price level fluctuations on asset values (the Pigou effect), or the effects of liquidity *per se* (monetary policy).

### Deferred Demand

In the immediate postwar period, there was much discussion of the extent to which consumer spending represented a backlog of pent-up demand resulting from wartime restraints on spending. As indicated earlier, consumer spending, at least relative to income, was abnormally low during the war years, for reasons that were quite obvious. If consumers are consistently prevented from buying what they would like to buy, do they then make up for this deprivation by spending at a higher rate relative to income once the obstacles are removed? Full discussion of this issue would take us farther afield than its importance for peacetime situations would justify. Nevertheless, some interesting theoretical points are involved. For example, it is closely tied in with our previous discussion of wealth and liquid assets.

Although taxes were greatly increased during the war, consumer disposable incomes nevertheless grew substantially in relationship to the limited available supply of consumer goods. Consumers got goods in an amount which, in effect, represented the residual between the total production of the economy and what was taken for government (i.e., mostly military)

[13] *Op.cit.,* pp. 185–6.
[14] *Op.cit.,* pp. 210, 245–7.

use and necessary investment. The difference between what consumers would have liked to have spent at the levels of disposable incomes they enjoyed and the amount of goods available was a measure of the "inflationary gap" in the consumer sector, which had to be "suppressed" by direct controls. Consumers came out of the war period holding an accumulation of saving substantially swollen by the "forced saving" of the war period. These savings constituted a growth in consumer wealth relative to the growth of incomes. Even though incomes grew, wealth had grown faster, as a result of the abnormally high percentages of income saved.

One might therefore identify the deferred demand for consumer goods with those "excess" wealth holdings relative to the level of income. This excess would be expected to result for some period in an elevation of consumption relative to income, until the previously excessive savings were eliminated through a sufficiently long period of abnormally low saving out of current incomes, or through an inflation which reduced the real value of the liquid portion of consumer assets.

Had taxes been increased sufficiently during the war to reduce consumer disposable incomes to the point at which consumers would not have wished to buy more goods than were available for them, there might have been no need for direct controls to avoid inflation, and there would surely have been no excess savings to be carried over into the postwar period. Also, with such high tax revenues, the government would have run little or no deficit. (Indeed a surplus might have resulted from so high a level of taxation.) We do not discuss here the question whether this would have been either a possible or a preferable way to have financed the war. We only point out that there would then have been no abnormal asset accumulation by consumers.

In the absence of this level of taxation there were, necessarily, abnormal asset accumulations. The particular *form* which these accumulations took depended on the extent to which government deficits were financed by borrowing from the non-bank public versus the extent to which they were financed by borrowing (directly or indirectly) from banks. In fact, a very large part of the borrowing was from banks, and consequently the assets which consumers accumulated were very heavily in the form of bank deposits. The excess consumer accumulation of assets could therefore be identified in important measure with a rise in the stock of money. This permitted many economists to "explain" the high postwar level of consumer spending in terms of a rise in the stock of money.

Yet it is not obvious that this explanation is satisfactory. Suppose, for example, that the same "inadequate" levels of taxation had been used, but, either through compulsion or by making their terms more attractive, more bonds had been sold to the public. Consumers would then have come out of the war period with the same abnormal increment of their wealth position, but its form would have been less liquid.[15] Would spending behavior have been different? This depends on the extent to which the *liquidity* of consumer assets instead of or in addition to their *volume* exerts an important influence on spending. It seems quite impossible, merely on the basis of the postwar experience, to reach any conclusion on this matter.

Suppose, however, that deficit financing whether in the form of money creation or the selling of bonds to the public had been avoided, and taxes had been raised sufficiently to avoid any excess consumer asset accumulation. Can we conclude that there would surely then have been no pent-up postwar demand? Although consumers would then have come out of the war period with no excess accumulation of assets, liquid or less liquid, they would still have come out of the war period unhappy and dissatisfied with the consumption levels to which they had been held. There might still have been a "bulge" of high consumer spending, as consumers tried to make up for previous deprivations. One might thus argue that the high postwar consumption was not necessarily associated with an increment either in total wealth position or in money holdings, but merely with a backlog of frustrated consumption desires. In fact, we had all three—higher wealth, higher liquidity, and a sense of deprivation —and their disentangling presents insuperable problems. Perhaps we can agree that, because postwar consumers had not only the accumulated *desire* but the accumulated *means* to consume, the postwar boom of consumer spending was, to some unknown extent, the greater than if only unsatisfied desires had accumulated. And, to some uncertain extent it was the greater because the accumulated means were in more rather than less liquid form. This still leaves the *relative* importance of these factors uncertain.[16]

[15] It should be pointed out that the "E-Bonds" sold to consumers had a fixed repurchase price, and could be cashed at any time without danger or loss. They were, therefore, practically as "liquid" as currency or bank deposits.

[16] When we refer to the "means" to consume we should not give the impression that there was, on balance, any net consumer dissaving after the war. The rate of saving was, to be sure, abnormlly low, particularly in 1946 and 1947. But there was not net asset decumulation. The "means" were not, on balance, drawn upon for purchases. It should, however, be recognized that the net saving of consumers as a group involved dissaving by probably a majority of individual consumers. The wartime asset accumulations (whatever their form) facilitated this, as did, of course, access to consumer credit (see below).

When we consider what we have called the backlog of unsatisfied desires, we need to sort out the nature of the goods whose normal purchase was deferred by wartime nonavailability, for the deprivation may have very different subsequent effects depending on where the shortages were concentrated. Some kinds of consumption—e.g., basic food intake in calories, vitamins, etc.—were not impaired, nor were there serious shortages of apparel and household textiles. But consumption of some particular foods and textile products was greatly reduced, e.g., beefsteaks, white shirts. Suppose a person who likes steaks has none for five years. Once they become available, he may eat beefsteak every night for a week, abnormally often for a month. But he does not, probably, now consume steaks in a number in excess of his normal consumption by an amount equal to his five-year deficiency; and he certainly does not consume this many extra steaks without reducing his consumption of other meats. In other words, we cannot assume that there can be any large deferred demand for nondurable consumer goods.

In fact, the greatest wartime deprivation for consumers was in durable goods. It was with respect to their materials (e.g., steel and copper) and productive facilities (e.g., automobile plants) where the greatest diversion to military production occurred. Consumers were therefore, in large measure, forced to postpone normal replacement of automobiles and appliances, and the normal growth in the use of these goods was prevented. To a much greater extent than for nondurables, this deferment of replacement and growth does represent a cumulative backlog of demand. By the end of the war there was not only the normal, continuing replacement demand for the durable goods that were relatively new at the beginning of the war, and whose replacement would normally have been expected in the postwar period, but, in addition, the deferred replacement demands of the war period. Thus it is in the durable goods area that the greatest importance of deferred demand must have been concentrated. This deferred demand supported durable goods markets at abnormal levels for a number of years after the war.[17] This brings us to the point at which special attention needs to be concentrated on the consumption of durables.

## THE INSTABILITY OF DURABLE CONSUMPTION SPENDING

It is an important fact that the short-run instability of consumption expenditures in relationship to income is largely concentrated in the area

---

[17] For efforts to calculate the extent of the deferred replacement demand, see articles by L. J. Atkinson, in the *Survey of Current Business,* for April 1948, pp. 15–21; and June 1950, pp. 5–10.

of consumer durables. This is certainly to be expected. The logic of the consumption function would suggest that it is the *current services* rendered by durable goods which are desired in an amount related to current income. A very modest change in the desired level of current services of durable goods can lead to sharp changes in their rate of purchase; and considerable irregularity in their purchase from year to year is consistent with only modest changes in the volume of current services rendered by consumers' stocks of durables, for these stocks are the accumulation of a number of years' purchases. Thus factors affecting the *timing* of purchase of durable goods can significantly affect aggregate demand without representing any considerable irregularity in the relationship of current consumption of the *services* of durable goods to income.

James N. Morgan has argued, indeed, that expenditures on consumer durables (including repairs and additions to houses) should be considered a separate category of income disposition, in contrast to (a) ordinary "down-the-drain" consumption spending, (b) contractual saving (life insurance, mortgage repayments, annuity purchase, etc.), and (c) liquid saving. He suggests that most of the year-to-year variability in consumption expenditure consists of shifts between durable expenditures and liquid saving. His research [18] suggests that expenditures on durables (a) constitute an almost uniform percentage of income for all income groups; (b) depend heavily, for the individual unit, on demographic factors, particularly age and number of years married; (c) fluctuate over time in response to external events and changes in consumer attitudes; (d) are sticky when income drops, but very flexible upward when income rises; (e) seem not to be importantly influenced by liquid assets or the family's expressed willingness to use consumer credit.

## Consumer Stocks of Durables

Although not a factor investigated by Morgan, other studies suggest that purchases of durables may be influenced significantly by the size of the existing stock of durable goods held by consumers, and by the precise age composition of this stock. These factors were implicit in our discussion of postwar deferred demand. Demand for durables was high in the postwar period because (a) consumer stocks of durables had either shrunk during the war or had grown less than in relationship to consumer demand for their services (based on income); and (b) the stock contained only relatively old units.

[18] "Consumer Investment Expenditures," *American Economic Review*, XLVIII (December 1958), 874–902.

Those who emphasize these factors in the explanation of consumer demand for durables in more normal times reason similarly. Suppose, for example, that consumers are heavily stocked with new automobiles, as a result of abnormally large sales during the one or two immediately preceding years. One can reason, therefore, that automobile sales will now be abnormally low quite regardless of income or any other factors.[19]

One need not accept this as an exclusive explanation to recognize its importance as a factor influencing the volume of durable goods sales. For example, a recent econometric study makes the stock of automobiles on the road a variable of considerable significance for explaining new purchases of automobiles, along with consumer incomes, relative prices of new and used cars and of cars relative to goods in general, and consumer credit terms.[20] Still others disparage the importance of stocks by emphasizing style and performance changes, and consumers' comprehension and acceptance of them, as important factors in the demand for durables. In other words, obsolescence can be as important as physical wearing out in creating a demand for new durable goods by persons who already own them.[21]

In the latest versions of the econometric model used at the University of Michigan for annual forecasts of the economic outlook, accumulated stocks appear as variables (with a negative influence on current demand) in the demand equations both for automobiles and for other consumer durables (as well as in the investment demand equations for housing, plant and equipment, and inventories). The equations used for 1959 forecasts are as follows:

$$A = .103Y - .145S_a + .383M_a + .607T + K_a$$
$$D = .116Y - .046S_d - .005M_d + .439T + K_d$$

where A is current demand for new and net used automobiles; D the current demand for other durables; Y disposable income; $S_a$ and $S_d$ the current stocks of automobiles and other durables, respectively; $M_a$ and $M_d$ the number of months' duration of average automobile and other durables installment terms, respectively; T time; and $K_a$ and $K_d$ are ap-

[19] K. E. Boulding, in "An Application of Population Analysis to the Automobile Population of the United States" (*Kyklos,* 1955, pp. 109–24), analyzes the automobile market in just these terms. Among other things, he argues that the absence of new car purchases during the war created a replacement vacuum 10 or 12 years later (the normal life of an automobile before scrappage is of about this duration).

[20] See D. B. Suits, "The Demand for New Automobiles in the United States, 1929–1956," *Review of Economics and Statistics,* XL (August 1958), pp. 273–80.

[21] See E. Mueller, "The Desire for Innovations in Household Goods," in *Consumer Behavior, Research on Consumer Reactions,* L. H. Clark, ed. (Harper Bros., 1958).

propriate constants. (All variables except $M_a$, $M_d$, and T are in billions of 1954 dollars.) [22]

## Terms of Consumer Credit

In discussing factors associated with automobile purchases, consumer credit terms were mentioned. The terms of such credit have often been considered to have a significant influence on consumer purchases of durables, and to constitute possibly a *strategic* variable because of their susceptibility to social control, both through general monetary policy and through direct regulation.

Consumer credit on reasonable terms, available to persons of moderate means, is a relatively new phenomenon in the United States. It is now extensively used (primarily in the purchase of durable goods), not only by persons who wish to spend beyond their incomes and have no assets to cash, but also by persons with substantial asset holdings—even "liquid asset" holdings. Perhaps more remarkable is the fact that it is used by persons who are not even dissavers—i.e., by persons who could purchase out of current income the items for which they use credit.[23] Because so many users of consumer credit would appear to be able to buy even if it were not available, there is debate as to how effective the regulation of consumer credit terms may be. No completely satisfactory conclusion has yet been reached as to the effectiveness of the controls used in the U.S. during and after World War II.[24] Nevertheless, the volume of consumer durable goods purchases so financed is now so great that few would deny the importance of the cost and availability or nonavailability of credit. Whatever the motives families have for the use of credit (and they are varied) instead of cashing assets or waiting until the full price has been accumulated, the desire and ability to purchase is surely subject to some degree of modification depending on the cost and availability of the use of consumer credit.

There is much agreement that the interest rate paid on installment credit—i.e., the pure cost—is of relatively less significance than such mat-

[22] See Daniel B. Suits, "The Outlook for 1960 as Forecast by an Econometric Model of the United States," *Seventh Annual Conference on the Economic Outlook* (University of Michigan, Department of Economics, 1959), pp. 53–65. For purposes of forecasting efficiency, the equations were actually estimated and applied in terms of first differences; however, if converted to the more customary form, the equations would appear as shown above.

[23] For details, see J. B. Lansing, E. S. Maynes, and M. Kreinin, "Factors Associated with the Use of Consumer Credit" in *Consumer Installment Credit*, Pt. II, Vol. I, Board of Governors of the Federal Reserve System, 1957, pp. 487–520.

[24] See, for example, the papers presented in *Consumer Installment Credit*, Pt. II, Vol. II (Federal Reserve).

ters as the size of required down-payments, the length of the period over which the balances must be repaid, and the credit standards employed in judging request for credit extension.

It should be recognized, first, that changes in these terms of availability can have only a temporary, one-time effect on the volume of consumer purchases. If the terms become easier, greater use can be made of credit, both by families who were previously unable to use it, and by families already buying on credit. This greater use permits an increased volume of consumer spending, as purchases occur earlier than they otherwise would. Eventually, however, everyone who is in a position to take advantage of the easier terms will have done so, and a new equilibrium may be established with a higher rate of new credit extensions offset by a higher rate of repayments resulting from the previous more liberal grants of credit. On the other hand, a tightening of terms will result in a smaller volume of new extensions while the burden of completing payments under already existing contracts continues to exercise its depressing effect on current expenditure. Eventually, however, a new equilibrium may be established with a lower volume of borrowing, of repayments, and of total credit outstanding. How long it would take for a new equilibrium to be established when terms change depends in part on the extent to which the same families continuously resort to use of credit rather than a constantly shifting group within the population. Much empirical research needs to be done before very reliable generalizations can be formulated.

The above argument shows that corresponding to each possible set of terms of availability of credit there is some maximum possible use of credit. What we do not know is the extent to which easing the terms of credit automatically results in a growth in the use of credit toward this maximum. That is, we do not know to what extent consumer credit operates as a *causal* as opposed to a *permissive* factor in consumer spending. Take, for example, the tremendous expansion in automobile purchases in 1955, a factor contributing to the "boom" conditions enjoyed by the U.S. economy in that year (and to some extent in 1956 and 1957, as capital facilities for the production of automobiles and of parts and materials for automobiles may have been expanded on the basis of the pressure on such facilities in 1955). The sale of 7.2 million new automobiles in 1955 (as compared with an average of 5.3 million units in 1949–54) involved a large expansion in the use of consumer credit. It is also clear that there was a substantial easing of credit terms in 1955— lower down-payments, longer periods for repayment—as opposed to previous years. But was the boom in sales *caused* by the easing of credit terms or merely permitted by it? That is, were there special factors (e.g., model changes) that led people to *want* substantially more new cars in that year, a desire which easy credit made it possible for them to fulfill (and which might even have been largely fulfilled had credit terms not been eased)? Or was it the easy credit alone that caused the expansion of sales? If, in another year, a similar easing of credit terms should occur, would the boom in sales automatically follow?

We can surely agree that the existence of consumer credit facilities *permits* a greater instability in the rate of purchasing of durable goods than would be the case were no consumer credit available. But we do not know to what extent *changes* in terms of availability *cause* changes in purchasing.[25]

## PSYCHOLOGICAL FACTORS

To isolate certain factors affecting consumption under the heading "psychological" is, of course, absurd. The relationships already considered between disposable income, wealth, etc., and consumer expenditures are relationships descriptive of behavior, presumably involving either consciously-adjusting or habitual forms of human action. That is, such causal factors as income, wealth, terms of credit, are specific, quantifiable "economic" variables, which affect the dependent variable, consumer spending, via some human comprehension and response. The contrast between these relationships and those here to be discussed presumably is that the latter involve as causal factors variables which are not themselves economic. They consist of basic values, attitudes, states of mind. To refer to one influence on consumption spending as economic and the second as psychological merely means that in the first case we think that we recognize some stable characteristics of human response, so that we can go from economic cause to economic effect without specific attention to the cognitive, emotional, and muscular processes which form the link. (However, the psychologist may show us that this neglect of the psychological process by which this link is made is often a source of error in our conclusions.) In the second case, we are unable to explain (i.e., have no acceptable theory about) which factors in the environment determine the states of mind, etc., which are the immediate precondition

[25] On the above issues, see the Federal Reserve study previously referred to, especially, in Pt. I, Vol. I, Chap. 7 (M. Moss), 9 (P. S. Taylor), 11 (P. F. Smith and others), and, in Pt. II, Vol. I, the papers by D. D. Humphrey, E. Miller, G. Katona, and J. Tobin.

of the behavior. Not knowing the more basic causes we settle upon the intermediate link in the chain and call it a "psychological" influence on consumption. We consider some such influences in this section.

### Keynes' "Subjective Factors"

Keynes discussed the various "motives" for saving, under such headings as "Precaution, Foresight, Calculation, Improvement, Independence, Enterprise, Pride and Avarice"; and corresponding "motives to consumption such as Enjoyment, Shortsightedness, Generosity, Miscalculation, Ostentation and Extravagance." He called these "subjective factors," and considered that the basic attitudes and values summarized under these headings were not liable to significant change in the short run. Few would argue with this judgment, but its converse—that these basic factors may alter significantly in the long run—is often ignored by those who search for a stable long-run consumption function. Economists are prone to seek some simple explanation which will link in a single formula the behavior of members of several successive generations, over time periods long enough for the standards of good taste, the cultural values, and the patterns of emulation to alter significantly. It would indeed be strange if the profound changes which have occurred in the American way of life between 1890 and 1960 had not also altered the relationship between consumption and income. Indeed, the very meaning of any comparison between incomes at two such distant points of time is questionable. No one expects to find any single formula which will explain consumption differences between such diverse civilizations as those of present-day U.S., China, Peru, and France. Yet the cultural differences between the U.S. of 1890 and 1960 are almost as profound as between any two of these contemporary societies.

Needless to say, these subjective and cultural factors cannot be reduced to any numerical scale and introduced as an additional variable in a consumption function, but must be considered as changing the shape and level of the function.

### Expectations and Attitudes

The simple logic of rational behavior suggests that a consumer who expects an increase either in his income or in the price level should consume more than one who expects no change or a decrease. Explanations of events based on income or price level expectations have occasionally figured in business cycle literature and, of course, also in the explanations for serious inflation. In case of the latter, for example, it has been suggested that continually rising prices engender strong expectations of further rise, causing consumers (as well as businesses) to attempt to increase the real volume of their spending, leading to increased aggregate demand, further upward movement of prices, more positive expectations of further rise, and so on in endless chain. The reverse possibility (hyperdeflation) follows with equal logic.

Keynes apparently accepted this logic but appeared to feel that expectations could be ignored in the analysis of aggregate consumption because, he said, with reference to income expectations, such expectations probably cancel out. At any given time, some families may expect higher incomes but others will expect lower (thinking, apparently, of the expectations that relate to the family life cycle or to the changing fortunes of individual industries or skills). Although he referred to price expectations as affecting business spending behavior, he made no such mention in the case of consumers. Perhaps he thought that these, too, cancelled out.

Theorists other than Keynes have not treated expectations in such cavalier fashion. Indeed, in the analysis of many members of the "Stockholm School" of Swedish economists, the relationship between income (or any other variable) and consumption spending is always explicitly formulated as a relationship between *expected* income and the behavior to be explained. To isolate expected income as the causal factor contributes to our analysis only if we can say something significant about expected income. Among the questions we must answer are these: (1) Is expected income frequently different from current income? (If not, we might just as well use current income.) (2) Does a consumer whose expected and current incomes are not the same spend differently than one for whom expected and current incomes are equal, and, if so, how? (Unless the expectations influence behavior it makes no difference that income expectations exist.) (3) Does the relationship between current and expected income change over time on the average for significant groups of the spending population? (If this relationship were reasonably stable, we could still ignore expectations for aggregate behavior even though we would need them to explain individual behavior.) (4) Finally, and most difficult, what determines changes in the relationship of current and expected income? (If we have no theory about the determination of expectations, we are left with expectations as an autonomous, "psychological" influence on consumption.) Parallel questions could be asked about price expectations.

Recent research, particularly at the University of Michigan Survey

Research Center, sheds considerable light on these questions. But in the process it raises many new problems. In answer to the first and third questions above, it is now abundantly clear both that expected incomes and prices are frequently different from current levels for many American consumers, and that the relationships between current and expected incomes and prices change materially over time. This is shown, for example, in Tables 12–1 and 12–2.

Table 12–1 compares people's expectations regarding their "financial situation" a year hence, at four selected recent dates. It shows considerable improvement between October 1954, at the end of the mild recession of that year, and June 1955, only eight months later. Thereafter successive surveys revealed a gradual downward shift of income expectations (although they remained very favorable in absolute terms), terminating in fall 1957, when the recession of that year was clearly

**TABLE 12–1.   Consumers' Expectations Regarding
Their Financial Situation a Year Hence**

| Expected Change in Financial Situation * | October 1954 | June 1955 | November– December, 1957 | May–June 1958 |
|---|---|---|---|---|
| Better Off | 31% | 37% | 28% | 30% |
| Same | 43 | 41 | 48 | 45 |
| Uncertain | 14 | 15 | 14 | 14 |
| Worse Off | 11 | 6 | 9 | 10 |
| Not Ascertained | 1 | 1 | 1 | 1 |
| Total | 100% | 100% | 100% | 100% |

* The question was: "Now looking ahead—do you think that a year from now you people will be better off financially, or worse off, or just about the same as now?"

Source: *Consumer Attitudes and Inclinations to Buy,* June 1958. Press release of Survey Research Center, University of Michigan, July 17, 1958.

underway. It is interesting to note that there was, on balance, no further deterioration of income expectations in the subsequent six months, despite an intensification of the recession.

Table 12–2 shows that price expectations are even more volatile than income expectations. This is illustrated even more dramatically by comparing price expectations for household goods and clothing in November 1951 and November–December 1952. Over this period the percentage expecting that prices would rise fell from 52 to 6 per cent, the percentage expecting no change rose from 19 to 40 per cent, and the percentage expecting that prices would fall rose from 6 to 26 per cent.[26]

[26] G. Katona and E. Mueller, *Consumer Attitudes and Demand, 1950–1952,* Survey Research Center, 1953, p. 25.

Thus, it is clear that expected prices and incomes do have an independent existence and that their relationship to current prices and incomes is subject to major alteration over time. But we still need to know

TABLE 12–2.  Price Trends for Household Goods and Clothing
Expected Over Next Year

| Expected Change in Prices * | October 1954 | June 1955 | November– December, 1957 | May–June 1958 |
|---|---|---|---|---|
| Will Rise | 14% | 27% | 44% | 28% |
| No Change Expected: or Some Rise, Some Fall | 49 | 46 | 33 | 39 |
| Uncertain, Depends | 4 | 9 | 9 | 13 |
| Will Fall | 32 | 18 | 13 | 19 |
| Not Ascertained | 1 | 0 | 1 | 1 |
| Total | 100% | 100% | 100% | 100% |

* The question was: "What do you expect prices of household items and clothing will do during the next year or so—stay where they are, go up, or go down?"

SOURCES: same as Table 12–1.

whether these expectations affect behavior and if so, how. Table 12–3 summarizes some evidence on differences of spending as between consumers whose income expectations differ.

As might be hypothesized, those expecting higher incomes dissaved more frequently and saved less frequently than those expecting incomes to fall. The differences are not striking, but they are consistent. Thus,

TABLE 12–3.  Relation Between Expected Changes in Income and
Proportions of Income Saved, 1948

(percentage distribution of nonfarm spending units in each group)

| Rate of Saving in 1948 | Next Year's Income Expected to be | | |
|---|---|---|---|
| | Higher | About the Same | Lower |
| Negative | 36% | 28% | 26% |
| Zero | 3 | 8 | 4 |
| Positive | | | |
| 1–19% of income | 41 | 47 | 47 |
| 20% or more of income | 20 | 17 | 23 |
| Total | 100% | 100% | 100% |

SOURCE: G. Katona, *Psychological Analysis of Consumer Behavior*, McGraw-Hill, 1951, p. 157. The source gives similar data for 1947.

we might conclude not only that consumers' income expectations do change independently of current income but also that these changes appear to influence spending behavior.

Evidence regarding the relationship of price expectations to spending and saving is, however, far less clear. Table 12–4 shows, in fact, that in 1950–52, more of those who expected prices would increase (these

TABLE 12–4.  Relation Between Price Expectations for the Coming Twelve Months and Opinions of Buying Conditions for Household Goods

(average of four surveys, 1950–1952)

| Opinions of Buying Conditions * | Expected Prices Over the Coming Twelve Months for Household Goods and Clothing † | | |
|---|---|---|---|
| | Increase | No Change Expected | Decrease |
| Good time to buy | 30% | 35% | 26% |
| Pro-con; uncertain | 25 | 24 | 21 |
| Bad time to buy | 45 | 41 | 53 |
| Total | 100% | 100% | 100% |

* The question was: "Do you think this is a good time or a bad time to buy such large household items (furniture, house furnishings, rugs, refrigerators, stoves, radios, and things like that)?"

† The question was: "What do you think prices of household items and clothing will do during the next year or so—stay where they are, go up or go down?"

Source: G. Katona and E. Mueller, *Consumer Attitudes and Demand, 1950–52,* p. 72.

constituted about 40 per cent of the sample) thought that this was a bad time than thought that it was a good time to buy. Among those who expected prices to decrease (about 20 per cent of the sample) only a slightly larger percentage thought that it was a bad time to buy than among those expecting price increases. While there is some differential impact of price expectations, it is striking that people can simultaneously (a) expect prices to increase, yet (b) think it a bad time to buy.

Further analysis shows that spending behavior and spending intentions (and judgments whether it is a "good time to buy") are influenced by a variety of attitudes and expectations other than simply expected incomes and prices. The consumer's general feeling of security or insecurity, his satisfaction or lack of satisfaction with recent economic (and political) developments, his longer term prognosis for general business conditions (including the likelihood of a severe depression) all enter into his willingness to make other than routine expenditures.

Study of the relationship between a general index of consumer attitudes (combining the responses to a half-dozen measures of consumer optimism or pessimism) and subsequent spending on durable goods has proceeded at several levels at the University of Michigan Survey Research Center. One level of analysis relates measures of these attitudes, obtained from successive cross-sections of the population, to changes in expenditures on durable goods, as measured by the Department of Commerce. Some results are presented in Figure 12–1. It is clear that the

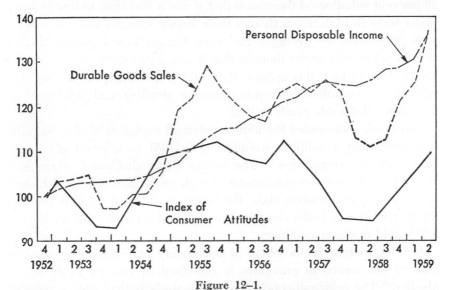

Figure 12–1.
(Copy of a figure prepared by the Institute for Social Research, University of Michigan, and reproduced with its permission.)

index of consumer attitudes is more closely related to durable goods expenditures than is disposable income; and, at least at times, changes in attitudes appear to have led changes in spending.

A second level of investigation relates to the attitudes and spending behavior of identical consumer units over successive reinterview periods. A study by Eva Mueller shows clearly that, at least in some periods, there is clear evidence of a positive association between the index of attitudes for individual units and the same units' spending on durable goods.[27]

One very important influence on consumers' willingness to buy appears to be their conception of what has been happening to prices (as op-

[27] "Effects of Consumer Attitudes on Purchases," *American Economic Review,* XLVII (December 1957), pp. 946–65.

posed to what is expected to happen in the future). Resentment over past price increases, or satisfaction with previous price stability appear to be closely associated with spending behavior. Thus, in June 1951, only 22 per cent of consumers thought it a good time to buy large household goods, and 53 per cent thought it a bad time to buy. This is despite the fact that 39 per cent of the same families expected further price increases in these items, and only 13 per cent expected prices to remain the same or fall. When asked to explain why it was a bad time to buy, 48 per cent volunteered the reason that it was a bad time to buy because prices were so high. Even though their money incomes had risen along with prices (on the average) and even though they expected further rises in prices, consumers thought that it was a bad time to buy durable goods. And, in fact, this opinion that 1951 was a bad time to buy was reflected in a considerable drop in consumer spending, and "soft" markets for almost all durable goods in 1951.

This result confounded the almost universal expectation of economists that inflationary conditions would exist in 1951 as a result of rapidly rising defense expenditures.[28] The Survey Research Center, whose surveys revealed consumer resentment at high prices and a general feeling of uncertainty and caution about the future, was almost alone in predicting that what was being described in mid-1951 as a "temporary buying lull" would probably continue.

A fuller analysis of the effect of inflationary or deflationary expectations of consumers on purchases is contained in another study by E. Mueller.[29] The principal conclusion of this study is that, during most of the post-World War II period in the United States, inflation has acted as a deterrent to consumer spending. That is, price increases have been resented, and this resentment has tended to curtail consumer spending. Although consumers' thinking about inflation is, of course, subject to change, as their experience with it multiplies, it seems clear that, up to the present, consumers have behaved in a stabilizing fashion. Had consumers reacted to inflation and to the expectation of inflation in the manner usually assumed by economists, their behavior would have added fuel to the flames of inflation. Instead, their behavior appears to have, in general, had a dampening effect.

Students interested in pursuing more closely the survey results regarding consumer attitudes and expectations will find a growing literature

[28] See John P. Lewis, "The Lull that Came to Stay," *Journal of Political Economy*, LXIII (February 1955), pp. 1–19.
[29] "Consumer Reactions to Inflation," *Ouarterly Journal of Economics*, LXXIII (May 1959), pp. 246–62.

to consult.[30] We can perhaps summarize the evidence both from aggregate data and from surveys in the following tentative propositions: (1) Consumer spending is not always a passive factor, rigidly linked to changes in incomes and other purely "economic" variables; it can and does fluctuate independently, on the basis of changes in consumer perceptions, attitudes, and expectations. (2) Consumer attitudes and expectations may sometimes merely reflect recent changes in the relevant economic variables, but they may also change "autonomously." (3) "We are not in a position yet to offer an answer to the basic question regarding the conditions under which autonomous changes in consumer attitudes occur. The *origin of changes in consumer attitudes* is still shrouded in uncertainty. But consumers are accessible; their attitudes and expectations can be measured; and there is reason to view these attitudes as advance indications of consumer action." [31] (4) Current research in the formation of attitudes and expectations and in the relation between attitudes and expectations on the one hand and spending behavior on the other promise to increase our understanding of consumer spending and thus our ability to forecast and to take measures to stabilize total spending and employment.

## STRUCTURAL FACTORS AFFECTING CONSUMPTION SPENDING

Up to this point most of our discussion has concerned factors which might affect the spending of individual consumer spending units. We have considered not only objective factors which influence the unit's spending, such as its income, its wealth, interest rates, and terms of consumer credit available to it if it wishes to borrow, but also psychological factors, such as the attitudes and expectations held by the unit. But over and above those factors which affect the behavior of individual units, we have to consider effects on aggregate consumption which arise from changes in the relative importance of different kinds of units in the total consumer population. If there are changes in this structure of spending units, consumption may change independently of changes in aggregate income (or of any of the other variables previously considered).

---

[30] In addition to works already cited, see *Contributions of Survey Methods to Economics*, L. R. Klein, ed. (Columbia University Press, 1954), esp. Chap. I and II; G. Katona and E. Mueller, *Consumer Expectations, 1953–56*, Survey Research Center, 1957; L. R. Klein and J. Lansing, "Decisions to Purchase Durable Goods"; *Journal of Marketing*, XX (October 1955), pp. 109–32; and G. Katona, *The Powerful Consumer* (McGraw-Hill, 1960).

[31] Katona and Mueller, *Consumer Expectations, 1953–1956,* p. 110.

Since most of these structural changes occur only rather slowly, they are of little importance in the short or medium-run analysis of consumption, and we shall devote little attention to them here.

## Income Distribution

One structural matter that has received considerable attention at the policy level is that of income distribution. Supposing it to be true (we will consider this question shortly) that the marginal propensity to consume of low-income families is substantially higher than that of high-income families, it would seem to follow that one important means of stimulating aggregate consumption (for example, in a period of slack employment) is to redistribute income from higher to lower income groups. This might be done by increasing tax rates on high incomes and reducing those applicable to lower incomes (or even by paying subsidies to the low income families, financed by taxes on the rich). This kind of action has frequently been advocated by "liberals" *on employment grounds* in periods of depression. It is not surprising that when, instead, inflation threatens, as the result of an excessive aggregate demand for goods, the same concern to maintain economic stability fails to suggest to these same persons that the burden of taxation be shifted from rich to the poor, in order more effectively to dampen the demand for consumer goods.

Actually, of course, the "full-employment" reasons for advocating more equal income distribution are rather thoughtlessly seized upon (in depression times) by persons whose real reasons for wanting a more equal income distribution are quite different. This is certainly unfortunate. If there are reasons (and there may well be very good reasons) for preferring a more equal income distribution, these reasons should stand on their own feet, quite independently of full-employment (or of anti-inflation) considerations. Relative tax rates (as between low and high incomes) should be determined on the basis of ethical considerations, or economic considerations that are quite independent of the current level of aggregate demand. Then, if demand is insufficient for full employment and it is desired to stimulate consumption (as opposed to investment) spending, *all consumers'* taxes can be reduced; or, if inflation threatens, and it is desired to repress consumption (instead of, or in addition to investment) spending, *all consumers'* tax rates can be increased. In our view, the *structure* of relative tax rates should be determined quite independently of stabilization objectives, and the *level* of rates (relative to government expenditure) varied to achieve an adequate and stable volume of consumption.

Still, there is a legitimate interest in the effects of changes in income distribution on the volume of consumer spending. For example, if the distribution of income alters as a result of changes in the private economy (i.e., independently of taxes), we may be interested in predicting the effect on total spending, and thus, perhaps, the need for an alteration of the general level of tax rates. Or, if we are considering a change in the relative structure of tax rates which is desirable on other grounds, we may also need to estimate the effect of this redistribution of the tax burden on total consumer spending.

Analyses which assume a considerable impact of income distribution on consumer spending sometimes carelessly confuse average and marginal propensities to consume. We know that there are very wide differences between average propensities at different income levels. Low-income families consume almost all of their incomes—they frequently dissave. The highest-income families may spend half or less of their incomes. But the marginal propensities are surely much less dissimilar. Assuming that we can judge the marginal propensities at different income levels from cross-section data, the *difference* in marginal propensities is reflected in the *curvature* of a budget-study consumption function. Musgrave and Painter, using such data, showed that even extreme redistributions of the total tax burden would have only very minor effect on aggregate consumption.[32] One may reasonably question, however, whether the appropriate marginal propensities can reliably be estimated from cross-section data, which, as we insisted above, are relevant to income *differences* and not necessarily to income *changes.*

Although there may be some systematic shifts in the distribution of income by income size that occur in the relatively short period (e.g., over the short-run fluctuations which we describe as business cycles), such changes are surely very minor. Kuznets' study of changes in the size distribution of income over the business cycle suggested that there was a slight tendency, on the average, for inequality to diminish slightly in booms and to increase in depressions; yet the contrary movement occurred in about half of the cases studied.[33] Much more important in Kuznets' study were the secular changes in income distribution between the twenties and thirties on the one hand, and the postwar period on the other. The sharp reduction in inequality (even *before* taxes) that developed during the thirties and forties may be *one* reason for the higher

[32] See R. A. Musgrave and M. S. Painter, "The Impact of Alternative Tax Structures on Personal Consumption and Saving," *Quarterly Journal of Economics,* LXII (1948), pp. 475–99.

[33] See S. Kuznets, *Shares of Upper Income Groups in Income and Savings* (National Bureau of Economic Research, 1953), pp. 48–62.

postwar relationship of consumption to income that we have commented on before.

Quite separate from changes in size distribution of income are the changes in "functional shares" that occur systematically over business cycles. By functional shares we mean the distribution as between wage and salary income, profits, interest, rents, and farm income. In depressions, interest and rent fall very little, wages and farm income fall more, and profits fall very sharply. There is considerable evidence that, even at the same income levels, farmers and small businessmen save much more than wage earners, for example. Thus, systematic shifts in functional shares over the business cycle may account for some of the short run changes in consumption that are observed. It was this fact that caused Klein and Goldberger to introduce the separate income shares in their consumption function, which we have previously several times considered.

### Demographic Factors

When we look at a cross-section study we find that consumption differences show up clearly by income levels. But even at any given income level, there are wide differences between the consumption spending of individual families. These differences can at least in part be explained by "demographic factors." These include such things as size of family (other things equal, spending of larger families is greater than of smaller), stage in the family "life cycle" (families with very young children— or children in college—tend to spend more than other families of the same size), place of residence (urban families spend more than rural), occupation (farmers and small businessmen are abnormally high savers), home ownership (renters save less than persons paying off a mortgage), race (nonwhites save more than whites at any given income level), and so on. Individual families may move from one of these categories to another in a relatively short period, but on the average for the whole population, changes in family size, in the percentage owning homes or businesses, in the proportions in different stages of the life cycle, in the proportions resident in urban areas, etc., change rather slowly. Thus these factors can properly be ignored in a short-run analysis confined to aggregate behavior. However, appreciable differences in (for example) average family size mark the postwar period in contrast to prewar, and may help account for differences in aggregate behavior. But, generally speaking, significant demographic changes occur only over periods of time long enough that we can hardly count on stability of the basic subjective factors, either. As previously indicated, we see little reason to suppose that we should expect completely to explain consumption expenditures over periods as long as a generation by any formula, however many demographic or other factors we may put into our consumption equation.

### Nonhouseholds

If we are trying to explain aggregate consumption or saving as estimated by the Department of Commerce (or similar) national income and product data, we must recall that certain nonhousehold groups are included in the personal sector. By way of example, private pension and welfare funds are treated as though all payments into such funds were payments to persons. In fact, in prosperous times the payments into such funds greatly exceed the outpayments to "natural" persons. Unless the wage earners who are accruing contingent claims against such funds adjust their private individual saving to take account of their share in the fund accruals, we should expect the institution and recent spectacular growth of such funds to affect the relationship between disposable income and consumption, as these magnitudes are measured in the national accounts. The other nonhousehold institutions, and the imputations that are made with respect to them in the national accounts, may further serve to introduce irregularities into the national account measurements of consumption and personal saving. There is no reason to suppose that any specific postwar irregularities are to be so explained; but it will be well for the student to be on guard for irregularities or changing relationships which reflect nothing more than the arbitrary accounting conventions that are inevitably necessary in any simple sector scheme of national accounts.

### CONSUMPTION AND GNP

We earlier insisted that the income concept relevant for consumer spending behavior is that of disposable income. Yet when we employ the consumption function in simple macroeconomic models we in fact need a different relationship—one between consumption and gross national product. Consider, for example, the simple Keynesian model which embodies the multiplier idea. It suggests that an increase in investment spending will raise income by a multiple of itself: at the new equilibrium level of income there will be more investment spending and, in addition, more consumer spending, too, induced by the higher level of income.

So long as we assume no government and no corporations, there is no problem. In this simple economy, national product equals national income equals disposable income. But once we introduce government, with its taxes, expenditure, transfers, interest payments, and subsidies; and corporations, with dividends which can diverge from current profits, the structure of national accounts becomes more complex. An increase in investment spending means an increase in GNP, but consumption spending does not depend on GNP, it depends on disposable income. If we want to find out what happens to consumption spending, and determine the size of the multiplier, we must find out what happens to disposable income as a result of added investment or consumption expenditure.

In the following chapter ("Simple Keynesian Model with Introduction of Government"), we will deal with these matters in the context of a formal algebraic model. Here, however, we deal with it in terms of the national income accounts, without use of equations.

The problem will perhaps become immediately apparent if we consider the relationship which exists in the national accounts between GNP and DI. The following table summarizes this relationship:

GNP   (gross national product)
  *minus* (a)   Capital consumption allowances *equals*
NNP   (net national product)
  *minus* (b)   Indirect business taxes
  *minus* (c)   Business transfer payments
  *minus* (d)   Current surplus of government enterprises minus subsidies *equals*
NI   (national income)
  *minus* (e)   Corporate profit taxes
  *minus* (f)   Corporate undistributed profits
  *minus* (g)   Corporate inventory valuation adjustment
  *minus* (h)   Contributions to social insurance
  *plus* (i)   Business transfer payments
  *plus* (j)   Government transfer payments
  *plus* (k)   Government interest *equals*
PI   (personal income)
  *minus* (l)   Personal taxes *equals*
DI   (disposable income)
  *minus* (m)   Personal saving *equals*
C   (consumption expenditures)

In increase in production of investment or consumption goods means an increase in GNP. What this means for DI (and thus for C) depends on what happens to DI as GNP changes. If a billion dollars added to GNP always meant a billion dollars added to DI, there would be no problem; but this is not the case. To find what happens to C (and therefore to GNP) when GNP changes, we first must establish what changes we can expect in each of the items that intervene in the above table between GNP and DI when GNP changes.

Of these intervening items we can first dispose of one minor one—Business transfer payments—which is first subtracted (c) and then added (i). Of the remaining items, seven (b, d, e, h, j, k, and l) are government items; three (a, f, and g) are business items. Consider first the government items. There are three classes of taxes, all of which are subtracted in going from GNP to DI. How do tax collections vary when GNP varies? Some taxes (e.g., property taxes, corporate franchise taxes) can be taken as independent of GNP. Most other taxes, to one degree or another, produce higher revenues as GNP expands. Some, such as sales taxes, expand roughly in proportion to GNP; others, such as personal income taxes, expand more than in proportion. Corporate profits taxes play a peculiarly strategic role. Such taxes are a roughly constant proportion of profits before tax, but profits of corporations are very sensitive to changes in GNP. A rise or fall in GNP tends to be accompanied by a proportionately much larger rise or fall in corporate profits. Thus a rise in GNP produces a more than proportional expansion in corporate profits taxes. Having much the same status as taxes are social insurance contributions, which, being based on payrolls, rise and fall with GNP.

Thus, the deductions from the private income stream associated with government *revenues* all expand when GNP rises and fall as GNP falls. Other things equal, this means that an expansion of GNP produces a notably smaller expansion in DI. The other things are not equal, and they strengthen this result.

*Added*, in going from GNP to DI, are Subsidies and Government transfer payments. Both of these tend to *fall* as GNP rises.

The net result of the government items, then, is to dampen severely the impact of a GNP change on DI. This dampening effect is commonly referred to as the "built-in stabilization effect" of our fiscal system. This is most frequently discussed in terms of recessions. When the value of total output (GNP) declines, disposable income is, in significant measure, protected by the fact that tax collections and social insurance contributions automatically decline and subsidies and transfer payments automatically increase. As a result of this built-in income protection, consumption expenditures will fall far less than were these stabilizers not working. Thus the cumulative impact of declining output is greatly reduced. What needs to be remembered is that these same stabilizers work on the recovery or expansion side, as well.

It is interesting to note that the intervening business items in our list also operate in a stabilizing fashion. One might suppose that capital consumption allowances would be independent of GNP, because their magnitude depends, not on current business conditions, but only on the already existing volume of depreciable assets. In fact, there is also some tendency for these allowances to be adjusted upward in good times and down in bad times, as accountants attempt to protect the reported profit position of their firms from undue fluctuations. The effect is probably small, but it again operates as a stabilizer. Corporate saving is one of the most important stabilizers. When corporate profits fall, businesses often fail to reduce dividends, or reduce them by much less. This means that corporate saving may easily go from a large positive figure in prosperous times to a negative figure in depressions; and *vice versa*. Because of the already mentioned sensitivity of profits to business conditions, this effect has considerable strategic importance as a stabilizer.

The total stabilizing effect of the intervening items is very considerable. With present tax rates and social insurance systems, and taking account of what appear to be the present marginal relationship of corporate profits to GNP, and of present corporate dividend policies, we get an effect that might be approximately summarized as

$$\Delta DI = .5\Delta GNP$$

That is, every increase or decrease of a billion dollars in GNP tends to produce an increase or decrease in DI of about a half billion.[34] If we take the marginal propensity to consume disposable income to be, for sake of argument, .8, this means that an increase of one billion in GNP will produce an increase of only about .4 billion in consumption spending (.5 billion times .8).

The significance of this should be clear. Looking only at the marginal propensity to consume disposable income, we might be tempted to conclude that the "multiplier" (which equals one divided by one minus the marginal propensity to consume) would be five (if the MPC is .8). But when we take account of the fact that a dollar's increased spending on

[34] Some studies place the (short-run) reflection of disposable income change as considerably lower than this. For example, a dynamic, short-run "recession model," constructed by J. Duesenberry, O. Eckstein, and G. Fromm, produces a disposable income change, two quarters later, of about 28 per cent of the GNP change, gradually increasing to 47 per cent after seven quarters. (To be published in *Econometrica*, 1960 or 1961.)

final output may produce only 50 cents additional disposable income, the multiplier becomes not *five* but only about 1.7. That is, the multiplier that is relevant to our model is based on the "marginal propensity to consume gross national product," which on our assumptions above is only .4.

Two additional points of great importance follow. The marginal propensity to consume that is relevant for our model must take account not only of the psychological propensities of consumers, but also of the institutional arrangements that determine how sensitive disposable income is to changes in aggregate spending. The first obvious conclusion is that even if the psychological propensities of consumers were perfectly stable, instability can be introduced into the relevant consumpton function at this other, institutional level. The "marginal propensity to consume gross national product" is not only considerably lower than the marginal propensity to consume disposable income, but it is also, presumably, less stable. The second point is, of course, that, by influencing the relationship between GNP and DI, public intervention can alter consumption spending independently of GNP. We consider this possibility more fully in the next section.

## FISCAL POLICY AND CONSUMPTION

In our analysis of how tax and transfer payment systems influence consumption spending, we assumed the operation of a given set of tax rates, and given arrangements regarding government transfer payments. But these rates and arrangements are in fact subject to change by deliberate policy decision, and such changes may be made deliberately in order to influence the volume of consumer spending. It is possible, also, that government policy (e.g., a special tax on undistributed profits) might influence corporate policies on dividend disbursement.

Suppose, for example, that there has been a decline in investment spending that threatens to create or has created reduced output and unemployment. The "built-in stabilizers" will already moderate the effect of this decline, as tax collections and corporate savings fall and transfer payments increase. But the built-in stabilizers cannot prevent a decline in total spending and income, for they come into play only because and to the extent that income falls. However, by lowering tax rates, and raising eligibility for transfer payments, a fall in GNP can actually be converted into a rise in DI, so that consumption spending may not fall but may even rise.

An example of the (somewhat accidental) use of fiscal policy to this end is provided by the 1953–54 recession. Using the quarterly series (seasonally-adjusted at annual rates) of the U.S. Department of Commerce, the peak of GNP was reached in the second quarter of 1953, and the trough in the second quarter of 1954. Table 12–5 presents the relevant figures for these two quarters and shows the changes between them.

Over this period, investment and government expenditures declined by a total of 14.6 billion. There was an increase in the export surplus of 1.5 billion, and an increase of consumption of 3.2 billion, producing the net decline of GNP of 9.9 billion. How did it happen that consumption *increased* in the face of a sizable decline in GNP? The subsequent detail in the table provides the answer.

An unfavorable factor was the rise in capital consumption allow-

**TABLE 12–5.** **Gross National Product and Related Items, Second Quarters of 1953 and 1954**

(seasonally-adjusted annual rates, in billions of dollars)*

|  | Second Quarter 1953 | Second Quarter 1954 | Change |
|---|---|---|---|
| Gross national product | 368.8 | 358.9 | −9.9 |
| Consumption expenditures | 233.3 | 236.5 | +3.2 |
| Gross private domestic investment | 52.9 | 47.2 | −5.7 |
| Government purchases of goods and services | 83.3 | 74.4 | −8.9 |
| Net exports | −.7 | +.8 | +1.5 |
| Capital consumption allowances | 26.2 | 28.5 | +2.3 |
| Indirect business taxes | 30.1 | 30.2 | +.1 |
| Statistical discrepancy | 2.0 | −.8 | −2.8 |
| Subsidies less current surplus of government enterprises | −.4 | −.3 | +.1 |
| Corporate profits taxes | 21.9 | 16.9 | −5.0 |
| Corporate undistributed profits | 14.5 | 11.1 | −3.4 |
| Corporate inventory valuation adjustment | −1.6 | 0 | +1.6 |
| Social insurance contributions | 8.9 | 9.6 | +.7 |
| Government transfer payments | 12.7 | 14.9 | +2.2 |
| Government interest | 5.1 | 5.4 | +.3 |
| Personal taxes | 35.9 | 32.8 | −3.1 |
| Disposable income | 252.8 | 254.8 | +2.0 |
| Personal saving | 19.6 | 18.3 | −1.3 |
| Consumption expenditures | 233.3 | 236.5 | +3.2 |

SOURCE: *Survey of Current Business,* July 1958, pp. 14, 15.

ances (reducing accounting profits). This primarily reflected the extra depreciation on new capital equipment added over the year. Despite some drop in output, and the reduction or removal of some Federal excise taxes, indirect business tax collections also rose, reflecting rate increases by state and local governments. A third unfavorable factor was the increase in social insurance contributions of .7 billion, instead of the expected (built-in) decline. This was the result of higher contribution rates which became effective during the period.

But these unfavorable developments were more than offset. Corporate profits taxes fell by five billion. This was the result of two factors: (1) corporate profits before tax fell considerably, carrying a (built-in) reduction of several billion in taxes; (2) the excess profits tax was abolished. Although after-tax profits still declined, corporations did not reduce their dividends; thus corporate undistributed profits fell by 3.4 billion. Personal taxes fell by almost 10 per cent, partly as a (built-in) result of lower tax base, and partly through a reduction of Federal income tax rates (perhaps partly offset by state and local increases). Transfer payments increased by 2.2 billion dollars, partly as an automatic result of unemployment, and partly through an upward revision of the benefit structure. Thus, as a result of built-in flexibility plus reductions of Federal tax rates and liberalization of transfer payments (more than offsetting state and local tax rate increases) consumer disposable income increased by two billion dollars. A further unexpected bonus came from a reduction of personal saving, so that consumption spending jumped by 3.2 billion.

Here is a clear example of how the fiscal system prevented what might have been a severe reduction of output (based on the decline in investment and government spending) from developing. Instead of a decline in consumption spending being piled on top of the decline in investment and government spending, consumption actually held firm, and led the way in the subsequent recovery. Federal fiscal policy also sharply moderated the recession of 1957–58, primarily through changes on the expenditure side of the budget.

## SUMMARY JUDGMENT ON THE CONSUMPTION FUNCTION

In the course of the previous and present chapters we have referred to a number of qualifications and uncertainties which must be attached to the use of the Keynesian consumption function. Clearly, the determination of aggregate consumption spending is a much more complicated matter than some early enthusiastic Keynesians realized. The relationship does not run simply from *current* income to *current* consumption, but rather involves some complex average of past and expected income and consumption. There are other factors than income to consider; even taking these factors into account may not fully explain certain irregularities of behavior, unless we fall back on the unsatisfactory description that these are caused by "psychological" factors. Much further research is needed, and some of it is underway.

But we should not go to the opposite extreme and reject altogether the Keynesian innovation. Certainly, no one today would assume (as the Classical economists in effect did) that consumption can be counted on automatically to vary in the opposite direction from and in the same amount as investment, producing a stable aggregate demand. A completely agnostic position might declare that we simply do not know what will happen to consumption when income rises or falls; but not that consumption changes will always exactly offset investment changes, and thus prevent income changes.

A much stronger than merely agnostic position is in fact justified. If disposable income falls or rises by only two or three or even five billion dollars, consumption expenditures might move in the opposite direction— or respond by an even larger movement in the same direction. Even this negative conclusion needs to be qualified by suggesting that if the income change were to persist for more than a quarter or two, a consumption adjustment might be expected in the same direction and in smaller amount than income had changed. Minor irregularities, which usually tend largely to cancel out over a period of a few quarters, preclude the kind of sharp short-run forecasts that we would like to be able to make. But if there should occur a major income movement—as a result of a considerable shift of investment or government expenditure—we can surely be confident that (unless fiscal measures insulate disposable income) consumption, too, will reflect and therefore intensify the income movement that had its origin in the investment or government sector.

Improved understanding of consumer attitudes and expectations will help us anticipate minor short-run movements of consumption (which, however minor, may be strategic for business cycle developments). Improved understanding of the role of wealth, liquid assets, consumer credit, stocks of durables and other factors will permit us to do a more accurate job of forecasting the extent of the larger movements of consumer spending. Perfect precision, of course, will never be obtained.

Yet even in the present state of knowledge, we must recognize that Keynes clearly put his finger on the major determinant of consumer spending; his "discovery" of the consumption function must be regarded as one of the major "breakthroughs" of modern economics. We may not fully subscribe to Alvin Hansen's judgment of the consumption function: "This is an epoch-making contribution to the tools of economic analysis, analogous to, but even more important than, Marshall's discovery of the demand function." [35] But we cannot fail to agree that any analysis of consumer spending (and thus any analysis of aggregate demand—for consumption makes up two-thirds of the total) which leaves out income as a primary determinant is not worth a moment's attention.

[35] *The New Economics* (Knopf, 1947), p. 135.

# Extensions and Applications of the Simple Keynesian Model

*Chapter XIII*

The three preceding chapters have considered the basic Keynesian thesis that consumption is a stable function of income. Our conclusion was a tentative and qualified acceptance of the hypothesis. We can admit the possibility of occasional unpredictable and major shifts in the consumption function, its probable inaccuracy as the basis for sharp short-run forecasting, and the undoubted relevance of other variables (without being entirely sure which these may be, nor how important their net effect). Yet we might still agree that a relationship exists which is of major importance for the understanding and prediction of movements of national income and output. Because the relationship is clearly not precise and unchanging, the theoretical model presented at the beginning of Chapter X, based on a consumption function, will offer, at best a simplified approximation of the behavior of the economy. Nevertheless such simplifications are often useful; indeed, it is the whole purpose of economic theory to simplify, to sort out the major from the minor influences.

Actually, there are other features of this simple Keynesian model which do even greater violence to reality than the assumption of a strictly regular consumption-income relationship. These include the assumptions of absolutely rigid wages and prices, of an interest rate which contributes nothing toward stabilizing aggregate demand, and of the complete absence of government. This last assumption will be lifted at the end of the present chapter, and the wage-price and interest rate assumptions, in the next.

308

Despite the crudity of the present model, it has found wide employment, especially in the discussion of public fiscal policies. Some of the debates which have arisen in connection with the interpretation and the applications of this model will be reviewed in this chapter. Equally important, this chapter will use this model to illustrate a number of methodological and analytical problems of rather general application.

## TAUTOLOGICAL VERSUS MEANINGFUL MULTIPLIERS

It will be recalled that the multiplier expresses the relationship which exists in the model between the quantity of investment (treated as autonomous) and the level of income. The magnitude of the multiplier turned out to be equal to the reciprocal of the marginal propensity to save, or $1/(1 - \text{MPC})$.

Professor A. G. Hart has insisted, no doubt correctly, that the multiplier concept is a useless "fifth wheel." It adds nothing to the ideas or results already implied in the use of the consumption function. Nevertheless, the multiplier idea has been widely used as a way of summarizing the workings of the Keynesian model, and a whole body of literature has grown up which employs this terminology. If the reader prefers, he can restate all of the discussion which follows without use of the objectionable term.

One of the first attacks on the multiplier idea was directed at a misuse of the concept—a misuse of which Keynes himself was occasionally guilty. It is useful to review this attack, and the misuse at which it was directed, because it illustrates a more general theoretical issue and an analytical trap into which many economists (present company probably *not* excepted) still occasionally fall.

The criticism of Keynes' multiplier occurred in a well-known article by Haberler which appeared in 1936.[1] Haberler, with some justice, accused Keynes of dealing in tautology when he discussed the multiplier— that is, of defining something as necessarily true, and then proclaiming as a discovery the "truth" of the relationship made inevitable by definition.

Suppose, for example, I assert the proposition that I can always predict exactly what the change in total enrollment in my beginning national income course will be from one year to the next merely by knowing the change in the number of *women* who enroll and a number called the "sex multiplier." The sex multiplier, $s$, is thus a number which shows the

[1] G. Haberler, "Mr. Keynes' Theory of the 'Multiplier': A Methodological Criticism," *Zeitschrift für Nationalökonomie*, 1936; reprinted in *Readings in Business Cycle Theory* (selected by a Committee of the American Economic Association), Blakiston, 1944, pp. 193–202.

relationship between the change in number of women enrolled and the change in total enrollment, i.e.,

$$s = \frac{\Delta N}{\Delta W},$$

where $N$ is the total enrollment, $W$ the enrollment of women, and $\Delta$ stands for change or difference. If $M$ represents the number of men enrolled, we know that

$$\Delta N = \Delta M + \Delta W.$$

Dividing both sides by $\Delta N$, we have

$$1 = \frac{\Delta M}{\Delta N} + \frac{\Delta W}{\Delta N}$$

or

$$\frac{\Delta W}{\Delta N} = 1 - \frac{\Delta M}{\Delta N}$$

The multiplier was defined above as the reciprocal of the expression on the left; i.e.,

$$s = \frac{\Delta N}{\Delta W} = \frac{1}{1 - \frac{\Delta M}{\Delta N}}$$

The term $\Delta M/\Delta N$ which appears in the denominator can be called the "marginal propensity of men to enroll in Economics 151." Given the magnitude of this propensity, I can predict, with absolute accuracy, the change in total enrollment merely by counting the change in the number of women. Since this number is always quite small, I can save a lot of time.

Suppose, for example, that the enrollment in Fall 1955 was: Total 30, men 25, women 5. In Fall 1956, the enrollment of women rose to 7. The "marginal propensity of men to enroll in Economics 151" in this year was 0.6. Thus, the multiplier theory predicted a change in total enrollment of $1/(1 - .6)$, or 2.5, times the change of 2 in women's enrollment, or a total change of 5. In fact, it turned out that the 1956 total enrollment was 35, an increase exactly as predicted.

Now some of my critics assert that this will not always work. "How about, for instance, during the War, when almost all able-bodied men of college age went into military service. Ackley's law must have failed then." This merely shows that my critics fail to distinguish between the logical theory of the sex-multiplier, which is always exactly and irrefutably true, and its application, in some particular exceptional circumstance. The facts about the period of the draft are as follows:

|          | *Total Enrollment* | *Men* | *Women* |
|----------|:---:|:---:|:---:|
| Fall 1941 | 28 | 21 | 7 |
| Fall 1942 | 16 | 5 | 11 |
| Change | −12 | −16 | 4 |

What was the marginal propensity in this period? It was

$$\frac{\Delta M}{\Delta N} = \frac{-16}{-12}, \text{ or } 1.333$$

This value for the marginal propensity yields a multiplier of

$$\frac{1}{1 - 1.333} \text{ or } -3.$$

If we multiply the change in women's enrollment of 4 by a multiplier of −3, we get a change in total enrollment of −12. This is exactly what happened. Therefore, it can be seen that the theory works perfectly even under the most exceptional circumstances.

Now the reader will immediately see what is the matter. This prediction of the multiplier theory *had to be borne out* because we have found the magnitude of the marginal propensity, and thus the size of the multiplier, simply by seeing what actually happens and then using what has actually happened to predict what must have happened. After all, it is not surprising that the change in the number of women, $\Delta W$, times the multiplier, $\Delta N/\Delta W$, should equal the change in total enrollment, $\Delta N$. It is quite often true that

$$\Delta W \cdot \frac{\Delta N}{\Delta W} = \Delta N$$

In fact, it is always true; and we hardly needed to have it demonstrated.

So perhaps the multiplier doesn't work perfectly under the unusual circumstances of war. But how about the 1955–56 prediction, which seemed so successful? Was there a trick to that, too? There was if the value of .6 for the marginal propensity was (as we suspect) arrived at by comparing the *actual* change in men's enrollment and in total enrollment between 1955 and 1956. Our theory would be worth something only if we had some other, independent basis for arriving at the size of this propensity than merely waiting to see what happened. If, by systematic observation over a period of years we had found a stable empirical relationship, we could use this relationship to predict. The prediction might then be correct, or, of course, it might not. But it would be a genuine prediction—i.e., one that was capable of being incorrect. Or, we might have some psychological theory of masculine behavior, based on experiments or observations in some different context, which, when applied to the context of Economics 151 would give us an independent basis for estimating the marginal propensity—that is, a basis independent of what actually happened to enrollments in any particular year. If we merely had some reason—based on a body of theory emerging from other contexts—to assert the probable *constancy* or *stability* of the marginal propensity, even though we could not determine its magnitude *a priori*, then our theory would still be an interesting and potentially useful hypothesis, even if not immediately available for predictions.

Given either an empirical or theoretical basis for asserting something about our marginal propensity, we have a useful hypothesis, which, if shown by repeated experience to be valid, might reach the dignity of being called a theory, or even a "law." But to be useful (that is, something other than a tautology), a hypothesis, theory, or law must be capable of being proved wrong. One that must always be true, by definition, is worse than useless—worse because it may delude us into thinking we know something when in fact we do not.

The relevance of the foregoing discussion is that the algebra by which we derived our multiplier relationship corresponds identically to the algebra used by Keynes in deriving the formula for his multiplier. And he asserted the inevitable and instantaneous nature of his multiplier relationship—even under special circumstances—in a way which is much reminiscent of our discussion of the war time case. Haberler rightly challenged this aspect. But the fact is that Keynes' multiplier theory was much more than tautology. For he was proposing a hypothesis about behavior—namely, the existence of a stable consumption function. His multiplier theory, properly interpreted, does have the nature of a refutable hypothesis; and in a very real sense Keynes was submitting this hypothesis to his fellow economists for their acceptance or rejection, depending on how well or how badly it worked out as an explanation of real events, and as a framework for organizing observations about the real world. It was only occasionally that his enthusiasm in defending his ideas allowed him to slip into tautology.

## PROBLEMS OF MULTIPLIER ANALYSIS

The first of the special situations which seemed to Keynes to call for defense of his theory was the situation of a time lag in the response of consumption spending. Actually Keynes was here departing from his static analytical framework to consider a dynamic problem, one to which his apparatus was not well suited. For the multiplier analysis (or the Keynesian consumption-investment model) is clearly a static—actually, *comparative* static—analysis. It asks how different will be the equilibrium levels of income that correspond to different given levels of investment. But when the model is expressed in multiplier form it is difficult to keep a discussion of it in static terms. Why is it, how is it, that an increase of one dollar of investment spending can possibly cause an increase of (say) two dollars of total spending? In trying to explain this to ourselves and others we tend to be unsatisfied with a graphic or algebraic solution of an abstract model (like those presented at the beginning of Chapter X, above); instead, we find ourselves explaining the matter in terms like these: "The original 'injection' of new investment spending causes the rate of production of investment goods to be increased in order to meet the enlarged demand. This leads to an equivalent increase in income in the capital goods industry. The recipients of this extra income may save some part of the increment, but will use most of it to enlarge their consumption spending. This will increase production and income payments in the consumer goods industries. The recipients of this further income increase will, in turn, save a part, but respend most of it, creating new income, new spending, new income, in an endless chain. When we consider the sum of all the successively smaller and smaller series of income increases, we find that the total increase in income (including the initial increase resulting from investment) is a multiple of the 'injection,' a multiple the size of which clearly depends on the percentage of each 'round' of income which is respent."

We often use numerical examples in the form of the one below, which is based on a marginal propensity to consume of .75, and an "injection" of 4 (billions). The arrows in the table call attention to the fact that each successive increase in consumption depended on an increase, earlier in the chain, of income. Thus, the rise in consumption in

|   | Original Equilibrium Level (Before Injection) | First Round: Injection | Second Round | Third Round | Fourth Round | Eventually Approaching (New Equilibrium) |
|---|---|---|---|---|---|---|
| *y* | 80 | 84 | 87 | 89.25 | 90.9375 | 96 |
| *c* | 70 | 70 | 73 | 75.25 | 76.9375 | 82 |
| *i* | 10 | 14 | 14 | 14 | 14 | 14 |

the "second round" from 70 to 73 depended on a rise of income from 80 to 84 (as a consequence of a rise of investment from 10 to 14); the rise of consumption from 73 to 75.25 depended on a rise of income from 84 to 87 (as a consequence of the aforesaid rise in consumption from 70 to 73); etc.

It is probably not possible to conceive of this whole process as being compressed into a single instant of time—all of the "rounds" occurring simultaneously. Only if consumers in the aggregate could know what the full effect on their incomes would be—not only the effect of the extra investment spending, but that of their own enlarged consumption spending, too—could we imagine the new equilibrium as being instantaneously established. Since this is absurd, we think of the process as one which occurs over time—as consumers repeatedly find their incomes rise, then increase their expenditures; again find their incomes higher, then again increase their spending; and so on. The "rounds" in our table then represent not merely analytical stages but temporal stages, too.

Suppose that we admit, therefore, the existence of a lag (however slight) between a change in income and the resulting change in consumption spending, and ignore, for the moment, the possibility of any other source of lag in the process. Income, then, will not rise instantaneously from 80 to 96, but will rise *toward* 96, at first faster and then by successively smaller increments. (Incidentally, we can think of this in terms of a "period analysis" if we wish, but we do not need to make the special assumptions of period analysis in this case, so long as we assume a uniform lag for all consumers.)

How did the consideration of this point get Keynes into trouble with a tautological defense of his multiplier? A moment's reference to our numerical example above will indicate the problem. If the marginal propensity to consume is .75, the multiplier is 4. This multiplier effect shows up in an *eventual* rise of income by 16—i.e., by four times the amount of the increment of investment. But if we consider the rise in income that has occurred at any point in time short of the termination of the process, we find the multiplier (up to that point) to have been less than four. At first it is 1, then 1.75, 2.3125, 2.734375, etc. But Keynes was not satisfied to have a multiplier that held true only after a period of time. He thought that it should hold true "always and instantaneously." Thus he would have it that the marginal propensity to consume, on which the multiplier is based, was at first zero (when income rose from 80 to 84 and consumption stayed—temporarily—at 70), then .43 (when income had risen from 80 to 87 and consumption only from 70 to 73), then .57, then .63, etc., approaching a value of .75 at the end of the process. This gives a multiplier that is always and instantaneously true, but also one that is a meaningless tautology, because the size of the marginal propensity to consume is calculated from the actual changes in consumption and income.

It would have been far better had Keynes been content to state the multiplier as a relationship which should hold approximately, and over periods of time long enough that consumption and income might be presumed to have adjusted fully to new conditions.

Another problem to which Keynes referred represented another possible source of lag in the multiplier process. In order to isolate this point, assume for the present no lag of consumption change behind income change. However, suppose that producers of consumer goods are unable to anticipate changes in the demand for their products but instead merely produce during any period (here it is most convenient to use a period analysis) at the rate at which sales were made in the preceding period.[2] This necessarily means that inventories are used as a buffer—if sales exceed production, inventories go down; if production exceeds sales, inventories rise. Making the same numerical assumptions as before (MPC = .75, injection of 4), we would get a sequence like that below:

| | Original Equilibrium Level (Before Injection) | First Round: Injection | Second Round | Third Round | Fourth Round | Eventually Approaching (New Equilibrium) |
|---|---|---|---|---|---|---|
| $y$ | 80 | 84 | 87 | 89.25 | 90.9375 | 96 |
| $c$ (sales) | 70 | 73 | 75.25 | 76.9375 | 78.203125 | 82 |
| $c$ (prod'n) | 70 | 70 | 73 | 75.25 | 76.9375 | 82 |
| $i$ | 10 | 14 | 14 | 14 | 14 | 14 |

In this example, the arrows call attention to the dependence of one period's production of consumer goods on the previous period's sales. Spending on consumer goods, however, depends on current income. Current income, in turn, is the sum of current investment spending (equals production) plus current production of consumers' goods. Again, in this case, we would prefer to say that the multiplier (of 4) holds only for the process as a whole. Keynes preferred to say that the multiplier held at every instant, but that the *multiplicand* changed. Investment did not

---

[2] We could also assume a lag in capital goods output; but capital goods are more typically produced to order, and limiting the lag to consumer goods will simplify exposition.

actually increase by 4 at once, because there was a partially offsetting decrease of inventories. In the first round this decrease was 3, constituting disinvestment which has to be subtracted to get a *net* increment of investment of only 1. This times the multiplier gives an increase of income of 4. By the next period, investment has risen from 10 to 11.75, as disinvestment in inventories drops to 2.25. Again the multiplier holds exactly and instantaneously. But the result does not answer the question which the multiplier theory supposedly asks—namely, what is the effect on income of a given increase in autonomous investment. The answer is that, ultimately, an income increase will have occurred, the size of which is determined by the marginal propensity to consume. In the interim, the amount of the increase will also depend on other factors having nothing to do with the marginal propensity to consume.

It is easy enough to incorporate the idea implied in the second of our above numerical examples into a dynamic multiplier analysis, and answer both questions at once: namely, the size of the ultimate increase in income, and its magnitude at various intervening times. We can do this with the following simple model:

(1) $$c_t = a + by_t$$

(2) $$y_t = \underline{c}_t + i_t$$

(3) $$\underline{c}_t = c_{t-1}$$

where $c$, $y$, and $i$ have their usual meanings, and $\underline{c}$ represents the *production* of consumer goods (distinguished from the sale or purchase of consumer goods, or consumer expenditures, $c$). The subscripts refer to time periods. Substituting gives us

(4) $$y_t = a + by_{t-1} + i_t$$

This is a "first order difference equation." It tells us that the income of any period depends on the current level of investment spending $(i_t)$ and on the previous period's income $(y_{t-1})$.

Corresponding to any constant level of investment, $i_0$, there is an equilibrium level of income. This level is characterized by the equality of successive incomes, i.e., by the situation

(5) $$y_t = y_{t-1} = y_E$$

Substituting from equation (5) into equation (4) gives us

(6) $$y_E = a + by_E + i_0$$

$$y_E(1-b) = a + i_0$$

(7)
$$y_E = \frac{a}{1-b} + \frac{1}{1-b}(i_0)$$

This level is, of course, the solution of the *static* Keynesian model. (See page 216.)

Suppose, for example, the consumption function is

(1a)
$$c_t = 10 + .75y_t$$

and $i_0$ is given as 10. We then have

$$y_t = 10 + .75y_{t-1} + 10$$

(4a)
$$y_t = 20 + .75y_{t-1}$$

If $y_{t-1} = 100$,

$$y_t = 20 + .75(100) = 95$$
$$y_{t+1} = 20 + .75(95) = 91.25$$
$$y_{t+2} = 20 + .75(91.25) = 88.4375$$

etc.

That is, income will continually change. It will, however, approach an equilibrium. We can find this equilibrium by substituting $y_E$ for both $y_t$ and $y_{t-1}$ in equation (4a).

(5a)
$$y_E = 20 + .75y_E$$
$$y_E = 80$$

If $y_{t-1} = 80$,

$$y_t = 20 + .75(80) = 80$$
$$y_{t+1} = 20 + .75(80) = 80$$

etc.

Suppose that from an equilibrium income level of 80, investment rises to 14, staying fixed at the higher level. Equation (4a) now becomes

(4a')
$$y_t = 24 + .75y_{t-1}$$

We can now trace the movement of income toward its new equilibrium

$$y_{t-1} = 80$$
$$y_t = 24 + .75(80) = 84$$
$$y_{t+1} = 24 + .75(84) = 87$$
$$y_{t+2} = 24 + .75(87) = 89.25$$

etc.

The level toward which this process is tending can be found as

(6a')                                $y_E' = 24 + .75 y_E'$

$$y_E' = 96$$

It will be noted that our numerical assumptions correspond to the results of the table on page 315. The student may wish to experiment with another consumption function, e.g.,

$$c_t = 30 + .5 y_t$$

He should also work out, in difference equation form, the simple dynamic model which incorporates a consumption lag, as in the table on page 313. Then he might wish to incorporate *both* lags into a single model—i.e., both a consumption and a production lag.

The assumption made above that producers always choose to produce just what they were able to sell last period is particularly artificial and unrealistic. Although we can replace it with somewhat more complicated and plausible behavior patterns, with interesting consequences (see the second appendix to this chapter), it is probably impossible to find any single pattern, however complex, which can summarize the short-period decision-making of firms with respect to their current output. This means that dynamic analysis of the multiplier process can probably never prove fully satisfactory.[3]

Before leaving these simple multiplier sequences, we should, however, consider the movement of income (and the meaning of the multiplier) in the case of "one-shot" changes in investment. That is, suppose investment to expand for one period, then to fall back to its initial level. Using the consumption lag (without any production lag) to illustrate, we might have:

|   | Original Equilibrium Level (Before Injection) | Round One: Injection | Round Two | Round Three | Round Four | Eventually Approaching (New Equilibrium) |
|---|---|---|---|---|---|---|
| $y$ | 80 | 84 | 83 | 82.25 | 81.6875 | 80 |
| $c$ | 70 | 70 | 73 | 72.25 | 71.6875 | 70 |
| $i$ | 10 | 14 | 10 | 10 | 10 | 10 |

[3] See G. Ackley, "The Multiplier Time Period: Money, Inventories, and Flexibility," *American Economic Review*, XLI (June 1951), pp. 350–68.

Obviously, the increase in income resulting from a "one-shot" increment of investment is of a transitory character, and income *never* reaches a level equal to the change in investment times the multiplier.

The multiplier can be given meaning even in this case, however, by recognizing that the total cumulative excess of income over its original level—i.e., $4 + 3 + 2.25 + 1.6875 + \ldots$—will necessarily be equal to the multiplier times the "one-shot" injection of 4.

Further consideration shows us that we can think of each period's investment (not just its investment increment) as creating a chain of subsequent effects—a diminishing stream of incomes trailing off into the future. Thus, if investment changes continually, from period to period, each period's investment creates its own peculiar "tail" of future incomes stretching ahead of it. We can then think of each period's total income as being the sum of all of the relevant portions of all of the previous tails. If investment should remain constant for many periods, income, too, would eventually become constant, for it would consist of successively smaller pieces of the income "tails" of all of the previous investments, as pictured in Figure 13–1, below. Thus the multiplier in the

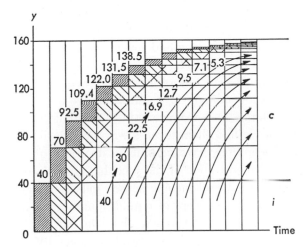

**Figure 13–1.**

"one-shot" case and in the constant investment case can be seen to be particular instances of a more general multiplier concept. Although this approach has been effectively used by others, we shall not pursue it further here.[4]

[4] See, for example, R. Goodwin, "The Multiplier," in *The New Economics* (ed. S. Harris), Knopf, 1947, pp. 482–99. For a general summary of multiplier analysis, see H. Hegeland, *The Multiplier Theory* (Gleerup, 1954).

Mention should also be made of the development and use of various kinds of multipliers in the analysis of international trade. Since this book assumes a closed economy, this subject will not be treated here. However, the student with a special interest in international trade theory will encounter these multipliers, and will see that they involve the problems discussed here as well as many new ones.[5]

## THE EQUALITY OF SAVING AND INVESTMENT AGAIN

It was seen in Chapter X that the model we are discussing can be described as one in which saving and investment determine the level of income. For some reason, the equality of saving and investment has been the subject of much confused discussion. Here there is little to do but to review and to bring together the discussions of earlier chapters.

There are clearly two senses (or more) in which we can speak of an equality between saving and investment. In the sense in which these terms are defined for national income accounting purposes, it is clear that saving and investment must always be identically equal. The student who is not convinced of this should review our previous discussion.[6] But, in the Keynesian model, we are using the equality of saving and investment as a *condition for equilibrium*. We are saying that the level of income must be such that saving and investment are equal; at any other level, they would be unequal. The source of confusion has been a failure to understand that when we talk of a possible inequality of $s$ and $i$, and of their equality as a condition for equilibrium, we must be defining one or both of these terms in a manner subtly different from the way we define them when we find them to be always identically equal. For the national income definitions have nothing to do with equilibrium or disequilibrium. The demonstration of the fact that $s$ and $i$ are always identically equal (in the national income sense) makes no reference to the level of income or to any concept of equilibrium.

The fact that we can use terms like these in different ways and for different purposes was thoroughly reviewed on pages 105–109, where we discussed the equality of supply and demand—first in a definitional sense, and then as a condition for equilibrium. Translating that discussion into the present context, we have it that $s \equiv i$, defining these terms in the national income accounting sense, of actual, realized saving (income less

[5] For an introduction to foreign trade multipliers see any recent standard textbook in international trade theory, for example, C. P. Kindelberger, *International Economics* (Irwin, 1953), Chap. 9, pp. 154–80.

[6] See pp. 71–73.

consumption) and investment (production not sold to consumers). But there is no necessity that $\bar{s} = s$, where $\bar{s}$ represents the saving that consumers intend to do, or would like to do (given the values of some other variables), or have planned to do; nor is it necessary that $\bar{i} = i$, where $\bar{i}$ is similarly defined in terms of intentions, preferences, or plans. However, *unless* $\bar{s} = s$ *and* $\bar{i} = i$—which means $\bar{s} = \bar{i}$—then either savers or investors or both will be doing what they did not intend, or do not prefer, or did not plan to do: that is, the situation cannot be one of equilibrium.

How might a difference arise between what savers prefer to do and what in fact they do? One source of such difference would arise from a lag in the adjustment of consumption to income. Consider, for example, the sequence discussed on page 313, which is reproduced without change in the first three rows below:

|  | Original Equilibrium Level (Before Injection) | First Round: Injection | Second Round | Third Round | Fourth Round | Eventually Approaching (New Equilibrium) |
|---|---|---|---|---|---|---|
| $y$ | 80 | 84 | 87 | 89.25 | 90.9375 | 96 |
| $c$ | 70 | 70 | 73 | 75.25 | 76.9375 | 82 |
| $i$ | 10 | 14 | 14 | 14 | 14 | 14 |
| $s \ (=y-c)$ | 10 | 14 | 14 | 14 | 14 | 14 |
| $\bar{s} \ (=-10+.25y_t)$ | 10 | 11 | 11.75 | 12.3125 | 12.734375 | 14 |
| $s_R \ (=y_{t-1}-c_t)$ | 10 | 10 | 11 | 11.75 | 12.3125 | 14 |

We have added three further rows showing saving. The first of these shows the value of saving as defined in national income terms—i.e., as the residual arrived at by subtracting consumption from income. Naturally, this has to be identical with investment. The second added row shows "desired saving"—the amount of saving which consumers would desire to make at the going level of income, assuming that level of income were to prevail long enough for them to adjust their consumption (and saving) to that level. During the period while the multiplier effect is working itself out, investment and saving (defined this way) are unequal, becoming equal only when equilibrium is restored by sufficient eventual rise in income. The difference between this and the previous measure of saving obviously consists (in this instance) of additional saving which occurs, and would be measured by a national income statistician, because, with a rise in income, consumption has not yet had time to adjust, and there is unintended or undesired saving. This saving is both the measure of disequilibrium and—because consumers try to readjust consumption to eliminate it—the cause of subsequent change in income, leading toward a new equilibrium.[7]

The final row shows a third saving concept, that of Robertson, who once chose to define saving as the difference between yesterday's income and today's consumption. This concept of saving agrees with neither of the others, but it shares with the second concept the property that it equals investment only when income is in equilibrium. This is because, whenever income is *changing*, today's income less today's consumption— which is today's investment—cannot possibly equal yesterday's income less today's consumption—which is what Robertson defines as saving. Thus we have equilibrium only when income is constant. Although many economists seem to confuse definitions two and three, it is clear that they are not the same. Specifically, the Robertsonian definition involves no "psychological" magnitudes at all.

It is possible to define saving in still other ways that permit it to be unequal to investment especially in disequilibrium. But if one chooses another definition, in accordance with which saving need not always equal investment, he must not criticise as wrong any statement which, using national income definitions, insists on the continuous and inescapable identity between saving and investment. No more should the person who prefers the national income definitions try to prove incorrect a statement involving inequality of saving and investment made by one who is using a different set of definitions. Yet this is just what has happened.

We must all be clear that different definitions are possible, under some of which $s$ and $i$ may be unequal. However, if we use one of the latter, we must also remember that the difference between $s$ and $i$ may represent a disappointment, a surprise, a frustration, a change of income from yesterday, but it cannot be identified as a fund. And unless the context makes the usage absolutely clear, one should always explain the sense in which he is using slippery terms such as these.

The production-lag case considered earlier in connection with the multiplier illustrates another source of potential difference (on some definitions) between saving and investment. We reproduce in the first four lines below the hypothetical example used above, on page 315, to illustrate this case.

---

[7] We could, of course, show a further row labelled $\bar{c}$. This would show desired or intended consumption—that which would occur at the going level of $y$ if it were to prevail long enough for consumers to adjust. It would be the complement of $\bar{s}$.

| | Original Equilibrium Level (Before Injection) | First Round: Injection | Second Round | Third Round | Fourth Round | Eventually Approaching (New Equilibrium) |
|---|---|---|---|---|---|---|
| $y$ | 80 | 84 | 87 | 89.25 | 90.9375 | 96 |
| $c$ (sales) | 70 | 73 | 75.25 | 76.9375 | 78.203125 | 82 |
| $\underline{c}$ (prod'n) | 70 | 70 | 73 | 75.25 | 76.9375 | 82 |
| $\bar{\imath}$ | 10 | 14 | 14 | 14 | 14 | 14 |
| $s\,(=\bar{s})$ | 10 | 11 | 11.75 | 12.3125 | 12.734375 | 14 |
| $i$ | 10 | 11 | 11.75 | 12.3125 | 12.734375 | 14 |

In line five, we show saving, which is, it will be noted, the same whether defined in the national income sense or as "desired" saving. This is so because we assumed away (for this example) any lag between income change and consumption change, that is, any possible difference between desires and their fulfillment. But it is clear, by comparison with the investment figures in row three, that there is divergence between $s$ and $\bar{\imath}$ except at equilibrium. This is because the investment figures relate not to actual, realized investment (in the national income sense) but to planned or intended investment. (This is why we have introduced the bar above the symbol.) Actual investment is shown in row six. It includes the change in inventories (as we do in national income accounting) whether this change was an intended, deliberate change, or whether—as in this case—the inventory change is an accidental result of a rise in demand which producers did not expect and had therefore not prepared for. Once again, there can be no escaping the equality of $s$ and $i$ at each and every point in the process, equilibrium or no equilibrium. But it is also not meaningless to talk about a *difference* between saving and investment (defining investment now in a different way), and their equality as a condition of equilibrium.

What we must not do is to confuse the definitions, and to argue, first, that saving and investment are always necessarily equal; then to propose their equality as a condition of income equilibrium, without indicating a change in the sense in which one or another of the terms is used. Keynes, and some of his followers, have occasionally been criticized for exactly this error. It should now not be too difficult to see that this error is, in a slightly revised context, exactly that involved in the tautological multiplier theory.

While dealing with the subject of the equality of saving and investment it is impossible not to say a little about still another set of saving and investment concepts, those identified with the "Stockholm School." [8] The Swedish economists of this school point out that one can define a concept (income, saving, investment, production, etc.) either *ex ante* or *ex post*— looked at "from before" or "from after." The *ex post* concepts are for all practical purposes the national income concepts—actual, realized income, investment, etc. *Ex ante* saving has frequently been incorrectly identified with Robertsonian saving, or with what we have called "desired" saving— i.e., that given by the consumption function ignoring lags. Actually, the Stockholm *ex ante* concepts, are in one sense much broader than any we have considered, although in another sense more restricted. What has to be understood is that the *ex ante* concepts are part and parcel of a rather different framework of analysis than is reflected in this volume, or indeed, in rigorous fashion, in most American or English theory. The Stockholm approach is to visualize all economic subjects as possessing, at all times, rather definitely formulated expectations about the future—at least with respect to many significant variables. These expectations relate both to variables not under one's own control, and, made consistent with these, to variables within one's control (the latter we can call "plans"). Thus, a producer may have an *expectation* of his sales and *plans* for his production and inventory change; a consumer may have an *expectation* regarding his income, and a *plan* for his consumption and saving. Although we can frame this in "period analysis" terms if we wish to suppose, or to assume for sake of simplicity, that these plans and expectations are revised only periodically, this is not necessary; we also can think of plans and expectations as being subject to smooth and continuous revision, and as related to time horizons of varying distances.

We also can suppose, as the Swedes do, that some kinds or parts of each subject's "plans" are always carried out as planned. However, all plans cannot always be carried out because these plans may be mutually inconsistent. For example, if the amount which consumers plan to, *and do*, spend, and the amount which investors plan to, *and do*, spend add up to more than the incomes consumers expected, then consumers' saving plans cannot possibly be carried out. That is, *ex post* saving will exceed

---

[8] See B. Ohlin, "Some Notes on the Stockholm Theory of Saving and Investment," *Economic Journal*, 1937, reprinted in *Readings in Business Cycle Theory*, pp. 87–130. These concepts, popularized in English by Ohlin's article, were not accepted as useful tools by all members of the "Stockholm School" at the time Ohlin wrote, and are even less universally accepted in Sweden today. Thus, when we refer in the text to concepts of the "Stockholm School," the reader should understand that we are discussing these particular ideas, but not implying that all Stockholm economists employ them.

*ex ante* saving. Since *ex post* saving must, by definition, equal *ex post* investment; and, since, by the assumption that investors' plans were carried out, *ex ante* and *ex post* investment were equal, then we could say that *ex ante investment exceeded ex ante saving*, and that this excess "caused" income to be greater than expected—i.e., caused income *ex post* to exceed income *ex ante*.[9]

We can complicate matters by assuming that investors' plans for capital expenditure are carried out but that their plans for inventory investment need not be. That is to say, we visualize producers having sales *expectations*, and *plans* for production and inventory change (assume planned inventory change zero for simplicity). If, now, we assume that production plans are always carried out, and, as well, that capital investment and consumption spending plans are carried out, then producers' inventory plans cannot also be carried out unless the expected sales of producers exactly equal planned consumption plus planned capital investment. If not, then *ex post* investment (which includes all inventory change) will diverge from *ex ante* investment.

On the basis of the above, we see that *ex ante* saving can diverge from *ex post* saving, which must equal *ex post* investment, which in turn can diverge from *ex ante* investment. All four will be equal only if all expectations are consistent with all plans; then expected incomes will equal actual incomes and expected sales equal actual sales. One can call this an "equilibrium." However, it is such only in a very special sense, for it is clearly possible that—if plans and expectations change together in a perfectly consistent way—incomes and sales could be continuously changing yet always in equilibrium.[10]

It should be noted that we have so far said nothing at all about the really crucial questions: (1) How are expectations framed? And (2) given the values of the expectations, how are plans made? Until we provide answers to these questions, we have not a model but only a framework for a model. We could, for example, answer question (1) by assuming that consumers' income expectations are always that future incomes will

[9] Reflection will show that no "causation" is involved. This merely *describes* what has happened. We cannot explain what "caused" income *ex post* to exceed income *ex ante* without explaining what "caused" income expectations and consumption plans.

[10] The assumption made above that consumers' spending (but not saving) plans, and investors' capital equipment spending (but not inventory) plans are always carried out is not a necessary feature of the Stockholm approach, although it is the assumption made in several Swedish analyses which are most familiar to English-speaking economists. These assumptions are not only inadequate but, under conditions of full employment, impossible. For a Swedish analysis which replaces them with other assumptions see B. Hansen, *A Study in the Theory of Inflation* (Allen and Unwin, 1951).

be the same as the present ones, and that producers' sales expectations are always that sales will be the same as at present. We could then assume, to answer question (2), that consumer spending plans derive from a consumption function, in which expected income (equals actual present income) determines planned (and actual) spending. We could further assume that producers' plans are always to produce just what they expect to sell. If so, we have a model identical in result with the Keynesian one implied in the discussion of the past few pages. But these results are not required by the Stockholm framework. The Stockholm definitions are also compatible with other theories regarding how plans are formulated, giving entirely different results.[11] Thus, it seems preferable to regard the *ex ante, ex post* concepts as simply a broad framework for analysis, into which any of a number of substantive theories might be fitted. The only common feature of these would be the view that expectations and plans are of crucial importance in economic life and are therefore crucial variables to be isolated in economic analysis. There is not room here for a critical discussion of this methodological presupposition of Swedish analysis. However, it should be noted that some Stockholm as well as non-Swedish economists have vigorously challenged this approach both as to its realism (in supposing that expectations are definite and important to behavior) and as to its analytical usefulness (because of difficulties of giving operational content to the concepts).

## DYNAMICS AND THE STABILITY OF EQUILIBRIUM

It will be recalled that Keynes laid great stress upon his assumption that the marginal propensity to consume, while greater than zero, *was also less than one*. We are now in a position to see clearly why this is important.

The simple Keynesian model has a static equilibrium solution even if the marginal propensity to consume is greater than one. Assume, for example, the following equations:

[11] For example, *consumer income expectations* might be based not only on currently received incomes, but also on the rate and direction of recent income change. Or they might be based upon consumers' interpretations of the business outlook and of government actions and international events. *Consumer spending plans* might depend not only on expected income but also (or instead) on the way in which present income differs from that previously expected; they could also (or instead) depend on other economic variables such as those listed in Chapter XII, or one could even use this framework of analysis *without any theory* of the determinants of consumer spending—taking an agnostic position that what consumers plan to spend must be considered autonomously determined.

$$c = -20 + 1.2y$$

$$c + i = y$$

$$i_0 = 10$$

We solve these as follows:

$$y_0 = -20 + 1.2y + 10$$

$$.2y_0 = 10$$

$$y_0 = 50$$

$$c_0 = -20 + 60 = 40$$

Graphically, we have the results shown by the solid lines in Figure 13–2.

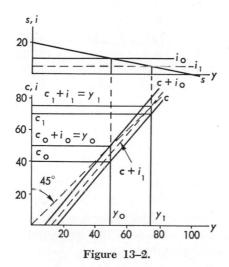

Figure 13–2.

This model has, however, the unexpected result that a drop of invest-ment will raise income, and vice versa. E.g., if

$$i_1 = 5$$

$$y_1 = -20 + 1.2y_1 + 5$$

$$.2y_1 = 15$$

$$y_1 = 75$$

$$c_1 = -20 + 90 = 70$$

The same results can be seen on the diagrams (broken lines).

This is consistent with the value of the (static) multiplier, which is

$$k = \frac{1}{1 - 1.2} = -5$$

Although all empirical data seem to suggest a MPC less than one, can we say that the Keynesian model would "work" just as well if it happened that the MPC were greater than one?

The answer is a definite "no." A Keynesian model with an MPC greater than one might have an equilibrium solution, but it would be an unstable equilibrium. This can easily be seen by assuming a time lag in the consumption function, spelling out the process of income change as below (using the numbers of the above example):

|   | *Original Equilibrium* | | | | | | | *New Static Equilibrium* |
|---|---|---|---|---|---|---|---|---|
|   | (1) | (2) | (3) | (4) | (5) | (6) | (7) | (8) |
| $y$ | 50 | 45 | 39 | 31.8 | 23.16 | 12.792 | 5 | 75 |
| $c$ | 40 | 40 | 34 | 26.8 | 18.16 | 7.792 | 0 | 70 |
| $i$ | 10 | 5 | 5 | 5 | 5 | 5 | 5 | 5 |

The drop of investment, and hence of income, of 5 (column 1 to column 2) causes a subsequent drop of consumption of $5 \times 1.2 = 6$, and therefore a drop of income of 6, as shown in column 3. This causes a still larger drop in consumption and income in the next "round," and consumption quickly reaches zero.[12] *Yet there exists a new equilibrium*, at an income of 75, with consumption of $-20 + 1.2(75) = 70$, and investment of 5. If only income could somehow get to 75, it could stay there; but it cannot. This new equilibrium—like the initial one—is "unstable." A Keynesian model with an MPC of one or greater could be set up in dynamic form as a theory of economic change or process; but there is no equilibrium in such case; the processes would approach no stable end.

To summarize this more formally, we have the dynamic model as follows:

$$c_t = -20 + 1.2y_{t-1}$$

$$c_t + i_t = y_t$$

If $i_t = 10$, we have

$$y_t = -20 + 1.2y_{t-1} - 10$$

$$y_t = 1.2y_{t-1} - 10$$

---

[12] The formula would give a negative figure for consumption in column (7). Since this has no economic meaning, we have substituted zero.

This has an equilibrium value of $y_t = 50$, as can be seen by setting

$$y_t = y_{t-1} = y_E$$

and substituting,

$$y_E = 1.2y_E - 10$$

$$.2y_E = 10$$

$$y_E = 50$$

But suppose that from an equilibrium of $y_t = 50$, $c_t = 40$, $i_t = 10$, there is a drop of investment to $i_{t+1} = 5$. We now have:

$$y_{t+1} = c_{t+1} + 5$$

$$y_{t+1} = -20 + 1.2(50) + 5 = 45$$

$$y_{t+2} = -20 + 1.2(45) + 5 = 39$$

$$y_{t+3} = -20 + 1.2(39) + 5 = 31.8$$

etc.

Yet there exists a new equilibrium (unattainable) of $y_E = 75$; for, if $y_{t-1} = 75$,

$$y_t = -20 + 1.2(75) + 5 = 75$$

$$y_{t+1} = -20 + 1.2(75) + 5 = 75$$

etc.

The above example illustrates in the simplest possible way the relationship between statics, dynamics, and "stability conditions." We have found a stability condition for the Keynesian model, that the MPC be less than one. Note that we found this condition *only when we specified (assumed) something about the dynamics of the model*. It could not be deduced from the static model alone, which is only capable of finding equilibrium positions, but not of determining their stability or instability. This general principle has, of course, an important corollary. Any static model can describe the equilibrium positions of a number of alternative dynamic models; thus the equilibrium of a static model may be stable with one set of dynamic assumptions, yet unstable with another.

For example, suppose that no lag exists in the adjustment of consumption to income change, but instead there is a lag in the adjustment of production of consumer goods to a change in their sales. If producer behavior is simply always to produce today at the rate of yesterday's sales (the assumption made in our previous discussion), then the stability condition is unaltered: equilibrium will be directly approached and will be stable so long as the MPC is less than one. But, as Professor Lloyd Metzler was the first to show, we can substitute other plausible assumptions regarding the (lagged) adjustment of production to a change in sales. These alternative assumptions give rise to a family of models, capable of producing both stable and explosive cycles and cobwebs in income and output. In some of these models, even quite low values of the MPC (e.g., MPC = .4) nevertheless make the equilibrium of the model unstable. Yet the equilibrium solution is exactly that of the elementary Keynesian model. The simplest of these models is presented in the second appendix to this chapter.

Thus it is an oversimplification to say that *"the"* stability condition for the Keynesian system is that the MPC be less than one. Rather, this condition obtains only for a model in which there is but a single lag— that of consumption behind income—and in which investment is truly autonomous. For example, in the next section we present a Keynesian-type (but not directly Keynesian) model in which investment, too, depends upon income. This model has a more restrictive stability condition (with an MPC < 1 it may still be unstable). Further, Keynes' own more complete model, which introduces the interest rate and the dependence of investment on the interest rate, can (under some dynamic assumptions) be stable even with a marginal propensity to consume of one or greater.[13]

The subject of stability conditions is sufficiently important that an appendix has been added to this chapter developing the subject somewhat further and more formally, with illustrations from the field of microeconomic price theory, as well as income theory.

## INVESTMENT, TOO, DEPENDS ON INCOME

We discuss in this section a model so often used by followers of Keynes that it has often, incorrectly, been called *the* Keynesian model (especially by critics). It is worth brief attention not only because it possesses certain plausibility as a model of the "real world," but also because it further illustrates the problem of stability of equilibrium and introduces other methodological issues of some general interest. In addition it will provide a springboard for our later discussion of the theory of investment.

---

[13] Briefly summarized, rising income will (given $M$) raise the interest rate, and discourage investment. Thus investment (*ceteris paribus*) depends inversely on income. The total "marginal propensity to spend" can thus be less than 1 even if the MPC exceeds 1.

The model involves the consumption function together with an explanation of investment which makes this, like consumption, depend on the level of income. Thus we have

$$c = a + by$$

$$i = e + fy$$

$$y = c + i$$

Substitution yields an expression for $y$ significantly different from that in the regular Keynesian "first model."

$$y = a + by + e + fy$$

$$y(1 - b - f) = a + e$$

$$y = \frac{1}{1 - b - f} (a + e)$$

The model is shown graphically in Figure 13–3.

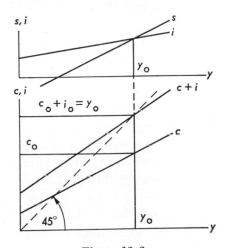

Figure 13–3.

Here the multiplier expression is modified. The addition of an amount of autonomous investment (represented by an increase in the constant term, $e$, in the investment function) will lead to an increase in income equal to the amount of the shift times a new multiplier $1/(1 - b - f)$. Since $f$ is necessarily positive, the size of the multiplier is larger than before. The common sense of this is easy to grasp. If a rise in income not only leads to increased consumption but as well to increased investment (creating the basis for further expansion of income, consumption, and investment, in endless chain), the ultimate increase in income will be greater than if only consumption so responded.

Suppose, for instance, that our functions were as follows:

$$c = 10 + .6y$$

$$i = 5 + .3y$$

$$y = c + i$$

$$y = 15 + .9y$$

$$.1y = 15$$

$$y = 150$$

If the constant in the investment function rose from 5 to 10, the new equilibrium would be found as follows:

$$y = 20 + .9y$$

$$.1y = 20$$

$$y = 200$$

Comparing the two solutions shows the multiplier to be 10, although the marginal propensity to consume of .6 would imply a multiplier of only 2.5. The enlarged multiplier is $1/(1 - .6 - .3) = 10$.

Among other things, this model is the source of the so-called "paradox of thrift." An increased propensity to save, in the simpler Keynesian model, left total saving (and investment) unchanged, although reducing income. In the present model the effort of the community to save more is actually self-defeating; the new equilibrium involves not only lower income but lower saving as well. Yet a community that loses its thrifty habits succeeds in saving more than it did previously. Although these results are more "interesting" and dramatic than those of the simple Keynesian model, this does not make it a "better" model, nor is the difference much more than one of degree.

It is also easy to see that the stability condition of this model is altered from the previous one. Instead of having it that the marginal propensity to consume must be less than one, we now have that the sum of the MPC plus the MPI (marginal propensity to invest, or slope of the investment function) must be less than one. Or, put otherwise, the MPS must exceed the MPI. Graphically this means that the saving function must cut the investment function from below. These results need not be labored.

One is tempted to criticize this model as doing too much; for if both consumption and investment depend on income, then there is no way to explain a variation in income except by reference to a *shift* in investment or consumption functions. But such shift involves a violation of the assumptions of the model, which are that both consumption and investment are meaningfully stable functions of income. One could with equal force criticize the supply-demand model of market price determination as invalid for the same reason. In this form, the criticism is hardly tenable. However, the same point, formulated somewhat differently, does bear upon the empirical usefulness of the model, and the possibility of its statistical verification, as we shall see below. One can surely admit, as do most who utilize this kind of model, that the investment function is not stable for long, but is rather subject to frequent shifts. This, in effect, says that investment can be thought of as having two components: a systematic component, which depends upon the level of income, and an autonomous component which varies, and whose variations account for shifting equilibrium levels of $y$, $c$, and $i$. Separate recognition of the systematic part would clearly constitute an improvement over the mere treatment of total investment as autonomous —if this theory does correctly describe the systematic elements at work, and if we are able to give empirical content to these systematic elements.

We now turn to a brief discussion of the plausibility of this model. We will consider first the matter of statistical verification from aggregative data; then we will consider, on a microeconomic level, whether the behavior which this theory implies on the part of the individual entrepreneur is consistent with other "knowledge" of how businessmen operate.

In Figure 13–4, we present data on GNP and gross private domestic investment in the United States for the years 1929–41, both measured in constant dollars. Although the points do not fall on, or even close to, a single line of relationship, it is clear that a strong correlation exists. Every time GNP rose, investment rose, and *vice versa*. The points for 1929–35 lie almost on a single line, as do the points for 1935–40, perhaps suggesting a shift in the relationship as the result of the New Deal. Alternatively, one might assume a single relationship for the whole period, with 1929 merely abnormally high and 1932–34 abnormally low.

Some attempts have been made to estimate a statistical investment function by just this method. But others have been quick to point out that the relationship shown is entirely specious, merely a misinterpretation of the direction of causation. For if, as we have generally accepted,

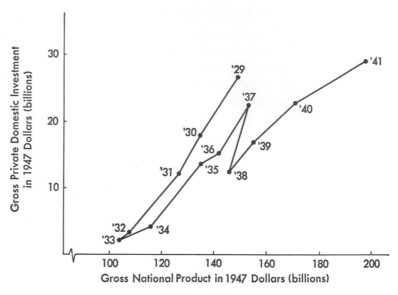

Figure 13–4.

consumption is a function of income, we should expect to get this kind of a relationship between investment and income, even if investment were entirely independent of income. Does not the causation run the other way: high investment causes high income (directly and via the multiplier), low investment, low income?

The criticism of statistical procedure is well taken; but reflection as to its import immediately suggests what may be a troublesome thought. The data are indeed consistent with the theory that investment is independent of income, while consumption depends on income; but they would also be consistent with the reverse theory: namely, that consumption is independent of income but investment depends on income! This is merely another way of saying that statistics can never "prove" a theory or hypothesis. The best that we can ever say is that statistics are consistent with a hypothesis. But they may be consistent with another hypothesis, too, as they seem to be here.

Clearly, the statistics could not be consistent with the hypothesis that *both* consumption and investment depend, in stable fashion, on the level of income. For if this were so (as we observed earlier) there could be no change in income: a *stable* saving function would always intersect a *stable* investment function at one point. If our model held, instead, that consumption is a stable function of income, and investment also a function of income, but subject to erratic shifts, the data could not help us identify the systematic part of investment—i.e., the slope of the investment function—for it would be impossible to separate the systematic from the nonsystematic component of investment. This last point can be seen from Figure 13–5. Here we have pictured the intersection of a stable saving

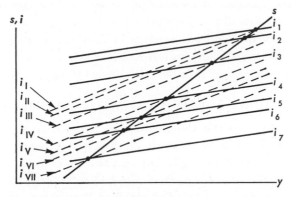

**Figure 13–5.**

function with a shifting investment function, producing a series of "data" on incomes and amounts saved and invested. Yet the same "data" might be produced by any of a whole set of shifting investment functions (two of which are shown), and the data would be incapable of indicating which set of shifting investment functions produced the observed intersections.

The problem here is like that involved in the statistical estimation of static supply and demand functions from a single set of data on prices and quantities exchanged over a period of time. If we hypothesize that the demand function were stable during this period while the quantity supplied depended on the weather or other "autonomous" factors, then the data could be interpreted as revealing the demand function (or testing its existence and stability). If we made the reverse assumption, the data must trace out the supply function. The assumption that both functions were stable would be inconsistent with observed *variation* of price and quantity. If, instead, our theory were that the demand function was stable while the supply function shifted—i.e., that supply consisted of a systematic plus an unsystematic element—the data would not permit us to distinguish the supply function.[14] Our conclusion must therefore be

---

[14] One familiar with modern econometric theory will recognize that we are talking here, in a most elementary way, about the problem of "identification" of a model. He will also be aware that, if we had an adequate dynamic theory of saving and investment (or of supply and demand for some good), the same data might permit us to identify both functions. He will also be aware that the introduction of addi-

that elementary statistical methods do not permit us to test the plausibility of a model involving both saving (consumption) and investment as functions of income. This does not mean that the investment theory is to be rejected—indeed, on this ground, one might equally well reject the consumption theory. Rather, it means that, as always, the economic theorist must first decide (on other grounds) what he considers to be a plausible model.[15] Then, if the model is capable of statistical testing (and not all models are), the statistician can tell him if it needs to be rejected. However, he can never "prove" it to be "the" correct theory.

## WHY INVESTMENT MIGHT VARY WITH INCOME

Is the "investment-a-function-of-income" hypothesis a plausible one, when analyzed in terms of the individual behavior which it implies? A clear-cut answer is not possible, but certain observations can be made with respect to the reasoning often supplied to support the hypothesis. The first support often employed is an allegedly technological one. More or less output requires more or less capital equipment to produce it, just as it requires more or less labor and material. Thus any increase in total output requires investment in additional plant and equipment with which to produce the added output. Investment is thus a function of output. Is this technological argument valid?

A higher aggregate income implies an increase in the demand for the product of almost every entrepreneur. In response to this increase in demand, he will need to employ more productive services of all kinds, and probably in amounts more or less proportionate to the level of output. Some of these productive services are purchased currently—labor, power, parts, raw materials, etc. A rise in demand will require greater purchases of all of them. The entrepreneur will also need a larger current flow of the services rendered by plant and equipment. Thus, a rise in demand

---

tional variables into our model may permit the data to be used for the statistical identification of functions otherwise not capable of identification. In the present example, our introduction of government expenditures and taxes (in the next section) provides a model which may be statistically identifiable, and thus would permit us to test the plausibility of the "investment-as-a-stable-function-of-income" hypothesis. However, we shall not make such a test.

[15] The "other grounds" which determine plausibility to a theorist presumably are its consistency with *a priori* postulates. In the last analysis, these postulates are either (1) the distillation of other empirical tests or observations, often casual rather than systematic; or (2) derived from the assumption of "rational behavior" and thus tacitly reflecting an empirical observation (more casual than scientific) that men behave "rationally," at least in certain spheres. These comments are not intended to derogate *a priori* analysis. In the present state of our knowledge such analysis may often be superior to such statistical tests as are available—which often means none.

(corresponding to higher aggregate income) may induce the entrepreneur to purchase more machinery. But with his purchase of a larger flow of machine services *NOW*, he must also purchase an enlarged flow for some period to come. This is what distinguishes the machine from the raw material "used up" in production. This means that, if demand rises and then merely remains at the higher level, the entrepreneur will probably not need, again, to buy still more new machines. Only if demand continually rises will he need to continue purchasing new machines. That is, it might be more plausible to assume, as a first approximation, that demand for machines (and thus investment) depends on the *change* of aggregate income rather than on its level. This is usually known as the "acceleration principle." It involves a very different theory of investment from the one presently under consideration. We shall investigate it in some detail later, and find it, also, to be subject to substantial reservations as to plausability. But the allegedly technological relationship which links an increased output to a greater requirement for capital goods does not, under examination, support a link between the *level of output* and the rate of investment.[16]

A second link sometimes proposed to support the connection of the level of income to the rate of investment is more plausible. It suggests that investment is, at least in part, determined by the internal availability of investible funds—that is, essentially, upon retained profits. As aggregate income rises, profit income rises, too, and, usually, more than in proportion. The funds that must be withdrawn to provide for the consumption expenditures of the proprietor (or the dividends which must be paid to keep stockholders satisfied) will ordinarily not vary in proportion to the variation in profits. Thus when total income, and total profits, are high, retained earnings are high, and *vice versa*, with retained earnings fluctuating rather violently (from negative to large positive quantities) in response to moderate output changes. Now it would be a crude version of the Classical Say's Law analysis to argue that all savings are automatically invested.[17] But there probably does exist some tendency for more to be invested when more is available to invest, quite apart from any other factor. This may be particularly true in the case of small businesses, whose

---

[16] The two ideas are, nevertheless, frequently confused, as for example by S. Weintraub, *Income and Employment Analysis* (Pitman, 1951), pp. 127–31. K. Kurihara, in *An Introduction to Keynesian Dynamics* (Columbia University Press, 1956), pp. 88 and ff., also calls the idea of this section the "acceleration principle," which seems unfortunate.

[17] Crude, because the better Classical analysis showed how the interest rate would vary to make the investment attractive.

access to the capital market is very limited, yet many of which are perennially starved for capital—i.e., unable to take advantage of clear opportunities to increase their profits. However, even the large corporation may sometimes prefer to reinvest extra profits in enlarging the business rather than to pile up useless bank accounts, to buy securities, or to give stockholders a taste of dividends at a rate that probably cannot be maintained. Likewise, even the large corporation may pass up or cut back promising investment projects when falling profits mean that they cannot be financed internally.

Again, this is a *tendency* only. Yet as a tendency, it may suggest a direct connection of profits (and therefore of aggregate income) to the rate of investment.[18]

An extension of this idea of financial limits to investment recognizes that a capital market exists, and that outside financing is also possible. However, we can still relate total investment to current (or recent) profits if we assume that the amount of outside capital which a firm can attract depends upon the amount of internal financing that its owners can supply (or that increases in the ratio of external to internal financing involve appreciable increases in the cost of the outside capital).[19]

There are still other links suggested between aggregate income and investment, either via profits or otherwise. For example, some hypothesize that investment is motivated by the hope or expectation of profits, and that the best information which the businessman has as to the level of profits to be expected is simply their current level. This, indeed, is the usual microeconomic explanation of how production is adapted to demand. If demand shifts from product A to product B, price changes will lead to profit changes which, in the short run, will cause output rates to be adjusted with given equipment, and, in the longer run, will induce extra investment in product B and disinvestment in product A. This investment and disinvestment will continue until profit rates are again

---

[18] Some statistical investment functions have included a profits term, with a "marginal propensity to invest" which is explained on the grounds set forth above. If it is so explained, the analyst usually rejects a "marginal propensity to invest" which, combined with the marginal propensity to consume profit income, exceeds a value of one. See, for example, L. R. Klein, *Economic Fluctuations in the United States, 1921–1941* (Wiley, 1950), p. 75. However, if the existence of an "investment depends on profits" connection is explained on other grounds—e.g., those suggested in the next paragraphs, there is no reason why the sum of the capitalists' MPI + MPC should not exceed one.

[19] This is the burden of the argument of M. Kalecki, "The Principle of Increasing Risk," *Economica*, IV, new series (1937), pp. 440–7. This is also an important element in the investment theory of A. Smithies, "Economic Fluctuations and Growth," *Econometrica* 25 (January 1957), p. 13, and of J. S. Duesenberry in *Business Cycles and Economic Growth* (McGraw-Hill, 1958)

equalized (assuming free entry and perfect competition) at zero pure profit.

Yet it is not always valid to apply a theory which is useful in explaining the internal structure of a variable to the determination of its aggregate amount. In the present case, for example, we should recall that the whole microeconomic discussion is carried out under the assumption of a constant level of total demand for the two products taken together and an income distribution which is constant. But the proposed use relates to a change in the aggregate demand for all products, and to a change in total income distribution. It is not that profits in one field are high or low relative to profits in other fields. Rather they are high or low relative to what they have been in the past—and by the same token relative to what they may be in the future. For example, if profits are currently high because business has reached a peak level following recovery from a previous depression, with threats in the air that the "boom" is near its end, investment plans may begin to be cut back no matter how high *current* profits may be. Nevertheless, to the extent that businessmen do not or cannot forecast the future other than by observing the present, the proposed connection of aggregate output and investment becomes more plausible.

Many business cycle theories have rested, explicitly or otherwise, on an assumed dependence of investment on profits, and of profits on aggregate output or income (or on the state of "business conditions"). In effect they have assumed a marginal propensity to invest so high that expansions and contractions cumulate in an unstable process. Turning points then come either (1) because the relation of profits to total output changes as the expansion or contraction proceeds (profit margins begin to shrink toward the end of expansions, begin to rise toward the end of depressions) for special reasons which the theorist may develop; or (2) because some external event or limit checks and reverses the process. We shall have a brief introduction to such theories in a later chapter.

The hypothesis that investment depends on the level of income or output is the simplest of all available theories of aggregate investment. This is insufficient reason to dismiss it. We have already indicated the difficulties of direct statistical testing of the theory. Further, even its supporters admit the relationship probably to be erratic and unstable. After examining other, more complicated theories at a later point, we may have to conclude that we have as yet no thoroughly satisfactory theory of investment.

## SIMPLE KEYNESIAN MODELS WITH INTRODUCTION OF GOVERNMENT

It is usual to develop abstract models for an economy without government—in fact the added simplicity thereby gained helps clarify the basic relationships to be discussed. But whenever we attempt to test the validity of these basic relationships by reference to data for an actual economy, we run into the problem that these data reflect the pervasive influence and activity of governments. Further, apart from mere intellectual curiosity, the principal reason why economists engage in model building is to help provide guidance of either a positive or negative sort on questions of public policy, which largely means government action or inaction. Thus, our simple models need to be complicated by the introduction of government. In particular, the simple Keynesian model has been widely adapted to explain the impact of government action and to justify certain lines of governmental intervention, while derogating other lines of action and inaction which had been justified by earlier models.

Since the application of macroeconomic theory to governmental fiscal policy is an important part of the subject matter of a specialized branch of economics—public finance—we shall not develop that application in detail. However, a brief development of this is essential. We shall limit our discussion to the specific case of an economy faced with unemployment (rather than inflation) and will develop it largely in a rather formal, if rigorous, algebraic form, without attempt at verification. However, in the previous chapter, we have dealt with the same matters in a less formal way, and have illustrated them with some data from the U.S. national income accounts.

If we recognize that all consumer earnings are not received as personal disposable income, and accept the view that consumption expenditures depend on disposable income rather than earnings, we can write our consumption function as

$$(1) \qquad\qquad c = a + by_D$$

where $y_D$ is disposable income. This income consists of several elements:

$$(2) \qquad\qquad y_D = y - d - t + r$$

where $y$ is gross national product, $d$ depreciation, $t$ the aggregate volume of tax collections, and $r$ the volume of transfer payments. To keep the model simple, we assume all corporate profits distributed in dividends, and ignore some other minor items. (In Chapter XII, we included all of these items, and emphasized the importance of undistributed profits.) Gross national product consists now of three parts:

(3) $$y = c + g + i$$

where $g$ is the volume of government expenditures on goods and services and $i$ is gross investment. A closed economy is assumed. We also assume unemployed resources to begin with.

Substituting yields

$$y = a + by - bd - bt + br + g + i$$

(4) $$y = \frac{1}{1-b}(a - bd - bt + br + g + i)$$

This expression indicates that a change in government expenditures ($g$) is subject to the regular Keynesian multiplier of $1/(1-b)$ (where $b$ is the marginal propensity to consume *disposable* income), on the assumption that the other variables within the parentheses ($d$, $t$, $r$, and $i$) do not change as $g$ and $y$ change. On the other hand, a change in $t$ (all other variables constant) will produce a change in $y$ equal to the change in $t$ times $-b/(1-b)$. This tax multiplier is negative, because an increase in taxes will reduce income, and it is necessarily smaller than the government expenditures multiplier, because $b$ is necessarily less than 1. An increase in transfer payments is subject to the same multiplier with reversed sign, namely, $b/(1-b)$.

Thus these elementary manipulations tell us that a one billion dollar increase in government deficit (or decrease in surplus) caused by an increase in expenditure (taxes and transfers held constant) will have a larger effect on income and output than the same change of deficit or surplus created by a tax reduction or transfer payment increase. The reason obviously is that a deficit increase of one billion dollars created by higher spending on current output creates *in the first instance* an increase of one billion in output (and income) which is subject to the multiplier. But if taxes are reduced by one billion, the initial increase in demand, and output, is for consumers goods. This increase will be not one billion but $b$ times one-billion, for $1 - b$ of the tax reduction will be added to saving by the initial beneficiaries. This in turn is subject to the usual multiplier, $1/(1-b)$, making the total increase $b/(1-b)$. Similar reasoning shows why the transfer payment multiplier is also lower.

Consideration could be given to the fact that the first round recipients of the tax cut or transfer increase may have a different marginal propensity to consume than that applicable to the population generally. This would presumably influence the size of the "first round" only, because thereafter the effects become fully diffused.

Suppose now that increased government expenditures are matched by an equivalent increase in tax receipts (transfers held constant), so that the surplus or deficit is not altered. An equal increase in $g$ and $t$ causes the total within the parenthesis of equation (4) to increase by $(1 - b)$ times the change in the size of the budget. Thus the increase in $y$ is equal to $(1 - b)$ times the multiplier, $1/(1 - b)$, or 1. The student should be sure that he can explain *verbally* why it is that a mere change in the size of the budget (with no change in surplus or deficit) is stimulating or deflationary—i.e., is subject to a multiplier of one rather than zero— on the assumptions made here.[20]

So far we have dealt with changes of *single items* within the parentheses of equation (4), other items within the parentheses held constant. But it is not reasonable to assume that the others will, in fact, hold constant if we take steps to alter one of them. For example, if income rises because of increased $g$ or $i$, $t$ will remain constant only if specific action is taken to reduce tax rates, by just the amount necessary to prevent any change in collections as the tax base rises. We can consider the case in which tax *rates* are left constant, and collections allowed to vary, by making, as a first crude approximation, tax collections a function of the level of $y$:

$$(5) \qquad\qquad\qquad t = h + jy$$

Substituting this expression in equation (2), and again solving, yields the following expression:

$$(6) \qquad\qquad y = \frac{1}{1 - b(1 - j)}(a - bd - bh + br + g + i)$$

This gives a multiplier of

$$\frac{1}{1 - b(1 - j)}$$

applicable to an increase in $g$ or $i$ (necessarily smaller than the multiplier previously derived), and a multiplier of

$$\frac{b}{1 - b(1 - j)}$$

for a transfer payment increase. A similar extension could take account of the probable inverse relationship of transfers to the level of income,

[20] For a good summary of the literature on this "balanced budget theorem," see W. J. Baumol and M. H. Peston, "More on the Multiplier Effects of a Balanced Budget," *American Economic Review* (March 1955), pp. 140–8.

but this will be omitted here (although it was considered in the numerical treatment of the previous chapter).

There remain two items within the parentheses, $d$ and $i$. We may reasonably assume $d$ constant (in the short run) with respect to changes in the other items. If we wish to accept the theory proposed in the previous section of this chapter—that $i$ is a function of $y$—we would add the equation

(7)     $$i = e + fy$$

Solving the system composed of (1), (2), (3), (5), and (7) yields the following expression:

(8)     $$y = \frac{1}{1 - b(1 - j) - f}(a - bd - bh + br + g + e)$$

If taxes, allowed to vary with income, reduce the value of the multiplier, the stimulating effect of higher income on investment of course operates in the reverse, to enlarge the multiplier applicable to an increase in government expenditures.[21]

Before reminding ourselves of the necessary qualifications of this analysis, a numerical example will be given. Assume the functions to be as follows:

$$c = 10 + .8y_D \qquad\qquad i = 5 + .11y$$
$$y_D = y - d - t + r \qquad\qquad d = 10$$
$$y = c + g + i \qquad\qquad r = 0$$
$$t = .2y$$

Solving this model yields the expression:

$$y = 28 + 4g$$

Thus, if $g = 30$, $y = 148$, $t = 29.6$, $y_D = 108.4$, $c = 96.72$, $i = 21.28$. But if $g$ should rise to 40, the other values would be: $y = 188$, $t = 37.6$, $y_D = 140.4$, $c = 122.32$, $i = 25.68$. Note that the increase of 10 in government expenditures had a multiplier effect of 4 on GNP, yet increased the government deficit only by 2. These particularly favorable results come from a combination of a rather high MPC and MPI together with a fairly high marginal tax rate, which dampens the multiplier, but protects the budget from excessive deficits. (The student may wish to experiment

---

[21] It can be seen that the stability condition for this model is that $b(1 - j) + f$ should be less than one. Thus, the sum of $b + f$ (i.e., the MPC + MPI) might exceed one.

with other values of the relevant functions which may seem more plausible.)

If we knew that the full-employment level of this economy was a GNP of 200, we could solve for the necessary level of $g$ as follows:

$$y = 200 = 28 + 4g$$
$$g = 43$$

We could similarly solve for the necessary tax reduction, expenditures held constant, in order to raise $y$ to 200. On the other hand, if we wanted to obtain this level with a balanced budget, by setting the average tax rate at the necessary level, we could solve as follows:

$$200 = c + g + i$$
$$g = t$$
$$c = 10 + .8(y - d - t)$$
$$c = 10 + .8(200 - 10 - g) = 162 - .8g$$
$$i = 5 + .11(200) = 27$$
$$200 = 162 - .8g + g + 27$$
$$.2g = 11$$
$$g = 55$$
$$c = 118$$

The necessary average tax rate would be $55/200 = .275$.

More elaborate models are possible, which recognize the fact that different tax functions apply to different types of income, as well as to introduce the corporate form and the important item of corporate saving. This requires extending the model by equations which embody theories as to the determination of the various income shares (including corporate profits) and as to corporate dividend policy. However, the foregoing provides sufficient general introduction to the subject.

Use of fiscal models of this general variety has proved helpful in analysis of many problems of public policy. Yet their applicability is specifically limited by the assumptions employed in the models used; failure to respect the limitations inherent in these assumptions has led to incorrect conclusions. Because of their importance, we therefore review these assumptions once again. They include the following:

1) As already noted, the specifically fiscal assumptions are crude (e.g., a single tax function applicable to aggregate income, a single average consumption function which is also applicable to limited groups—e.g., taxpayers, etc.). Yet refinement requires more elaborate theories—regard-

ing income distribution, corporate saving behavior, and similar matters—introducing new sources of error.

The remaining assumptions relate to more general aspects of the Keynesian model.

2) The model is static. The assumption, therefore, implied in its use is that an equilibrium analysis can be relevant to policy matters. Specifically, the analysis compares an initial equilibrium situation with a new equilibrium which results from the introduction of given changes in taxes or expenditures. But is the situation of the economy in which such changes may be introduced ever an equilibrium one? Does a new equilibrium result, and within a time interval that makes the analysis meaningful?

3) The analysis is specifically limited to situations of less-than-full employment.

4) Closely related to the above, the analysis is conducted either on the assumption of constant wages and prices or else that wages and prices can change without affecting any of the relationships of the model. To assume that wages and prices can remain unchanged in the face of substantial changes in levels of demand, output, and employment is probably not realistic. Although we may think that the consumption relationship is stable in real terms, is this also true of investment? And most fiscal determinations are made in money rather than real terms; consequently, they change in real terms with every change in the price level.

5) The rate of interest is assumed not to vary, or else that its variation makes no difference. The assumption of an invariant $r$ either requires a completely elastic liquidity preference schedule (quite improbable) or a very unlikely kind of monetary policy; yet a variation in $r$ might affect consumption, and traditional analysis has argued that it certainly would affect investment. If there are systematic rate-of-interest effects, they are omitted from the model.

6) The assumption is made that real consumption expenditure is a stable function of real disposable income. This means that the price level, rate of interest, quantity of money or total assets, the distribution of income, etc., are of little or no moment.

7) The assumption is made that real investment is either (a) autonomous or (b) a function of real total output. As already pointed out, this assumes away any effects via the price level, interest rate, etc. It also assumes, more specifically, that private investment is either (a) unaf-

fected by the volume of government expenditure and by the levels of tax rates or (b) is affected only through the net effect of these on the level of income. The possibility that changes in tax rates may affect the willingness of entrepreneurs to assume investment risks is thus assumed away. Also assumed away is the possibility that government spending may in some sense compete with private investment (or affect the "confidence" of investors). According to some, who emphasize these effects, changes in government spending may be offset or even more than offset by changes in private investment.

8) A closed economy is assumed. For an economy in which international transactions are important, this will never do.

9) It is implied in the previous assumptions that purely financial aspects of government fiscal operations make no difference. That is, if there is a government deficit, it matters not whether the deficit is financed by borrowing from the public or from the banking system (or whether the banks have excess reserves), or by printing money. Monetary policy makes no difference. This is sometimes treated as more than an assumption of the model. Some argue that finance *can* make no difference. If government deficits and/or investment increase, saving must increase in an identical amount, they point out. If the government deficit is financed by selling bonds, the public can buy these bonds with the enlarged saving. If the deficit is financed by the printing press, the new money (instead of the new bonds) becomes the asset form in which the enlarged saving is embodied.

Whether finance *really* makes no difference can only be seen when we enlarge the analysis by readmitting such things as the quantity of money and the rate of interest into our model. Naturally they can make no difference if we assume them out of the way. To consider these as variables, along with the wage and price level, is the task of the following chapter.

It is striking, however, to note that the models employed in the present chapter reach precisely opposite conclusions as to the roles of fiscal and monetary policy from those of the Classical model. As pointed out earlier (pages 164–167), in the Classical model monetary policy was all-powerful in overcoming any unemployment which might occur because of rigid wages or a failure of the interest rate, while fiscal policy (except as a mere instrument of monetary policy) was powerless. Only as we bring together into one enlarged model the considerations involved in both models can we judge whether or to what extent either of these extreme views on policy may be broadly correct. Just as the simple Keynesian models developed in Chapter X and expanded in the present chapter assume away the instruments (flexible wages, prices, and interest rates) which formed the heart of the Classical analysis, so did the Classical analysis assume away (by failing to consider them) such fundamental relationships as the speculative demand for money and the consumption function. We must now throw all of these elements into a single pot, stir well, and taste the resulting stew.

## APPENDIX

### Stability Conditions

On page 329, we showed that the stability condition of the simple Keynesian model, incorporating a consumption lag, was that the MPC be less than one. No rigorous demonstration was provided for this finding. However, it can be derived quite directly, by simple algebra. We generalize the model, as follows:

$$y_t = c_t + i_t$$

$$c_t = a + by_{t-1}$$

By substitution,

$$y_t = by_{t-1} + (a + i_t)$$

The equilibrium consistent with any given constant level, $i_0$, of investment is found by letting

$$y_t = y_{t-1} = y_E$$

or, substituting in the previous expression,

$$y_E = by_E + (a + i_0)$$

$$y_E = \frac{1}{1-b}(a + i_0)$$

which is, of course, the familiar formulation obtained earlier for the static model.

If, for any period, income is at its equilibrium level, it will remain there, for

*if*
$$y_{t-1} = y_E = \frac{1}{1-b}(a + i_0)$$

*then*
$$y_t = by_{t-1} + (a + i_0)$$

$$= \frac{b}{1-b}(a + i_0) + (a + i_0)$$

$$= \left(1 + \frac{b}{1-b}\right)(a + i_0)$$

$$= \frac{1 - b + b}{1 - b}(a + i_0)$$

$$= y_E$$

This condition obtains whether or not the equilibrium is stable. However, suppose that income is, for one period, different from its equilibrium level. That is, suppose that

$$y_{t-1} = y_E + X$$

where $X$ is either positive or negative, but not zero. Then, in the following period,

$$y_t = by_{t-1} + (a + i_0)$$

$$= b(y_E + X) + (a + i_0)$$

$$= \frac{b}{1-b}(a + i_0) + bX + (a + i_0)$$

$$= \frac{1}{1-b}(a + i_0) + bX$$

$$= y_E + bX$$

In the period which follows, we have

$$y_{t+1} = b(y_E + bX) + (a + i_0)$$

$$= \frac{b}{1-b}(a + i_0) + b^2X + (a + i_0)$$

$$= \frac{1}{1-b}(a + i_0) + b^2X$$

$$= y_E + b^2X$$

And, in the following period:

$$y_{t+2} = y_E + b^3X$$

The income series, then, is,

$$(y_E + X), \ (y_E + bX), \ (y_E + b^2X), \ (y_E + b^3X), \ \text{etc.}$$

If $X$ is positive, that is, if income in period $y_{t-1}$ exceeded equilibrium, then it is clear that the excess will grow if $b$ is greater than one. That is, the equilibrium is unstable. But the excess will shrink toward zero if $b$ is less than one. If $X$ is negative, which means that income in period $y_{t-1}$ was less than equilibrium, then the deficiency will grow if $b$ is greater than one, and shrink toward zero if $b$ is less than one.

Consider now the case $b = 1$. In this case our difference equation becomes

$$y_t = y_{t-1} + (a + i_0)$$

If $(a + i_0) = 0$, then we have the result that income always equals its previous value. Although this is a kind of equilibrium ("neutral equilibrium"), it implies no economic explanation for the level of income. Income is whatever it has been. But if $(a + i_0)$ is either positive or negative, no equilibrium is possible: successive values of $y_t$ will differ by a constant amount —income either shrinking toward zero (if $[a + i_0] < 0$) or growing without limit (if $[a + i_0] > 0$).

Our conclusion thus is that stable equilibrium requires that the marginal propensity to consume be less than one.

The principle that stability conditions can only be derived from dynamic assumptions is an important one. Consequently we shall illustrate it from another field of economics. Consider, for example, the market for a single commodity, whose static supply and demand curves (assumed to depend on price alone) are shown in the following equations, and in Figure 13–6.

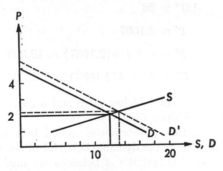

**Figure 13–6.**

Generalized equilibrium formulation:

$$\begin{cases} S = r + sP \\ D = u - vP \\ S = D \end{cases}$$

$$r + sP = u - vP$$

$$P(s + v) = u - r$$

$$P = \frac{u - r}{s + v}$$

Specific example:

$$\begin{cases} S = -4 + 8P \\ D = 20 - 4P \\ S = D \end{cases}$$

$$-4 + 8P = 20 - 4P$$
$$12P = 24$$
$$P = 2$$
$$S = -4 + 8(2) = 12$$
$$D = 20 - 4(2) = 12$$

We now suppose an upward shift in the demand function, which now becomes

$$D' = 22 - 4P'$$

(This is shown as the broken line in Figure 13–6.)

Solving, we have

$$-4 + 8P' = 22 - 4P'$$
$$12P' = 26$$
$$P' = 2.1667$$
$$S' = -4 + 8(2.1667) = 13.333$$
$$D' = 22 - 4(2.1667) = 13.333$$

The new equilibrium involves a higher price and a somewhat larger quantity exchanged, as shown in Figure 13–6.

But are we sure that the equilibrium identified here is a stable one? We can be sure only if we specify the dynamic behavior of the market participants. There are numerous possible varieties of behavior we might specify, each corresponding to some particular set of technological and institutional conditions. Suppose that we specify, for example, that suppliers adapt to price changes only with a lag. Because of the time consumed in production, an alteration in the rate of input creates an altered rate of output only some time later. This is true in agriculture, but also in many industrial processes. We may suppose no lag in the response of buyers to price change. We further suppose that the good is nonstorable, that the quantity produced is all put upon the market immediately as it is produced, with the price immediately adjusting to clear the market. This gives us the following dynamic model:

Generally:

$$\begin{cases} S_t = r + sP_{t-1} \\ D_t = u - vP_t \\ S_t = D_t \end{cases}$$
$$r + sP_{t-1} = u - vP_t$$
$$P_t = \frac{u - r}{v} - \frac{s}{v} P_{t-1}$$

Specifically:

$$\begin{cases} S_t = -4 + 8P_{t-1} \\ D_t = 20 - 4P_t \\ S_t = D_t \end{cases}$$

$$-4 + 8P_{t-1} = 20 - 4P_t$$

$$P_t = 6 - 2P_{t-1}$$

Suppose that price was initially at its equilibrium level. This level is:

$$P_E = 6 - 2P_E$$

$$3P_E = 6$$

$$P_E = 2$$

Then (as before), introduce an upward shift of the demand curve to

$$D_t' = 22 - 4P_t$$

$$S_t = D_t'$$

$$-4 + 8P_{t-1} = 22 - 4P_t$$

$$P_t = 6.5 - 2P_{t-1}$$

$$P_t = 6.5 - 2(2) = 2.5$$

$$P_{t+1} = 6.5 - 2(2.5) = 1.5$$

$$P_{t+2} = 6.5 - 2(1.5) = 3.5$$

$$P_{t+3} = 6.5 - 2(3.5) = -.5$$

$$P_{t+4} = 6.5 - 2(-.5) = 7.5$$

etc.

There is a new equilibrium price, which is $P'_E = 2.1667$, but instead of reaching this new equilibrium, the price and quantity fluctuate more and more widely back and forth, from above the equilibrium to below it. Figure 13–7 exhibits this "undamped cobweb" movement.

Once again, we can easily ascertain the stability condition for this model. Its equilibrium price is found as

$$P_E = \frac{u - r}{v} - \frac{s}{v} P_E$$

$$P_E \left(1 + \frac{s}{v}\right) = \frac{u - r}{v}$$

$$P_E = \frac{u - r}{s + v} \text{(compare above, p. 349)}$$

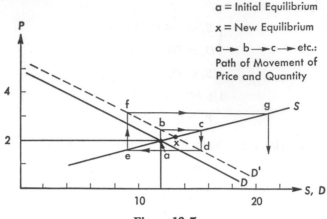

**Figure 13–7.**

If the price in any particular period $t - 1$ differed from equilibrium by an amount $X$ (positive or negative), then

$$P_t = \frac{u - r}{v} - \frac{s}{v}(P_E + X)$$

$$= \frac{u - r}{v} - \frac{s}{v}\left(\frac{u - r}{v + s} + X\right)$$

$$= \frac{u - r}{v} - \frac{s}{v} \cdot \frac{u - r}{v + s} - \frac{s}{v}X$$

$$= \frac{u - r}{v + s} - \frac{s}{v}X$$

$$= P_E - \frac{s}{v}X$$

and, by similar derivation,

$$P_{t+1} = P_E + \left(\frac{s}{v}\right)^2 X$$

$$P_{t+2} = P_E - \left(\frac{s}{v}\right)^3 X$$

etc.

From this series:

$$[P_E + X],\ [P_E - \frac{s}{v}X],\ [P_E + \left(\frac{s}{v}\right)^2 X],\ [P_E - \left(\frac{s}{v}\right)^3 X],\ \text{etc.}$$

it can easily be seen that the divergence from equilibrium (1) always fluctuates from a plus to a minus to a plus figure in successive periods, and (2) becomes greater, remains constant, or shrinks toward zero as $s/v$ is greater than, equal to, or less than one—i.e., depending on whether $s > v, s = v, s < v$. Interpreting the algebraic condition in graphic terms, we have the result that market equilibrium is stable or unstable depending on whether the slope $(v)$ of the demand curve (ignoring sign) is numerically less or greater than the slope $(s)$ of the supply curve.[22] The student can test this conclusion by working out (algebraically, or by an accurately drawn graph) the dynamics when the model takes these values:

$$S_t = 5 + 6P_{t-1}$$

$$D_t = 33 - 8P_t$$

Here again, it was impossible to determine from the static model whether equilibrium was stable or unstable. This could only be determined by reference to the dynamic properties of the model.

However, the reader will recall that we assumed only one of a number of possible dynamic pattern of market behavior. Suppose that the basic (static) supply and demand curves were exactly as before, but that market dynamics were as follows:

1) Suppliers (perhaps a price leader) determine an announced market price, established at the beginning of each market period and prevailing throughout the period whether or not amounts supplied and demanded are equal. The difference between these amounts is absorbed by sellers' inventories.

2) This price will be the same as, greater than, or less than the last period's price depending on whether, last period, supply just equalled, fell short of, or exceeded demand. The greater the excess of supply over demand (or *vice versa*) last period, the greater the reduction (increase) that will be announced for this period. Algebraically:

$$P_t = P_{t-1} + x(D_{t-1} - S_{t-1})$$

where $x$ is the coefficient of price adjustment.

3) As before, buyers adjust their amounts purchased to the current price without lag. That is,

$$D_t = u - vP_t$$

---

[22] The student will often find this condition expressed in just the opposite way: namely, that stability requires that the slope of the supply curve be greater than the slope of the demand curve. This is the correct statement if we think in terms of a conventional graph. In that case, we must rearrange our supply and demand curves from:

$$S = r + sP$$
$$D = u - vP$$

into the following:

$$P = 1/sS - r/s$$
$$P = -1/vD + u/v$$

The condition for stability is that $1/s$ be greater than $1/v$, which means, of course, that $v$ is greater than $s$.

4) Sellers adjust their output to the announced price, without lag. That is,

$$S_t = r + sP_t$$

To illustrate, suppose that the values of $r$, $s$, $u$, and $v$ are the same as before, so that we have

$$S_t = -4 + 8P_t$$

$$D_t = 20 - 4P_t$$

$$P_t = P_{t-1} + .05(D_{t-1} - S_{t-1})$$

The coefficient .05 (for $x$) measures the intensity of sellers' adjustment to a previous supply-demand gap. This intensity could range from zero (no price adjustment no matter how large the gap) to a very sharp reaction (in this case, a coefficient of the order of .2 would represent a sharp response). Solving the model gives us:

$$P_t = P_{t-1} + .05(20 - 4P_{t-1} + 4 - 8P_{t-1})$$

$$P_t = .4P_{t-1} + 1.2$$

If

$$P_{t-1} = 2$$

$$P_t = .4(2) + 1.2 = 2$$

That is,

$$P_E = 2$$

But if

$$P_{t-1} = 3$$

$$P_t = .4(3) + 1.2 = 2.4$$

$$P_{t+1} = .4(2.4) + 1.2 = 2.16$$

$$P_{t+2} = .4(2.16) + 1.2 = 2.064$$

etc.

obviously a stable result.

However, if $x$ equaled .1, we would have:

$$P_t = P_{t-1} + .1(20 - 4P_{t-1} + 4 - 8P_{t-1})$$

$$P_t = -.2P_{t-1} + 2.4$$

Again, if

$$P_{t-1} = 2$$

$$P_t = -.2(2) + 2.4 = 2$$

But if

$$P_{t-1} = 3$$

$$P_t = -.2(3) + 2.4 = 1.8$$

$$P_{t+1} = -.2(1.8) + 2.4 = 2.04$$

$$P_{t+2} = -.2(2.04) + 2.4 = 1.992$$

etc.,

also obviously a stable result, although in cobweb pattern.

The general form of the difference equation for this model is

$$P_t = P_{t-1}[1 - x(v + s)] + x(u - r).$$

This equation can easily be shown to produce a stable or unstable result depending on the magnitude of the term $[1 - x(v + s)]$. Since this term cannot be greater than one ($x$, $v$, and $s$ are all defined as positive), a progressive monotonic (i.e., one-directional) movement away from equilibrium is ruled out. If $x(v + s)$ is less than one, then the quantity $[1 - x(v + s)]$ will be positive but less than one, and a monotonic movement toward equilibrium is generated. However, if $x(v + s) > 1$, the quantity $[1 - x(v + s)]$ will be negative, and a cobweb movement will result, becoming unstable if $x(v + s)$ reaches a value of 2 or greater.

Whether this model is more or less realistic than the previous one, or is so for some kinds of markets but not others, or whether still another set of dynamic equations should be used, is beside the point for our present purpose. That purpose is to illustrate the corollary to the general principle previously established. The general principle was: *Stability of equilibrium cannot be deduced from a static (equilibrium) model, but depends on the dynamics of the model.* The corollary is this: *The same static model can describe the equilibrium positions of a number of alternative dynamic models; thus the equilibrium position of a static model may be stable with one set of dynamic assumptions, unstable with another.*

# APPENDIX

## An Inventory Cycle Model

In the text of this chapter, we considered one possible variety of inventory policy by sellers—an entirely passive one. We suggested that sellers might always produce in any period whatever they sold in the previous period. Thus, if this period's sales differ from those of last period, inventories will either increase or decrease. No provision was made for any attempt to restore the previous level of inventories by altering production plans. Lloyd Metzler was the first to investigate the consequences of an effort by sellers to maintain a desired stock of inventories, through appropriate correction of production plans.[23] His simplest model assumes that sellers produce this period what they

[23] See his "The Nature and Stability of Inventory Cycles," and "Factors Governing the Length of Inventory Cycles," *Review of Economic Statistics*, XXIII (August 1941), 113–29, and XXIX (February 1947), 1–5.

sold last period, plus such additional amount as may be necessary to restore last period's unintended decline of inventories, or minus last period's unintended accumulation of inventories.

That is, we assume that there is some desired level of inventories, which we shall here designate as $x$. Production of consumer goods in any period, $\underline{c_t}$, is thus:

(1) $$\underline{c_t} = c_{t-1} + (x - n_{t-1})$$

where $c_t$ represents sales, and $n_t$ is the actual end-of-period stock of inventories. We add the definition

(2) $$n_t = n_{t-1} + (\underline{c_t} - c_t)$$

that is, ending stock equals beginning stock plus production and minus sales.

(3) $$c_t = a + by_t$$

that is, sales depend on current income.

(4) $$y_t = \underline{c_t} + i_t$$

We substitute as follows:

$$y_t = c_{t-1} + x - n_{t-1} + i_t$$

$$= c_{t-1} + x - n_{t-2} - \underline{c_{t-1}} + c_{t-1} + i_t$$

$$= c_{t-1} + x - n_{t-2} - c_{t-2} - x + n_{t-2} + c_{t-1} + i_t$$

$$= 2c_{t-1} - c_{t-2} + i_t$$

$$= 2a + 2by_{t-1} - a - by_{t-2} + i_t$$

(5) $\qquad y_t = 2by_{t-1} - by_{t-2} + a + i_t$

This reduced-form difference equation has the usual static multiplier solution. If we substitute in equation (5)

$$y_E = y_t = y_{t-1} = y_{t-2}$$

we find the familiar

(6) $$y_E = \frac{1}{1-b}(a + i_t)$$

But if investment increases, the new equilibrium is not established immediately but only by a cyclical path of income change, in which income first overshoots the new equilibrium, then falls below it, rises above, but less than the first time, and so on.

We can illustrate by assuming the following values for our parameters:

$$a = 5$$

$$b = .75$$

$$i_{t-1}, i_{t-2}, i_{t-3} \cdots = 20$$

$$i_t, i_{t+1}, i_{t+2} \cdots = 25$$

The initial equilibrium income is

$$y_E = \frac{1}{1 - .75}(25) = 100$$

The new equilibrium is

$$y'_E = \frac{1}{1 - .75}(30) = 120$$

But the path of movement is as follows:

$$y_t = 2by_{t-1} - by_{t-2} + a + i_t$$
$$= 1.5(100) - .75(100) + 30 = 105$$
$$y_{t+1} = 1.5(105) - .75(100) + 30 = 112.5$$
$$y_{t+2} = 1.5(112.5) - .75(105) + 30 = 120$$
$$y_{t+3} = 1.5(120) - .75(112.5) + 30 = 125.625$$
$$y_{t+4} = 1.5(125.625) - .75(120) + 30 = 128.4375$$
$$y_{t+5} = 1.5(128.4375) - .75(125.625) + 30 = 128.4375$$
$$y_{t+6} = 1.5(128.4375) - .75(128.4375) + 30 = 126.32825$$

etc.

The common sense of all this is not too difficult to disentangle (once it has been demonstrated mathematically).

With an unexpected increase in sales (which depletes inventories), producers respond not only by raising their production to the new higher level of sales, but also by attempting to restore the depleted inventories. This effort to restore inventories is, of course, self-defeating, because the higher income resulting from the greater production causes a further increase in sales, which depletes inventories again, leading to further expansion of production, income, and sales. But so long as the MPC is less than one, this cannot go on for ever. Income eventually rises above the level which the multiplier (operating on the new higher level of investment) can support, except as it is maintained above this level by the effort to restore previously depleted inventories. At some point these inventories are restored. When this happens, inventory investment is no longer positive, and income drops toward its equilibrium level. But this drop in income leads to a drop in sales, and inventories begin to pile up. This leads to a further reduction of production, as producers try to use up their excess stocks instead of producing all that they expect to sell. This attempt is also self-defeating because it reduces income and thus further reduces sales. Again, however, there is a limit, and excess inventories will finally be worked off, but only after income has fallen below its equilibrium level.

Now it can be proved that equilibrium in this model is stable, in the sense that the amplitude of the resulting cycles will diminish toward zero. Metzler, however, complicates the model further (perhaps in the direction of realism) by introducing two further assumptions. One is to make the desired stock of inventories not constant but a proportion of current sales. The other is to have producers assume that when sales have been rising they will continue to rise. Instead of producing the amount that they actually sold last period (plus an inventory correction), they will extrapolate rising (or falling) sales into the future.

Metzler shows that either amendment of the simpler model (or both in combination) can produce *unstable* cycles (as well as more complex forms of movement), *even with MPC < 1*. That is, there may exist an equilibrium which cannot be attained.

# The Complete
# Keynesian Model

*Chapter XIV*

The complete Keynesian model can be approached from either of two directions. (1) We can add the consumption function and the "speculative demand for money" to the Classical model (a task already half-completed in Chapter IX). Or, (2) starting from the simple Keynesian model of the last chapter, we can add the necessary relationships involving wages and prices and the supply and demand for labor, and those involving money, the interest rate, and the response of investment (and possibly saving) to a variable interest rate. It is clear that the first route would be simpler and more direct. Nevertheless, we shall follow the second because it may throw into sharper relief certain relationships that are often the subject of confusion. We shall work with a formally defined algebraic model (supplemented by diagrams); but we will also attempt to describe verbally the logic and the relevance of each step. In the following chapter, we shall summarize our findings as to what, if anything, the "Keynesian revolution" added to or changed in the Classical macroeconomics, remembering always that the Classical structure was seldom, if ever, completely specified in the form of a rigorous and static model.

## COMBINING CLASSICAL AND KEYNESIAN SAVING
## AND INVESTMENT THEORIES

The simple Keynesian model can be set up either in the "$c + i$" form or the "$s = i$" form (see pages 210–216). We shall work with the latter, only for convenience of transition from Keynesian to Classical ideas (although in many respects the former method of statement leads one away from some common logical traps which surround the latter method and invite the unwary). Our model then begins with a saving function

(1) $$s = s(y)$$

For our simple Keynesian model we can either represent investment as autonomous, or we can make it a function of income. To obtain greater generality, we will adopt the latter:

(2) $$i = i(y)$$

We specify that $ds/dy$ (marginal propensity to save) is greater than zero, and greater than $di/dy$ (marginal propensity to invest). Graphically, this means that the saving function cuts the investment function from below, as in Figure 13–3. We have the equilibrium condition

(3) $$s = i$$

Suppose that we now begin the enlargement of the model by admitting an influence of the rate of interest on investment, and, for formal completeness, on saving, too. The influence on investment is inverse, on saving direct; i.e., $\delta i/\delta r < 0$, $\delta s/\delta r > 0$ (investment slope is negative, saving slope positive). This means that equations (1) and (2) must now be broadened, as follows:

(1') $$s = s(y, r)$$

(2') $$i = i(y, r)$$

It should be clear that equations (1'), (2'), and (3) do not form a complete system—that is, we cannot solve them for all four variables ($s$, $i$, $y$, and $r$). If $y$ were given, we could solve for $s$, $i$, and $r$; that is, we could find the rate of interest that would equate saving and investment. If $r$ were given, we could solve for $s$, $i$, and $y$; that is, we could find the level of income that would equate saving and investment. But if *both* $y$ and $r$ are free to vary, there will be a whole family of possible combinations of $y$ and $r$ at which $s$ and $i$ are equal.[1]

---

[1] This result is not affected if we prefer to make saving a function of income only and investment a function only of the interest rate:

(i) $$s = s(y)$$

(ii) $$i = i(r)$$

(3) $$s = i$$

There are still four unknowns and but three equations.

Graphically, we can represent the matter as in part A of Figure 14–1. If $i$ depends both on $y$ and $r$, then we can show the dependence on $y$ by the upward slope of an investment function in a Keynesian-type diagram,

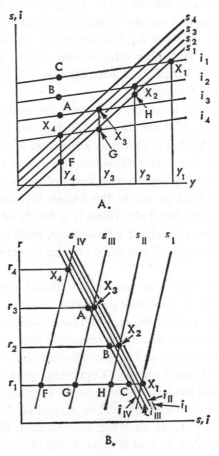

Figure 14–1.

with axes $i$ (or $s$), and $y$. But if it *also depends on $r$*, there is not one investment function in this diagram but a whole family—one for each possible level of $r$. Here we show only four of these. Function $i_1$ assumes a given interest rate, $r_1$; function $i_2$ shows how investment varies with income when the rate of interest is somewhat higher, at $r_2$ (less would be invested at every level of income); function $i_3$ assumes a still higher rate of interest, $r_3$; etc. Similarly with the saving function. If the rate of interest should be $r_1$ (the same rate assumed in drawing function $i_1$), saving would vary with income along function $s_1$; but at a higher rate, $r_2$, more would be saved at every level of income—this function would shift to $s_2$; etc. If the rate of interest is predetermined at $r_1$, then the relevant functions are $s_1$ and $i_1$; these intersect at $X_1$, leading to the equilibrium income $y_1$. But for other rates of interest (e.g., $r_2$, $r_3$, and $r_4$, shown), there are other levels of income that equate saving and investment. These intersections are labeled $X_2$, $X_3$, and $X_4$. Obviously, we could select still other rates of interest, and find other intersections. These will fall on a line which passes through $X_4X_3X_2X_1$. Each point on this line corresponds to some particular rate of interest.

It is equally possible, however, to picture the matter as in part B of Figure 14–1. Here the axes are those made familiar in Classical saving-investment analysis. Saving is shown as a function of the rate of interest. But, if we add that saving is *also* a function of income, we have a separate saving function corresponding to each level of $y$. Suppose that $s_{IV}$ corresponds to income level $y_4$, $s_{III}$ to the higher income level $y_3$, $s_{II}$ to a still higher level $y_2$, etc. Similarly, there is a family of investment functions.[2] Again, we have a family of intersections, such as those marked $X_1$ through $X_4$ in the diagram. These trace out the movements of $s$, $i$, and $r$ with changes in $y$.

The relationship between the two figures should now become evident. It can be illustrated by considering the points labeled A, B, and C in the second or "Classical" part of the figure. These points show the different amounts of investment (measured horizontally) that correspond to three different interest rates, $r_3$, $r_2$, and $r_1$, *given* level of income $y_4$. These same points can now be located on the "Keynesian" part A. Given level of income $y_4$, we can find the levels of investment (here measured vertically) which correspond to each interest rate, $r_3$, $r_2$, and $r_1$. Another set of common points is the set F, G, H, showing, in each part, the levels of saving at a single rate of interest, $r_1$, and at three levels of income, $y_4$, $y_3$, and $y_2$.

It should also be easy to see that points $X_1$, $X_2$, $X_3$, and $X_4$ in part A correspond exactly to points $X_1$, $X_2$, $X_3$, and $X_4$ in part B. In part A, for instance, $X_1$ shows that the equilibrium level of income is $y_1$, if the rate of interest is given at $r_1$ ($s_1$ and $i_1$, which intersect at $X_1$, are the appropriate income functions when $r$ is given at $r_1$). In part B, $X_1$ shows that the equilibrium rate of interest is $r_1$, if income is given at $y_1$ ($s_I$ and $i_I$ are the appropriate interest functions when income is given at $r_1$). It can be

---

[2] If we assume $\delta i/\delta y = 0$, then there is only one investment function in part B, and a family of parallel *horizontal* "functions" in part A. If saving is a function only of $y(\delta s/\delta r = 0)$, then in part B the $s$ "functions" are a family of parallel vertical lines; while in part A there is a single $s$ function rising to the right.

seen that the saving and investment coordinate of $X_1$ is the same in each figure, at level $s_1$, $i_1$. In short, these two figures contain exactly the same information, merely arranged in different ways. They show that $r$ will equate $s$ and $i$, but only if $y$ is given; or, equally well, that $y$ will equate $s$ and $i$, if only $r$ is given. There are, indeed, an infinite number of possible combinations of $y$ and $r$ that will equate $s$ and $i$.

We can now derive a description or a graph of these combinations. For example, the $y_4$ which appears on the horizontal axis of part A corresponds to the $r_4$ on the vertical scale of part B, and similarly for the income and interest coordinates of the other X-points. Figure 14–2 trans-

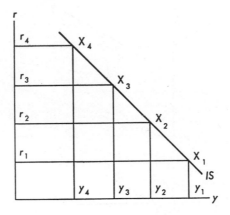

Figure 14–2.

fers this information to a single diagram with these two axes. The curve which connects these points in the new figure is labeled "*IS*," following the notation of Professor Alvin Hansen, who popularized this kind of diagram.[3]

Can we explain in words why the relationship between $r$ and $y$ must be of the kind shown in this figure? If we neglect the dependence of $s$ on $r$ and of $i$ on $y$ (both presumably secondary), we can explain it quite easily, in either of two ways. If $r$ is high, $i$ will be low, for high $r$ discourages investment. If $i$ is low, so will be $y$, via the multiplier. And vice versa. Or, we can put it that if $y$ is high, so will be $s$, for saving is a

[3] See his *Monetary Theory and Fiscal Policy* (McGraw-Hill, 1949), Chap. V. Actually, the analytical technique stems directly from an article by J. R. Hicks, "Mr. Keynes and the Classics," *Econometrica* (1937), reprinted in *Readings in the Theory of Income Distribution*, selected by a committee of the American Economic Association (Blakiston, 1946), pp. 461–76. See also a similar analysis by Oskar Lange, in the first part of his "The Rate of Interest and the Optimum Propensity to Consume," *Economica* (1938), reprinted in the AEA *Readings in Business Cycle Theory*, pp. 169–78.

direct function of income. In order for $i$ to equal a large $s$, the rate of interest must be low. And vice versa. If we reintroduce the further dependence of $s$ on $r$ and of $i$ on $y$, the verbal argument becomes more complicated. The student should probably attempt to state it, finding it both difficult and lengthy. Perhaps he will then be more grateful for the graphs, which put the matter so neatly.

More elegant, but probably no easier to visualize, is a representation of these relationships in a single three-dimensional diagram, as in Figure 14–3. Here we show two surfaces, an investment surface (the lined sur-

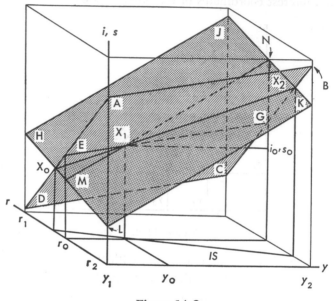

**Figure 14–3.**

face in the figure), and a saving surface (stippled), intersecting along the line $X_0 X_1 X_2$. In attempting to understand the diagram, the first thing is to get the axes clearly in mind. Vertically, we measure amounts of saving or investment. From left to right, we measure levels of income. Going away from the viewer is the interest axis, with the highest rates in the background. The investment surface is bounded by the letters $ABCD$. As we move along this surface from left to right, from lower to higher incomes, its level rises—i.e., the amount of investment increases—whatever the level of interest rate. This is shown, for example, by the cross section $DC$ which shows the rate of investment for each level of income, given rate of interest $r_1$. Cross section $EX_1G$ shows investment varying with income, when the interest rate is $r_0$. And $AB$ is an income cross section at $r_2$. But the investment surface sinks as we move along it in the direction of higher interest rates, whatever the level of $y$. For example, cross-sections $AED$ and $BGC$ exhibit this characteristic, at income levels $y_1$ and $y_2$, respectively.

The saving surface, bounded by letters $HJKL$, slopes upward away from the viewer and upward to the right. That is, it shows more saved as the rate of interest rises, and more saved as income rises. Cross-sections $LMH$ and $KNJ$ exhibit the former characteristic at two given income levels, $y_1$ and $y_2$, respectively. Cross-sections $HJ$, $MX_1N$, and $LK$ represent the increase of saving as income rises, at levels of interest $r_1$, $r_0$, and $r_2$, respectively.

If a viewer saw this figure from directly in front of it, so that the interest dimension were not visible, he would see three investment functions ($AB$, $EX_1G$, and $DC$) each rising gradually to the right; and three saving functions ($HJ$, $MX_1N$, $LK$) each rising more rapidly to the right. The middle pair ($EX_1G$ and $MX_1N$) would intersect within the figure (at $X_1$). If he stood at one "end" of the figure—say, the left end—looking directly toward it so as to collapse its income dimension—he would see a diagram like Figure 14–1, part B, except that it would be rotated one quarter turn to the left. (If the viewer turns the page so that the right edge becomes the bottom, he will see, in the two "end" planes of the figure, familiar Classical saving-investment diagrams.)

If we trace on the "floor" of the diagram the projection of the intersection between the two planes, we have a line which connects all of the possible combinations of rate of interest and level of income that will equate saving and investment. This is the $IS$ curve previously derived.

Although our model is still incomplete, it is obvious that we can no longer describe it as one in which "saving and investment determine the level of income." It could with equal correctness (or error) be described as one in which "saving and investment determine the interest rate" (as Classical economics held). Actually, we can see that saving, investment, income, and interest rate must bear certain relationships one to another, all being mutually determined in a system of interdependence, but that single and simple lines of causation are now ruled out.[4]

[4] A numerical example may help the reader to grasp the relationships involved. Suppose that the saving and investment functions are

(1)                             $s = .25y + r$

(2)                             $i = .05y - 3r + 40$

Given $r$ at some particular figure (e.g., 5), these become the equations of the simple Keynesian saving-investment model, and can be solved for equilibrium income ($y = 100$). Changing the assumed $r$ shifts the equations and alters the equilibrium $y$. But

## INTRODUCTION OF SUPPLY AND DEMAND FOR MONEY

To continue with the expansion of our model we may look for some other macroeconomic relationship involving one or more of the variables already considered. One that immediately suggests itself is the relationship between the rate of interest and the other factors involved in the supply and demand for money. We add the following equation:

$$(4) \qquad\qquad M = lPy + L(r)$$

where $M$ is the total supply of money, $lPy$ the transactions demand, and $L(r)$ the speculative demand. This equation should be familiar from previous use. Since $M$ is assumed to be an exogenous variable (and $l$ is determined by economic structure), we add only one new variable, $P$; but this still leaves the model incomplete, for we previously had one more unknown than we had equations. Now there are five unknowns and four equations.

However, a system in which $P$, also, is taken as given is not completely without interest, in view of the known "stickiness" of many prices—and of wage rates, which are the chief determinant (on the cost side) of the price level. In fact, a system consisting of these four equations is often represented as "the" Keynesian system (something of an exaggeration in the light of Keynes' own lengthy discussion of the relation of wages, prices, and the marginal product of labor). Such a system has some interest, then, in itself. In any case, we can use it as a *stage* in the transition toward our larger model, which will attempt to "explain" the price level, rather than to take it as given. For the moment, however, let $P$ have the same "autonomous" status as $M$.

If prices and money are given, equation (4) tells us that there are certain combinations of $y$ and $r$ that are possible—i.e., certain combinations that will equate the supply and the demand for money. The nature of this relationship has been indicated previously (pages 180–182). We

---

if $y$ is instead given (e.g., at 120), the equations take the form of the Classical saving-investment intersection, determining the equilibrium interest rate ($r = 4$). Changing the assumed $y$ shifts the equations and alters the equilibrium $r$. Both Classical and Keynesian saving-investment theories are thus seen as special cases.

Solving the equations simultaneously gives

$$(3) \qquad\qquad y = 200 - 20r$$

or

$$(4) \qquad\qquad r = 10 - .05y$$

This is the *IS* curve, and produces the whole family of possible $r$ and $y$ combinations.

can recall it by introducing some diagrams previously used, as in Figure 14–4. We can read this pair of diagrams in either of two ways. We can start in the upper one with some rate of interest—say $r_0$—and at this rate find the corresponding speculative demand for money, $M_{s_0}$ (given the

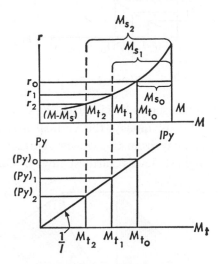

**Figure 14–4.**

prevailing interest rate expectations of wealth-holders). Subtracting $M_{s_0}$ from the total supply of money, $M$, leaves an amount $M_{t_0}$ to satisfy the transactions demand. Reading down to the lower half of the diagram, we can discover what level of $Py$—and, since $P$ is given, therefore what level of $y$—is necessary to yield just this transactions demand (in this case, $Py_0$). Conversely, we can in the lower diagram assume some level of $y$—say, $y_1$—which, given $P$, produces a transactions demand $M_{t_1}$. This demand, transferred to the upper diagram, shows how high the interest rate must be (in this case $r_1$) to reduce speculative holdings to a level which makes total demand just equal to the supply of money.

Again, we can combine the information from these two parts into a single diagram, Figure 14–5. This shows directly the possible combinations of $r$ and $Py$, given some particular supply of money. We label this $LM$, following Hansen's usage. This line connects each interest rate (read from the vertical axis of the top half of Figure 14–4) with the corresponding level of money income (read from the vertical axis of the lower half of Figure 14–4).

The information shown in the two parts of Figure 14–4 and in Figure 14–5 can all be combined into one three-dimensional figure, as in Fig-

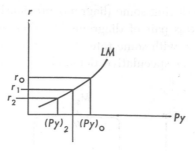

Figure 14–5.

ure 14–6. This figure again shows two intersecting surfaces. The horizontal axis represents quantities of money, the vertical axis interest rates, and the axis which moves away from the viewer represents levels of money income, with the highest levels farthest away. One surface is the

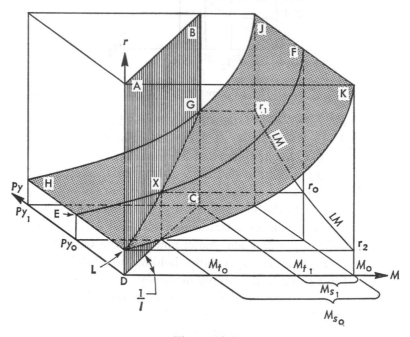

Figure 14–6.

transactions demand for money, labeled *ABCD*. This shows the transactions demand increasing with higher income, but independent of the interest rate. The stippled surface *HJKL* represents the speculative demand for money, subtracted from the given total supply of money $M_0$. (If the total supply increases, this whole surface moves to the right; if $M$ decreases, it moves to the left.) These two surfaces intersect along line *LXG*. If we project the image of this surface onto the (right) end plane of the figure, we get the line labeled *LM*. This shows the possible combinations of $Py$ and $r$ which will equate the supply and the demand for money. For example, if income is $Py_1$, the transactions demand will be $M_{t_1}$, requiring an interest rate $r_1$ in order to reduce the speculative demand to $M_{s_1}$, where $M_{t_1} + M_{s_1}$ just equal the total supply. Likewise, if money income is $Py_0$, the interest rate will be $r_0$; if income is zero, the interest rate would be $r_2$.[5]

## THE HICKS-HANSEN ANALYSIS

The supply and demand for money thus give us a relationship between $Py$ and $r$, which, on the assumption of a given $P$, is also a relationship between $y$ and $r$. We bring together, in Figure 14–7, the results of our

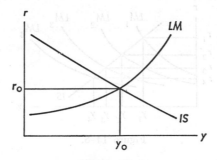

**Figure 14–7.**

previous analysis. It will be recalled that the *IS* curve shows the various combinations of $y$ and $r$ that are consistent with an equality between $s$

[5] A numerical example is more complicated, if we insist on a curvilinear $M_s$ function. Suppose we represent the two demands as

(5) $$M_t = .4y$$

(6) $$M_s = \frac{100}{r - 1} - 10$$

and fix the supply of money as

(7) $$M = 55$$

If $y$ is taken as given (e.g., at 100), we can solve for $r$ (equals 5). We thus see that $r$ is "determined" by $M$, which is the Keynesian theory of interest (e.g., increase $M$ to 80, $r$ becomes 3). But we cannot take $y$ as given. Rather, $r$ and $y$ are interrelated through the LM curve:

$$55 = .4y + \frac{100}{r - 1} - 10$$

or

(8) $$y = 162.5 - \frac{250}{r - 1}$$

and $i$ (given the $s$ and $i$ functions). The *LM* curve shows, for some given quantity of money and price level, the various possible combinations of $y$ and $r$ that make the public just willing to hold the stock of money that exists. Clearly, at $r_0 y_0$, *both* equilibrium conditions are satisfied: that saving equal investment and that the supply equal the demand for money. Any point on line *IS* satisfies the first of these; any point on line *LM*, the second; but only their intersection satisfies both conditions.[6] It represents, then, the "solution" of the system. (If we also wish the values of $s$, $i$, $M_t$, and $M_s$, we can go back to the original figures and read them off.)

This solution is, of course, displaced by any change in the data or functions which lie behind either curve. For example, an increase or decrease in the quantity of money would give rise to changes both in $y$ and $r$ as shown in Figure 14–8 (and, of course, also in the other variables).

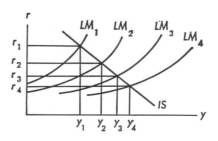

**Figure 14–8.**

As the supply of money successively increases by equal increments, the *LM* curve shifts from $LM_1$ to $LM_2$ to $LM_3$ to $LM_4$ (these curves are equally distant, *horizontally*, one from the next). Further equal increases in $M$ provide successively smaller reductions in $r$ and increases in $y$. Similarly, we can consider the effect of upward or downward shifts in the saving or investment function. In Figure 14–9 we show the effects of a reduced propensity to save (represented by a uniform reduction in $s$

---

[6] To continue our numerical example: we found the *IS* curve as

(3)                                     $y = 200 - 20r$

and the *LM* curve as

(8)                                     $y = 162.5 - \dfrac{250}{r - 1}$

Solving these simultaneously (that is, finding their intersection) gives

$$r^2 - 2.875r - 10.625 = 0$$

the only economically meaningful solution of which is

$$r = 5$$
$$y = 100$$

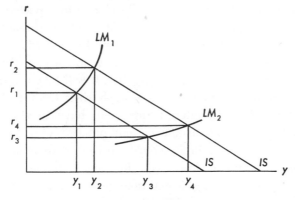

**Figure 14–9.**

for every combination of $y$ and $r$). Going back to Figures 14–1 and 2, it can be seen that this will raise the *IS* curve by a uniform amount along its whole length. The effect on $r$ and $y$ depends on whether the initial intersection of the *IS* curve was with a steeply rising or a relatively flat portion of the *LM* curve. If the former, the effect would be to raise income moderately (as from $y_1$ to $y_2$) and interest substantially ($r_1$ to $r_2$). But if the initial intersection were with a flat portion of the *LM* curve, the effect on income would be large (as from $y_3$ to $y_4$), on interest slight ($r_3$ to $r_4$).

Let us see now whether we can translate the analysis of this section into verbal terms. Considering the case of a reduction in the propensity to save, we might begin as follows: A reduced propensity to save means an increased demand for consumer goods, thus higher income and employment. The extra income will cause further increases in consumption, and in investment, too. However, with a larger volume of output, it is necessary for larger quantities of money to be tied up in transactions balances. If the total stock of cash is unchanged, this means that funds must be diverted from speculative balances, leading to a rise in interest rates. This rise, by checking investment and stimulating saving, will tend to check the expansion of output.

The next-to-last sentence of the preceding certainly needs further enlargement, perhaps in this way: The requirement for larger transactions balances will lead not only to a reduced market demand for securities, as some current savings are used to build cash balances, but an increased supply on the market, as some security holders sell in order to accumulate working balances. The fall of security prices will proceed to the point at which enough persons, *previously holding idle cash,* now decide that security prices are safe—i.e., low enough relative to expected future price levels—to make security-holding preferable to idle-cash-holding. To this we can add: If security prices are quite low to start with, so that there are few who are holding idle cash and few others close to the margin of indifference between cash and securities, it will take a rather substantial fall in security prices to induce much shift from cash-holding to security-holding. That is, interest rates will have to rise quite a bit, meaning that the rise in income cannot proceed very far. But if the initial situation is one of high security prices, with many who prefer idle cash, including many close to the line of indifference between cash-holding and security-holding, it will take only a moderate fall in security prices to induce a substantial shift from cash-holding to security-holding. That is, interest rates will not need to rise very much, even though income rises substantially—which it can do because there will be little rise in interest rates to check it.

As is always the case with verbal "stories," we tread perilously close to misleading statements in the foregoing, as well as being forced to bring dynamic considerations into what is supposed to be a static analysis. Nevertheless, such stories may help us to keep in mind the reality that presumably lies behind the arid curves in our diagrams.

The student should not only analyze in diagrammatic terms the effects of other changes—e.g., in investment propensities, or in the institutional determinants of velocity (i.e., in $l$)—but should also try to tell a "story" about his conclusions.

## AN ALTERNATIVE DIAGRAMMATIC ANALYSIS

The Hicks-Hansen diagram has elegant simplicity which appeals to many. It has the disadvantage, however, that most of the "works" are out of sight. This means that we need to use another diagram (or an extra mental calculation) to determine the effect of a displacement of the equilibrium on the other variables of our system. Likewise, it means that if we wish to consider the effect of a change in some one of the functions which lie behind the *IS* or *LM* curve, we need another diagram (or mental process) to determine how the assumed shift will affect the *IS* or *LM* curve. Other less elegant apparatus is possible, which exposes more of the relationships to view. One rather simple diagram is shown as Figure 14–10. To make things easy, we have assumed that saving depends only on $y$, but not on $r$, and investment only on $r$ but not $y$. This simplifies matters greatly, with little change in results if (as many assume) neither omitted relationship is quantitatively very important.

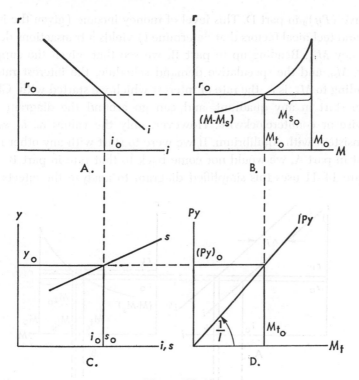

**Figure 14–10.**

All elements in this figure are familiar, although part C may appear strange at first. It shows the Keynesian saving-investment diagram with axes reversed (income measured vertically instead of horizontally, and amounts of saving and investment horizontally instead of vertically), and with the income scale compressed—i.e., a given distance on the vertical scale represents many more dollars of income than the same distance on the horizontal scale (e.g., $i_0$, $s_0$ may be 10 and $y_0$, 100).

Since the variables are all interdependent, we can "start" our analysis anywhere, so long as we realize that there is no single direction of causation implied by our description. For simplicity, start in part A. Given rate of interest $r_0$, and the investment schedule shown, the amount of investment will be $i_0$. Reading down to part C, we see that, given the saving schedule, and investment at $i_0$, income will be $y_0$. Since prices are assumed to be given, any change in $y$ produces a proportionate change in $Py$. Thus we can select our units for money income in such fashion that a given vertical measurement of $y$ in part C corresponds (given $P$) to the same vertical distance in part D. Corresponding to $y_0$ in part C, we therefore have $(Py)_0$ in part D. This level of money income (given the institutional and technical factors that determine $l$) yields a transactions demand for money $M_{t_0}$. Reading up to part B, we see that, given the supply of money, $M_0$, and the speculative demand schedule, the interest rate corresponding to $M_{t_0}$ is $r_0$, the rate of interest which we started with. Clearly, we can start in any quadrant, and can go around the diagram either clockwise or counterclockwise. However, only the values $r_0$, $i_0$, $s_0$, etc., are consistent with equilibrium. If we were to start with any other rate of interest in part A, we would not come back to that rate in part B.

Figure 14–11 uses this simplified diagram to analyze the effects of an

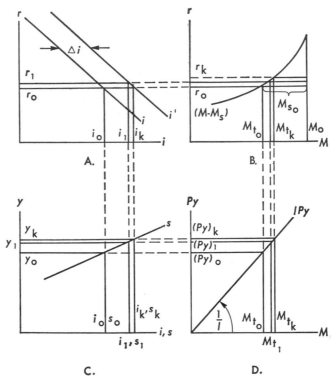

Figure 14–11.

upward shift in the investment function, from $i$ to $i'$. As compared with the initial position, the new schedule shows a willingness to invest more than before, in the amount of $\Delta i$, at every interest rate. If we wish, we can think of this as new government spending, with no change in tax collections. If there were no change in the interest rate, investment would rise from $i_0$ to $i_k$—i.e., by $\Delta i$, leading (via the multiplier) to an increase of income from $y_0$ to $y_k$. This would mean an enlarged transactions demand, from $M_{t_0}$ to $M_{t_k}$. If the quantity of money remained unchanged at $M_0$, the interest rate would obviously have to rise to $r_k$. This means that the whole chain of effects just traced *could not occur;* for it started with a change in investment which would occur only if the rate of interest stayed the same as before. But obviously the rate of interest cannot stay the same. Thus the new equilibirium, shown by $r_1$, $i_1$, $y_1$, $M_{t_1}$, $M_{s_1}$, involves less of an increase of investment and of income than would have been predicted by the multiplier effect alone [i.e., $\Delta i \times 1/(1 - MPC)$].

The extent to which higher interest rates will check the increase in demand resulting from improved investment prospects will depend on the slopes of the several schedules. If the MPC is high (MPS low), a small change in investment will lead to a large change in income. If $l$ is high, a small change in income will lead to a large increase in transactions demand. If the speculative demand schedule is steep, a small increase in the demand for money will lead to a large increase in the rate of interest. Can we not even imagine a case in which a low MPS, a high $l$, and a steep speculative demand schedule might lead to an interest rate so much higher than the original one that the net effect would be a decline in investment, in spite of the upward shift in the schedule? The answer is no, and the reader can test his understanding of the model by explaining why. He should also analyze, using this diagram, the effects of shifts in each of the other schedules—or even simultaneous shifts in two of the schedules. Again, the explanations should be put in words that make no reference to diagrams.

It should be clear that we have already achieved significant modification of the conclusions of the simple Keynesian model. For example, the multiplier effect tends to be reduced, as we have just seen. A shift in $i$ or $s$ schedule tends to be partly self-correcting, through the effects of a changing transactions demand, operating via the interest rate. Also, it now appears to make some difference how new investment is financed— whether through bank loans that increase the supply of money, or through borrowing from the public. If the former, the increase of $M$ will offset the tendency for $r$ to rise as $y$ increases. More generally, monetary policy—which obviously had no place in the simple Keynesian model— now acquires a *raison d'etre:* namely, that of influencing $r$, and thereby $i$ and $y$.

These modifications of the simple Keynesian model are matters of *degree* only, except in a limiting case. The nature of this limit depends upon the fact that, at some interest rate, the speculative demand disappears. That is, there is some interest rate so high that no one expects a further rise (i.e., security prices so low that no wealth-holder would expect any further fall); and at this rate—or higher rates—no one prefers to hold idle cash. Once the rate of interest is at or above this level, any further increase in the transactions demand for money (as a result of increased output or prices) cannot be accommodated through a reduction of speculative balances, for such balances do not exist. If aggregate demand (either investment or consumption) nevertheless tended to increase, the attempt to acquire the additional transactions balances by selling bonds, or by retaining current saving in cash form, would drive up the interest rate, but would not make more transactions cash available. Hence the interest rate would necessarily move up sufficiently that the net increment of aggregate demand would be choked off to zero (although investment might rise at the expense of consumption, if saving responds to the interest rate). Under these circumstances the results of the simple Keynesian model are not merely modified, they are completely invalidated. The multiplier is zero (so long as $M$ is constant). But any increase in $M$ would lead to a proportionate increase in $y$ (if output were less than its full-employment limit).

Hicks and Lange,[7] and others who have considered this circumstance, were tempted to label this as "the Classical case"—i.e., a special limiting case of a more general analysis (which also includes the simple Keynesian case as its opposite limit: see below). The results of this case have certainly a Classical character. It is perhaps incorrect, however, to say that the Classical writers were (unconsciously) considering only one limiting case out of a possible range—that case in which $r$ is so high that no one expects a further rise. Rather, the Classical analysis did not consider a speculative demand for money at all. Its (tacit) assumption was either that wealth-holders have no interest rate expectations at all, or, more likely, that they expect that, whatever today's rate may be, such rate will likewise prevail in the future.

There is another "limiting case" often pointed out by users of this model. It is the case in which the speculative demand for money schedule is horizontal in the relevant range—i.e., the interest-elasticity of the demand for money is infinite. In this case, the conclusions of the *simple* Keynesian model of Chapter X hold without modification. The transactions demand and the rate of interest put no limitation on the operation of the multiplier; monetary policy is powerless; etc. Since these conditions are likely to be even approximated only in the depths of a severe depression, when monetary policy has already so increased the supply

[7] For references, see fn. 3, this Chap.

of money (and shrinking income so reduced the transactions demand) that liquidity preference is completely satiated, the conclusions of the *simple* Keynesian model have often, with justice, been labeled "depression economics."

## WAGES AND PRICES

The assumption under which all of our Keynesian analysis has so far been conducted is that of a given level of prices. The assumption of rigid prices is not completely unrealistic, at least in some periods and places. Nevertheless, we cannot be satisfied with such an analysis, for at least two reasons: (1) the price level is not, in fact, ever truly rigid. Since it is not, we wish to understand the forces determining price level movement. We are interested in the price level not only for its own sake, but also to permit us to understand movements of the *money* as well as the *real* national product and national income. (2) Further, there are interactions between price level and real output or income. Since the price level does, in fact, vary, we cannot have a full understanding of the determinants even of *real* output and income unless we bring in price level effects.

We approach an analysis of the price level in two stages: first, we assume a given money wage rate but with prices free to vary; then we assume the money wage, too, to be free to vary.

The wage and price level theory which we shall use is essentially that of the Classical school, as already outlined in Chapter VI. This theory rests upon the assumptions of (a) diminishing marginal returns in production as aggregate employment increases; (b) profit maximizing behavior by employers; (c) for convenience only, pure and perfect competition in the sale of products; and, when we allow money wages to vary freely, (d) perfect competition among workers for jobs.

A graphical analysis which incorporates these new elements is shown in Figure 14–12. Parts A, B, C, and D of the figure are taken directly from the set used earlier in this chapter (Figures 14–10 and 14–11). Parts E, D, F, and G, relating to wages, employment, and the price level, were used in exactly this form in Chapter VI to illustrate the Classical theory of wages and prices. Part E is the aggregate production function, showing output as a function of employment; part F shows the demand for labor as a function of the real wage (this is the marginal product of labor, or the slope of the production function); part D shows the transactions demand for money; while part G shows the various combinations of money wage and price level associated with any given real wage.

To understand the figure, we can start, as before, in part A. The equi-

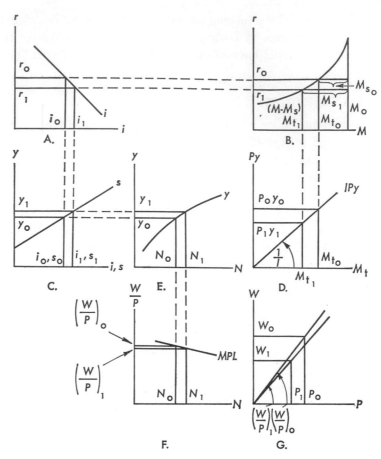

**Figure 14–12.**

librium values are plotted with subscripts zero. (For the present ignore
the variables with subscript one.) Given $r_0$, investment will be $i_0$. In part
C, we find that $i_0$ is associated with income $y_0$. Since prices are no longer
given, we cannot use $y_0$ alone to find, in part D, the transactions demand
for money. We need also the price level. Part E shows that output level
$y_0$ will require an employment level of $N_0$. In order for employers to be
willing to hire this number of workers, we find (in part F), that the real
wage must be $(W/P)_0$. Given this real wage and the assumed money
wage level $W_0$, we can find (part G) the necessary price level, $P_0$. Having $y_0$ (from part E), and $P_0$ (from part G), we can now, in part D, find
the corresponding transactions demand, $M_{t_0}$. This, given the speculative
demand schedule and the stock of money, $M_0$, produces (part B) a rate of
interest, $r_0$, which was where we started. If we were to start with any
other rate of interest (or value of any other variable except that with

subscript zero), and were to trace corresponding values in all other diagrams, we would not come back to where we had started. For example, if the interest rate in (A) were higher than $r_0$, the level of income (C) and employment (E) would be lower, and the real wage higher (F). This would mean lower prices (G), a smaller transactions demand (D), and a *lower* interest rate (B)—inconsistent with our assumed *higher* rate.

The student should be certain that he can trace the effects on the equilibrium levels of all variables of any of the kinds of shifts we have previously considered: e.g., a shift in the investment or saving schedules, a change in $M$, a shift in the production function, etc. We shall confine our analysis for the moment to the effects on equilibrium values of the variables of two kinds of changes: an increase in the investment schedule, and a reduction of the money wage. For the first of these, see Figure 14–13.

A shift of the investment schedule by $\Delta i$, from $i$ to $i'$, would, if $r_0$

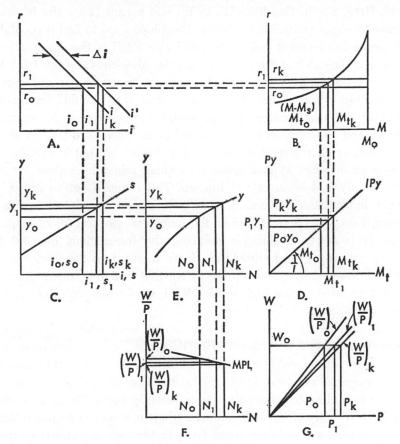

**Figure 14–13.**

were unchanged, have led to the full multiplier effect on income, i.e., $\Delta i[1/(1 - \text{MPC})]$, or a rise to $y_k$. This result is impossible, for the rate of interest cannot stay at $r_0$. It cannot because the transactions demand for money will increase. Notice that the increase in transactions demand as income rises now comes not only from the fact of higher output ($y_0$ to $y_k$), but also from the fact that prices would have to rise ($P_0$ to $P_k$), given the money wage, in order to offset diminishing returns. Instead of this full multiplier effect, the new equilibrium (shown in all cases by subscripts 1), involves a higher rate of interest and a rise in income, saving, investment, prices and transactions demand. It can be demonstrated, however, that except in certain special limiting cases (noted later) the multiplier effect will always be positive. That is, income will always rise with an increase in the investment schedule, and fall in the case of a downward shift.

For the effects of a change in the money wage, we return to Figure 14–12. Here, a reduction from $W_0$ to $W_1$ will permit (a) a rise in prices relative to wages (which is necessary if employers are to find it profitable to increase employment and output; and (b) a fall in the absolute level of prices sufficient that $Py$ will fall even though $y$ rises. $Py$ must fall because, in order for the larger output to be sold, investment must increase. Why must investment increase if a larger output is to be sold? An increase in output—and therefore real income—will bring an increase in consumption demand. But such an increase would be insufficient to take all of the added output off the market—i.e., the MPC is $< 1$. That is why investment must increase. With a given investment schedule, investment can increase only at a lower rate of interest. This requires (given $M$), a reduction in transactions demand, i.e., a reduction of $Py$ while $y$ increases.

How, then, does a reduction of the money wage level affect employment? It increases it through reducing the transactions demand for money, lowering $r$, and stimulating $i$. An increase in the money wage would decrease employment to the extent that a higher transactions demand, associated with a higher price level, would tend to raise the rate of interest and check investment.

What determines the level of the money wage? Keynes' treatment assumed the money wage level to be dependent upon institutional and historical forces, subject to some influence also by the state of the economy. Money wages at any point in time are at the level where they are, mostly because it is close to where they have recently been. To be sure, they may have recently risen or fallen somewhat in response to institutional pressures, such as minimum wage laws, or through the efforts of trade unions, or public opinion. Further, the state of employment will make some difference. As an economy moves closer to full employment, the strength of trade unions is likely to increase, and the resistance of employers to wage increases to fade. Further, as full employment is approached, particular employers, in certain localities or occupations, will encounter a shortage of labor—they will be unable to hire as many men as they need at the going rate of wages. They will, therefore, tend to seek additional employees by offering slightly higher wages, quite apart from trade union efforts. Conversely, when employment is very slack, trade unions will press less hard for wage increases, employers will find no need to bid against each other for labor and may even try to get their workers to accept lower money wages in order to reduce costs and strengthen their competitive position. There may even be some competition, open or concealed, among workers for the available jobs.

Thus, Keynes saw the wage level as tending to rise (from wherever it had been) when employment was nearly full, rising perhaps faster the closer the economy was to full employment and the stronger and more efficient was trade union organization. Money wage rates would tend to sag when unemployment was widespread, again perhaps sagging faster the weaker were unions and the greater the level of unemployment. But at any given time and place the money wage rate level was, more or less, a matter "autonomously" determined. Since the money wage was not absolutely rigid, its variations over time might affect somewhat the levels of other variables. But aside from the effect on the price level, further induced changes would be small, since speculation tended to stabilize the interest rate, and investment demand was only moderately sensitive to such interest rate changes as did occur. For all practical purposes, we could speak of the economic system as having an "equilibrium" even when employment might be less than full.

This concept of the money wage level is a very different one from the "flexible" wage level assumed by Classical writers. If the wage level is truly flexible, it falls continuously and without limit, whenever there is any unemployment, and is stable only if all workers seeking jobs can find them. Keynes' concept has the money wage level stable at some point below full employment, a point at which upward and downward pressures are in balance. At lower levels of employment, wage rates may sag, but only at a limited, predictable rate—a rate which depends on the *extent* of unemployment, which would not be the case with truly flexible wages.

## FLEXIBLE WAGES AND EMPLOYMENT

What is the consequence for the Keynesian model if we introduce truly "flexible" money wages? It is that we add a new condition of equilibrium in the model, namely, that the supply and demand for labor be equal—i.e., that full employment prevail. There has been, and remains, much doubletalk about whether Keynes (or anyone else) could demonstrate the possibility of equilibrium at less than full employment except with rigid money wages. We can clear away a lot of the nonsense merely by being sure about our terminology. If wages are truly flexible—i.e., fall without limit whenever there is unemployment—then, by definition, there can be no equilibrium short of full employment. This conclusion follows directly from the meaning of the term equilibrium. Surely, an economic system is not in equilibrium with one of its important variables —the money wage—falling continuously. If the money wage falls continuously whenever there is unemployment, then equilibrium at less than full employment is not possible with flexible wages.

But this is a tautological kind of conclusion. What we want to know is whether, if wages are flexible, a decline in wages will lead to the achievement of equilibrium—i.e., to full employment. For we can agree that equilibrium at less than full employment is impossible with flexible wages (how could anyone deny it?), yet still not believe that falling money wages will succeed in eliminating unemployment. That is, it could be argued that flexible wages would, at least in some circumstances, simply perpetuate a disequilibrium which falling wages did nothing to eliminate. Whether falling wages will tend to increase employment and restore equilibrium is a question of *substance,* in contrast to the purely semantic question considered a moment ago. What answer can we give to this question of substance?

Figure 14-14 deals with this question, at least in the static terms to which we have so far largely confined our analysis. This figure is like the two preceding ones, with one exception. In part F, we have introduced the supply of labor function. For if wages fall whenever there is less than full employment, then they fall whenever the supply of labor exceeds the demand for it, that is, whenever the real wage is higher than $(W/P)_F$, shown by the intersection of the two schedules in part F. If, in parts A and B, the investment and liquidity preference schedules are those shown by the solid rather than the broken lines, then it can be seen that full employment equilibrium is possible, at the values of all variables shown by the subscripts $F$. If the values shown by the subscripts 0 should

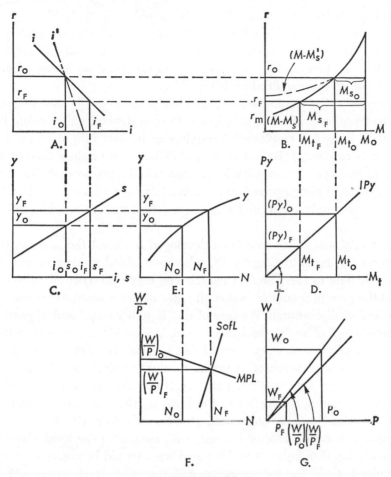

**Figure 14–14.**

prevail, there would be disequilibrium, because, with a supply of labor in excess of demand, money wages would fall. This fall would terminate only at level $W_F$ of money wages, with a real wage now equal to $(W/P)_F$. In this case, the answer to the substantive question is this: not only is equilibrium at less than full employment not possible (by definition) when wages are flexible, but also, flexible wages will lead to equilibrium at full employment.

Suppose, however, we make one change. Let the investment schedule be that shown by the broken line in part A. It is not hard to see that full employment cannot result from flexible wages. For full employment to be achieved, it is necessary that investment be in the amount $i_F$. But now investment cannot reach $i_F$, except at a negative interest rate. But at an

384                                                      *Macroeconomic Theory*

interest rate below zero, no wealth-holder would willingly hold a security in preference to cash. Thus we have the situation identified in Chapter IX as an "inconsistency between saving and investment" at full employment. Clearly, here, falling wages could not eliminate the cause of their further fall, and no equilibrium is possible.

Or suppose that the investment schedule is as originally assumed, but that the liquidity preference schedule is the one shown by the broken line in part B. Here, full employment requires an interest rate of $r_F$ (so that investment can be $i_F$). But no amount of deflation can reduce the interest rate that far. Even if the price level approached zero, so that the transactions demand also approached zero, the interest rate would still be too high for full employment, and wages (and thus prices) would continue to fall.

The model which has now been developed is almost the same as that which was set forth in Chapter IX, where we added the speculative demand schedule to the Classical model. The only difference of substance is that the present model embodies the idea of the consumption function. In the earlier discussion of the case of the "liquidity trap," and of possible "inconsistency" of saving and investment, we could only conclude that, if flexible, prices and wages would fall indefinitely; but we could say nothing about what levels other variables might reach during this process. Now we can provide the missing answer. If the "liquidity trap" prevailed, the rate of interest would fall to the level at which the speculative demand schedule became horizontal, investment would rise to the level corresponding to this rate of interest, with income at the level given by the multiplier. Employment and the real wage would be correspondingly determined. Only the money wage and the price level would not be determined, falling without limit, at a rate determined by the speed of the downward wage revision.

In the "inconsistency" case, deflation would reduce the rate of interest toward zero (or toward the level which $r$ would assume if the transactions demand were zero—$r_m$ in part B of Figure 14–14), with investment and income rising toward the corresponding limiting values.

The principal difference between the present model and that of Chapter IX is, however, that if money wages do not fall, or stop falling, we can find an equilibrium for income, employment, and the other variables even at levels below full employment. Or, put otherwise, we can predict the levels of other variables corresponding to any given level of the money wage. The Classical model, with or without liquidity preference, would predict unemployment at any level of the money wage above some crucial figure; but how much or how little unemployment, whether rising, falling, or stable, was beyond its scope.

Returning now to the present case, it is easy to see that we need not press the plausibility of either *extreme* case (the "liquidity trap," or an "inconsistency") to appreciate the possible difficulties in the way of attempting under all circumstances to secure full employment by the route of wage and price deflation. The flatter the speculative demand schedule (even though it never becomes infinitely elastic), and the steeper the investment schedule (even though it is not vertical), the greater is the necessary fall in wages and prices. So great a fall may be impossible to accomplish in any reasonable period of time. Thus wage flexibility may be a theoretical but not a meaningful or practicable solution to unemployment.

This is reinforced when we recall the additional considerations advanced in Chapter IX—the institutional difficulties of securing rapid wage flexibility, and the possibility (this is a dynamic rather than an equilibrium consideration) that falling wages and prices will create an expectation of further fall, and thus lead to a postponement of investment expenditures and consumer durable goods expenditures, intensifying rather than mitigating the problem.

There are further "indirect effects" of wage flexibility as a cure for unemployment that should now be mentioned, which have not so far been included in our diagrams or other analyses of wage flexibility. For example, if we abandon our assumption of a closed economy, wage and price reductions relative to levels prevailing abroad can be a most important source of additional demand for a nation which relies heavily on international trade.

Other effects involve the possible impact on consumption expenditures of a falling wage-price level. Wages and entrepreneurial incomes will tend to fall in similar proportion as wages are cut, for prices will follow wages down. A somewhat lesser fall in profits than wages would be implied, but only to the extent that deflation has a net favorable effect. If wage earners have a higher marginal propensity to consume than profit recipients (particularly when we take account of corporate saving), a greater fall of wages than prices may reduce the consumption associated with any given level of income, thus requiring somewhat further absolute fall in wages and prices than would have been required to produce any given increment of employment had the marginal propensities been equal.[8] However, the effects of redistribution between wages and profits come about only to the extent that *for other reasons* wage reductions have a favorable effect on aggregate demand. Thus they can either augment or partially neutralize a favorable effect arising from another source, but can have no independent influence in determining whether the deflationary process will have a favorable result.[9]

However, to the extent that there are fixed incomes in the economy (interest, rents, pensions, royalties, etc.), there also takes place a redistribution of real income from the employer-employee group in favor of the fixed income group. This occurs *per se* as a result of deflation. To the extent that there is an appreciable difference between the marginal propensities to spend of the fixed income and variable income groups, the effect of deflation will be favorable or unfavorable depending on the direction of this difference. If we think of the fixed income groups in terms of one cliche—the "widows and orphans"—the effect of deflation on consumption might appear favorable. If our image of the fixed income groups is the bloated, silk-hatted coupon-clipper, the effect would be unfavorable. We probably do not know enough for a judgment on this point, and should in any case recognize that the net effect would probably be slight in either direction.

Another consumption impact that must be considered when we deal with a real rather than an abstract economy is the impact through taxation and transfer payments. Since tax and transfer payment rates are expressed in dollar rather than real terms, the effect of a deflation on after-tax incomes must be considered. A mere fall in wages and prices will increase the real benefits implied in any system of transfer payments, thus stimulating consumption (as opposed to the situation if wages and prices did not fall). But tax rates are also fixed in money terms. Their burden on consumption will increase to the extent that they are fixed-sum taxes like property or poll taxes, or specific taxes like five cents per gallon on gasoline; it will remain unchanged if they are *ad valorem* taxes (e.g., percentage sales taxes); and it will decrease to the extent that they are progressive income taxes, whose income brackets are fixed in dollar terms. Since most taxes are in one of the latter two categories, the net effect of deflation on consumption via a given system of tax rates

[8] On the other hand, we should really consider the total "marginal propensity to spend" (to consume *plus* to invest) of the two groups. A positive marginal propensity to invest by profit recipients might well offset the difference in MPC's, and thus require somewhat less of a deflation.

[9] The reason for this may not be intuitively obvious. A mathematical demonstration is not given, but a numerical example which illustrates this conclusion is given in the appendix to this chapter (pp. 395–398).

and transfer payments is probably slightly favorable. To the extent that some government expenditures may be fixed in dollar rather than in real terms, government demand may also be somewhat increased through deflation. It should be noted, however, that any such favorable effects of deflation could be alternatively achieved—if that were feasible—by tax rate reductions, and expenditure and transfer payment increases, without change in the price level.

Still another consumption impact of deflation might arise through the "Pigou effect." Since this has already been extensively considered in Chapter XII (see pp. 270–273), we shall not add anything further here, beyond recalling a generally skeptical judgment as to the empirical importance of this effect.

Attempting to bring together all of the considerations so far advanced would probably lead to a judgment that the effect of falling wages and prices on employment tends to be favorable (unless the dynamic effect on expectations is rather strong). These favorable effects arise through the impact of a reduced transactions demand on the interest rate, possible favorable effects through the balance of payments, through some redistribution in favor of fixed income groups, some lessening of the real burden of taxation, and some increase in the real volume of consumer wealth. Each of these is individually subject to question, but their net impact might well be judged favorable.

This conclusion is not, however, the only one we need for policy purposes. For there are alternative routes to full employment, and we presumably should choose the best one. A full judgment on the question of policy would demand comparing the advantages and disadvantages of wage and price flexibility with the advantages and disadvantages of various programs of fiscal or monetary policy, direct stimulus or control of consumption and investment, and perhaps others. This is not the place for a consideration of the relative merits of these several policies. The comment is, however, necessary because some writers seem to believe that if they can only show a presumption to the effect that wage and price flexibility will tend to stabilize employment, then it automatically follows that public policy should be directed toward maximizing the degree of wage and price flexibility.

## SOME MISTAKEN VIEWS ON WAGE AND PRICE FLEXIBILITY

Both those who favor and those who oppose flexible wages and prices as a means for stabilizing employment have used arguments as to the effects of wage cuts on consumer demand which can easily be shown to be unsound or misleading in the light of the previous analysis. A review of some of these arguments may help further to clarify the theoretical points involved. It must be emphasized that, for the present, we are confining our discussion to a static equilibrium model. The arguments which we consider here have all been advanced in that context.

Each of these arguments assumes that there can be some *direct effect* of wage rate changes on aggregate consumer demand. For the present, therefore, we are ignoring all of the possible "indirect effects" via the rate of interest, foreign trade, Pigou effect, etc.

One line of argument is frequently used by those who feel that flexible wages are not a good means to stabilize demand. It is often put forward by them in the mistaken impression that they are thereby explaining Keynes' analysis of wage cuts. The argument runs this way. "From the standpoint of employer incentives, wage cuts would appear to be favorable to the employment of labor. But this neglects the demand side. For wages are not only a cost but an element of income. If wages are cut, incomes fall, and so, therefore, the demand for consumer goods will fall. As a result of the drop in demand, prices must fall, too, perhaps even as much as wages, thus eliminating the employer incentive." Now this is a strange doctrine, indeed. Whether *total wage income in money terms* ($W$ times $N$) falls or not depends not only on what happens to money wages, $W$, but also on employment, $N$. Only by assuming no increase, or a lesser (percentage) increase in employment than the cut in wages can one be sure that there is a fall in money wage income. But we should not *assume* what it is that we want to discover. Further, what is relevant to demand for consumer goods (and thus, indirectly, demand for labor) is not money income, but real income. If prices fall, then that is relevant, too. Indeed, if prices fall in the same proportion as wages (which is the conclusion of the above argument) there will be no reduction in *real* wage income even if employment does not increase!

This argument also seems to imply that wage income is the only kind, or the only kind that is relevant to the demand for consumer goods. In fact, nonwage income, for example, profits, must also be considered. Entrepreneurs eat, too. If prices fall in the same proportion as wages, then there has been no redistribution between wage and nonwage income; if they fall by less, any loss by wage earners is a gain by someone else, *relatively*. But what happens to *total* income, and total demand, remains dependent upon what happens to employment and output—which is exactly what we are trying to discover and therefore must not assume.

We cannot reach any conclusion about total demand for goods except by considering all of the relationships in our model, which this argument attempts to short cut.

A second line of argument has been used by those who have supported flexible wages as a means of stabilizing demand. This argument is one stage superior to the previous one, for it recognizes that what happens to total wage income depends on what happens to employment as well as what happens to wages. There must be cases, this argument insists, in which the demand for labor has an elasticity greater than one. If so, then total wage income will increase as a result of a wage cut. Even if prices do not fall, this means an increase in the *real* as well as the money income of labor, and therefore an increase in the demand for consumer goods. Thus, we do not have to rely on an "indirect" effect, operating on investment through the demand for money and the interest rate, or through taxation or foreign trade. A wage cut may have a direct effect on aggregate consumer demand.

Now this argument is all right as far as it goes, but it does not go far enough. To see what is missing, refer to Figure 14–15.

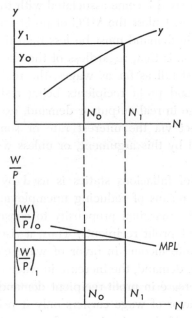

**Figure 14–15.**

In the lower half of the figure is an elastic demand for labor schedule. A cut in $W/P$ will increase real wage income, for the product $(W/P)_1 \times$

$N_1$ is greater than $(W/P)_0 \times N_0$. If wage-earner demand for consumer goods depends on real wage income, then wage-earner demand for goods will rise when the real wage declines. We may even assume that the marginal propensity to consume of wage-earners is one. But the argument is incomplete unless we compare this potential increase in *demand* with the increase in *supply* of goods. The increase in supply is equal to $y_1 - y_0$. Will the increase in demand be that great, even with a wage-earner MPC $= 1$? It will be *only if the entire increment of income earned from the production of this increment of output goes to wage earners.* But this is impossible under the assumption of profit-maximizing behavior by entrepreneurs. Output $y_1$ and employment $N_1$ were chosen by entrepreneurs, we assume, as a point of maximum profit, this optimum point of operations having been shifted from the previous one involving output $y_0$ and employment $N_0$. Unless output $y_1$ involves a larger profit income, it will not be chosen; for employers still have the option of producing the previous output $y_0$, which, with lower wages, would clearly mean a greater profit than originally. Thus, for employers to prefer output $y_1$, it must offer greater profit than the previous output. This means that some part of the increased income associated with the larger output must go to nonwage-earners. Unless the MPC of profit recipients is also equal to one, the increase in demand must be less than the increase in supply. The correct conclusion is that, regardless of the elasticity of the demand for labor, prices must fall as far as wages, the real income positions of both wage earners and profit recipients being restored to their initial levels with no change in real output or demand, except as there may be some "indirect" effect via the interest rate or some similar "indirect" route not considered by this argument, or unless we use some dynamic argument.

Still a third line of fallacious statics is used by those who support wage *increases* as a means of reducing unemployment. It relies on the probable fact that the marginal propensity to consume of wage-earners is higher than that of profit recipients. Thus, a rise in wages, which is assumed to redistribute income in favor of wage earners, will cause an increase in aggregate demand, the increase in wage-earner demand being greater than the decrease in profit-recipient demand. Now there will be a redistribution in favor of wage earners only if prices rise less than in proportion to wages. If they rise in equal proportion, everything is as before, in real terms. Why is it assumed that employers will not raise prices in the same proportion? Without going through the argument in detail, it can be shown that the assumption of profit maximizing behavior by entrepreneurs will require an equal percentage increase, unless there is some "indirect" effect—e.g., via the interest rate or the Pigou effect. If prices were at first advanced in smaller proportion, the real wage would be higher than initially, and employment and output therefore lower. This reduction in real income would reduce demand, but by less than the decrease in supply (because the MPC is less than one). Prices would therefore rise, until the initial wage-price ratio was restored. If there were any "indirect" effect, it would presumably be unfavorable, causing prices to rise by less than wages, and employment to decrease rather than increase as the argument tried to prove. If there were no "indirect" effects, the wage increase would merely inflate prices in equal proportion.

These, and other similar erroneous lines of argument all try to prove that wage changes can have some *direct* influence, favorable or otherwise, on aggregate consumer demand. The fact is that no direct effects on consumer demand are possible so long as we accept three assumptions: (a) that real consumption, in total and of each group, is a function of *real* income; (b) that the average MPC of the community as a whole (wage earners and nonwage-earners taken together) is less than one; and (c) that employers maximize profits; and so long as we reason in terms of a static model.

A specific numerical model in terms of which the problem can be analyzed is presented in an appendix to this chapter. Each of the three mistaken analyses here considered can be tested through this example, which incorporates the three assumptions listed above.

We have been concerned in this section with some incomplete or mistaken analyses, each of which has been used as the basis of a policy recommendation. Although we think it important to show the errors of these arguments, we do not necessarily reject or approve any particular policy recommendation merely because a certain argument proceeds or does not proceed logically from assumptions to conclusions. The static Keynesian analysis appears to be *logically* faultless, and argues that, although wage reductions can have no direct effect on demand, they should probably have some favorable indirect effects, except in limiting cases. But Keynes himself rejected general wage cuts as a policy for increasing employment, largely on the grounds that whatever good wage cuts might accomplish could be obtained more quickly and efficiently in other ways. To be sure, Keynes did not consider the Pigou effect. Some who have considered it believe that this should reverse Keynes' conclusion. Others remain profoundly skeptical. It is probably well to remain skeptical of any easy conclusion for social policy on a matter so complex as this. The conviction of Classical thought that unemployment could arise only from too high a money wage and could always be cured by wage cuts obviously rested on an oversimplified and unrealistic analysis. The crude "underconsumptionist" arguments of trade unions for money wage increases are equally suspect.

Nevertheless, it is probable that there may be particular times and places where a general wage cut would (if it could be secured) have a pronounced favorable effect, and be the most efficient among alternative policies. There may even be times and places where a general wage increase would be helpful. But the justification of any such policy must rest on more complex and subtle considerations than are incorporated in the static theories so far analyzed, as well as upon findings of fact and administrative or strategic considerations which may be of crucial significance. In particular, dynamic relationships, which our static theories neglect, are of overriding importance in the design of short-run economic stabilization policies. Thus our interest has been primarily that of indicating erroneous or incomplete arguments in support of one or another policy; not in arriving at a particular recommendation.

For example, once we introduce expectations and a dynamic analysis, the effect of a wage cut might be highly favorable. We know that a wage cut for one firm (all other wages and prices unchanged) will lead that employer to expand output [10] in the (correct) expectation that the demand curve for his own product will be unaffected. Total output in the economy will not necessarily rise, for his increased sales will be at the expense of other products; but a wage cut will raise *his* production, sales, and profits.

Suppose that, even though a wage cut is general in the economy, each employer (not having learned "Keynesian economics") *assumes* that he will be able to sell more, and steps up his production. If the consumption function is stable and investment does not increase, we know that the increased output cannot all be taken off the market. Increased output means more income and hence more consumer buying; but so long as the marginal propensity to consume is less than one, demand will expand by less than supply. Suppose, however, that the desired stock of inventories of each employer (or, at least, of many employers)—or even his desired stock of plant and equipment—is tied to his output level. Then increased output (in the *expectation* of increased sales) will engender investment in inventories or plant and equipment, and hence an increase in demand that may, in the aggregate, justify the increased output.

---

[10] Unless his demand curve has zero elasticity or his marginal cost curve is vertical.

Since we postulated that this investment depended on an *increase* in output, it may only be maintained if there is now a further increase in output. Thus, in the absence of another favorable "shock," the economy might then fall back, after this short spurt, to its initial position. But this is not the only possibility. If, for example, investment depends heavily on business confidence, a rise, once begun, may easily cumulate. In effect, the marginal propensity to spend (MPC + MPI) may exceed unity during expansion periods, once the expansion is touched off.

What we have sketched above is only one of numerous possible developments, not a general dynamic theory of the effect of wage cuts in a depression. As indicated above, the effect might equally well be highly unfavorable; to decide when one might expect favorable and when unfavorable results takes us far beyond the scope of this book (and, one may suggest, far beyond the firm "knowledge" of economists).

It is, nevertheless, fair to state that the theoretical developments of the past twenty-five years have probably brought about as complete a reversal of the general tenor of informed judgment on the matter of wage cuts as on any other single major question of stabilization policy. Thirty or forty years ago the opinion of economists would have been close to unanimous that wage cuts (if they could be achieved) would have a favorable effect on employment—when there was general unemployment. Today the overwhelming judgment would be to leave money wages alone, or to put a heavy burden of proof on one who would propose to remedy unemployment by any kind of manipulation of the general level of wage rates.

## FULL EMPLOYMENT AND INFLATION

The discussion of this and the preceding several chapters has concentrated almost exclusively on situations involving unemployment, and a national income and output short of what the economy is capable of producing. It should be easy to see, however, that there is nothing inherent in the Keynesian model that makes unemployment inevitable. What Keynesian theory stresses is rather the absence or weakness of those *automatic stabilizers* relied upon in Classical theory to prevent deficient aggregate demand or quickly to eliminate a deficiency if it should arise. Keynesian doctrine suggests that the external forces shaping aggregate demand—the position of the *c* and *i* functions, and the level of *g*—*may be such* as to yield less than full employment. But, by the same token, they *may yield* a level of aggregate demand sufficient for full employment, or even a level of demand more than sufficient. Actually, a level of demand just sufficient for full employment would represent an unusual case, for this is only one possible point in a wide band of possibilities, a dividing line between the case of unemployment and inflation. For aggregate demand more than sufficient for full employment would imply inflation.

We shall consider the analysis of inflation in detail in a later chapter; but the outline of the Keynesian analysis of inflation is implicit in all that has been developed for the unemployment case. If the demand for final goods, and therefore for resources (including labor) which produce final goods, should exceed the supply when all workers are employed, there will be a bidding up of both $P$ and $W$. That is, there will be if we assume prices and wages flexible to upward pressure, whether or not they may be so to downward pressure. Such upward flexibility (with full employment) was what Keynes assumed; and, in general, one can take little exception to this asymmetry of his hypothesis.

The question then arises as to the possible effects of rising wages and prices on aggregate demand. Will inflation tend to remove the excess demand that causes it, or will it leave the excess untouched, causing prices and wages to rise in endless spiral?

Keynes argued that flexible wages, *on the downside,* might remove a "deflationary gap"—a margin between actual demand and full employment—but that the effects were uncertain and weak. By the same token, an "inflationary gap"—an excess of demand over the full-employment level—will generate an upward price and wage movement which might have some tendency to remove the excess, or might not. The analysis of effects in the inflation case is exactly parallel with that in the deflation case. They include (1) interest rate effects, (2) income redistribution effects, (3) Pigou effects, (4) foreign trade effects, (5) tax and transfer payment effects, (6) expectational effects. These will be considered later.

Mistaken analyses are as dangerous and as easy to arise in the inflation case is in that involving deflation. If one argues that higher prices will directly reduce real consumer demand, he is reasoning illegitimately from a single commodity to the aggregate economy. For money incomes rise in whatever proportion prices rise, leaving consumers in the same real income position as before. Unless it affects expectations or interest rates, inflation of the cost of capital goods should not deter real investment demand, for the prices of the final products made with capital goods will have risen, too. A rise in money wages will not reduce employer demand for labor if prices also are moving up. Attempting to derive some "direct" effects on consumption or investment or on the willingness of employers to bid for labor by introducing particular elasticities of demand for labor, or differences in MPC between workers and owners can be no more successful in this case than in the analysis of deflation, so long as we assume no money illusions, and the maximization of profit.

If the net effect of the indirect effects (1) through (6) above should be for aggregate real demand to fall as prices rise, there may be some rise in prices just sufficient to eliminate the entire excess, producing a level of demand just equal to productive capacity when all resources are employed, and a cessation of the price rise, with prices stable at their new, higher level. If the net effect of (1) through (6) is not to reduce real demand, then aggregate demand in excess of full-employment output can only create a disequilibrium *process* of continuing inflation. With our static tools we can say little or nothing about the speed or nature of that process.

One final paragraph on the relation of the quantity of money to inflation will terminate this discussion. Given equilibrium at full employment, an increase in $M$ will ordinarily lead to a rise in prices. It will do so by causing $r$ to fall, thus stimulating investment and creating an *excess* of demand, in place of the previous just-adequate level. If the only source of the excess demand is a reduced $r$ arising from an expanded $M$, a cessation of the increase in $M$ should cause the inflation to terminate, with a price level higher in the same proportion as $M$. This higher price level will generate an increase in transactions demand equal to the increase in $M$, allowing only the previous level of speculative balances, and thus the same interest rate as initially. If prices had risen by less than $M$, there would remain idle balances to depress $r$ and manufacture further inflation. Wages, too, must have risen in the same proportion. If they had risen by less, employers would be trying to hire more workers (at the lower real wage) than were willing to work. One may note that this analysis of inflation is practically identical to that which, in Chapter VII, we attributed to Wicksell. The identity between quantity theory and Keynesian reasoning in this particular case should not, however, confuse us. The Keynesian analysis might have inflation with no increase in $M$, or an inflation the extent of which would bear no necessary relationship to the extent of any increase in M.

## APPENDIX

### A Numerical Model for the Analysis of Wage Changes

This model is designed only to make it easier to see that the *direct* effects of a money wage increase or decrease on consumer demand are nil, given certain basic assumptions, no matter whether the demand for labor is elastic or inelastic, and whether the marginal propensity to consume of wage earners is or is not higher than that of profit recipients. This conclusion follows so long as our argument is static and we accept the three basic assumptions: a consumption function stable in real terms; an average MPC $< 1$; and profit maximizing behavior.

The model consists of six equations and an (autonomous) money wage level.

(1) $$\frac{C_w}{P} = \frac{WN}{P} \, (\text{or}, \, C_w = WN)$$

This equation describes the consumption of wage-earners $(C_w)$. We assume that both marginal and average propensities equal one; workers spend their entire money incomes—i.e., the entire money wage bill $(WN)$.

(2) $$\frac{C_r}{P} = 10 + .6 \frac{Py - WN}{P}$$

This equation describes the consumption of profit recipients $(C_r)$.[11] We assume their real consumption to be a function of their real income, with a marginal propensity to consume of six-tenths. Profit in money terms is equal to the money national income $Y$ or $(Py)$ less the wage bill $(WN)$.

(3) $$\frac{I}{P} = 30$$

This embodies the assumption of constant (intended) real investment.

(4) $$Py = C_w + C_r + I$$

Total expenditure or income consists only of consumption plus investment.

(5) $$y = 50 + 7N - .02N^2$$

This is the aggregate production function. It shows diminishing marginal returns as employment increases.

(6) $$\frac{dy}{dN} = \frac{W}{P}$$

This is the familiar assumption of profit maximization, assuming perfect competition. Given the production function of equation (5), $dy/dN = 7 - .04 \, N$.[12]

(7) $$W = \$5$$

This is the initial money wage, which we can alter to find the effects on other variables.

It can be seen that we assume only a single commodity, one which can either be consumed or invested. This is equivalent to using an index number of outputs of a number of commodities on the assumption that the *composition* of output either remains constant, or at least makes no difference.

---

[11] Profit here really means nonwage income. Specifically it includes interest and rent; we are assuming no government transfer payments, pensions, etc.

[12] The student who is not familiar with the rules for differentiation will have to take this on faith.

Simultaneous solution of these seven equations is possible by successive substitutions. This process yields a cubic equation, which has, however, only a single solution with economic meaning (that is, a single solution involving positive prices and quantities). The student need not attempt to reproduce the solution, but he may wish to test the values shown below to see that they satisfy each of the equations. He can take it on faith that there is no other set which will also satisfy all of them.

$$N = 50$$

$$y = 350$$

$$\frac{W}{P} = 5$$

$$P = \$1$$

$$Y = \$350$$

$$WN = \$250$$

$$Y - WN \text{ (profits)} = \$100$$

$$C_w = \$250$$

$$C_r = \$70$$

$$I = \$30$$

This system involves an elastic demand for labor. If the real wage could be reduced from 5 to 4.4, employment would expand from 50 to 65 [substitute in equation (6)], causing real wage income $(WN/P)$ to increase from 250 to 280.[13] Suppose that the money wage were cut from \$5 to \$4.40. Suppose, further, that prices did not change. (In a moment we shall show that they must change, but assume that they do not in order to see why they must!) This would mean a reduction in the real wage from 5 to 4.4. Such a reduction would, as already noted, lead to an increase in employment from 50 to 65, and an increase in money wage income from \$250 to \$286. Wage earner consumption would therefore also increase from 250 to 286 units of output [see equation (1)]. But how much would output increase if employment went from 50 to 65? It can be seen that $y$ would rise from 350 to 420.5 [equation (5)], and the money national income, $Y$, from \$350 to \$420.50 (still assuming unchanged prices). Wage earners, then, would provide a market for 36 additional units, but production would have risen by 70.5 units. Could profit recipients be counted on to consume the balance? Profit income has risen from \$100 to \$134.50 (\$420.50 − \$286). On this basis, $C_r/P = 10 +$ .6(\$134.5/P) $= 90.7$. This is an increase of 20.7 units from their previous demand of 70, but it is not enough. Total demand is now $(C_w/P)$ 286 + $(C_r/P)$ 90.7 + $(I/P)$ 30 $= 406.7$, compared with a total supply of 420.5. If, in fact, employers had assumed that prices would stay unchanged when wages

[13] At the equilibrium point, the elasticity of demand for labor is 2.5.

were cut, and had immediately raised employment from 50 to 65 in this expectation, they would now find unsold goods piling up. This (unintended) investment in inventories, together with the intended investment of 30, equals the saving by profit recipients.

Suppose that, in response to this inability to sell what they produced, entrepreneurs reduced prices, but in smaller proportion than wages had fallen, say, to $.94. This means a real wage of 4.68, employment of 58 [equation (6)], and output of 388.72 [equation (5)]. With a money national income of $365.40 (388.72 × $.94), the wage bill would be $255.20 (58 × $4.40), leaving a profit income of $110.20. Wage earner consumption would be 271.5 (255.20 ÷ $.94), and consumption from profits 80.3 [10 + .6($110.20/$.94)]. Adding investment of 30 gives total demand of 381.8. This is still short of the output of 388.7. The gap has been reduced by half, from 13.8 to 6.9. But a gap remains, and will remain at any price level higher than $.88, at which point prices will have fallen in the same proportion as wages, the real wage will again be 5, with employment back to 50, and output back down to 350. Wage income will be $220 (50 × $4.4); the money national income $308 (350 × $.88); and profits $88. Consumption by wage earners will be 250 ($220 ÷ $.88); by profit recipients 70 [10 + .6($88/$.88)]; making total demand 350, once again equal to the supply.

The student can test the effect of a money wage increase by an analogous procedure.

# Keynesian and Classical Models Compared and Evaluated

*Chapter XV*

## A COMPARISON OF FORMAL MODELS

To begin this comparison of Keynesian and Classical macroeconomic models, let us retrace very briefly the steps through which we developed our Classical model, in Chapters V through VIII.

We started with the simple idea of the "quantity theory," expressed symbolically as

$$(1) \qquad\qquad M = lPy$$

This idea, that money is held only so long as necessary to bridge the necessary time-gap between transactions, and then moves along against goods, provides not only a theory of the price level, but necessarily incorporates, as well, a simple explanation for the volume of output (and by implication) employment. If prices $(P)$ are flexible, then they will always rest at the level which permits output $(y)$ to be at the maximum level permitted by resource supplies and technology. Only with this assumption is it possible to explain why prices (in the short run) vary proportionately with the supply of money.

This theory might do well enough in an economy where each man produces what he sells and sells what he produces. But if labor is hired by a specialized agent, an entrepreneur, we need to expand this simple analysis by recognizing that employment decisions depend on the relationship between two kinds of price levels—the price level of goods and the price level of labor (the money wage). To have an employment theory, therefore, we added the equation, already implicit,

(2)                    $y = y(N)$   (the production function)

together with

(3)          $\dfrac{dy}{dN} = \dfrac{W}{P}$   (the condition for profit maximization)

and

(4)                    $N = N\!\left(\dfrac{W}{P}\right)$   (the supply of labor function)

Equilibrium in the labor market requires equality between the supply and demand for labor (a real wage equal to the marginal supply price of labor and as well to the marginal product of labor). Equilibrium in the market for goods requires equality between the supply and demand for goods (a price level at which the entire output can be sold which it is profitable to produce, given the state of technique and the wage level). These conditions of equilibrium are added to the first one—that equilibrium in the public's money holdings requires equality between the supply and demand for money (a price level for the goods exchanged just high enough so that there are no idle balances).

Since the theory that all money which is received automatically gets spent does not square with the fact that many people save who do not themselves invest, we added the notion that the market rate of interest fluctuates to keep investment spending equal to the nonspending of income by consumers. For the rate of interest to perform in this way it was necessary to revise the interpretation of equation (1) to imply only that wealth holders always prefer to hold earning assets rather than barren cash, and to round out the system with:

(5)                                        $s = s(r)$

(6)                                        $i = i(r)$

(7)                                        $s = i$

The resulting model had certain properties of which the following summary will remind us: (a) the only equilibrium is with full employment; (b) changes in $M$ can influence only the price level, not the rate of interest, the real wage, nor the levels of output and employment; (c) only in the disequilibrium process, as explained by Wicksell, is there any tie between the rate of interest and the rest of the model; but this explanation is necessary to make good sense out of the theory of prices and for us to understand how the banking system fits into the picture; (d) if money wages are rigid at too high a level, or fail to fall fast enough, full employment is impossible; but the theory is not clear whether the result would be a continuously falling employment and output level, or some quasi-equilibrium at less than full employment, and, if the latter, at how much less.

From the standpoint of subsequent students of economics, it was in some ways unfortunate that Keynes did not see how he could graft his ideas on to this Classical model, but felt that he had to reject it, and to start over again. It should be recorded that he tried the older approach. This two-volume *Treatise on Money* (published in 1930) was a long and painstaking development along the lines pioneered by Wicksell and others in the Classical tradition. But Keynes ended his work on the *Treatise* deeply dissatisfied. He wrote, in the preface:

> This book . . . has occupied me for several years, . . . during which my ideas have been developing and changing. . . . The result is, I am afraid, that there is a good deal . . . which represents the process of getting rid of the ideas which I used to have. . . . I feel like someone who has been forcing his way through a confused jungle. Now that I have emerged from it, I see that I might have taken a more direct route. . . .

Five years later, his new approach appeared, his *General Theory of Employment, Interest and Money.* In this he attacked the Classical theory as unrealistic in its assumptions and incorrect in its logic. Rather than to modify and correct it, he started over again, developing his own theory in about the order in which we have done, in Chapter X, XIII, and XIV. That is, he started with the idea of a consumption function, and the recognition that total income was derived from (and, on simple assumptions, equaled) total spending for consumption and investment:

(I) $$c = c(y)$$

(II) $$y = c + i$$

(III) $$i = i_0$$

As we have seen, (I) and (II) can equally well be rewritten:

(Ia) $$s = s(y)$$

(IIa) $$s = i$$

From this model derive the multiplier, and the basic Keynesian fiscal policy conclusions. We found that we could substitute for (III)

(IIIa) $$i = i(y)$$

without making any real difference, so long as the modified stability condition was observed.

But Keynes was too good a Classical economist really to assume investment autonomous (or dependent only on income); rather, he accepted (with certain qualifications that we shall refer to in a moment) the Classical idea that investment depends on the rate of interest:

$$\text{(IIIb)} \qquad\qquad\qquad i = i(r)$$

or, combined with the notion embodied in (IIIa),

$$\text{(IIIc)} \qquad\qquad\qquad i = i(r, y)$$

His principal qualifications were, one, that the investment schedule was relatively steep: even at zero $r$, investment would be at a finite rate, not necessarily sufficiently high for full employment; and, two, that the position of the investment schedule was highly unstable (he emphasized psychological reasons for its instability) and subject to wide swings that (for purposes of his formal theory) must be considered autonomous.

These latter qualifications play an important role; nevertheless the admitted dependence of $i$ on $r$ made the model incomplete without a theory of the interest rate. It had to be a theory other than the Classical one, or the rate of interest would admit by the back door the Classical doctrines of automatic stabilization of aggregate demand. In his interest theory he embodied ideas which derived from his own earlier work and which had been at least partially foreshadowed in Wicksell's disequilibrium analysis. (By stating his theory in stock rather than flow form, however, he failed himself fully to see the exact nature of his innovation, nor could many subsequent economists—even down to the present—see through his novelty of form of statement to appreciate both its link with the past and the nature of its substantive innovation.) Thus we have:

$$\text{(IVa)} \qquad\qquad\qquad M = M_t + M_s$$
$$\text{(IVb)} \qquad\qquad\qquad M_t = lPy$$
$$\text{(IVc)} \qquad\qquad\qquad M_s = L(r)$$

or simply

$$\text{(IV)} \qquad\qquad\qquad M = lPy + L(r)$$

So long as prices are assumed as rigid, and no account is taken of the necessity for employers to find a profit margin between the wage and price level, equations (I), (II), (IIIb), and (IV) define a "complete" model, in the sense that there are as many equations as unknowns.

But Keynes was also too good a Classical economist to assume away the price and profit mechanism. Thus we add

(V) $$y = y(N)$$

(VI) $$\frac{dy}{dN} = \frac{W}{P}$$

Realizing that addition of the Classical supply of labor function would imply a full-employment solution, and believing that in any case money wages are not flexible, Keynes substituted an autonomously determined money wage

(VII) $$W = W_0$$

In his verbal discussion, he admitted some departure from the assumption of a completely rigid money wage, as already indicated.

Keynes did not reject the logic of the Classical supply of labor schedule

(4) $$N = N\left(\frac{W}{P}\right);$$

in fact he retained it to define the position of full employment. But he argued that this equation could not always be fulfilled simultaneously with the others—i.e., that equilibrium at less than full employment is possible.

It should not be difficult to see that the two models, Keynesian and Classical, overlap considerably. Bringing them together for purposes of comparison (with the order rearranged in the Keynesian model) we have

| Classical | | Keynesian | |
|---|---|---|---|
| (1) | $M = lPy$ | (IV) | $M = lPy + L(r)$ |
| (2) | $y = y(N)$ | (V) | $y = y(N)$ |
| (3) | $\dfrac{dy}{dN} = \dfrac{W}{P}$ | (VI) | $\dfrac{dy}{dN} = \dfrac{W}{P}$ |
| (4) | $N = N\left(\dfrac{W}{P}\right)$ | (VII) | $W = W_0$ |
| (5) | $s = s(r)$ | (Ia) | $s = s(y)$ |
| (6) | $i = i(r)$ | (IIIb) | $i = i(r)$ |
| (7) | $s = i$ | (IIa) | $s = i$ |

The differences that show up on the surface are only three:

a) Keynes added the speculative demand for money to the Classical transactions demand [equation (1) versus (IV)].

b) Keynes suppressed the supply of labor function and assumed rigid wages; [(4) versus (VII)].

c) Keynes assumed saving (consumption) to depend on income rather than upon the interest rate [(5) versus (Ia)].

Which of these constitutes the really crucial difference between Classical and Keynesian analyses? Some economists have said that it is the first of these differences, others that it is the second, others the third, while still others say it is none of these but something else that does not show up directly in this formal structure.

To show that the crucial difference is not the consumption (saving) function, some economists correctly point out that, if the only modification in the Classical model were the substitution of (Ia) for (5), the conclusions of the Classical model would hardly be altered at all. This can be seen by recognizing that (2), (3), and (4) still define a full-employment equilibrium of $y$, $N$, and $W/P$. Adding equation (1) solves for the absolute price and wage level. With $y$ already determined, then, by (Ia), so is $s$. Given $s$ and equations (6) and (7), $r$ and $i$ are determined. If $M$ is changed, only prices and wages are altered. If the $s$ or $i$ schedules shift, only $r$ will be altered. The only difference is that, now, a shift in either the production function or the supply of labor will alter the rate of interest, because, by altering $y$, they will change the level of saving relative to investment. But this is a minor difference, of little importance for short-run economic policy, because the aggregate production function and labor supply change only slowly and steadily.

Others go on to argue that the speculative demand for money is not very important because we can add this, too, to the Classical model without changing its basic conclusions (this is true whether we add this alone or with the consumption function as well). We saw in Chapter IX that the speculative demand schedule did not necessarily spoil the Classical full-employment equilibrium. We saw in Chapter XIV that if we insert flexible wages [i.e., equation (4)] into the Keynesian model, we may still find an equilibrium at full employment. Ignoring many necessary qualifications (contained in the analyses referred to in the two previous sentences), one can then go on to argue that the really crucial Keynesian innovation was the introduction of rigid wages. Only if rigid wages are assumed can there be any "equilibrium" at less than full employment. Since Keynes' principal claim was to have demonstrated this possibility, it is clear that wage rigidity is his crucial assumption. This, some critics add, is nothing very original; for even the Classical economists fully recognized that rigid wages would cause unemployment; in fact it was the only possible cause of unemployment. It is merely that Keynes was the first to write a whole book about the special case in which wages are rigid.

Keynes himself anticipated this criticism, and went to great pains to argue that his conclusions did not depend on the assumption of rigid wages. Many (perhaps most) later Keynesians have agreed with Keynes' own apparent judgment that the really crucial cause of unemployment was the speculative demand for money.[1] It was this which prevented the interest rate from stabilizing aggregate demand, thus throwing an insupportable burden upon wage and price flexibility, which were actually far from perfect anyway. Further, if the speculative demand schedule were very elastic, almost no amount of deflation would work. Rigid wages are thus not the *cause* of unemployment; they merely prevent unemployment from creating a painful, largely useless, even bottomless deflation.

Another view argues that neither the consumption function, liquidity preference, nor rigid wages is the really crucial Keynesian innovation. Suppose that we accept the Classical model in full, except to specify that, at least at times, there may be an inconsistency between saving and investment; that is, equations (5), (6), and (7) may have no solution at a positive rate of interest. This can occur if the interest elasticity of saving is slight—and Keynes argued that saving depended primarily on $y$ and only secondarily, if at all, on $r$—and if the interest elasticity of investment is also limited, and this was also something Keynes stressed. If such an inconsistency exists, wages and prices would fall without limit, unless wages are sticky. If such an inconsistency exists, the rate of interest would fall toward zero, except to the extent that the speculative demand for money would cushion its fall. But wage rigidity and the speculative demand are mere details. The fundamental cause of unemployment lies in the insufficiency of investment relative to saving, and the inability (quite apart from speculation) of the interest rate to do much about it. In this view, then, the fundamental Keynesian ideas are contained in the simple three-equation model; the rest is mere window dressing. The

[1] "Men are unemployed . . . because people want the moon;—men cannot be employed when the object of desire (i.e., money) is something which cannot be produced and the demand for which cannot be readily choked off. There is no remedy but to persuade the public that green cheese is practically the same thing and to have a green cheese factory (i.e., a central bank) under public control." (*General Theory,* p. 235.)

simple model ignores the interest rate, but the interest rate is not very important anyway.

We do not have to choose one among these competing views as correct, rejecting the others. They are matters of emphasis, and of degree.

One striking fact, however, emerges. Whether we emphasize that unemployment is caused by wage rigidity, by speculation, or by inconsistency, the primary determinant of the *extent* of unemployment, and therefore of the level of national income and output, is the slope of the consumption function. For if neither the interest rate nor the wage and price level is able to equate saving and investment (at full employment), the level of income will (at less than full employment). *How far income must fall below the full-employment level to do this depends on the slope of the consumption function.* Thus the consumption function, insufficient *by itself* to explain anything, becomes the kingpin of the Keynesian structure after all. This is what justifies Hansen in calling it the "heart of the Keynesian analysis," and which supports the extensive and continuing efforts to define, refine, and to measure statistically the nature and stability of the relationship of income and consumption.

## PROBLEMS OF EVALUATING THE KEYNESIAN SYSTEM

Professor Joseph A. Schumpeter, along with Keynes one of the few great economists of the twentieth century, writing a memorial article on Keynes,[2] refused to "grade the *General Theory* as though it were a student's examination book." Nor will such an attempt be made here, particularly because our subject has not been Keynes' ideas as such, and even less his own exposition of his ideas. But the macroeconomic model set forth in the present chapter is in all important respects Keynes' model. We have compared it with the Classical model, over which it is quite obviously an improvement. But we cannot avoid some responsibility also for evaluating it not merely by comparison with the past but as an analytical instrument, taking account of the controversy which the *General Theory* generated, and of subsequent improvements and developments in economic thought.

[2] *American Economic Review*, XXXVI (September 1946), 495–518, reprinted in *The New Economics*, S. E. Harris, ed. (Knopf, 1947). For other important evaluations of Keynes' work see Chap. VIII–XIV of *The New Economics*; A. F. Burns, *Economic Research and the Keynesian Thinking of Our Times* (Twenty-sixth Annual Report of the National Bureau of Economic Research, June 1946); "Keynesian Economics after Twenty Years" (papers and comments by W. Fellner, D. Dillard, D. Mc. Wright, W. A. Salant, and T. Scitovsky), *American Economic Review*, XLVII (May 1957), 67–95; J. R. Schlesinger, "After Twenty Years: The General Theory," *Quarterly Journal of Economics*, LXX (November 1956), 581–602; and the article by Wright cited in the next footnote.

Such judgment is made difficult by the fact that Keynes' book included not only an analytical model, but, as well, Keynes' own use of this model (together with the "facts" as he saw them) for the purpose of prediction; further, on the basis of his predictions, he suggested or implied certain social policies.

It is at least possible that the model might have been quite adequate, but the "facts" wrong, leading to wrong predictions. And, even if the predictions were correct, the suggested social policies might be subject to criticism as badly designed or ineffective. We are here primarily concerned, of course, with Keynes as model-builder (i.e., as economic theorist), not as model-user or policy maker. It has been difficult for critics of Keynes to distinguish among the three roles; in fact, in evaluating the *General Theory* as such it is not necessarily appropriate to make the distinction. Clearly, however, much of the opposition to Keynes and to Keynesian ideas has centered about Keynesian forecasts and Keynesian policies.

Keynes' forecast, never fully spelled out but quite apparent in the background of his discussion, is that the wealthy, advanced countries of the West faced, in the twentieth century, a more or less chronic deficiency of aggregate demand. This would result from a combination of a fairly high average propensity to save (and an even higher marginal propensity) in combination with investment incentives that were substantially less strong than in the nineteenth century. Thus the mature economies of Western Europe and North America could expect a continuing threat of unemployment and "stagnation." This theme was developed in more detail by the American economist Alvin Hansen, but its origin is clearly apparent in the *General Theory*.

Now this forecast conceivably might have been correct had not World War II and the subsequent "cold war" intervened; some economists are still inclined to support this view. The recurrent fears of what might happen to the American economy if a major reduction of government defense spending should become possible are an echo of the stagnation reasoning of the late thirties. More economists today, however, would call the forecast incorrect, arguing that Keynes' gloomy prospect merely reflected a short-sighted projection of the depression conditions of the early thirties.

The error of the forecast (if it was erroneous) could, as suggested earlier, reflect a wrong judgment of the "facts"—i.e., a poor estimate of the probable strength of aggregate demand. Or, it could reflect a bias of the analytical model. Keynes' view that the MPS was substantially higher than the APS (and thus that a wealthy economy had to find "offsets to saving" which were a higher percentage of total output than for a poor economy, was probably wrong (see above, pp. 236–246). Some might choose to call this an error as to the "facts," rather than of the model, for the postulated relationship of MPS to APS is in no way fundamental to the Keynesian model. Perhaps this is leaning over backward to defend Keynes as theorist. His forecast as to investment incentives in part merely represented (from hindsight) a bad guess as to future technological and demographic developments; however, it also reflected an analytical error in his investment theory. This matter is most appropriately discussed below, in Chapters XVII and XVIII, so that we are not in a position to develop it at this point. The error, however, can be remedied without impairing any other part of the Keynesian model. The model developed in this and the preceding chapters has only a very rudimentary investment theory, and does not incorporate this error.

As to the validity of the social policies suggested or implied by Keynes we shall not enter. One could and can accept the analytical model—and even, perhaps, the forecasts—yet possibly reject completely the Keynesian policies.[3] As we indicated in the opening paragraphs of this book, choice of social policies involves far more than theoretical models.

We confine our discussion, then, to Keynes as economic theorist or model-builder. In this context, we can indicate certain weaknesses and inadequacies. Some of these have previously been presented, and only need review. Others represent an introduction to problems considered in the remaining chapters, and in the post-Keynesian macroeconomic literature in general.

First of all, we should recognize that Keynes was not always a fair critic of Classical analysis, nor was he fully aware of the relationship of his own ideas to the body of thought that preceded him. In particular, he was far less of a revolutionist than he sometimes appeared to consider himself. His model might yield very different predictions in any given set of hypothetical facts than the Classical model; yet it can better be considered an extension and improvement of, rather than a substitute for, the macroeconomic thinking of his predecessors. Some of his accusations of logical errors on the part of the Classical writers are clearly unfair, at least if the Classical system is given sympathetic interpretation. As we have seen, it is possible to construct a logically valid Classical model, which produces a full-employment equilibrium, what-

[3] For an interesting discussion of these several elements in Keynes' position, as well as an excellent review of the significance of Keynes' work, see David McC. Wright, "The Future of Keynesian Economics," *American Economic Review*, XXXV (June 1945), 284–307.

ever one may think of the assumptions that underlie this model. But it is the assumptions that are mainly to be criticized, not the logical consistency of the argument which rests upon these assumptions.

Further, Keynes was himself occasionally guilty of logical errors, at least in some statements of his position. For example, we have already commented at length upon his tautological defense of his multiplier idea, and upon his failure to be clear about the senses in which he was using the terms saving and investment. Further, it is of course impossible to argue, as he sometimes appeared to do, that, if wages and prices were fully flexible, there could still be "equilibrium" at less than full employment. His appreciation of the difference between his own form of statement of interest theory and the loanable funds form of statement was surely quite inadequate, and his criticisms of the former theory not always well taken. The confusions in his investment theory referred to above will be developed in a later chapter.

But, as is the case with the Classical theory, it is possible to give the Keynesian analysis a sympathetic rather than a hypercritical interpretation. So interpreted, his system must at least be recognized as internally complete and consistent. Given his assumptions, the analysis proceeds logically to the conclusions which it reaches.

But the validity of an economic model does not rest alone or even principally on its logical consistency. In this respect, the reconstructed Classical model scores as well as Keynes'. What then is the test of a "good" model? It is its usefulness—its ability to help us to understand and perhaps to influence the "real world"—to see behind the incredibly complex tangle of surface manifestations to the basic forces which principally shape the broad current of events; to enable prediction as to the major effects of any proposed social action (or failure to act).

To see what makes a model useful or not useful for understanding or control, we need to consider further the nature of a model and the ways in which we employ it. A model consists of certain selected *variables* and certain postulated *relationships* among these variables. All variables not selected for inclusion become unspecified parameters—they merely influence the shape and nature of the *relationships* which are included in the model. Values of some of the included variables are determined autonomously—i.e., outside the model; values of others are determined within the model. We use the model to make "conditional predictions," as follows: given the values of the autonomous variables and the nature of the relationships, there is some set of equilibrium values (or type of movement) of the variables; if we change one or more of the autonomous variables, or the shape or position of one or more of the relationships, there is a new set of values (or type of movement). Our "conditional prediction" thus takes the form: "If A changes, there will be the following changes in B, C, and D." When we feed new information into our model, and observe what happens, we perform an "intellectual experiment," somewhat analogous to but essentially different from a laboratory experiment.

The results of this experiment can then be compared with the "real world," to see how well the model predicts. This test may involve forecasting, or it may only be a test against history. Some models (e.g., those without lags) have no usefulness for forecasting because we know the (real world) outcome as soon as we know the (real world) values of the autonomous variables. Such models may still be highly useful for understanding what has happened and for guiding attempts to influence what is currently happening.

To be sure, such tests of models can rarely be conclusive. In the "real world," we almost never have a neat change of one (or two) variables (or relationships), the others staying put for us to get a precise comparison with the results of our "intellectual experiment." Imperfections of measurement contribute to the difficulty. Further, several alternative models may give "conditional predictions" which our rough tests show to be about equally good (or bad). We cannot yet rely only upon statistical tests to establish the usefulness of a model. What are some of the other characteristics of a "good" model?

First, it is almost needless to say that a model can be found to be useful or not useful, to give good, fair, or poor predictions, only if its variables are so defined as to have some "real world" counterpart. That is, its variables must be capable of empirical approximation or measurement, directly or indirectly. A model whose variables are not "operationally defined" can never be tested, and, certainly, it cannot be "used."

Second, a model is more useful (other things equal), the more specifically formulated are its relationships, and therefore the more detailed its predictions. If we describe our relationships only in broad terms—e.g., that a "slope" is positive rather than negative—then we can make only qualitative predictions, or maybe none at all. (If the result depends on two or more "slopes" then we may not be able to give a prediction even as to the direction of a result unless we know whether one slope is greater or less than another.) The more we can specify as to the shapes and positions of our relationships, the more detailed and therefore (if accurate) the more useful our model's predictions.

Third, the model is more useful the more stable (in the "real world") are the relationships it includes. It is this stability which permits the discovery and description of the nature and quantitative measure of the relationships, which in turn make the model useful. The degree of this stability is related to the time horizon of the model: some models are short run, others pretend to longer run usefulness. Obviously, however, relationships stable only in the very short run make a model of little use (even for very short-run predictions), for it becomes too difficult, if not impossible, to give such relationships empirical content. Since the shape and nature (and therefore the stability) of a relationship depends on the variables *not isolated*, this means that a "good" model isolates as explicit variables those which change most and whose change makes the most difference, leaving as unspecified parameters those which, in the time period relevant to the model, change least. It cannot isolate too many variables or the model becomes unmanageable. But it cannot hope for stable relationships if it isolates too few. The "best" or "correct" number is thus a compromise.

But among the variables we particularly wish to isolate are those which are "strategic"—that is, those which are or might possibly become subject to social control. Since what is or might be subject to social control depends in part on the mores or value system of the community as well as upon the availability of administrative machinery or other means, the distinction between good and bad theory becomes somewhat relativistic.

This recognition is strengthened when we consider further that the *problems* on which the theory focuses (or permits one to focus) differ and change in the importance with which they are perceived by society, thus making theories obsolete or timely, depending on their problem focus. For example, the physical and psychic misery of unemployment may be considered a small matter in one society, a matter of overwhelming concern in another. A theory about unemployment would be judged trivial in the one society, significant by the other. Needless to say, changes in economic and social structure as well as in social values will contribute to the changing importance of problems and thus to the judgment as to the usefulness of a theory.

Of course, a theory does not have to focus on *all* important economic problems of a society—we can have a division of labor, one theory being useful for (say) problems of income distribution and another for problems of income level. These can safely be entrusted to separate models, of course, only if there is little or no mutual interaction between the variables of the two models.[4] But any given theory is more useful or more adequate as it focuses on those problems with which the society finds its greatest concern.

We have thus suggested some tests of the usefulness of a theory—that its variables be operational, that its relationships have empirical content and be reasonably stable, that it include strategic variables, and that it be relevant to important problems of a society. Other tests might be proposed, or these rearranged or restated. This is not a matter on which all economists will agree. However, let us see how we might evaluate the Keynesian model in the light of these criteria. First let us consider some of the criticisms which have been made of the Keynesian analysis; then we will summarize our evaluation in terms of the criteria we have just developed.

## CRITICISMS OF THE KEYNESIAN MODEL

The first criticism we shall consider is that the Keynesian model is "too aggregative." By this it is presumably meant that the model should contain more variables and more relationships than it does. We have already seen that an increase in these numbers can (if the additions are properly selected) increase the stability of the relationships and thus improve the predictions of the model. So far as is known, the criticism that the Keynesian model is "too aggregative" has not been made because of any belief that the model fails to isolate strategic variables.

Certain disaggregations are often made in applying the Keynesian model. For example, investment is broken down into plant and equipment, residential housing, and inventory change. This permits us to take better account of the effect of autonomous factors affecting these narrower categories—for example, special governmental measures directed toward encouragement or restriction of housing expenditure, special supply situations for capital goods, etc. Or, we may break out consumer durable goods from other consumption expenditures (supplying separate consumption functions for durables and for all other consumption), in order to permit us to take account of changes in the availability of consumer credit, or of special factors affecting the market for automobiles, etc. When we do this we do not, however, introduce any new relationships of interaction; we do not really expand the model.

What some critics assert is much more fundamental. It is that the very use of aggregative expenditure concepts like consumption and in-

---

[4] There can be one way interaction. For example, if national income influences income distribution, the level of national income can be taken as autonomous for the distribution model. But not if distribution in turn influences level; then we need one model instead of two.

vestment (or even their major subcategories) dooms the model to give wrong or seriously misleading advice. The unit of analysis must be the individual commodity, or commodities grouped in some other manner, e.g., by degree of elasticity of supply (contrasting, perhaps, agricultural products, whose output has little short run elasticity; many services, which may have great elasticity of supply but almost zero employment effects; some manufactured goods, production of which can be expanded easily but in proportion to labor input; manufactured goods using imported raw materials, etc.). The issue involved here is a complex one. It does appear that, *particularly for some economies,* the criticism has merit. A later chapter considers the problem in more detail. For the American economy, however, our judgment will be that this point is on the whole not well-taken.

The further disaggregation which the Keynesian model does seem most to require, even for an economy like the American, relates to the problem of income distribution. By implication, the formal model presented in the previous section has two income shares: wages and profits. Even these two shares are not used in the consumption analysis—the assumption is either that recipients of these two income shares have identical consumption patterns, or else that the distribution of income between them is either stable or a stable function of aggregate income. Certainly, the model would be improved by the introduction of a farm sector (this relates also to the previous point); but one can easily exaggerate the importance of agriculture in the American economy. More serious is the absence of the corporation and corporate saving, an interest share in the national income, proprietorships and professional practice, etc. But we must realize that introduction of these new variables implics the introduction of new relationships, which permit the *determination* of these income shares as well as their impact on consumption and investment. One may easily agree that "it would be nice" to have this disaggregation, without having any satisfactory idea how to provide it. The dilemma becomes particularly apparent when we consider (see below) the inadequacies of even the simple income-distribution theory implied in the unexpanded Keynesian model. Although we can agree that an expansion of the model in these directions would be desirable, it has not been clearly demonstrated that the explanation of the volume of consumption can be greatly improved by disaggregation. It is possible that the most significant improvements would come in the explanation of investment expenditure.

A second general criticism of the Keynesian model is that it is "too static." This may mean almost opposite things. On the one hand, the model cannot deal with the short-run dynamics of income change; on the other, it is not suited to the analysis of problems of long-term growth.

To be sure, the Keynesian model can be given some short-run dynamics merely by the introduction of certain lags—for example, of consumption behind income, of investment behind interest rate, of transactions demand behind money income, and so on. A whole class of dynamic models can be so constructed, some of which can produce interesting cycles, growth patterns, etc. The problem is not that the Keynesian model cannot be made dynamic, but is rather that we need to know which lags (if any) are empirically important, and whether, once the model is made dynamic, *rates of change* of some variables do not need to be introduced into some of our functions. In equilibrium, rates of change of all variables are zero; hence their influence disappears in the functions applicable to equilibrium positions. It cannot be forgotten that the dynamic counterpart of a static model introduces new problems of substance, having no place in the static model. Specifically, we would argue that the crucial factor in the short-run dynamics of the so-called "business cycle" relates to the adjustment of production to changes in sales—that is, to the dynamics of inventories. In the static model, production and sales are equal—inventories are constant. Empirical evidence shows clearly, however, that the largest single item in the short-term income fluctuations designated as "business cycles" is the change of inventory investment.[5] The static Keynesian analysis can offer us few clues to the understanding of these movements.

On the other hand, the Keynesian model is, by its own terms, limited to the short run. Keynes specifically assumed a given stock of capital equipment. Making output a function only of employment reflects this assumption. It is often pointed out that Keynes' analysis is self-contradictory, for the analysis deals with situations in which (net) investment may be positive or negative. This means that the stock of capital is changing. Keynes' assumption can be defended by arguing that, in the short run, changes in the stock of capital can only be very small—even annual net investment is only a small fraction of total capital stock. Still, an assumption of stable production or investment functions over any considerable period of time is obviously deficient. In particular, any analysis of economic growth or development must take specific account of capital accumulation.

Another side of this phenomenon of growth of capital stock is the growth of consumer wealth, as claims accumulate to the increased stock.

[5] See M. Abramovitz, *Inventories and Business Cycles, with Special Reference to Manufacturers' Inventories* (National Bureau of Economic Research, 1950). The relationship found by Abramovitz is even more pronounced in post-war business fluctuations in the United States.

That this may affect consumption is a possibility several times noted. More subtle, perhaps, is the point that the *form* in which wealth accumulates—whether equities or debt certificates, whether reflected directly or through financial intermediaries—may also influence consumption and perhaps particularly investment. This relates to the criticism, considered below, that the Keynesian model, even in its static formulation, pays insufficient attention to the details of business financing.

Clearly, the Keynesian model is "too static" for the analysis either of the business cycle or of problems of economic growth. It needs to be expanded and supplemented in substance (and not merely in form) to deal with these problems.

We may turn from these general criticisms of the Keynesian model to criticisms of specific parts. We shall not repeat our consideration of the consumption function hypothesis, that having been the subject of considerable previous discussion. Neither shall we consider here the Keynesian investment theory, which, for several reasons, seems best considered separately and at a later point. Keeping in mind these gaps in the evaluation here presented, we begin with criticisms of the wage-price-production segment of the model.

There are three relationships involved in this segment; that of employment to output (the production function), that of profit maximization (a relationship among wage rates, prices, and output), and that of the determination of the money wage level. The notion of a stable aggregate production function is, in the short run, fairly reasonable, at least for an economy like the American, where labor mobility is high and where no one or a few industries are of dominating importance. Some disaggregation, especially of farming, and perhaps of capital goods and some services might improve the relationship; but these are not serious problems for most purposes. However, the assumption that the production function involves diminishing returns seems more questionable (see Chap. IV).

The profit maximization hypothesis is, moreover, quite unsatisfactory, at least as a short-run principle. Perhaps the trouble is that output and employment decisions must reflect, not actual, known ratios of wages to prices, but the ratio of known wages to expected future prices (this relates to the short-run dynamics of inventory formation, a problem mentioned earlier). Equally serious, however, is the fact that industrial price decisions (and those in the distributive and service trades) often reflect rules of thumb, longer-run strategic considerations, the delicate balance of oligopolistic power, much inertia but occasional attempts to "beat the gun," and so on. It should be noted that the deficiencies of the wage-price analysis are also the deficiencies of the income-distribution theory implied in the model. It may be that for many kinds of problems the inadequacy of the profit-maximizing hypothesis makes little difference. It surely does make a difference, however, for an analysis of problems of short-run wage-price policy, and of situations of inflation. But, as is frequently the case, it is much easier to criticize than to suggest improvements.

The theory of money wage determination either of the Classical or Keynesian model is quite inadequate. To assume money wages completely flexible to changes in employment is only slightly more absurd than to assume them rigid—or, rather, autonomously determined.

Making the *rate of change* of money wages a function of the level of employment is slightly better (indeed this is what Keynes' incidental discussion implied). But a tie to the cost-of-living is also important. Here is the principal reason why it becomes highly useful to split off a farm sector: the cost-of-living and, therefore, money wages are particularly sensitive to changes in farm prices. Trade union wage policy and the state of employer resistance to wage inflation do not, however, seem to be matters easily reduced to any stable function of anything.

A further criticism of the Keynesian model relates to its money and interest rate analysis; first, as to what it includes, then as to what it omits. Perhaps the most valid criticism of the speculative demand for money analysis is the implication sometimes supplied that the speculative demand schedule possesses any degree of permanence or stability. Its position and shape clearly depend upon the level and dispersion of the interest rate expectations of wealth-holders. While it is conceivable that these might be stable and unchanging, this is hardly plausible. Major revisions in the actual level of interest rates (as, for instance, between 1929 and the mid-thirties, or between the end of World War II and the nineteen-fifties) must certainly give rise to entirely different speculative demand curves. And even in the short run, one might well suppose that the level of interest rate expectations trails along after the movement of actual rates. The idea that wealth-holders speculate with respect to the interest rate (i.e., bond prices), and that their expectations prevent the adjustment of the rate to changes in the level which would equate current saving and investment is entirely reasonable, and surely calls attention to a phenomenon of crucial importance. But to reduce this idea to a schedule considered to have any stability or permanence is to carry the idea further than seems reasonable or necessary. Taking account of this objection increases considerably the complexity of the analysis, something which the actual importance of the interest rate for aggregate demand may not justify.

But if our analysis focuses on the interest rate, this and other elaborations seem to be called for. The further elaborations relate to the existence of assets other than the Keynesian triad of money, bonds, and goods. Not only are there bonds (and loans) of varying maturity and risk, but there are shares and various hybrid securities, and there are the various forms of equities and debts created by the structure of financial intermediaries. Institutional, psychological, and structural factors create, on the one hand, a complex of opportunities for business to finance its expansion and re-equipment, and on the other a complex of types of claims to be held—both by natural persons and by financial intermediaries. It is quite clear that the differential availability of various forms of finance and the structure of financial costs may affect investment as much as does the level of "the" interest rate. The structure of current financing also determines, in the longer run, the accumulating structure of claims and debts, with possible further impact on the behavior of consumers and firms.

The view that disparages the importance of the interest rate (or of financial considerations in general) on the level of economic activity has, perhaps, as good claim to empirical support as the opposite view. Keynes, himself, however, appeared to attribute considerable importance to the interest rate. It can be argued, therefore, that his interest analysis was too imperfect to bear the weight which he wished it to carry.

Another whole group of critics belabors Keynes' failure to take account of the "Pigou effect" (which some choose to call the "real balance effect"); or continues to harp upon the impossibility of less-than-full employment equilibrium if wages and prices are perfectly flexible. One can easily agree that Keynes may have incorrectly stated his position, yet not accept the *substance* of this criticism. Wages are simply not and could not be made flexible enough for the question to have much relevance, *unless the Pigou effect were very powerful.* There is surely no evidence to support the view that the Pigou effect is or ever has been of appreciable significance to any real economy.

In summary, we can note no criticisms that Keynesian variables are nonoperational. On the contrary Keynesian economics has stimulated a vast effort to collect and organize data around the concepts of national income and output, consumption, investment, employment. One might qualify by noting that the Keynesian concepts call for desired or intended consumption, saving and investment.[6] He might also object that Keynes' key investment concept (the "marginal efficiency of capital") is

---

[6] The inability to measure unintended investment (in inventories) creates particular difficulties for business cycle analysis, but indirect approaches even to this are developing, through the measurement of output plans.

non-operational. But, all told, the operational character of Keynesian variables represents the greatest strength of the Keynesian system. Likewise, the variables strategic for monetary and fiscal policy are nicely isolated by the Keynesian analysis. The key relationship, the consumption function, has (as modified by subsequent research) a quite detailed empirical content, permitting quite specific predictions. And, surely, the analysis has direct relevance to what remains a problem of great social concern, that of unemployment.

But none of the other relationships has the empirical content of the consumption function, and their stability is subject to severe question, in particular those relating to income distribution and price formation, labor supply or wage determination, and those involved in the theory of money and assets. Improvements seem to require added (or substitute) variables and relationships.

Finally, even in the postwar world, unemployment (or the fear of unemployment) remains an ever-present danger. But the greatest macroeconomic problems of today appear to be connected with economic growth and inflation. By its own terms Keynesian analysis is not directly applicable to problems of growth. Although the model can be applied to inflation, and provides notable insights previously lacking, it is inadequate for complete understanding or for the guidance of policies to deal with inflation.

Yet with all its acknowledged deficiencies, the Keynesian analysis still stands as the most useful point of departure in macroeconomic theory. Itself incomplete and imperfect, it remains the foundation of the great majority of the significant theoretical works in macroeconomics of the past two decades. It has also long provided the basic framework for most governmental analyses of economic conditions and forecasts, and, increasingly, of the analyses and forecasts made by private groups and firms. As J. R. Hicks once put it, "the General Theory is neither the beginning nor the end of Dynamic Economics"; but it is perhaps significant that almost no single extension, amendment, or elaboration of the Keynesian model yet commands sufficient agreement among economists that it, rather than the Keynesian element it is designed to replace, has become the common starting point for the work of others.

Thus, in the chapters that follow, we are dealing with ideas still very much in flux.

# Some Extensions

## PART FOUR

# The Theory of Inflation [1]

*Chapter XVI*

## INTRODUCTION

Up to this point we have had little to say, at least explicitly, concerning the significant problem of inflation, which we may define as a persistent and appreciable rise in the general level or average of prices. Yet it may well be argued that inflation is currently, has been for a decade or more, and threatens to be in the future one of the most crucial macroeconomic problems for most countries of the world. In this chapter we shall review the standard theories of inflation, finding them, in large part, merely further extensions of analytical tools already thoroughly developed. We shall, however, also suggest that the kind of inflation that seems most relevant to today's world may require some concepts not contained in the preceding analysis—indeed, some that depart rather sharply from notions accepted in the analysis up to the present chapter.

Before proceeding to this review of theories, we should first make the rather obvious point that inflation *per se* is a process: we define inflation as *rising prices*, not as "high" prices. In some sense, then, inflation is a disequilibrium state; it must be analyzed dynamically rather than with

---

[1] The sixth, eighth, ninth, and tenth sections of this chapter are taken with little change from the author's paper "A Third Approach to the Analysis and Control of Inflation," in *The Relationship of Prices to Economic Stability and Growth,* Compendium of papers submitted by panelists appearing before the Joint Economic Committee, Congress of the United States, March 31, 1958, pp. 619–36. Beginning with "Markup Inflation," the presentation involves somewhat unorthodox ideas of the author, which probably would not find wide acceptance.

the tools of statics. The latter may tell us something about the conditions under which an inflation may emerge, or possibly define its limits (by describing the conditions of price level equilibrium). But to analyze the rate of inflation—to explain why it is one per cent rather than 15 per cent per year—is essentially a problem of macrodynamics. As with other parts of dynamic analysis, the study of rates of inflation is both complex and relatively underdeveloped.

## DEMAND INFLATION

The first theory of inflation discussed or implied in our previous chapters is that of the Classical school. In this analysis the price level depends directly and proportionately on the quantity of money. Inflation occurs when the quantity of money increases, and stops when the quantity of money is stabilized. The rate of inflation presumably depends on the rate of new money creation; if $\Delta M/M$ is 3 per cent per year, prices will tend to rise at 3 per cent per year.

In its cruder forms, the quantity theory is defective in failing to explain the channel by which an increase in $M$ produces an increase in money spending, which, with constant output (at the maximum level permitted by the economy's resources), bids up prices. This deficiency was remedied by Wicksell, who saw new money flowing into the economy in the forms of bank loans to businessmen to finance investment in excess of the current rate of saving. This represented, then, a net increase in the aggregate demand for an unchanged total supply of goods (since the economy was already at full employment), bidding up the prices of goods (and of the resources to produce goods), and at the same time extracting "forced saving" from the consumers, whose money incomes were based on an earlier price level. Wicksell clearly saw that the rise in prices would not itself reduce aggregate demand, because, after a brief lag, money incomes would rise in proportion to prices, leaving consumers in the same position as before to compete with investors for the limited supply of goods. If the banks stood ready to supply the investors with further new loans, the process would continue. If, on the other hand, the banks ceased to expand the money supply, the market rate of interest would have to rise to the "natural rate," choking off the extra investment demand (and perhaps stimulating saving—i.e., reducing consumption demand), thus halting the inflation.

The theory of inflation implied in Keynes' analysis is little more than a modification and generalization of Wicksell's. Suppose that there is already full employment and investment demand increases. This means a total demand for goods in excess of the available supply. Prices are bid up. Since consumer demand depends on real income, which is not reduced by rising prices because the sale of output at higher prices creates an equivalent rise in money incomes, the excess of demand is not eliminated. Keynes, however, broke the close tie between the quantity of money and the level of aggregate demand. An economy might experience some inflation even with a constant money supply. It is useful to recapitulate how and why. If $M$ were constant, an increased level of prices would raise the transactions demand and thus push up interest rates, tending to choke off the extra investment demand, and to moderate the inflationary pressure. But it would not eliminate it. The reason is that the rise in interest rates would free some cash from speculative balances to supply the added transaction needs. As security prices fell, some previous cash holders would wish to hold securities instead. This would moderate the fall in security prices (rise in interest rates), which would thus be insufficient to remove all of the excess demand. Only if there were zero speculative balances would the result correspond to Wicksell's, for in this case, a larger transactions demand (resulting from higher prices) could not be accomodated, and, interest rates would necessarily rise sufficiently to choke off the entire excess of aggregate demand (perhaps partly through reducing consumption, if saving were affected by interest rates).

The two analyses, and the difference between them, can also be illuminated by considering the case of increased government demand in a situation of full employment. If government spending increases with no rise in taxes, the difference (deficit) must be financed either (a) by borrowing from the general (nonbank) public, or (b) by running the printing press, or borrowing from banks with excess reserves, thus indirectly increasing the money supply. In Wicksell's analysis, solution (b) would raise the price level but not solution (a). In the case (b), the new government demand is not matched by an equivalent reduction in private demand, so that excess demand appears. But if the government borrows from the nonbank public [solution (a)], it must compete with private investors, bidding up the rate of interest to the point at which private demand is reduced by as much as public demand increases. But in Keynes' analysis, even solution (a) will be inflationary, because speculation will moderate the rise in interest rates: the cheaper securities will induce some former cash-holders to become security holders instead. To be sure, solution (b) would be more inflationary because it need produce no rise in interest rates. If solution (b) were continually followed,

inflation would proceed without limit. However, if bonds were sold to
the public with no increase in $M$, the rise in prices would ultimately increase transactions demands sufficiently to bid up the rate of interest
to the point at which excess demand would disappear, and the inflation
would terminate.

There is thus a significant difference between Keynes' and Wicksell's
treatment of inflation. For the latter, any increase in $M$ (except that which
paralleled a rise in total productivity of the economy) is necessarily
inflationary. This would be true even if the initial increase in $M$ occurred not through direct bank lending to business or government, but
merely through central-bank open-market purchases of securities. For
Keynes, the rise in prices might occur even with no increase in $M$; yet
an increase in $M$ secured through open market operations might have no
impact on prices, particularly if the economy started from a position of
less-than-full employment.

Still, despite the differences, both explained inflation, when it occurred,
as arising from an excess of aggregate demand over the full-employment
capacity of the economy. It is merely that Keynes broke the tight tie-up
between aggregate demand and money supply (and, of course, considered also situations of less-than-full employment, under which increased demand could have its primary impact in raising production,
rather than in bidding up the price level for a fixed output).

Keynes' demand-inflation analysis has frequently been expressed in
terms of the concept of an "inflationary gap." This can easily be pictured as in Figure 16–1. Here we represent consumption as a function

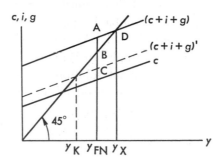

Figure 16–1.

of *real* income, $y$, in the customary manner. Assuming a "large" level of
$i + g$ (investment plus government spending), and assuming this level of
real spending to be independent of the price level, the total desired real
expenditures at each possible level of income are shown by the solid line,

$c + i + g$. If there were no limit on real output, income would rise to $y_x$, where real expenditure would equal real output, as shown by the intersection (point $D$) with the 45° construction line. But suppose there exists a full-employment limit on real output, $Y_{FN}$. Real income cannot reach $y_x$. At $y_{FN}$, total demand $(c + i + g)$ exceeds total output, leaving an "inflationary gap" equal to $AB$ in the figure. This inflationary gap would cause prices to rise, but, on our assumptions, this does nothing to eliminate the gap. Inflation proceeds without limit, unless or until there are indirect effects of rising prices either on $c$, $i$, or $g$, sufficient to eliminate the gap.

As noted in Chapter XIV, the Keynesian analysis of the possible "indirect effects" of rising prices on real demand are precisely parallel with the Keynesian analysis of deflation. Suppose, as Keynes assumed would ordinarily be the case, the aggregate of real demands were insufficient to create full employment, as represented by the broken line labeled $(c + i + g)'$. Here we have, at full-employment income, $y_{FN}$, what we might call a "deflationary gap," in the magnitude $BC$. If such a situation created no tendency for prices to fall, or if their fall made no difference, income would settle at the less-than-full employment level, $y_K$. This, in general, is the Keynesian result. Keynes did acknowledge, however, that, if wages and prices were flexible downward, there might be some indirect effects of deflation which could tend to lift real demand, conceivably, even, lift it sufficiently to restore full employment and remove the deflationary gap. In an earlier chapter we reviewed what these effects might be.

In considering the "inflationary gap" case, we need only turn our previous analysis around. Suppose an "inflationary gap" like $AB$ exists and prices do rise. What will be the effect on real demand?

1) If $M$ is constant, or rises in smaller proportion than prices, $r$ will rise, tending to reduce $i$ (conceivably also shifting the $c$ function downward).

2) There will be a redistribution of real income against fixed income groups. If the latter's consumption propensity is higher than average, this will tend to lower the aggregate $c$ function (but if lower than average, it will raise it).

3) If there is international trade, higher domestic prices will tend to encourage imports and reduce exports (an effect which can be put into the diagram by including "net foreign investment" in $i$).

4) To the extent that the "Pigou effect" exists, higher prices may reduce $c$.

5) If tax collections rise faster than prices (as they are almost certain to do through the effect of the progressive income tax), this in effect shifts the $c$ function downward, by reducing the disposable income associated with any given level of $y$. Transfer payments fixed in dollar terms also become less significant, further reducing the $c$ function.

6) If rising prices engender expectation of further rise, leading consumers to step-up their normal buying of durable goods and investors to try to "beat the rise" by investing more or sooner than otherwise, the inflationary gap may be widened. If speculators try to build up inventories this will further widen the gap. On the other hand, if the current rise in prices is expected to be temporary and to be followed by later reductions in prices, consumer buying of durables and investment in plant and equipment may be delayed, and inventories drawn down, thus narrowing the gap.

7) We have left to the last the effects on the distribution of income between wages and profits. If money wage rates were fixed, the higher prices would go entirely to profits. Unless the MPC + MPI of profit recipients exceeded the MPC of wage earners, this would tend to reduce aggregate demand, and to narrow the gap. A wage ceiling without price ceilings might have this effect. However, on customary assumptions of profit-maximizing behavior, and a free labor market, there should be no permanent redistribution against labor. For any fall in the real wage should make individual employers anxious to increase their employment and output, resulting in a competitive bidding for labor which (with full employment) would cause money wage rates to rise along with prices. If there were a lag of wage adjustment, income would be temporarily redistributed against labor, *during the inflation,* thus narrowing the inflationary gap. The wage lag could not, however, eliminate the gap and bring price stability. For, if prices stabilized as a result of reduced consumer demand arising from a wage lag and a redistribution toward profits, wages would then "catch up," reopening the gap.

Although inflation from excess demand might easily occur during a strong investment boom (such as might result from massive innovations, opening of new territory, etc.), surely the important cases of demand inflation result from government expenditures, especially those associated with war or war preparations. Government programs of heavy investment in "social capital," particularly in underdeveloped areas seeking rapid economic development, may also create strong inflationary pressure.

## THE CONTROL OF DEMAND INFLATION

Since government wartime expenditure is almost inevitably financed at least in large part by new money creation, it is obvious why war inflation is closely identified with an expansion of the money supply. But, it can be seriously questioned whether war inflation could be fully controlled exlusively by an avoidance of monetary expansion. Suppose, for example, that the United States in World War II had taken measures to prevent any expansion of bank credit. This would have meant that the government deficit would have had to have been financed solely by the sale of bonds to the general nonbank public. Obviously, this would have created an extremely strong upward pressure on interest rates. Only at very high interest rates (very low bond prices) could the public have been persuaded to hold the very large volume of new issues required. Whether such high interest rates—e.g., 20 per cent—could have eliminated excess demand seems highly questionable. It is unlikely that high interest costs would have reduced government spending appreciably. Nonessential government spending, including state and local spending for capital improvements, was already cut to the bone. Investment spending—except for programs required for the production of war goods—was also already pared to the minimum. Heavy disinvestment was in fact occurring in the nonwar sectors, as replacement expenditures were postponed. The primary effect of high interest rates would necessarily have been on consumer spending. While it is conceivable that sufficiently high interest rates might have had significant effects, high and *fluctuating* interest rates (i.e., unstable capital values) might have deterred saving.

One obvious answer, of course, was to have had smaller deficits through higher tax rates. Tax rates were, of course, increased very substantially (although they were still lower than in some other war economies). Fiscal measures—i.e., taxation—can repress consumer demand more surely than high interest rates. But tax rates sufficiently high to avoid a deficit (or even to create the surplus that might have been required to eliminate the inflationary gap) threaten to interfere with work incentives. Also, the higher rates are advanced, the greater the problems of equity that are created, and the greater the pressures on taxpayers to avoid payment, by means legal or illegal.

Thus many argue that the best policy for a wartime economy is not one which seeks to eliminate the inflationary gap, but rather one that attempts to reduce it as far as is feasible and politically acceptable through taxation, leaving some gap to be "repressed" through direct controls. Such controls (a) reduce demand directly, as through consumer rationing, prohibition of manufacture or use of materials in the manufacture of nonessential goods, direct controls of investment, etc.; and (b) suppress the remaining pressure of excess demand through wage and price ceilings. J. K. Galbraith has thus argued that the "disequilibrium system" used by the U.S. in World War II represented something close to an optimum arrangement.[2] By spreading the pressures for evasion between taxes, rationing, production controls, and price ceilings, each remained reasonably effective, although no single instrument could have carried the job alone.

There is one other aspect of wartime inflation which cannot be neglected even in the most cursory treatment such as this. The massive expansion of government demand in wartime is not a demand for "goods in general." It is a demand highly concentrated in particular fields. Much of its impact focuses back on a few key raw materials, supply of which is quite inelastic. The demand for copper, for example, became fantastically inflated by wartime requirements. Even if fiscal and monetary controls had been applied with sufficient vigor to stabilize the general average of prices, the price of copper would have risen enormously, meaning that many other prices would have to have been forced *down*, through reduced demand, so as to stabilize the average level of prices. Thus even with a stable average level of prices, there would have been tremendous shifts in *relative* prices, creating, of course, marked changes in income distribution. Such changes in relative prices are surely desirable, to the extent that they automatically redirect expenditure and shift resources. Extremely high prices, profits, and wages in copper mining accompanied by depressed prices, profits, and wages, in, say, dressmaking, would have caused consumers to have shifted expenditures from copper-using goods to items in relatively more abundant supply, such as dresses, while causing such resources as were mobile to shift from less essential—i.e., less demanded—occupations to the more critical areas.

But it can well be argued that the primary effect of such relative price changes would not have been effectively to have shifted resources or even to have redirected purchases, but rather to have created vast windfalls for persons fortunate enough to be in the favored industries, and substantial hardships for others, who might have faced significant earnings declines, or even unemployment, while being forced to pay higher prices for at least some essential goods whose purchase was necessary to

[2] See his article, "The Disequilibrium System," *American Economic Review,* XXXVII (June 1947), 287–302.

even a minimum standard of life. It can be argued, in short, that massive readjustments of production and consumption simply cannot be accomplished in a short time through the price system, and that the primary effect of attempting to do so would have been the quite fortuitous creation of windfall incomes ("profiteering") for some and hardships for many.

These microeconomic considerations are ignored when one deals in aggregate terms with the concept of an inflationary gap, total expenditures, and the average price level. But they should not be ignored, even in a macroeconomic analysis; for the distortion of relative prices might well reduce aggregate supply considerably, by creating unemployment of resources (including manpower) that could not under any circumstances be shifted into war production.[3]

This is another argument for the "disequilibrium system," and for the use of direct controls not only to repress total demand but as well to obtain those shifts of resources that are feasible. For example, instead of allowing the prices of consumers durables (using scarce materials) to rise sufficiently to price all except the wealthiest out of the market, it may be both more efficient and more equitable simply to prohibit their manufacture. Instead of bidding manpower from nonessential to essential employments by depressing wage rates in the former and letting them soar in the latter, one can perhaps more effectively place employment ceilings on the former industries (e.g., prohibit new hiring) and direct manpower into the more essential employments. A full system of direct manpower controls never was implemented in the United States, although it was used in other belligerent countries.

Such considerations as these suggest the more general thesis, to be briefly considered in the final chapter of this book, that a purely macroeconomic approach, both in analysis and in policy, while perhaps quite adequate and useful for an economy with general "slack"—e.g., under conditions of cyclical less-than-full employment—has severe limitations for an economy pressing against limitations of "capacity." This is because capacity limitations are necessarily "spotty" in their impact. Certainly this is so in wartime, when aggregate demand is both extremely great, and its *composition* is also very much altered from its normal pattern and thus differs markedly from the specialized distribution of productive resources.

[3] Further, since the prices of the scarcest goods would still rise, there would be incentive to speculate in wastefully large inventories of such goods.

## THE DYNAMICS OF DEMAND INFLATION

Inflationary gap analysis is essentially static. It defines a condition for price level stability—i.e., a macroeconomic equilibrium—but it contributes nothing directly to analysis of the time rate of inflation. Various models have been or might be constructed which would throw light on the dynamic behavior of an economy with excess demand. None of these is particularly adequate.

Suppose we assume the existence of an inflationary gap. How fast will prices rise? We may believe that, under certain conditions, a price rise of 20 or 50 or 100 per cent would remove the gap, through (for example) the effect of rising interest rates (if $M$ is constant), the Pigou effect, tax effects, or international trade effects. The fact that each of these may be questionable, that other effects may be offsetting, etc.; is not relevant here. The point is that these theories provide the definition of a price level equilibrium; what we also need is some theory of disequilibrium behavior. The latter may even be far more useful than the former. We know that prices will not rise 20, 50, or 100 per cent at once, but only over a period of perhaps several years. By that time it is almost certain that the basic conditions determining the size of the inflationary gap, and the circumstances under which it might be closed, will have altered, so that our static analysis has little relevance. But a useful theory of the inflationary process could contribute to an understanding of current price movements. One may object that the static theory is more basic because it tells us (ideally) by how much we would need to raise taxes, reduce government expenditures, or manipulate the money supply in order to eliminate an inflationary gap. But in this case we are talking about closing the gap by manipulating some policy variable other than the price level. What we argued above was that, *assuming that the gap is not eliminated in one of these ways*, it is more interesting to know how rapidly inflation will proceed, and what factors might influence that rate, than it is to know what ultimate rise in the price level might theoretically close the gap.

One hypothesis might be that the rate of price increase is functionally related to (perhaps proportional to) the size of the inflationary gap. The larger the gap, the faster prices rise; the smaller the gap the more slowly they rise. In some very general sense this must be true. However, it is not at all clear that the relationship even approaches proportionality. It may be that prices rise approximately as fast with a 3 per cent gap as with a 30 per cent gap. In any case, such a proposition as that the rate of price increase is a function of the size of the gap is only an empirical hypothesis; it does not rest upon any analysis of individual firm or consumer behavior. On a microeconomic level, it would imply that firms with unsatisfied customers raise their prices more frequently or by larger amounts the larger the number of their unsatisfied customers. This may well be true, although for many firms, it is not clear how they know the size of their unsatisfied demands. Moreover, this hypothesis is superficially inconsistent with the demand inflation hypothesis, which asserts that prices are bid up by buyers, rather than advanced by sellers. If we stick strictly to the idea that prices are bid up by buyers, it is hard to see why prices should not be bid up to the point at which markets are cleared. With a general inflationary gap, this would mean that the price level should immediately "explode" upward to the point (if such exists) that the gap would be closed by the indirect effects we have discussed. That is, it would unless the ability of buyers to bid prices up is, at any one time, limited. Some theories of the rate of demand inflation imply just this kind of limit to the rate of price inflation.

Implicit in Wicksell's analysis, for example, is the idea that market demand for goods is at any one time limited by the money income accruing from *previous* production. Consumers come into the market with money incomes based on the previous sale of output at the price level then prevailing. Their demand competes with that of businessmen supplied with new bank money. Given this available purchasing power, prices at any given time are bid up to the point at which all markets are cleared—that is, the point at which there are no unsatisfied demands: "excess demand" is zero. However, after some lag, money incomes rise as a result of the sale of output at the new higher prices, requiring a still higher price level for the goods market to remain cleared. The speed of inflation then depends on (a) the length of the lag between the sale of goods at higher prices and the corresponding receipt of higher money incomes; and (b) the real income elasticity of the demand for goods in general (higher prices and temporarily fixed incomes limit buying, but the extent of the rise in prices thus depends on whether higher prices reduce demand little or considerably).

We may formulate a simplified version of this model as follows:

$$(1) \qquad\qquad y_t = c_t + i_t = y_0$$

where $y_t$ is current real demand for output, made up of real consumer demand, $c_t$, and real investment demand, $i_t$, and where $y_0$ is the maximum (full employment) real output of the economy. We can, if we wish, include government spending in $i_t$. Putting $y_t = y_0$ means that we are assuming no unsatisfied demand—i.e., markets are cleared.

(2) $$c_t = a + b \, \frac{Y_{t-1}}{P_t}$$

where $a$ is a constant component of real consumption, $b$ is the marginal propensity to consume, and $Y_{t-1}$ is the money income arising from sale of output at an earlier date, and $P_t$ the current price level.

(3) $$i_t = i_0$$

This assumes that real investment demands are carried out regardless of current prices. That is, in Wicksellian terms, the banks currently provide whatever new funds are necessary to buy the investment goods demanded. Alternatively, we might have assumed that the banks supply a fixed amount of purchasing power to investors (and/or government), and that the extent of investors' current real purchases depends on the rise in prices. That is,

(3a) $$i_t = \frac{I_{t-1}}{P_t}$$

where $I_{t-1}$ is a predetermined amount of purchasing power. However, for simplicity, we use equation (3).

(4) $$Y_t = y_0 P_t$$

By substitution we obtain the following result:

(5) $$\frac{P_t}{P_{t-1}} = \frac{b y_0}{y_0 - (a + i_0)}$$

This result tells us that the rate of price increase depends positively both on $b$ (the marginal propensity to consume) and positively on $(a + i_0)$, which is the portion of full employment output that is demanded independently of current real income (previously-generated money income divided by current prices). It depends negatively on $y_0$, for an increase in $y_0$ will raise the numerator by less (since $b < 1$) than it will raise the denominator.

For example, if $y_0 = 100$, $a = 20$, $b = .5$, and $i_0 = 40$,

$$\frac{P_t}{P_{t-1}} = \frac{.5(100)}{100 - 60} = 1.25$$

That is, prices rise by 25 per cent per period. What *annual* rate of price increase this implies depends on the length of the income-payments lag.

If this is six months, prices rise by (approximately) 50 per cent per year. If it is two years, it is (approximately) 12.5 per cent per year.[4] Obviously, the longer this lag, other things equal, the slower the rate of inflation.

Now this model gives the result that the rate of inflation is directly (but not proportionally) related to the size of the inflationary gap. But this does not depend upon any assumption that the rate at which individual businessmen increase their prices depends on the size of their unsatisfied demands; there is no unsatisfied demand at any time. There *would be* an unsatisfied demand if there were no payments lag. In that case the consumption function would be

$$(2a) \qquad\qquad c_t = a + b \frac{Y_t}{P_t}$$

We can measure the size of the inflationary gap by gap by using this consumption function.[5] But the gap never actually exists in the market for goods: it is translated into "forced saving" by consumers.

A variant of this theory of the rate of inflation is to postulate a wage rate adjustment lag. Wicksell's lag recognizes the fact that although the current *earned* income, in monetary terms, depends on current prices,

---

[4] It may appear strange that the rate of inflation depends positively upon the marginal propensity to consume. Actually, this is true only if we take $a$ (the constant part of consumption) as given. But if we raise $b$ and lower $a$ so as to leave equilibrium real consumption unchanged at the given full-employment level of income, we actually reduce the rate of inflation. For example, if we make $b = .6$ and $a = 10$ (which would yield the same consumption as before at an equilibrium $y = 100$), the rate of inflation is reduced to 20 per cent per period.

[5] That is, the inflationary gap can be measured as

$$\text{I.G.} = a + b \frac{Y_t}{P_t} + i_0 - y_0$$

or

$$\text{I.G.} = a + by_0 + i_0 - y_0$$

which reduces to

$$\text{I.G.} = a + i_0 + (b - 1)y_0$$

It can easily be seen that any parameter change which enlarges the I.G. will also raise $P_t/P_{t-1}$. The gap is zero when

$$y_0 = \frac{a + i_0}{1 - b}$$

It can also be seen from equation (5) that $P_t/P_{t-1} = 1$ when the same condition is satisfied:

$$\frac{P_t}{P_{t-1}} = 1 = \frac{by_0}{y_0 - (a + i_0)}$$

or

$$y_0 = \frac{a + i_0}{1 - b}$$

this income is available for spending only when it is (some time later) paid out, or, at least, recognized by the accounting process. Wicksell may have been thinking, in fact, about the actual physical circulation of dollars. The dollars received by business, he assumed, could not be paid out until after they were received. His analysis—at least as we have presented it—either implies that money wages paid rise proportionately with money profits, or that this makes no difference: if wage earners don't get higher money wages, money profits will advance the more. Actually, the flow of dollars is probably not the crucial determinant of the income lag, anyway. But there may very well be a differential lag in the advance of money wages and money profits, and this may influence the speed of inflation.

Suppose that we assume that price increases swell profits immediately (and, through continuous accounting, are recognized as such immediately). But assume that wage rates are advanced in some relation to the price level (cost-of-living), but with a lag. If this is the case, the emergence of an inflationary gap will immediately raise prices and profits, but until wage rates are raised, it will reduce real wage income. The "clearing" of the goods market at any given time might then be secured by sufficient temporary redistribution of real income against labor (assuming a lower marginal propensity to spend by profit recipients than by workers).

A model of this sort has been developed by Arthur Smithies, in a well-known article.[6] Smithies' model of war inflation includes two other lags in addition to the wage lag. One is the lag between appropriations of government funds and their expenditures. That is, he assumes that the government attempts to purchase a (constant) amount of physical output, and appropriates a sum sufficient to purchase this at then current prices. But, under inflationary conditions, rising prices erode the purchasing power of the appropriation, which is then continually adjusted upward, but always lags behind. (This lag corresponds to that implied in our alternative investment equation (3a) of the Wicksellian system.) We ignore this lag in the simplified model presented below. In fact, in wartime, government procedure comes close to being one in which government's physical demands are always satisfied, and the appropriation adjusted to whatever amount may be necessary to pay the bill. Smithies' further lag is in consumption out of profits. This, he explains, is due to the lag in the recognition and distribution of profits; but it might also

---

[6] "The Behavior of Money National Income under Inflationary Conditions," *Quarterly Journal of Economics*, LVII (November 1942), 113–28; reprinted in American Economic Association, *Readings in Fiscal Policy* (Irwin, 1955), pp. 122–136.

reflect a psychological lag. We also ignore this in our simplified model. Smithies' model further postulates that consumption depends on money income rather than real income, which he justifies on the basis of the operation of a progressive tax system. Again, we stick to the simpler formulation.

Our simplified wage-lag model can thus be constructed as follows:

$$(1) \qquad y_t = c_t + i_t = y_0$$

(where $i_0$ includes government expenditure).

$$(2) \qquad c_t = c_{W, t} + c_{R, t}$$

where $c_{W, t}$ and $c_{R, t}$ are the current consumption expenditures of workers and non-workers respectively.

$$(3) \qquad c_{W, t} = a + b \, \frac{W_t}{P_t}$$

where $W_t$ is current money wage income.

$$(4) \qquad c_{R, t} = m + n \, \frac{R_t}{P_t}$$

where $R_t$ is current nonwage income. It is necessary for the model that $n < b$.

$$(5) \qquad i_t = i_0$$

$$(6) \qquad Y_t = y_0 P_t$$

$$(7) \qquad Y_t = W_t + R_t$$

$$(8) \qquad W_t = N_0 w_t$$

where $N_0$ is the (constant) full-employment volume of employment, and $w_t$ the current money wage rate.

$$(9) \qquad w_t = x P_{t-1}$$

which assumes that wage rates are kept proportional to prices but with a lag.

By simple substitution, this system can be reduced to the following formula which indicates the rate of inflation:

$$(10) \qquad \frac{P_t}{P_{t-1}} = \frac{(b - n) N_0 x}{y_0 (1 - n) - (a + m + i_0)}$$

Comparison will show that this expression, although containing more elements, parallels closely that obtained from the quasi-Wicksellian model. As in that model, the market for commodities is continuously

cleared: the inflationary gap is latent, never apparent. Income is redistributed from workers to nonworkers (through higher prices and a wage
lag) to whatever extent is necessary to clear the market.

It is clear from (10) that the rate of inflation per calendar period
depends on the length of the wage payment lag and on the size of the
(latent) inflationary gap. We can also see the effect on the speed of
inflation of changes in the various parameters.

## BENT HANSEN'S DYNAMIC MODEL
## OF DEMAND INFLATION

In an interesting and important book by the Danish economist Bent
Hansen, a somewhat different dynamic model is presented.[7]

Hansen criticizes what he calls the Keynesian analysis of inflation as
failing to portray the pure case of demand inflation. By assuming that
wage rates are tied to prices, or are otherwise autonomously determined,
we are mixing up the cases of demand inflation and what he calls "spontaneous inflation"—more commonly now referred to as "cost inflation" (see
below). Although this criticism may be appropriate for a model like
Smithies', it is not clear that it is appropriate for the Keynesian model,
at least as this is implicit in the *General Theory*. In any case, Hansen
wants wage rates in a pure model of demand inflation to be *market-
determined*, by supply and demand for labor. He provides an interesting
dynamic analysis incorporating two separate market-determined price
levels—one for goods and one for labor. His analysis can easily be summarized in Figure 16–2.

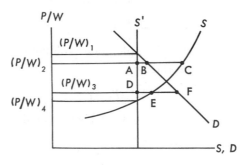

Figure 16–2.

It must be noted at once that our vertical axis here is the price-wage
ratio (inverse of the real wage). The S curve indicates the amounts of
aggregate output that firms would want to supply at each price-wage

[7] *A Study in the Theory of Inflation* (Allen and Unwin, 1951), especially Chap. VII.

ratio. It is, in some sense, an aggregate of the supply curves of all firms in the economy. Although a shortage of labor relative to the demand for it does not restrict the output of any given firm (each firm can always bid labor away from other firms, or at least attempt to do so), the aggregate output of all firms cannot increase beyond the total availability of labor. This fact is indicated in our figure by the vertical line $S'$, which shows the output corresponding to full-employment of the labor supply. If we thought that the supply of labor were a function of the real wage we could reflect this by an appropriate curvature of the $S'$ line.

The horizontal difference between lines $S$ and $S'$ can thus be taken as an *index* of the "inflationary gap in the factor market." At all levels of $P/W$ higher than $(P/W)_4$, such a gap is seen to exist.

Curve $D$ shows the aggregate demand for output. We have drawn it as sloping downward to the right, reflecting the assumption that the marginal propensity to spend of wage-earners exceeds that of nonwage recipients. As Hansen points out, this need not be the case, and a reverse slope is possible. Such a slope might alter some of the results presented below. We will, however, confine ourselves to the simpler case shown in the figure. The reader will see that Hansen's analysis (to this extent) rests in part on a factor considered in the Smithies' model.

The horizontal difference between lines $D$ and $S'$ can obviously be taken as a measure of the "inflationary gap in the goods market." At all price/wage ratios below $(P/W)_1$, such a gap exists.

Hansen now assumes the following dynamic relationships:

(1) $$\frac{dp}{dt} = f_1 \ (D - S')$$

and

(2) $$\frac{dw}{dt} = f_2 (S - S')$$

These assumptions are that the time rate of change of the price level is a function of the size of the inflationary gap in the goods market, and the time rate of change of wages is a function of the size of the inflationary gap in the factor market. Although these functions do not have to be linear, they are given the property that they pass through the origin and are monotonic—i.e., when $D - S'$ is zero, $dp/dt = 0$; and when $S - S'$ is zero, so is $dw/dt$. When the gaps are positive, the rates of price and wage change are positive.

Suppose we have the situation pictured in Figure 16-2, and $P/W =$

$(P/W)_1$. In this case, there is no goods gap, and goods prices do not rise. But there is a large factor gap, so that wages rise rapidly. This necessarily means a fall in $P/W$. As $P/W$ falls, however, the size of the factor gap is reduced, and a goods gap begins to open up. At $(P/W)_2$, the goods gap, $AB$, would produce a certain rate of price increase, while the factor gap $AC$ would produce a certain rate of wage increase. If these rates happened to coincide, the $P/W$ ratio would thereafter remain unchanged. That is, $(P/W)_2$ would represent a "quasi-equilibrium" position. Suppose, however, that, at $(P/W)_2$, the small goods gap produced only a slow rise in prices, while the still relatively large factor gap produced a somewhat higher rate of wage increase. This necessarily means a further fall of $P/W$. If it fell as far as $(P/W)_3$, the factor gap would be narrowed to $DE$, and the goods gap raised to $DF$, producing a more rapid price rise and a slower wage rise. At $(P/W)_4$, the factor gap would be eliminated and wages would be stable, while the large goods gap would raise prices, thus raising $P/W$.

It is clear that somewhere between $(P/W)_1$ and $(P/W)_4$ there must exist some quasi-equilibrium at which both wages and prices move together. This will be at a relatively high $P/W$ if wage rates are sluggish and prices volatile, while quasi-equilibrium $P/W$ will be relatively low in the opposite case. The actual speed of the inflation in quasi-equilibrium will depend on the absolute sensitivity of wage and price change to the size of the relevant gaps. If both are relatively volatile, inflation will be rapid; if both are relatively sluggish, inflation will be slower.

Hansen's analysis proceeds to consider a number of complications (including imperfect competition) and the effects of a number of policy alternatives.

A basic assumption of this approach is one that we have already questioned. It is that equations (1) and (2) have some independent meaning as descriptions of behavior. By merely assuming these relationships Hansen has begged most real questions regarding the speed of inflation. To be sure, he has some interesting things to say about the participants' comprehensions as to the size of these gaps, and with respect to factors which "artificially" alter them. (For example, if, in an inflationary situation, buyers find themselves unable to purchase all that they wish, they may begin to place duplicate orders, thus increasing the size of the apparent gaps. On the other hand, if they become reconciled to their inability to buy or hire the amount of goods or labor that would be optimum for them, they may simply give up trying to buy the excess, thus reducing the apparent excess demand.) Still, the basic assumption remains that there is some (largely unspecified) relationship between the size of gaps and the time rate of price increase. If, for example, the relationship were as pictured in curve A of Figure 16–3

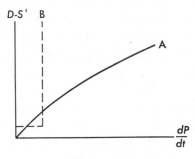

**Figure 16–3.**

(for the goods market only), the conclusion would be quite different than if the relationship were curve B.

The basis for either relationship is far from obvious, and it would appear that the explanation for its shape needs to be sought not in some inherent logic of a free-market situation, but rather in institutional behavior patterns. If true, this suggests that Hansen's analysis contains a basic contradiction: he wishes to describe a situation of demand inflation, free from such institutional elements as "wage policy," "administered pricing," or trade union pressures; but his functional relationships of the rate of inflation to the sizes of the gaps necessarily rest upon some kind of institutional behavior in situations in which markets are not "cleared" by price variation. It may be suggested, therefore, that some analysis of the general sort presented in a later section of this chapter may provide more useful insights than does Hansen's analysis, however interesting it may be. First, however, we need to examine the pure case of "spontaneous" or "cost" inflation, before attempting to bridge this analysis with Hansen's elegant but perhaps rather empty analysis of demand inflation.

## COST INFLATION

Cost inflation has almost invariably been described as stemming from labor union pressure on wage rates. It is wage-cost inflation. This analysis starts from the recognition that wage rates in the modern economy are not strictly market-determined prices. They do not adjust quickly and freely and automatically to whatever level may be necessary to "clear" the labor market. They are "administered prices," and, as such, do not rise only when the demand for labor exceeds the supply. This recognition carries one step further the concession usually made to realism when we assume that, although wages and prices may rise in response to excess demand, they do not fall whenever there exists any unemployment. We shall argue at a later point that this wage-cost inflation analysis is still lopsided, and thus misleading, by recognizing that wage rates are administered prices but failing to recognize that most prices for goods and services are also administered. (The term "administered prices" is used in a completely neutral sense: they are not necessarily bad or good, high or low, collusive or competitive; they are merely prices that are set by a seller—or buyer—and maintained unchanged for a considerable period, rather than being determined like prices of wheat or cotton or General Motors shares by continuous bid and offer.) But first we will review the usual analysis of wage-cost inflation.

We now recognize that rising wage rates are not exclusively the product of an excess demand for labor. We observe that collective bargaining produces wage rates that may rise even when there is no excess demand for labor—perhaps even an excess supply. Wage rates tied to the cost-of-living fall in this category, as do wages which automatically rise in reflection of some presumed (or even measured) rise in productivity. Wage rates which rise because employers can afford to pay them are in this group, or which rise because employers want their workers to be happy. Wage rates which rise to preserve parity with wages elsewhere or for other kinds of labor are also in this class, as well as wage rates that rise simply because organized workers are able, by successful strike or threat of strike, to compel employers to pay the higher rates. The crucial difference from the demand inflation case is that, here, rising wages are not, for each and every type of labor and in each and every labor market or even in the typical case, confined to the situation in which there is an actual, experienced market scarcity of labor, which forces employers to compete for workers by bidding wages upward.

Suppose that employers generally should agree to or be forced to raise wage rates even when there was no scarcity of labor. If the rise exceeds the slow improvement of productivity, this raises employers' costs of production and, on normal assumptions, would reduce their willingness to supply goods at the previously prevailing price level. A reduction of supply would not be accompanied by an equivalent reduction of demand, and prices for products would thus rise. Unless and until prices rose in the same proportion as wage rates there would exist a tendency for the supply of goods to fall short of demand, thus causing the price rise to continue until the previous ratio of wages to prices was restored.

The reasoning which supports this result should now be familiar and need only be summarized. Briefly, the usual treatment assumes that (a) employers determine prices and outputs in a way which continually maximizes short-period profits; and (b) the "marginal revenue product" of labor declines for each firm as employment and output increase. These assumptions mean that if wage rates are raised, employers will not offer the previous volume of employment (producing the previous volume of output) unless or until prices rise in equal proportion, restoring the previous "real wage." The conclusion that demand for total output will fall by less than output, and thus assure the necessary rise in prices, assumes (a) that the marginal propensity to consume real income is less than unity, and (b) that any change in current wages and prices revises investors' expectations of future wages and prices in the same degree (i.e., the "elasticity of expectations" is unity). It however ignores the possible effect on aggregate demand—presumably via interest rates—of a failure of the quantity of money to expand proportionately, as it ignores other "indirect effects" of inflation on demand.

In fact, we know that what is more likely to happen is that autonomous wage increases will lead employers directly to post higher prices, rather than first to reduce their supply and let the market bid prices up. But even if prices of goods rise only in response to an actual excess of demand over supply, one can reach the conclusion (based on the assumptions summarized above) that prices would be bid up in the proportion that wage rates rose.

This is spontaneous inflation. It requires no excess demand; it can even occur when there is some or perhaps considerable unemployment. It arises because wage rates increase even with no excess demand for labor.

Now there are two objections often made to this argument. One is that wages cannot and will not rise unless there is a genuine excess demand for labor—that the labor market really behaves like the purely competitive market of economic theory—that the demand inflation case is the only case. This view argues that labor gets wage increases only when there exists a true scarcity of labor. To be sure labor does get wage increases when there is a labor scarcity; but the economist who fears cost inflation observes that wage increases also occur for classes of labor for which there is no excess demand, and perhaps even when there are no classes of labor in excess demand.

The second objection is that any rise in the general level of wages and prices, unless it is accompanied by at least a proportional expansion of the money supply (or an increase in government deficit) will reduce the total demand for goods. This reduction in demand will create unemployment, and the development of unemployment will quickly put an end to inflationary wage hikes. This argument puts the stress on the "indirect effects" through the interest rate, which we have discussed at length in earlier chapters in connection with wage decreases. The argument is theoretically correct, but of how much practical importance? In the first place, it can be questioned whether the reduction in demand accompanying a moderate inflation of the price level will be very great, even if the money supply does not expand.[8] Second, even if there is a reduction of demand which creates unemployment, the level of unemployment sufficient to eliminate inflationary wage increases is probably fairly high. Thus, even if inflation should eventually curb itself, it would have to proceed rather far before the curb would work. We might find both the extent of the inflation and the degree of the necessary unemployment socially intolerable.

It is commonly agreed that this kind of inflation is much more difficult to control by traditional monetary or fiscal means than demand inflation. For to avoid it, aggregate demand must be kept or pushed low enough, and sufficient unemployment created, that unions will not seek or else employers will refuse to grant—strike or no strike—wage increases in excess of productivity increases. This may mean a very considerable body of unemployment. Even if it does not, it may require a sacrifice of the rate of economic growth that we want. For, according to this view, fiscal and monetary measures can control inflation only by putting pressure on the employer, in order that he may in turn put pressure on the union. Employers' profits are thus caught between the upper millstone of a restrictive monetary or fiscal policy, operating to reduce aggregate demand, and the lower millstone of upward wage pressure. Profits must be squeezed until employers are able and willing to squeeze the inflation out of wage demands. This may be disastrous for investment and thus for growth.

Recognition of these difficulties seems to have led some businessmen

---

[8] Some argue that the monetary authorities will necessarily have to "ratify" the inflation by increasing the money supply; or even that the "necessary" increase in money will come more or less automatically. Since we do not consider the change in money supply of much short run importance (there was no change for example, from 1955 to 1957 although prices rose considerably), we prefer not to stress this aspect. Of course, there are limits to the increase in "velocity" that occurs if prices rise and output does not fall while money supply is constant. But these limits are likely to be reached or to have their effects at a point in time sufficiently remote from the wage increase as to be for all practical purposes an independent event.

to decide that they would prefer a little inflation. Others have concluded that control of upward wage pressure must come not from fiscal or monetary policy, but from a direct attack on the strength of unions, through new labor legislation. One may question whether proposed changes in labor laws (short of abolition of collective bargaining) would have much effect on upward wage pressures: for example, "right-to-work" laws may only make unions more aggressive in seeking wage increases; and prohibition of industry-wide bargaining may weaken employers as much or more than unions.

Although we do not propose to undertake any important empirical study at this point, some reference needs to be made to evidence which indicates that the cost inflation case has relevance, in the face of repeated assertions by some theorists that cost inflation is meaningless or impossible, and in the face of public policies that often seem to assume that any inflation is necessarily of the demand variety.

If wage rates rose only as the result of an excess demand for labor, then we should expect to find a close relationship between the extent of unemployment and the rate of change of money wages. Yet data for the U.S. for the period 1900–58 show almost no relationship at all between the extent of wage change in a given year and the unemployment rate of that year; even when we take relatively short, homogeneous periods, such as 1900–15 and 1947–58, the relationship is far from close.[9] For what it is worth the data suggest that "a 4 per cent unemployment rate roughly implied a 3 per cent wage increase in the earlier period, whereas it seems to imply an annual increase of some 5 per cent in the postwar period. In general, however, the relationships after the First World War are so poor as to warrant drawing few conclusions—except that the level of unemployment required to keep wage increases below 2½ to 3 per cent [10] appears to be quite substantial."

If one is willing to stretch the data a bit further than they perhaps warrant, the postwar relationships . . . suggest one additional hypothesis. Fairly sizeable levels of unemployment do affect the magnitude of the annual increases in

[9] See Charles Schultze, *Recent Inflation in the United States* (Study Paper No. 1, Joint Economic Committee, Congress of the U. S., September 1959), pp. 60–1, where these data are plotted. See also: J. W. Garbarino, "Unionism and the General Wage Level," *American Economic Review* XL (Dec. 1950); O. Eckstein, "Inflation, the Wage-Price Spiral and Economic Growth," *Relationship of Prices to Economic Stability and Growth*, Joint Economic Committee, *op. cit.*; P. A. Samuelson and R. M. Solow, "Analytical Aspects of Anti-Inflation Policy," *American Economic Review* L (May 1960); A. W. Phillips, "Money Wages and Unemployment in the United Kingdom," *Economica* (Nov. 1958).

[10] Judged to be roughly the average increase in productivity (footnote supplied).

average hourly earnings. However, the relationship between wage rates and unemployment breaks down once unemployment falls below 5 per cent. The rate of increase in average hourly earnings then seems to depend very little on the level of unemployment, and much more on the rate of change in the cost of living and other factors.[11, 12]

The extent of any relationship between employment (if not unemployment) and wage rate increases can also be tested on a cross-section basis, using data for different industries for a single year or other short periods. This has been done by Levinson, in a study for the Joint Economic Committee.[13] Simple cross-section regressions for 19 manufacturing industries between percentage change in straight-time hourly earnings and percent-

---

[11] Schultze, *op. cit.*, pp. 61–2.

[12] Schultze does not present a statistical regression covering this relationship. But this can easily be done. For example, on the theory that the rate of change of wage rates depends negatively on the volume of unemployment and positively on the change in the cost-of-living, we can set up a regression equation in the form

$$\Delta W_t = aU_{t-1} + b\Delta P_{t-1} + c$$

where $W$ is the average wage rate, $U$ the volume of unemployment, and $P$ the cost-of-living index. Of several statistical regressions in this form which I have tried for U. S. manufacturing, 1946–58, the best, so far, is one in which $\Delta W_t$ is the difference in cents between this (calendar) year's average straight-time hourly earnings for manufacturing production workers, and last year's average; $U_{t-1}$ is average level of unemployment in thousands for the year ending with the previous June; and $\Delta P_{t-1}$ is the difference in points between the levels of the Consumers Price Index of the previous June and of the June before that. The resulting equation is:

$$\Delta W_t = -.001376U_{t-1} + .4945\Delta P_{t-1} + 10.228$$
$$\phantom{\Delta W_t = }(.00057)\phantom{xxx}(.114)\phantom{xxxx}(1.63)$$

Standard errors are shown in parentheses under each coefficient (all are significant). The coefficient of correlation ($r$) is .87.

This equation can be interpreted as follows:

(a) During this period, wage rates tended to increase by 10.2 cents per hour per year, if the cost-of-living was stable and unemployment was zero.

(b) This increase in wage rates was reduced by 1.4 cents per hour for every one million unemployed during the previous year; for example, a rise of unemployment from 2 million to 3 million (prices constant) would result in a reduction of the annual wage increase from 7.5 cents to 6.1 cents; while (with stable prices) unemployment would have had to be 7.43 million to keep wage rates stable.

(c) Every increase of one "point" in the Consumers Price Index (on the average, a point was a little less than one per cent in this period) tended to raise the subsequent wage increase by about .5 cent per hour.

It is clear from the above that neither unemployment nor the change in the cost-of-living was the primary cause of wage rate changes during this period. Rather, unidentified forces tended consistently to raise wage rates almost regardless of either unemployment or price changes.

One criticism of the above regression is that the periods of the wage change and the price change comparisons overlap. Thus it is not entirely clear that, to the extent that wages change with the cost-of-living, the causation runs from cost-of-living to wages rather than the other way.

[13] H. M. Levinson, *Postwar Movement of Prices and Wages in Manufacturing Industries*, Study Paper No. 21, Study of Employment, Growth, and Price Levels, Joint Economic Committee, January 30, 1960.

age change in production worker employment showed no significant or even consistent relationship over the years 1947–58. (In some years the relationship is negative, in some years positive.) Using a multiple regression of wage rate change upon a number of other variables confirmed the absence of significant relationship between wage change and employment change. The principal factor explaining differences between industries in wage rate change was found to be differences in profit levels.[14]

These tests do not quite directly deal with the relationship of *unemployment* to wage rate change, which would seem to be the crucial relationship required by the theory that wage rates are market-determined prices. This test would be difficult on a cross-section basis, unless perhaps *areas* rather than industries might be used as the units of analysis. But casual observation leads one to doubt that short-run wage rate changes differ significantly between areas in relation to differences in unemployment rates.

That money wage rates can rise significantly even when and where there is no excess demand for labor would seem to be not merely a boast of trade union leaders and a complaint of employers, but a well-documented fact.

## MIXED DEMAND-COST INFLATION

Obviously, we need not preclude interactions of cost and demand elements, or hybrid forms of inflation. For example, some argue that inflation can only originate from excess demand, but that the excess need not be a general one. Suppose, for example, that under conditions of reasonably full employment, but no excess demand for goods-in-general, there is a strong increase in the demand for one particular good or class of goods. This may even be associated with an equivalent reduction in demands for other goods. The resulting demand pressure on the particular industry or industries will bid up its prices and profits. It will also induce these producers to attempt to expand output. Because of imperfect labor mobility, additional workers can only be recruited at higher wage rates, and these are bid up by competition of employers. (In an alternative version, the excess profits provide a strong "target" for wage demands, which the particular employers are not inclined to resist, particularly since their prices are rising and because they hope that it will ease their employment problems.) The initial rise in wages in the particular industry is thus described, without too much stretching of the term, as demand-induced. But workers in other industries, seeing that wage rates have risen

[14] *Ibid.*, pp. 2–4.

in the first industry, seek, successfully, to have their wage rates adjusted "in line" with the initial increase, even though, in their industries, there is no excess demand for labor. By this process, generalized inflation is induced without any general excess demand, but as the result of excess demand in a sector of the economy. "Cost" forces do not originate the inflation, but they generalize it from the original locus.[15]

Another popular hybrid model of inflation lays particular stress on agricultural prices, and on the link of wage rates to the cost-of-living. Again, suppose no general excess demand, but let food prices rise, for example as the result of a poor harvest. Because of the large weight which food has in the cost-of-living index, and because the notion that real wages should not be permitted to decline has a strong public appeal, wage rates in industry are adjusted upward to match the increase in living costs. Again, inflation results, but neither from any general excess of demand, nor from independent wage cost pressures.

In summary, what most of these hybrid models of inflation contemplate is that forces which should, theoretically, produce a change only in relative prices, produce instead a rise in absolute prices, because of the existence of institutional factors which refuse to permit a change in relative prices to occur—in the first instance, an obstacle to changes in relative wage rates in different industries, in the second instance an obstacle to a change in prices of agricultural goods relative to industrial wage rates.

These hybrid theories stress elements of rigidity which are no doubt of considerable strategic importance in explaining peacetime inflation. Still, one can argue that these are merely particular cases of cost inflation. Their essential feature is that wage rates can and do rise, even in the absence of any general excess demand for labor. We still have, then, a dichotomy between demand inflation (prices in general are *bid* up by excess aggregate demand) and cost inflation (the average wage rate is *pushed* up without any general labor shortage, and this raises prices).

## DISTINGUISHING DEMAND AND COST INFLATION IN PRACTICE

Economists have talked so much about the distinction between demand and cost inflation in recent years that it may seem strange that they have not been able to reach wider agreement about what has been happening in the United States since World War II. To what extent has the inflation

---

[15] This is the essential explanation advanced by Schultze for the inflation of 1955–58, in his excellent study referred to above.

in the United States since the war been demand inflation and to what extent, if any, has it been wage-cost inflation? There is little agreement on this question. We may agree to place the price increases of 1945 to 1947 and of 1950–51 in the demand inflation category, although it is very hard to prove this to be the case. These three years account for about half of the total inflation of 62 per cent in the cost of living over the period 1945–59. What about the other years of smaller price increase: 1948, 1952, 1953, and 1956 through 1959? Why is there debate about these years? Why is it hard to prove that even in 1946, 1947, and 1951 the rise in prices was demand-induced?

Let us review how we should expect wages and prices to behave in a year of demand inflation and how this behavior would differ in a year of cost inflation. In the demand inflation case, presumably it is an excess demand in the product markets that pulls or bids prices upward. The increased profitability of production in turn creates an excess demand in the labor market which bids or pulls wage rates upward. In short, in demand inflation, excess product demand *pulls up* goods prices, creating excess labor demand which *pulls up* wages.

In the wage-cost inflation case, the causal sequence is reversed. Wage rates rise without excess demand, which creates an actual or potential shortage of goods at the old price level. This shortage bids up prices (or would bid them up if sellers did not automatically advance them).

There are several reasons why it is difficult in practice to distinguish these two cases. In the first place, the above distinction has to do with direction of causation, and not necessarily with a time sequence of events. Even though excess demand bids up prices, which leads to a bidding up of wages, it is not necessary that there be any significant lag between price and wage changes. Nor, in the opposite, cost-push case, is it implied that wages should rise significantly before prices.

Nor, though this is often suggested, can we conclude that simply because a wage advance may exceed the rise in productivity, this proves a cost push. The same would be true in a demand inflation. Nor does the relative *extent* of the rise in wages and prices necessarily tell us much about causation. Wages rise more than prices when productivity is advancing; and we would expect this whether the origin of price rises was from excess demand or cost. And the rise in productivity neither proceeds smoothly over time, nor is it measurable independently of wage and price changes.

There is one crucial test that should throw a good deal of light on the matter. If wages and prices rose when there was less than full employment, we should be able to rule out demand inflation (although the presence of full employment does not necessarily preclude cost inflation). But "full employment" is a slippery concept. It clearly does not mean zero unemployment, for there is always "frictional unemployment." Even with an excess demand for labor, (a) some workers are idle for seasonal reasons; (b) some workers, having lost a job in a firm, industry, or locality of declining employment, have not yet moved to the firm, industry, or locality where there are unfilled vacancies; (c) persons who voluntarily give up one job in search of another are unemployed between jobs; (d) new entrants into the labor force need some time to find their slots; (e) workers retiring from the labor force appear for a time as unemployed; (f) some workers are marginal by reason of mental, physical, or emotional handicap, and cannot hold a steady job, yet because they sometimes work they are included in the labor force. There is no reason to suppose that these circumstances are constant over time or between economies. Particularly, the extent of unemployment of type (b) depends on the extent of *divergence* of movements within the economy: we can imagine periods when the division of total production among firms, industries, and localities remains fairly stable; other periods when there is considerable redistribution of demand and "churning around" within a fixed total output. Frictional unemployment will be substantially greater in the second period than the first. Likewise, the extent of frictional unemployment will depend on the flows of information about job opportunities, and the mobility of labor (which is influenced by seniority provisions, family and emotional attachments, and so forth).

When we say that an excess of demand for labor over supply bids up wages we mean an excess of demand over supply net of frictional unemployment. But how extensive is frictional unemployment? We can beg the question (and some do) by saying that if wage rates rise when there is 5 per cent unemployment, this means that frictional unemployment is more than 5 per cent. If at another time (or in another country) wage rates are stable when unemployment is 3 per cent, then frictional unemployment is less than 3 per cent. But by this procedure, we automatically get the answer that the only kind of inflation is demand inflation!

Only an extremely detailed study could reach even tentative guesses whether we should categorize the wage movements of a particular year as demand-induced or cost-determined. The reason is, of course, that wages are not set in a way which permits us to make the distinction that our theory requires. Wages are not set by impersonal supply and demand forces, in a continuously operating market, but are changed at infrequent intervals, by an administrative process, and reflecting many criteria other than supply and demand. (One such criterion, which seems to be almost automatically accepted, is that wage rates should rise at least as much as the cost of living, quite independently of labor supply and demand.)

The fact that wage rates are administered prices does not mean that wages might not rise to reflect demand forces, but only that we cannot ever really tell whether or to what extent this is the case. Even in years in which demand forces are clearly extremely strong we probably cannot answer the question: Would the rise in wage rates that actually occurred this year have occurred if wages had been set in a perfect market by an auction process? In fact, as we shall argue below, while such a question may have some meaning for a single industry, it is conceptually meaningless for a whole economy. About the best we can say is that there is some evidence that wage rates tend to rise somewhat faster when unemployment is lower than when it is higher. But a part of this can be explained by the fact that years of low unemployment are also years of increasing living costs; and, as already observed, the administrative tie between wages and the cost of living is not only widely accepted, but even made automatic for many workers.

It seems plausible, moreover, that the administrative character of the wage-setting process may, in years of strong excess demand, considerably slow down the advance in money wage rates that would occur otherwise (i.e., if wages were set in a more-nearly-perfect market).

But if we cannot tell much about whether the inflation of a particular year resulted from demand or cost forces by looking at wages, can we not tell by looking at individual prices? The answer is that this evidence is almost equally difficult to interpret.

The fact is that most prices are not set by impersonal supply and demand forces any more than wage rates are. For some farm products and raw materials, prices do respond directly and almost daily to demand and supply considerations. Prices rise when and only when demand exceeds supply and fall in the reverse case. But for most manufactured goods and for almost all goods and services at the retail level, prices rise and fall not in any direct or automatic reflection of impersonal supply and demand forces, but instead as a rsult of some manager's decision, applying some rule or formula, or using his informed judgment as to the best way to behave in the current situation.

The general price level rose in 1956 and 1957. This general rise consisted of increases in millions of individual prices, which more than offset reductions in a few thousand prices and stability in many others. Was the rise in most of these prices in response to an excess of demand over supply? How do we know? How could we ever find out? The very concept—clear enough in the textbook—is almost impossible to apply in most markets.

Among others, prices of steel and of automobiles rose. Were these particular increases the result of excess demand? That is, had the price of steel not been revised upward by a deliberate policy decision, would the market have *bid* prices up? And would the increase have been by the particular number of dollars a ton that actually occurred? To ask the question in this form is to show that it is not fully answerable. We can certainly look for some *indicators* of the presence of excess demand in each of the postwar years—as revealed, for example, in order backlogs. However, we would need to know not only whether there were order backlogs (there are always some), but how general they were, how extensive, and for how long they were expected to last. With this information, and knowledge of the extent to which productive capacity was currently employed, we might be able to determine that some of the price increases that have occurred in steel since the war were probably in response to excess demand; others clearly occurred with no excess of demand over supply; regarding still other instances, it would be impossible to reach a conclusion.[16] In hardly any case could we guess whether the particular price increase that did occur was of a magnitude approximating what would have occurred in a market in which price adjusted automatically to supply and demand.

In some ways the steel case is a relatively easy one, for the concept of "capacity" may have fairly definite meaning in steel. But consider automobiles. Not only does the output of each make of automobile often move independently of other makes, but what does "capacity" mean for any single make? With how many assembly lines operating, at what speed, for how many shifts, and for how many months (prospectively) of the year?[17] The concepts required by the contrast of demand and wage

[16] Eckstein and Fromm reach the conclusion that demand forces played a minor role in postwar steel price movements (O. Eckstein and G. Fromm, *Steel and the Postwar Inflation*, Study Paper No. 2, Joint Economic Committee, Congress of the U. S., November 6, 1959, p. 33).

[17] It is well-known that the concept of a "supply curve" has no meaning under oligopoly conditions. However, even if we measure "supply" by a curve of average or marginal costs, we could give clear meaning to an assessment of the presence of excess demand only if the cost curve were rectangular, or nearly so; flat up to some limit of output where it rises vertically, or at least with a sharp discontinuity. One finds it difficult to conceptualize the supply for automobiles. But even the marginal cost curve (of each make) is surely not rectangular, and we cannot merely compare demand with "capacity."

cost inflation are no easier to apply to most other manufactured products —appliances, clothing, processed foods, chemicals, rubber products, etc.

We find it extremely difficult to conclude that, in 1957 for instance, prices would have gone up even if wages had not, thus wages in 1957 were *pulled* up; or on the contrary, prices in that year would not have gone up if wages had not risen—the wage inflation forced prices up. It is not only that we cannot conclude that one or the other was true of most markets; it is even very hard to say which was the case in any single market.

But the problem is even worse. It is not merely that we cannot reach conclusions regarding the nature of inflation in a particular time and place. The distinction itself tends to break down when we bring the real-world processes of price and wage setting into our consideration. What does it any longer mean to say that in 1951 we had demand inflation because wages rose no more than they would have been bid up in an auction-type labor market (given the rises in goods prices that were occurring), when the rises in goods prices that were occurring were predicated in most instances, through "pricing formulas" or the exercise of "good business judgment," on the simultaneous and expected rise in wage rates? Or what does it mean to say that in 1957 we had cost inflation because prices rose no more than they would have been expected to rise in response to demand-supply forces, given the rise in wage costs that occurred in 1957, when this very rise in wage costs was at least in part tied (through cost-of-living clauses or the cost-of-living principle in wage negotiation) to the rise in prices that was occurring or was expected to occur in 1957?

In short, the dichotomy between demand and cost inflation appears impossible of application. The principal reason is that neither in the labor market nor in most commodity markets are wages or prices set in automatic response to supply-demand forces, rising when and only when there is an immediate current excess of demand over supply. Instead, prices are largely administered in both kinds of markets. Is it not necessary, therefore, to find a theoretical framework for the analysis of inflation which assumes administered wages and prices?

In such an analysis aggregate demand must play an important role. It would be absurd to argue that aggregate demand has no relevance to inflation. We have merely argued that the concept of excess aggregate demand is not useful—not operational—in the form in which it is usually presented. We can perhaps meaningfully compare two states of aggregate demand. Within limits, we can agree that demand was greater in one year than another. But can we meaningfully—i.e., operationally—compare demand with supply to find which was in excess? As will be seen below, our suggested treatment, in effect, makes demand inflation a matter of *degree*, not of *kind*.

The usual wage-cost inflation analysis has the advantage that it recognizes, realistically, that wage rates are administered prices; but, unrealistically, it assumes at least tacitly either that prices of goods and services are market-determined rather than administered, or that this makes no difference. Also, it seems frequently to ignore the fact that not only do prices follow wages but that wages also follow prices. Today's wage increase may seem to require tomorrow's price increase. But, to labor, today's wage increase is often seen as an important measure required by yesterday's increase in the cost-of-living. Our theory of inflation should consider not merely the effect of wages on prices but should give equal weight to the influence of prices on wages.

We turn, therefore, to an alternative theoretical approach which may provide a better insight into the nature of the inflationary process and the policies necessary to control it, an approach usually condemned by economists as unsound.

## MARKUP INFLATION [18]

We present below a very simplified version of what we can call the "markup" analysis of inflation, indicate certain criticisms made of this approach and why they miss the point, then elaborate the analysis slightly. Finally, we may consider its implications for economic policy.

Suppose that all business firms have the practice of pricing the goods and services which they sell on the basis of some standard markup over their costs of direct materials and direct labor. (This markup therefore covers both overhead costs and profit.) For the moment, assume constant efficiency or productivity. Suppose further, that labor seeks and is able to get wage increases to match any increase in the level of consumer prices. In effect, labor, too, then prices its services on the basis of a fixed markup over its cost of living.

Now it is easy to see that this model can generate either a stable, a rising, or a falling price level, depending on the markups which business and labor respectively employ. The markup pattern by business may be

[18] A formal model of pure "markup inflation" is provided by F. D. Holzman, "Income Determination in Open Inflation," *Review of Economics and Statistics*, XXXII (May 1950), 150–58. A model combining markup and demand elements is presented by J. Duesenberry, "The Mechanics of Inflation" in the same issue of this journal, pp. 144–49.

such that a wage level of $2.00 an hour yields a price index of 100, which was just the index level which led workers to demand a wage level of $2.00. But this need not be the case. Suppose that a wage level of $2.00 leads to a price index of 104, and that a price index of 104 leads workers to seek and to get a wage of $2.08, which in turn requires a price index of 108.2, a wage level of $2.164, and so on. Clearly an endless upward spiral of wages and prices would ensue so long as these bases for setting wages and prices prevailed. If the markup on one or both sides is a percentage markup, the inflation will proceed faster than if one or both of the markups is fixed in dollars and cents. Further, depending on the magnitudes of the two markups, the spiral may eventually taper off into stability (in the absence of a new push) or may have no termination. These are matters of detail, of no great relevance here. The important fact is that, if each participant prices on the basis of a markup over the prices he pays, we can have a spiralling process of very considerable magnitude and duration.

This spiral works within the business sector as well as between business as a whole and labor. Most sales by the "average" business firm are made to another business firm. If one firm raises its prices in order to preserve its desired markup, this raises the costs of other firms, which in turn raise their prices, increasing the costs of still other firms (including perhaps the initial firm), in an endless chain. Some of the sales of some of these firms are also made to consumers. This raises the cost of living, and, by causing wage costs also to rise, intensifies the spiral. Nevertheless, it should be noted that the dollar value of sales between business firms is much greater than the dollar value of sales of labor to firms. Even if wage rates were stable, we could have a considerable round of markup inflation entirely within the business sector, if the initial conditions and the markups applied by firms were such as to produce it.

Now it is also clear that even if the markups applied by business and by labor were such as to produce an inflationary spiral, a gradual improvement of efficiency and productivity might eventually bring the spiral to a halt. For a rise in efficiency means that a rise in wage rates or prices of purchased materials produces a smaller rise in labor and materials costs. Thus markup patterns which were initially inconsistent with stable prices can become consistent with stability through the growth of productivity.

But this happy result would, of course, be lost, if the several parties to the game each tried to appropriate the gains of rising productivity, through expansion of their markups. Indeed, if the desired shares of the productivity gain add up to 100 per cent—or, as they easily might, to more than 100 per cent—of the gains of productivity increase, the spiral might still go on indefinitely. And this effort to expand the markups to appropriate some of the gains of rising productivity is just what we observe. Labor seeks not merely to maintain a constant "real wage," but to achieve a rising standard of living; business, too, would like to enjoy some of the benefits of the increasing productivity which, one must agree, arise primarily from business investment and managerial skill and ingenuity. (One time-honored way in which this occurs is through the application of customary markups to "standard" costs, using current wage rates and materials prices. Unless the "standards" are revised to reflect the rising productivity, management appropriates the entire productivity gain.)

The model is dreadfully oversimplified. But we can expand it without changing the conclusions. For example, we can add an agricultural sector. However, if we have agricultural prices supported at some percentage of parity, this only adds to the inflationary race, particularly because our parity index assumes that farmers should receive 100 per cent of the gains that occur in agricultural productivity. There should also be added a free-market sector, in which prices respond freely to supply-and-demand forces, a sector largely identified with raw materials.[19] Imports and exports may also be added. These greatly complicate the analysis and succeed primarily in obscuring rather than altering the primary engine of inflation. This engine is the struggle between labor and business to preserve levels of return and to achieve gains in return that cannot be accommodated out of the total national income. It is as if the two parties were demanding shares of the national income that added up to more than 100 per cent of the total national income. The attempt of each party to get its desired "fair share" produces only an indefinite inflationary spiral.

There is no evidence to show that either labor or business wants inflation as such; indeed each deplores it. The goal of business in setting prices is not to get higher prices; it is to obtain what it considers a "fair" markup over costs; if costs went down so would prices. When businessmen raise prices they often do it apologetically, explaining that they are no more than reflecting the rise that has occurred in their costs—or even showing that the price increase falls short of the increase in their costs.

[19] An attempt to build the free market prices into the model and to spell out further the dynamics of markup inflation is provided in G. Ackley, "Administered Prices and the Inflationary Process," *American Economic Review* XLIV (May 1959), 419–30.

The implication is clear that the passing on of cost increases (or decreases) to buyers—i.e., the preservation of a markup—is taken as the normal and obvious standard by which the propriety of a price change should be judged.

Nor does labor seek inflation. What it wants is a standard of living protected against erosion from higher prices, and rising gradually to reflect labor's "fair share" of the gains of rising productivity.

One thing that is appealing about the markup hypothesis is that it places the emphasis where unions and businessmen place it—not on the level of price, *per se*, nor on supply and demand, but on the preservation of "fair" relationships between buying prices (including the cost-of-living), and selling prices (including wage rates).

The hypothesis that most prices are set by markup over cost is often rejected as meaningless by economists. This may be the superficial form that pricing takes, they agree; nevertheless, the markups used are not just any numbers that come into the seller's minds. The markups employed merely reflect the operation of more fundamental supply and demand forces, and change as these forces change.[20] If sellers in a given field try to use markups that are too high, they will find themselves unable to sell what they expected to be able to sell at the prices they are charging; inventories will pile up; prices (and thus markups) will have to be adjusted downward.

In an analysis of the structure of relative prices—in connection with problems of resource allocation and income distribution—the markup hypothesis may not be useful, even as a starting point. But different considerations apply to an analysis of the inflationary process. If sellers typically set prices by applying customary markups to their costs, then in an inflationary setting of generally rising costs, markups may not change appreciably as the price level rises. And even if they do change, some markups are as likely to be revised upward as others downward. As a description of the way in which price levels change, the markup hypothesis is neither meaningless nor far from the truth; it is certainly a more realistic and useful hypothesis than the assumption that prices adjust immediately and directly to a "clear-the-market" level set by supply and demand.

Nevertheless, the fact is that markups do vary, and their variation may be significant. If our interest is in *price structure* we are concerned (in

[20] See Richard Heflebower, "Full Costs, Cost Changes, and Prices," in *Business Concentration and Price Policy*, A Conference of the Universities—National Bureau Committee for Economic Research (Princeton University Press, 1955), pp. 361–392.

effect) with variations in *relative* markups—how markups fall in those fields in which supply tends to exceed demand and rise where demand tends to exceed supply. Our hypothesis is that this is precisely how total *demand* becomes relevant to an analysis of the price level: specifically, we suggest that the average level of markups employed by business firms tends to rise as total demand increases and to fall as demand declines, but only moderately so.[21]

The second related hypothesis is that the "markup" which unions (and employers) apply to the cost-of-living in setting wage rates also tends to rise and fall as the volume of unemployment falls and rises.

This modification of the markup analysis of inflation makes it a more fruitful tool. It shows how inflation may occur, through inconsistent markups, even with some slack in the economy; but it also indicates why inflationary difficulties become more intense as total demand increases. It provides a framework which embraces elements both of the demand and of the cost analyses.

Too much of our thinking about inflation has concentrated on how it starts rather than with how it proceeds. Inflation might start from an initial "autonomous" increase either in business or labor markups. Or it might start from an increase in aggregate demand which first and most-directly affected some of the flexible, market-determined prices. But however it starts, the process involves the interaction of demand and markup elements.

A fuller elaboration of our simple model should take account of additional elements, including particularly the role of expectations, both as to demand and as to cost, and by consumers as well as businessmen. One principal relevance of expectations—except perhaps in hyperinflations—is with respect to the cost base to which business markups are applied, or the rising cost of living assumed in wage negotiations. When demand is moderate, markups may be applied to historical, experienced costs. As

---

[21] This is not just another way of saying that prices rise in response to excess demand. The question is not *whether* prices rise with excess demand but when and by how much they rise and how this amount is determined. If prices were completely market-determined, varying daily or hourly to clear the market, then the excess demand theory would answer our questions. But if this is not the case, we can talk meaningfully about the extent and pace and mechanics of inflation only by taking account of the particular ways in which prices are set. To say that prices rise "in response to" excess demand doesn't help much unless we know how far or how fast or how often they rise. Our thesis is that the best simple and general description is to say that they rise when costs rise, usually not before, that the price rise tends to be about equal to the rise in costs at "moderate" levels of demand, somewhat greater (but not "much greater") when demand is at a higher level, somewhat (but not much) less when demand is lower.

demand increases and the pace of price rise accelerates, there is an increasing tendency to project rising labor and material prices into the future and to apply the markups to these. Workers assume that the cost of living will rise, and try to anticipate it in their wage settlements. The projection of rising costs is perhaps the principal reason why business markups (over *actual* cost) rise with increases in aggregate demand. An additional reason why business markups may expand with aggregate demand is that the extent of discounts from and "shading" of quoted prices decreases with improving conditions. At retail, this takes the form of fewer special "sales" at "markdown" prices. Nevertheless, there is much evidence to show that the initial markups applied by sellers in computing their announced prices vary little between conditions of moderate prosperity and boom. The principal difference in realized markups occurs through the greater tendency for projection of cost increases during boom periods and through the greater prevalence of "sales" and special deals when demand slackens.[22]

## CONTROL OF MARKUP INFLATION

In the light of the markup analysis, the tools of monetary and fiscal policy obviously can have some effect on inflation. A reduction of total demand for goods may tend to reduce slightly the general level of markups which sellers apply to their costs; as a reduced total demand for goods is translated into reduced employment, the wage demands of trade unions tends to be scaled somewhat downward—or, if not the demands, the wage increases for which they are willing ultimately to settle.

But it is also clear that there is no neat relationship between full employment and inflation. Inflation may be a troublesome problem even (as in 1956 and 1957) with no general pressure on the labor supply, inflation may even survive in weakened form (as perhaps in 1958) in a period when there is considerable slack in the economy.

In view of this unhappy state of affairs, is there nothing that can be done to avoid a gradual upward creep of the price level—a creep that becomes uncomfortably rapid whenever the economy is sustaining vigorous growth and full utilization of its potential, and which stops only when the economy performs badly in these other respects?

To answer this question, we need to remind ourselves why it is that the process of wage and price determination seems to be inconsistent

[22] Some evidence as to the relative stability of business margins is provided in G. Ackley, *American Economic Review*, XLIV, esp. pp. 426–28.

with price stability, at least at full employment. The mere fact that both business and labor set their prices on the basis of a markup over costs, with an effort to capture some part of the gains of rising productivity, does not inevitably mean inflation. It means inflation only if the markups are inconsistent—if one or both of the markups is too high.

The usual cost inflation analysis necessarily places the blame solely and squarely on labor. Inflation occurs when labor makes inflationary wage claims. The markup analysis qualifies this conclusion, by pointing out that it is the *combination,* the *interaction,* of wage claims and business pricing policies that may produce inflation.

It is not hard to see why labor is usually given the sole blame for inflation. First, in the usual cost inflation analysis, prices (but not wages) are assumed to be set by impersonal supply and demand forces. This leaves no one to blame (except labor) if prices rise. We see wages set in a conflict situation—by bargaining between workers (the inflationists) and employers (who are fighting for price stability). Prices, on the other hand, are traditionally set by unilateral determination. Both buyers and sellers formally participate in setting wage rates; only sellers in setting most other prices. We tend to see conflict only in a formal context of conflict. Second, most analyses of wage cost inflation gloss over the relation of the cost of living to wage demands. This is like asserting that the chicken necessarily comes before the egg. Thus, Vice President Yntema of the Ford Motor Company, in testimony before the Senate Monopoly Subcommittee in 1958, pointed to the wage increases of 1956 and 1957 which raised the costs of Ford cars, and forced price increases. But had Ford prices not increased (and prices charged by most other manufacturers similarly situated) wage rates would have increased very much less, because the cost-of-living escalator would not have operated.

Although labor gets most of the blame for inflation, labor stubbornly refuses to accept the villain's role. Its wage demands are reasonable, its spokesmen insist, and consistent with price stability, if only the cost of living were controlled, and if business did not insist on exorbitant profit demands.

The markup analysis of inflation requires us at least to face labor's question. We can no longer hide behind "supply and demand" as the determinants of all prices except the price of labor. We have inflation if the markups are inconsistent, but is only labor's markup too high?

How might one judge whether business markups are too high? We would have had a standard for this judgment if all industries were organized in accordance with the model of pure and perfect competition. But they are not so organized, and few would be satisfied if they were. For the markups which purely competitive sellers are able to apply to their costs would provide profit margins probably quite insufficient for the massive reinvestment of earnings which is so important to economic growth, and the vast expenditures on research and development which are crucial to economic progress.

Although we have no easy standard to judge the propriety of business markups, and although these markups serve an economic function related to growth and progress (as well as provide the incomes of the owning and managerial classes), we can not assume that business markups are necessarily correct and above examination, whatever they may happen to be. *A priori*, it may be as sound to claim that business markups may be "too high" as to claim that wage demands may be excessive; as sound to blame business as labor for inflation.

What needs to be recognized is that it is the *attempted* or *desired* markups by labor and business which are "too high," individually or in combination. The actually realized markups can never be inconsistent. The two interest groups can lay claims that add up to more than 100 per cent of the national income; but they can never receive more than 100 per cent. It is inflation which chisels away the excess. To say that social policy should find a better way of reconciling these inconsistent claims is not to say that either group must *necessarily* take a smaller share of the national income than it is in fact getting. But it is not at all clear what this "better way" may be.[23]

[23] Some tentative suggestions, advanced with great hesitation, are made in the author's testimony before the Joint Economic Committee (see fn. 1, this chapter), pp. 633–36.

# The Theory of
# Investment

*Chapter XVII*

Investment has been assigned a position of crucial importance in almost all macroeconomic theories. This is true not only of modern Keynesian and post-Keynesian theories, but as well of most earlier "business cycle" theories. This primary role must surely reflect the observed great instability of investment, which (in net terms) fluctuates from negative to large positive amounts. On the average, (deflated) gross private investment has accounted for about 11.4 per cent of (deflated) gross national product in the United States during the past thirty years, ranging from a minimum of 2.0 per cent in 1933, to a maximum of 17.1 per cent in 1950. Of course, if Keynes' idea of a stable consumption function has any validity, the importance of fluctuations in investment is greatly understated in the percentages just cited; for, with a reasonably stable consumption function, investment fluctuations give rise to fluctuations in consumption, too. A drop or increase in investment may thus produce only a minor change in the percentage of investment to total output, because it will produce a similar fall or rise in output.

Our theory of investment is therefore of crucial importance in understanding income fluctuations. But, as we shall see, much of our theory is rather formal and sterile of empirical content; that portion that has empirical content finds wide disagreement and difference of emphasis among economists.

We begin our discussion by considering some analytical problems associated with the conventional or Classical theory of investment. As
460

we have previously indicated, Keynes took over this theory in substance, introducing some refinements, continuing some existing confusions, but adding certain qualifications and emphases of his own.

## THE MARGINAL PRODUCTIVITY OF CAPITAL

Classical theory has always held that capital is employed in an amount determined by its marginal productivity in comparison with the rate of interest. Stated otherwise, the "demand schedule for capital" shows amount demanded to be an inverse function of the rate of interest, a function which reflects capital's declining marginal productivity.

This macroeconomic schedule reflects the profit-maximizing behavior of individual firms. A firm maximizes profit (under perfect competition) when it uses labor to the point where labor's marginal product equals labor's price—i.e., the real wage rate; it likewise maximizes profit if it uses capital to the extent where capital's marginal product equals capital's price—i.e., the interest rate. If we accept the assumption that the marginal productivity of capital declines with increasing employment of capital, both for the firm and for the economy, then the pursuit of maximum profit will lead to a greater employment of capital the lower the rate of interest.

One may object that the price of capital is not the interest rate but the price of capital goods. Given the interest rate (as one of the costs of using capital goods), then we can think of the comparison which the firm makes as being a comparison between the productivity (in dollar terms) of capital goods and price (in dollars) of the capital goods used. This, however, can easily enough be translated into a comparison of the *percentage* productivity (or yield) of capital goods and the rate of interest (which, of course, is also expressed in percentage terms).

The relationships among these various magnitudes, namely, dollar yield, cost of capital goods, percentage yield, and the interest rate are often a source of confusion. It is therefore necessary to analyze carefully the nature of these several concepts.

The yield of capital goods is available only in the future, over a period whose length depends on the durability of the capital goods. The dollar yield attributable to a particular capital instrument in any future period is the excess of the sale value of goods produced by use of the capital instrument over all of the costs associated with its use— for example, labor, materials, power, selling expense. We could also deduct depreciation if we wished to make our yield comparison on a net basis, but the gross basis is simpler and is customary. We do not deduct interest, if we wish to compare the yield with the rate of interest. (If we deducted interest, we would have to revise our criterion to say that investment is profitable if the net yield is positive, rather than if it equals or exceeds the interest rate.)

The nature of the computation which the profit-maximizing entrepreneur must hypothetically make can perhaps best be understood if we first take a simple example. Suppose a potential investment will yield (we expect) $100 at the end of one year, and another $100 at the end of each of the next three years; thereafter, nothing. (The case of continuous yield—monthly or daily—is more complicated mathematically, although not in principle.) These expected yields are computed after deduction of all costs except depreciation and interest. If the asset being considered costs $400, it is clear that its yield, both in dollars and per cent, would be zero. It would not pay to make such an investment if the interest rate were positive, for the $400, if owned by the potential investor, could be loaned out, returning the same $100 per year at the end of each of four years, *plus something more*. If the funds have to be borrowed, the capital investment will cost in excess of $400, but will return only $400.

If, however, the cost of the asset is some figure less than $400, e.g., $354.60, it has a positive yield. In dollar terms, this yield is $45.40, over a four-year period, but what is the percentage yield? We cannot merely divide the dollar yield by 4 (making it $11.37 per year), and find what percentage this is of the original investment of $354.60, for this latter amount will not be invested for the whole period, but only for a single year. The second year's investment is less: it is equal to ($354.60) plus ($354.60 times $m$) minus ($100), or $354.60 \times (1 + m) - \$100$, where $m$ is the percentage yield we are seeking. This expression recognizes that the original investment of $354.60 for the first year will be increased by some return ($354.60 times $m$), but $100 will have been withdrawn at the end of the first year. The third year's investment will be equal to the second year's investment plus $m$ times this amount minus another $100:

$$[\$354.60 \times (1 + m) - \$100] + [\$354.60 \times (1 + m) - \$100] \times m - [\$100]$$

with an even more complicated expression for the fourth year's investment. From the above, it appears that we need to know the percentage yield before we can determine the base on which to calculate the percentage. Fortunately, the calculation is not an impossible one. It can be shown that $m$, the percentage yield that we are seeking, can be obtained by solving this equation:

$$(1) \qquad \$354.60 = \frac{\$100}{1+m} + \frac{\$100}{(1+m)^2} + \frac{\$100}{(1+m)^3} + \frac{\$100}{(1+m)^4}$$

More generally, the expression is

$$(2) \qquad C = \frac{y_1}{1+m} + \frac{y_2}{(1+m)^2} + \frac{y_3}{(1+m)^3} + \cdots + \frac{y_n}{(1+m)^n}$$

where $C$ is the cost of the asset, and $y_1, y_2, y_3, \ldots y_n$ the gross dollar yields of the asset at the ends of years $1, 2, 3, \ldots n$.

The above equation (2) leads us to the formal definition of the percentage rate of return or yield, $m$, of an asset as *that rate of discount which, when applied to the series of expected dollar yields from the use of the asset, will just reduce their sum to equal the cost of the asset.* Using as illustration the hypothetical data given above, we can find this rate by trial and error as follows:

| | Value Discounted at | | | |
|---|---|---|---|---|
| *Expected Dollar Yield* | 3% | 4% | 5% | 6% |
| $100 at end of one year | $ 97.09 | $ 96.15 | $ 95.24 | $ 94.34 |
| $100 at end of second year | 94.26 | 92.46 | 90.70 | 89.00 |
| $100 at end of third year | 91.51 | 88.90 | 86.38 | 83.96 |
| $100 at end of fourth year | 88.85 | 85.48 | 82.27 | 79.21 |
| Sum of discounted yields | $371.71 | $362.99 | $354.60 | $346.51 |
| Cost of asset | $354.60 | $354.60 | $354.60 | $354.60 |

The numbers in the first four rows of the columns of the above table can be found by use of a discount table (which shows the present value of $1 at the end of years 1 through 50, at various rates of discount). To say that the value discounted at 5 per cent of $100 one year from now is $95.24 is, of course, to say that $95.24 invested at 5 per cent will return $100 in one year. To say that the value discounted at 5 per cent of $100 two years hence is $90.70 is to say that $90.70 invested at 5 per cent (with first year's interest reinvested) will return $100 in two years.

What the above calculations show is that the yield on this particular potential investment is just 5 per cent. Only if the prospective dollar yields are discounted at 5 per cent will their discounted sum just equal the cost of the asset. Clearly, if the market interest rate (i.e., bond yield) is less than 5 per cent, this investment would be better for a man possessing $354.60 than would be the purchase of a bond. If the interest rate is just 5 per cent, then it is a matter of indifference whether he buys the bond or buys this asset; while if the interest rate exceeds 5 per cent, he had better buy the bond. In other words, we can say that it pays to invest in any capital good if the percentage rate of return or yield from the capital good exceeds the market rate of interest.

We could, of course, express our criterion differently. We could say that it pays to invest in a capital good if its cost, plus interest on the investment at the going market rate of interest, is less than the dollar yield expected from the asset. Although this way of putting it is more natural for an investment which has a single one-time yield rather than a series of yields, we can still give it application in the latter case. Continuing to refer to the same hypothetical investment costing $354.60, we have the calculations shown in the following table:

|  |  | $r = 4\%$ | $r = 5\%$ | $r = 6\%$ |
|---|---|---|---|---|
| (a) | Original cost: 1st year's investment | $354.60 | $354.60 | $354.60 |
| (b) | Interest on 1st year's investment [(a) $\times r$] | 14.18 | 17.73 | 21.28 |
| (c) | Investment at end of 1st year [(a) + (b)] | 368.78 | 372.33 | 375.88 |
| (d) | 2nd year's investment [(c) $-$ $100] | 268.78 | 272.33 | 275.88 |
| (e) | Interest on 2nd year's investment [(d) $\times r$] | 10.75 | 13.62 | 16.55 |
| (f) | Investment at end of 2nd year [(d) + (e)] | 279.53 | 285.95 | 292.43 |
| (g) | 3rd year's investment [(f) $-$ $100] | 179.53 | 185.95 | 192.43 |
| (h) | Interest on 3rd year's investment [(g) $\times r$] | 7.18 | 9.30 | 11.55 |
| (i) | Investment at end of 3rd year [(g) + (h)] | 186.71 | 195.25 | 203.98 |
| (j) | 4th year's investment [(i) $-$ $100] | 86.71 | 95.25 | 103.98 |
| (k) | Interest on 4th year's investment [(j) $\times r$] | 3.47 | 4.76 | 6.24 |
| (l) | Investment at end of 4th year [(j) + (k)] | 90.18 | 100.00 | 110.22 |
| (m) | Yield at end of 4th year | 100.00 | 100.00 | 100.00 |

Comparison of the last two lines shows that by the end of the fourth year, the cost-plus-interest still invested in the capital good is almost $10 less than the remaining final yield if $r$ is 4 per cent; just equals the yield if $r$ is 5 per cent; and exceeds the yield if $r$ is 6 per cent. It obviously pays to invest if $r$ is 4 per cent, is a matter of indifference if $r$ is 5 per cent, and does not pay if $r$ is 6 per cent.

There is still a third way of expressing the criterion. The first was that it pays to invest if the percentage yield of the asset exceeds the interest rate; the second that it pays to invest if the cost plus interest is less than the yield; the third is that it pays to invest if the expected yield discounted to the present at the market rate of interest exceed the cost of the asset. The first compares two percentage rates; the second compares cost-plus-interest with yield; the third compares cost with discounted yields. They obviously all express the same principle and would give identical advice in any given instance.

It can be seen that there are three elements in the calculation, however we combine them: cost level of capital goods, expected dollar yields, and market rate of interest. Obviously, a change in any one of the three will change the calculation of profitability. We can combine any two of these three elements for comparison with the third. Which two we choose to combine will depend on what we wish to make an explicit variable in our further analysis—e.g., if the rate of interest is a strategic variable in our analysis we will use the first comparison (as did both the Classical writers and Keynes). On the other hand, if we wish to isolate as the strategic variable in our analysis the present level of cost of production of capital goods we will prefer the third comparison; while if the expected future price level is the variable we wish to isolate we will take the second formulation.

For the individual firm, the rate of interest can be taken as given, regardless of the scale of its employment of capital.[1] Likewise, for all except the largest firms, it is probably correct to take the level of the cost of capital goods as independent of the firm's own employment of capital. The third element, the expected dollar yields, might be assumed to decline as the firm used more capital. At least this is inherent in the usual assumption that the long-run cost curve of the firm (all purchased factors of production variable) is U-shaped. Thus, for an analysis of a single firm, we might assume that any disequilibrium—i.e., nonequality between percentage yield and interest rate—would be removed through

---

[1] In a few cases, an increasing cost schedule of borrowed funds to a firm has been included as a strategic element of an analysis. This would seem to be of principal relevance, at least in the longer run, to an explanation of the size of firms. In any case we neglect this element in our subsequent analysis. See, however, M. Kalecki, "The Principle of Increasing Risk," *Economica,* IV, new series (1937), pp. 440–47. J. Duesenberry, *Business Cycles and Economic Growth* (McGraw-Hill, 1958), also makes this an important element. Particularly in a business cycle analysis, ignoring the rising cost of borrowed funds *to the firm* (even if "the" rate of interest is constant) probably constitutes a serious deficiency. See, however, the section on financial considerations in investment theory, below.

an adjustment in the extent of the firm's employment of capital, which would cause sufficient change in unit operating costs and thus in expected dollar yields to eliminate the inequality. Another reason for declining expected yields as the scale of the firm expands arises on the demand side. Larger output by the firm will, at least under conditions of imperfect competition, require lower selling prices and hence lower expected yields. If our analysis were on an industry basis (rather than a single firm), this would be a source of declining expected yields even in the case of pure competition.

However, when we consider the economy as a whole, these particular sources of declining yield to the capital of an individual firm can be ignored. Through an adjustment in the number of firms (each of which operates at its optimum scale), the use of capital could increase or decrease without affecting expected unit costs. Further, if all firms and industries expand output together, there need be no change in relative prices of the several products, and no prospective loss of sales on this account.[2]

Although increasing unit costs or declining sales prices have sometimes been used [3] to explain the decline in expected yields as the total social output expands with the use of more capital, this seems often merely an illegitimate extension from the firm or the industry to the economy as a whole. Rather, when we consider the economy as a whole we can take as variables things that are given for the individual firm (the interest rate, and the cost level of capital goods). And, although we will assume the expected yields from investment to decline as more capital is used in production, it will be for a different reason than is relevant to the decision of any single firm. This reason relates to the fact that more capital can be used by the economy as a whole only by making productive methods more "roundabout," more "capital-intensive," more

---

[2] Actually, since there exist (a) certain scarcities of specialized natural resources, together with (b) different income elasticities of demand for different goods, there will have to be changes in relative prices as total output expands; but every rise in the relative price of one good is a fall in the relative price of another.

[3] Especially by Duesenberry, *op.cit.*, esp. pp. 49–85. Duesenberry's whole analysis of the marginal efficiency of capital is curiously microeconomic in character. Thus, although he assumes that the cost of funds to the firm rises with its own increased use of funds, he does not take account of the effect of changes in the total use of funds by all firms on this cost. Nor does he take account of the effect of the scale of total investment on the cost of capital goods. Yet he stresses the role of rising costs and declining average revenues to the firm without recognizing that the former could be avoided by an increase in the number of firms and that the latter is an illegitimate generalization of partial analysis to the total economy.

Perhaps we can defend Duesenberry by arguing that individual firms act on the basis of the assumption that the environment is unchanged; that in the modern world of oligopolies the number of firms is relatively fixed. But these seem weak reasons for dealing with a macroeconomic matter in such completely microeconomic terms.

"indirect." The comparison involved here is between different (known) methods of production. Methods using more capital are, in general, and perhaps up to some limit, lower-cost methods of production than those using less capital. That is, for the same total annual expenditure on the purchase of materials and factors of production (including, of course, the cost of the capital goods) a larger physical (and dollar) yield can be expected from more capital-intensive methods.[4]

Some hypothetical examples indicating this relationship are shown in the table which follows. Lines A, B, and C relate to three different methods of producing some commodity. Method A involves little capital investment, method B more, and method C still more. In each case, the capital equipment is assumed to have the same durability, i.e., 10 years' life. The difference in investment, then, is solely in terms of the greater elaboration or complication of the capital goods used in methods B and, especially, C. Each of the first three rows involves spending $100 annually in the production of the commodity. Although each method thus has the same total cost (exclusive of interest), the more capital-intensive methods are seen to produce greater output. Exclusive of interest, unit costs are therefore lower the more capital-intensive is the method of production employed. (The data can, of course, be restated as in the last three lines of the table, which translate them into the production costs of an identical 1,000 units by each method.)

The relationship shown is that which is assumed will, in general, prevail: namely, more capital-intensive methods produce more at the same cost (exclusive of interest) than less capital-intensive methods. (Or, to say the same thing differently, they produce the same output at lower cost.)

Certain economists have attempted to describe the essence of capital as a lapse of time between inputs and outputs; use of more capital-intensive methods means longer lapse of time between "original" inputs ("labor" and "land") and output. In some sense this identification of time and capital is correct; but it does not imply that more capital-intensive methods necessarily involve capital instruments of greater durability. However, more capital-intensive production may well involve greater durability of capital goods. Lines D, E, and F in the table relate to methods of production that are intrinsically the same. To produce 1,000 units requires, in

---

[4] The fixity of the supply of natural resources ("land") could also perhaps be used to explain a tendency for yields to decline as more capital is used. This was apparently the primary source of Ricardo's tendency for "profits" to decline as capital accumulated. We prefer to minimize this factor, at least in the aggregate, and to rest the explanation on other grounds.

TABLE 17–1. Hypothetical Unit Costs by Different Methods of Production and Different Degrees of Durability of Capital Instruments

| Production Method | Investment Required | Annual Depreciation | Costs of Labor, Materials, etc. | Total Cost (Excluding Interest) | Annual Output (Units) | Unit Cost (Excluding Interest) | Total Cost, Including Interest | | | Unit Cost, Including Interest | | |
|---|---|---|---|---|---|---|---|---|---|---|---|---|
| | | | | | | | at 20% | at 10% | at 1% | at 20% | at 10% | at 1% |
| A | $200 | $20 | $80 | $100 | 1000 | $.100 | $140 | $120 | $102 | $.140 | $.120 | $.102 |
| B | 500 | 50 | 50 | 100 | 1300 | .077 | 200 | 150 | 105 | .154 | .115 | .081 |
| C | 800 | 80 | 20 | 100 | 1500 | .067 | 260 | 180 | 108 | .173 | .120 | .072 |
| D | 70 (1 year) | 70 | 50 | 120 | 1000 | .120 | 134 | 127 | 121 | .134 | .127 | .121 |
| E | 200 (4 yrs.) | 50 | 50 | 100 | 1000 | .10 | 140 | 120 | 102 | .140 | .120 | .102 |
| F | 600 (30 yrs.) | 20 | 50 | 70 | 1000 | .07 | 190 | 130 | 76 | .190 | .130 | .076 |
| A | 200 | 20 | 80 | 100 | 1000 | .100 | | | | | | |
| B | 385 | 38.5 | 38.5 | 77.0 | 1000 | .077 | | | | | | |
| C | 533 | 53.3 | 13.3 | 66.7 | 1000 | .067 | | | | | | |

each case, $50 of expenditure on current inputs of labor and material. The capital instruments used, however, can be constructed of different materials, or with different degrees of care, so that they last for different periods. The greater durability involves greater original cost; but the *annual* cost of the more durable instruments is shown to be lower.

Whether the more capital-intensive method represents a process in which capital substitutes for labor and materials, or merely one in which the capital instruments are more durable, the principle is the same: that the cost of production (exclusive of interest) tends to be lower for more capital-intensive than for less capital-intensive methods.

This relationship does not, however, mean that more capital-intensive methods are always to be preferred to less capital-intensive ones, as the last six columns show. For interest is also a cost. If interest rates are high (e.g., 20 per cent) the methods involving greater investment per unit of output are heavily penalized. Indeed, method D (the least capitalistic of all) is the cheapest method at an interest rate of 20 per cent. A lower rate, e.g., 10 per cent, provides less of a penalty for more capital-intensive methods: B is now cheaper than A, and C as cheap; E is cheaper than the less durable D. While if the interest rate is low, e.g., 1 per cent, the advantage of the more capital-intensive methods finds little offset in higher interest cost; C and F are the cheapest methods. As between A, B, and C, method A would be preferred if the interest rate were 20 per cent, B if it were 10 per cent, and C if it were 1 per cent. As among D, E, and F, the cheapest method is D at an interest rate of 20 per cent, E at 10 per cent, and F at 1 per cent.

In general terms, we can picture the relationship between capital intensity and cost as in Figure 17–1.

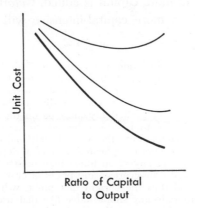

Figure 17–1.

Here the heavy line shows the presumed reduction of unit cost (exclusive of interest) as more capital-intensive methods of production are employed. The two lighter schedules show total unit costs including interest—at a higher rate (upper line) and at a low rate. Clearly, even though unit costs exclusive of interest decline continuously, unit costs including interest (in an amount proportional to the amount of capital employed) do not decline continuously. However, the point of minimum cost always involves a more capital-intensive method when the interest rate is low than when it is high.

The data presented in the table merely indicates which is the cheapest way to produce at each interest rate; they do not indicate whether any method would be profitable at any interest rate or what would be the most profitable method. For example, if the price per unit of output which could be obtained were $.30 (and were expected so to continue over the life of the asset), then any method could be profitably employed, at any interest rate shown; if it were $.02, no method would be profitable at any interest rate. At intermediate prices, some methods would be profitable at some interest rates, while other methods would be less profitable or unprofitable. Given any expected price and any interest rate some one method is most profitable and will be selected. If, then, there occurs a decline in the interest rate, a more capital-intensive method becomes the most profitable.[5]

However we may choose to make our comparison of costs and yields, it is clear that more capital-intensive methods are the most profitable the lower the interest rate. Additional use of capital, by more capital-intensive methods, adds to output (or reduces its unit cost, exclusive of interest), but the added product (or cost reduction) is of finite magnitude, and decreases as more and more capital is added. *Ceteris paribus,* the lower the rate of interest the more capital-intensive will be the structure of production.

[5] One cannot use a crude calculation such as that of Table 17–1 to select (in a close case) the most profitable method, nor to find at what interest rate the unit cost by any method would just equal the price. For the unit costs are shown in the table inclusive of depreciation, using, for convenience, a straight-line method of spreading original cost. The correct calculation of profitability must be on the basis of expected *gross* yields (excluding depreciation from cost), using one of the three methods described at the beginning of the chapter. Put otherwise, the rational calculation of maximum profit implies a considerably more complicated method of depreciation (i.e., of determining the amount invested at any given time) than the straight-line method. Thus, even with constant expected selling prices and prices of current inputs, the unit costs *including depreciation,* and thus the current unit profit, will vary from one year to the next, making inappropriate any simple table like that used above. However, for our purpose here—that of illustrating the empirical assumption regarding the costs of different methods—this kind of crude calculation is much the simplest, and not seriously misleading.

It should be recognized, of course, that this relationship is not presumed to be smooth and continuous. For some products, some one among the currently available techniques of production may be the cheapest, *regardless of the interest rate*. That is, the unit cost line, instead of being continuously declining like that shown in Figure 17–1, is like that of Figure 17–2. In this example, the method indicated by letter A is cheaper

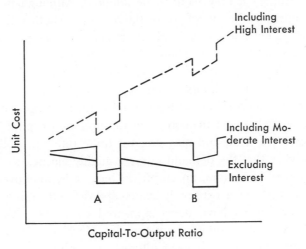

**Figure 17–2.**

than any other almost regardless of interest rate. Only if the interest rate fell very low would it be profitable to adopt method B. All other methods are out of the question at any interest rate. However, the principle need not depend on the existence of a smooth continuous relationship for each commodity. All that the principle asserts is that more capital-intensive methods tend, *in general,* to be cheaper than more direct methods.

How do we know this to be true? We do not have any clear and logical proof that it must be so. Rather, confidence in the correctness of the principle is based upon a general observation that in regions where and at times when interest rates are high, more direct methods are preferred; where or when they are low, more capital-intensive methods are chosen. To be sure, some economists attempt to find this a general "law" of the natural world, and resort to what in the last analysis are metaphysical arguments in support of their contention that more roundabout methods are always and without limit cheaper (excluding interest) than less roundabout. Keynes, on the other hand, held that there was no general reason why this must be so; this was also the position of some earlier economists, e.g., Wicksell. Beyond some point, they argued, increases in the capital intensity of production may cease to reduce unit costs (exclusive of interest); in fact, after some point, more capital-intensive methods may even be more expensive than less capital-intensive. Thus, Keynes argued, at a zero rate of interest, the best methods of production would not be those of infinitely high capital intensity. Rather, even if capital were interest-free, some finite degree of capital intensity would be preferred. More capital-intensive methods than these would require a negative interest rate (i.e., a subsidy) if they were to be adopted. Although the issue is, in a sense, academic when it relates to the question whether the demand for capital would become infinitely elastic at zero or some rate of interest above zero, it is not academic when it reflects a divergence of views as to the relative degree of interest-elasticity of the demand for capital at rates of interest within the limits of our experience. Keynes' view that (at least at times) the demand curve for capital is fairly steep (i.e., interest reductions have little effect in increasing the optimum capital-intensity) is at sharp variance with, and may suggest quite different policies than the opposing view that the demand curve is highly elastic.

The question is, at bottom, an empirical one. It is, moreover, one on which relevant evidence is extremely scarce and difficult to interpret. The metaphysical arguments have never appeared convincing, and Keynes seems as entitled to his opinion as anyone else. However, the question as to the importance or effectiveness of interest rate policy does not rest on this question alone, as will be evident later.

To the direct effect of interest rate on the choice of productive methods, we can also add an indirect, interindustry effect. A reduction of interest cost has a greater effect in reducing total unit cost and therefore prices of those goods produced by more capital-intensive methods. A reduction of the interest rate will tend to reduce the price of electric current or the level of house rents much more than it will reduce prices of goods which use little capital, and it will have almost no effect on the price level of personal services. To the extent that goods produced by more capital-intensive methods compete either in consumer budgets or in production with other goods produced by less capital-intensive methods, a reduction in the relative prices of the former will cause their partial substitution for the latter, thereby further increasing the "demand for capital." Thus, for example, in a country with high interest rates, more personal services and fewer consumer durable goods are used; laundresses (almost zero capital cost) substitute for washing machines (produced with capital goods and also themselves durable).[6]

---

[6] There is a popular derivation of the investment schedule, making no explicit reference to capital intensity, which needs to be disposed of before we proceed. The

## SOME PROBLEMS IN CAPITAL THEORY

Before proceeding to consider some major problems concerning the applicability of the above analysis to the theory of investment, it is necessary to consider briefly two subsidiary problems. One is the effect of uncertainty upon the calculations reviewed above; the second is the question whether firms, in fact, make such calculations as these.

argument, briefly summarized, runs somewhat as follows. We can imagine that, at any given time, a firm (or an economy) is presented with numerous alternative investment opportunities. These vary in the return which they promise. Some, such as emergency replacement of a crucial machine which has broken down, the installation of safety equipment newly required by law, the exploitation of newly invented machines which sharply reduce cost, investment in general in rapidly growing industries, promise very high returns. Other investments of a more conventional or routine sort promise only moderate returns; while the prospective returns from investment in still other lines— for example, the duplication of equipment of which the supply is already in excess of probable need—may be very low, or even negative. We can array these investment opportunities from highest return to lowest. This gives us a schedule, with quantities of investment on the horizontal axis and rates of return on the vertical. Naturally, the opportunities offering highest yields are exploited first—in fact, ideally, all opportuni- ties whose promised yields exceed the interest rate will be exploited. The lower the rate, the more investment opportunities which it will pay to exploit. Investment de- pends on the rate of interest.

The above is correct enough. But it should not take much consideration to realize that the schedule we have described has nothing to do with the marginal productivity or efficiency of capital (or the marginal efficiency of investment), and that such a schedule (array) cannot serve as the basis for any theory of investment.

Why do prospective yields *differ* in different industries or types of investment? One reason is that past investment has not been properly directed. It has flowed too heavily into some areas, depressing their yields to low (even negative) levels, while it has been insufficient in other areas, due to lack of knowledge or barriers to entry. To the extent that present investment is now properly directed, it will tend to erase these yield differentials. It will be sufficiently large in the high yield areas to reduce yields to equal the rate of interest, and it will be negative in the areas in which current yields fall short of the interest rate, to an extent, or for a period, sufficient to bring yields in these areas up to equal the rate of interest.

This current investment "straightens out" the array—in the limiting case, makes yields in all fields in which any capital exists the same, and equal to the interest rate. The *slope* of this investment schedule at any given time, then, depends only on the extent to which past investment has been or has not been properly directly. And this slope tells us nothing at all about what will happen to the average of all yields as the total stock of capital or rate of investment either rises or falls.

A second reason for an array of differential yields is that new events—inventions, shifts of demand, "breakdowns," legislation, etc.—have not affected all types or lines of investment equally. Thus we have an array of unequal yields, which current invest- ment will tend to "straighten out"; but, again, the *slope* of this array has nothing to do with the marginal efficiency or productivity of anything, and it offers no basis for a prediction of what will happen to net investment (the positive investment in the high- yield areas, plus the negative investment in the low-yield areas) as the rate of interest may fall.

The question at issue is what happens to the (average) yield on capital as the total amount of investment, directed optimally, or directed however it is directed, is in- creased or decreased. There is no avoiding hard questions of capital intensity if we are to answer this question.

The calculation as to the profitability or lack of it of a proposed invest-ment requires a forecast of (a) the sale value of the output resulting from the use of the capital good over its whole life (the extent of its life is likewise a forecast), and (b) the variable costs associated with the production of this output. Physical magnitudes (rates of output and input, length of life) as well as future price levels are involved in these esti-mates. Since such forecasts are uncertain, must we not modify the analysis to take account of this fact? Obviously we must, but we shall here take account of it only in a formal way, avoiding the really significant sub-stantive problems. What we must say is that the expected dollar yields—which enter into the calculation of profitability—may represent something other than the "objectively" best forecast that the firm can make. Thus, in the numerical example with which we began the chapter, the expected yields of $100 per year at the end of each of four years summarize the firm's subjective valuations of all of the possible developments which might occur.

One way of representing the effect of uncertainty is to conceive of the entrepreneur as visualizing a frequency distribution of possible yields. This distribution might indicate that, for the second year, the chances were two in one hundred that the yield might exceed $240, 5 in one hundred that it might be in the range $200–$240, 10 in one hundred in the range $160–$200, 18 in 100 between $120 and $160, 30 in 100 between $80 and $120, 18 in 100 $40 to $80, 10 in 100 zero to $40, 5 in 100 zero to −$40, 2 in 100 a loss in excess of $40. (The distribution obviously need not be symmetrical, as is this one.) Such a distribution has an average value (weighted probability) of $100. This is also the single most prob-able value (mode of the distribution). But to say that this prospect is "worth" $100 to an entrepreneur is to ignore the effect of uncertainty itself. For many (most?) individuals, uncertainty is presumably a deter-rent: if offered a choice between $100 and a lottery having the above chances of yield, they would prefer the $100. By finding what lower *certain* figure (say $85) would induce one to prefer the distribution hav-ing an "objective" value of $100, we could find the amount of his "un-certainty discount." For some persons, it is presumed, the uncertain pros-pect is actually preferred: such persons, enjoying the stimulation provided by uncertainty, might pay a premium for the uncertain prospect—might prefer our lottery to a certain figure of, say, $105. Indeed, it is hard other-wise to explain gambling.

Further, we could imagine that certain portions of the distribution of possible outcomes have large strategic importance to some individuals in determining the value to them of the whole distribution. The distribution presented above is shown (in smoothed form) in Figure 17–3, as line A. Other lines show other possible types of distributions. Distribution B is symmetrical like A, and has the same average and same mode ($100). To a person disliking uncertainty this is worth more than A; to a gambler it is

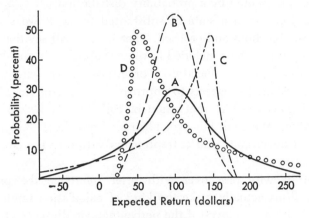

Figure 17–3.

worth less. Distribution C has a higher modal value ($150)—that is, $150 is the single most probable outcome. But its chance of large gain is nil, and the chance of large losses appreciably greater than distribution A. Yet it has the same average—i.e., $100—as A. A person attracted by the possibility of large gains, as well as one repelled by the possibility of large losses, would discount heavily the fact that the single most probable outcome (40 chances in 100) is a yield of $150. Others might prefer it to A. Distribution D is similarly unsymmetrical. Although its most probable outcome is a small gain of $50, its weighted average outcome is almost $100, and it offers fairly considerable possibility of large gain.

Formally, we can try to dodge the problems raised by uncertainty by saying that the figure for expected yield which enters into the entrepreneur's calculation is the "certainty equivalent" of the range of uncertain values—that is, it is the "objective value" of the distribution (is this the average or the mode?), less any discount or plus any premium for uncertainty. There are two things wrong with this solution. One, it is purely formal; it ignores the important empirical problem of how, in fact, people react to uncertainty and to its various forms. For example, suppose a tax or subsidy scheme is proposed which alters the probabilities involved—either in some symmetrical or unsymmetrical way. What effect will this have on investment? Without some empirical hypotheses as to the effects of uncertainty we cannot answer. (Are most entrepreneurs gamblers, or the reverse? Are they peculiarly sensitive to absolute losses, to the prospect of large losses, to the possibility of large gains, etc.?)

An even more serious objection to the "certainty equivalent" solution is made by those who refuse to agree that a subjectively uncertain situation can even be represented by a probability distribution.

Since this topic is in a state of substantial ferment, we shall merely register these objections and proceed. That is, we shall say that the effect of uncertainty is somehow included in the entrepreneur's calculation; that changes in the degree of uncertainty or in attitudes toward uncertainty can cause investment prospects to improve or to deteriorate without any change having occurred in what might be called the "physical" attributes of the situation. We shall however abstract from these matters: "*Given* the degree of uncertainty and entrepreneurs' attitudes thereto, such and such will be the case." [7]

We shall likewise pass over with brief reference the problem of realism. Do firms actually make the kind of calculation implied above? The rule that it pays to invest if the percentage yield exceeds the interest rate (or in its other formulations) is a rule of rational behavior; but are firms rational? Do they behave this way? There is plenty of evidence that they do not. The opinions of well-informed observers, plus some scanty evidence from surveys, indicate that, in fact, investment decisions are often based on hunch or whim or prejudice, on noneconomic factors, or, where calculations are made, on rules of thumb that occasionally cause the selection of unprofitable alternatives or, more frequently, rejection of profitable investments; and in general are systematically biased in their choice of the best among several possibilities. [8]

There is obviously room both for a significant study of how firms actually make their investment decisions and for educational efforts to show firms how to make better—i.e., more rational—decisions. Neither of these is called for here. However, the question that is raised is whether a theory that is based upon the assumption of rational behavior will give incorrect predictions if in fact firms behave otherwise.

Obviously, it will give incorrect predictions of individual firm behavior. But the important question is whether such predictions will be systematically biased when we consider investment as a whole. The answer

[7] For summaries of the rapidly growing literature on decision-making under uncertainty see W. Edwards, "Theory of Decision Making," *Psychological Bulletin* (July 1954), esp. pp. 390–403; and H. A. Simon, "Theories of Decision Making in Economics," *American Economic Review*, XLIX (June 1959), 253–83.

[8] See Simon, *op.cit.*

is that, at the present stage of our knowledge, the error is probably not significant. The kinds of *changes* (e.g., reduction of $r$, increase in cost of assets, expected increase in future selling price level) that might affect the rational calculation of profitability in a certain direction will almost surely affect actual calculations in the same *direction*, if not to the same extent. This is a casual kind of judgment, but no other kind is currently possible. Again, more research on actual decisions, and more education as to the rational formula, are needed, to help make our theories of investment more useful for prediction.[9]

## FROM THEORY OF CAPITAL TO THEORY OF INVESTMENT

The theory of capital, as sketched above, explains how the optimum stock of capital employed by the firm depends upon the relationship between the cost of assets, their expected yields, and the interest rate. This follows from the assumption of rational—i.e., profit-maximizing—behavior. If we add the empirical observation that, in general, more capital-intensive methods involve lower unit cost (exclusive of interest) than less capital-intensive methods, then we should expect to find that the lower the rate of interest, the more capital-intensive will be the productive methods that firms employ, that is, the higher will be the ratio of the value of their capital to the value of their output. This proposition relates to the explanation of differences over time or place in the productive methods employed by economies with different interest rate levels. Or, if there should be systematic differences *among firms* at a given time and place in either the cost they must pay for assets or in the rates of interest they must pay (e.g., by size of firm) we would expect to find differences in these firms' degrees of capitalization.

However, these propositions relate to firms which are in equilibrium with respect to their use of capital—i.e., to firms whose capital structure has been adjusted to the going rate of interest, cost of capital goods, and expected yields. None of the propositions so far developed is *directly* relevant to the theory of investment. For investment occurs only when firms are not in equilibrium with respect to their capital structure—when they have less (or more) capital goods than the optimum. Despite the

[9] For discussion of the problem considered in this and the preceding paragraphs, see J. F. Ebersole, "The Influence of Interest Rates upon Entrepreneurial Decisions in Business—a Case Study," *Harvard Business Review* (Autumn 1938), pp. 35–39; J. Dean, "Better Management of Capital Expenditures Through Research," *Journal of Finance* (May 1953), pp. 119–28; and *A New Method of Return on Capital Expenditures* (Privately printed, Berwyn, Pa., 1953, distributed through Joel Dean Associates). The last of these references implies that its author has himself "discovered" the correct calculation of maximum profit.

fact that many economists have carelessly identified the theory of investment and the theory of capital (or have mixed into a single confused
presentation considerations relevant to both), it is clear that we have not
one but two problems: first, to explain the optimum—that is, the equilibrium—stock of capital for a firm and an economy; and, second, to
explain at what rate investment occurs when the capital stock is not at
its optimum. What we need is a theory relating first to the size of the
*stock*—capital—and second to the size of the *flow*—investment—by which
the stock grows or shrinks.

An analogue may help us to see the difference. The use of labor by the
firm is optimum when the value of the marginal product (assuming perfect competition) equals the money wage. A firm is in equilibrium when
so operating. But when so operating its rate of *hiring* (net) is zero. Suppose a wage rate change alters the optimum size of the firm's labor force.
We then have the question of how fast the firm will increase (or decrease)
its force—that is, a theory of the rate of hiring. This is precisely analogous
to the question to be answered by the theory of investment. Although the
theory of hiring (men) is probably of trivial importance—in contrast to
the theory of investment—it is clear that it would rest upon considerations
quite apart from those involved in the theory of the optimum *use* of labor.

If we limit ourselves to the single firm, it is not too difficult to pass
from theory of capital to theory of investment. It becomes more difficult
when we consider the economy as a whole. If a firm has less capital than
the optimum appropriate to the going rate of interest, cost of capital
goods, and expected yields, and if the capital goods it needs are in the
stock of its supplier, the investment can occur very rapidly. If we enlarge
the analysis to include the supplier, or, if the capital goods must be made
to order, then the rate of investment will be determined by the production
period of the particular capital goods. Suppose, for instance, that the
optimum stock of capital for a certain firm were previously $1,000,000,
and, following a reduction of the interest rate, all other factors remaining
the same, the optimum stock becomes larger, say $1,300,000, because it
now pays to mechanize a process formerly performed manually. Suppose
further that it takes eighteen months for the new equipment to be built
and installed. Then (assuming the cost of the new goods is incurred
evenly over the eighteen months), the firm's investment will be at the
rate of $200,000 per year for one and one-half years; thereafter, zero. But
if the period of production were cut in half, to nine months, investment
would be at the rate of $400,000 per year (for nine months).

It is important to recognize that in this example the rate of investment was determined by a factor which does not enter at all in the theory of capital—namely, the speed of construction of capital goods.

Suppose, to take another example, that the firm's actual stock of capital exceeds its optimum stock. What determines the rate of its (dis)investment? If the investment is in plant or equipment, it is determined by the rate of wearing out or obsolescence of the particular capital goods. If in stocks, by the rate of their sale or use in production. In either case, considerations outside of the orbit of capital theory determine the rate of investment.

Approaching complications one at a time, we can develop several alternative theories of investment for the economy as a whole. The first one is very simple. Instead of the production time of capital goods, which is relevant to a single investment, we have, as a limit on the rate of investment for the economy as a whole the productive capacity of the capital goods industry. If this industry can turn out capital goods at an annual rate of 50 billion dollars, then *gross* investment cannot exceed 50 billion per year (at least in real terms). Net investment cannot exceed this figure less the amount of annual depreciation and obsolescence. If the latter is 10 billion, then net investment cannot exceed 40 billion, nor fall below minus 10 billion. Gross investment (which cannot be negative) can range from zero to 50 billion, net investment from −10 to 40 billion.

Further, so long as our theory is strictly aggregative (i.e., takes no account of the fact that separate firms and industries may be in different situations), it can be shown that the model would produce only three possible rates of investment; −10, zero, 40. For the optimum stock of capital must always either exceed, fall short of, or just equal the actual stock. If the optimum *exceeds* the actual, firms must be clamoring for new capital goods, and the capital goods industry, trying to fill its orders, will be operating at capacity. But unless the optimum stock of capital grows as fast or faster than the actual stock accumulates through investment, the actual stock must gradually "catch up" with the optimum. If, then, the optimum stock just equals the actual, net investment would be zero. Capital goods would be replaced as they wore out, but no more. The third possible rate of investment would reflect a situation in which the optimum stock fell short of the actual stock. In this case gross investment would be zero, and net investment would be negative, at a rate determined by the rate of depreciation. Again, unless the optimum stock were to shrink as fast as the actual, a point of equality should eventually be reached, and the rate of net investment should rise from negative to zero.

The model is obviously very crude, but it does correspond at least very roughly with the frequent observation that the capital goods industries are industries of "feast or famine"—they oscillate rather violently between conditions of feverish activity and stagnation. This model helps us see in part why this may be so. Each of these conditions corresponds to a *disequilibrium* for industry in general (including, of course, the capital goods industries) with respect to the stock of capital goods. Either kind of disequilibrium may be rather slow to correct itself, since the production of capital goods (even at the maximum rate) cannot add significantly to the stock except over a considerable period of time, nor can depreciation reduce the stock very rapidly. A relatively slight disequilibrium (percentagewise) between actual and optimum stocks may thus engender a fairly considerable period of intense activity or stagnation in the capital goods industries.

One might add the fact, long recognized, that, for psychological reasons, the boom may lead to overbuilding, so that what was a shortage of capital (actual stock less than optimum) frequently leads to an excess, and vice versa.

Another, more subtle and systematic point was made in some of the earlier business cycle literature, particularly by the German writer Spiethoff. He pointed out that when industry in general was short of capital, so that the capital goods industry was working at capacity, the capital goods industry was itself under pressure to add to its capacity (i.e., the size of its optimum stock was enlarged). Thus, the capital goods industry's efforts to increase its own capacity intensified and prolonged the boom that resulted when other industries were trying to add to their capacities. In the depression, when the capital goods industry was shut down, it, too, had excess capacity that needed to be worked off through failure to replace.

But a still more important intensifier of boom and depression is added by the Keynesian consumption function. When the capital goods industries are working at capacity, a considerable amount of income is being generated in the capital goods industries. Consumption spending will therefore also be abnormally high, generating further incomes in the production of consumer goods, and further consumption spending. Thus, during the boom when the stock of capital goods is below its optimum size, income and output will be raised not only by the amount of production of capital goods at their capacity rate, but by a multiple of that. Once production of new capital goods at a capacity rate, over a sufficient period of time, has caused the stock of capital to catch up with the optimum level, and net investment then drops to zero, income will fall, not only through the reduction of investment, but by that amount times the multiplier.

Thus, if we start from an equilibrium position in which the stock of capital is at its optimum, and something happens—e.g., a reduction of the interest rate or a technological innovation—to increase the optimum stock, a boom of considerable consequence may ensue during the period in which the capital stock is growing toward its new optimum. On the other hand, if the optimum stock should become less than the actual, a period of zero replacement investment will occur, during which time the capital goods industries are completely shut down, while depreciation gradually reduces the capital stock; this will, of course, also bring a period of depression in the consumer goods industries.

In equilibrium, we may again stress, when the capital stock is fully adjusted to its optimum level, net investment is zero. Nevertheless, replacement investment, equal to depreciation, would maintain a certain level of activity in the capital goods industries, and consumption spending would be at a level appropriate to this level of income originating in the investment trades.

## THE COST OF CAPITAL GOODS AS A SYSTEMATIC ELEMENT IN INVESTMENT THEORY

One objection to the kind of theory developed above relates to the concept of capacity to produce capital goods. Instead of capacity being a fixed amount, economists often prefer to think of a flexible limit to output, with more output always forthcoming, but always at a higher (marginal) cost. The fixed capacity concept implies a supply schedule like that of part A of Figure 17–4. Instead, the usual concept of supply is

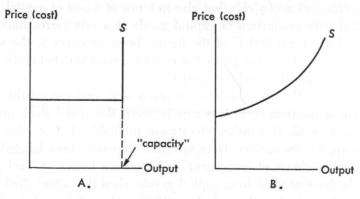

Figure 17–4.

that of part B. Here there is no single point which can be labeled that of "capacity." If the curve at some point becomes vertical, that point might merit the label; but that point may be entirely academic, the high cost of supply causing output, under normal circumstances, to be carried only to a much lower point. Or, if there were a sharp discontinuity in the curve (as may sometimes occur), we might call this the point of "capacity." In general, however, the notion of rising supply cost has traditionally been preferred to that of capacity.

Suppose we substitute this idea of a rising cost schedule for the capacity concept in our investment theory. We then have the cost of capital goods dependent on their rate of production. Let us assume again that, given the rate of interest, the optimum stock of capital exceeds the actual stock, and consider what will be the rate of investment.

We can see, however, that there is now an ambiguity in our concept of the optimum stock of capital. For one of the elements in the determination of the optimum stock is the cost level of capital goods. To any single firm this can be taken as given. But we are now hypothesizing that for the economy this cost level is variable, and depends on the total rate of investment. That is, the cost can be considered as given to the firm, but must be considered to vary with the decisions made by all firms taken together.

Suppose that we remove this ambiguity by defining the demand curve for capital (which shows the optimum stock at each rate of interest) in terms of *that level of cost of capital goods which would prevail if investment were at a net rate of zero*. In part A of Figure 17–5, the optimum stock of capital is shown by the curve labeled MEC (abbreviating the phrase "marginal efficiency of capital," popularized by Keynes). Each point on this curve must be understood to be defined in terms not only of a given expectation of yields, but also in terms of a cost of capital goods associated with production of capital goods at a rate corresponding to zero net investment. Part C of the figure shows, as curve S, the supply curve of capital goods. The particular cost level used in defining the MEC curve in part A is the level $x$ of part C.

If, in part A, the rate of interest is given at $r_0$, and the existing stock of capital is $K_0$, then there is a gap between the actual stock and the optimum stock $\overline{K}$. This makes investment profitable; but at what rate? Part B supplies the answer. Here we have drawn a curve labeled MEI ("marginal efficiency of investment"). This curve begins at level $i_1$, for this is the level of yield from capital goods when the actual stock is $K_0$ (see part A) and when the cost of production of capital goods is at level

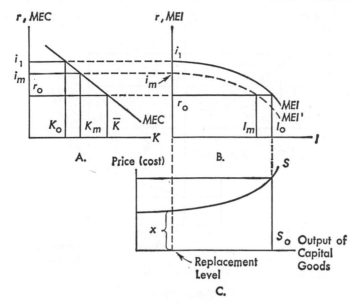

**Figure 17–5.**

$x$. The MEI, however, declines as the rate of investment rises, reflecting the fact that higher investment rates will raise the cost of production of capital goods. In fact, the MEI of part B falls at the same (percentage) rate as the supply cost, shown in part C, rises; it is, in a sense, a mirror image of the supply curve (although the vertical units are different). What rate of investment then occurs? Clearly rate $I_0$. For at this rate the cost of capital goods is bid up to a level high enough that a further increase in the rate of investment would reduce the percentage yield from capital goods below the rate of interest. $I_0$ is thus the *short-run* equilibrium rate of investment.

But it is the equilibrium rate only in the *short run;* for investment at any rate above zero causes the actual capital stock $K_0$ to increase. This increase causes the whole MEI schedule to shift downward. For example, when the capital stock has grown to $K_m$, the MEI schedule will have shifted downward to the level of the broken line in part B, leading to a lower rate of investment, $I_m$. This means that the further growth of $K$ proceeds more slowly toward $\overline{K}$.

The relationship of the present analysis to the preceding one can easily be visualized by the solid curves in Figure 17–6. Under the assumptions of the previous model, the supply curve is infinitely elastic at a given cost level, up to some point of capacity. The MEI schedule is thus horizontal

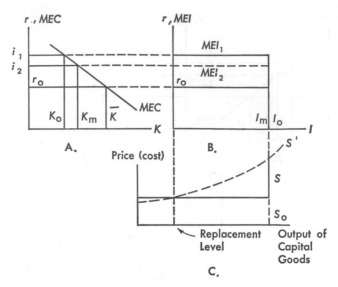

Figure 17–6.

up to that same point, and investment will always occur, if it occurs at all, at rate $I_0$. As it occurs at this rate, capital accumulates, reducing the MEI curve (but not the rate of investment) until investment at zero rate is suddenly called for.

If we merely "round off" the sharp corner of the supply curve of the simple model of the last section, the theory is only slightly modified. If, however, we substitute a supply curve such as the broken line in part C of Figure 17–6, then the theory seems to become almost a different kind of theory. Both, however, reflect the same phenomenon—namely, the existence of barriers to an indefinite increase in the rate of investment. (It is interesting to note that if the supply curve is like the broken line of part C of Figure 17–6, the equilibrium stock of capital $\overline{K}$ can theoretically never be obtained, only approached. For the nearer the actual stock comes to the optimum, the lower will be the rate of investment, and thus the slower the approach toward $\overline{K}$. The point is, however, not an important one.)

The theory of investment developed in the preceding paragraphs is in substance, essentially that of Keynes. Keynes, however, presented this substance in a confusing (perhaps one should say confused) way. He defined a schedule which he called the "marginal efficiency of capital schedule." This showed the amount of investment which would occur at each rate of interest. It declined, he said, for two reasons: one, the larger the stock of capital, the lower the expected return from the use of capital assets; and, two, the greater the rate of investment, the higher the cost of assets. Investment was carried to the point at which the M.E.C. equaled *r*. The second of the reasons for declining M.E.C. was more important, he said, in the short run and the first in the longer run.

This reflects an unfortunate confusion of factors relating to the size of the *stock of capital* with those relating to the *rate of investment*. It led to various contradictions and ambiguities that are easily enough resolved when one separates the two sorts of considerations, as we have done above. This was first clearly achieved by Lerner.[10]

Although the notion that the limitation on the output of capital goods occurs in the form of rising costs rather than in a sharp capacity limit is substantially more "elegant," one may doubt the practical importance of this "improvement" in the analysis. This is particularly the case when we recall the rather high cyclical stability of the prices charged by most capital goods industries. Costs of production of steel and machinery may rise as these industries move to higher rates of production, although even this can be challenged.[11] But prices charged certainly do not respond in any very systematic way. In a boom, the chief means by which the available production of capital goods is rationed among customers is not through price increases but through "queuing." New orders go to the end of a steadily lengthening waiting list. The backlog of orders is gradually worked off, at which point the boom may collapse.

Whether or not the rising cost of capital goods idea relied upon by Keynes is more "realistic" than the capacity analysis, it probably adds little that is essential to our investment analysis, and the capacity concept substitutes an analytical simplicity that could more than compensate for any slight loss of realism. At least, in the section "A Simple Capital Accumulation Model of the Business Cycle," we shall develop a business cycle theory which uses the capacity concept rather than the rising supply cost notion of Keynes.

## "ACCELERATION" THEORIES OF INVESTMENT

The optimum stock of capital, as we have developed it above, in line with a tradition which includes most "Classical" economists up to and including Keynes, involved, as we have seen, three elements: the rate of interest, the cost of capital goods, and expected yields from the use of capital goods. An alternative notion, referred to briefly at an earlier point,

---

[10] See A. P. Lerner, *The Economics of Control* (Macmillan, 1944) Chap. 25.
[11] For example, recall the argument of pp. 95–101.

suggests that the most important factor determining the size of the optimum stock of capital for a firm is the level of demand for its product. Although this element can be included in our earlier analysis under the "expected yields" heading, the point is a much more specific one. Suppose we assume, not too unrealistically perhaps, that, given the rate of interest, the cost of capital goods, and the price level of final output, there exists for each good some fixed proportion between the rate of production of that good and the stock of capital needed for its production. Each machine, that is, can turn out only so many units of output; to turn out more units requires more machines. Abstracting from all other influences, then, the necessary stock of capital (in physical terms) depends on the rate (in physical terms) of demand for final output. Then any change in the level of final output will call for a change in the stock of capital in an amount $x$ times the change of output, where $x$ is the value of capital necessary to produce one dollar's worth of output. That is, investment equals $x\Delta y$.

If $i = x\Delta y$, then $i$ will equal zero when $\Delta y$ equals zero—that is, when income is constant. But if income changes, by a positive or negative amount, investment (or disinvestment) will occur, at a rate which is small or large depending on whether the change of income is small or large.

One of the simplest and best known models of the business cycle comes from the mere introduction of the acceleration principle idea into the simple Keynesian multiplier model. It was developed in mathematical form by Paul Samuelson on the basis of a suggestion by Alvin Hansen.[12] Since it is both one of the simplest and best-known of the "difference equation" models of the business cycle, we shall present it briefly here, before indicating some of the analytical shortcomings of the model.

As usual, we start with a definition of income as

$$(1) \qquad\qquad y_t = c_t + i_t + g_t$$

together with a lagged consumption function

$$(2) \qquad\qquad c_t = a + by_{t-1}$$

and an investment function

$$(3) \qquad\qquad i_t = w + x(c_t - c_{t-1})$$

We are obviously using a period analysis, in which the period is defined as having the length of the consumption lag. Equation (3) asserts that

[12] P. A. Samuelson, "Interaction between the Multiplier Analysis and the Principle of Acceleration," *Review of Economic Statistics*, XXI (May 1939), pp. 75–78 (reprinted in the AEA *Readings in Business Cycle Theory*, pp. 261–69).

investment will occur in this period at a level sufficient to supply the added capital goods required to produce the increment of consumer goods output which has occurred since last period, plus a constant, $w$, which may be zero.

Substituting from (2) into (3) and then from both into (1) gives these results:

$$i_t = w + x(a + by_{t-1} - a - by_{t-2})$$

$$i_t = w + xby_{t-1} - xby_{t-2}$$

$$y_t = a + by_{t-1} + w + xby_{t-1} - xby_{t-2} + g_t$$

(4) $$y_t = b(1+x)y_{t-1} - xby_{t-2} + a + w + g_t$$

Equation (4) tells us that this period's income depends on the incomes of the two previous periods, plus the current level of government expenditures. The equilibrium income level of this model associated with any given values of $a$, $b$, $w$, and $x$, and any given level, $g_0$, of government expenditures can be found by setting

$$y_t = y_{t-1} = y_{t-2} = y_E$$

or,

$$y_E = b(1+x)y_E - xby_E + a + w + g_0$$

$$y_E(1-b) = a + w + g_0$$

$$y_E = \frac{1}{1-b}(a + w + g_0)$$

This is, of course, the usual multiplier formulation, in which income equals the expenditures which are independent of income, times the multiplier. It should be noted that the acceleration coefficient, $x$, drops out of the expression for equilibrium income. The reason is simple enough: investment occurs as a result of the acceleration principle only when income is changing; equilibrium means stable income, therefore no role exists for the acceleration principle in equilibrium.

For example, if $b = .5$, $a = 10$, $w = 0$, and $g_0 = 0$, equilibrium income is

$$y_E = \frac{1}{1-.5}(10) = 20$$

If $g$ now changes from 0 to 2, regardless of the magnitude of the accelerator, $x$, the new equilibrium is

$$y_E = \frac{1}{1-.5}(12) = 24$$

Suppose, however, we start with $y_{t-2} = 20$ and $y_{t-1} = 20$ (corresponding to an equilibrium with zero government expenditure); then cause g to increase to 2 and trace the movement of income through successive periods. This requires that we know the magnitude of $x$. Assume it is 2. Substituting our assumed numerical values in equation (4) above gives

$$y_t = .5(1+2)y_{t-1} - 2(.5)y_{t-2} + 10 + 0 + 2$$

or

$$y_t = 1.5y_{t-1} - y_{t-2} + 12$$

Substituting 20 for $y_{t-1}$ and $y_{t-2}$, we have

$$y_t = 30 - 20 + 12 = 22$$

$$y_{t+1} = 1.5(22) - 20 + 12 = 25$$

$$y_{t+2} = 1.5(25) - 22 + 12 = 27.5$$

$$y_{t+3} = 1.5(27.5) - 25 + 12 = 28.25$$

$$y_{t+4} = 1.5(28.25) - 27.5 + 12 = 26.875$$

$$y_{t+5} = 1.5(26.875) - 28.25 + 12 = 24.0625$$

$$y_{t+6} = 1.5(24.0625) - 26.875 + 12 = 21.21875$$

$$y_{t+7} = 1.5(21.21875) - 24.0625 + 12 = 19.765625$$

$$y_{t+8} = 1.5(19.765625) - 21.21875 + 12 = 20.4296875$$

Continuing to trace out the income movement for successive periods we would find that income turns up again, rises above the new equilibrium, reaches a maximum, declines, reaches a minimum, rises, in a never-ending cycle. The amplitude of the fluctuation (which is centered on the new equilibrium level of 22), however, will neither increase nor shrink.

This particular result depends, however, on our selection of values for our several variables. Specifically, it depends on the absolute and upon the relative magnitudes of $b$ (the marginal propensity to consume) and $x$ (the acceleration coefficient). The student can test this by trying, instead, the following pairs of values: $b = .8$, $x = .1$; $b = .5$, $x = 1$; $b = .8$, $x = 4$; etc. Trial and error is a rather painful way of discovering the possible solutions of this model. However, a mathematician can solve the generalized equation [(4) above], to determine the possible types of movement and the conditions under which each type occurs. The results for this model are summarized in Figure 17–7.

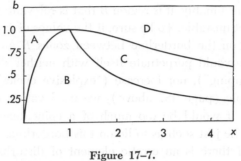

Figure 17–7.

Figure 17–7 shows a number of possible combinations of values of $b$ (the marginal propensity to consume), measured vertically, and $x$ (the accelerator), measured horizontally. Any point in the quadrant represents some pair of values of the two variables. For any such combination of values that falls in region $A$, the equilibrium of the model is a stable one, and is approached by a monotonic path, as is shown by line $A$ in Figure

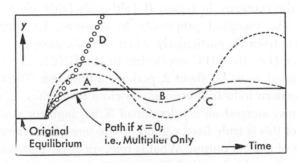

Figure 17–8.

17–8. In region $B$, the path to equilibrium is that of a damped cycle, as line $B$ in Figure 17–8. In region $C$, the equilibrium of the model is unstable: if income is at its equilibrium level it will stay there; but if there is a change in any of the determinants of equilibrium (e.g., in $g$, $a$, or $w$), a cyclical movement will be generated, which, centering on the new equilibrium value, will oscillate around it in ever widening cycles, as in line $C$. In region $D$, the movement is simply an explosive one. Also shown in the figure is the path of adjustment if the accelerator is zero—i.e., if only the multiplier is operating (through a lagged consumption function).[13] Again we have an example of the principle that a system may have an equilibrium, yet be dynamically unstable.

This model (or a variant) has had great appeal for economists, as offering a simple yet logical explanation of the essential mechanism of the business cycle. Presumably, it is region $B$ that is relevant; for cycles in the real world are not unstable. To be sure, if the values of $b$ and $x$ were such as to lie exactly on the borderline between zones $B$ and $C$ (in Figure 17–7), the cycle would perpetuate itself with neither diminution of its amplitude ("damping"), nor increase ("explosive cycles"). [In our first numerical example (page 487 above), we used values that lay on this borderline.] But it would be too much of a coincidence for the "real-world" values to be just such as to lie on this borderline. However, it can be shown that if there is an erratic element of disturbance, a damped cycle can be kept oscillating. In fact, in an interesting experiment, using a set of random numbers for his "disturbance," G. H. Fisher showed how this cycle model would produce a synthetic "time series" that looks convincingly like the familiar series used to show the business cycle, and with no apparent tendency for the cycle to die out, even after several hundred successive periods.[14]

Further, Hansen argued that the probable values of $b$ and $x$ were such as to place the economy in region $B$ (although fairly close to the $B$–$C$ boundary). The marginal propensity to consume, he suggested, was surely not far from .5, particularly when we take account of the drain through taxes (i.e., the MPC applicable to the GNP). The accelerator's value, he argued, must be about 2, perhaps a little less. The total capital stock of a modern industrial economy is close to 3 times its national income. This may suggest an accelerator of 3, too high for stability. However, much of this is truly fixed capital, in the sense that its value is quite independent of current output. What is relevant is the *marginal* capital to output ratio—the added capital necessary to produce an added dollar's worth of output. This might reasonably be expected to be close to $2.

This reasoning is fairly convincing, at first sight. But more careful examination discloses a serious fallacy. When we say that the ratio of capital to output is two (or any other number), we must specify the period over which the rate of output is to be measured. The comparisons Hansen had in mind were between the capital stock and *annual* output. The same data would make the ratio not 2 but 4 if output were expressed

---

[13] With MPC $< 1$.
[14] See "Some Comments on Stochastic Macroeconomic Models," *American Economic Review*, XLII (September 1952), 528–39.

in half-yearly rates; or it would be 8 if output were expressed per calendar quarter; 24 if output were expressed in monthly rate. Which manner of expression is called for by the model? The answer is that the way in which the rate of output must be expressed depends on the length of the period of the model. What is the length of the period in this model? It is the length of the consumption lag. This lag is certainly not a year. At most, it might be a calendar quarter. This would convert an accelerator of 2 expressed in terms of annual output into an accelerator for model purposes of 8. But this puts us into the unstable region—actually into region $D$ where there is not even a cycle.

We can reduce the apparent instability somewhat by correcting one feature of the model which reflection shows to be quite implausible. This is the requirement that the investment called for by the accelerator be completed in the same period as that in which the additional consumer goods output occurs which required the investment. Suppose the output is of shirts. If income rises, people buy more shirts. To make more shirts requires more sewing machines. But what our last model required was that, when *this* quarter's demand for shirts turned out to be higher than last quarter's demand, more sewing machines (and more steel, etc. to make sewing machines) had to be made, this *quarter,* in time to be used, *this quarter,* to make the extra shirts. This seems to require an impossible speed of construction and installation of plant and equipment. To get away from this difficulty, some have *lagged* the accelerator effect, making it

$$(3')\qquad\qquad i = w + x(c_{t-1} - c_{t-2})$$

This turns out to reduce the instability of the model—i.e., the levels of $b$ and $x$ consistent with the achievement of the equilibrium position.

However, another modification which many prefer works in the opposite direction—to make the stability requirements more restrictive. This change involves making the accelerator apply to changes in *total output,* not merely in the output of consumer goods. For added output of capital or government goods should, by the same logic, also require added investment (unless we assume that the capital goods industry always has excess capacity). Thus we have:

$$(3'')\qquad\qquad i = w + x(y_t - y_{t-1})$$

or

$$(3''')\qquad\qquad i = w + x(y_{t-1} - y_{t-2})$$

It is likewise possible to work with an unlagged rather than a lagged consumption function. Thus we have a choice of several models, involving different combinations of accelerator and multiplier. However, almost all have the problem that, if we make realistic assumptions about lags and the size of $b$ and $x$, we seem to get an unstable result.

One trouble perhaps is that the accelerator relationship is given too fixed and rigid a form. The acceleration principle is sometimes presented as a technological or engineering relationship: more output requires more machines, and more output is thus impossible until more machines have been produced. The difficulty with this technological formulation is apparent when we consider, as we did a few paragraphs back, the necessity for some lag in the relationship. Without such a lag, the implication is that the customer's order (if it involves *added* business) cannot be filled until the new machines are built, installed, and operating. Actually, the relationship is much looser; and, once its looseness is recognized, we see that it is not strictly a technological relationship at all, but a truly economic one. Even if all regular equipment is in use when there is a rise in demand, the rise can still be met, temporarily, by drawing down inventories, by working overtime, by extra shifts, by pressing into service standby equipment. But inventories cannot be drawn down below zero, and production through overtime, extra shifts, or standby equipment is more costly. If the rise in business is expected to endure long enough to make it worth while, new equipment will be ordered. On the other hand, if the rise in business is not expected to be permanent, the added demand will be met in the ways already suggested, or perhaps by raising the price. Only if the rise in demand is considered to be permanent will the pursuit of maximum profit lead the entrepreneur to install the added equipment.

This way of thinking about the accelerator is obviously more realistic; but it also shows us that the value of the accelerator is not necessarily fixed over the period of the business cycle, and that its value will be affected by calculations of future profitability extending over the life of the new assets. The strict accelerator theory calls for the entrepreneur to assume, in these calculations, that future demand (in physical terms) is always precisely equal to current demand. Instead, we know that entrepreneurs may expect future levels of demand to differ materially—in either direction—from the current level. These economic calculations also involve expectations as to future price levels, as well as (as we have seen) the cost level of assets, their availability, and the interest rate.

Mention of the cost and availability of assets brings us to what may be the biggest fault of the strict accelerator theory. The accelerator theory ignores any limit on the rate of production of capital goods. No matter how rapid the increase in the demand for final products, the necessary capital goods can be immediately produced, so that the optimum stock and actual stock always coincide. In our previous consideration of the Keynesian theory we stressed the difference between a capital theory (relating to the optimum stock of capital) and an investment theory (describing how the optimum is approached). The acceleration principle in a sense uses a single theory for both jobs. Suppose, instead, we use the basic idea of the accelerator—that the optimum capital stock depends on output—only as our theory of capital. We then recognize that when the optimum stock and the actual stock diverge, investment will occur, at a rate governed by supply conditions in the capital goods industry (if investment is positive), and at a rate governed by the speed of wearing-out of existing capital goods (if investment is negative).

## A SIMPLE CAPITAL ACCUMULATION MODEL OF THE BUSINESS CYCLE [15]

Suppose we start from a situation of complete equilibrium, in which all firms [16] have just the stock of capital necessary to produce the amount of output currently demanded. Net investment is thus zero; the capital goods industry is producing only for replacement purposes, and has idle capacity. Suppose that this equilibrium is disturbed by some increase in the optimum stock (or decrease in the actual stock) of capital. This could result, for example, from technological change. Will equilibrium be restored?

A shortage of capital will lead to an immediate increase in orders to the capital goods industries, and therefore to an increase of production by these industries up to their capacity level. The increased employment and income in these industries will lead to a higher level of consumption demand, *and thus to an increase in the optimum stock of capital, intensifying the capital shortage,* and prolonging the period of capacity operation in the capital goods industries. Eventually, however, the shortage of capital is made up. At this point optimum stock and actual stock are equal. Is this not a new equilibrium for the economy? Obviously it cannot be. For, once the actual stock reaches the optimum level, orders for new capital goods must decline to a mere replacement level. This means re-

---

[15] The model developed in this section is essentially that first presented by Richard Goodwin in *Econometrica*, 19 (1951), 1–17. However, an essentially similar mechanism figured in earlier business cycle theories of M. Kalecki and N. Kaldor.

[16] Except firms in the capital goods industry.

duced employment and income in the capital goods industries, and therefore reduced consumption demand. A drop in total demand must therefore necessarily occur once the actual stock of capital has accumulated to its optimum level. This drop of demand itself reduces the optimum level of the capital stock. Thus, to get *enough* capital goods means to get *too many*.

Production of capital goods now drops to zero, for not even replacement expenditures will now be made. Consumption, income, and total demand drop further, causing still further shrinkage in the optimum stock of capital, thus intensifying and prolonging the redundancy of capital, which can only slowly be worked off through depreciation.

Finally, however, the stock of capital will have shrunk to the point at which, even with low total demand, it is no longer redundant. Normal replacement expenditures are now in order. But this means a rise in income and employment (as operations commence in the capital goods industries), and thus an increase in total demand, and an immediate rise in the optimum stock of capital, turning what had been a just adequate capital stock into one that is too small, leading to increased orders for capital goods, further rises in income, total demand, and in the optimum stock, and so on.

Assuming no lags (except the necessary lag in capital accumulation or capital shrinkage), we can represent this model graphically as in Figure 17–9. Here time is measured on the horizontal axis, and, in the three parts, investment, income, and capital on the vertical axis. We start with a hypothetical period of equilibrium in which the actual and optimum stocks are equal. At time $A$ this condition is disturbed, we assume, by a very slight increase (say to $X$) in the optimum stock. This sets off a boom, as investment, income, and thus the optimum stock rise. The limit of the boom is set by the productive capacity for capital goods. During the boom, while investment continues at the maximum possible level, the actual stock of capital gradually accumulates up to the point of saturation of backlog demands for capital goods (at time $B$), and thus to the crisis.

The student can easily see some violently unreal aspects of the model (e.g., the rectangular shape of the cycle; the necessity for depressions to be longer than booms; etc.). He may also be able to see intuitively, however, that introduction of lags—e.g., in consumption—and of an upward trend in investment, representing technological progress, can eliminate these objectionable features. Another complication, easily enough introduced, is to allow the capacity of the capital goods industry itself to vary, through investment and disinvestment in this industry.

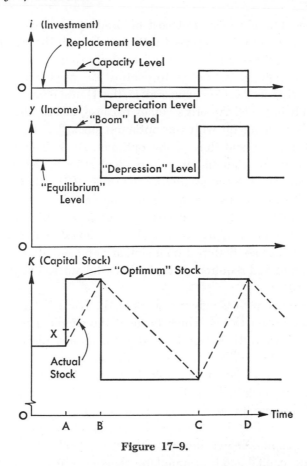

**Figure 17–9.**

One modification which changes the time-shape of the cycle produced by this model is to substitute the Keynesian rising cost schedule instead of the fixed capacity limit in capital goods industries. We shall not de-velop such a model here, but it has been developed by Goodwin.[17] Full equilibrium in such a model, as in the previous model, would involve, of course, a stationary stock of capital—i.e., zero net investment. In such equilibrium, capital goods would be being produced at the replacement rate. At this rate, both their production cost and the level of returns ex-pected from their use when the economy was operating at the level of income appropriate to zero net investment would be such that replace-ment investment (but nothing more) would be profitable at the going rate of interest. This equilibrium would be stable only if a positive rate of

[17] See the chapter by Goodwin in A. H. Hansen, *Business Cycles and National Income* (Norton, 1951), esp. pp. 442–59.

net investment would raise unit cost of production of capital goods by more than it would raise expected returns (through the effect of higher investment—via the multiplier—on the total demand).[18]

It is interesting and instructive to contrast the mechanism of the business cycle crisis in the Goodwin and in the Hansen-Samuelson models. In the Goodwin model the crisis comes because, at last, the actual stock of capital has caught up with the optimum stock, leading to a drop of investment, income, and thus of the optimum stock. This is clearly not the problem in the Hansen-Samuelson accelerator model, for there the optimum and actual stocks are always the same. It is rather that (at least in regions B and C) the *increase* of income and demand must at some point begin to taper off. This means that the *increase* in optimum stock begins to taper off, leading to a decline in investment and, with one period lag, in income. Both rest on a similar notion—that of a relationship between output and required or desired capital stock. But they are very different theories.

Simultaneously with Goodwin's work, J. R. Hicks [19] had developed a modified accelerator theory which brought the simple accelerator model much closer toward the Goodwin model. In the first place, Hicks incorporated a limitation on the operation of the accelerator that many earlier writers on the acceleration principle had noticed—namely, that it does not operate symmetrically in the upward and downward directions if changes of demand are at all large. That is, if the level of final demand drops sufficiently fast that the optimum stock of capital declines more rapidly than capital depreciates, then the strict accelerator relationship is upset. Excess capital goods accumulate; then, even if final demand levels off or rises, investment will not occur until the idle machines are brought back into use. This lower limit on the rate of investment is, of course, one element of the Goodwin theory.[20]

Goodwin's theory also had an upper limit on the rate of investment— one set by the productive capacity of the capital goods industry. Hicks does not recognize this limit, but instead its first cousin. Hicks postulates a ceiling on total output—of $c + i + g$—a limit set by the size of the total labor force. When, through the operation of the accelerator and multi-

18 Goodwin assumes that this would not be the case—that is, that the equilibrium would be unstable, generating continual cyclical oscillation. However, Goodwin is incorrect in asserting that this is a necessary consequence of the model.

19 *A Contribution to the Theory of the Trade Cycle* (Oxford, 1950).

20 As Duesenberry later demonstrated, recognition of this lower limit on investment can by itself convert a model with values of $b$ and $x$ which would otherwise lead to an explosive result into a cycle of limited and nonincreasing amplitude. See "Hicks on the Trade Cycle," *Quarterly Journal of Economics*, LXIV (August 1950), 464–76.

plier, demand would occur at a rate beyond this limit of productive capacity, the limit would in fact prevail. This is not, of course, a specific limit on investment as such, but only on the total of investment plus other kinds of output. When consumption was low (early in the recovery phase), investment could occur at whatever rate was called for by the strict operation of the accelerator.

The importance of this limit on total output for Hicks' theory can easily be seen. If physical output can no longer rise (or can rise only very slowly) because the "ceiling of full employment" has been reached, then investment must decline, because investment depends on the rate of change of total output. A reduction in the rate of change (which must occur when the "ceiling" is "hit") will lead to a drop in investment, and thus to a drop of income, etc. Thus, even with high values of $b$ and $x$—which would otherwise call for a region $D$ type of movement—the "explosion" is contained, and instead a "limit cycle" occurs.

Both Goodwin and Hicks have minimized this difference between their two theories. Yet the difference seems considerable; and, because it involves at least one further stage of disaggregation, the Goodwin idea seems the better of the two. However, we shall not enter further into the details of Hicks' theory or into the relative merits of the two.

## FINANCIAL CONSIDERATIONS IN INVESTMENT THEORY

The accelerator and capital accumulation theories of investment seem to omit any consideration of the rate of interest or, more generally, any financial considerations. Keynes' stress on the rate of interest, on the other hand, had merely continued an ancient and respected tradition in economic theory. If the quantity of money is fixed (e.g., by a rigid tie to gold), then any rise in income tends (through the transactions demand) to raise the rate of interest, or fall of income to reduce it. To whatever extent that expenditures depend on the rate of interest, this will constitute an additional check on the extent of boom or depression arising from investment changes. Further, as Hawtrey and others have postulated,[21] a money supply derived from commercial bank lending may increase during the earlier stages of an income expansion, until further rise in $M$ is curbed by the exhaustion of excess reserves, causing the rise in the rate of interest to come later in an income expansion and to play perhaps a more important role in its termination. Conversely,

[21] For a review of "monetary theories" of the business cycle see any standard business cycles text, or G. Haberler, *Prosperity and Depression* (third, enlarged edition, League of Nations, 1941), pp. 14–28.

the money supply may shrink as fast or faster than income in the earlier stages of an income decline, so that interest rates fall only later, providing some spur to revival. Delayed flows of currency between bank reserves and public circulation were also an element in Hawtrey's theory.

These systematic interest rate effects could be introduced as additional elements in the acceleration or the Goodwin capital accumulation models, by making the ratio of (optimum) capital to output vary inversely with the rate of interest. In effect, these models, as previously presented, abstract from changes in the interest rate. Many economists would argue that this abstraction is entirely justifiable, because they doubt the importance, in practice, of interest rate changes. The historical and probable future range of variation in interest rates, they argue, is too small to be of much importance relative to the wide variations which occur in the other elements determining the optimum stock of capital; and, as Keynes himself argued, the possibilities for reducing unit costs through further increases in capital intensity are at any time quite limited—that is, the optimum $K/y$ ratio is little effected by moderate changes in $r$.

But the importance of financial considerations may exceed the traditional concern with the rate of interest. The emphasis on the interest rate as an investment determinant essentially assumes a nearly perfect capital market. In such a market, the cost which any firm must pay to acquire outside funds is much the same as the return which an individual or firm with excess funds can obtain by lending his excess. But suppose this is not the case.[22] Suppose that the true cost of outside funds substantially exceeds the "market rate of interest." Then the opportunity cost of using internally-generated funds (depreciation allowances and retained earnings) is substantially less than the cost of outside funds. Investment in excess of internal funds by rapidly expanding firms will then be justified only if the return exceeds the high cost of outside funds, and this will tend to maintain a marginal rate of return on real capital investment well above the market rate of interest. This means that it is ordinarily more profitable to invest internally generated funds than to lend them, even when external factors may reduce somewhat the return on real capital investment. And even a considerable increase in this rate of return on investment in real assets may not stimulate much greater investment than can be internally financed. This makes investment de-

[22] Imperfections of the capital market may in part be inherent in the nature of specialization and private enterprise; in part also, they may reflect imperfect knowledge, elements of monopoly, or non-economic behavior. We do not discuss them here.

pend in important measure on the volume of internally-generated funds.[23]

This emphasis on the availability of internal funds was introduced above, on pages 337–339, in connection with the hypothesis that investment was a function of the level of income. The reader should refer back to those pages for a further exposition of this idea.

The theory that investment depends (for financial reasons) on income, however, contained two hypotheses. The first hypothesis was that, with an imperfect capital market, investment depends significantly upon the flow of depreciation allowances and retained earnings. The second and quite separate hypothesis was that the volume of such internal funds is a function of the level of national income. The reasoning in support of the second hypothesis was that the volume of profits fluctuates sensitively with changes in total output. Since dividends tend to be stable over time (responding only slowly and partially to rising or falling profits), the volume of retained earnings is an even more sensitive reflector of business conditions, as measured, e.g., by national income.

Duesenberry, however, suggests a different hypothesis.[24] It is that profits $(\pi)$ depend positively on national income (as above), but negatively on the stock of capital, or, in a linear version:

$$(1) \qquad \pi_t = ay_t - bK_t$$

or

$$(1a) \qquad \pi_t = ay_{t-1} - bK_{t-1}$$

If dividends depend positively both on profits and previously retained earnings, then it can be seen that retained earnings (and thus investment) depend in a complicated way upon income (positively) and upon capital stock (negatively). Simplifying greatly the lag structure, Duesenberry arrives at the following basic investment equation:

$$(2) \qquad i_t = ay_{t-1} - \beta K_{t-1}$$

The above investment theory can thus be derived from purely financial considerations.[25] But it is instructive to recognize that such a theory is extremely similar in form, if not in derivation, to investment theories

---

[23] There is much evidence in partial support of this hypothesis. For example, see J. Meyer and E. Kuh, *The Investment Decision* (Harvard University Press, 1957).

[24] *Business Cycles and Economic Growth.*

[25] The form of Dusenberry's own investment equation does not, however, depend solely on financial considerations.

based upon the fundamental idea of the acceleration principle—that of an optimum relationship of capital to output.

Suppose we rewrite the above equation as

$$(3) \qquad\qquad i_t = \beta \left( \frac{\alpha}{\beta} y_{t-1} - K_{t-1} \right)$$

Investment will then be zero when $\alpha/\beta y_{t-1} = K_{t-1}$. We can identify $\alpha/\beta y_{t-1}$ as the optimum capital stock and $\alpha/\beta$ as the optimum capital-to-output ratio. And what is the role of the $\beta$ outside the parentheses? It indicates how rapidly any gap between the optimum stock $(\alpha/\beta y_{t-1})$ and the actual stock $(K_{t-1})$ is exploited. If $\beta$ has a value of .25, it means that investment is at a rate which would make up one quarter of any such gap within a single time period. If $\beta = 1$, we have the case of the strict acceleration principle (with a one-period lag): investment occurs in whatever amount is necessary to raise actual capital stock to its optimum level (of last period).

The simple Goodwin model presented in the last section cannot quite be cast in the form of equation (2); but if we replace the rectangular cost curve in the capital goods industry by a linearly rising supply schedule for capital goods, we can derive exactly this formulation: the extent to which any gap between optimum stock (which depends on income) and actual stock is made up in any one period is proportional to the size of the gap.[26]

Economists have frequently used investment equations like equation (2) in empirical studies, and have derived their hypotheses entirely from "accelerator-type" reasoning—i.e., based essentially upon technological considerations. Investment depends positively on income: given the capital stock you already have, the higher income is the more additional capital you need. Investment depends negatively on the capital stock: at any given level of income, the more capital you already have, the less additional capital you need.

In a sense, then, this investment theory is an extremely general one, comprehending either or both accelerator-type and financial elements, and including as a special case ($\beta = 1$) the strict accelerator.

## SUMMARY

In the foregoing sections we have surveyed several models of the investment process. Here we bring them together for review and comparison.

---

[26] Exactly such a formula is described by Goodwin, on p. 461 of the reference given above.

The simplest theory of investment was introduced in an earlier chapter—that investment, like consumption, depends on the level of income. Our conclusion was, however, that, by itself, this theory seemed inadequate to explain many of the most striking features of investment history. In particular, it cannot be used to explain the turning points of the business cycle: high income can only produce high investment, and low income low investment.[27]

The simplest theory considered in the present chapter is that of the acceleration principle, which makes investment depend on the change in income (or consumption). Combined with a lagged consumption function, the simple accelerator produces a model which can generate cyclical fluctuations of income. However, as a technological relationship (often the basis on which it is presented) it involves the entirely implausible requirement that investment must occur (instantaneously) before added output can be forthcoming in response to an increase in demand. But if we break the technological link by introducing a lag, then we convert the acceleration principle into a simple and far from plausible theory of business expectations—namely, the assumption by businessmen that future demand levels will always just equal the present level (no matter how high or low the present level nor how much it may just have changed from preceding levels).

The other major and clearly fatal flaw in the simple accelerator theory is its ignoring of limits on the rate of investment—limits either on disinvestment or upon positive investment. In effect the supply curve for capital goods is taken as infinitely elastic, regardless of the level of demand (and this in the *short run*).

The Goodwin hypothesis marks a great improvement on the simple acceleration principle in this respect. It recognizes limits both on investment and disinvestment—the capacity of the capital goods industry on the one hand, and physical depreciation on the other. Although this makes the theory sharply different from the acceleration principle, it retains the other weakness of the latter. In the Goodwin model, the optimum stock of capital depends on the current level of demand; this implies, again, the assumption by businessmen that present output levels—whatever these may be—will persist in the future. During depressions, businessmen assume that they will continue forever; during booms, the same.

Keynes' theory, which substitutes the idea of an increasing-cost supply schedule for capital goods instead of the capacity concept, is more elegant and complex. It is not for this reason necessarily superior, however. For

[27] Even introduction of a lag in the dependence of $i$ on $y$ cannot create a cyclical movement.

it is to be doubted that a strong systematic relationship exists between output of capital goods and the prices at which these are sold. Perhaps the Goodwin "capacity" concept is not only simpler but also just as realistic. However, the serious shortcoming of the Keynesian investment theory is its ignoring of the "feedback" from current income to the optimum stock of capital. We have argued above that this "feedback" cannot be taken as simple and mechanical, because the link runs via businessmen's expectations, and it is absurd to suppose that businessmen always expect current demand levels to continue.

To be sure, Keynes stressed the importance of businessmen's expectations in the determination of investment. In a way, he even anticipated the criticism presented above against the simple theory of expectations embodied in the acceleration hypothesis (although his analysis was not so directed): he argued specifically that businessmen could not be taken as assuming current levels of demand to persist into the future. But despite some sparkling observations, he provided no theory of how business expectations are formed *and revised*. He stressed only their sensitivity and volatility, and their tendency to sharp and simultaneous revision by many businessmen. In this connection he emphasized (perhaps overemphasized) the importance of the level of share prices as an influence on the investment decisions of entrepreneurs, and showed, quite brilliantly, how this level of prices in an organized stock market is influenced by speculative considerations having little or nothing to do with the "real" business outlook. His Chapter 12 is a classic which every student should read.

About the only systematic element appearing in Keynes' discussion of expectations is an idea with a long history in English business cycle literature.[28] This is the notion that good times breed overoptimism, bad times overpessimism. It should not need to be demonstrated, however, that this idea, *by itself*, cannot explain turning points.

What seems to be one of the greatest gaps in investment theory is the absence of one or several sets of testable hypotheses about how current (and immediately past) income and output levels generate expectations for the future; hypotheses systematic enough to constitute the framework for a useable theory, yet not so simple as to do such violence to reality as is evidently the case with the acceleration hypothesis.

The other element in the Keynesian analysis which is missing in the

[28] It finds its earliest clear expression (in 1867) by John Mills, and its fullest formulation by Pigou. See the discussion of Mills in A. H. Hansen, *Business Cycles and National Income* (Norton, 1951); and A. C. Pigou, *Industrial Fluctuations* (Macmillan, 2nd ed., 1929).

simpler theories so far covered in our summary is the introduction of the rate of interest as a variable in the determination of investment. Although we can introduce the rate of interest as a determinant of the optimum capital-intensity used in accelerator-type models,[29] recent theory has emphasized instead the existence of capital market imperfections, which makes the availability of funds more important than the market rate of interest. If we combine with this the idea that profits depend positively on income and negatively on the capital stock, we come back to something very much like the acceleration-type hypothesis: investment depends positively on income and negatively on the capital stock.

Indeed, in the last analysis, the financial and the acceleration hypotheses may not be as remote in ultimate derivation as we have made them appear. One can argue, in a most general way, that the technological considerations which basically underlie the accelerator model operate not so much as direct technological restraints or spurs to entrepreneurial behavior, but rather, primarily, as determinants of profitable business operations. Although the acceleration principle makes no reference to the price and profit system, this is merely a short-cut: the technological relationships that underlie the accelerator actually guide behavior through their effect on prices and costs and ultimately on profits.

Perhaps the real conflict in investment theory that we have not tried to reconcile is the conflict between theories that stress capital "deepening"—that is, investment which increases the capital-intensity of production; and those that stress capital "widening"—investment which accompanies a growth of total output. Keynes and his Classical predecessors essentially emphasized the former. Modern theory, in its concern with growing economies, has stressed the latter. Keynes and most pre-Keynesians saw investment as a means of using more capital to produce the same output—the substitution of capital for other factors of production. Post-Keynesian theories stress the adjustment of the capital stock to the growth of total output with no change in capital-intensity.

Yet, at least in a formal way, the simple investment function

$$i = \alpha y - \beta K$$

can be interpreted to include the cases both of widening and of deepening.

On the one hand, we can interpret a fall in $K/y$ as stimulating to investment, because it means that rising demand is getting ahead of productive

[29] This is, in effect, what Hayek tried to do in his several business cycle models, reviewed, e.g., in Haberler, *op.cit.*

capacity—capital widening is now in order. Or a rise in $K/y$, particularly if due to a fall in $y$, depresses investment because it means idle facilities. Yet if we think of $K/y$ as a measure of capital-intensity in the sense of the "degree-of-roundaboutness" of productive techniques, our function above gives the Keynesian result that the higher the existing capital-intensity, the less the opportunities for further investment (i.e., for further increases in $K/y$).

Thus, in a most general sense, our function

$$i = \alpha y - \beta K$$

can be seen to summarize any or all of the several approaches to investment theory.

We shall continue with the subject of investment theory in the subsequent chapter, in connection with our discussion of economic growth. At this point we need only warn the reader that three very significant elements of investment theory have been deliberately omitted from our discussion. One is the theory of investment in residential housing. Another is the theory of *inventory investment* (although this was touched on in the Appendix to Chapter XIII). In effect, we have concerned ourselves with investment in plant and equipment. The third element, principally relevant to plant and equipment, is *technological change*. We have, in the foregoing, taken technical knowledge as given. Yet it could well be argued that the principal dynamics of investment relate to technological change.

# Economic Growth: The Problem of Capital Accumulation

*Chapter XVIII*

## THE SEVERAL KINDS OF GROWTH

The study of "economic growth" or "development" has become almost a fad in recent years. Colleges and universities have introduced new courses and "institutes" in this subject, books by the dozen have appeared, and conferences, speeches, and articles on growth are continually increasing in number. The topic of "growth" is extremely broad, and, as the term is often used, covers several quite dissimilar kinds of phenomena. We should surely distinguish at least two broad categories, only the second of which concerns us here. Both of these kinds of growth are covered by a single definition—"the case of steadily increasing per capita income." But the primary source of the increase is very different in the two cases.

The first type of "growth" or "development" is that involved in the shift from an "underdeveloped" to a "developed" economy. The second kind is the growth of the already "developed" economy. Obviously, the growth phenomena is, for many economies, a blend of both elements. Still, it is useful to separate them analytically.

The former type of change, which is associated with some of the most pressing social, political, and ideological problems of the modern world, is in many ways far more crucial, and its encouragement or guidance perhaps far more difficult than the second. In many areas of the world vast populations seek to transform their economies overnight to resemble (at least in results) the economies of Western Europe and North

505

America, an accomplishment that social scientists know is impossible, except over a considerable period of time.

This kind of economic development involves many aspects of culture and social organization. One important aspect is the change from non-economic to economic motivation—from habitual or customary ways of behavior, from political or religious dominance in economic affairs, to a rational, goods-centered concept and measurement of personal and social welfare. This accompanies a transformation from simple to complex forms of economic organization—from a subsistence or barter economy to a market economy, using money, and employing credit facilities and a capital market. Almost invariably the process involves the abandonment of primitive, inefficient techniques of production and the adoption of techniques already widely employed elsewhere. To permit these developments, there often must be supplied large bodies of "social capital" in the form of roads, communication facilities, and public works, as well as improved government services. There must also be the acquisition of new skills by the population, not only of the production but of organization, communication, and management. The process, further, almost inevitably involves a relocation of population, as work moves from farms, forests, and mines to urban factories. These and many other basic changes take place along with the capital accumulation, population growth and technological change which are the earmarks of the further growth of an already developed economy.

The latter kind of growth is clearly a far simpler phenomenon, and it is at least plausible to assume that it can be analyzed by purely economic tools. Study of the former type of growth—which involves a transformation of the total culture—demands also the concepts, theories, and insights of sociologist, political scientist, anthropologist, psychologist, engineer, and educator.

We are thus concerned, in this chapter, with the growth of an economy already employing modern productive techniques and highly-developed economic institutions. Its concern is further limited, it may be added, to the essentially free-market, free-enterprise system of organization. Although growth of such an economy can be assumed usually to include population growth and continuing technological change, some recent theoretical models have ignored these two aspects and concentrated only on the accumulation of capital and claims. While this may provide a simple first approximation, it is obviously quite incomplete.

In the following sections we review several simple models of economic growth of the second type, i.e., of a developed economy.

## THE CLASSICAL PROGRESS TOWARD A STATIONARY STATE

In his excellent book *Economic Dynamics*,[1] William Baumol provides a neat summary of what he calls the "magnificent dynamics" of the early Classical school. The basic concern of this model is with the growth of population toward its maximum size—a size at which per capita income is just sufficient to permit the population to reproduce itself at the physical (or cultural) minimum level of subsistence. If the population should be below this size, per capita income would exceed subsistence, permitting a margin which will be divided between (a) payment of wages in excess of subsistence, thus encouraging population growth, and (b) profits in excess of the capitalists' living expenses, a difference which can (and will) be invested to equip the growing population with the necessary tools (or at least to provide the enlarged investment in work-in-process or payrolls associated with a larger working force). In the simplest formulation, in which capital is nothing but a "wages-fund," the accumulation from profits need provide merely the added working capital—i.e., the payrolls (or, in real terms, consumption for workers during the "production period")—associated with a larger employment.

But growth of labor and capital necessarily encounters diminishing returns, owing to the scarcity of natural resources. Thus, with population growth, the margin between production and subsistence steadily narrows and eventually disappears, eliminating both profits and above-subsistence wages. With zero profits, accumulation ceases—the stock of capital is stationary. With wages at subsistence level, population growth also ceases.

The model has many deficiencies. It is sometimes suggested that its predictions have (so far) been prevented from realization because improved technology has continually lifted the production function. The race between technological improvement and diminishing returns has (so far) been won by technology. But one can point to a more crucial short-coming of the model itself which may have contributed to the failure of its predictions. This is a deficiency of its concept of capital. In this model, capital is no more than a "wages-fund," or, at best, consists of the necessary new tools (just like those already in use) for workers newly-added to the labor force. Instead, we know that use of capital in production can provide each worker—old and newly-added— with *more* and *better* tools, enabling him to increase his productivity. Thus, if capital accumulation can occur *at a faster rate* than population

[1] New York, Macmillan, 1951, Chap. 2, pp. 11–19.

growth, we might escape the limits of natural resource capacity, even without technological change, and the stationary state would not be the inevitable goal toward which an economy must progress.

Baumol's presentation of the "magnificent dynamics" is in a figure like 18–1. Line *P* is the economy's aggregate production function, which displays diminishing returns as labor (and its associated capital) are increased. Line *S* shows the necessary volume of subsistence for the labor force, proportional to population. At populations less than *OC*, output can exceed subsistence. For example, at population *OA*, output will be *AN*, and necessary subsistence *AM*. Wages can (and will) be higher than subsistence, with the marginal output *MN* being divided between above-subsistence wage payments to workers and entrepreneurial profits.

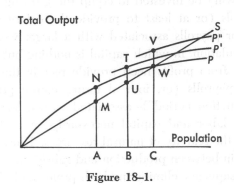

**Figure 18–1.**

The former induce population growth and the latter both permit (i.e., finance) and motivate the investment which provides the growing population with its wages-fund and tools. This process continues until population reaches *OC*, at which point wages cannot exceed subsistence, so population growth ceases; nor are there any profits, so investment ceases.

What we pointed out above as a defect of the model is the possibility that *investment which raises capital per worker* can lift the whole production function, by making each worker more productive. Thus, by the time population has grown to *OB*, a more rapid capital accumulation may have lifted production to *BT* (on schedule *P′*); when population is *OC*, further investment may have raised the production function to *P″*, giving output *CV*; and so on.

However, we shall not pursue further the Classical model. For its principal dynamics relate to the growth of population. Although purely economic factors are important in the explanation of population dynamics, most of us now think that other factors are more important. A model that concentrates exclusively on these two simple relationships—of wages to population growth, and of diminishing aggregate returns to labor (and capital) as a result of the limitation of natural resources—seems not very relevant to Western society.

## KEYNES AND THE STAGNATIONISTS

The second simple model which we shall consider is that of the stagnationists, whose prediction, like that of the Classical model, is a pessimistic one, but for quite different reasons. The foundation of the stagnationist position has already been indicated, in the previous chapter. It was Keynes' view that the marginal productivity of capital schedule was fairly inelastic, at least in the highly developed economies of the West. Thus the growth of capital through investment must ultimately lead toward capital "saturation," a deficiency of investment opportunities relative to full-employment saving, and a necessary decline in income and employment to the extent necessary to eliminate the excess of saving. Figure 18–2 summarizes Keynes' vision of the problem.

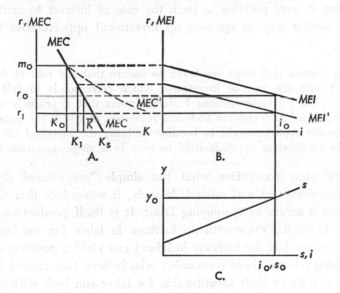

**Figure 18–2.**

Parts A and B of this figure come from the previous chapter (see Fig. 17–6). We add, in part C, a saving schedule, and the determination of income.

With an initial capital stock $K_0$ (part A), the marginal yield on capital $m_0$ exceeds the rate of interest $r_0$. Given the cost schedule of capital goods production (not shown) we have the "marginal efficiency of investment schedule" in part B, with investment initially at $i_0$, producing (part C) income level $y_0$.

Positive investment (as at $i_0$) causes the capital stock to grow from $K_0$ toward the optimum stock $\bar{K}$. At some point the actual stock has reached $K_1$, causing the MEI schedule to have shifted downward to MEI′. This means declining investment and income. This could be avoided only if the rate of interest should simultaneously fall to $r_1$.

Keynes had two pessimistic points to make. (1) The rate of interest will not *automatically* fall to $r_1$, as Classical analysis had assumed. Speculation, based on obsolete expectations, would prevent this result. It would take an active monetary policy to *push* the rate of interest down to its new full employment level. But even more pessimistic was the next point: (2) If the MEC schedule looks like the solid curve in part A, and this is how Keynes thought it looked, there were limits to how long income could be supported even by a policy of progressive reduction of the rate of interest. When the capital stock reached $K_s$ (assuming it were possible to push the rate of interest to zero), there was no further way of opening up investment opportunities to offset saving.

Let us assume that steps are taken to ensure that the rate of interest is consistent with the rate of investment which corresponds to full employment. . . . On such assumptions I should guess that a properly run community equipped with modern technical resources, of which the population is not increasing rapidly, ought to be able to bring the marginal efficiency of capital in equilibrium approximately to zero in a single generation.[2]

Keynes' view recognizes what the simple "magnificent dynamics" model just reviewed had missed. Namely, it recognizes that capital is more than a means of employing labor. It is itself productive, and an increase in capital even with no increase in labor (or an increase in capital greater than the increase in labor) can yield a positive, although diminishing return. Those economists who believe that capital is indefinitely and without limit substitutable for labor can look with optimism on capital accumulation. They visualize an MEC curve like the broken curve of part A of Figure 18–2. In this case, accumulation would, of course, be accompanied by a decline in interest rates, as the marginal yield of capital declined. But the rate would never approach zero; the marginal productivity of capital is always positive regardless of the

[2] *General Theory*, p. 220. See also pp. 217 ff., and 374–77.

amount of capital used. The demand for capital would be infinite at some interest rate above zero.

Keynes saw no reason for this optimism. The best (i.e., cheapest) method of producing anything would involve only a limited use of capital even if use of capital were free of any interest cost. It would take a Rube Goldberg[3] to devise still more capitalistic methods of production, and their inefficiency would require a negative rate of interest to make them pay.

We have already considered the basic error of this Keynesian position. It is a failure to realize that a growth of income—a growth which the very act of investment permits—can prevent capital saturation. There is twice as much capital in use in the United States today as two decades ago. But we are not for that reason necessarily closer to capital saturation than we were then. For the whole economy has grown, too. An economy twice as big in annual output can use twice as much capital. To be sure, if we were trying to use twice as much capital to produce the *same output* as that of two decades ago, we would have to be using capital in ways such that the marginal yield would be very low, perhaps negative. But this is not our problem, and Keynesian stagnation is not the *inevitable result* of capital accumulation. This is not to say that there can never be a problem of too much capital; merely that today's investment (to solve today's full employment problem) does not *necessarily* make it harder to find profitable investment outlets tomorrow, as Keynes frequently argued. What is missing from Keynes' analysis is the "feedback" from income to investment, which is stressed in the acceleration principle, or in the Goodwin model, although in a form that is obviously much too rigid.

As expanded by the stagnationists under the leadership of Hansen, there are other elements in the argument than that just indicated. Hansen stressed the importance of *population growth* and *territorial expansion* as factors opening up new investment outlets. (Note the reference to population growth in the quotation from Keynes on page 510.) Each source of investment outlets seemed to be about exhausted at the time Hansen wrote (1938).[4] Of course, the subsequent "population explosion"

---

[3] Rube Goldberg is a cartoonist who used to design complicated and amusing machines to perform simple tasks—machines having a very high capital investment per unit of output.

[4] Hansen's Presidential address to the American Economic Association in December 1938, "Economic Progress and Declining Population Growth," appeared in the *American Economic Review*, XXIX (March 1939), and is reprinted in *Readings in Business Cycle Theory* (Blakiston, 1944), pp. 366–84. This is the best short statement of the position.

in the United States—which marks a sharp and perhaps unpredictable break in the trend on which Hansen relied—has since eliminated or postponed one strand in the stagnationist argument. However, the causal link from population growth to investment, clear enough for public investment and perhaps even for housing and basic utilities, is far from obvious with respect to private investment in facilities to produce ordinary consumer goods. An increase in population increases *potential* consumption, and thus the potential size of the economy and the capital stock which it can use without reducing the rate of return. But perhaps only if the investment first occurs and incomes rise as a result can the *potential* consumption be translated into actual demand and thus provide a justification for the investment. Because of this deficiency, Hansen's argument that rapid population growth is an *automatic* stimulus to investment (and the cessation of such growth an automatic damper of investment) was never thoroughly convincing.

Other subsidiary strands of the stagnationist position related to (a) an alleged change in the nature of technical innovation, and (b) certain financial developments, both matters which will be briefly discussed in the following chapter.

To the extent that the stagnationist position rested on Keynes' failure to see that the size of the capital stock can only be considered "large" or "small" in relation to the size of the national income, and that it is possible for the two to grow together, the position embodied an analytical error.[5] The stagnationists could argue that capital accumulation necessarily and inevitably leads a wealthy, progressive economy either into stagnation and unemployment or into massive deficit financing, only if it could show reasons why private demand—including investment—must inevitably fail to grow in proportion to productive capacity. On balance, one must conclude that the stagnationists failed to make their case, if this case is understood as arguing the inevitable progress of capital accumulation into capital redundancy. If it argued merely that stagnation is a *possible* state for a wealthy economy, it was arguing little more than Keynes had already demonstrated, quite without reference to long run capital accumulation.

[5] To avoid misunderstanding, it should be made clear that Hansen's position recognized—indeed, it emphasized—growth, along with technological change, as being the primary source of investment opportunities. But this growth was tied essentially to autonomous population growth and territorial expansion. For a clear statement of Hansen's views see pp. 138–40 in his "The *General Theory*" in *The New Economics*, S. Harris, ed. (Knopf, 1947).

## DOMAR'S FORMULATION OF THE PROBLEM OF GROWTH

An understanding of one fundamental relationship between capital accumulation and growth stems perhaps most clearly from the work of Evsey Domar.[6] Domar starts from Keynes' recognition that today's investment competes, at least potentially, not only with yesterday's but with tomorrow's investment. It provides new productive capacity, which, if it is not adequately used, will discourage further investment tomorrow. And if investment declines tomorrow this will increase the surplus of idle capital, making the problem more difficult. But, unlike Keynes, Domar saw that there was nothing inevitable about this outcome. If total demand tomorrow should be sufficiently greater than today's demand, the newly added productive capacity could be fully employed, and there would be room for new investment again tomorrow, creating productive capacity that might in turn find full outlet if only demand would continue to grow day-after-tomorrow.

Domar asked at what rate demand would have to grow—and how might this growth come about—in order to maintain full use of the rising productive capacity provided by capital accumulation. The simple essence of the answer, disregarding a number of subtleties also considered by Domar, can be summarized as in the following paragraphs.

If consumption demand depends on real income, consumer demand will grow if income (output) does, absorbing the larger part of any increase in output. But consumer demand alone cannot supply the entire market for additional output, for the MPC is less than 1; further, consumption's role is entirely passive—consumer demand will grow if income does, but it cannot itself initiate the growth. This active role must be taken by investment. If investment will grow, income will rise and consumer demand will expand. If investment fails to grow, consumer demand, too, will fail to grow. By how much must investment grow in order to use the new capacity added by each period's investment?

Assume a constant marginal propensity to save, $\alpha$. Assume, further, that every dollar's worth of investment makes a net addition to productive capacity (measured in dollars' worth of potential output) which is also roughly constant. Represent this ratio of added capacity to added capital stock by the symbol $\sigma$. Then the necessary rate of growth of investment is a constant, equal to $\alpha\sigma$. The demonstration of this is simple.

[6] Evsey D. Domar, "Expansion and Employment," and "The Problem of Capital Accumulation," *American Economic Review*, 37 (March 1947), 34–55 and 38 (December 1948), 777–94. These and related essays are republished in Doman's *Essays in the Theory of Economic Growth* (Oxford University Press, 1957).

If one dollar's investment adds $\sigma$ dollars of added capacity, then the cumulative investment of any period adds capacity in the amount $\sigma i_t$. The *additional* aggregate demand required tomorrow to use the *added* capacity created by today's investment is the same, i.e., $\sigma i_t$. Of this added capacity, added consumption can account for $(1 - \alpha)\, \sigma i_t$. The balance, $\alpha \sigma i_t$, must represent *additional* investment demand. That is, tomorrow's investment, $i_{t+1}$, must exceed today's, $i_t$, by the added amount $\alpha \sigma i_t$:

$$\Delta i = \alpha \sigma i_t$$

or

$$\frac{\Delta i}{i_t} = \alpha \sigma$$

Thus, if investment grows at a constant percentage rate, $\alpha \sigma$, productive capacity, although continually growing, will be fully used. On the other hand, if investment should grow, but at a lesser rate, added productive capacity would not be fully utilized; instead, an increasing margin of idle capacity would accumulate. Thus, we have the paradox that if only productive capacity grows fast enough, no idle capacity will develop. But too small a growth of capacity will produce a surplus of capacity.

The above argument can be illustrated by Figures 18–3 and 18–4.

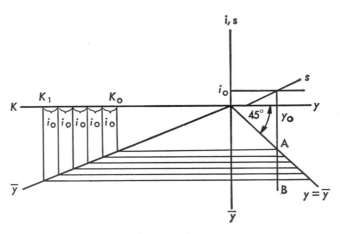

**Figure 18–3.**

In each figure we show the Keynesian saving-investment diagram in the upper right-hand corner: $i$ determines $y$. Along the axis extending to the left are measured quantities of capital. If, in Figure 18–3, we start with $K_0$ and invest the identical amount $i_0$ in successive periods, $K$ will grow toward $K_1$ as shown. In the lower left-hand quadrant we show the relationship of capital stock to productive capacity $\bar{y}$. We have shown capacity as proportional to capital: $\bar{y} = \sigma K$. As seen on the right-hand side, if investment occurs continually at rate $i_0$, income will stay at $y_0$ (upper quadrant), but (lower quadrant) capacity will continually grow. Thus, if the initial situation were one of full use of capacity (point $A$), the growth of idle capacity can be seen as the horizontal distance between the line $AB$ and the 45° line which would correspond to continued full use of capacity.

Presumably, investment could not long stay at $i_0$ with this growth of idle capacity.

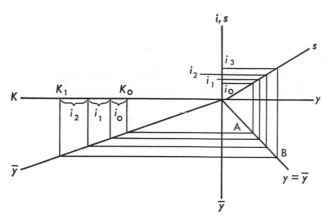

**Figure 18–4.**

In Figure 18–4, investment does not remain at $i_0$, but grows at the rate necessary for output continually to use the capacity provided by previous investment.

We can derive graphically this necessary rate of growth of investment. Compare any two investment rates, e.g., $i_2$ and $i_3$. Call the difference $\Delta i$. The corresponding $\Delta y$ equals $\Delta i$ divided by the slope of the saving schedule

$$\Delta y = \frac{\Delta i}{\alpha}$$

The change in capacity associated with investment at rate $i_2$ is seen as equal to $i_2$ times the slope of the capacity schedule

$$\Delta \bar{y} = i\sigma$$

For there to be equality between output and capacity,

$$\Delta y = \Delta \bar{y}$$

it is clear that

$$\frac{\Delta i}{\alpha} = i\sigma$$

or

$$\frac{\Delta i}{i} = \alpha\sigma$$

The foregoing relationships can also be illustrated by numerical sequences, such as those below. These assume that the marginal propensity to save is .25, and that one dollar's investment will create additional productive capacity of $.10. Thus, σ has a value of .1.

| t<br>Quarter | K<br>Capital<br>Stock | ȳ<br>Capacity<br>output | y<br>Actual<br>output<br>(c + i) | c<br>Consumption<br>(= .75y) | i<br>Investment<br>(exogenous) |
|---|---|---|---|---|---|
| A. Investment grows at the necessary rate (2.5%): | | | | | |
| 1 | $400 | $40 | $40 | $30 | $10 |
| 2 | 410 | 41 | 41 | 30.75 | 10.25 |
| 3 | 420.25 | 42.025 | 42.025 | 31.51875 | 10.50625 |
| 4 | 430.75625 | | | | |
| B. Investment is constant: | | | | | |
| 1 | $400 | $40 | $40 | $30 | $10 |
| 2 | 410 | 41 | 40 | 30 | 10 |
| 3 | 420 | 42 | 40 | 30 | 10 |
| 4 | 430 | | | | |
| C. Investment grows at too slow a rate (1%): | | | | | |
| 1 | $400 | $40 | $40 | $30 | $10 |
| 2 | 410 | 41 | 40.4 | 30.3 | 10.1 |
| 3 | 420.1 | 42.01 | 40.804 | 30.603 | 10.201 |
| 4 | 430.301 | | | | |

It can be seen that if investment grows at a rate of 2.5% (case A), actual output will grow hand-in-hand with capacity. If investment is merely constant (case B), or grows at a slower rate (case C), an increasing margin between capacity and output will develop.

While dealing with numbers, there is a dimensional problem that needs to be mentioned.

The parameter σ (here .1) needs to be understood as a ratio with the dimension of a flow. We compare two dollar flows—two productive capacities measured in terms of potential output ($\bar{y}$). These potential outputs differ in that one represents the output from a larger capital stock than the other. The parameter $\sigma$ is the ratio of the flow difference ($\Delta\bar{y}$) to the stock difference ($\Delta K$ or $i$). The dollar sign appears in both numerator and denominator, and thus cancels. But the time unit in which the flows are expressed (in the numerator) remains in the quotient. In terms of our example, capital stocks of $400 and $410 can produce potential flows of $40 and $41 per quarter; $\sigma$ is equal to ($1 per quarter $\div$ $10) = .1 per quarter. Had $\bar{y}$ been expressed per year, the difference of flows would have been ($164 — 160) = $4, and $\sigma$ would be .4 per year.

We likewise have the dimensional problem of relating investment to capital stock. If we express investment as $10 per quarter, then, in the course of a quarter during which investment has been at this rate, the capital stock will have risen by $10. But even if we had expressed investment as $40 per year or $3.33 per month, in the course of one quarter the capital stock would still have risen by $10, and productive capacity by $1 per quarter (or $4 per year or $.333 per month). Thus we could convert the numbers in the last four columns to rates expressed in terms of another time period, without having to change the numbers for the capital stock.

We need not frame this model in period analysis terms, except for the difficulties of working with rates of growth compounded continuously. For simplicity, therefore, we may assume investment and income flows are at constant rates within each interval (quarter), changing only at the ends (beginnings) of the quarters.

The above dimensional problems relate not only to the Domar model but as well to models subsequently to be discussed. Before proceeding to these further models, we should point out again that Domar did not pretend to provide a theory of growth, but only to indicate one significant aspect of the *problem of growth,* and to compute, on simplified assumptions, what the necessary rate of growth would have to be in order to avoid the accumulation of excess capacity which would inhibit growth. That is, *Domar described an equilibrium growth path,* but indicated little about what might cause the economy to follow or to depart from that path. This equilibrium growth path is defined by the condition that all of the capital provided by previous investment is utilized, yet neither is there any capital shortage.

## HARROD'S GROWTH MODEL

R. F. Harrod had a more ambitious aim. Not only did he recognize the *problem of growth,* but also he tried to provide a theory which explained how steady growth occurred in an economy; and also how, if this growth were interrupted—if growth once diverged from its equilibrium path—the economy might either "explode" into too rapid growth, producing inflation, or cease to grow altogether, producing depression.

Harrod's own presentation [7] leaves certain crucial points quite unclear; consequently, in summarizing his argument, we are necessarily going somewhat beyond his own formulation. Although not all commentators on the Harrod model accept our formulation, we are strengthened in our view by the fact that several distinguished students have reached parallel interpretations.[8]

Whereas Domar had no theory of what investment *would be* (but only what it *must be* for growth to be sustainable), Harrod adopts the acceleration principle as a theory of investment. The aggregate demand for current output can then be expressed by

$$(1) \hspace{3cm} c_t = ay_t$$
$$(2) \hspace{3cm} i_t = b(y_t - y_{t-1})$$

It will be noted that this form of the acceleration theory is the one which (pages 491–492, above) we have characterized as untenable because it implies that capital goods must be produced simultaneously with the increased output which requires their production (including in this increased output the capital goods themselves).

Accepting the above as a theory of aggregate demand for output, we must now consider the aggregate supply of output. The essence of Harrod's view here is that the supply of output must be planned and undertaken in advance of its sale. Consequently, there is the possibility of a divergence between supply and demand.

Harrod's theory about supply is as follows. If producers guessed correctly last period about demand, and their supply just equalled mar-

[7] "An Essay in Dynamic Theory," *Economic Journal* XLIX (March 1939), 14–33, reprinted in *Reading in Business Cycles and National Income,* A. H. Hansen and R. V. Clemence, eds. (Norton, 1953), pp. 200–19, expanded and revised in *Towards a Dynamic Economics* (Macmillan, 1949), esp. pp. 63–100.

[8] Especially S. S. Alexander, "Mr. Harrod's Dynamic Model," *Economic Journal* LX (December 1950), 728–29; and W. J. Baumol *Economic Dynamics* (Macmillan, 1951), pp. 36–54. On the other hand, our interpretation departs widely from that given by, for example, all three of the commentators on Harrod whose articles are reprinted in the Hansen and Clemence *Readings:* D. M. Wright, Joan Robinson, and J. R. Hicks (pp. 220–66).

ket demand, they will, this period, plan to increase their output by the same percentage as they increased it last period. Note that the assumption is not that if they guessed right last period they will repeat *last period's output*, but rather that they will repeat *last period's growth rate of output*. On the other hand if they guessed wrong last period, and produced too much, they will reduce *last period's growth rate of output* (not necessarily last period's output). If they produced too little last period, so that demand exceeded their supply, they will put into effect this period a larger rate of growth of output than last period. Harrod does not specify by how much they will alter last period's growth rate if it turned out to have been incorrect. A general formulation[9] of their behavior might be:

$$(3) \qquad \frac{y_t}{y_{t-1}} = \frac{y_{t-1}}{y_{t-2}} + f(u_t)$$

$$(4) \qquad s_t = c_t + i_t$$

$$(5) \qquad u_t = y_{t-1} - s_{t-1}$$

$$(6) \qquad f(u_t) \gtrless 0 \text{ as } u_t \lessgtr 0$$

where $y$ means total output, $s$ is sales, and $u$ therefore is the unintended addition to inventories. The condition (6) is that, if $u$ is zero, $f(u)$ will be zero—that is, in equation (3), this period's rate of growth of output will equal last period's; while if sales exceeded output ($u_t$ negative), $f(u)$ will be positive and the previous rate of growth of output will be increased. But if output exceeded sales last period ($u_t$ positive), last period's growth rate of output will be reduced.

In order to develop the argument more specifically (and to use numerical examples), we may provide a more specific formulation of equation (3) that is consistent with the general formulation given above. It is

$$(3') \qquad \frac{y_t}{y_{t-1}} = \frac{y_{t-1}}{y_{t-2}} \cdot \frac{s_{t-1}}{y_{t-1}}$$

It can be easily seen that, if last period's sales equalled output, the previous growth rate will be repeated (for the second fraction on the right will be unity); while if sales exceeded output, the previous rate of growth will be increased. This formulation is thus consistent with Harrod's general "law" of producer behavior.[10]

[9] Suggested by S. S. Alexander, *op.cit.*
[10] It should be emphasized that Harrod nowhere provides equation (3) or (3') or any other. However, he does describe the producer behavior summarized in such an equation.

We have, then, a model consisting of the equations of demand, (1) and (2), the equation of output (3′), and the definition of sales (4).

Solving these four equations gives:

(7)
$$\frac{y_t}{y_{t-1}} = (a+b)\frac{y_{t-1}}{y_{t-2}} - b$$

That is, the current growth rate of output in any period depends in linear fashion on the previous period's growth rate of output. This is the general dynamic equation for the Harrod model using (3′) as our formulation of producer behavior.

Suppose, for example, $a = .9$, and $b = 2.1$. Then

$$\frac{y_t}{y_{t-1}} = 3\frac{y_{t-1}}{y_{t-2}} - 2.1$$

If $\frac{y_{t-1}}{y_{t-2}} = 1.02$, $\frac{y_t}{y_{t-1}} = .96$    If $\frac{y_{t-1}}{y_{t-2}} = 1.05$, $\frac{y_t}{y_{t-1}} = 1.05$

If $\frac{y_{t-1}}{y_{t-2}} = 1.04$, $\frac{y_t}{y_{t-1}} = 1.02$    If $\frac{y_{t-1}}{y_{t-2}} = 1.06$, $\frac{y_t}{y_{t-1}} = 1.08$

There is, as seen above, one rate of growth (1.05) which, if it prevailed last period, will prevail again. But if growth in one period is at a lower rate than 1.05, then it will be at a still lower rate in the next period, while if growth in any period exceeds 1.05, it will exceed it by more in the subsequent period. This rate of 1.05 is also the "equilibrium rate" of growth—the growth rate at which sales expectations will always just be satisfied, and production and sales be equal. It is where

$$s_t = y_t$$

or

$$ay_t + b(y_t - y_{t-1}) = y_t$$
$$y_t(1 - a - b) = by_{t-1}$$

(8)
$$\left(\frac{y_t}{y_{t-1}}\right)_E = \frac{b}{a+b-1}$$

That is, the equilibrium growth rate is constant. With the above numerical assumptions, it is a growth rate:

$$\left(\frac{y_t}{y_{t-1}}\right)_E = \frac{2.1}{.9 + 2.1 - 1} = 1.05$$

If the rate of growth happens to diverge even once from its equilibrium path, it will thereafter diverge increasingly. For example, if

$$y_{t-2} = 100,$$

and

$$y_{t-1} = 104$$

then, from equation (7):

$$\frac{y_t}{y_{t-1}} = 3 \cdot \frac{104}{100} - 2.1 = 1.02$$

$$y_t = 1.02 \times 104 = 106.08$$

$$\frac{y_{t+1}}{y_t} = 3 \cdot \frac{106.08}{104} - 2.1 = .96$$

$$y_{t+1} = 106.08 \times .96 = 101.8368$$

$$\frac{y_{t+2}}{y_{t+1}} = 3 \cdot \frac{101.8368}{106.08} - 2.1 = .78$$

$$y_{t+2} = 101.8368 \times .78 = 79.43$$

etc.

Harrod's formulation happens to be in terms of *percentage increments* of growth:

$$\frac{y_t - y_{t-1}}{y_t}$$

and he identifies a "warranted rate" of growth, $G_w$. Our "equilibrium rate" can easily be converted to this form. If

$$\frac{y_t}{y_{t-1}} = \frac{b}{a+b-1}$$

then

$$-\frac{y_{t-1}}{y_t} = \frac{1-a-b}{b}$$

and

$$1 - \frac{y_{t-1}}{y_t} = \frac{1-a-b}{b} + 1$$

or

$$G_w = \frac{y_t - y_{t-1}}{y_t} = \frac{1-a}{b}$$

Harrod uses the marginal propensity to save, s, which is $1 - a$; and the capital coefficient $C$, which is the same as $b$. Thus he writes his formula for the "warranted rate of growth" as

$$G_w = \frac{s}{C} \qquad {}^{11}$$

Before introducing further complications, let us see if we can express in words what this is all about. Harrod's vision is of a growing, expanding economy, in which businessmen are always, in effect, "betting" on growth, but not always sure how much growth to count on. Since they must produce in advance of sale, they have no choice but to make a "bet." Having made their production decisions, the carrying out of these decisions (a) generates consumer incomes, and, through consumer spending, a market for part of the output they have decided to produce; and (b) requires additions to productive capacity in the form of capital goods and extra inventories, the magnitude of which additions depends on the growth of output they have decided (collectively) to provide. (Note that the production increase decision comes first, and the investment decision follows from it.) There is one production decision—i.e., one rate of growth of output, but only one—which is correct, in the sense that it will generate just enough demand to permit them to sell all they have produced. This is the "equilibrium," or "warranted" rate. If the collective "bets" of sellers happen to hit this rate, all is well. Behaving as they do, if they once hit the correct rate of growth it will perpetuate itself.

But if the collective "bets" should involve an output increase which exceeds this warranted rate, demand will be generated which is even greater, so that shortages appear, leading sellers to try a still larger rate of growth, creating still larger shortages, and so on. If producers are "too optimistic," and plan too much growth (more than is "warranted"), their overoptimism makes things turn out even better than their overoptimistic expectation. But if they are insufficiently optimistic, and make production plans involving insufficient growth, their pessimism will be more than confirmed.

---

[11] The resemblance to Domar's formula is apparent when we recognize that Harrod's $C$ is closely related to the reciprocal of Domar's $\sigma$. The latter is the ratio of added capacity (in terms of added output) to added capital stock. The former, $C$, is the ratio of necessary added capital to an output increase. The similarity of the Domar formula and the Harrod formula for the warranted rate of growth has made many confuse the two ideas into one, and to refer casually to the "Harrod-Domar growth model." In fact, as we have seen, the approaches are quite different.

The aspects of all of this that seem particularly implausible are two. In the first place, one empirical generalization on which all of this rests is that producers behave in the manner described by equation (3): *when they find production just right* (in the sense that it can all be sold, but no more could be), *they will repeat last period's growth rate of output.* Harrod has not a word to say in support of this empirical "law," nor any explanation why this particular assumption is more plausible than a much more conventional one, which is that when producers find that their output was "just right," they will repeat that output (not the rate of growth that produced that output). On *a priori* grounds there is no particular reason to prefer either of these versions; and it is a question of fact, not of logic, whether either of these or some other mode of behavior is followed in making production plans.

Second, the notion that production plans come first, and that these, then, through the accelerator, determine investment, quite reverses the more usual (and *a priori* more plausible?) sequence. This holds that investment decisions determine the rate of growth of aggregate demand, which in turn determines output.

Many commentators on the Harrod model (as earlier noted) fail to interpret it as requiring either of these questionable elements. They describe the model as one in which the accelerator determines investment, and (by their silence concerning production decisions) one in which output merely adjusts to demand. That is, they describe the model as

(1)
$$c_t = ay_t$$
(2)
$$i_t = b(y_t - y_{t-1})$$
(9)
$$y_t = c_t + i_t$$

By substitution we get

$$y_t = \frac{b}{a + b - 1} y_{t-1}$$

or

$$\frac{y_t}{y_{t-1}} = \frac{b}{a + b - 1}$$

which is identical with our previous solution for the warranted rate of growth in the Harrod model as we understand it.

But this formulation has none of Harrod's properties of instability. Output is always (on these assumptions) a constant multiple of last

period's output. If, in any one period, output differed from this, there
would be no serious consequence. If $b/(a + b - 1)$ were 1.05, each
period's output (and demand) would always be five per cent above that
of the previous period, whether or not the previous period's output was
five per cent above that of the period before.

Further, this model lacks all plausibility, for it implies perfect forecasting for all concerned. Producers always forecast perfectly their sales,
and produce to meet them; and this forecast of sales includes the sale
of capital goods in an amount determined by the simultaneous growth
of sales. Consumers perfectly forecast their incomes. There is no lag—
no chance for error either in the investor's forecast of production, the
producer's forecast of sales, nor the consumer's forecast of income. If we
agree that this is unrealistic, and introduce a lag in any of these reactions,
except in Harrod's very special way, we get a completely different model,
with none of Harrod's properties.

We might assume that producers can be wrong about sales, and adjust
production with a one period lag. This is the conventional output assumption: when production turns out just right, repeat that production. That is,

$$(1) \qquad\qquad c_t = a y_t$$
$$(2) \qquad\qquad i_t = b(y_t - y_{t-1})$$
$$(3'') \qquad\qquad y_t = s_{t-1}$$
$$(4) \qquad\qquad s_t = c_t + i_t$$

This produces an accelerator model analogous to the one described above
(on pages 485–493), with the same four possible kinds of time paths of
output as shown in Figure 17–8, *and with equilibrium income constant.*

If we either lag consumer behavior so that we substitute instead of (1)

$$(1') \qquad\qquad c_t = a y_{t-1}$$

alternatively, if we lag the accelerator response, so that we substitute,
instead of (2)

$$(2') \qquad\qquad i_t = b(y_{t-1} - y_{t-2})$$

we again get, not Harrod's result of a "warranted" rate of steady growth
with cumulative instability on either side, but an accelerator model permitting various kinds of fluctuations, *but whose equilibrium solution is
always a constant income, not a steadily-growing one.*[12]

---

[12] J. R. Hicks, *A Contribution to the Theory of the Trade Cycle* (Oxford University
Press, 1950), has presented an accelerator model using an investment equation like
(2'), but superimposed upon a steadily growing (at a constant percentage rate) level

We must have Harrod's special output assumption—or some substitute—
to produce his very special results.[13]

In summary, Harrod tried to do considerably more than Domar. Domar
defined a sustainable growth path in which all of the capital provided
by previous investment is utilized, yet without any deficiency of capital.

---

of autonous investment. As a result, the equilibrium income of the economy, instead
of being constant, grows at this same percentage rate. Superimposed on this equilibrium income there are the various possible patterns of accelerator-multiplier interaction typified in Figure 17–8, except that they are tilted upward around the equilibrium path. Hicks (in the article reprinted in the Hansen-Clemence *Readings*)
identifies his equilibrium path with Harrod's warranted growth rate. There seems to
be no justification for this identification. Hicks' equilibrium path of growth arises from
the assumption of growing autonomous investment; Harrod's arises from his assumption that producers will repeat a successful experiment in the growth of planned
production.

[13] It can also be demonstrated that Harrod's unique results depend on his further
assumption of no constants in either consumption or investment functions. If we
insert such constants, equation (7) is altered to become

$$(7') \qquad \frac{y_t}{y_{t-1}} = (a+b)\,\frac{y_{t-1}}{y_{t-2}} - b + \frac{m+n}{y_{t-2}}$$

where $m$ and $n$ are constants in the consumption and investment functions, respectively. This differs from (7) by the inclusion of the final term on the right. Again,
there is an equilibrium growth rate, at which sales $(s_t)$ and output $(y_t)$ are always
equal. It is:

$$(8') \qquad \left(\frac{y_t}{y_{t-1}}\right)_E = \frac{b}{a+b-1} - \frac{m+n}{(a+b-1)y_{t-1}}$$

This is obviously not a constant but rather an increasing rate of growth. But the
actual path of growth (7') cannot possibly coincide with this equilibrium rate. This
can most easily be seen by considering the case in which sales in one period are
assumed to equal production. Under our assumption about producer behavior, an
equality of production and sales will cause producers to repeat last period's growth
rate of output. But in order for sales this period to grow as fast as output, output
must grow at an increasing rate, as equation (8') shows. Or, to put it otherwise, an
equality of sales and production one period will cause producers to repeat last period's
growth of output. But if there are constants in either consumption or investment
functions, aggregate demand (i.e., sales) will grow in smaller proportion than production, creating an excess of production over sales, leading to a reduction in the rate
of growth of production, which will cause an even greater excess next period, and
so on.

The only feasible path of growth of output that can be maintained in Harrod's
system with constants in the demand equations is one of zero growth—a constant
level of income. Harrod remarks that his model (without constants) seems unable
to include the case of zero growth. Actually it does include it; but with no constants,
the no-growth level of income is also a zero income. With constants inserted, the
no-growth level is a positive level, and is the only level at which equilibrium between
sales and production is continuously possible. If income is at the level equal to the
sum of the constants times the multiplier, demand (sales) will equal income (production). If income does not change, accelerator investment remains at zero. If production equaled sales last period with zero growth, producers will repeat zero growth
this period, maintaining the equality of production and sales. If, however, the equilibrium is disturbed, income will never return to its equilibrium level, but will increasingly diverge from it.

Harrod's warranted growth rate also embodies this concept of equilibrium. His use of the accelerator implies this right from the start, for the accelerator (used without lag) necessarily precludes either deficient or surplus capital: investment is made in just the amount that is required to produce each period's output. Rather his warranted growth rate is additionally concerned with *another kind of equilibrium:* that between demand and supply for current output. Harrod assumes, with little apparent foundation, that producers always expect sales to grow by the same per cent as they have been growing, and plan their production in this expectation. Given the capital-to-output ratio (accelerator) and the marginal propensity to consume, there is only one rate of growth of sales that can satisfy this particular kind of expectation. An equilibrium between demand and supply of current output is the crucial element of his growth theory.

## A REINTERPRETATION OF HARROD'S MODEL

There is a reinterpretation of Harrod's model that avoids the features to which we have made primary objection. This interpretation does not require that producers repeat "successful" growth rates of output, but merely that production should follow sales; and it gives the major dynamic role to investment rather than to production decisions. In some ways, this model is closer to the spirit of Domar than of Harrod.

We begin by accepting the basic idea underlying both Domar's and Harrod's (as well as Goodwin's and all accelerator) models—namely, that the size of the capital stock should bear some relationship to output. In its most general form, it can be expressed as

$$\overline{K} = by$$

where $\overline{K}$ is the "optimum" stock of capital. Somehow, investment is designed to push the actual capital stock toward the optimum stock $\overline{K}$. If we ignore (as all of the growth models we have so far considered do ignore) possible limits on the production of capital goods (see above, pages 492–493), then we can assume that each period's investment is in an amount necessary to build the capital stock from $K$ to $\overline{K}$. But there are necessary lags. Suppose that businessmen decide on the investment that would be necessary to bring the capital stock up to what would be, this period, its optimum size. But such investment can only be carried out next period. Then

$$i_t = \overline{K}_{t-1} - K_{t-1}$$

or

(2'') $$i_t = by_{t-1} - K_{t-1}$$

We combine this with a consumption function,

(1) $$c_t = ay_t$$

the assumption that production adjusts at once to demand,

(9) $$y_t = c_t + i_t$$

and the definitional relationship of investment to capital,

(10) $$K_t = K_{t-1} + i_{t-1}$$

By substitution, we can derive

(11) $$y_t = \left(1 + \frac{b}{1-a}\right)(y_{t-1} - y_{t-2})$$

This particular solution has precisely the properties of Harrod's warranted growth model: namely, there exists one rate of growth which, if attained, will perpetuate itself: while if growth exceeds or falls short of this rate it will increasingly diverge. A generalized algebraic solution for the equilibrium growth rate is somewhat complex, and unnecessary for our present purpose. However, the following numerical sequences, which assume $a = .8$ and $b = 2.22$ can be easily followed. First, an example of equilibrium growth, at 10 per cent per period: [14]

| $K$ | $\overline{K}(= 2.22y_t)$ | $y(= 5i_t)$ | $c(= .8y)$ | $i(= \overline{K}_{t-1} - K_{t-1})$ |
|---|---|---|---|---|
| 200 | 222 | 100 | 80 | 20 |
| 220 | 244.2 | 110 | 88 | 22 |
| 242 | 268.62 | 121 | 96.8 | 24.2 |

However, if this growth is interrupted it will not be resumed. For example, suppose that investment in period 2 is not 22 but for some accidental reason 21.5. The subsequent development is a sharp drop in investment and income:

[14] If we assume that the period (i.e., the lag in the investment adjustment) is 2 years, this gives an *annual* growth rate of less than 5 per cent, and a desired ratio of capital to *annual* income of 4.4, not completely beyond the range of plausibility.

| K     | $\overline{K}$ | y      | c     | i        |
|-------|--------|--------|-------|----------|
| 200   | 222    | 100    | 80    | 20       |
| 220   | 238.65 | 107.5  | 86    | 21.5     |
| 241.5 | 207.015| 93.25  | 74.6  | 18.65    |
|       |        |        |       | negative |

On the other hand, if investment is excessive, the system explodes. Suppose investment in period 2 is 22.2 instead of 22:

| K     | $\overline{K}$ | y     | c      | i      |
|-------|---------|-------|--------|--------|
| 200   | 222     | 100   | 80     | 20     |
| 220   | 246.42  | 111   | 88.8   | 22.2   |
| 242.2 | 293.262 | 132.1 | 105.68 | 26.42  |
|       |         |       |        | 51.062 |

The extreme instability shown by these simple examples is, of course, quite unrealistic. Nevertheless, the simple case illustrates the mechanics of the model. How would we describe in words the nature of this growth process?

The above model is one in which steady growth—at an equilibrium rate determined by the capital coefficient and the propensity to save—can keep the optimum stock of capital always just far enough above the actual stock to motivate further investment which will perpetuate steady growth. (Note that the optimum $K/y$ is 2.22, but that in equilibrium growth the actual $K/y$ stays at 2.0.) But should growth once falter, producers will find less pressure on them to increase their productive capacity. Investment will decline, there will be still less pressure on capacity, leading to further declines of investment, and so on.

In this model, the capital coefficient, together with the expected level of output, determines the optimum capital stock. But a given capital stock can always produce more output than that consistent with its optimum utilization. Such extra output, however, leads to pressure to add to capacity—in the attempt to restore the optimum ratio of capital to output.

The sequence of decisions in this model seems, on the whole, somewhat more realistic than in Harrod's model. It starts with investment decisions, based on current utilization of capacity. These determine aggregate demand, which in turn determines output. This is in contrast to Harrod's sequence, which goes from output decisions to aggregate demand to the investment necessary to produce the planned output. The possibility of favorable or unfavorable surprise that leads to instability is here a surprise with respect to the rate of utilization of productive capacity, rather than a surprise with respect to the salability of current output.

Although this sequence puts its emphasis on a process that may seem more realistic, it should be stressed that either model does extreme violence to reality. Either model, in strict form, implies a greatly oversimplified theory of expectations. Harrod's expectational model can be reduced to the notion that if producers find that sales have grown by some particular percentage this period, they will assume that the same rate of growth will occur again. (It is this assumption that leads them to plan to repeat that growth of output.) Our version implies that producers who find that current output (i.e., sales) requires a utilization of capacity beyond its optimum will try to expand capacity to the extent necessary to take care of that (present) rate of sales, presumably in the expectation that future sales will be no greater. In fact, continually growing sales may induce producers to expand capacity not just to the extent necessary to take care of current sales but to take care of an expected further growth of sales.

## DUESENBERRY'S GROWTH MODEL

Recently, James Duesenberry [15] has developed a growth model much more sophisticated and realistic than this simple quasi-Harrodian one, but which operates on the same principle: growth occurs because the actual capital-to-output ratio remains sufficiently far below the optimum ratio to induce sufficient investment to keep income growing as fast (or faster) than capital accumulates. In order to see what is involved, it is first necessary to point out that the above model (like Harrod's original one) has not one, but two, equilibrium growth rates. Given the numerical values which we have assigned above, this second equilibrium "growth" rate is at a fantastic 1,000 per cent per period. Following are some illustrative values for this second equilibrium sequence:

| $K$ | $\overline{K}(= 2.22y_t)$ | $y(= 5i_t)$ | $c(= .8y)$ | $i(= \overline{K}_{t-1} - K_{t-1})$ |
|-----|------|--------|-------|--------|
| 2   | 222    | 100    | 80    | 20     |
| 22  | 2,442  | 1,100  | 880   | 220    |
| 242 | 26,862 | 12,100 | 9,680 | 2,420  |
|     |        |        |       | 26,620 |

---

[15] *Business Cycles and Economic Growth.*

Duesenberry has invented an excellent device for exhibiting the two equilibrium growth rates of this kind of model. He shows that we can calculate and plot the separate growth rates of income and of the capital stock. Our model consisted of the following equations:

(2″)                                            $i_t = by_{t-1} - K_{t-1}$

(1)                                                  $c_t = ay_t$

(9)                                                  $y_t = c_t + i_t$

(10)                                                $K_t = K_{t-1} + i_{t-1}$

From the first three we derive

$$y_t = \frac{b}{1-a} y_{t-1} - \frac{1}{1-a} K_{t-1}$$

From this, we can easily calculate the percentage growth rate of income, as follows:

$$r_y = \frac{y_t - y_{t-1}}{y_{t-1}} = \frac{y_t}{y_{t-1}} - 1 = \frac{b}{1-a} - \frac{1}{1-a} \frac{K_{t-1}}{y_{t-1}} - 1$$

(12)                          $$r_y = \frac{a+b-1}{1-a} - \frac{1}{1-a} \frac{K_{t-1}}{y_{t-1}}$$

Similarly, from equations (10), (9), and (1), we can derive the growth rate of capital:

$$K_t = K_{t-1} + i_{t-1}$$
$$= K_{t-1} + y_{t-1} - ay_{t-1}$$

$$r_k = \frac{K_t - K_{t-1}}{K_{t-1}} = \frac{K_t}{K_{t-1}} - 1 = 1 + (1-a) \frac{y_{t-1}}{K_{t-1}} - 1$$

(13)                              $$r_k = (1-a) \frac{y_{t-1}}{K_{t-1}}$$

Each growth rate is seen to be a function of the (lagged) capital-to-output ratio. If we plot these growth rates in a quadrant in which growth rates are measured vertically and $K_{t-1}/y_{t-1}$ horizontally, it is clear that (12) is a straight line of negative slope, and (13) a rectangular hyperbola, asymptotic to the axes. If these lines interesect at all, they must intersect twice. In fact, with the numerical values we have used, the construction is as appears in Figure 18–5, with the intersections coming at the values indicated.

What is the significance of an intersection of $r_y$ and $r_k$? Obviously, where $r_y = r_k$, capital and income are growing in identical proportion, and therefore, both the subsequent values of $r$ and of $K/y$ will remain unchanged. It is an equilibrium rate of growth.

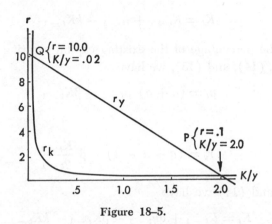

Figure 18–5.

As our first numerical examples (page 528) show, the intersection at $P$ is unstable. For, at levels of $K/y$ less than 2, $r_y$ exceeds $r_k$, income grows faster than capital, further reducing $K/y$, leading to ever-accelerating income growth. For levels of $K/y$ greater than 2, $r_k$ exceeds $r_y$, causing capital to grow faster than income, further increasing $K/y$. Hence, while $P$ represents an equilibrium rate of growth, it is unstable in just the way Harrod described. However, the student can easily verify that the equilibrium growth rate at $Q$ is stable.

Now, what is the relevance of this second equilibrium growth rate? None, directly. But suppose, following Duesenberry, that we build numerous stabilizers into our model, a few of which are as follows:

(a) When $bY_{t-1} > K_{t-1}$ assume that only a fraction of the "gap" is made up at any one time; i.e., put the investment equation in the form

(14) $$i_t = \alpha y_{t-1} - \beta K_{t-1} \, ^{16}$$

where $\alpha/\beta$ is the optimum capital-to-output ratio, but where $\beta$ is less than one.

(b) Introduce a lag in the consumption function, making it

(15) $$c_t = a y_{t-1}$$

(or, in a more complex version,

16 See pp. 499–500.

(15′)                          $c_t = a y_{t-1} + b c_{t-1} + d K_{t-1})$

(c) Introduce depreciation explicitly

(16)                          $K_t = K_{t-1} + i_{t-1} - k K_{t-1}$

where $k$ is the percentage of the existing capital expiring in any period.
From (9), (14), and (15), we have

$$y_t = (a+\alpha) \; y_{t-1} - \beta K_{t-1}$$

or

(17)                          $$r_y = (a+\alpha-1) - \beta \, \frac{K_{t-1}}{y_{t-1}}$$

From (16) and (14) we have

$$K_t = K_{t-1} + a y_{t-1} - \beta K_{t-1} - k K_{t-1}$$
$$= a y_{t-1} + (1 - \beta - k) \; K_{t-1}$$

or

(18)                          $$r_k = a \, \frac{y_{t-1}}{K_{t-1}} - (\beta + k)$$

Again, (17) is a straight line of negative slope and (18) a hyperbola,
asymptotic to the vertical axis and to $-(\beta + k)$. If the two lines intersect—i.e., if there exists any equilibrium rate of growth—they will intersect
twice. Again, one of these intersections (the one corresponding to the
larger $K/y$ and the lower rate of growth) will be unstable and the other
stable.

We can now choose numerical values for our parameters which will
produce plausible rates of growth, *even at the stable intersection.* For
example, assume the following values:

$$\alpha = .4$$
$$\beta = .045$$
$$a = .77$$
$$k = .06$$

The two equilibrium rates of growth are as follows:

at $Q$ (stable equilibrium): $r_y = r_k = .0624$ (approx.)
  equilibrium $K/y = 2.39$ (approx.)

at $P$ (unstable equilibrium): $r_y = r_k = .0024$ (approx.)

equilibrium $K/y = 3.72$ (approx.)

Given the same values, the *optimum* capital-to-output ratio can also be computed by finding at what $K/y$ net investment would be zero, as follows:

$$i - kK = \alpha y - \beta K - kK = 0$$

$$\alpha y = (\beta + k)K$$

$$\frac{K}{y} = \frac{\alpha}{\beta + k} = \frac{.4}{.105} = 3.81$$

With these numbers in mind, we can easily grasp Duesenberry's essential argument.

Suppose that the actual $K/y$ at some particular time is between $P$ and $Q$, e.g., at 3.0. Under these circumstances, $r_y$ (.035) exceeds $r_k$ (.028). Income grows faster than capital. Thus the $K/y$ ratio tends to fall, eventually reaching, if nothing happens, the stable equilibrium value $(K/y = 2.4)$. From time to time, however, the economy is subject to "shocks," which may temporarily reduce $y$, thus raising $K/y$. Unless such shocks reduce income sufficiently that $K/y$ is driven beyond the point of unstable equilibrium $(K/y = 3.7)$, no serious depression will result; and once the effects of the shock are worn off, growth can resume. It is Duesenberry's judgment that most historical depressions represent the effect of shocks which have not been sufficiently serious to raise $K/y$ into the unstable range.

However, should $K/y$ be driven above 3.7 before the shock wore off, capital would then be so abundant that income growth (even if positive) would fall short of capital growth, and adjustments to this would only make the situation worse.

Note again the essential feature of the growth mechanism. In the area of stable growth, *actual* $K/y$ is less than 3.7. Yet the *optimum* $K/y$ (at which $r_k = 0$) was found to be 3.81. That is, growth occurs because the *actual* $K/y$ is kept sufficiently far below the *optimum* to stimulate new investment at a rate high enough for income to grow. That is, growth occurs because, and so long as, a continued capital shortage is maintained.[17]

---

[17] This interpretation is not strictly accurate, because it is technically possible, under some circumstances, for $r_y$ to be positive (and stable) even with $r_k$ negative; or for both $r_y$ and $r_k$ to be negative, yet no major depression to follow. However, the above description fairly conveys, I hope, the substantive, economic *essence* of the Duesenberry model.

Duesenberry does not argue that values of the parameters must inevitably be such that stable growth is possible—indeed, at some points he seems to suggest that only fortunate developments in technology and rapid population growth have blessed the American economy with the stability properties that he thinks he observes. Essentially what is needed is a reasonably high propensity to consume, protected against income decline by some form of lag, or better, ratchet; and a low sensitivity of investment to a gap between optimum and actual stocks—but not too low: the sum of the marginal (income) propensities to consume plus invest $(a + \alpha)$ must somewhat exceed one or no growth is possible.

Duesenberry's book has much more that is important and relevant to say about both growth and cycles (as well as some things whose relevance and correctness may be challenged). But his fundamental vision of the growth process is essentially new, and it explains some aspects of historical processes that no other theory explains as well.

## SUMMARY

With this we leave the *demand approach to economic growth*. Keynes, Harrod, and Duesenberry were all concerned with the question whether, or under what conditions, a modern economy might generate sufficient aggregate demand to permit continued growth. All were concerned with the role of capital accumulation as a possible inhibitor of growth, but they came up with quite different answers as whether this threat was serious.

Keynes, failing to grasp clearly that growth of demand and output could create investment opportunities for capital "widening," and pessimistic about the possible extent of capital "deepening," saw an inevitable impasse for an economy disposed to save a large fraction of a full-employment income. Capital accumulation might cause it to run out of investment opportunities "within a generation."

Harrod clearly saw the possibilities for widening investments; he built the accelerator (without lag) into his model. This made one particular rate of growth of output self-justifying if it occurred; but it became necessary to provide some mechanism to make it occur, and his mechanism surely leaves something to be desired. In any case, his model was also essentially pessimistic as to steady growth: it was a tightrope from which the slightest slip in either direction was fatal. Of these three, only Duesenberry could be truly optimistic about growth. Given the right set of parameters an economy might well grow in a way which was proof against all but the most serious shocks, by staying always sufficiently far behind its optimum capital requirements that even a considerable reduction of income would find capital still not redundant but scarce.

Yet despite their differences, all three approached the growth problem from the demand side. Output, and its ability to grow, were seen to be limited by aggregate demand. The problem of growth is the problem of demand.

In the first sections of the next chapter, we return, in effect, to the simpler problem posed by Domar: what kind of a rate of growth of demand (if it did occur) would fully utilize an economy's growing productive facilities? We do not worry about demand. Either we assume that it is naturally buoyant, or that government can make it so. The important question then is, how fast does capacity grow? But now, for the first time, we are prepared to recognize that an economy's productive capacity depends on something more than just the size of its capital stock.

*Chapter XIX*

## FULL USE OF A GROWING LABOR SUPPLY

The "magnificent dynamics" of the Classical economists, summarized earlier, found the essence of growth in a growing labor force. Capital's role was purely subsidiary: it was seen as necessary to provide (as a minimum) the "wages fund" to employ a growing population, or to equip it with the tools necessary for its employment. Population growth entered into Keynesian stagnationist thinking also, but as a factor influencing aggregate demand rather than as providing a growing labor force to help produce a growing output. Domar and Harrod seem to have ignored labor force growth altogether.

Actually, this element is not absent from Harrod's analysis. For Harrod described another rate of growth besides his "warranted rate." He called it the "natural rate" and defined it as follows: [1]

The maximum rate of growth allowed by the increase in population, accumulation of capital, technological improvement and the work/leisure preference schedule, supposing that there is always full employment.

This "natural rate" of growth presumably sets a limit on the actual growth rate. And if this natural rate were less than the warranted rate, even if equilibrium could be maintained along the warranted path, it must eventually collide with the limit imposed by the natural rate, with

---

[1] Hansen-Clemence *Readings*, p. 216. Domar ("The Problem of Capital Accumulation") also refers to something of the same kind, when he talks of the "can" as opposed to the "will" of growth.

presumably serious consequences. For if growth of output were limited by a full employment (of labor) ceiling,[2] the accelerator would then generate less investment, aggregate demand would fall, and when output likewise declined, the accelerator would generate negative investment.

Now, however, we are no longer worrying about the *demand* for aggregate output, but rather concentrating attention on the ability of the economy to produce. We see what appears to be a dual limitation on output. One arises from the size of the stock of available capital equipment, the other from the available supply of labor. This dualism, first brought into growth discussion by Harrod's contrast of the warranted and natural rates of growth, stimulated subsequent contributions by other economists.

Daniel Hamberg, for example, suggested that we identify two alternative equilibrium growth paths.[3] One is the equilibrium path (Domar's) which would fully use the existing (but growing) plant capacity provided by past capital investment. The second is the equilibrium path which would fully use the existing (but typically growing) labor supply. He pointed out that there is no reason to suppose that one rate of growth of output would simultaneously fully utilize both factors.

We assume that our existing technology involves some (constant) capital-to-output ratio $(K/y)$. If this is so, then, once capacity is fully utilized, output can grow only in strict proportion to the further growth of the capital stock. But this technology also involves some (constant) labor-to-output ratio $(L/y)$. Once the labor supply is fully utilized, output can then grow only in strict proportion to the growth of the supply of labor. These two rates need not be the same.

For example, suppose that the labor supply were growing at a rate of 1 per cent per year. If there must be strict proportionality between employment and output, output could then grow no faster than 1 per cent per year. But if the population desired to save 10 per cent of a full employment income, and the investment of 10 per cent of income would cause plant capacity to grow by more than 1 per cent per year (say by 4 per cent), investment of 10 per cent of income would quickly create idle capacity, depressing investment, and preventing maintenance of

[2] Although Harrod's definition, quoted above, makes reference to capital accumulation as one of the factors determining the natural rate, this is obviously a mistake; for, through Harrod's accelerator, capital is always provided in the necessary amount for any period's production; nor can the propensity to save be an additional limit on growth in Harrod's model because this, too, enters into the formula for the warranted rate.

[3] "Full Capacity vs. Full Employment Growth," *Quarterly Journal of Economics* LXVI (August 1952), 444–49.

full employment. On the other hand, if population and labor force growth were at 3 per cent per year, and the propensity to save were only 2 per cent at full employment, and if the investment of 2 per cent of income would not permit a 3 per cent growth of plant capacity (but say only 1 per cent growth), maintenance of full-employment would again be impossible, for there would be insufficient plant and equipment to employ the annual labor force increment.

If the propensity to save were freely adjustable, it could fit the requirements of the dual equilibrium, and there would be no problem; but presumably it is not.

Harold Pilvin pointed out, however, that there is something else that might "give" in this situation—namely, the proportions in which capital and labor are combined.[4] Our assumption of a fixed $K/y$ and a fixed $L/y$ implies also a fixed $K/L$—that is, no possibility of substitution of capital for labor or labor for capital. Instead, he suggested, such subsiitutability is, at least within limits, possible.

Suppose, as a first approximation, we represent potential maximum output ($\bar{y}$) as a linear function of both labor and capital, where $L$ and $K$ represent total available capital and labor.

$$\bar{y} = aL + bK$$

This is a production function in which the marginal products of labor and capital—$a$ and $b$—are both constant, and each is independent of the input of the other factor. In other words, there is free substitutability between labor and capital.

We may add a linear saving function

$$s = cy + d$$

where $y$ is actual income (as opposed to $\bar{y}$) and $c$ is the marginal propensity to save.

Given $L$ and $K$, there is a certain level of total capacity, $\bar{y}_0$. Then there is some level of (net) investment, $i_0$, such that $y = \bar{y}$—i.e., the economy is operating at capacity. Assume that this level of investment is positive. This means that the capital stock is growing.

At the end of a period of unit length, the capital stock will have grown by $i_0$. Assume that during the same period $L$ has grown by an amount $\Delta L$. Then the increase in productive capacity is

$$\Delta \bar{y} = a\Delta L + bi_0$$

---

4 "Full Capacity vs. Full Employment Growth," *Quarterly Journal of Economics* LXVII (November 1953), 545–52.

In order for $y$ (i.e., aggregate demand) to grow by this amount, investment must also grow, to $i_1 = i_0 + \Delta i$. The size of this necessary increase of investment is

$$\Delta i = c \Delta y = c \Delta \bar{y}$$

Substituting, we find

$$\Delta i = ac \Delta L + bci_0$$

or

$$\frac{\Delta i}{i_0} = \frac{ac \Delta L}{i_0} + bc$$

This formula says that investment must grow at a (nonconstant) percentage rate which depends on the marginal products of labor and capital ($a$ and $b$), the marginal propensity to save ($c$), and the increment of labor supply ($\Delta L$).

In the special case in which either $\Delta L = 0$ or $a = 0$ (that is, either the labor force fails to grow, or its growth makes no difference in potential production), and in which the marginal product of capital ($b$) is equal to the average product of capital (which is then the inverse of the ratio $K/y$), this formula is exactly the same as Domar's (or Harrod's). The necessary (or equilibrium) rate of growth of investment is the product of the marginal propensity to save and the inverse of the capital coefficient. But in case the labor supply is also increasing, and has a positive marginal product, and if the marginal product of capital (and of labor) is not equal to the average product, the rate of growth necessary for full utilization of both factors is the more complex expression given above.

The aggregate production function that we have used above is at an opposite extreme from that implied in Hamberg's analysis. Hamberg's implied production function is one of fixed proportions among inputs, and between input and output. Graphically, it can be represented as in Figure 19–1.

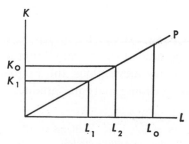

**Figure 19–1.**

Here only the combinations of $K$ and $L$ that lie along the diagonal line $P$ through the origin are possible. If capital is available in amount $K_0$ and labor in amount $L_0$, only $L_2$ of labor can be utilized, and $L_2L_0$ would necessarily be idle. If the factor supplies were $K_0$ and $L_1$, only $K_1$ of capital could be used and $K_1K_0$ would be idle.

The production function

$$y = aL + bK$$

however, has no such restriction. Any point in the quadrant is as possible a combination as any other.

The more conventional assumption lies between these extremes. It implies substitutability between $K$ and $L$, but not with constant marginal products. The more conventional production function can be represented as in part A of Figure 19–2.

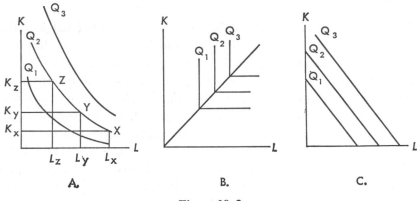

**Figure 19–2.**

In part A output $Q_1$ can be produced with any combination of inputs along "isoquant" $Q_1$; the larger output $Q_2$ with any combination along $Q_2$; etc. Factor substitution is imperfect, however. To move from combination $X$ to combination $Y$ in producing $Q_2$, it is necessary to substitute an added quantity of capital $K_xK_y$ for reduced labor $L_yL_x$. If labor input is further reduced to $L_z$ (the further reduction $L_zL_y$ equals the previous reduction $L_yL_x$), capital input must be increased by $K_yK_z$ (which is larger than $K_xK_y$). It can be shown that the slope of the isoquant at any point is the ratio of the marginal products of the two factors. If this slope changes as we move along the isoquant, this is equivalent to saying that we have declining marginal products as one factor input is increased.[5]

[5] For a fuller explanation of this kind of diagram, the student who is unfamiliar with it should consult any standard intermediate text in price theory, for example, K. Boulding, *Economic Analysis,* 3rd ed. (Harper, 1955), Chap. 34, pp. 733–59.

In contrast, the assumption implied by Hamberg is like part B. Here no substitutability of inputs is possible. The free substitutability implied by our first production function

$$y = aL + bK$$

produces isoquants like those of part C.

If, now, we make the more conventional assumption of part A, how should we represent Pilvin's path of growth involving full employment both of capital and labor?

We can easily adapt the figure used to illustrate the Domar model (Figure 18–4) to fit this case.

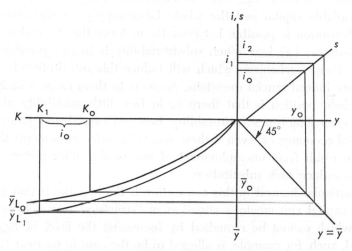

Figure 19–3.

The departure from the earlier figure is in the lower left-hand quadrant. Here we must represent potential output ($\bar{y}$) as a function both of $K$ and of $L$. Production function $\bar{y}_{L_0}$ shows how potential output varies with capital input, given labor supply $L_0$. But with a larger labor supply $L_1$, potential output varies along curve $\bar{y}_{L_1}$. Each of these functions shows diminishing marginal returns to capital as it is increased with constant labor input.

If we start with labor supply $L_0$ and a capital stock $K_0$, potential output is $\bar{y}_0$. For actual output to equal potential output, income must be $y_0$, which, given the saving function, requires investment of $i_0$. Investment at rate $i_0$ for a unit period will raise $K_0$ to $K_1$. If labor supply is unchanged at $L_0$, investment must rise to $i_1$ in order for output to be at the capacity level. But if labor supply has also risen, to $L_1$, the still larger investment of $i_2$ is necessary in order to utilize fully both the capital stock and the labor supply. We can now generalize further by recognizing the possibility of technological change, which will have the effect of shifting the production function—necessarily in such fashion that the new potential output is higher than before for any given combination of $K$ and $L$. (In considering technological change, however, we neglect a number of rather profound problems, including the fact that capital embodied in given instruments may be made obsolete by technological change, and in general the problem of the meaning and measurement of the "quantity" of capital when techniques change.)

Recognition that there always exists some level of investment which can produce sufficient aggregate demand so as fully to utilize both the total available capital and the whole labor supply, on the assumption that substitution is possible between them, turns the discussion to the real questions: (a) how much substitutability is in fact possible? And (b) are there mechanisms which will induce this substitution to occur? These are indeed crucial questions. Answers to them range widely. One widely held position is that there is, in fact, little possibility of short-run or even long-run substitutability between capital and labor in an industrial economy; or, even if there were, the price movements that are likely to result from unemployment of one or the other factor are not likely to induce such substitution.

Of particular interest in this connection is the hypothesis that a shortage of capital can create a situation of "structural unemployment" of labor, which cannot be remedied by increasing the level of aggregate demand. Such, for example, is alleged to be the case in postwar Italy. In the following section this case is briefly examined. Its discussion raises, in rather concrete form, some of the most interesting theoretical issues in modern macroeconomics. We do not attempt to arrive at any "correct" solutions to the Italian case—either on the level of theory or policy. We do not even attempt any accurate or detailed presentation of the "facts" of the case; indeed, we deliberately oversimplify the facts in order to sharpen the theoretical questions that arise.

## STRUCTURAL UNEMPLOYMENT

By 1949–50, extensive war damage to Italian industry and transportation had been essentially repaired, and output was back at prewar levels. Since then, output per capita has grown at a rather steady rate averaging 5 per cent per year, faster than that of the U.S., or that of any major country of Western Europe except West Germany. Yet overt unemployment has continually remained at between 8 and 10 per cent of the labor force, and there is admittedly a large margin of "concealed unemployment"—workers on farms and in small family enterprises who would quickly seek better jobs if jobs could be found. Likewise, Italy's percentage of labor force participation is phenomenally low, and it seems obvious that many potential workers, women particularly, would enter the labor force if there were adequate opportunities for employment.

The explanation for this unemployment held by most Italian economists, and more or less officially accepted by government economic policy, runs in terms of a shortage of capital. Total output is limited by shortages of plant and equipment, which are inadequate to employ the potential labor force. Schematically, $K/y$ is fixed by the techniques employed (and these are the only "efficient" techniques). However, over time, technological change is tending to raise this ratio. Labor requirements are related to total output—i.e., $L/y$ is fixed in the short run, although it has a significant downward trend over time, reflecting growing productivity. Given $K$, $y$ is limited; given $y$, $L$ is limited, and to a figure well below the number who seek jobs (or would seek them if they were available). And the number seeking jobs is continuing to rise as a result of population growth. Thus the only solution to unemployment is an extremely rapid growth in $K$.

Knowing $K/y$ and its trend, $L/y$ and its trend, and $\Delta L$, we can compute how fast $K$ must grow in order that, by any specific date in the future involuntary unemployment will be eliminated. The "Vanoni plan," more or less officially embodied in government policy, is a calculation showing how unemployment might be eliminated by 1965, through a sufficiently rapid growth of capital.

But capital can grow rapidly enough only by the investment of an exceptionally high percentage of current national income. This means that economic policy (particularly fiscal policy and wage policy) must be directed toward repressing consumption. Investment is already a much higher percentage of national income (20 to 25 per cent of gross product) in Italy than in the United States or many other Western countries; yet it must become an even higher percentage in order to solve the unemployment problem within any reasonable time period.

The Keynesian remedy for unemployment is obviously not applicable in this presumed state of affairs. An increase in aggregate demand (e.g., increased government expenditure, or encouragement of consumption expenditures or exports) would not increase employment, it would only create inflation, because increased demand cannot call forth extra output.

Unemployment is structural, not the result of inadequate demand. What is required to eliminate it is not less but more saving.

Although this prescription for unemployment seems to be just the opposite of Keynes' prescription, actually the two are not inconsistent. No one argues that more saving will create higher employment at once, but in the future. Rather, it is argued that present aggregate demand (consumption plus investment) is adequate to take off the market all that can be produced, and therefore to employ all the workers that can be employed. A substitution *today* of more investment at the expense of less consumption would, however, permit output (and therefore employment) to be greater *tomorrow* than would be the case were consumption not reduced today. Implied by the argument is that investment demand is (at present) practically unlimited, and any reduction of consumption would be more or less automatically offset by increased investment. If this were not so, reduced consumption would reduce output and employment *today,* and it would not make possible larger output and employment *tomorrow,* either.

For this line of argument to be completely valid either one or the other of two propositions must be accepted. The first is that unemployment of labor does not lead to a reduction of the real wage rate, relative to the rate of interest. The second, alternative, proposition is that any such reduction in the cost of labor would not induce any substitution of labor for capital in the production process.

Let us consider the second proposition first. In conventional theory, a reduction in the price of one of two factors of production will induce a substitution of the now cheaper factor for the now more expensive one, because employers attempting to maximize profits will carry the employment of each factor to the point at which its marginal value product equals its price (under pure competition). The simplest graphic representation is of the sort presented in Figure 19–4.

The lines labeled $Q_1$, $Q_2$, etc., are isoquants, each representing some particular quantity of output, and each showing all of the combinations of capital (measured vertically) and labor (measured horizontally) which will produce that output. Isoquant $Q_2$ represents a larger output than $Q_1$, $Q_3$ larger than $Q_2$, etc. Assume, in fact, that these outputs are equally spaced—e.g., that $Q_1 = 10$, $Q_2 = 20$, $Q_3 = 30$, $Q_4 = 40$, $Q_5 = 50$. The way in which the line parallel with the $K$ axis at $L_0$ is cut by the successive isoquants shows how successively larger increments of capital are necessary to achieve given increments of 10 of output—i.e., a diminishing marginal product of capital as capital input is increased with

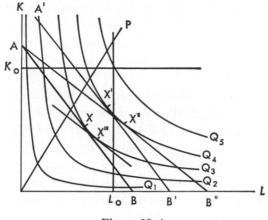

Figure 19–4.

constant labor input. The line $K_0$ shows a diminishing marginal product of labor as labor input is increased with constant capital input. The diagonal line $OP$ shows roughly constant returns to scale (at least between $Q_1$ and $Q_5$), for it shows that successive equal increments of $L$ and $K$ in fixed proportions produce equal increments of output.

Line $AB$ connects all of the combinations of inputs that can be purchased with some particular given sum, at certain prices for the two factors. If this entire sum were spent on purchasing capital, it would buy amount $OA$. If it were all spent on purchasing labor, it would buy $OB$. It will also buy any combination of labor and capital along line $AB$. If this sum is to be spent, it should obviously be used to purchase the combination of labor and capital indicated by $X$; for this is the largest output which this sum spent on factors can achieve. Given the same prices of the two factors, a larger sum would buy any of the input combinations along $A'B'$ (parallel with $AB$). The best combination is obviously $X'$. Whatever the sum to be spent (and this construction does not permit us to determine what that will be), it is obvious that it will involve a combination of factors like $X$ or $X'$—i.e., a point of tangency between the *expenditure line and an isoquant*.[6]

Consider now the impact of a change in one of the factor prices, say, for example, a reduction in the price of labor. This reduction, with no change in the price of capital, produces a new expenditure line, $AB''$, for the expenditure of the initial sum. The new best combination is

[6] It can easily be shown that at this combination, the *ratio* of the factor prices equals the *ratio* of the marginal products. The best *total* amount spent on purchase of factors by a firm under pure competition cannot be shown by this construction; but it involves the *equality* of each factor price and marginal (value) product.

shifted to $X''$, involving a substitution of labor for capital, in the sense that the new combination is more labor intensive than the method used when labor was relatively more expensive. If one were now to produce output $Q_3$ with the new factor prices, the best factor combination would be $X'''$ instead of $X$.

It is obvious that the extent to which a given change in factor prices will produce factor substitution depends on the degree of curvature of the isoquants. If they are very flat, as in part A of Figure 19–5, then a change in relative factor prices will produce a large change in combining proportions. If, as in part B, the isoquant is very sharply bent, only a small change of combining proportions results. If the isoquants are rectangular, no change in relative factor prices can alter the proportions in which factors are combined.

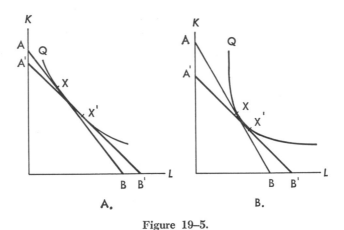

Figure 19–5.

What is alleged in the Italian and in similar cases, is that the isoquants approach the rectangular form (at any given time). Further, over the course of time, technological change is rapidly displacing the isoquants to the left, so that more and more capital is required in order merely to employ a fixed amount of labor, while the labor supply is constantly growing. Consequently, factor price changes can do little to secure full employment of labor; rather, full employment of labor in the reasonably near future is possible only with the most rapid capital accumulation.

The notion that *no* factor substitution is possible (i.e., that the isoquants are perfectly rectangular) is obviously too extreme, and almost no one would so argue. Further, even if combining proportions were perfectly rigid for each product, it would still not be true that the use of factors by the whole economy would have to be in fixed proportions, unless the proportions in which factors were used were identical for each and every product. Through international trade, a country can specialize in the production of those products using the relatively abundant factor, importing those which require relatively large proportions of the scarce factor. A country with abundant labor and scarce capital should have relatively low wages and high interest rates, making prices of domestically produced labor-intensive goods cheap relative to imported goods of this kind, and prices of domestically produced capital-intensive goods expensive relative to imports.

But this same process of indirect factor substitution, through inter-commodity substitution, operates even within the domestic economy, to the extent that labor-intensive and capital-intensive goods compete with each other for the consumer's (or investor's) dollar. If, for example, an excess supply of labor tends to depress wages relative to interest rates, this will reduce the prices of labor-intensive goods relative to prices of those goods using less labor in their production. To the extent that this alteration in relative prices induces substitutions in the purchase of *goods*, it indirectly brings about substitution between factors, even if the proportions in which factors are used in producing each good are absolutely rigid.

Further, in the production of many individual commodities there may be alternative techniques of production, which use factors in different proportions. Given the use of each technique, factor proportions may be fixed; but there may be alternative techniques ("processes") which may become more profitable at other combinations of factor prices. This gives rise to discontinuous factor substitutions as relative prices change—that is, no substitution will be induced until some critical threshold is reached, at which point it pays to introduce an alternative process.

Finally, in some areas of production, e.g., agriculture and many services, more or less continuous factor substitution is surely possible, in the manner envisaged in the conventional continuous isoquants represented in Figure 19–4.

Nevertheless, Eckhaus has argued [7] (with reference to economies like the Italian) that factor supplies may be so far out of balance that even though there are some industries with continuous factor substitution, the supply of one factor may still be redundant at all possible combinations of factor prices. The essence of his argument rests on the possibility that even in the industries of continuous factor substitution, there are limits

[7] "This Factor Proportions Problem in Underdeveloped Areas," *American Economic Review*, XLV (September 1955), 539–65.

to the use of either factor. That is, in agriculture, for instance, a point may be reached at which the marginal product of labor becomes zero. In diagrammatic terms this means that the isoquants at some point become parallel with the $L$ axis. If labor is already used to the point that its marginal product approaches zero, even a real wage rate which approaches zero will not induce appreciable further use of labor in agriculture. And even at prices for agricultural commodities approaching the minimum level at which they cover only the nonlabor costs, consumers would not transfer sufficient consumption expenditure from nonagricultural goods to permit full employment of the excess labor supply. More capital is needed, both in agriculture and in nonagricultural industries, in order for output and employment to expand.

A further complication, certainly in the Italian case, is that introduction of new goods and changes of consumer taste have produced a continuous trend in consumer demand toward products that are highly capital-intensive.

Thus, even if some factor substitution is possible, either direct or indirect, or both, there may still be a real problem of structural unemployment of labor in a capital-poor economy, which cannot be solved either by increasing aggregate demand in the economy or by any socially tolerable decline in the real wage.

This reference to socially-tolerable wage levels brings us back to the second of the two alternative explanations for structural unemployment referred to above, on page 544. We said that factor substitution would fail to occur in the face of surplus labor either because such substitution was not technically feasible, or because unemployment might fail to produce sufficient decline in real wages.

There are several possible types of limits on the decline of real wages. One, which is probably not relevant in Italy but may be in other more primitive economies, arises from the typical family organization of subsistence agriculture. Since family income is shared equally among family members, the income level for a family member will equal the *average* product of labor on the family farm, rather than the *marginal* product. If the *marginal* product of labor in industry is lower than the *average* product on the farm (even though the farm *marginal* product may be zero), there will be no inducement for workers to move from farm to industry even though total output and real income and employment would be thereby increased. This is probably not the case in Italy. The marginal product of labor in industry is surely above the average product in family-organized agriculture. But there are institutional factors which perpetuate a permanent and substantial wage difference between farm and industry.

These institutional supports to real wages in industry arise from trade union and government action, both reflecting a social judgment of what are tolerable, "decent," minimum standards. Social insurance and social services are an important part of this social minimum level of industrial wages. This concept of social minimum is further reflected in automatic formulas tying wage rates to the cost of living. These effectively prevent a substantial reduction of the real wage rate even through inflation.

It is quite natural, therefore, and not necessarily irrational, that primary efforts to solve the problem of structural unemployment should center on efforts to encourage the most rapid possible accumulation of capital. It is obvious that the end result of the elimination of unemployment through forced rapid capital accumulation will be a higher standard of life than one secured primarily through a reduction of real wages so as to encourage the labor-intensive industries. It is interesting and important, however, to note that, to some extent, the same measures promote both types of absorption of the unemployed—a restrictive national wage policy, which tries to keep real wages from advancing as fast as productivity, both (a) tends to repress consumption, setting more resources free for investment, and (b) encourages the use of labor in production to whatever extent its substitution for capital is possible.

## TECHNOLOGICAL CHANGE AND ECONOMIC GROWTH

In most of our previous discussion of growth, we have abstracted from technological change. This reflects a long tradition in economics of abstracting from "changes in the state of the arts." Yet one may well argue that to discuss growth on such assumptions is to miss the essence of the matter. The economics of technological change is just now beginning to receive the serious attention of a number of economists, belatedly following up leads provided by Schumpeter [8] and a few other pioneers.

We make no attempt in this section at systematic development of the

---

[8] J. A. Schumpeter, *The Theory of Economic Development* (Harvard University Press, 1949). Schumpeter's classic thesis, first published in 1911, found the mainspring of economic growth in the activities of entrepreneurs, or innovators. These agents of change were not inventors, but businessmen possessing the peculiar and scarce talent of seeing the possibilities for profit in introducing new methods, new products, new types of organization. Schumpeter also argued that business cycles were a necessary consequence of the process of innovation: that an inherent mechanism required that innovation produce waves of investment. One can reject his explanation of cycles and still agree with most of Schumpeter's doctrine regarding economic growth.

topic. Rather, we merely indicate a few of the ways in which techno-logical change is relevant to growth analysis. One may regard this dis-cussion as serving primarily the purpose of reminding the reader that our treatment omits a whole range of vitally important considerations.

We may think of technological change as affecting both the supply and the demand sides of the growth problem. Technological change of the kind that has economic significance necessarily raises the total pro-ductivity of the economy. An invention is meaningful if it raises output with given input, or lowers input for given output. An innovation may reduce input per unit of output of both labor and capital, though not necessarily in equal proportions. Or it may, of course, lower the required input per unit of output for one factor—e.g., labor—and raise the required input of another—e.g., capital. But the innovation will not be adopted unless the reduction of labor input is greater (in value) than the increase in capital input (or *vice versa*). Thus innovations may be, in an absolute sense, capital-saving but labor-using, labor-using but capital-saving, or both labor-saving and capital-saving (but not both labor-using and capital-using). Even innovations that are *absolutely* capital-saving and labor-saving may be *relatively* capital-using (or labor-using or neutral), while innovations that are absolutely capital-using but labor-saving are *a fortiori* capital-using in a relative sense.

Actually, a great fraction of innovations involves the introduction of new or altered goods. If these yield higher sale return per dollar of com-bined expenditure on factors of production, they can be said to raise output relative to input. And if their production is more or less labor-intensive or capital-intensive than the goods they displace we can also classify such innovations as relatively or absolutely labor-saving, capital-saving, or relatively neutral. Although innovations which change the product offer many difficulties of measurement and evaluation that do not arise in the case of innovations which reduce cost, we shall not consider these problems here.

Considering the effect of technological change in terms of the Domar statement of the growth problem makes clear that technological change which is capital-using in an absolute sense reduces the growth rate of investment necessary for full use of capacity, for it reduces the addition to capacity associated with any given amount of investment; while tech-nological change which is capital-saving increases the necessary rate of growth of investment.[9] This is crudely illustrated by the following se-

---

[9] On the other hand, as noted above, capital-using innovations heighten the prob-lems of structural unemployment in a capital-poor economy.

quences, which assume that the average capital-to-output ratio has been 4/1, while the marginal capital-to-output ratio is 5/1 in case A and 3/1 in case B:

### Case A

| $K$ | $\bar{y}$ $(= .25K_0 + .2\Delta K)$ | $y$ | $c$ $(= .5y + 40)$ | $i$ (necessary for $y = \bar{y}$) |
|---|---|---|---|---|
| 400 | 100 | 100 | 90 | 10 |
| 410 | 102 | 102 | 91 | 11 |

### Case B

| $K$ | $\bar{y}$ $(= .25K_0 + .333\Delta K)$ | $y$ | $c$ | $i$ |
|---|---|---|---|---|
| 400 | 100 | 100 | 90 | 10 |
| 410 | 103.333 | 103.333 | 91.667 | 11.667 |

As part of the "stagnation thesis" of Alvin Hansen, it was suggested that the nature of innovation, which had earlier been predominantly capital-using, had, more recently, become of a capital-saving character. This meant that even greater population growth would be necessary to absorb full-employment saving. Illustrations of recent innovations which were capital-saving could easily enough be found (for example, air transportation would appear to be far less capital-using than railroad transportation). However, atomic energy and the whole movement summarized as "automation" are examples of still more recent innovations that are obviously capital-using. In any case, one cannot characterize the process of innovation by way of examples. Now that we are beginning to acquire some reasonable estimates of the capital stock, it may be possible to discover trends in the nature of past innovation, but this is a complex task.[10]

[10] This cannot be accomplished merely by comparing the historical movement of capital and output, however. For even without any technological change, the accumulation of capital at a faster rate than the growth of labor would tend to raise the $K/\bar{y}$ ratio, and, of course, the average productivity of labor. That is, the data we observe are the result of a number of simultaneous changes, and we must attempt to sort out that part which is due to technological change. Among others, an interesting contribution to this task has been recently made by Robert Solow, "Technical Change and the Aggregate Production Function," *Review of Economics and Statistics,* XXXIX (August 1957), 312–20.

We are even farther away from understanding the nature of the process of technological change itself. Although we are accustomed to treat such change as purely autonomous, actually such change is itself endogenous: the growth of technology is tied up, both as cause and effect, with the whole process of economic, social, and cultural evolution. Some economists have proposed the concept of "induced" technological change, suggesting that its relatively capital-saving or labor-saving character may in part derive from changes in relative factor prices. Although an interesting hypothesis, it seems unlikely that we shall be able to find any stable empirical parameters for such a relationship.

In the present state of our knowledge it seems probable that the best representation of technological change, as it relates to the "supply side" of the growth problem, is as a steady autonomous "trend factor," affecting both capital and labor requirements per unit of output (although not necessarily in equal proportion). This is the usual treatment.[11]

The effect of technological change on the "demand side" of the growth problem has attracted greater attention in the past than its effect on aggregate supply. It is relatively easy to see that major waves of investment demand often have their origin in revolutionary changes in technology. The railroad, electricity, and the automobile, for example, have each been responsible for a great burst of investment, both in the industries directly involved and in subsidiary industries. In part, these waves of investment, extending over several decades, have created boom conditions because they have inserted new forms of production far more capital-intensive than those they have displaced. But even if an innovation is not of the capital-using variety, its rapid introduction is almost sure to stimulate investment, for the alternative forms of production which are displaced are not given time to withdraw their capital by failure to replace as it wears out. Rather, much existing capital is quickly made obsolete, and the investment of the new industry far exceeds disinvestment in the old. Thus we can be quite sure that a technically progressive economy, and one which continually creates new products,

---

[11] For some kinds of problems, however, it may be important to disaggregate projections of capital and labor requirements for growth, taking account of the very different capital and labor requirements of different types of production. If, for example, we are projecting the capital requirements and employment opportunities for a capital-poor economy, it will be important to separate out not only the growth of the more capital-using heavy manufacturing sectors, but also the public utility industries and housing. These industries (housing, in the extreme) have the characterisitic of very high capital-to-output ratios, and very low labor requirements per unit of current output. (We need, of course, to recognize that the construction of the capital goods themselves need not always be highly capital-intensive: a dam, or housing, can be constructed by highly labor-intensive methods.)

will have a higher level of net investment than an economy in which the pace of innovation is more leisurely. The only offset to this is that, in the technically progressive economy, entrepreneurs will tend to expect early obsolescence, and thus to provide depreciation allowances high enough to "write off" their investment in a shorter time than purely physical depreciation rates would suggest. This, of course, reduces reported profits and tends to repress consumption. It seems doubtful, however, that this is a complete offset.

Reference to depreciation allowances requires mention of a further aspect of the growing economy that has received attention in recent writing.[12] Assuming that depreciation is on a straight-line basis, that growth proceeds at a steady rate and with consumption a stable function of income, it is possible to work out certain algebraic relationships between depreciation, replacement, and investment. Assuming stable prices, it can be shown that depreciation allowances will exceed replacement requirements in a growing economy, and that the excess will be the greater the faster the rate of growth and the more durable the assets. Although inflation will reduce the excess, it requires considerable inflation to eliminate it; accelerated depreciation, on the other hand, raises the excess.

The reason for these relationships can easily be understood. In a growing economy, replacement requirements in any year relate to capital goods acquired $m$ years earlier, where $m$ is the average life of capital goods. But during the intervening years, investment has been occurring at a rate in excess of that of $m$ years ago; and depreciation allowances of the current year reflect the larger investment of the years in between.

Recognition of this relationship requires some modification of growth models of Harrod or Domar variety, which we shall not here undertake, and it is of obvious relevance for models in which investment is a function of the net flow of internal funds.

In addition, however, we should now recognize that technological improvement, if it is capital-saving in an absolute sense (whether or not it is relatively capital-saving) will further reduce replacement requirements relative to depreciation allowances.

---

[12] Two articles appearing almost simultaneously contain the basic considerations. See R. Eisner, "Depreciation Allowances, Replacement Requirements and Growth," *American Economic Review*, XLII (December 1952), 820–31, and, for a fuller presentation, E. D. Domar, "Depreciation, Replacement, and Growth," *Economic Journal*, 63 (March 1953), 1–32. See also the latter's "The Case for Accelerated Depreciation," *Quarterly Journal of Economics*, 67 (November 1953), 493–519.

## THE GROWTH OF WEALTH AND CLAIMS

In an earlier section, we recognized that a growing economy is one in which the capital stock steadily accumulates, and considered some of the problems involved as the proportions between accumulating capital, growing labor supply, and output might change in the course of an economy's development.

In the present section we recognize a closely related aspect of growth: namely, that as capital accumulates in the form of physical goods—plant, equipment, and inventories—this accumulation is necessarily matched by a growth of consumer wealth, in the form of claims to the ownership of this physical capital. The growth of total claims includes, however, not only the claims representing ownership of the accumulating physical wealth, but includes also any increment of claims issued by the government, in the form of cash and bonds, which do not necessarily parallel any increase in productive wealth. For example, if a government finances a deficit resulting from war by issuing bonds or money (directly or indirectly), there will be a growth of claims to which no accumulation of productive assets corresponds. On the other hand, government enterprises may build capital facilities, yet pay for them from current tax revenues, thus creating no increment of claims to match the growth of the capital stock. Or, government may consistently run a surplus, thus reducing the total claims outstanding in the hands of the public,[13] while maintaining or increasing the stock of governmental capital goods. What needs to be understood is that a government deficit necessarily produces an increase in the public's claims and a surplus a decrease. A surplus, for example, means that tax receipts exceed expenditures. This surplus might be held in cash, thus reducing the public's money supply; or it might be used to retire debt, thus leaving the money supply unchanged but reducing public holdings of debt. Choices made as to the financing of a deficit or the disposition of a surplus affect the *composition* of claims; but the fact of deficit or surplus governs the change in the combined volume of debt plus money claims. Of course, the *composition* of government claims in the public's hands can be altered without deficit or surplus, and thus with no change in the aggregate of the two kinds of claims, through central bank open-market operations, which exchange debt for money, or *vice versa*. The differences between the two forms of claims are, of course, that one is interest-bearing and the other not; and

---

[13] It should be recalled that here we are including the banking system as part of the "public." For many purposes it is important to treat the banking system as a separate sector, and to be concerned with the stock of claims of particular types in the hands of the *nonbank public*. This is the province of monetary theory.

that one is and the other is not used as a medium of exchange. Except for government bonds like Type E, the price of the one form of claim in terms of the other can fluctuate.

We have already considered, at least in a static context, the effect of changes in the *composition* of a given volume of government claims. A relative increase in money claims tends to lower interest rates; a relative decrease in the volume of money claims raises interest rates. In a later section we shall refer to the changing composition of a growing body of claims; but our first interest is in the effect of changes in the total volume, which includes the two kinds of government claims plus the net volume of private claims.

We may note that there are also several significant classes of private claims, and that the composition of private claims can also change, either along with a change in their aggregate volume, or even independently thereof. For example, capital spending by business can be financed by reinvestment of earnings, thus increasing the equity of the original owners; it can be financed by new share issues, thus bringing in new ownership; it can be financed by bond issues sold to the general public; it can be financed by bank loans. In the last case, we have a simple example of the pyramiding of claims. The business owes the bank, which in turn owes the holders of the new deposits created by the loan (assuming that it is a net new loan). Total *gross* claims in the economy have increased by twice as much as the amount of new investment; but net claims have increased only by the amount of the investment. More complex forms of pyramiding involve financial intermediaries other than banks—e.g., insurance companies. Still, whatever the method of financing private investment, we can be sure that net private claims will grow with the total of net private investment. Gross claims will multiply with the growth of "financial intermediaries." Our first interest, as previously indicated, is in the effects of a growth in the net volume of total claims. Following that, we will have a little to say regarding changes in the composition of claims that may accompany a growth in their volume.

## THE WEALTH EFFECT ON CONSUMPTION: PRIVATE CLAIMS [14]

The possible effect of changes in the volume of wealth on the consumption function was considered above (see page 269) in connection

[14] This section and the next depend heavily upon the author's article "The Wealth-Saving Relationship," *Journal of Political Economy*, LIX (April 1951), 154–61. I am grateful to the University of Chicago Press, publisher of this journal, for permission to use these materials.

with the so-called "Pigou effect." Pigou's interest, like that of others who have considered the matter (such as Patinkin) was with the effect of changing price levels on the real value of a given volume of claims, to the extent that such claims had fixed money prices. But there are other contexts in which the changing volume of claims might influence consumption.

As Patinkin has noted,[15] Keynes was aware of the relationship between assets and saving. In his discussion of the secularly falling marginal efficiency of capital, which, to him, was the prospect for rich, mature economies, Keynes asked what would happen to an economy whose capital stock became so great that further investment yielded no net return even at a zero rate of interest. One possibility was that such an economy would stumble along at a low level of employment, the community becoming "so impoverished that the aggregate of saving has become zero, the positive saving of some individuals or groups being offset by the negative saving of others . . . the standard of life sufficiently miserable to bring saving to zero." [16]

But there is another possibility. "The only alternative position of equilibrium would be given by a situation in which a stock of capital sufficiently great to have a marginal efficiency of zero also represents *an amount of wealth sufficiently great to satiate to the full the aggregate desire on the part of the public to make provision for the future*, even with full employment." [17] Here, clearly, is a recognition that consumption depends not only on income but upon consumer assets as well. In the article referred to in the note on p. 555, the writer has christened this the "Keynes (wealth) effect." It would seem obvious that this effect may have some relevance to the secular growth of an economy in which capital is accumulating.

Yet it can easily be shown that, under the *simplest* circumstances of long-run growth, the dependence of saving on a growing stock of consumer assets would not reduce the propensity to save. Let us suppose that economic growth takes place through capital accumulation but with no change in the "capital coefficient"—the ratio of capital stock to capacity output. This growth in capital and income may or may not involve any new technology, but, if it does, the technological innovations must be "neutral" in the sense that they require no change in the capital coefficient at any given rate of interest. Assume, further, no secular change in the rate of interest. Under these circumstances the capital

[15] See Don Patinkin, "Price Flexibility and Full Employment," *American Economic Review*, XXXVIII (September 1948), 555.
[16] *The General Theory*, pp. 217–18.
[17] *Ibid.*, p. 218 (Italics mine).

stock and the level of capacity output will necessarily grow in the same proportion. Assume, further, that the assets of consumers consist only of claims to ownership of productive physical assets. Then consumer assets and consumer income will necessarily grow in identical proportion. At least, the last statement is correct on the assumption that over the entire period investment incentives are such as to maintain full use of capacity, or some roughly constant percentage of full use. If this happens, the percentage of income that the community desires to save will not be affected by the growth of assets.

To illustrate this conclusion, assume that consumption depends linearly on current income and on accumulated savings. For the numerical examples that follow, assume that the consumption function is

$$c = .8y + .05A$$

where $c$ is consumption, $y$ income, and $A$ accumulated assets. Assume further, as we have indicated, that the accumulated assets of consumers consist only of claims to ownership of productive wealth—i.e., equities in or indebtedness of business firms. Assume, in addition, that there is a constant ratio between the stock of productive capital and the level of full capacity income, such that $2.00 worth of added capital will raise the full-capacity level of income by $1.00. Thus if the accumulated assets of consumers are $200, the productive capital of the economy is also $200, and the level of full-capacity income is $100. Constant prices are assumed throughout.

If investment incentives are such that over a relatively long period investment is sufficient to maintain full use of capacity (or some roughly constant percentage of full capacity), the growth of income and consumer assets might look as they do in lines (years) 1 through 4 of Table 19–1. Although the marginal propensity to consume (income) is

TABLE 19–1.  Assumed Growth with Consumption
Dependent on Assets

| Productive Wealth (= consumer savings) (1) | Full-capacity income (= .5 col. 1) (2) | Actual income (= col. 4 + col. 5) (3) | Consumer expenditures (= .8 col. 3 + .05 col. 1) (4) | Investment expenditures (assumed to grow autonomously) (5) |
|---|---|---|---|---|
| 200 | 100 | 100 | 90 | 10 |
| 210 | 105 | 105 | 94.5 | 10.5 |
| 220.5 | 110.25 | 110.25 | 99.225 | 11.025 |
| 231.525 | 115.7625 | 115.7625 | 104.18225 | 11.57625 |

only .8, and the average propensity is .9, the secular growth of accumulated savings in the same proportion as the growth of income causes
consumption to grow exactly in proportion to income.

And if capital accumulation at the rate necessary to maintain full-use
of capacity should tend to saturate investment opportunities, the asset-
saving relationship appears to offer no rescue. Was Keynes wrong in
suggesting that the effect of assets on saving might rescue an economy
from stagnation?

There does appear to be one possible route through which asset accumulation might have a favorable effect. As we have previously seen,
Keynes considered at length the effects of a falling interest rate on
capital requirements. In accordance with traditional capital theory, falling
interest rates should permit—i.e., make profitable—the use of more
roundabout means of production. As already indicated, we encounter a
fundamental difference of opinion between most Keynesians, who feel
that the opportunities for such added roundaboutness are definitely
limited, and those like Knight who insist they are unlimited. If they are
indeed unlimited, falling interest rates (whether this occurs "naturally"
or must be induced, at least initially, by monetary action to overcome
the obsolete expectations of speculators) are the answer to all problems
of capital accumulation. If, with Keynes, we reject this possibility, falling
interest rates may provide some added investment opportunities but only
some. What is most important to note is that it is *falling* interest rates,
not *low* interest rates, which open up added investment opportunities.
Each fall in the interest rate makes profitable the deepening of capital,
and this deepening, while it proceeds, requires net investment. But corresponding to any given rate of interest there is an optimum stock of
capital (in the absence of innovations, population growth, etc.), and, once
this stock is achieved, no further net investment is required.

But the same is not true of the effect on saving. A deepening of the
capital stock means a growth in the capital stock relative to income, and
consequently a growth in the aggregate of consumer assets relative to
consumer income.[18] Hence, if consumption depends positively on assets
as well as on income, capital-deepening should reduce the propensity
to save. This Keynes appreciated, but it appears to have been largely

[18] Actually, a fall in the rate of interest means a growth of capital values relative
to income even if no "real" deepening occurs. Directly or indirectly, immediately or
ultimately, a fall in the rate of interest will raise the aggregate value of income-
yielding assets relative to income. The rise in the value of bonds would gradually
be wiped out through maturity and refunding, but the same is not true of private
equities.

overlooked in the subsequent discussion of capital accumulation. Whether the "Keynes effect" provides a complete and unassailable final bulwark against stagnation from excessive capital accumulation (in an economy with a high saving propensity) rests essentially on two questions of fact: (1) "How much capital-deepening can be secured by the progressive lowering of the interest rate to its lowest practicable level?" and (2) "How strong is the relationship between assets and income—to what extent does wealth accumulation reduce the desire to save?" Although it seems over-optimistic to conclude that asset accumulation through private investment should inevitably yield an eventual full-employment equilibrium even if all else fails, Keynes was surely correct in suggesting its relevance to the problem.

## THE WEALTH EFFECT ON CONSUMPTION: PUBLIC CLAIMS

Our treatment of a growing volume of claims has so far been confined to the private claims that accompany net private investment. We need now to consider the growth of money claims and government debt. Money claims are of two kinds: the obligations of private banks (formerly largely bank notes, now, in the U.S., at least, primarily demand deposits), and the noninterest-bearing obligations of the government (in which we include the central bank). Bank deposits can constitute a part of the growth of private claims, to the extent that the debts of business are assumed by the banks, which in turn issue their own liabilities in the form of notes or deposits. In this way some fraction of the growing volume of private debt resulting from investment becomes "monetized." [19] Such monetization of private debt can provide a growing economy with the enlarged volume of money needed to accomplish the enlarged volume of transactions, together with the larger cash balances which the public may wish to hold idle for precautionary or speculative purposes as population and income grow. Although such a monetization of private debt can alter the composition of private claims, it cannot increase their total net volume.

Only a growth of government claims (currency and bonds) can inde-

---

[19] One necessary prerequisite of this growth of bank notes or deposit currency is, of course, that banks receive also a growing volume of reserves (in what is now roughly one-fifth the amount of the volume of notes or deposits). In a banking system like that of the U.S., these can be provided in two ways—through monetization of a growing stock of a nonproductive asset, gold; or, more importantly, through the action of the Treasury or central bank. In such a banking system, therefore, growth of bank money depends on the growth of government (or central bank) claims.

pendently add to the volume of total wealth-claims in the economy. (Some of the growth of public debt can, of course, be monetized by the banks, just as with private debt.) Suppose that government continually runs a current deficit, thus adding to the net volume of the public's stock of claims. But if the stock of government claims grows only in equal proportion to the stock of private claims, productive capital, and current output, then, as in the previous case, the fact that consumption depends on wealth as well as income again makes no difference. If, however, government claims grow at a faster rate than current production and the capital stock, there may arise an effect on consumption which we may call the "Lerner effect," after A. P. Lerner, who first explicitly related the growth of government claims to the problem of general economic growth.[20]

Lerner's argument, briefly summarized, was this. Suppose that there exists a shortage of private investment opportunities, so that full-employment requires more or less continuous government deficits. Nevertheless, sooner or later, this situation will be self-correcting. The necessary deficits will have to be financed by creating new claims for the public to hold—either debt or money. Eventually, the growing stock of these claims would sufficiently increase the public's propensity to consume as to eliminate any excess of saving over investment at full-employment income.

From our previous consideration of the case of private investment it should now be clear why, and to what extent, this result might be anticipated. In the case of claim accumulation from private investment, an increase in productive capacity went hand-in-hand with the accumulation of claims. Although the accumulation of claims did raise consumption, it did not raise it relative to full-capacity income, which grew in proportion to the accumulation of productive capital, except in the case in which technological change or a lower interest rate led to an increase in the capital/output ratio. Lerner's case therefore must depend on the fact that government deficits are used nonproductively—that is, fail to raise the level of full-capacity output in the same proportion. Government deficits associated with plant and equipment expenditures by government enterprises would not produce the "Lerner effect"—unless the new enterprises had a higher capital-to-output ratio than the previous ratio for the economy, or unless the government enterprises would operate

[20] See his "The Burden of the National Debt," in *Income, Employment and Public Policy: Essays in Honor of Alvin H. Hansen* (Norton, 1948), pp. 255–75, esp. pp. 264 ff.

at increasing losses. But if government deficit-financing is essentially un-productive—that is, does not add to future productive capacity—the Lerner effect should operate.

In Chapter XII, we implicitly considered the Lerner effect as an aspect of the postwar legacy of wartime deficit finance. Because consumers emerged from the war with an extra accumulation of assets, the consumption function may have been raised above its prewar level, contributing to postwar inflationary pressure. What was missing from the earlier discussion was a clear notion of a productive capacity which depends (in important degree) on the stock of productive capital, and which had not grown during the war.

Consumer assets had grown relative to producer assets, and consumption may thus have risen *relative* to full-capacity income. The war-time savings had made consumers feel wealthy and may have raised their desire to spend, without the productive capacity of the economy having grown in proportion, as it would have done had the savings been "offset" by productive investment rather than unproductive deficits. The legacy of war finance in this model is inflationary quite independently of whether the deficits were financed by money creation or bond sales. Even if bonds were non-marketable, consumers, believing them to be part of their wealth, would behave in the way suggested. Only when the price level rose, and the real value of the accumulated saving fell sufficiently, would the difficulty be surmounted.

All of the above discussion has rested on the assumption that there exists some significant connection between consumer assets and consumer spending, something which is difficult to establish empirically, and can even be disputed on *a priori* grounds. If the effect were insignificant, all of the above would be of little relevance to the growth problem: the accumulation of claims accompanying the growth of production and the deficits of government would have no significant "feedback" to private demand.

However, whether or not the aggregate volume of claims affects consumption spending, it is further possible that changes in the composition of claims may have significant effects. We turn in the next section to a brief discussion of some of these possible composition effects.

## THE STRUCTURE OF CLAIMS

Consideration of the structure of claims in the context of economic growth is only beginning to receive the consideration of economists.

Important classificatory and empirical work has been done by Raymond Goldsmith; [21] and the beginnings of a theoretical approach have been made by J. G. Gurley and E. S. Shaw.[22] But as the latter remarked, "The complexities of a growth model that incorporates the financial as well as the real conditions of growth appear, for the present at least, to defy simple or even systematic formulation." Gurley and Shaw's particular formulations are controversial, and not necessary for an elementary presentation of the problem with which they are concerned. This problem, briefly, is that of adjusting the growing volume of claims to the changing asset preferences of wealth holders, and, as well, to the changing needs and desires of investors in real assets.

Any growth in the net total of claims which accompanies the accumulation of physical assets can take a bewildering variety of forms. Of the varieties of what Gurley and Shaw call "direct debt" or "primary securities," equities of various types, mortgages, and bonds (again of various types) are the outstanding examples. But there are also many forms of "indirect debt" or "financial assets"; these are the obligations of financial intermediaries. These take such forms as bank money, arising from the purchase of "direct debt" by banks in exchange for demand deposits; savings deposits and saving and loan shares; insurance policies; shares of investment trusts or mutual funds; equities in retirement systems; and many others.

In addition, savers may hold "direct debt" issued by governments (ranging from treasury bills to the long-term bonds of local governments); together with government currency (non-interest-bearing government debt). Financial intermediaries also purchase the direct debt of governments, exchanging for it their own, "indirect" obligations.

There are many attributes of these potential forms of wealth-holding that are attractive in various ways to wealth-holders. These attractions consist of liquidity (greatest for currency and deposits, least for low grade bonds); return (ranging from zero on currency and deposits to relatively high and fluctuating returns on speculative shares); stability of return over time; auxiliary services (such as insurance, annuity or

[21] R. W. Goldsmith, *Financial Intermediaries in the American Economy since 1900* (Princeton University Press, 1958).

[22] See especially their article "Financial Aspects of Economic Development," *American Economic Review*, XLV (September 1955), 515–38. See also their "Financial Intermediaries and the Saving-Investment Process," *Journal of Finance*, XI (May 1956), pp. 2557–76; and "The Growth of Debt and Money in the United States, 1800–1950: A Suggested Interpretation." *Review of Economics and Statistics*, XXXIX (August 1957), 250–62.

pension guarantees, or opportunities to participate in management, etc.); and in other ways.

With growth in the total volume of claims to be held, with changes in the public's "taste" as between such aspects as liquidity or security, the desired "mix" of wealth-holdings as among these instruments will almost certainly change (at least at any given set of relative prices of these instruments).

Direct investors have choices among the types of primary securities they may issue to finance investment. Some forms of finance cost more, others less; some involve obligations for steady payment of interest or repayment of principal, others do not; some dilute the existing control of the enterprise, but not others; and so on. With growth in the cumulative total of real investment, changes in institutional forms of business organization, and alterations in the "tastes" of entrepreneurs, the proportions in which the alternative methods of finance are desired to be used may also change.

Changes in both the structure of the demand for assets by wealth holders, and the structure of the supply of claims by direct investors will influence relative asset prices. In addition, there is the changing supply of claims of different types issued by governments. But the price structure of claims is not only the outcome of the demands of wealth holders and the supply by government and direct investors. Sitting in the middle of the market are financial intermediaries of all kinds. In general, their effect is to narrow and moderate price fluctuations arising from changes in the structure of the ultimate demands and supplies. If business wants primarily to issue bonds, but many wealth-holders prefer a diversified holding, which does not fluctuate in capital value, and which promises a steadier if lower return, savings banks may mediate, keeping bond interests rates lower than would be possible if all bonds had to be sold directly to somewhat reluctant individual savers.

All wealth-holders need some, and varying, cash balances. Ordinary business firms cannot issue non-interest bearing debt which serves as money. Commercial banks mediate by taking at least some forms of business debt in exchange for deposit balances. And so on.

The extent of the moderating influence of the intermediaries is, of course, limited by institutional rules, and, in part, by the monetary policies of central banks. Insurance companies could not, until recently, hold shares; banks must keep reserves consisting of the liabilities of the central bank; and so on. New forms of financial intermediaries may arise, or institutional rules may be altered, better to perform the mediating function, but there may be a considerable lag of such response. Intermediaries profit from the existence of rate differentials between the kinds of obligations they hold and those they issue; but there are costs, too, that must be covered. The pursuit of profits by intermediaries, and competition among them, together with the costs of operation (including the risks) of various types of financial intermediaries, the structure of the demand for assets by wealth-holders, and the structure of the supply of claims issued by direct investors and governments, produces the "mix" of assets that we observe, and the relative prices among them. ("Demand" and "supply" in the above sentence should, of course, be interpreted as "schedules.")

Now all of this is by way of framework or background for a theory of growth, and, in itself, provides little insight. Only as we develop further empirical hypotheses can we hope to contribute to growth economics. Some hypotheses are possible and plausible. A very simple one relates to the demand for money in a growing economy. It might be hypothesized that the demand for money grows in proportion to the growth of output. In this case, failure of the central bank to provide an adequate growth of bank reserves would prevent growth in the money supply, leading to a fall in the prices of other claims (rise in the yields necessary to make the public willing to hold the growing supply of them), with possible serious consequences for investment. Gurley and Shaw argue that this is too simple an hypothesis. They suggest that growing income may be accompanied by a more than proportional growth in the demand for other (indirect) obligations of financial intermediaries. They observe that claims against such intermediaries have grown considerably more rapidly than claims against banks. A growing demand for such indirect assets accompanying growing income and wealth, if it is satisfied by the development and expansion of the intermediate financial institutions, may create indirect demand for the debts of real investors sufficient to lower the interest rate, even though the stock of money may be growing less rapidly than income.

Changes in the extent of "external financing" by business (as opposed to reinvestment of earnings and depreciation allowances) will also affect the structure of interest rates. Thus, if enterprises fear dilution of control through new share issues, and are averse to borrowing, and if the number of enterprises does not grow but only their average size, it may be difficult to satisfy the demands of individual savers for a diversified growth of claims except at continually falling interest rates. If falling interest rates should succeed in depressing saving, full employment may be maintained, but the rate of growth is reduced. If it fails to depress saving, unemployment may result. (This assumes that falling interest rates will fail to change the preferences of existing firms for internal financing, and that new firms, taking advantage of the low rates, would still be unable to compete with established firms because of imperfections of competition in the goods markets.)

Something of this sort seems to have been in the minds of the Hansen stagnationist school when they argued that an alleged growing preference for internal financing by business left the savings of individuals "no place to go." Thus, because no investment was forthcoming to match such saving, income would have to be low enough to choke off such saving. If this was to have been a separate and additional reason for stagnation—over and above the presumed shortage of investment opportunities—it had to imply that the structure of financial markets was inadequate to transfer saving, in the forms in which savers wished to make it, into investment, financed in the way in which businessmen wished to finance it. We shall not attempt to evaluate this hypothesis; we present it merely as an example of the kind of hypotheses one may make concerning the role of finance.

Although such speculative hypotheses about the role of finance in economic development are not difficult to invent, it must be admitted that careful empirical support for few such hypotheses has so far been adduced.[23] Thus, we simply do not know whether or to what extent or in what way if any the changing structure of claims—i.e., the "financial problems"—associated with growth in turn affects the growth process.

Perhaps the one generalization which can be best supported is that "innovations" in the financial field have made important "autonomous" contributions to growth.

When financial innovators develop and promote new kinds of indirect financial instruments attractive to wealth-holders, they permit direct investors to float new securities on more favorable terms (lower necessary yields), yet at the same time make saving not only no less attractive but rather even more attractive than before. The *"yield"* to savers can be made to *rise* (measured not—or not merely—in terms of percentage return but more importantly in terms of safety, convenience, liquidity, or desirable services), while at the same time the *cost* to investors *falls*. By promoting both saving and investment, financial institutions promote

---

[23] For a number of such hypotheses, and some controversial implications for monetary and debt management policy, see Gurley and Shaw. *op. cit.*

growth. Even trade union pressure for the development of private pension funds can thus be seen as a possible important promoter of economic growth, on the plausible assumption that saving in the form of pension reserves does not displace other saving by the beneficiaries.

## NONPROPORTIONAL GROWTH

We usually measure economic growth by the size of certain *flow* magnitudes—income, output, or consumption. But a growing economy usually also accumulates certain *stocks*. In this chapter we have considered a few problems involving stock growth. These problems have in common that they involve *nonproportional* accumulation of stocks.

Keynes' vision of the growth process assumed a necessary growth of capital in excess of output growth. In the previous chapter we showed that this kind of nonproportional growth was not inevitable, and we explored some simple growth models in which capital and output (the only two variables considered) might grow together.

In the present chapter, we have raised other possible problems of nonproportional stock accumulation. First, we took into account the growth of the labor force, and, in particular, the possibility that its growth in a particular economy might have outstripped the accumulation of capital, at least in the light of the currently relevant technology. We considered the difficulties of relying upon market changes in real wage rates and interest rates to accomplish the necessary adjustments of the capital-labor ratio. We concluded that there might well be circumstances in which market adjustments were inadequate to preserve a smooth and continuous development involving steady full employment of both capital and labor. Technological change has aided in the adjustment for the wealthier economies, in which capital tends to accumulate faster than labor; but it has complicated the problem for the poorer economies which have faced the opposite problem.

We then briefly considered some aspects of the accumulation of claims, both those private claims associated with the growth of productive capacity, and the government claims which are not so associated. The significance of any conclusions from this analysis is qualified by our ignorance of the extent to which the growth of wealth affects consumption spending. Finally, mention was made of the possible effects of changes in the composition of a growing volume of claims—that is, the nonproportional growth of the various types of claims—and of the role of financial intermediaries in this process.

We are very conscious that we have touched on only a very few facets of the theory of economic growth, and that our allocation of attention to these facets has in all probability been "nonproportional" to their true importance. We have said practically nothing about the basic cultural determinants of growth, including the factors of motivation, values, economic organization, the skills of workers and managers, and ingenuity of innovators and promoters, the willingness to invest resources in basic "pure research" and in education, and a host of other factors. But discussion of these probably belongs more appropriately in a treatment devoted not merely to the economic growth of an already "developed" economy, but as well to the problems of transition from an underdeveloped to a developed economy. As we remarked at the beginning of our discussion of growth economics, these problems are not only more difficult than the ones we have discussed, but require the skills and insights of anthropologist, sociologist, psychologist, historian, educator, and engineer as much as they do of the economist.

# Macroeconomics and Microeconomics

*Chapter XX*

In this final chapter we propose to examine, although in a manner neither complete nor fully systematic, a problem first raised in Chapter I—the problem of how macroeconomic theory is related to micro-economics. In large part this will consist of bringing together observations that have been made in previous chapters. One "practical" conclusion that will be stressed is that a purely macroeconomic approach, while reasonably reliable for economies operating with some "slack," has more severe limitations when it deals with economies operating at or close to "full employment" of their resources, and especially when the limit on aggregate output stems from a shortage of capital rather than labor resources. We begin, however, with some more general matters.

Macroeconomic theory deals with an economy as a whole. The variables on which its interest is focused are aggregates or averages covering a whole economy, extending only to such subdivisions of these aggregates as may be required to explain the behavior of the economy-wide aggregates. The crucial question, of course, is how much "disaggregation" is "required" in order to explain the behavior of the aggregates. If our conclusion were that an extreme degree of disaggregation was required, macroeconomics would lose most of its value, degenerating into a general equilibrium analysis which has little or no useful empirical content. The value of macroeconomics lies precisely in the fact that it purports to have some empirical content: that it can make predictions, not precise, but useful predictions regarding the behavior of such significant variables as total employment and total output and their rates of growth,

568

and the general price level and its movements. "Practitioners" of macro-economics believe that they can make such predictions on the basis of the presumed stability of a reasonably small number of relationships among broad aggregates or subaggregates. The usefulness of macro-economics thus depends on the stability and measurability of these macroeconomic relationships.

Now it might be possible to discover such relationships on a purely empirical basis, simply by trying all possible combinations until those are found which have the best "fit" (in some statistical sense). Actually, the number of possible combinations involving aggregates and subaggregates constructed in various ways is so large that some kind of theory or hypothesis is almost necessary to know what relationships to look for (although the capacity of modern electronic computors is so great that it is becoming almost possible to try all imaginable combinations). Further, we are usually not content with "purely empirical" relationships. We want to understand "why" things are as they are. One reason is that we want to be able to predict the effect of "autonomous" events—such as wars, strikes, changes in foreign supplies or demands, technological changes and changes in "tastes," growth of populations, institutional changes in business structure, and the whole range of government actions undertaken for reasons unconnected with any effort to influence the macroeconomic variables in which we are interested. Another reason is that we want to be able to tinker with the mechanism. If we do not like the results (in terms of unemployment or inflation, or insufficient growth, for example), we may want to consider government measures which would alter the relationships. In order to predict the effect of autonomous changes, including the effects of proposed policies, we must understand directions of causation, and thus know which empirical relationships will remain stable, which will be altered, and how, when something happens or is made to happen.

This means that we need more than a finding that certain relationships have been stable in the past. We want to understand why they have been stable in terms that relate in the last analysis to human choices, technology, or institutional rules. Essentially, this means that we want our macroeconomic relationships to be consistent with, or to be explainable in terms of, microeconomic theory.

A simple example will help clarify our point. We might find that, over a considerable period in which tax rates and the volume of government expenditures had been roughly stable, consumption, investment, and national income varied together in a systematic way. We could interpret the existence of these empirically rather stable relationships to mean that national income determines both (or either) investment and consumption. But if, in fact, investment were determined or even significantly influenced by other variables, and consumption depended on *disposable* income, the previously stable relationships would be upset when tax rates were considerably changed or the volume of government expenditures underwent large alteration.

The relationship between macroeconomics and theories of individual behavior is a two-way street. On the one hand, microeconomic theory should provide the building blocks for our aggregate theories. But macroeconomics may also contribute to microeconomic understanding. If we discover, for example, empirically stable macroeconomic generalizations which appear inconsistent with microeconomic theories, or which relate to aspects of behavior which microeconomics has neglected, macroeconomics may permit us to improve our understanding of individual behavior.

But in order to proceed in either direction—either to develop the macro theories implied by microeconomics, or the micro theories implied by macroeconomic generalization—we need to be aware of some rather technical "problems of aggregation."

## THE PROBLEM OF AGGREGATION

Microeconomic theory has developed on a largely *a priori* basis, resting upon a concept of maximization or optimization of position, together with some presumed physiological or technological relationships of inputs and outputs. Although we may sometimes "test" or measure these relationships on a purely microeconomic basis, by studying individual firms or consumers, most of our data relate to some combinations of units. Thus aggregation problems arise even with respect to the testing of conventional so-called "microeconomic" theories of price and income distribution. Intuitively, we suppose that these problems are the more serious the broader is our aggregation over families, firms, or products.

Aggregation problems are of several orders. One order of problems is statistical in the narrow technical sense. It arises essentially from the fact that there is a certain element of "randomness" or "indeterminacy" in individual behavior and/or a certain inaccuracy in any *measurement* of individual behavior. Our statistical method must make certain (and preferably explicit) assumptions regarding this random element. Although these statistical problems are important, we shall neglect them here, thus, in effect, assuming that all measurement is perfect and that there is no random element in individual behavior. Another statistical

problem which we shall here ignore (although we have briefly discussed one example of it at an earlier point—Chapter X, pages 223–224)
is the question whether and to what extent we can use cross-section relationships as proxies for aggregative relationships.

But apart from these statistical questions, there are conceptual problems in aggregation which we can ignore only with peril.[1]

We recall, first, one simple proposition, introduced in Chapter I, that
the stability of an aggregative relationship between macrovariables
depends on the stability of the composition of our aggregates. To use a
simple example, different from the one used in Chapter I, suppose that
our micro theory should tell us that investment by a firm is a function
(*inter alia*) of its profits. Suppose, however, that we find no relationship
between aggregate investment of a group of firms and the total profits
of the group. Does this disprove the hypothesis? It may not.

Assume, for example, that we have three firms, whose profits are $R_A$,
$R_B$, and $R_C$, and whose investment is $I_A$, $I_B$, and $I_C$. Assume that the
separate investment functions are:

*Case A*

$$I_A = 100 + .1\ R_A$$
$$I_B = -20 + .8\ R_B$$
$$I_C = R_C$$

For each firm, investment is linearly related to profits, with a positive
slope. Suppose that, at two different times, profits are as follows:

| Time 1 | Time 2 |
|---|---|
| $R_A = 100$ | $R_A = 300$ |
| $R_B = 100$ | $R_B = 200$ |
| $R_C = 200$ | $R_C = \ \ \ 0$ |
| $\Sigma R = 400$ | $\Sigma R = 500$ |

Investment will then be:

| Time 1 | Time 2 |
|---|---|
| $I_A = 110$ | $I_A = 130$ |
| $I_B = \ \ 60$ | $I_B = 140$ |
| $I_C = 200$ | $I_C = \ \ \ 0$ |
| $\Sigma I = 370$ | $\Sigma I = 270$ |

[1] For a more general and more sophisticated treatment of aggregation problems
than this (including statistical problems), see H. Theil, *Linear Aggregation of Economic Relations* (North-Holland, 1954). For a review, largely based on Theil's work,
see R. G. D. Allen, *Mathematical Economics* (London: Macmillan, 1959), pp. 694–
724.

$$\frac{\Delta\Sigma I}{\Delta\Sigma R} = \frac{-100}{100} = -1$$

Although aggregate profits have increased, aggregate investment has fallen. Yet it remains true that, for each firm, investment is positively related to profits. The reason, of course, is that the distribution of aggregate profits has radically changed.

One might conclude from this example that if the distribution of the aggregate "independent" variable shifts widely and erratically, we can derive no stable or meaningful macro functions; and, conversely, using aggregative data, we cannot "discover" the "true" micro relationship. This apparent conclusion is, however, subject to several reservations. We obtained the result we did in the previous example partly because the distribution of aggregate profits among firms changed sharply, and partly because the individual micro relationships which we used had widely different slopes. In fact, had the micro slopes been identical, the changing distribution of profits would have made no difference what-soever. This can be seen by considering the following example.

## Case B

$$I_A = \ \ 60 + .5R_A$$
$$I_B = \ \ 10 + .5R_B$$
$$I_C = 100 + .5R_C$$

(These functions have been chosen to produce the same distribution and same total of investment as in case A with the initial distribution of profits.) Our comparison now shows:

| Time 1 | | Time 2 | |
|---|---|---|---|
| $R_A = 100$ | $I_A = 110$ | $R_A = 300$ | $I_A = 210$ |
| $R_B = 100$ | $I_B = \ \ 60$ | $R_B = 200$ | $I_B = 110$ |
| $R_C = 200$ | $I_C = 200$ | $R_C = \ \ \ \ 0$ | $I_C = 100$ |
| $\Sigma R = 400$ | $\Sigma I = 370$ | $\Sigma R = 500$ | $\Sigma I = 420$ |

$$\frac{\Delta\Sigma I}{\Delta\Sigma R} = \frac{50}{100} = .5$$

It will be noted that a change of total profits of 100 produced a change of investment of 50, exactly the marginal relationship which held for each of the three firms. We would get this result for any possible combination of profits having a different sum than at time 1. It should be obvious that even if the slopes of the relationships were not identical for all firms, but were, instead, all close together—ranging, say, between .45 and .55—an increase in aggregate profits would tend to produce an increase in aggregate investment of *roughly* half of the increase of profits, almost no matter how the profits were distributed, although even in this case, the slope of the aggregative relationship could easily fall outside of the .45 to .55 range, and in an extreme case, could even be negative, or in excess of 1.0.

For example, assume:

## Case C

$$I_A = 200 + .45 \; R_A$$
$$I_B = -40 + \phantom{0}.5 \; R_B$$
$$I_C = -20 + .55 \; R_C$$

| Time 1 | | | Time 2 | | |
|---|---|---|---|---|---|
| $R_A = -200$ | $I_A = 110$ | | $R_A = -100$ | $I_A = 155$ | |
| $R_B = \phantom{-}200$ | $I_B = \phantom{0}60$ | | $R_B = \phantom{-}250$ | $I_B = \phantom{0}85$ | |
| $R_C = \phantom{-}400$ | $I_C = 200$ | | $R_C = \phantom{-}350$ | $I_C = 172.5$ | |
| $\Sigma R = \phantom{-}400$ | $\Sigma I = 370$ | | $\Sigma R = \phantom{-}500$ | $\Sigma I = 412.5$ | |

| Time 3 | |
|---|---|
| $R_A = \phantom{-}500$ | $I_A = 425$ |
| $R_B = \phantom{-}100$ | $I_B = \phantom{0}10$ |
| $R_C = -100$ | $I_C = -75$ |
| $\Sigma R = \phantom{-}500$ | $\Sigma I = 360$ |

As between times 1 and 2, the aggregate marginal propensity to invest is .425; but as between times 1 and 3, it is −.1.

Our first conclusion is, then, that aggregation is a legitimate procedure when the behavior of the individual units subject to aggregation is basically similar, and when the distribution of the independent variable does not vary in an excessively violent manner. This suggests, therefore, that it is important, in aggregation, to group together units whose responses can be assumed to be roughly the same, and that aggregations covering widely dissimilar forms of individual behavior may be dangerous, unless we can be sure that the independent variables change in roughly the same way for all units. The latter condition is, of course, often satisfied. If the independent variable is a particular price (or price level) or an interest rate, all firms or consumers may be assumed to experience roughly the same change at any given time. But where the independent variable is an income, we can be less sure. When aggregate disposable income (or profits) rises or falls, the individual recipients may have experience quite different from the average or aggregate. If this is combined with a considerable variety in the individual responses ("micro slopes"), there may be trouble.

Actually, where we deal with large numbers, wide variety of individual income experience may still not be serious, provided that this variety of experience is random—that is, that there is no systematic tendency for individuals experiencing one particular kind of income movement to have response rates (micro slopes) substantially different from the average for other groups. Thus the fact that individual profit experience varies widely is not serious for our presumed investment function unless the firms whose profits (say) fall when aggregate profits rise can be assumed to have significantly different investment responses than other firms.

Suppose, however, that we have reason to believe that changes in the distribution of the independent variable are not merely random, but instead that different subcategories experience changes that are systematically different from the total (or average) movement. For example, if one group of firms should have very stable profits, and another group (which might be concentrated in certain industries, or be typically of a different size than the others) had highly volatile profits, so that changes in aggregate profits were primarily the result of changes in the profits of the latter group, the slope of the macro function would reflect primarily the (possibly untypical) response rates of this group.[2]

This last point can be illuminated by considering in more general fashion the case in which the distribution of the independent variable depends systematically upon its aggregate size. Consider a simple case in which we have three micro relationships for three individual units, as follows:

$$y_a = a_0 + a_1 x_a$$
$$y_b = b_0 + b_1 x_b$$
$$y_c = c_0 + c_1 x_c$$

Assume, further, the following "distribution functions"—i.e., relationships between the movements of the individual independent micro variables ($x_a$, $x_b$, and $x_c$), and the aggregate $x$, which is the sum of the micro variables:

---

[2] Thus Thiel (*op. cit.*), pages 24–6, argues that, because high incomes are more volatile than low incomes, the aggregate marginal propensity to consume will reflect primarily the presumably lower individual MPC's of the high-income families.

$$x_a = A_0 + A_1 \; x$$
$$x_b = B_0 + B_1 \; x$$
$$x_c = C_0 + C_1 \; x$$

We are interested in the relationship between the aggregate dependent variable, $y$ (equal to $y_a + y_b + y_c$) and the aggregate independent variable, $x$.

By simple substitution, we derive the following expression for the dependence of $y$ on $x$:

$$y = (a_0 + b_0 + c_0) + (a_1 A_0 + b_1 B_0 + c_1 C_0) + (a_1 A_1 + b_1 B_1 + c_1 C_1) \; x$$

Examination of this equation shows that, in the general case, the intercept (constant term) of the macro relationship equals the sum of the corresponding micro intercepts (first parentheses), *plus* a weighted sum of the intercepts of the distribution functions, each weighted by the appropriate micro slope (second parentheses). The macro slope (third parentheses) is a weighted average of the individual micro slopes, each weighted by the slope of the appropriate distribution function. (We call it a weighted average rather than a weighted sum, because the sum of the weights—$A_1 + B_1 + C_1$—should equal unity.) Thus the macro function depends, in a fairly complicated way (more complicated, if the number of the independent variables exceeds one) on both the individual corresponding micro functions, and upon the form of the distribution functions.

We can also see that (in this simple case) the macro intercept will equal the sum of the micro intercepts only if the constants in the distribution function are all zero (as would be the case if the percentage distribution of the independent variable were constant). We can further see that the macro slope is a weighted average of the micro slopes, in which the systematically more volatile units have the greatest weight. We can also note that, if the micro slopes are identical ($a_1 = b_1 = c_1$), the weights (that is, the distribution of the independent variable) make no difference. Essentially similar results hold for the case in which either $y$ or $x$ is a fixed-weight index number rather than an aggregate of the corresponding macrovariables.

The general conclusion, that the shape of the macrorelationship reflects both (a) the shapes of the corresponding microrelations, and (b) the systematic elements in the distribution of the independent variables is of considerable importance for macroeconomics. For it means that even where we find a reasonably stable macrorelationship, its future stability may depend upon the continuation of one or more distribution relationships. If changes in population distribution, consumer tastes, business structure, or government policy should alter the distribution relationships, our macrorelation may be altered, even though the corresponding microrelations (that is, the behavior patterns of the individual units) are unchanged. Since most macroeconomic models do not explicitly include distribution functions, changes in the latter can upset predictions based on an assumed stability of the macrofunctions.

As discussed in Chapter XIV, this fact leads many "model-builders" to introduce some significant degree of disaggregation into their models. For example, it may be quite important to disaggregate the consumption function, by considering separately the disposable incomes of wage earners, farmers, independent businessmen, and profit recipients. But this means that the model must then include explanations of the separate income shares of these groups ("distribution functions"). To do this requires explicit consideration of industrial pricing behavior, the movement of wage rates, the special factors influencing farm prices, and so on. Thus, disaggregation of income shares in a macroeconomic income-expenditure model, must introduce matters which are at the heart of microeconomic price and income-distribution theory. It should be noted, of course, that the price and distribution theories needed for such a disaggregated macroeconomic model are themselves highly aggregative in the sense that they must deal not with individual prices, profits, wages, etc., but rather with broad aggregates covering numerous industries, products, firms, and workers. At several points in the preceding chapters we have commented on the weakness of conventional price and income-distribution theories for this purpose.[3] Perhaps we can conclude this phase of the discussion, then, by suggesting that, while it is surely important for the progress of macroeconomics to be able to incorporate explicit theories of pricing and income distribution at least on a broadly aggregative basis, present microeconomic theory does not appear to supply entirely satisfactory hypotheses for this purpose. Progress in macroeconomics thus depends on further progress in the microeconomic theory of prices and distribution of incomes.

## THE CANCELLATION OF RELATIVE PRICE EFFECTS: DEMAND

In the above discussion we have been concerned with aggregation over individual units (firms or families). Although aggregation over

[3] See especially, pages 415–416.

commodities has been implied, no attention has been paid to this aspect. Yet specific attention to aggregation over commodities clarifies another aspect of the relationship between micro and macroeconomics.

Macroeconomic analysis, whether of the Keynesian or of the simpler quantity-theory sort, treats aggregate output (or, perhaps, aggregate output of consumer goods or of investment goods) as though it were a single commodity. It also suggests that it is produced by combining one homogeneous factor of production, labor, with another homogeneous factor, capital. There are perhaps two circumstances in which this treatment might be fully legitimate. One circumstance would be that in which the composition of aggregate output never changed. If a "unit" of aggregate output always consisted of *a* units of commodity A, *b* units of commodity B, and so on, then we might legitimately speak of an aggregate like "total real consumption" as though it were a single good instead of a vast conglomeration of diverse goods and services. The other circumstance in which this procedure might be legitimate would be in the case in which, although the "mix" of products changed, the relative prices of all goods in the mix were perfectly stable, so that the terms at which each commodity or service might be translated, in the market, into any other commodity or service were always the same. In this case, a "dollar's worth of output" (corrected for changes in the absolute level of prices) would seem to have a clear enough meaning.

But neither condition fully obtains, and we need to investigate the consequences of a changing distribution of aggregate output, or of changing terms of exchange between outputs. Although the problem is much broader, we can illustrate it by the case of consumer demand. For this we assume that all consumer units have identical demand patterns, so that problems of aggregation over different income units disappear. But consumers are confronted with opportunities to buy not one single consumption good (or a fixed "mix" of consumption goods); rather they can purchase different commodities, in varying proportions.

Microeconomic theory tells us that the amount of consumer purchases of any commodity is a function of its price, given consumer income and prices of other commodities. A reduction of the price of any commodity (other than an "inferior good") will increase its sales for two reasons: (a) a "substitution effect," and (b) an "income effect." The substitution effect occurs because the price is now lower relative to the prices of other commodities, leading to its substitution (at the margin) for the purchase of other goods. Purchase of this good is increased, while purchases of other goods are reduced. The income effect operates because a price reduction (with constant money income) increases real income. This leads to increased purchases, both of the particular commodity and of all other commodities (except of "inferior goods," in which case the income effect will be negative). Thus the effect of a price reduction on purchases of the particular good is ordinarily positive for both income and substitution reasons. The effect on purchase of other goods will be negative through the substitution effect, but positive through the income effect.

Now it is not difficult to see how the income effect of microeconomic theory is related to the consumption function of macroeconomics. The latter holds that a rise in real income (which can come either through a rise in money income, the price level constant or rising by less; or through a fall in prices, money income constant or falling by less), will increase consumer demand for commodities in general—the amount of the increase in demand for each commodity depending on its individual income elasticity. The aggregate marginal propensity to consume is thus the sum of all of the individual commodity "income effects."

But how is the substitution effect handled in macroeconomic theory? If all individual prices rise or fall in the same proportion as the general price level, then there are no substitution effects to worry about. But suppose prices rise or fall unequally. This will produce substitution effects on the demands for particular commodities. How does it affect aggregate consumer demand?

To keep our treatment of the problem as simple as possible, assume that consumers can buy only two commodities, quantities of which are indicated by $c_a$ and $c_b$, and their prices by $p_a$ and $p_b$. Micro theory then tells us (in a linear approximation) that the following relationships hold:

$$c_a = a_0 + a_1 \frac{Y}{p} + a_2 \frac{p_a}{p_b}$$

$$c_b = b_0 + b_1 \frac{Y}{p} + b_2 \frac{p_b}{p_a}$$

Where $Y$ is total money income, $p$ is the average price level, $a_1$ and $b_1$ are the income coefficients of demand, and $a_2$ and $b_2$ are the coefficients of relative price response. Ruling out inferior goods, we assume that $a_1$ and $b_1$ are each positive (macroeconomic theory adds that their sum is less than one), while $a_2$ and $b_2$ each are negative.

Now we wish to derive an aggregate consumption function, using $c$ as the sum of $c_a + c_b$. By substitution we derive:

$$c = a_0 + b_0 + (a_1 + b_1) \frac{Y}{p} + a_2 \frac{p_a}{p_b} + b_2 \frac{p_b}{p_a}$$

Except for the final two terms, this is the customary Keynesian consumption function. It would appear from this, however, that relative prices should also be included in this aggregate consumption function, unless we could be sure that the sum of the final two terms were constant.

In order to isolate the substitution effect, let us suppose that $p_a$ and $p_b$ both change, but in such fashion that $p$ remains unchanged. (This assumption is not necessary, but it avoids confusing income and substitution effects.)

It is clear that any such change in relative prices will produce results that are at least partly offsetting, for a rise in $p_a/p_b$ necessarily means a fall in $p_b/p_a$. Consumption demand for one commodity will increase, and for the other will decrease. But is there any reason to suppose that the two effects are completely offsetting? Is it necessary that the values of $a_2$ and $b_2$ should be such that any change in relative prices leaves total $c$ unchanged? The answer is that there is no *a priori* reason why this should be the case.[4] Yet apparently this has, at least roughly, been the case, so far as the record of experience indicates. At least, no statistician has improved the "fit" of an aggregate consumption function through including any term for relative price effects (it should be added, however, that few have really tried!).

One reason why no effect of relative prices on aggregate consumption has shown up in the data in a way that would suggest its inclusion in statistical work may well be that relative prices of the important categories of goods change very little, at least in the short run. Although, in the past several decades, the general price level has several times changed rather strikingly, most important groups of prices have changed in roughly the same extent. To be sure, there are significant secular movements of relative prices; but these seem to occur sufficiently slowly that any possible effect on the volume of aggregate demand would be swallowed up in other "trend" factors. Nevertheless, there are some systematic short-run variations in relative prices, over the business cycle. For example, farm prices are considerably more volatile than those of manufactured goods, and prices of most services are little affected by short-run changes in the economy. But to the extent that relative prices change in a way that is systematically related to movements in total out-

[4] See G. Ackley and D. B. Suits, "Relative Price Changes and Aggregate Consumer Demand," *American Economic Review*, XL (December 1950), 785–804.

put, any effect on aggregate demand of a systematically changing distribution of prices gets "picked up" in the coefficient of the income term in the aggregate consumption function.

## SUPPLY EFFECTS IN A CAPITAL-ABUNDANT ECONOMY [5]

We might now ask why it is that relative prices of different consumer goods change much less than the absolute price level, and why such short-run change as does occur is, to a significant degree, related systematically to changes in aggregate income or output. The answer to this question must bring in the supply side, as well as demand. Here, again, we have an opportunity to clarify our understanding of the relationship between micro and macroeconomics.

In the simplest Keynesian income-expenditure model, the supply of aggregate output is assumed to be automatically expansible (in response to aggregate demand) up to a full-employment limit on output. Keynes' analysis did, of course, assume diminishing returns as output increased in the short run. This meant that prices must rise at least somewhat relative to wages during an expansion of output (with certain possible repercussions through the transactions demand for money and the interest rate). Keynes' analysis, being short run in character, assumed a fixed stock of capital (and "land"); any increase in aggregate output was thus secured by increasing the employment of labor, up to a limit of "full employment" of the labor force. Keynes' assumption clearly was that total output was limited not by shortages of plant and equipment and natural resources, but by a shortage of labor. As we have previously noted, he was concerned with the problems of an economy already well-endowed with capital, and with a stationary or slowly growing population and labor force. We shall first consider this case, before tackling (in the next section) the alternative possibility, perhaps typical of the poorer, less-developed economies, that the effective limitation on aggregate output comes not from labor but from the supply of capital and land.

The notion of diminishing returns implies that more or less labor is used along with a given stock of fixed capital. We have considered (in Chapter IV) an alternative view, that labor and capital have to be used in fixed proportions, and increased use of labor is thus possible only by activating previously idle capital equipment. In this case, no diminishing

[5] In this and particularly in the subsequent sections I have drawn upon my article "The Keynesian Analysis of Italian Economic Problems," *Banca Nazionale del Lavoro Quarterly Review,* No. 42 (September 1957). I am grateful to the Banca Nazionale del Lavoro for permission to use brief excerpts from this article.

returns need attend a rise in employment and output. Let us first consider microeconomic supply aspects on the assumption that all individual production functions are of this type, and that sufficient capital facilities exist for each good to produce the amount of that good demanded at the full-employment level of income.

A rise in aggregate demand means a rise in the demands for most individual products. If the expansion has its origin in, say, a reduction in the rate of interest, demand for many kinds of capital goods will increase. Rising income in the production of capital goods will result in increased demand for most consumer goods, expanded through the multiplier process. Not all goods will experience the same (percentage) increase in demand. Capital goods of the more durable type will be affected more by an interest rate reduction than more short-lived capital goods. The income-elasticity of demand for some consumer goods is greater than for others, and, for a few (inferior goods), demand may even decrease with rising income. In the limiting case, however, we might assume that the labor supply was already distributed, by occupation, skill, and location, in accordance with the structure of the demand for it in a full employment situation. In this case a fully-aggregative analysis has no limitations.

If the only variations in output and employment that ever occurred consisted of cyclical fluctuations, in an economy with constant technique and constant tastes, such a distribution of the labor force might exist. However, this is unlikely to be the case in the real world. No two expansions or contractions of aggregate demand are ever precisely the same in their composition. If the expansion has its origin in increased investment resulting from technological change it will involve a different composition of demand for capital goods than if the origin is a reduced interest rate or improved "confidence," or a reduction in business taxes. If the origin of the increased demand is in the government sector, a somewhat different pattern of demand may develop. If the origin is in an increased propensity to consume or a tax reduction on consumers it will be still different. Further, consumer "tastes" change, new products emerge which appeal to consumers, and so on. Thus the distribution of idle labor in a situation of less-than-full employment will never be precisely in accordance with the demand for it at full employment. In extreme cases—e.g., when the origin of increased demand is in government war procurement, severe local and particular labor shortages may arise even while there is considerable idle labor in other areas or occupations. The significance of local labor shortages thus depends on

(a) how vigorous may be expansions of aggregate demand—i.e., how close to full employment the economy may be pushed; and (b) how much change occurs in the microstructure of demand.

If local labor shortages do emerge, the prices of the goods whose production is limited by labor shortage will then rise in response to rising aggregate demand. At the same time, producers of these goods will tend to offer higher wages in an effort to attract labor from other areas or occupations. If labor can be induced to move from surplus to deficit areas or industries by modest wage differentials, full employment of the entire labor force might be achieved with only modest changes in relative wages and prices. But the less mobile or the more highly-specialized is the labor supply (and the greater the divergence of the existing pattern of labor supply from the pattern of its demand) the greater will be the change in relative prices (and wages) that will be required. Also, of course, the greater the *average* rise in prices (and wages) that will occur, even if prices and wages are stable in the areas and products having surplus labor.[6]

The extent of the changes in relative (and hence absolute) prices that occur will thus be determined by both demand and supply effects: on the demand side, by the ease with which buyers can be induced to switch their purchases to other products as the relative prices of these commodities rise (through the substitution effect of relative price change); and, on the supply side, by the extent to which a rise in relative prices can attract new variable resources into production of these goods. The rise in relative prices will be less the greater the "mobility" of buyers —i.e., the more perfect the substitutes that are available—and the greater the mobility of resources. If either mobility were perfect, only infinitesimal changes in relative prices would occur as the economy approached full employment.

The picture is further complicated when we admit the possibility that even though there is no general shortage of plant and equipment, a rise in demand may nevertheless cause some industries to encounter "bottlenecks" of plant capacity while most other industries still have idle facilities and while there is still considerable unemployed labor. In these cases, the prices of the bottleneck products will be bid up, but with no

---

[6] We have already noted that prices and wages in other areas are likely to rise, too, in resistance to a change in relative prices. Three particular channels of resistance are important: the upward adjustment of wage rates "in line" with "patterns" set elsewhere; the use of standard "productivity" adjustments; and the tie of wage rates to the cost-of-living. These mean that the rise in average prices will be the greater.

short-run supply response. This is in contrast with the labor shortage case, where some short-run supply response can be accomplished through labor mobility. Prices for the bottleneck products must rise sufficiently to divert demand from these products to others not in a bottleneck position (through the substitution effect of relative price changes). If these products have close substitutes, only a moderate change of relative prices (and only a moderate rise in the average price level) need occur. If, however, there are no close substitutes, increased aggregate output may require a very considerable rise in the prices of these bottleneck goods.

Now we may complicate still further by recognizing that all production functions are not of the fixed proportions type. For some, perhaps many, products and services, the proportions in which labor and capital may be employed are widely variable, with either increasing or decreasing returns. For example, increased demand for movies as incomes rise can be met (within the capacity of existing theaters) at diminishing average cost. Increased demand for food will, in general, evoke no immediate supply response (because of the production cycle in agriculture), although with some lag there may be increased intensity of cultivation, at higher costs. And so on.

We can be confident, then, that any short-run expansion of aggregate demand will involve the following aspects:

(a) There will not be equal expansion of demand for all individual commodities.

(b) Whatever the structure of the demand expansion, different supply conditions will be met for different products, ranging from one extreme of complete short-run inelasticity of supply in the case of fixed-capital bottlenecks, all the way to the other extreme of perfect elasticity of supply in the case of production at constant cost together with either excess labor or perfect mobility of labor; many products will fall in an intermediate category as a result of either: (i) labor shortage and imperfect labor mobility, or (ii) variable proportions of inputs and increasing marginal costs.

(c) This will necessarily lead to changes in relative prices, and some rise in the average price level relative to wage rates.

(d) Although money incomes may rise to keep pace with the rise in the average price level (because the sale of goods at higher prices generates higher money incomes) and thus the partial supply obstacles need not necessarily block the expansion of demand and of aggregate output, the change in relative prices may react upon the volume of aggregate demand at any given level of real income or output.

(e) Changes in the structure of demand (or supply) from one expansion or contraction to the next may lead to different relative price changes and thus a different aggregate relationship of demand to output.

(f) Depending on the structure of the demand expansion and the obstacles it meets on the supply side, the expansion of total employment associated with a given increase in aggregate output may differ from one expansion to another.

(g) Broadening the analysis to take account of induced effects upon investment demand, the differing obstacles to supply of various commodities may induce very different patterns of investment response.

Thus the *microeconomic* aspects of the expansion or contraction process threaten to alter such fundamental macroeconomic relationships of a macroeconomic model as the consumption function, the relationship of employment and aggregate output, and any induced investment effects of rising output.

All of this does not, however, add up to the conclusion that macroeconomics must be abandoned. On the contrary, looked at in another way, it suggests, within certain limits, a stronger theoretical basis for macroeconomic models. Note especially the following considerations:

(a) Because of the consumption function, any major expansion or contraction of aggregate demand—whatever its origin—will involve, in large measure, an expansion or contraction of consumption, too. That is, investment and consumption demand tend to move together rather than inversely.

(b) The structure of the income elasticities of demand for particular commodities probably has reasonable stability; that is, the same commodities tend to experience relatively larger or smaller swings in demand.

(c) The labor force and the stock of plant and equipment are usually distributed in rough relationship to the full-employment demand for their employment—severe labor or plant bottlenecks are rare in an "ordinary" business expansion.

(d) In an economy like the American there is reasonable labor mobility at the margin.

(e) Even if bottlenecks occur either from plant or labor shortages, there are few products for which reasonably good substitutes do not exist in a wealthy, diversified economy, so that relative price changes will not often be extreme.

(f) The existence of rather large inventories in a wealthy economy helps ease the particular strains that may occur.

If we are dealing with movements of aggregate demand and output of the sort associated with the "business cycle," changes in composition of output and in relative prices will thus be both (1) *moderate*, and (2) will tend to be *systematically related* to changes in the aggregates. The latter means that empirical macroeconomic relationships may reflect not only individual behavior but also systematic distribution effects; but this does not necessarily disturb the stability of the aggregate relationships.

One final point needs to be added to this qualified defense of macroeconomics: the more sophisticated macroeconomic models involve, or can be made to involve, sufficient disaggregation to take care of some of the principal irregularities of behavior. For example, investment in housing is subject to peculiar influences, both demographic and institutional; its swings are often somewhat independent of changes in other investment demand. For this reason it is frequently split off from other investment. Another example: the relationship of consumption to GNP is strongly affected by taxes and transfer payments, subject to autonomous change through government policy. A more complex model, using a consumption function based on disposable income, can thus be expected to predict better than a simpler model using consumption as a function of GNP.

While these considerations may underline our confidence in reasonably disaggregated macroeconomic models, they also help us to understand their limitations. These limitations relate primarily to circumstances in which the structure of an expansion (or contraction) of aggregate demand may be expected to differ significantly from previous patterns; and to any circumstances in which total output is pushed close to full-employment limits.

We have already referred in our discussion of the control of wartime inflation to a good example of these limitations. A purely macroeconomic analysis—using the concept of an inflationary gap—may be extremely helpful in understanding the general source of wartime inflationary pressure. Yet it serves quite inadequately for the design of policy. Purely macroeconomic measures of fiscal and monetary policy might conceivably succeed in stabilizing the general price level even in wartime. Yet they might in the process produce quite intolerable strains on the social fabric, and result in substantial and unnecessary reductions of output. The *structure* of demand calls for massive transfers of resources; yet the relative-price system may be quite unable to produce such transfers. Direct controls, judiciously used, may effect as much or even more of a transfer than could the relative-price system, and with considerable less personal hardship and unnecessary waste of resources.

Up to this point, our discussion has assumed that, in general, and apart from occasional specific bottlenecks of plant capacity, the basic limitation on aggregate output arises from a shortage of labor. In a previous chapter, however, we considered the possibility that the effective limitation on output might arise from a shortage of capital—a stock of plant and equipment insufficient to permit employment of the entire labor supply. We consider the implications of this in the following section.

## SUPPLY EFFECTS IN THE CAPITAL-POOR ECONOMY

Again, in this case, we need to make more specific assumptions about the nature of the production functions for individual products. Suppose that we make the traditional assumption that any given stock of plant and equipment can be used with varying amounts of variable input, but that increased "doses" of variable input produce, after some point, less than proportional, *but always positive* increments of output. That is, we assume the conventional continuous cost curves of part A of Figure 20–1.

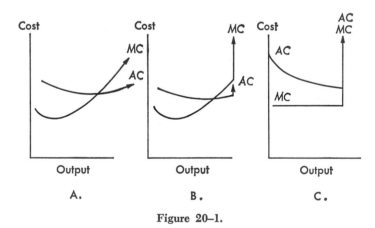

Figure 20–1.

But if all individual cost curves were of the sort pictured in part A, the notion of an aggregate output limited by plant capacity would have no clear meaning. More output could always be obtained, in every industry, although at increasing cost. It should, therefore, always be theoretically possible to obtain full employment of the total supply of labor. In fact, however, the necessary level of the real wage might be so low as to make this solution not a meaningful one; so that, in a practical (if not in a theoretical) sense, it would be correct to say that full employment could not be secured by an expansion of demand, but would instead require sufficient new investment to displace the individual cost curves far enough to the right (or to multiply their number sufficiently) that all labor could be employed at a tolerable wage level.

If the typical cost curve were of the sort pictured in part B of Figure 20–1, a limitation of aggregate output based on capital shortage would now have more precise meaning. In this case there is an absolute limit on output in each production unit. If the total labor supply were more than sufficient to permit every production unit to operate at its absolute limit, we could clearly say that total output was limited by shortages of plant and equipment. This would also be the case if the typical cost curve were like that of part C.

In either of the latter two cases, as aggregate demand increased, more and more products would reach their capacity limits. Absolute and thus relative prices of these products would therefore rise in the face of further increase in demand, diverting demand to other products, until, finally, all products had reached the point of capacity operations, and no further increase in demand could raise any output.

Now it is conceivable that in an economy plagued by a general shortage of capital, cost conditions in all industries might be quite "symmetrical," in the sense that all industries would tend, when aggregate demand increased, to approach limits on production, or sharply rising marginal costs, at about the same point. In this case, the structure of relative prices and the distribution of total output might change but little, or change only in a systematic and predictable way.

However, casual observation, as well as the testimony of careful students of capital-short economies, suggests a different model. It is one in which true bottlenecks of plant and equipment exist in certain highly strategic materials—for example, steel, cement, or electric power. Yet there are other goods for which supplies may be quite freely expansible— e.g., raw materials like stone or timber, or final products like textiles, housefurnishings, or personal services. Yet the goods whose production can easily be expanded are such imperfect substitutes for the bottleneck goods that no practicable rise in the relative prices of the strategic goods (and of the final products which use them) could have much effect in shifting intermediate demand to other raw materials or final demand to other end products whose production is not limited. We may be able to

conceive of changes in relative prices which would accomplish the adjustment of demand to available plant capacity. But to secure such changes
in relative prices without an elaborate system of subsidies might require
an impossible inflation of the price level and a socially intolerable redistribution of personal incomes. Barring such changes in relative prices,
we cannot say that total output is limited by a *general shortage of capital*,
but rather by *specific shortages of plant and equipment* in a few
strategic lines.

The capital-poor economy may perhaps differ from the capital-rich
economy only in degree rather than kind. But the difference may be
extremely significant. In a capital-rich economy, in which the limit to
aggregate output is basically set by labor supply, an expansion of aggregate demand may run into particular bottlenecks based primarily on
local or particular shortages of labor, requiring an adaptation of the
structure both of demand (through relative price changes) and of supply
(through relative wage changes) as the expansion proceeds. But one
should certainly suppose that a limit to aggregate output set by a shortage
of capital would be much more uneven in its impact than one set by a
shortage of labor, for labor is certainly more mobile and adaptable than
fixed plant. Further, the capital-poor economy is likely to be one undergoing rapid transformation in the structure of its demands, so that
plant capacity is woefully short in just the industries undergoing most
rapid growth.

Suppose that such is the case. Then a purely macroeconomic analysis
might lead to a most inappropriate design of economic policy. We referred in Chapter XIX to the diagnosis that said that Italy must restrict
consumption (or the increase in consumption), in order to divert resources to investment so as to permit a closer approach to full employment in the future. Suppose such restriction of consumption were undertaken by general tax increases, or perhaps by a generally restrictive wage
policy leading to an income distribution favoring profits. Such policies
might effectively depress the consumption of automobiles and appliances
(or the increase in their consumption), and thereby free steel to build
more steel plants, cement factories, and power stations. This is exactly
the shift from consumption to investment that will permit greater output
and employment at a later date. But general measures to restrict consumer demand will also restrict the consumption of textiles and personal
services. The resources released in these latter industries will not help
break the steel or cement shortages. Many of the resources will be released into unemployment, rather than diverted to investment. Likewise,

any *generalized* inducement to invest, e.g., through a lowering of interest rates, may stimulate investment in *all* lines, not merely in the bottleneck areas. Thus steel may be diverted from the construction of steel plants, prolonging the period of shortage. What is needed is not more investment in general nor less consumption in general. Rather, what is needed is the provision, by appropriate investment, of more plant capacity in just the right places, and in just the proper sequence, adapted to the present and emerging future pattern of demand. It is less consumption not of all goods but of those final products which use the particular commodities whose output is already at capacity and of which more needs to be diverted for investment purposes. Neither indiscriminate encouragement of investment nor of saving will achieve the objective of permitting increased employment in the future, except with a large waste of potential current output—if, as we have argued, the shoe does not pinch everywhere, but only in spots.

It is clear that this case is strikingly parallel to the case of wartime inflation in a capital-rich economy. As in that case, our uncomfortable conclusion seems to be that intervention—in this case to secure the objectives of rapid growth and future full employment—may have to take a more direct and detailed character than general measures of fiscal and monetary policy.

Keynesian aggregative analysis suggests and supports aggregative policies—generally of a fiscal or monetary nature. These policies are not directed toward individual products or industries or localities. They are "indirect" rather than "direct" controls. To most economists this is one of their great advantages. This preference reflects a recognition of the fact that the successful design of policies of the more direct variety requires a vastly greater amount of detailed information, and that such policies are infinitely more difficult to administer or enforce; and also a feeling that the more detailed interventions involve the public administration in more specific and personalized decision making—in favor of this person or firm or group over another—with its possibilities for petty tyranny, favoritism, and corruption.

A general increase or decrease in the level of personal taxation, for example, can be expected to depress or to stimulate the demand for consumer goods in general. No administrator need decide whose consumption will be reduced, nor of what products. To be sure, because there are different income elasticities of demand, the depression or stimulus will have an unequal impact upon different goods. But if all goods are produced under conditions of approximately constant marginal cost, and labor is highly mobile, the structure of relative prices need not be greatly affected; the composition of output will adapt itself to the composition of demand, and only modest shifts in relative incomes will secure the necessary rearrangements of consumption and production. Similarly, a tightening or loosening of monetary controls will affect interest rates and the availability of loans and thus discourage or stimulate investment, the commodity composition of which can be easily adapted to the structure of demand.

But we have argued that the microeconomic assumptions which justify our macroeconomic theoretical analysis are very unlikely to be satisfied in the capital-poor economy. Thus the use of policies which derive from a macroeconomic analysis may also be quite mistaken, or, at least, highly inefficient.

## CONCLUSION

Modern macroeconomics finds its origin in the ideas of J. M. Keynes, although building upon a long tradition of monetary theory. The theories of Keynes and of his predecessors are highly aggregative, and focus primarily on problems of short-run instability in the highly-developed and essentially free-market economies of the Western world. This has been, in an important sense, an analysis of the "business cycle problem"—of relatively short-run fluctuations of output and employment. These are precisely the problems for which, we have argued, a relatively simple, highly aggregative macroeconomic model is most appropriate. The composition of aggregate demand, and the structure of incomes, can be taken to be reasonably stable during such movements, except for variations that are systematically related to changes in the size of the aggregates. Serious obstacles to the expansion of particular outputs are not likely to arise either from particular labor shortages or from bottlenecks in plant and equipment. In such economies, the agricultural and mineral sectors, whose supply conditions are in many respects unique, are relatively unimportant. Labor supply is relatively limited, capital relatively abundant. Unemployment of labor is typically associated with an underutilization of plant and equipment. An approach toward full employment involves only moderately diminishing returns for most products.

But if our concern is with capital-poor economies, in a state of rapid or forced development, the usual macroeconomic assumptions may be more seriously violated. And even for the wealthier, already well-developed economies, a concern with secular problems of growth poses a different set of analytical and policy problems, perhaps requiring a different framework of variables and relationships. For in a growth context, no economy is more than temporarily capital-rich. To analyze growth problems using a Keynesian model which explicitly assumes a given stock of capital, and employment as the variable associated with changes in output is obviously inappropriate. The stock variables of capital and claims, and their structure, assume primary importance. And changes in the structure and composition of output inevitably accompany its growth.

This does not mean that macroeconomic analysis must be abandoned, but perhaps rather that greater disaggregation is required, or disaggregation on some alternative bases. We cannot avoid the fact that many of our most pressing economic problems are unalterably macroeconomic in character, and that some kind of macroeconomic analysis is therefore indispensable in the design of public policy. The macroeconomic models stemming from the work of Keynes have the great virtues that the number of variables isolated for analysis is small enough to be manageable, that its hypotheses are (mostly) framed in terms that permit empirical testing and measurement, that among the variables isolated are those which are strategic at least for the traditional instruments of monetary and fiscal policy. If the models or the policies are inappropriate, they need to be improved; but the use of macroeconomic models is unavoidable, in a world in which public policy is irrevocably committed to the maintenance of reasonable short-run stability of output and prices, and continuing rapid economic growth.

# Index

Abramovitz, M., 414n
Acceleration principle, 337, 485–493, 496–497, 500–503, 518–529
Ackley, G., 23n, 205n, 245n, 269n, 270n, 318n, 421n, 454n, 457n, 555n, 579n, 580n
Administered prices, 439–440, 449–459
Aggregation problems, 20–24, 223, 412–413, 570–591
Alexander, S. S., 518n, 519n
Allen, R.G.D., 571n
Arrow, K., 78n
Atkinson, L. J., 282n
Balanced budget multiplier, 342–344
Banks. *See* Central bank; Commercial banks
Baumol, W. J., 342n, 507–508, 518n
Boulding, K. E., 284n, 540
Brown, E. C., 229n
Brumberg, R., 246
Budget studies, 221–224, 244–245, 277–279, 297–298
Built-in stabilizers, 301–302, 305
Burns, A. F., 406n
Business cycle theory, 5, 17, 339, 355–358, 414, 485–497, 502, 533–534
Business sector in national income accounts, 39–47
Capacity, 97–101, 450, 479–485, 493–497, 513–517, 526–534, 537–549, 580–591
Capital consumption allowance, 67–68
Capital deepening, 503–504, 508–512, 557–558. *See also* Investment, theory of: marginal productivity of capital

Capital-labor substitution, 539–549
Capital-short economies, 542–549, 586–591
Capital, theory of, 461–479. *See also* Investment, theory of
Capital widening, 503–504. *See also* Acceleration principle
Central bank, 165, 198–201
Claims, composition of, and economic growth, 554–555, 561–566
Claims, volume of, 554–561. *See also* Consumption function: effect of wealth; Pigou effect
Clark, J. M., 218
Clark, L. H., 245n
Clemence, R. V., 518n, 536n
Cobweb theorem, 349–355
Colm, G., 73n
Commercial banks, 63–64, 149–151, 165–166, 198–201, 497–498, 555, 559, 563
Concealed unemployment, 543
Consumer credit, 285–287
Consumer durable goods, 282–287, 293
Consumer expectations and attitudes. *See* Consumption function
Consumption function: algebra and geometry of, 210–217; durable goods expenditure, 282–287; effect of consumer credit, 285–287; effect of deferred demand, 279–281; effect of demographic variables, 298–299; effect of expectations and attitudes, 288–295, 326, 426; effect of income distribution, 296–298, 385–393, 395–398, 413, 426, 434–437, 574n; effect of liquid assets, 273–281;

**593**

DATE DUE